D0848521

Textile Science

Textile Science

Kathryn L. Hatch

UNIVERSITY OF ARIZONA
TUCSON

WEST PUBLISHING COMPANY

Minneapolis/Saint Paul New York Los Angeles San Francisco

Library of Congress Cataloging-in-Publication Data

Hatch, Kathryn L.
    Textile science / Kathryn L. Hatch
        p. cm.
    Includes Index.
    ISBN 0-314-90471-9
    1. Textile fabrics. 2. Textile fibers. I. Title.
TS1445.H334 1993
677—dc20   91-25761
                                            CIP

PHOTO AND ART CREDITS

Unit I opener   Artwork courtesy of Dow Corning Corporation of Midland, MI.   **Table 3.1**   Data courtesy of The Polypropylene Council of America, Inc., of New York, NY.   **Table 3.2**   Data reprinted from *Textiles*, Vol 1(1), 1972, p. 13 with permission of the British Textile Technology Group of Manchester, England.   **Table 4.1**   Table reprinted from ASTM, *1990 Annual Book of ASTM Standards—Section 7—Textiles*, Vol 7.01, p. 69 with the permission of the American Society for Testing and Materials of Philadelphia, PA.   **Table 5.1**   Table reprinted from "IFI Fabricare News," July 1987, with the permission of the International Fabricare Institute, 12251 Tech Road, Silver Spring, MD 20904.   **Figure 5.1**   Photographs reprinted from *Textiles*, Vol 8(3), 1979, p. 70 with permission of the British Textile Technology Group of Manchester, England.   **Figure 5.7**   Photographs reprinted from "The Proceedings of the 31st Annual Meeting of the Electron Microscopy Society of America," 1973, pp. 58 and 59 with the permission of Claitor's Law Books, 3165 S. Acadian, Baton Rouge, LA 70808. Phone: 800-274-1403; Fax 504-344-0480.   **Figure 5.8**   Photograph reprinted from *Textiles*, Vol 5, p. 47, 1976 with permission of the British Textile Technology Group of Manchester, England.   **Figure 5.9**   Drawings reprinted from P. Hadlington and J. Gerozisis, *Urban Pest Control*, 1988, p. 137 with permission of NSW University Press of Kensington, Australia 2033.   **Figure 6.1**   Photograph reprinted from J. Foussereau, C. Benezra, and H. I. Maibach (eds.), *Occupational Contact Dermatitis*, 1982 with permission of Munksgaard Publishers of Copenhagen, Denmark.   **Figure 6.2**   Photographs reprinted from the *Textile Research Journal*, Vol 57, 1987, p. 27 with permission of the Textile Research Institute.   **Figure 6.4**   Drawings reprinted from S. Watkins, *Clothing: The Portable Environment*, 1984, pp. 43 and 51 with permission of the Iowa State University Press.   **Figure 6.5**   Drawings reprinted from S. Watkins, *Clothing: The Portable Environment*, 1984, pp. 115, 135, 137, and 140 with permission of the Iowa State University Press.   **Figure 6.6**   Drawings reprinted from S. Watkins, *Clothing: The Portable Environment*, 1984, p. 85 with permission of the Iowa State University Press.   **Figure 6.7**   Drawings reprinted from L. R. Sauvage, M.D., "Grafts for the 80s," 1980, with permission of the Hope Heart Institute of Seattle, WA.   **Unit II opener**   Artwork courtesy of Boehme Filatex, Inc., of Reidsville, NC.   **Figure 7.1**   Data obtained from the *1992 AATCC Technical Manual* (Test Method 20A—1981) and used with permission of the American Association of Textile Chemists and Colorists, P.O. Box 12215, Research Triangle Park, NC 27709.   **Figure 7.4**   Wool fiber structure reprinted from *Industrial & Engineering Chemistry*, Vol 44 (9), 1954, p. 2158 with permission of the American Chemical Society of Washington, DC.   **Figure 7.9**   Drawings reprinted from *Textiles*, Vol 16(2), 1987, p. 50 with permission of the British Textile Technology Group of Manchester, England.   **Figure 7.10**   Drawing and captions reprinted from *Textiles*, Vol 16(2), 1987, p. 52 with permission of the British Textile Technology Group of Manchester, England.   **Figure 7.11**   Drawing and captions reprinted from *Textiles*, Vol 16(2), 1987, p. 53 with permission of the British Textile Technology Group of Manchester, England.   **Figure 7.12**   Drawings reprinted from Hoechst Celanese, *The Dictionary of Fiber and Textile Technology* (2nd ed.), 1990, pp. 146–147 with permission of Hoechst Celanese Corporation of Charlotte, NC.   **Figure 7.14**   Drawing reprinted from *Textiles*, Vol 16(3), 1987, p. 82 with permission of the British Textile

(Credits continue after Index)

To Mom and Dad
the Forester
the Fisherman
the Artist and his Wife
the Dermatologist and his Wife
the Appraiser and his Wife
and my dearest women friends
(Connie, Geummi, Harriet, Kay,
Linda, Nancy, Norma, Sandra,
Suzanne, and Virginia)

CONTENTS IN BRIEF

UNIT I
THE WORLD OF TEXTILES

UNIT II
FIBER STRUCTURE AND PERFORMANCE

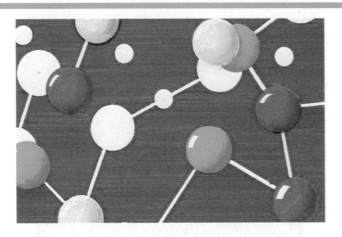

UNIT III
YARN STRUCTURE AND PERFORMANCE

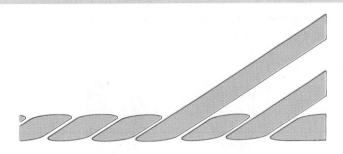

UNIT IV
FABRIC STRUCTURE AND PERFORMANCE

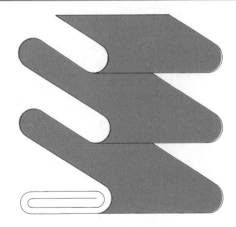

UNIT V
CHEMICAL, MECHANICAL, AND THERMAL
TREATMENTS AND PERFORMANCE

CONTENTS

CHAPTER 5

MAINTENANCE

CHAPTER 6

HEALTH/SAFETY/PROTECTION

CHAPTER 7

CHAPTER 8

DETAIL VIEW 21
SPECIAL-USE MANUFACTURED FIBERS AND ASBESTOS

CHAPTER 21

SPECIAL-USE MANUFACTURED FIBERS AND ASBESTOS

UNIT 3
YARN STRUCTURE AND PERFORMANCE

OVERVIEW 3
YARN STRUCTURES

DETAIL VIEW 22
SPUN YARNS

CHAPTER 22

SPUN YARNS

CHAPTER 30

PREPARATORY AND FINAL
FINISHES   387

CHAPTER 31

COMFORT AND PROTECTION
FINISHES   393

CHAPTER 32

AESTHETIC APPEAL FINISHES   401

DETAIL VIEW 33
MAINTENANCE FINISHES   412

DETAIL VIEW 34
DYED TEXTILES   426

CHAPTER 33

MAINTENANCE FINISHES   413

CHAPTER 34

DYED TEXTILES   427

Most of the fabrics shown in the Table of Contents were provided courtesy of Cranston Print Works Company, Cranston, RI. © Cranston Print Works Company.

TEXTILE SCIENCE is the study of the structure and performance of fabrics. It includes the examination of fibers (the fundamental units of all fabric), the yarns manufactured from fibers, and the manner in which fibers and yarns are structured into fabric. It also encompasses knowledge about dyestuffs and pigments, which provide an incredible array of color in textiles, and about the many chemicals used to enhance both the aesthetic and functional aspects of fabric.

Fabric performance is integral to the study of textile science. In the twentieth century, scientists discovered how to "engineer" fibers—to build the performance features needed for a particular application directly into a fiber. This discovery so improved the quality of life in the United States—indeed, in much of the world—that in the 1980s, The National Science Foundation recognized manufactured fiber development as one of the six scientific discoveries in the twentieth century that had the greatest impact on our way of life. By the late 1980s, textile scientists had expanded the ability to engineer performance into fibers to the ability to engineer performance into complete fabric systems. Jogging, bicycling, skiing, and aerobics outfits, as well as spacesuits, are some of the results of applying textile science to specific performance needs. The stain-resist carpets first made available to consumers in the mid-1980s also represent an engineered textile system.

Why Study Textile Science?

Knowledge about textile science is particularly important for individuals who are working or who plan to work in soft-good retail merchandising, interior design, apparel and fabric design, or positions linked to the production and distribution of fibers, yarns, and fabrics. An understanding of textile science should help buyers to act responsibly: to select textiles that fulfill needs but that do not introduce harm into the environment. As Stanley Marcus, chairman emeritus of Neiman Marcus, so aptly said

I'm not sure what buyers know about fiber content and fabric structure. Too many buyers have been taught merchandising, not merchandise. The power of management should be exercised. It's like a withered arm that has atrophied when it fails to do what it's supposed to do. It is up to management to decide not whether the article will sell but whether it should be sold in the first place.[1]

Individuals working in professions in which textiles are produced, distributed, marketed, and sold increasingly find that they must have product knowledge—particularly knowledge about how one product compares to similar products in performance.

On a personal basis, a knowledge of textile science can add significantly to our lives. We can develop a great appreciation for the fabrics that surround us each day. We can improve our ability to make choices in the textile marketplace, so that we can maximize our satisfaction with a textile product. We can learn to more fully evaluate the information that manufacturers of expensive, high-tech textile products provide on product hangtags and in magazine ads. We also can become more expert at selecting textiles that meet our need to be environmentally conscious consumers (fabrics that are made with renewable rather than nonrenewable resources; textiles that are biodegradable; textile production processes that do not pollute the environment). Lastly, we can gain an appreciation of the continuing impact of textile science on our everyday life, as we follow new developments in textile science.

---

[1] Stanley Marcus, "Still Minding the Stores," *Womens Wear Daily* (May 9, 1984), pp. 6–7.

Goal

The primary goal of *Textile Science* is to enable you to select the textile that best serves a specific end-use application—the textile that best matches the performance criteria established by the purchaser. The key elements in working toward this goal are: (1) knowledge of the variety of textile materials; (2) knowledge of the type and level of performance that can be achieved in a textile material; and (3) the ability to link knowledge of fabric performance and fabric structure during the decision-making process.

Other objectives include developing communication skills by gaining an understanding of the language of textile science, an appreciation for the beauty and technology of textiles, a sense of the role of legal requirements in the production and sale of textiles, and an interest in continuing to explore developments in textile science.

The Language of Textile Science

The language of textile science is extensive and unique. A portion of the language communicates the many textile forms (for example, the types of fibers, yarn structures, and fabric structures). Another portion of the language communicates the performance of the textile (for example, its tenacity, resilience, and pilling propensity). Still other words communicate aspects of textile production. You must be familiar with the precise scientific meaning of each term, so that misunderstandings do not arise needlessly.

Information technology is at the hub of international trade and requires a "controlled terminology." Richard Stehlow tells us that

No longer can we generally enjoy the leisurely luxury of negotiating meaning with friendly discourse. To communicate effectively, we need a controlled vocabulary—an agreed on list of terms used in a specific application or field, along with a single definition for each term.[2]

In textile science, certain organizations have been developing a controlled vocabulary, which is used in this textbook. Different organizations focus on different segments of this textile vocabulary; the sources of various terms and definitions are carefully referenced in each

---

[2]Richard Stehlow, "Standardization News," ASTM, Vol. 18 (August 1990), p. 18.

section. Be aware that changes in the vocabulary (mainly through expansion) are likely to occur as this vocabulary is further developed.

At times, you may feel overpowered by the number of new words presented in this textbook, but do not delay learning them. If a textile structure is being defined, take the time to "connect" the words in the definition with the drawing or photograph of the structure provided. Ask yourself whether or not you see the features described in the definition; if you do not, ask your instructor for clarification. Think carefully about each word or phrase in the definition of a textile performance property, and associate the definition with that performance property to help you recall it later. Just memorizing is not meaningful.

As you read the text, you may occasionally forget the meaning of a term that was introduced earlier. The Index will direct you to the page where the term was originally defined. Many key terms are defined in the Detail Views at the beginning of each chapter.

Textbook Organization

The text is organized into five units. Unit I focuses on the distinction between textile structure and performance, as well as on the nature of the interrelationships between them. Units II–V emphasize the great variety of fibers, yarns, fabrics, and mechanical, chemical, and thermal treatments available in the textile marketplace today. Take a few minutes to scan the Table of Contents to give yourself a perspective on how the textbook is organized.

Overview and Detail Views. An Overview at the beginning of each unit provides the most fundamental concepts examined in that unit and relates them to one another. The introductory text to each unit explains the major concepts outlined in the Overview. Take a moment to look at the five overviews in the book. As you begin each unit, study the Overview first; then return to it when you have finished reading the chapters in that unit.

A Detail View at the beginning of each chapter provides the major topics to be discussed in the order of their presentation in the chapter and usually relates them to each other. Often the key words introduced in a chapter, as well as their definitions, appear in a Detail View. Take five or ten minutes to become familiar with the format and intent of the Detail Views throughout the textbook. Study each Detail View before you begin to read a chapter; then return to it when you have finished that chapter. Be sure you understand how the topics relate to each other.

Summaries. Each chapter contains a great quantity of detailed information—more facts than a student can or should be expected to absorb all at once. Some detail is included because it is interesting and provides you with the incentive to read further, such as discussions of how the generic group names for the manufactured fibers were determined. Other detail is included because it makes a concept more meaningful or realistic. For example, you are informed that a seatbelt should be replaced following an automobile accident in which the belt was instrumental in saving an individual's life, because that belt has been taken beyond its ability to recover from stress and would not provide the required amount of protection if a second accident were to occur.

To help you sort out the basic concepts from the detail, several learning tools are provided in addition to the Overviews and Detail Views. Tables summarizing the properties of various fibers, yarn structures, and fabric structures are one of the tools. For example, in Unit II, Fiber Structure and Performance, you will find that Table 1 in each chapter summarizes the performance of the fiber discussed in that chapter. Study Table 1 in Chapters 10 to 20 to familiarize yourself with fiber property summaries. Also look at Tables 1, 2, and 3 in Chapter 22 within the Yarn Structure and Performance Unit to see how yarn properties are summarized. A Chapter Summary, which ends each chapter, is another learning tool. Often it directs you to the key learning tools in the chapter.

Illustrations. Great effort has been made to illustrate and photograph as many textile structures as possible and to include color photographs of dyed and printed textiles. Part of your success in working in the fiber, textile, and related industries is dependent on your ability to visualize a structure, associate it with the appropriate name, and use the correct term to communicate information about a specific textile to others.

To make the illustrations as useful as possible, a description of the distinguishing feature(s) of a structure appears in the figure as well as in the text discussion. Be sure that you can recognize the distinguishing features of each textile that is illustrated.

Structures and manufacturing processes are presented in a consistent manner within a chapter. For example, a textile is shown entering a manufacturing process on the left side of the page and emerging from the process on the right side of the page. In some chapters, the textile enters the process at the bottom of the page and exits at the top. The method of entry and exit depends on the particular machinery used. The text discussion will tell you how a particular group of figures are presented.

Student Preparation

It is difficult, if not impossible, to study textiles without some background in the natural sciences, because it is simply not enough to discuss the "what" without the "why." An introductory chemistry and/or physics course at the university level is a recommended prerequisite. The basic scientific principles presented in the text are meant to serve either as a review for those of you who have already studied the natural sciences or as a supplement for those of you who have not had instruction in certain areas.

Save This Book

At the end of your course, you may be tempted to return your *Textile Science* text to the bookstore for a refund. When you begin working in your chosen career, you will know that this was a mistake. You will find yourself returning to the bookstore to purchase another basic book on textile science. The fundamental concepts presented here will remain intact for years to come and serve you well into the future. The fundamental fiber data will not change. Each of you will need to subscribe to textile trade journals to keep up-to-date on new textile developments on a daily or monthly basis.

Help to Improve This Book

Since my sole intent was to write a book that would make learning about textile science as organized, technically correct, up-to-date, and interesting as possible, I welcome your comments about where you became confused or bored and what stimulated you to study further. If you find any technical errors, please point them out. Send in any questions that you think should be addressed in this textbook. There are no better reviewers than the users of the text—that is you.

Mail your comments to Professor Kathryn L. Hatch, The University of Arizona, College of Agriculture, Building #33, Room 116, Tucson, AZ 85721. You will be assisting future students who enroll in this course and in similar courses across the country. Several hundred textile science courses translate into thousands and thousands of students each year. Let's work together to make this course one of great value.

And now enjoy your adventure into the world of textile science. The fundamental principles and applications that you learn here will serve you well throughout your career and personal life.

*T*HIS BOOK never would have been written if it had not been for the opportunity provided by Iowa State University to study Textiles and Related Sciences. This program involved me in a scientific field that has direct application to the needs of people. The university's philosophy, "Science with Practice," has always served me well in my professional life. Special appreciation is extended to Harriet Lewis and Jane Saddler, from whom I took my first courses in textiles as an undergraduate student.

It has been a pleasure to teach college students for the last 16 years. Several students have become great friends. Many I still recall from time to time; some have faded from memory, but their names are listed in my student file. To each, I extend a very special thanks. In the past several years, students in my textile science course have patiently used xeroxed chapters from this textbook as I produced them. Their suggestions for improvements have been invaluable.

The following faculty reviewers helped to eliminate technical errors and provided thoughtful direction: Ira Block, University of Maryland; Jeanette Cardomone, Virginia Polytechnic State University; Lenore Cheek, Louisiana State University; Billie Collier, Louisiana State University; Shirley Cox, Georgia State University; Elizabeth Easter, University of Kentucky; J. Nolan Etters, University of Georgia; Maureen Grasso, University of Texas, Austin; Kay Grise, Florida State University; Christine Ladisch, Purdue University; Joan Laughlin, University of Nebraska; Mary Lou Rowley, Eastern New Mexico University; Nancy Markee, University of Nevada, Reno; Shirley Medsker, University of Idaho; Robert Merkel, Florida International University; Gary Mock, North Carolina State University; Charles Noel, Ohio State University; Sylvia Phillips, Phoenix College; Alvertia Quesenberry, Ball State University; Marsha Stein, Post College; Kristen Swanson, Northern Arizona University; Carol Tuntland, California State University–Los Angeles; Mary Warnock, University of Arkansas; and Patricia A. Wilson, Colorado State University.

Several colleagues deserve special mention: S. Kay Obendorf, Cornell University and Roger Barker, North Carolina State University who were always willing to talk through topics that confused me; Oscar Blazquez, University of Arizona, who miraculously transformed my ideas for illustrations into sketches; and Roger Kramer, University of Arizona, for his suggestions during the development of illustrations and selection of fabrics to be photographed. The Science and Engineering Library reference librarians helped from beginning to end—from obtaining research materials to finding publishers' and authors' addresses so that permission to reprint forms could be sent.

I wish there were space to name every individual working in some capacity in the textile field who so generously and graciously assisted by answering my questions, providing photographs, sending fabrics that could be photographed, and supplying technical literature. I was continuously amazed and thankful for their quick and accurate responses to my requests.

To Tom LaMarre, who somehow convinced me five years ago to write this book and to Poh Lin Khoo, Emily Autumn, Doris Cadd, Jan Fisher, and Shelley Clubb, who took the manuscript and transformed it into this volume, my very special thanks. May a gentle breeze be at their back and a calm sea lie before them.

To all my dear friends and family who patiently—and impatiently—waited for this book to be finished, my heartfelt appreciation. The book is finished and I am looking forward to renewing my interactions with them.

Kathryn L. Hatch

The World of Textiles

Textile Materials and Their Performance

Textile materials are "fibers, yarn intermediates, yarns, fabrics, and products made from fabrics which retain more or less completely the strength, flexibility, and other typical properties of the original fibers or filaments."

STRUCTURE

is knowledge about a physical entity or a description of objects and their arrangement or location.

PERFORMANCE

is knowledge about the way in which or the efficiency with which the textile reacts or fulfills its intended purpose.

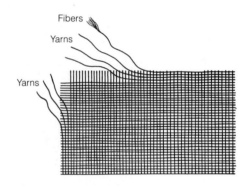

Fibers

Yarns

Yarns

Durability

The ability of the textile to retain its physical integrity under conditions of mechanical stress for a reasonable period of time.

Comfort

The ability of the textile to provide the body with freedom from pain, freedom from discomfort, the ability to maintain a neutral state.

*T*EXTILES ARE an integral part of our world. When we wake up in the morning, we raise our head from pillows covered with fabric and often filled with fibers and climb out from under sheets and blankets. We step into slippers and slip into robes. We wash our bodies with washcloths and dry them with towels. We brush our teeth with toothbrushes; the bristles are synthetic textile fibers. We drink coffee or tea, and the coffee grounds and tea leaves are filtered through nonwoven textiles. We dress in knit and woven apparel fabrics.

When we get into a car or bus, we sit on upholstered seats and the vehicle moves on tires reinforced with strong textile yarns. We stand on carpets, sit on upholstered furniture, and look out of curtained (draped) windows in our living and working spaces. Fiberglass insulation in our buildings reduces heating and cooling bills.

The golf clubs, tennis rackets, and ski poles we use in recreational sports may be reinforced with lightweight textile fibers. The roads and bridges we travel over may be stabilized or reinforced with textiles. The stadiums we sit in may be covered with a fabric roof. Some of us have artificial arteries made of textiles. Many of us have had wounded tissue closed and held together by textile sutures after surgical procedures.

Throughout the day, we use other types of manufactured products; most of them would have been more difficult to manufacture and distribute without rubber conveyor belts, in which textiles are embedded. Even the processed foods we eat have passed through textile filters.

Our increased knowledge of space is partially due to the development of strong, heat-resistant textile fibers that prevent the exhaust cones of space satellites from melting and disintegrating under the tremendous heat they are exposed to when launched. The ability of physicians to diagnose internal medical problems without surgery is due to the use of specially developed optical fibers. No aspect of our lives seems untouched by textiles.

According to the American Society for Testing and Materials, *textile materials* are "fibers, yarn intermediates, yarns, fabrics, and products made from fabrics which retain more or less completely the strength, flexibility, and other typical properties of the original fibers or filaments." This definition of textile materials contains two key elements that you will be studying in this text: structure of textiles (fibers, yarns, fabrics, and products), and performance of textiles (strength and flexibility).

WHAT IS TEXTILE STRUCTURE?

Textiles are objects; they are fibers, yarns, and fabrics. The drawing in Overview I shows a fabric, the yarns

Aesthetic Appeal

The degree of pleasantness of the textile to the eye, hand, ear, and nose (to the sensory mechanisms of the human body).

Maintenance

The ability of the textile to remain in the same state of cleanliness, size, physical integrity, and color as when purchased, following wear, use, and/or care procedures.

Health / Safety / Protection

Those aspects of textiles that make them potentially hazardous substances or that protect the human body and the environment from a variety of harmful substances (includes properties that make textiles appropriate for use in the diagnosis, prevention, and treatment of medical problems).

from which a fabric is composed and, in turn, the fibers from which the yarn is made. As objects, fibers, yarns, and fabrics have definite structural features that can be described following observation. Many aspects of textile structure can be identified after looking closely at the textile with your eyes or the aid of a magnifying glass: as examples, how the yarns are arranged within the fabric, what the yarn looks like, and whether the fibers are long or short. It is necessary to use a light microscope to view the surface features of fibers because they are so small. Even finer structural detail can be observed through an electron microscope. Other scientific instrumentation is required to discern certain internal features of fibers.

WHAT IS TEXTILE PERFORMANCE?

Textile performance deals with what the textile can do; that is, what needs it can help to fulfill. The *Random House Dictionary of the English Language* defines "performance" as "the manner in which or the efficiency with which something reacts or fulfills its intended purpose."

Performance is discovered by actually using the textiles or by subjecting them to conditions that simulate the ones to which they will be applied. Consumers of textiles find that they prefer certain shirt fabrics over others because of differences they note in the comfort provided; they discover that they prefer certain jeans or certain upholstery fabrics because of differences they observe in the wearlife. Textile scientists evaluate the performance of a textile by using laboratory instruments that bend, pull, rub, heat, wet, and otherwise manipulate the textile and quantify the effects of such treatments. In other words, they quantify the performance of the textile.

Performance can be specified on two levels of precision: performance attributes and performance properties. *Performance attributes* (the more general of the two) specify the five major needs or requirements that *fabrics* generally meet: durability, comfort, aesthetic appeal, maintenance, and health/safety/protection (see Overview I):[1]

---

[1] Additional performance attributes may arise after the fabric has been sewn or constructed into the end-use item; for example, fit, style, and design are performance requirements for apparel. Other performance requirements, such as sewability, are necessary to construct an end-use product. However, the discussion in this textbook focuses primarily on the fabric performance attributes required by the ultimate purchaser.

■ *Durability:* The ability of the textile to retain its physical integrity under conditions of mechanical stress for a reasonable period of time.

■ *Comfort:* The ability to provide the body with freedom from pain, freedom from discomfort: the ability to maintain a neutral state.

■ *Aesthetic appeal:* The degree of pleasantness of the textile to the eye, hand, ear, and nose (to the sensory mechanisms of the human body).

■ *Maintenance:* The ability of the textile to remain in the same state of cleanliness, size, and physical integrity, and to be the same color as when purchased, following wear, use, and/or care procedures.

■ *Health/safety/protection:* The aspects of textiles that make them potentially hazardous substances or that protect the human body and the environment from a variety of harmful substances (includes properties that make textiles appropriate for use in the diagnosis, prevention, and treatment of medical problems).

Although performance attributes provide valuable information about needs that may be fulfilled by textiles, these attributes are difficult to quantify or measure. Each performance attribute can be clarified by considering specific performance properties. For example, a durable textile does not tear, break, wear out, develop holes, or otherwise fall apart too quickly. Durability therefore includes strength (the ability not to break under a pulling force), abrasion resistance (the ability to withstand rubbing forces), and flexibility (the ability to bend repeatedly and not break), as well as elongation and elastic recovery, which influence how well a textile can absorb mechanical stress.

UNIT ORGANIZATION

Chapter 1 highlights the basic structural features of a textile fabric and compares it with three closely related materials: paper, leather, and fur. Detail View 1 illustrates and defines the major components of a textile fabric.

Chapters 2–6 develop the idea of fabric performance by examining the performance properties that contribute to fabric durability, comfort, aesthetic appeal, maintenance, and health/safety/protection, respectively. Detailed Views list and define the performance properties considered in each chapter. These sections not only provide "at-a-glance" views of key performance property words but also serve as convenient references for reviewing performance words used throughout the text.

TERMINOLOGY

The definitions used throughout Unit I are primarily taken from the American Society for Testing and Materials (ASTM), "Standard Terminology Relating to Textiles" (D123-88b) and "Burning Behavior of Textiles" (D4391-87), *1990 Annual Book of ASTM Standards,* vol. 07.01 (Philadelphia: ASTM, 1990). In many cases, the ASTM performance definition is quoted. In others, the ASTM definition has been paraphrased to assist the beginning student.

OBJECTIVES

The objectives of Unit I are that you:

1. Understand what textiles are.
2. Correctly interpret the meaning of textile performance attributes and properties.

The minimum expectation is that you will be able to:

1. Define textile, fiber, yarn, fabric, colorant, and textile chemical.
2. Describe the components of fabric.
3. List the five performance attributes.
4. Name and define the performance properties of fabrics.

Textile Fabrics

A *textile fabric* is "a planar structure consisting of yarns or fibers." It may also consist of dyes and pigments (colorants) and chemicals. The fabric is generally a porous material. The description of a fabric includes a description of each of these aspects.

GENERAL FEATURES

Fiber

"Unit of matter having an extremely small diameter and a length at least 100 times this diameter." Cylindrical or ribbon-shaped units. The basic structure of textile yarns and fabrics.

Yarn

"A continuous strand of textile fibers, filaments, or material in a form suitable for weaving, knitting, or otherwise intertwining to form a textile fabric."

Fabric construction

The manner in which yarns are interlaced, interlooped, knotted, or otherwise intertwined to form the fabric; when yarn is not present, how the fibers are distributed and held to form a coherent fabric structure.

Interstices (voids)

Spaces between fibers within yarns and between yarns in the fabric.

Colorants

Dyes and pigments that "modify the perceived color of objects or impart color to otherwise colorless objects."

Chemicals

Chemicals of various types that alter the fibers, yarns, and construction of a fabric during or after their formation.

ANATOMY OF A COTTON FABRIC

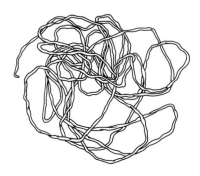

Magnified view of one cotton fiber.

Magnified section of a yarn made from cotton fibers.

Magnified section of a woven fabric made from cotton yarn, showing the interlacing of the yarns and the interstices in the fabric.

Magnified view of a section of cotton fiber, showing the location of a colorant and a durable-press reactant between the fiber's polymers.

*T*extile Fabrics

Our world is filled with countless types of materials: concrete, steel, linoleum, stone, paper, wood, plastic sheets, and molded plastics, to name just a few. Textile fabrics are also materials. Specifically, they are materials characterized as "planar structures consisting of yarns or fibers." They also may contain dyes and pigments (colorants) and chemicals. They are usually porous materials.

Generally, textile fabrics are relatively thin and flexible (pliable, bendable) sheet materials. Fabric thinness ranges from sheer curtain and blouse fabrics to carpeting and blanketing. Most fabrics bend or fold easily when held in the hand; others are more difficult to bend but usually are not as hard to bend as steel and molded plastics.

The major components of textile fabrics are listed and defined in Detail View 1. A durable-press-treated cotton fabric is "dissected" to illustrate each of the components.

COMPONENTS OF TEXTILE FABRIC

Fibers

Textile fiber is "a generic term for the various types of matter that form the basic elements of textile fabrics and other textile structures." More specifically, a textile fiber is "a unit of matter that is characterized by having a length at least 100 times its diameter or width and which can be spun into yarn or made into a fabric. . . ." The diameter of textile fibers is small—generally, 0.0004–0.002 inch (in), or 11–50 micrometers (μm). Their length varies from $\sim\frac{7}{8}$ in or 2.2 centimeters (cm) to many miles.

On the basis of length, fibers are called staple fiber or filament. Textile filament is "a variety of fiber having extreme length, not readily measured." Staple fibers are "natural fibers or cut lengths of filament," the latter being $\sim1\frac{1}{2}$–8 in (3.75–28.5 cm) in length.

Detail View 1 shows a magnified view of one fiber taken from a durable-press-treated cotton fabric. Cotton fiber is one of the shortest textile fibers. Note how long it is in relationship to its width. Take a cotton fiber from a 100% cotton garment (the label should identify the fiber content) and observe the size of the fiber. Then take fibers from some other fabrics and observe their lengths and widths.

Many different types of fibers (cotton, polyester, nylon, wool, and olefin, to name a few) form yarns and fabric. Fibers differ from each other in polymeric substance (chemical nature), cross-sectional shape, and surface contour, as well as in length and width. Figure 1.1 shows some of the variations in the surface features and cross-sectional shapes of textile fibers. In Unit II, the great variety of fibers and their performance properties are discussed at length.

Yarns

Yarn is "a generic term for continuous strands of textile fibers, filaments, or material in a form suitable for weaving, knitting, or otherwise intertwining to form a textile fabric." Yarns are recognized by their cylindrical or ribbon-like shapes. They are generally larger structures than fibers. A yarn usually can be subdivided into smaller

FIGURE 1.1   Some structural variations in the surface features and cross-sectional shapes of textile fibers.

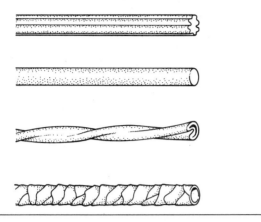

parts; that is, fibers can be separated from it.[1] Most fabrics are made from yarns, and the yarns often can be easily pulled from the fabric.

---

[1]Three exceptions are monofilament, tape, and network yarns. Monofilament yarn is composed of one filament, a tape yarn is a flat ribbon like filament, and a network yarn resembles a three-dimensional wire netting. All are discussed in Chapter 24.

In Detail View 1, a yarn has been taken from a cotton fabric and magnified. Note that the cotton fibers in the yarn are fairly well aligned with the axis of the yarn; that is, they lie along the yarn length. In this yarn (as in most yarns), the fibers are not so intermeshed that they cannot be separated. The yarn illustrated is called a spun yarn because it is made from short or staple fibers.

There are many different types of yarns (Figure 1.2). Yarns differ in size and in uniformity along their length. They also may differ in the length of their fibers, in the arrangement of these fibers within the yarn, and in fiber composition (the specific type of fibers in the yarn). Examine several yarns from different fabrics, and note the structural differences you can detect. Additional yarn structures are shown in Unit III.

Fabric Construction

Fabric construction focuses on the arrangement of yarns or fibers within a fabric. In Detail View 1, yarns are seen crossing over and under each other in the cotton fabric. This arrangement of yarns is called interlacing; when the yarns are interlaced at right angles to each other, a woven fabric is formed. In the cotton fabric, the crosswise yarns cross over one lengthwise yarn and then under the next lengthwise yarn. This specific arrangement in a woven fabric is called plain weave.

FIGURE 1.2   Some structural variations in yarns.

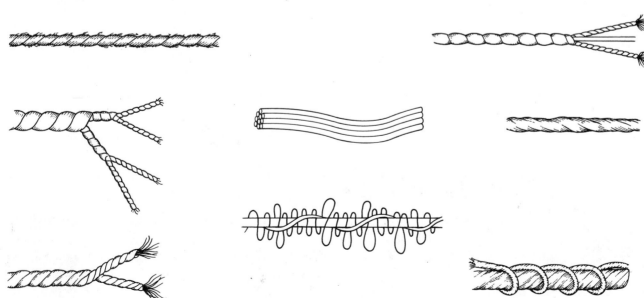

Many of the fabrics shown in Figure 1.3 have yarns interlaced at right angles, but the pattern of interlacing differs. In some fabrics, the yarns interloop to form knit fabrics. How the yarns interloop is important in describing the construction of a specific knit fabric. Nonwoven fabrics do not have yarns; the arrangement of fibers is important in describing the construction of nonwoven fabrics. Select fabrics with woven, knit, and nonwoven constructions. Additional fabric constructions are considered in Unit IV.

Interstices (Voids)

A substantial portion of a fabric is *interstices* or *voids*. According to the *Random House Dictionary of the English Language*, interstices are "small or narrow spaces or intervals between things or parts, especially when one of a series of alternating uniform spaces and parts." In fabrics, interstices are not necessarily uniform in size and shape. Most fabrics exhibit a broad distribution of pore sizes and shapes. In Detail View 1, the woven cotton fabric has been magnified so that the amount of space between yarns is readily seen. The interstices in a fabric or yarn may be observed by holding it up to the light. Fibers, too, have internal voids, but they are not visible to the naked eye.

Surprisingly, little volume of a fabric is composed of "solid" material. Fabric is highly porous—typically, 60–90% air by volume (Figure 1.4). (Note that the percent is by volume, not by weight.) Fabrics can be made nonporous by filling the interstices with resins.

Textile scientists are quite interested in these interstices because they influence the flow of water vapor and heat through fabrics. Therefore, much of the comfort provided by textile fabrics is due to their porous structure. Air trapped in interstices contributes heavily to the ability of fabric to act as an insulator. Textiles are said to be permeable because of their degree of porosity.

Colorants and Chemicals

Colorants and chemicals can constitute a substantial portion of the finished textile. In many cases, 10% or more of a fabric's weight may be due to the chemicals that have been used to improve one or more of the fabric's properties.

Colored textiles contain dyestuffs and pigments. These *colorants*, the physical entity in a fabric, are chemicals that "modify the perceived color of objects or impart

FIGURE 1.3 Some variations in fabric construction.

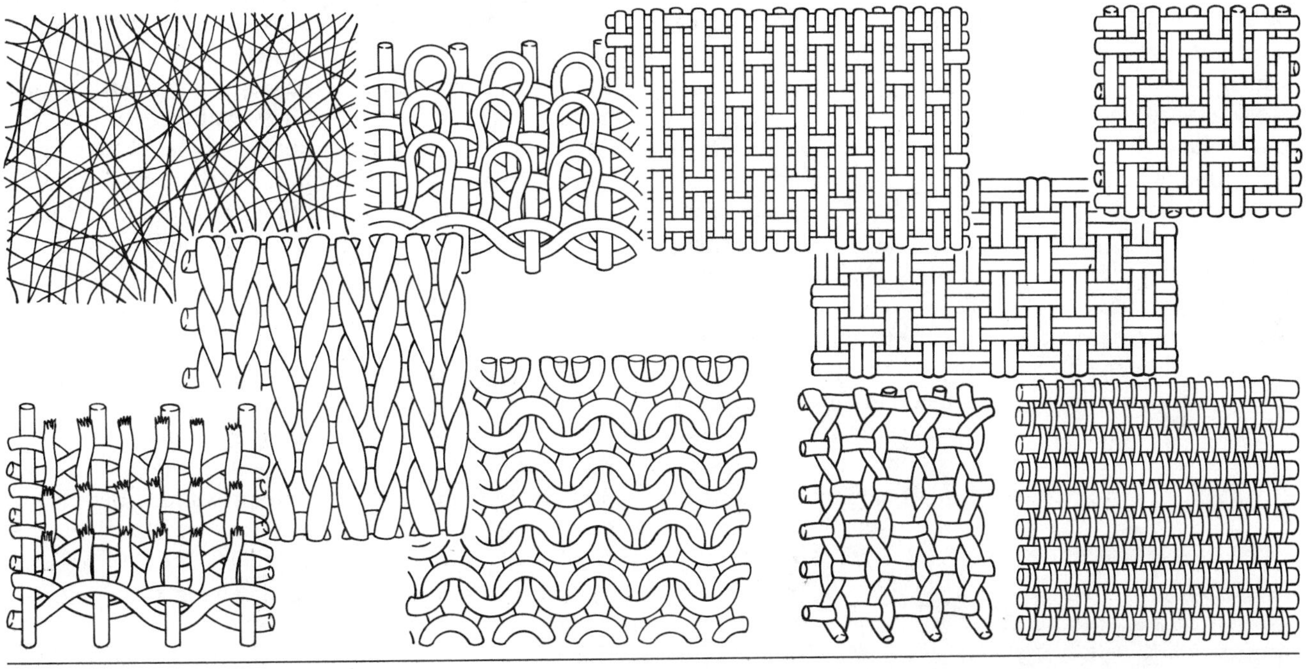

FIGURE 1.4 The proportions of fabric volume filled with fiber and air.

Suit fabric is 25% fiber and 75% air.   T-Shirt fabric is 13% fiber and 87% air.   Winter coat fabric is 5% fiber and 95% air.

color to otherwise colorless objects."[2] *Color,* the result of the modification of light by colorants, is not a physical entity. The presence of colorants in a textile is generally known because the textile appears colored to the observer. In Detail View 1, a portion of a fiber has been magnified to show the absorption of colorant into the fiber. The molecular structures of several dye molecules are shown in Figure 1.5; note that one dye is indigo, which is used to dye the warp yarns of denim fabric. Colorants are fairly large molecules. Their descriptions can include chemical name, Colour Index number, application method or class, and the color imparted.

Fabrics may contain *chemicals,* such as flame retardants, delustrants, sizings, softeners, antioxidants, stain repellents, water repellents, and bacteriostats. There are many different chemical compounds in each category. Detail View 1 shows the location of an N-methylol compound, which renders the cotton fabric relatively wrinkle-free. The molecular structure of dimethyloldihydroxyethyleneurea (DMDHEU)—the most frequently used cellulosic, durable-press reactant—is shown in Figure 1.5.

Chemicals can be found within fibers or may form a

more-or-less continuous, solid film around yarn and individual fibers. Chemicals may fill the interstices in the fabric. In some fabrics, a chemical (usually an adhesive) holds layers of material together.

Laboratory analytical procedures can determine the presence and nature of chemicals in a fabric when observation is not sufficient. A description of a chemical contained in a fabric might include its specific chemical name and a trademark designation. The amount of chemical contained in the fabric may be specified as a percent of add-on (the change in the weight of the fabric prior to and following chemical application divided by the original weight of the fabric). Different types of colorants and finishing chemicals are considered in Unit V; chemicals added to manufactured fibers during their formation are discussed in Unit II.

FABRICATED TEXTILE PRODUCTS

Once fabric is manufactured, it is formed into a *fabricated textile product*—the *end-use product,* such as apparel items, tents, carpeting, draperies, or filters, which is purchased by the ultimate consumer. Most fabricated textile products are formed by cutting appropriately shaped pieces from fabrics and sewing them together. The formation of these "sewn" products is accomplished

[2] F. W. Billmeyer, Jr., and M. Saltzman, *Principles of Color Technology,* 2d ed. (New York: John Wiley, 1981), p. 111.

FIGURE 1.5 Molecular structures of some colorants and textile chemicals.

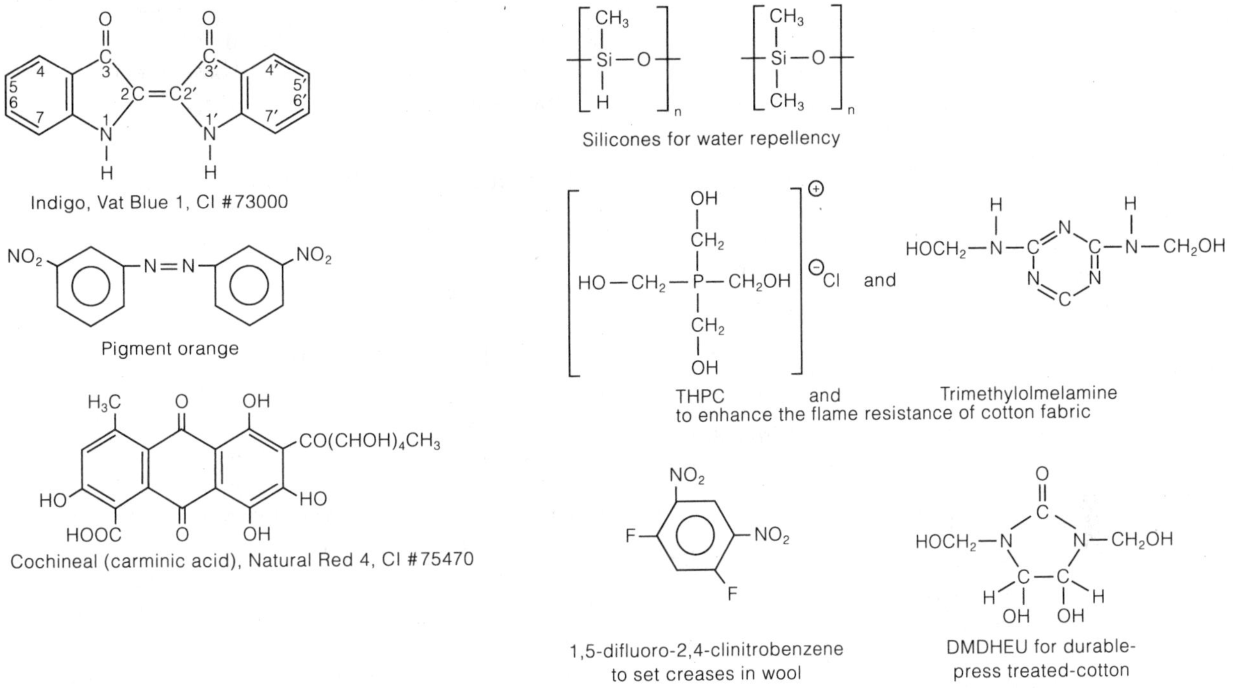

Indigo, Vat Blue 1, CI #73000

Pigment orange

Cochineal (carminic acid), Natural Red 4, CI #75470

Silicones for water repellency

THPC   and   Trimethylolmelamine
to enhance the flame resistance of cotton fabric

1,5-difluoro-2,4-clinitrobenzene
to set creases in wool

DMDHEU for durable-
press treated-cotton

within the apparel manufacturing and sewn-products industries. Fabricated textile products are sold in four major domestic markets: apparel, interior textiles, household and institutional textiles, and industrial and consumer textiles. These are the ultimate markets for all fibers, yarns, and fabrics.

Apparel

The *apparel market* includes items that will be worn. Fabrics are fabricated, sewn, or constructed into infant's wear, children's wear, girl's and boy's wear, and men's and women's wear. Skirts, blouses, pants, shirts, lingerie, underwear, T-shirts, socks, hosiery, coats, scarves, mittens, gloves, sweaters, warm-up suits, swimsuits, jogging shorts and tops, as well as many other apparel items, constitute this market. Although protective garments for fire-fighters, pilots, pesticide applicators, and similar hazardous occupations, as well as uniforms for military and airline personnel, are items that are worn,

they are considered part of the industrial and consumer market rather than part of the apparel market.

Interior Textiles

Carpeting, draperies, curtains, upholstery, and wall coverings are the products in the *interior textiles market*. All are used as surface treatments within homes and commercial buildings. Textiles destined for use in public buildings, such as hospitals, nursing homes, movie theaters, government buildings, and corporate offices, are generally designed to withstand more vigorous wear and tear than that encountered in a home. These textiles form a *contract* interior textiles market.

Household and Institutional Textiles

All textile products used within the home, except carpets, drapes and curtains, wallcoverings, and upholstery, are usually considered *household textiles*.[3] Bedsheets, pillowcases, mattress pads, towels, blankets, tablecloths, and the like constitute this category. These same items, when used in hospitals, nursing homes, restaurants, and other public places, form an *institutional textiles market*.

Industrial and Consumer Textiles

For centuries, "textile products" meant only apparel items, household products, interior textiles, and a limited list of diverse industrial products. Over the last 20–25 years, however, the list of products in the industrial and consumer textiles market has increased dramatically. This growth is attributed to the fact that engineers and others concerned with the development and utilization of materials have increasingly recognized some of the unique and exceptional properties of textiles and worked to design specific textiles for specific applications.

Donald Keen defines the industrial and consumer textiles market by saying, "If you don't wear it, sit on it, or walk on it, it is an industrial textile."[4] *Industrial textiles* include filters, automobile safety belts, and enormous structures, such as storage tanks, tents, and roofs. *Geotextiles* are generally used in soil and soil-based applications, such as road building, dam construction, and erosion control. Protective clothing worn in hazardous work situations, as when pouring molten metal, fighting fires, and cleaning up chemical spills, is part of the industrial textiles market. The construction, mining, sanitation, fishing, aerospace, and transportation (shipping, sailing, automotive, etc.) industries, as well as the medical community and the military, purchase diverse industrial textile products.

Consumer textiles include recreational items, such as tents and backpacks. Textiles are used in the manufacture of other recreational products; as examples, tennis rackets and golf clubs may be reinforced with fibers, balls are covered with fabrics, and baseballs are filled with wool yarn. These recreational products are not textile products, however. Book packs, awnings, and umbrellas are further examples of consumer textile products.

---

[3] Sometimes the household textiles market includes interior textile products as well. Interior textiles are separated here because many interior design students enrolled in textile courses are primarily interested in the narrower interior textiles market.

[4] J. Donald Keen, "Celanese Fibers," presentation to the New York City Chapter of the American Association for Textile Technology (January 14, 1985).

CLOSELY RELATED MATERIALS: OTHER THIN, FLEXIBLE, FIBROUS MATERIALS

Closely related to textile fabrics are other thin, flexible, sheet materials that are fibrous. These materials include paper, leather, and fur.

Paper and Paper-like Textiles

Paper is "a material made from flexible cellulose fibers which, while very short (0.02 to 0.16 inch or 0.5 to 4.0 millimeter) are 100 times as long as they are wide."[5] Any fibrous raw material, such as wood, straw, bamboo, hemp, sisal, flax, cotton, jute, or ramie, can be used in paper manufacture. The fibers are separated during a pulping process. Wood is the major source of fiber for pulping. Pulped fibers have a strong attraction for water and for each other; when suspended in water, they swell. If many, suspended fibers are filtered onto a wire screen, they adhere weakly to each other. As more water is removed from the fibers on the screen by suction, they are forced closer together and the sheet becomes somewhat stronger but is still relatively weak. As the sheet dries, it becomes much stronger and paper is produced. The largest use for paper is paperboard (sheets of varied thickness used in packaging), followed by printing and writing papers and sanitary tissues.

The textile structure most closely related to paper is a *wet-laid fiber web*, also called a disposable nonwoven (Chapter 28). A wet-laid fiber web is composed of randomly distributed cellulose fibers; a portion of these fibers are of "textile length" (longer than fibers used to manufacture paper). As the name "wet-laid" indicates, the short and "textile length" fibers are suspended in water and filtered as they are in papermaking. The "textile length" fibers are often rayon fibers: a type of manufactured cellulose fiber (Chapter 14). The fibers in the web generally must be bonded by glue or adhesive to provide structural integrity. The greater the proportion of rayon fibers in the web, the less paper-like (the more textile-like) the fibrous sheet material becomes. Wet-laid fiber webs with which you may be familiar are patient examination gowns used at a doctor's office, disposable bedsheets and pillowcases, and surgical packs and gowns.

It is difficult to distinguish wet-laid fiber webs from

---

[5] *McGraw-Hill Encyclopedia of Science and Technology* (New York: McGraw-Hill, 1987).

some types of paper. Several criteria are applied to help make this distinction. Compared to paper, wet-laid fiber webs usually are more silent (they rustle less), softer, and, in some cases, washable. Wet-laid fiber webs, when extended over the edge of a surface, generally bend in more than one direction (they are said to "drape"). In contrast, paper bends in only one direction when extended over the edge of a surface. As a general rule, paper holds a crease and a wet-laid textile does not.

Leather and Leather-like Textiles

Leather is "the pelt of an animal which has been transformed by tanning into a nonputrescible, useful material."[6] Cattle are usually the source of the hide, but pigs, horses, goats, and other animals may be sources. Hides are perishable; if left untreated, they begin to decompose within hours after being removed from a carcass. Leather is a stable product that is no longer susceptible to rotting (putrefaction). Suede is leather that has been given a soft, napped surface.

Leather is a thin material composed of collagen fibers. When used for apparel items, such as coats, vests, shoes, boots, belts, and as upholstery material, it is flexible. Leather is usually not considered a textile, even though it is fibrous. Its fibers do not have a separate identity in the textile sense.

Leather-like textiles are synthetic materials that are used as substitutes for leather. Some leather-like fabrics are coated fabrics, consisting of a woven base to which a solid and expanded vinyl substance has been added (Chapter 29). They are often used in upholstery as well as in apparel and accessory applications. Some suede-like fabrics are composed of extremely fine fibers surrounded by nonfibrous, polyurethane foam. Fabric trademarks are Facile®, Ultrasuede®, and Belleseime®; the first two are distributed by the Skinner Division of Springs Mills; the third, by the Kanebo Company in Japan.

The surfaces of woven and knit fabrics can be modified so that they appear to be suede or chamois-like. Mechanical treatments, such as emerizing, sanding, and sueding (Chapter 32), are often used for this purpose. These fabrics are easy to distinguish from leather. When the edges of leather or leather-like applique are hidden from view, it is difficult even for experts to tell the materials apart. This fact has caused problems for drycleaners, who often are unable to judge the correct drycleaning procedure for such items.

Furs, Animal Fibers, and Fur-like Textiles

Fur "means any animal skin or part thereof with hair, fleece, or fur fiber attached. . . . ."[7] The pelt has been converted to leather, but the beautiful hair fibers are carefully preserved. Furs are not considered to be textiles. The use of furs has become a controversial and heated issue between animal-rights activists and the fur industry. Fur-like fabrics, many of which are pile-knit fabrics (Chapter 27), closely resemble furs in appearance and feel.

When the hair is removed from the pelt, the hair fiber is considered to be a textile fiber. Angora rabbit hair fibers can be processed into yarns and the yarns can be made into fabric (angora sweaters). Some hair fibers (for example, mink and reindeer) may be combined with other textile fibers (generally wool or silk) and made into fabrics. It is difficult to spin some hair fibers because they are either too short or too slippery to process successfully into yarns and fabrics.

CHAPTER SUMMARY

A textile fabric is "a planar structure consisting of yarns or fibers." Both fibers and yarns are cylindrical structures; they are very long in relation to their widths. Fibers form the fundamental unit of yarns and therefore of fabric. A fabric's construction depends on how the fibers and yarns are arranged to form the cohesive planar structure. Fabrics tend to be highly porous due to the interstices (voids or spaces) between fibers (the fundamental units) and yarns. Fabrics also may contain colorants and finishing chemicals. All these aspects of fabric structure impact on the performance of the fabric.

Fabrics are manufactured into products that are purchased by ultimate consumers. Fabricated textile products can be grouped into four major markets: apparel, household and institutional textiles, interior textiles, and industrial and consumer textiles.

Paper, leather, and fur are thin, flexible structures that are fibrous but are not textile fabrics. The fibers in paper are significantly shorter than fibers that can be converted into textile fabric, the fibers in leather cannot be separated from each other, and fur fibers are attached to a pelt.

---

[6] New England Tanners Club, *Leather Facts: A Picturesque Account of One of Nature's Miracles*, 1st ed. (Peabody, MA: New England Tanners Club, 1965).

[7] *Rules and Regulations Under the Fur Products Labeling Act* (Washington, DC: The Federal Trade Commission, effective August 9, 1952; amended July 4, 1980).

Durability Properties

Durability is the ability of a textile to retain its physical integrity under conditions of mechanical stress for a reasonable period of time.

PERFORMANCE PROPERTY	DEFINITION
Strength	Ability of a textile to withstand rupture as pulling, tearing, and bursting forces are encountered.
Breaking/tensile/tenacity	Ability to withstand a longitudinal pulling force.
Tearing	Ability to resist further rupture when a lateral pulling force is applied at a cut or hole in a fabric.
Bursting	Ability to retain integrity under a distending force.
Elongation*	Ability of a textile to extend when mechanical forces (particularly longitudinal pulling forces) are encountered, thereby retaining its physical integrity until a force of sufficient magnitude causes rupture.
Elastic recovery† (elasticity)	Ability of a textile to return to its original dimensions after being stressed (generally elongated), enabling the textile to readily absorb the next applied stress.
Abrasion resistance	Ability of a textile to withstand rubbing (frictional force) on its surface. The three types of abrasion are *flat, edge,* and *flex.*
Flexibility**	Ability of a textile to retain its physical integrity when subjected to repeated bending forces.

*Elongation is also a component of stretch and plays important roles in body-movement comfort and in shape retention—an aesthetic aspect of textiles (see Detail Views 3 and 4).

†Elastic recovery is necessary for shape retention in both stable and stretch textiles (see Detail Views 3 and 4).

**Flexibility also indicates the amount of force required to bend or flex a fiber, yarn, or fabric (finished or unfinished); in this context, flexibility is related to the softness or stiffness (flexural rigidity) of the textile (see Detail View 4).

2

$\mathcal{D}$urability

Much has been written about the stresses that people are exposed to during their lifetimes and the effects of such stresses on them. Textiles must also cope with different types of stress, many of which are mechanical, as they are worn, used, and laundered. Textile fabrics are pulled, twisted, bent, and rubbed. These stresses may be mild and infrequent or they may be harsh and continuous. Textile scientists have studied the effects of mechanical stresses on fibers, yarns, and fabrics and used this knowledge to develop fabrics that will be durable in use.

Fabrics in formal evening wear worn to a dinner or cocktail party encounter small, but repeated, mechanical stresses. Similarly, fabric in an infant's christening gown or upholstery fabric on an antique chair, which is to be admired solely for its beauty, does not need to be very durable in its environment of mild use and wear.

Sportswear fabrics must withstand harsher mechanical stresses, such as pulling and bending, as wearers run, swing, bend, twist, and otherwise move their bodies while playing games or enjoying the sporting events. The fabric in a road-construction worker's clothing or in a physically active five-year-old's outdoor play clothing must withstand considerable rubbing against rough surfaces and resist tearing when it comes into contact with machinery or playground equipment. A carpet in a school hallway must withstand the abrasive action of sand embedded within the pile and constant treading on its surface.

Textiles in tire cords must withstand constant flexing. In aircraft tires, the shock of landing must be withstood

time after time. Ropes for all purposes, such as mountain climbing and parachuting, must not fail when sudden forces are applied. The fabric layers in bulletproof vests, which are designed to prevent a high-speed bullet from penetrating, must not completely rupture.

Most textiles "wear out" over time because mechanical forces cause the structure to disintegrate. How long a textile should maintain a minimum physical integrity depends partially on the product. Generally, carpets and draperies are expected to be durable (not "wear out") for a longer time period than apparel items are. Nonwoven, disposable textiles, such as gowns worn at the doctor's office, are expected to be durable for a very short period; they must retain their physical integrity for a few minutes or hours at most.

Textile durability is the ability of the textile to retain its physical integrity under conditions of mechanical stress for a "reasonable" period of time.[1] A durable textile does not tear, break, rupture, develop holes, become thin, or completely wear away when it is exposed to pulling, rubbing, flexing, and twisting forces during wear, use, and care procedures. A textile that is not durable enough to resist these mechanical forces is of little value, no matter what other performance attributes it may have.

An understanding of strength, elongation, elastic recovery, abrasion resistance, and flexibility is required to evaluate the durability of fabrics. Data regarding these

---

[1] M. Joseph, *Introductory Textile Science*, 5th ed. (New York: Holt, Rinehart and Winston, 1986), p. 363.

performance properties reveals the ability of the textile to withstand specific types of mechanical forces. The definitions of durability performance properties are given in Detail View 2.

Nonmechanical factors in the environment, such as ultraviolet light, chemicals, and microorganisms, also may alter the durability of a textile. The effects of these nonmechanical factors on textile durability are considered in Chapter 5.

STRENGTH

The *strength* of a textile is its ability to withstand rupture as pulling, tearing, and bursting forces are encountered. Three types of textile strength are breaking, tearing, and bursting.

Breaking (Tensile) Strength

Breaking (tensile) strength is the ability of a textile to withstand a longitudinal pulling force (Figure 2.1). To determine breaking strength, two places (ends) on a fi-

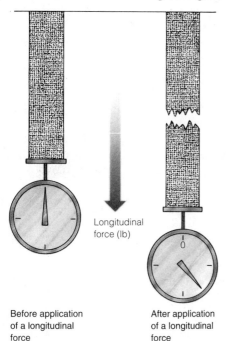

FIGURE 2.1 The application of a longitudinal pulling force to determine breaking strength.

Longitudinal force (lb)

Before application of a longitudinal force

After application of a longitudinal force

ber, yarn, or fabric are held securely while a longitudinal pulling force is applied. The greatest longitudinal force that the textile (fiber, yarn, or fabric) can bear without rupturing is its breaking strength. Textile professionals use the term "tensile," rather than "breaking," when discussing the strength of fibers.

How Much Strength? The relative breaking strengths of textiles, particularly fibers and yarns, can be determined with hands and muscles. Differences in the amount of exertion required to rupture the fiber or yarn can be felt. The breaking strengths of many fabrics may be beyond the maximum force that many people can exert. In the laboratory, an instrument called a tensile tester records the force (pounds, grams, newtons, etc.) necessary to rupture the textile. The higher the force required, the greater the breaking strength.

It is customary to express breaking strength in terms of force per unit area or force per unit width to permit the comparison of breaking strengths of equal amounts of textile material. For fibers and yarns, tensile or breaking strength is given as force per cross-sectional area because fibers and yarns are basically rodlike structures. Specifically, grams per denier (g/den) or newtons per tex (n/tex) are generally used. Grams and newtons are units of force; denier and tex are indications or measures related to the unit area. For fabrics, breaking strength is normally reported as force, with an indication of the width of fabric tested. Generally, the width is one inch.

Further, breaking strength data is usually only provided for woven fabrics. A strength measurement is reported for the crosswise and for the lengthwise direction of these fabrics.

Longitudinal Forces in Use Situations. Considerable breaking strength is required for end uses in which the fabric will be subjected to large, longitudinal forces. Wall-to-wall carpets must have a high enough breaking strength to withstand the carpet installer's forceful pulls to make the carpet, which is tacked along the wall at the opposite side of the room, lie flat and smooth. In draperies, the weight of the fabric itself provides a downward pulling force. If the drapery fabric is not stronger than this downward force, it will rupture. Although a drapery is not likely to rupture under its own weight, the effect of the downward pulling force can sometimes be seen in a lengthening of the drapery over time.

The tighter that garments fit and/or the more difficult they are to put on, the greater the breaking strength of the fabric must be. When a person sits down in a pair of

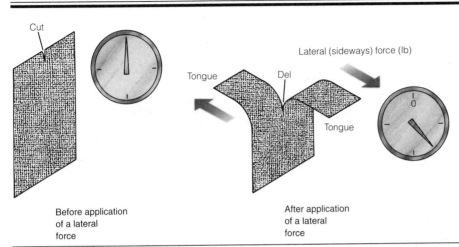

FIGURE 2.2 The application
of a lateral pulling force at a cut
to determine tearing strength.

Cut

Lateral (sideways) force (lb)

Tongue   Del

Tongue

0

Before application
of a lateral
force

After application
of a lateral
force

pants, especially tight ones, the fabric is pulled forcefully between knee and hip as well as across the hip. Pulling a tight-necked T-shirt over the head and putting on pantyhose are other examples of sizable longitudinal pulling forces being exerted on a garment fabric. Fabric lacking sufficient breaking strength will rupture if its breaking strength is exceeded by the pulling force. More often, a garment seam, rather than the fabric itself, ruptures because the seam is weaker than the fabric.

Safety belts, parachute harnesses and fabric, cargo slings, and ropes are examples of consumer and industrial textiles that must withstand large, longitudinal forces. Failure to maintain physical integrity in these end use situations is more disastrous than the mere embarrassment of a rupturing garment or interior textile fabric. People can be critically injured and/or monetary loss can be sustained if the textile should fail.

As a Predictor of Wearlife. Breaking strength is accepted as one of the most important textile properties because it provides a comprehensive check of most features of fabric composition and finishing. Breaking strength can be an indication of the coherence of a textile; without a sufficient amount of coherence, all other textile properties would be of little value. Breaking strength is of greatest value in checking the effect of manufacturing on the ultimate strength of the fabric. A minimum breaking strength specification restricts the manufacturer to the use of a minimum-quality fiber and yarn. The resulting fabrics have less mechanical and chemical damage at point of sale.

Breaking strength is not the best indicator of the serviceability of apparel and interior textile fabrics, even though certain applications do demand a minimum breaking strength. Longitudinal forces encountered in use are rarely great enough to break these fabrics. The amount of breaking strength provided by the manufacturer is usually sufficient for the intended use of the fabric.

Tearing Strength

Tearing strength is the ability of a fabric to resist further rupture when a lateral (sideways) pulling force is applied at a cut or hole in the fabric. *Tearing* refers to the progressive rupture of a fabric along a line. In woven fabric, the tear progresses yarn by yarn. The position of the yarns at the del, the triangular distortion at the active region of tearing, and the position of the yarns just ahead of the tear are distorted during tear action on a woven fabric. The yarn distortion and tearing action illustrated in Figure 2.2 can be confirmed by cutting a small slit in the edge of a woven fabric, observing the initial positions of the yarns at the end of the cut, then exerting a sidewise or lateral force to begin a tearing action, and finally observing the position of the same yarns again.

In fabrics that do not contain yarns, tearing occurs as the fibers are separated by the lateral pulling force. The action is quite similar to tearing a piece of paper. Tearing a nonwoven, interfacing fabric illustrates the mechanism of tear in a fabric composed directly of fibers.

Tearing strength is more directly related to serviceability than breaking strength, because tearing strength is a reflection of the individual strength of yarns. Yarn strength is considerably lower than fabric strength. Therefore, fabrics are more likely to rupture when tear-

FIGURE 2.3 The application of a distending force—a force perpendicular to a fabric surface—to determine bursting strength.

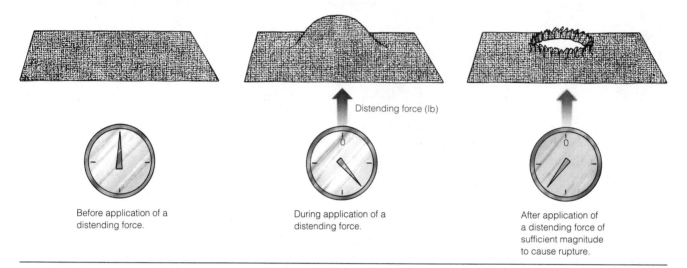

Distending force (lb)

Before application of a distending force.

During application of a distending force.

After application of a distending force of sufficient magnitude to cause rupture.

ing (lateral) forces are applied than under longitudinal forces.

How Much Tearing Strength? In the laboratory, the ends (tongues) of a piece of cut fabric are clamped into an instrument (Figure 2.2).[2] A lateral force is exerted, and the instrument records the force (in grams, newtons, pounds, etc.) required to tear the fabric. The greater the force, the greater the tearing strength of the fabric.

Tearing Forces in End Use. Insufficient tearing strength is a more common reason for the failure of fabric in use and wear than insufficient breaking strength. In World War I, the tearing strength, rather than the breaking strength, was the cause of concern in selecting the fabric used to cover airplane wings. It was essential for the fabric to retain its integrity if it was ruptured by a bullet during combat. Considerable research was conducted at that time to develop suitable fabrics that would withstand such tearing phenomena.

Fabrics used to cover stadiums and other large structures must have excellent tear resistance. Should a hole develop in the fabric, the fabric must not split. The fabric covering on the U.S. pavilion at the 1970s World's Fair in Spokane, Washington, continuously tore.

Sufficient tear resistance allows apparel fabrics that develop holes from cigarette ashes or abrasive action to remain intact for further use. Fabric apparel may also tear when pockets or ornamentation are caught and pulled away from the base fabric.

Bursting Strength

The *bursting strength* of a textile is its ability to retain physical integrity when subjected to a distending or swelling force; a force applied perpendicular to the fabric surface. When a fabric is held taut and a force is brought to bear on its surface, the fabric may distend. The yarns in a fabric change positions and lengthen as the force increases. If the distending force becomes great enough, the fabric will give way or burst (Figure 2.3).

To confirm the action of a distending force on a fabric, place a nonwoven, interfacing fabric in an embroidery hoop, suspend the hoop over a glass, and then push down on the fabric with your middle finger. Observe that the fabric "swells," becoming rounded under the area of pressure; when the downward distending force is great enough, the fabric ruptures. You also can feel this distending force when you bend your arm while wearing

---

[2] The instruments are either a tensile tester or an *Elemdorf tearing strength tester.* The methods for quantifying tearing strength can be found in the *American Society for Testing and Materials* (ASTM) *Annual Book of Standards,* Section 7 (Philadelphia: Methods D2261-83, D2262-83, and D1424-83, 1990).

a close-fitting, long-sleeved shirt; your elbow pushes against the sleeve fabric.

How Much Bursting Strength? The number of pounds, grams, or newtons of distending force required to rupture the fabric is its bursting strength. The greater the force, the higher the bursting strength of the fabric.

Bursting Strength in End Use. Bursting strength is an important property when a fabric must withstand a force perpendicular to its surface. This occurs at the knees of tight pants when the wearer stoops down. Trampoline and parachute fabric are subjected to repeated forces of considerable magnitude perpendicular to their surfaces.

ELONGATION

Elongation is the ability of a textile to extend when subjected to mechanical forces, particularly pulling, tearing, and bursting forces (Figure 2.4). Such extension, or "give," permits the textile to absorb the force attempting to rupture it. During the time the textile is extending, it does not rupture. If the force is removed before maximum extension is reached, the textile does not rupture. If maximum extension is reached and the force is still applied, however, the textile will probably rupture.

How Much Elongation?

Elongation is determined by marking a distance on the fiber, yarn, or fabric and then applying a pulling force. The distance extended is noted (see Figure 2.4). Percent elongation is calculated as

$$\frac{\text{Extended Length} - \text{Unextended Length}}{\text{Unextended Length}} \times 100$$
$$= \% \text{ Elongation}$$

If the force is great enough to extend the textile to its maximum, to the point at which rupture occurs, the percent elongation calculated is called elongation at break.

Consider the percent elongation at break of a swimsuit fabric. A 10-inch (in) or 25.4 centimeter (cm) line is marked on the fabric (the unextended length). The fabric is grasped at the 10-in mark and pulled with considerable force. Just at the point of break, the length of the line is 20.5 in (52.1 cm)—the extended length. The percent elongation at break of the swimsuit fabric is therefore

$$\frac{20.5 - 10.0}{10.0} \times 100 = 105\%$$

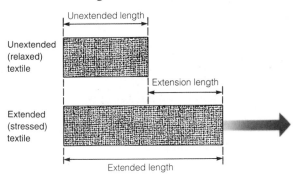

FIGURE 2.4   The application of a pulling force to determine elongation.

In comparison, consider the elongation in the crosswise direction of a woven shirt fabric. Again, a 10-in line is drawn on the fabric and the fabric extended to its rupture point. At the point of rupture, the length of the line is 10.25 in (26 cm). Therefore, the percent elongation at break of the woven shirt fabric is

$$\frac{10.25 - 10.0}{10.0} \times 100 = 2.5\%$$

Swimsuit fabric extends considerably farther than woven fabric before the force breaks it. The higher the percent of elongation at break, the greater the extension under force.

Elongation in End Use

Fibers and yarns must have some ability to elongate to withstand the stresses placed on them in yarn and/or fabric manufacture. The minimum amount of elongation a fiber may have is ~1%. Rupture occurs continuously without minimum elongation. Glass fibers, even though they are strong, are difficult to form into yarns and fabric because their elongation is so low.

Fabric to be used in a high-impact application, such as a bullet-proof vest or a trampoline, will be engineered to have a specific degree of elongation. The fabric then will extend when the force is applied, preventing the buildup of an excessive force that could cause it to rupture.

Knit fabrics are often made with low-twist yarns. These yarns are not as strong as the yarns used in woven fabrics. Soft yarns can be used successfully in knit fabrics because the loops of yarn reposition themselves into a straighter configuration as a knit fabric is pulled, permitting it to elongate. The yarns do not need to withstand the applied force until they are repositioned as much as possible in the knit structure.

Elongation Related to Other Fabric Properties

As has been emphasized, elongation is an important aspect of fabric strength. A textile will not rupture under a longitudinal, lateral, or distending force until it has extended to its maximum length.

Elongation is also an important consideration in the shape retention of fabrics. Fabrics with low elongation tend to keep their original dimensions during use; they do not bag or sag. Fabrics with a high degree of elongation, on the other hand, may not retain their shape while in use. Of course, shape retention also depends on whether the fabric will return to its original length when the force is removed. This property, called elastic recovery, is examined in the next section.

Elongation is also related to elastic recovery and to stretch. To determine elastic recovery, the textile first must be elongated. Elongation is one of the two components used to determine stretch. The relationship of elongation to stretch, elastic recovery, and shape retention is clarified further in Chapters 3 and 4.

Textile stiffness, discussed in Chapter 4, is also related to elongation. Generally, textiles with less elongation tend to be stiffer than those with more elongation.

ELASTIC RECOVERY (ELASTICITY)

Elastic recovery, or *elasticity*, is the ability of a textile to return to its original dimensions after being stressed or elongated (Figure 2.5). A key word in this definition is "return." Elastic recovery is an important aspect of textile durability. The more fully a textile can recover from an applied stress, the more likely it will be to withstand the next stress it encounters.

How Much Elastic Recovery?

Elastic recovery can be determined for fibers, yarns, and fabrics. The textile is extended (a force is applied), and the force is then removed. Generally, a length is marked on the textile before extension; the textile is extended a specific amount (say 10% of its original length), and the length is measured again after the force is released (see Figure 2.5). These length measurements are used

FIGURE 2.5   **The application of a pulling force and release of that force to determine elastic recovery.**

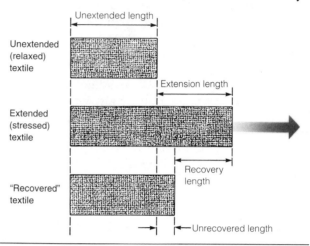

to calculate the elastic recovery, which is expressed as a percent:

$$\frac{\text{Extended Length} - \text{Unrecovered Length}}{\text{Extended Length} \times 100}$$
$$= \% \text{ Elastic Recovery}$$

Let's consider the elastic recovery of nylon fiber and polyester fiber when each has been extended 3%. The length marked on each unextended fiber is 100 in (254.0 cm), although any length could be marked. A force is applied so that each fiber lengthens to 100.3 in (261.6 cm), which is 3% elongation. When the stress is removed and the length of each fiber is determined, the polyester is 100.72 in (255.78 cm) long and the nylon is 100.33 in (254.84 cm) long.

The calculation of percent elastic recovery for nylon is

$$\frac{3.0 - 0.33}{3.0} \times 100 = 89\%$$

because the extended length is 103 − 100 and the unrecovered length is 100.33 − 100.

The calculation of percent elastic recovery for polyester is

$$\frac{3.0 - 0.72}{3.0} \times 100 = 76\%$$

because the extended length is 103 − 100 and the unrecovered length is 100.72 − 100.

FIGURE 2.6 The application of a rubbing force to determine abrasion resistance.

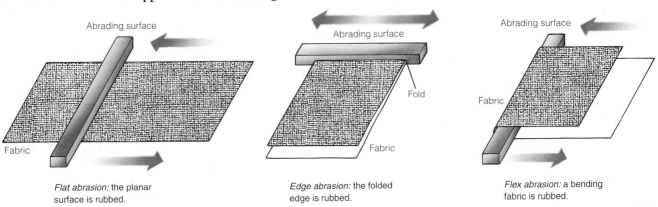

Flat abrasion: the planar surface is rubbed.

Edge abrasion: the folded edge is rubbed.

Flex abrasion: a bending fabric is rubbed.

Nylon fiber recovers more fully than polyester fiber when elongated 3%. The closer the percent of elastic recovery is to 100%, the greater the recovery is to the original length. The closer the percent of elastic recovery is to 0%, the smaller the recovery is to the original length. At 0%, the textile remains at the extended length after the pulling force is removed.

It is always important to know the amount of elongation when considering the elastic recovery of a textile. In general, the greater the elongation (stress), the lower the elastic recovery; the smaller the stress, the better the elastic recovery. However, some fibers recover better from higher elongation than from lower elongation.

Importance in End Use

Polyester and nylon fibers have almost equal breaking strengths but differ substantially in ability to recover from a stress that elongated them by 3%. This difference in elastic recovery leads to quite different end uses for polyester and nylon. For example, nylon fibers dominate the market for women's sheer hosiery. Fine nylon yarns can be used in sheer hosiery because the nylon fiber not only extends during leg movement but recovers well from this extension over time. Hosiery can fit close to the leg, move with the leg, and recover from pulling stresses. The nylon fibers do not break; the hosiery does not bag or sag. Nylon also is used far more extensively in ropes and cordage than polyester, because nylon fibers absorb repeated large stresses better.

Polyester fiber is used far more extensively in clothing than nylon fiber because it recovers better from low repeated stresses. This performance is required in apparel fabrics, which are subjected to only small repeated stresses when worn and laundered.

Relationship to Other Fabric Properties

Elastic recovery is not synonymous with stretch. Elastic recovery is, however, an important aspect of the stretch performance of a textile. Further clarification of the relationship of and distinction between these performance properties is given in Chapter 3. Elastic recovery is also related to the property shape retention (Chapter 4).

ABRASION RESISTANCE

Abrasion resistance is the ability of a textile to withstand rubbing (frictional force) applied to its surface (Figure 2.6).[3] Fabrics with high (excellent) abrasion resistance retain their physical integrity. Fabrics with low (poor) abrasion resistance become thin and/or develop holes.

Frictional Damage in End Use

Deterioration occurs continually as a fabric is subjected to friction during wear, use, and laundering. The sever-

---

[3] The American Society for Testing and Materials does not define "abrasion resistance." The *ASTM Annual Book of Standards* defines *abrasion* as "the wearing away of any part of a material by rubbing against any other surface" (p. 12).

ity of abrasive action received by a fabric depends on the roughness of the rubbing surface, on the frequency of rubbing, and on the pressure applied during rubbing. Manufacturers devote considerable effort to the development of high abrasion resistance in textile materials that are to be subjected to considerable rubbing such as carpeting used in high traffic areas.

Inflicted Fiber Damage. Mild frictional wear occurs as a fabric slides over a flat, relatively slick surface. Little distortion of the fibers, yarns, or fabric occurs. The continual movement of long sleeves over a desk surface and the movement of an iron over fabric represent smooth frictional wear. The action is mild, so long periods of time pass before the fibers and, consequently, the fabric show signs of wear.

More severe frictional wear occurs during laundry. Fabrics rub against one another and against the sides of the washer and dryer.

Fabric movement over rough surfaces causes even faster fabric deterioration. A fabric becomes noticeably thinner after a short exposure to a high abrasive force. Loss of fibers from the fabric and damage to the fiber surfaces generally occur. The abrasion suffered by denim fabric in the knees and seat of children's blue jeans is largely due to fiber damage, breakage, and loss.

Abradants may become embedded within the fabric in use and even during laundry. Sharp abradants, which are small relative to fiber diameter, may cut or grind fiber surfaces. For example, calcium carbonate deposits can accumulate on fabric during laundry, usually when non-phosphate detergents are used in hard water and no water softening product is added. The calcium carbonate particles can cut into fiber surfaces as the fabric is worn, causing abrasive damage.

Carpet fibers may be abraded by sand and other small particles that become embedded within the pile. Walking over the carpet causes these particles to grind away at fiber surfaces. Eventually, the fibers break away and the pile becomes less dense. Periodic vacuuming is recommended to reduce this type of abrasive damage to carpets.

Other Harmful Effects. The effect of frictional force on the textile is not limited to deterioration due to fiber damage and loss; a frictional force can cause undesirable changes in fabric appearance. Abrasion can significantly alter the position of yarns in the fabric, cause fabric distortion, and otherwise injure the fabric structure. A smooth fabric may develop a hairy surface; a napped fabric, such as flannel, may lose its raised fiber surface and appear threadbare. Worsted suiting may develop an unpleasant shine, but other cloths may lose their lus-

trous appearance. *Pilling,* the development of small balls of fuzz on the fabric surface, is a direct result of abrasion. When colorants are rubbed from a fabric by another material, the abrading fabric can become stained.

For most modern apparel fabrics, with the exception of some uniforms and other workclothes, the change from a new to a "used" appearance is probably more important than the mechanical breakdown of the fabric. A change in fabric appearance usually occurs sooner than actual fabric damage and therefore is the limiting factor in how long the garment is worn. A further discussion of changes in fabric appearance is included in Chapter 4.

Flat, Edge, and Flex Abrasion

Textile products are subjected to abrasion on their flat fabric surface and where the fabric is folded. Abrasion damage also occurs within the fabric as it flexes and bends during use. These types of abrasion are called flat, edge, and flex, respectively (see Figure 2.6).

Flat abrasion occurs when the fabric is flat—for example, on bedsheets, when sleepers lie on them; in jackets, at the elbows; in trousers, at the knees, seat, and inside the legs; and in socks at the heels and toes. The arms and seat cushions of upholstered furniture "wear out" largely due to flat abrasive action. Carpet "wears out" in traffic paths, due to both flat and flex abrasive action.

Edge abrasion occurs at fabric folds. Fabric damage in shirts tends to appear around the collar and cuff folds long before abrasive damage occurs on the shirt front, elbows, or sleeves. "Wear" is usually visible at the cuff and pocket edges in trousers before it occurs on the seat of the pants.

Flex abrasion results from unidirectional bending. Bending creates internal friction in the fabric, which causes fiber deterioration or breakage. In a laboratory, a fabric is flexed (pulled) over a bar or other wear surface. The passage of the fabric over the bar creates friction between the fabric and bar edge. This type of abrasion occurs when carpet fibers rub against each other as the yarns flex and bend under the compressive forces of people walking over them. Embedded abradants often do their damage when the fabric is flexed.

How Abrasion Resistant?

Abrasion resistance is usually determined for fabrics but also may be determined for yarns. It is extremely difficult to quantify abrasion resistance in a meaningful way. Abrasion resistance is often specified by giving the number of times a fabric must be rubbed until a hole forms in it. The conditions under which the fabric is rubbed are

FIGURE 2.7 The application of a bending force to determine flexibility.

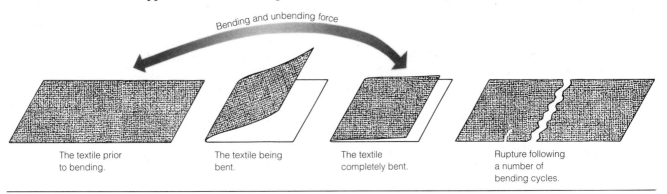

Bending and unbending force

The textile prior to bending.

The textile being bent.

The textile completely bent.

Rupture following a number of bending cycles.

stated: the type of abrading material, the amount of the downward force, and the direction of abrasive action (back and forth or circular). Fabrics that can be rubbed a greater number of times have higher abrasion resistance.

Another method of quantifying abrasion resistance is to calculate the percent of fabric weight or strength lost due to abrasive action. The fabric is initially weighed, or its strength is determined. A fabric sample is then rubbed a predetermined number of times, its weight or breaking strength is determined again, and the percent of weight or strength lost is calculated. The greater the percent loss of strength or weight, the lower the resistance of the fabric to abrasion.

FLEXIBILITY

The *flexibility* of a textile is its ability to retain physical integrity when subjected to repeated bending forces (Figure 2.7). Failure to withstand repeated bending results in fatigue; the fabric splits, and the fibers break away.

Bending Forces in End Use

One reason textile materials are used in numerous products is because they are flexible. Flexibility is part of the definition of a textile. Without rupturing, textiles (fibers, yarns, and fabrics) can bend, twist, and flex.

When garments are worn, the degree of bending in the apparel fabric is usually small but occurs continuously. A skirt fabric and the fabric behind the knees of pant legs bend back and forth when a person walks. The fabric in the crotch and behind the knees of pants is more severely bent when the person sits down or stoops. Quite severe bending occurs when creases or pleats are pressed into pant legs or skirts; in such cases, the fabric is completely folded over on itself.

Pile yarns and fibers in carpeting must withstand the repeated bending and crushing that takes place as people continuously walk over them. Drapery fabric must flex—particularly at the header, where the fabric is folded and straightened each time the drapery is opened and closed.

Textiles with low or no flexibility can be useful. For example, carbon fibers and fabric break readily when bent or flexed. One severe bend and the fabric splits. Carbon fibers are very strong and very lightweight, and these performance properties can be advantageous if the fiber or fabric is not allowed to bend. Embedding the carbon fibers or fabric in a resin yields a highly rigid material. Carbon fibers are embedded in the shanks of many golf clubs; carbon fabric in a resin material is used for automobile and aircraft bodies.

How Flexible?

Flexibility can be quantified as the number of times a fiber, yarn, or fabric can be bent before breaking occurs. For example, wool fibers can be bent 20,000 times before rupturing, but cotton fibers rupture after about 2500 bends.[4] Therefore, wool fibers are said to have higher flexibility than cotton fibers.

Bending and Other Fabric Properties

What happens to a textile when it is bent is an important consideration in most end-use applications. Here, our

---

[4] *The World Book of Wool* (London: International Wool Secretariat, Department of Education, 1952).

concern has been how many times a textile can be bent before it breaks—the aspect of bending related to *wearlife,* or *durability.*

In addition, it is important to determine the ease with which a textile can be bent and can recover when the bending force is removed. The ease with which a textile bends is related to sensorial comfort, softness/stiffness, body, and drapability. Resistance to bending is called flexural rigidity, or simply flexibility. Most often, when the term "flexibility" is used in textiles, it refers to the ease of bending rather than to the ability to bend without breaking. The ability of the textile to recover from bending, so that it does not remain folded, is related to resilience, loft (compressional resilience), wrinkle recovery, and shape retention. These properties are discussed in Chapter 5.

USE OF LABORATORY DATA TO PREDICT WEARLIFE

There is poor correlation between laboratory determination of various aspects of fabric durability and actual fabric performance. In other words, it is not possible to say that due to a difference of so many pounds between the breaking strengths of two fabrics, one fabric can be expected to retain its physical integrity for a specifically longer time. One reason for the poor prediction from laboratory data lies in the magnitude of force applied in each situation. In the laboratory, fabrics are generally subjected to a force large enough to cause rupture on initial application. In most end-use situations, fabrics are exposed to repeated small forces.

Another important reason for poor prediction of durability is that the fabric is subjected to all types of forces in use (longitudinal, lateral, distending, frictional, and bending) all at the same time. In the laboratory, the textile scientist is only capable of exerting one or a few of these forces on a fabric at one time.

Wear studies, in which textiles are put into actual use for a period of time, are extremely important. The fabric receives the type of "wear" expected in consumer use. However, these studies require a long time to complete and are expensive.

CHAPTER SUMMARY

It is difficult to think of any textile application or end use for which a degree of durability is not essential. Even for fashion apparel, the fabric must have enough physical integrity to save the wearer from potential embarrassment created by fabric rupturing. At the other extreme, textile durability is of the highest priority when failure could result in loss of life. Strength (breaking, tearing, and bursting), abrasion resistance (flat, edge, and flex), elongation, elastic recovery, and flexibility are performance properties that comprise the durability of a textile. Fiber composition, yarn structure, fabric structure, and mechanical and chemical treatments all play an important role in determining the durability of a textile product. The definitions of each of the durability properties are given in Detail View 2.

Comfort Properties

Comfort is freedom from pain, freedom from discomfort. It is a neutral state.

PERFORMANCE PROPERTY	DEFINITION
Thermophysiological Comfort	**Attainment of a comfortable thermal and wetness state; involves transport of heat and moisture through a fabric.**
Insulative ability (thermal resistance)	Degree of resistance to heat transfer.
Water vapor permeability (breathability)	Rate of diffusion of body-generated water vapor through a fabric.
Wickability	Dispersion or spread of water through a given fabric area, vertically or horizontally, by capillary action.
Water content/regain	The total amount of water in a fabric.
Absorbency	Ability to take water internally into fibers.
Adsorbency	Ability to hold water on surfaces of fibers.
Imbibed water	Water contained within fabric interstices.
Drying rate	Time necessary for a fabric to dry.
Water repellency	Ability of a fabric to shed environmental water but to allow insensible perspiration to pass through.
Water resistance and Waterproofness	Ability of a fabric to resist wetting and penetration by water; ability of a fabric to provide a complete barrier to the penetration of water.
Sensorial Comfort	**The elicitation of various neural sensations when a textile comes into contact with the skin.**
Prickliness/Itchiness/Inflammation	Ability of a textile to trigger pain receptors in the skin.
Roughness	Ability of a textile to trigger the touch group of sensory receptors.
Thermal character (warm/cool feeling)	The apparent difference between the temperatures of the fibers and the skin of the observer touching them.
Electrical conductivity (cling and shock)	Ability of a textile to conduct electrons along its surface.
Body-movement comfort	**Ability of a textile to allow freedom of movement, reduced burden, and body shaping, as required.**
Stretch	Ability of a textile to extend under tension and then to recover relatively quickly and fully to its original dimensions.
Weight	Mass per unit area; determines the amount of burden to be carried by the wearer.
Pressure/compression	Ability of a textile to produce a compressive force sufficient to permit wearer comfort and body shaping.

3

Comfort

In Duluth, Minnesota, a third-year medical student steps into a tank of water which is maintained at a chilly temperature of 50° F (10° C). There he will spend the next 30 minutes as a human guinea pig so that data can be collected concerning how a person in street clothes responds physiologically to extreme cold. The Duluth scientists will compare this data with similar readings for volunteers in survival gear. The goal is to develop outerwear that will protect pilots and other wearers from hypothermia if they are dumped into icy waters.

A great deal of knowledge about the ability of fabric to provide *thermophysiological comfort* under more "normal" environmental conditions, as people relax and work, has been gained through experiments conducted under extreme weather conditions. Due to a greater emphasis on fitness in recent years, human volunteers have exercised for scientists in hot, humid environments and in hot, dry ones. Additional information has been gathered about heat and moisture flow through a variety of exercise-garment fabrics and the resulting effect on the fitness enthusiast's performance. Data about heat flow through draperies and carpeting has also been gathered.

In this chapter, we discuss the performance properties of fabrics that provide thermophysiological comfort. We also address two other important aspects of comfort: sensorial and body-movement comfort. Detail View 3 lists and defines each of the textile performance properties examined in this chapter.

WHAT IS COMFORT?

Comfort is defined as freedom from pain, freedom from discomfort. It is a neutral state. Textile scientists say that people are "comfortable" in their garments when they are unaware of them both psychologically and physiologically. In this textbook, only *physiological comfort* is addressed. Awareness of clothing usually leads to an expression of discomfort (too hot, too cool, too wet, too prickly, too heavy, too constraining). It is unusual to hear expressions of "positive" comfort.

In general, people consider themselves to be thermally comfortable when they do not need to take off or put on additional clothing (or, conversely, to change the room thermostat) to feel cooler or warmer. When a textile scientist questions subjects about their state of thermal comfort while sitting or exercising in a room at a set temperature and humidity, they usually indicate the degree of coolness or warmness away from a central point. That central or neutral point is "comfortable"; the state of "very comfortable" cannot be assessed. The same situation occurs when degree of wetness is of interest. When wetness is not sensed, people judge the fabric they are wearing to be comfortable; otherwise, they indicate some degree of wetness from the neutral state. The wearer is either comfortable or experiencing some degree of discomfort.

TEXTILE PERFORMANCE PROPERTIES AND THERMOPHYSIOLOGICAL COMFORT

Humans must maintain an internal body temperature close to 98.6° F (37° C). A rise or fall in this "core" temperature of ~9° F (5° C) is usually fatal. The body constantly generates heat from the metabolism of food and muscle activity and loses this heat to the environment. A balance must be maintained between the rates of heat production and heat loss. When the external temperature is 84° F (29° C), the heat production and heat loss of an unclothed human at rest are in balance.

The temperature range of the environment in which an unclothed human can survive is relatively small. Slightly cooler environments than 84° F (29° C) can be tolerated by increasing the amount of body heat produced through the consumption and metabolism of food and more vigorous physical activity. In addition, the human body will adjust the loss rate of body-generated heat by constricting the blood capillaries lying within the skin, so that blood carrying internal body heat is not circulated to the skin as rapidly. Shivering generates more body heat through muscle contractions and friction. In cold air, this is a plus. In cold water, however, shivering is a mixed blessing; the additional splashing that results drains away more body warmth than it produces. As the internal body temperature declines, the body takes more drastic action and limits the supply of blood to the arms and legs which are not essential to its survival. If a net heat loss occurs, the body core temperature drops and *hypothermia* may result.

An unclothed body in a hot environment is faced with cooling itself. It needs to dissipate body-generated heat as well as the heat the skin absorbs from the environment. Under these circumstances, the body dilates the blood capillaries. The evaporation rate of water diffusing from the body's interior to the skin surface increases and greater cooling takes place. As external heat increases, the body activates sweat glands and the liquid water (sweat or *sensible perspiration*) is evaporated for better cooling. An increase in activity level brings about the same physiological responses. Failure to dissipate sufficient heat may result in *hyperthermia*.

Surrounding the body with fabric extends the range of environments in which humans can work, live, and be thermally comfortable. In cold environments, the insulative capability of a fabric is of paramount importance. In hot environments, the resistance a fabric provides to the flow of heat from the body to the environment is detrimental to thermal comfort, but the ability of the fabric to prevent external heat from reaching the skin is highly important. When activity level is high in both cold and hot environments, the ability of fabric to transport moisture is essential to thermal as well as "wetness state" comfort.

Attainment of a Comfortable Thermal State

Heat is always being transferred in one way or another, wherever there is any difference in temperature. Just as water will run downhill, always flowing to the lowest possible level, heat (if left to itself) flows down the temperature hill, always warming the cold objects at the expense of the warmer ones. When considering heat flow through fabric, we must remember whether the body or the environmental temperature is higher, because this will determine the direction of heat flow. In a cold environment, heat will flow from the body to the environment. In a hot one, environmental heat will place a heat load on the body.

The rate at which heat flows depends on the steepness of the temperature hill as well as on the properties of the materials through which the heat has to flow. The difference in temperature per unit distance is called the *temperature gradient* (an analogy to steepness of grade which determines the rate of water flow).

Heat is transferred from a hotter object to a cooler object in one of three ways—by conduction, convection, or radiation.

Heat can flow by *conduction* only when collisions of neighboring molecules occur in stationary matter, as they do in fibers, metals, water, wood, or air. The outside surface of a teacup becomes warm because the heat of the water inside is conducted through the metal or clay forming the cup.

Convection is the transfer of heat from one place to another by actual motion of the hot material. Heat can be transferred by convection through gases (such as the air) and liquids (such as water). When cool air comes into contact with a heated surface, it expands in volume; being lighter than the surrounding air, it rises, drawing a cooling current of air over the warm surface. Air in a room is heated by convection. Air near the radiator is warmed; it moves upward to the ceiling, where it cools, and then moves downward to be heated again.

Radiation involves the transfer of heat by energy waves. Loss of heat by radiation does not require a material medium. Radiation occurs only from the surfaces of objects. Any object constantly emits radiation of a certain character and intensity, depending on its temperature. Objects differ in their ability to absorb, transmit, and reflect incident radiant energy on their surfaces. Objects that are excellent radiators are also excellent absorbers of incident radiant energy. The heat of the sun is transferred to the earth by radiation.

Heat Transfer from an Unclothed Body. In an environment at a lower temperature than skin temperature, an unclothed body loses body-generated heat to the environment. About 90% is emitted from the skin surface (80% by conduction, convection, and radiation and 10% by evaporation); the other 10% is lost through respiration. The skin, acting as a radiator, warms the immediately surrounding air by conduction. The heated air rises due to buoyancy, forming an envelope of air that moves upward and surrounds the unclothed body (Figure 3.1).

The convective upflow of air is thin and slow-moving at the ankles and lower legs, but quickly increases in velocity and thickness until it becomes vigorous over higher parts of the body. The plume of hot air above the head extends at least 5 feet (1.5 meters) before dispersing into the general room air.

In an indoor environment, the nude human body loses ~60% of its heat by radiation. The body is an excellent radiator. The walls or other nearby objects that receive this radiation also emit radiation, some of which is received and absorbed by the human body.[1] In an environment cooler than the human body, a net loss of radiated heat occurs which the individual can detect. For example, in a newly heated room where the air temperature is at a satisfactory level for thermal comfort, thermal discomfort can be noticed because the walls and furniture are still cold.

When an unclothed person is exposed to a source of radiant heat greater than that of the body, net thermal load is experienced. Radiant heat from a fire, molten metal, a room radiator, and the sun all increase skin temperature and create thermal load. Each source emits different wavelengths of thermal radiant energy, all of which are readily absorbed by the skin. The skin is a good absorber of energy over a wide spectral range.

Heat Transfer from a Clothed Body. The modes of heat transfer are the same for a clothed body as for an unclothed body—by conduction, convection, and radia-

FIGURE 3.1   Heat dissipation from an unclothed body in an environment of 77°F (25°C).
Some heat is radiated (⌇⌇➤) to cooler surfaces in the environment. Other heat is conducted (– – ➤) through the boundary layer of air which is 6–8 inches (0.15–0.20 meters) thick. Natural convective currents (⌣), with air velocities as high as 1.3–1.6 feet (0.4–0.5 meters) per second, move ~ 160 gallons (600 liters) of air per minute over the body surface. A plume of heated air rises ~ 5.0 feet (1.5 meters) above the head.

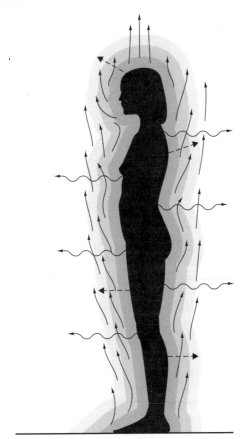

tion (Figure 3.2). Heat loss is due in part to the conduction of heat along the fibers having direct contact with the skin surface and in part to fiber-to-fiber contact. Heat may also be conducted through a boundary layer of air at the skin surface and then transferred to the fabric outer surface by (1) conduction through the fibers and air, and (2) by convection of air through the fabric interstices. At the fabric surface, the heat dissipates into the surroundings (1) by conduction through a layer of air close to the outer fabric surface and then by convection, and (2) by radiation to cooler surfaces of the en-

---

[1]Remember that good radiators are also excellent absorbers of incident radiant energy. The absorption of this energy raises the temperature of the object.

FIGURE 3.2 Heat flow through a fabric when skin temperature is higher than external temperature.

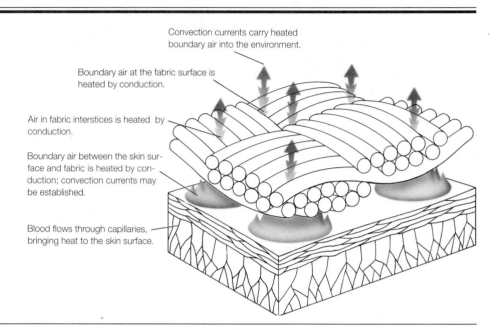

Convection currents carry heated boundary air into the environment.

Boundary air at the fabric surface is heated by conduction.

Air in fabric interstices is heated by conduction.

Boundary air between the skin surface and fabric is heated by conduction; convection currents may be established.

Blood flows through capillaries, bringing heat to the skin surface.

vironment. However, the fabric provides resistance to the flow of heat; it slows the rate at which heat is transferred from the skin to the environment.

Heat Transfer to and from Building Interiors. The greatest heat loss from a building interior to the exterior environment is through windows (that is, through glass). Glass does not prevent the transmission of the sun's radiant energy—an advantage in winter, when radiant energy is welcome, but not in the summer. As air is warmed at the surfaces of radiators by conduction, it expands and rises. Convective currents are established in the room, and the air in these currents is cooled as it moves over the cold glass surfaces of the windows. This air must then be reheated, increasing energy costs.

Heat is also lost through floors, particularly when the building is built on a slab. In this case, warm air heats the concrete, which conducts the heat away.

Why Fabrics Serve as Insulators. First, the ability of *fibers* to resist the flow of body-generated heat is excellent, because they have high resistance (low conductivity) to conductive heat flow compared to most other types of materials (Table 3.1). When fibers contact the skin, heat is not rapidly transferred to the external environment. If aluminum were placed on the skin, the heat flow would be 1000 times greater than the flow of

heat through an equal thickness of textile fibers. Heat flow is three times greater through water than along textile fibers.

Air is even more resistant to the flow of body-generated heat than fibers are. The thermal conductivity of air is eight times less than that of fibers, so heat flow is eight times slower through air than through textile fibers. Air is the best thermal insulator available. Since fabrics are composed of fibers and air, two materials that

TABLE 3.1 Thermal Conductivities of Different Materials.

	Metal	Glass	Water	Fiber	Air
Conductivity*	200,000	1000	600	200	25
Relative to Fiber		1000	5	3	1	−8
Relative to Air		8000	40	25	8	1

Cotton	Nylon	Wool	Polyester	Silk	Polypropylene
17.5	10.0	7.3	7.0	7.0	6.0

*In milliwatts per meter (mW/m) at 70° F (21° C).

have low thermal conductivities, they can be excellent thermal insulators.

Second, fabrics are effective insulators because they slow the rate of convective heat loss from the body. The fibers and yarns within a fabric divide the volume of air into discrete, small spaces. When the interstices are less than $\frac{1}{4}$ inch across, air movement is prevented (convective currents are not established) and the air becomes "dead." The air between yarns and between fibers within yarns is heated by conduction, but convective heat movement does not occur readily.

Third, a fabric is an effective insulator because it contains a large surface area to which air can adhere. For example,[2] the total surface area within the fabric composing a man's suit is 299 square yards (yd²) or 250 square meters (m²), the area of a tennis court; the amount of fabric is 6 yd² or 5 m². Boundary layers of air form at the fabric surfaces as well as at the fiber surfaces. The boundary-layer theory states that moving air (or water) that comes into contact with a solid object will adhere to the surface of the solid due to a frictional force. Within $\frac{1}{8}$ inch, there is almost no movement at all. Also, the density of the boundary-layer air is higher than the air further away from the object. The denser the air, the greater its insulative ability. When a fabric is placed over the skin, there is a boundary layer of air at the skin surface and another boundary layer at the outer fabric surface. Both layers of air provide considerable resistance to the loss of body-generated heat.

Further, boundary layers of air are believed to form at the fiber surfaces, assuming that the boundary-layer theory applies to air in a static (nonmoving) condition. The amount of air within the fabric would consist of the trapped air held between the fibers as well as denser air bound by friction to the fiber surfaces. Based on this theory, "microfibers" are used in fiberfill batts to increase insulative ability without increasing fabric weight.

Lastly, radiative heat loss is less. Fabric is not as effective a radiator as the skin, even when both are at the same temperature. Fabrics are not good heat radiators and do not absorb large quantities of radiant heat. Little heat is lost from the outer fabric surface as radiant heat. Fabrics therefore provide protection from the radiant heat of the sun.

How Much Resistance to Heat Flow? The role of fabric is to provide resistance to the flow of heat from the body (that is, to provide insulation). The total resistance is a combination of the resistance provided by the fabric itself, the resistance of the layer of air between the skin surface and the inner fabric surface, and the resistance of the layer of air between the inner and outer fabric surfaces.

The thermal resistance of a piece of fabric can be determined in a laboratory and is expressed in units called togs. A fabric has a thermal resistance of 1 tog when a temperature difference of 0.1° C between its two faces produces a heat flow equal to 1 watt per square meter (W/m²). As a general rule, which is also much easier to comprehend, fabric thermal resistance is more or less proportional to fabric thickness. The thicker the fabric, the greater its thermal resistance and therefore the greater the retention of body heat.

The selection of fabrics with appropriate tog values is important but is not the only consideration in the development of an effective, thermally comfortable clothing assembly. Clothing design is also highly critical because it influences the flow of heat. Garments with collars, cuffs, and waists, for example, dramatically alter the flow of natural convective currents. Garment fit is an important factor, too: the closer the garment fits to the skin, the thinner the stationary boundary layer of air and the more slowly this air moves by convective currents. Close-fitting garments generally provide greater thermal comfort than loose-fitting garments of the same style and fabric.

Attainment of a Comfortable State of Wetness

The human body loses moisture continuously. People are not conscious of this loss of water, called *insensible perspiration*, in a resting state. On average, a sedentary individual loses about 1 ounce or 30 grams of water as vapor per hour which translates into 1½ pints or 0.71 liters every 24 hours. Two-thirds of this moisture is lost through the skin; one-third is expelled from the lungs into the air.

Water diffuses from the underlying layers of skin to the skin surface and evaporates.[3] Since heat is required to convert the liquid water to vaporous water, the loss of

---

[2]E.E. Clulow, "Thermal Insulation Properties of Fabrics," *Textiles* 7/2 (1978): 47–52.

---

[3]Water vapor is composed of individual water molecules. Each molecule is ~0.0004 micrometers (μm) in diameter. In comparison, a liquid drop of water consists of hundreds of thousands of individual molecules held together by hydrogen bonds. A water droplet with a diameter of 100 micrometers (μm) contains ~1.75×10^{16} molecules of water; a drop (at least 20 per milliliter) contains ~1.67×10^{21} molecules of water.

FIGURE 3.3 Diffusion of water vapor through a water-vapor-permeable fabric.

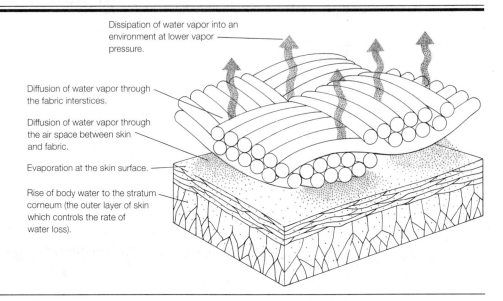

Dissipation of water vapor into an environment at lower vapor pressure.

Diffusion of water vapor through the fabric interstices.

Diffusion of water vapor through the air space between skin and fabric.

Evaporation at the skin surface.

Rise of body water to the stratum corneum (the outer layer of skin which controls the rate of water loss).

the diffused water cools the body. At room temperature, a sedentary individual gives up ~10% of total body heat to evaporate this diffused water.

The rate of loss of insensible perspiration is governed by a *vapor pressure gradient.* For a clothed body, a vapor pressure gradient exists when the vapor pressure on one side of the fabric is higher than it is on the other. The higher the vapor pressure at the skin surface relative to the environment, the more rapid the rate of insensible perspiration loss. Similarly, when the air is humid on one fabric face and dry on the other, water molecules diffuse from the damp side to the dry side. Thus, the rate of water loss increases as the skin temperature and the surrounding temperature rise.

When the body needs to lose more heat than it can by the evaporation of diffused internal water and by conduction, convection, and radiation, insensible perspiration stops and the body begins to sweat, or to produce *sensible perspiration.* Sweat (primarily liquid water exuded by sweat glands in the skin) is brought on by a marked increase in activity level, air temperature, and/or humidity. The evaporation of sweat from the skin surface is a cooling mechanism for the body because a considerable amount of body-generated heat is required to convert the quantity of sweat present on the skin surface to water vapor. The evaporation of 1 gram of water at skin temperature produces ~0.6 kilogram calories of cooling. As long as sweat does not run from the skin surface, the cooling process proceeds.

In most situations, a fabric should provide no resistance to the flow of insensible perspiration from the skin surface to the environment and allow liquid water to move rapidly away from the body. Fabric placed over the skin, however, interferes with the loss of body-generated water. As vaporous and liquid water pass through a fabric, the fibers and the trapped air in the fabric interstices can become moisture-laden, reducing the insulating ability of the fabric. A state of wetness, as well as of thermal discomfort, can be produced.

In other situations, such as fabrics to be worn in inclement weather, the primary role of the fabric is to form a barrier to the passage of liquid water to the skin surface. However, some passage of water from the body to the environment must continue to take place for maximum thermal and wetness comfort to be realized.

Water Vapor Permeability. When fabric is placed over the skin of a sedentary individual, the water evaporated from the skin surface will diffuse into the fabric (Figure 3.3). Specifically, it diffuses into the interstices between the yarns and between fibers composing the yarns, and may diffuse into and out of fibers comprising the fabric, depending on the type of fiber.[4] In *water-*

---

[4] Water vapor can more easily diffuse through absorbent (hydrophilic) fibers than through nonabsorbent (hydrophobic) fibers. Fabrics composed of nonabsorbent fibers have slower diffusion rates than those composed of absorbent fibers if the fabrics have similar interstices.

vapor permeable fabrics, the vaporous water makes its way to the fabric surface and diffuses into the environment. The rate at which water vapor diffuses through a fabric is called its *water vapor permeability.*

Fabrics that allow water vapor to be transmitted from the body to the environment are often referred to as "breathable" fabrics. Since water vapor diffuses through fibers and fabric interstices, both the fibers and the fabric can be said to "breathe." As water vapor is evaporated from the skin surface, it continues to diffuse through water-vapor-permeable fabrics. The fabric and skin remain "dry."[5]

In *water-impermeable fabrics,* vaporous water is prevented from diffusing into the environment. Certain finishes (films) over a fabric, for example, prevent vaporous water molecules from escaping. (It is estimated that for vaporous water molecules to pass through a fabric, its pores must be at least 3 micrometers in diameter.) Water vapor that continues to be evaporated from the surface of the skin fills the fabric interstices. Liquid water then begins to form on the surface of the skin, and the upper layers of the skin hydrate (fill with additional water). A sensation of wetness occurs.

Placing a 2-inch square of apparel fabric (representing a water-vapor-permeable material) and a 2-inch square of plastic wrap (representing a water-vapor-impermeable material) on the skin surface dramatically illustrates the diffusion of water vapor from the skin. Tape the edges of both squares to the skin, so that the moisture is directed through the materials and does not escape at the edges. Remove both materials after 30 minutes. You will see that the skin that has been under the plastic wrap is glistening. Water diffusing through this skin has not been permitted to diffuse to the environment. If you had taken your skin temperature before you placed the materials on it and again just before you removed them, you would have found that the skin temperature under the plastic wrap was higher than it was under the apparel fabric. Evaporative cooling did not take place under the plastic wrap. The cool sensation you feel when you remove this wrap is due to the rapid evaporation of the accumulated water from the skin surface.

Garments for everyday use must have a degree of water vapor permeability. The hotter the environment or

the greater the activity level, the higher the water vapor permeability must be to keep the skin dry and to permit evaporative cooling.

In a tent or other textile enclosure, it is necessary to allow the water that evaporates from the body to pass through the roof. Otherwise, water will condense on the inside of the roof and drops may fall inside the tent. Many nylon tents have a separate "rain fly," made of water-impermeable fabric, that sits above a water vapor permeable tent roof.

When sitting on a chair or sofa, body water must pass through the upholstery fabric as well as garment fabric. Sitting on a vinyl upholstery fabric on a hot day may cause a person's skin to become wet because the fabric blocks the passage of water from the body to the environment.

Wickability. Liquid water can be transported through fabric by *wicking,* or *capillary action* (Figure 3.4). Capillary action is observed when a blood sample is taken: the end of a small hollow tube is placed into a drop of blood, and the blood is drawn up into the tube. *Vertical wicking* is observed when oil moves up a cotton wick in an oil-burning lamp: as the oil burns, additional oil is brought to the flame by wicking. *Horizontal wicking* is observed when a water drop spreads over the surface of a fabric.

In fabrics, capillary action may occur along the outside of fibers (rather than inside, because most fibers are not hollow) and through the interstices (capillaries) in the fabric. Water content needs to be high for wicking to occur; the fabric needs to "wet out" with sweat. The capillaries (interstices) in the fabric must form a continuous "route" from one side of the fabric to the other.

WICKABILITY IN END USE. Wickability is desirable in garments worn in hot environments, where high temperatures cause sweating, and is even more important in fabrics designed for vigorous exercise in hot or cold environments. The wicking of liquid water through a fabric essentially draws water away from the skin surface, keeping it as "dry" as possible. "Wet" skin presents a number of problems. The movement of fabric on wet skin is more abrasive to the skin than the movement of the same fabric over dry skin. Wet skin is prone to fungal infections. Joggers who select socks that wick moisture away from their feet as it accumulates on the skin are less likely to get blisters or athlete's foot.

Wicking also prevents evaporative cooling from taking place on a person's skin surface when that cooling would

---

[5] All layers of the skin contain water; the deeper layers are much moister than the outer boundary layer. The water content of the boundary layer, called the stratum corneum, increases when the diffusion rate of water from the underlying skin layers is greater than the evaporative rate of water from the skin surface. The water content of the boundary layer also may increase when water from sweating is absorbed.

FIGURE 3.4 Wicking of liquid water (sweat) through and across fabric.

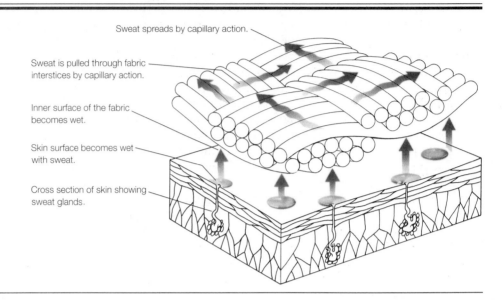

Sweat spreads by capillary action.

Sweat is pulled through fabric interstices by capillary action.

Inner surface of the fabric becomes wet.

Skin surface becomes wet with sweat.

Cross section of skin showing sweat glands.

be detrimental. Individuals exercising or working in cold environments may become so warm in their garments that sweating is triggered. A layer of wicking fabric at the skin surface will wick the sweat and delay the onset of chilling. Skiers often select thermal underwear that will wick.

Manufacturers continue to develop fabrics with the enhanced ability to wick moisture from the body, making synthetic-fiber garments intended for everyday wear more and more comfortable. Wickability is obviously not desirable for garments designed to keep rain from the body surface or textiles used to keep interior living or working spaces dry.

HOW WICKABLE? The rate at which fabric vertically wicks water can be observed by immersing the end of a strip of the fabric in water. The distance that water travels up the fabric within a certain time period indicates the rapidity of wicking. The rate of horizontal wicking can be determined by measuring the area over which a water drop spreads on the fabric surface.

Water Content. Vaporous water that does not diffuse through the fabric and liquid water that is not wicked through the fabric is held within the material until it reaches its *saturation point*. Water may be held within fibers (*absorbed water*), on the surfaces of fibers (*adsorbed water*), and in fabric interstices (*imbibed water*), as shown in Figure 3.5.

ABSORBED WATER. Absorption is the incorporation of one substance into another at the molecular level. The fibers in absorbent fabrics allow water molecules to penetrate into them. Fibers differ substantially in the amounts of water they can absorb.

ADSORBED WATER. Adsorption occurs when a substance is attracted to the surface of a solid. An adsorbed layer can be held to the surface of a fiber by intermolecular forces, the forces of chemical bonding, or a combination of the two. Fibers differ in amounts of water they can adsorb. When the surface area of a fabric is increased, the amount of water that its fibers can adsorb also increases. Therefore, the structure of the yarn or fabric is significant in terms of the amount of water that a fabric can adsorb. For example, cotton towels with looped surfaces are far more adsorbent than cotton towels with cut pile surfaces (velour towels).

IMBIBED WATER. To "*imbibe*" means to soak or saturate. If a person exercises strenuously or it is an extremely hot day, sweat may saturate the apparel fabric. Saturation also may occur when the fabric next to the skin is covered with a water-vapor-permeable layer; examples are glove liners under rubber protective gloves and garments under conventional waterproof rainwear. The water-vapor-impermeable layer does not allow the water continuously emitted by the body to escape to the outside environment.

FIGURE 3.5 The location of liquid and vaporous water in a fabric.

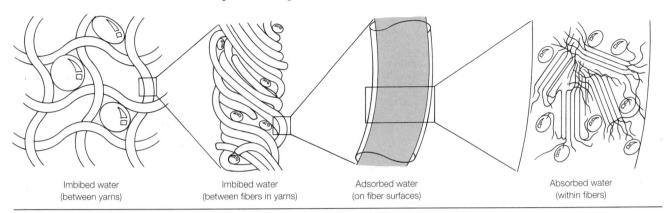

Imbibed water
(between yarns)

Imbibed water
(between fibers in yarns)

Adsorbed water
(on fiber surfaces)

Absorbed water
(within fibers)

HOW MUCH WATER IS HELD? The total amount of water in a fabric or fiber is expressed as its *moisture content* or *moisture regain*. Moisture regain is calculated as a percent of dry weight; moisture content, as a percent of moist weight.

In the case of moisture regain, the fiber or fabric is dried to remove any moisture it may contain. It is then weighed, exposed to a source of moisture, and reweighed. The calculation for moisture regain is

$$\frac{\text{``Wet'' Weight} - \text{Dry Weight}}{\text{Dry Weight}} \times 100 = \% \text{ Moisture Regain}$$

In the case of moisture content, the fabric or fiber is not dried; its initial weight includes any moisture it may contain. The calculation for moisture content is

$$\frac{\text{``Wet'' Weight} - \text{Moist Weight}}{\text{Moist Weight}} \times 100 = \% \text{ Moisture Content}$$

Drying Rate. How quickly or slowly a fabric dries is important to thermophysiological comfort. A fabric that remains wet causes the body to cool to a lower temperature than a fabric that dries quickly does. Fabrics composed of fibers such as cotton, wool, and rayon hold more moisture and hold it more tenaciously than fabrics composed of fibers such as nylon, polyester, and olefin. Therefore, when rapid cooling is desired, fabrics such as cotton are better than nylon or polyester, for example. Wet fabric, however, tends to cling, places a greater burden on motion, and is more abrasive than dry fabric.

Water Repellency. Water-repellent fabrics cause water to bead up on their surfaces while allowing insensible perspiration to pass through the fabric interstices. Water-repellent fabrics resist wetting. Water beads up and rolls off a water-repellent fabric; water spreads and wets fabrics that are not water-repellent (Figure 3.6).

Water repellency is a surface phenomenon. Water is a high surface tension fluid which means that the water molecules have high attraction for each other. Fabric surfaces differ in surface energy due to fiber content and type of chemical finish applied. Water beads up on a fabric with a surface energy lower than water; it spreads and wets a fabric with a surface energy greater than water. For example, water sprinkled onto wax paper beads up but on regular paper it spreads and wets. Likewise, water sprinkled onto a fabric finished with a wax beads up because these treatments have lowered the surface energy of the fabric below that of water. The water molecules have greater attraction for each other than for the surface of the fabric.

HOW WATER REPELLENT? To determine how water repellent a fabric is, water may be sprinkled onto the fabric surface and one observes the proportion of the surface that has been wetted, which can range from no wetting to complete wetting. It is also possible to weigh a sample of dry fabric, immerse it in water for a specified period of time, remove it slowly to allow excess water to drip from it, and then reweigh it. The degree of water repellency (wetting) is calculated as a percent of dry weight.

FIGURE 3.6   Water repellent and nonwater repellent fabrics.

Light rain

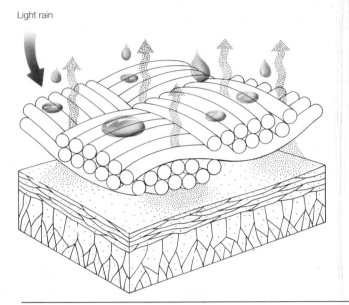

Light rain

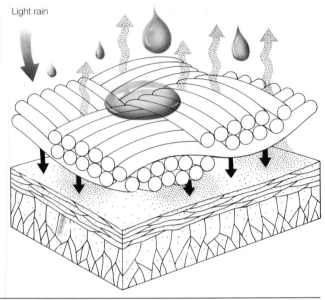

Water repellent: Rain drops bead up on the fabric surface and water vapor is dissipated.

Not-water repellent: Rain drops spread and wet the fabric; water vapor is dissipated.

Water Repellency in End Use. Many upholstery fabrics are water-repellent so that liquids (cola, wine, water) spilled on them can be wiped away before they wet and stain. Many raincoat and jacket fabrics are water-repellent. In a gentle rain, a water-repellent fabric usually resists water penetration. In a torrential rain, the wearer of a water-repellent fabric may get wet because the force of the falling water may be sufficient for penetration to occur.

Water Resistance and Waterproofness. *Water-resistant fabrics* are those that resist the penetration of water. The greater the force of impact as water hits the fabric surface, the greater the likelihood that it will penetrate and wet surfaces under it. Compactness of the fabric structure is an important consideration in how water resistant a fabric is. The most water resistant fabrics are called waterproof fabrics.

Waterproof fabrics provide a complete barrier to liquid water (Figure 3.7). They are impervious to rain, even under the most severe conditions.[6] The wearer of a rain-

coat made from a waterproof fabric does not need to worry about getting wet. Depending on the type of waterproof fabric, conventional or breathable, water vapor (insensible perspiration) may or may not be allowed to diffuse to the environment.

HOW WATER RESISTANT? The degree of water resistance is a function of how much force is required to cause water falling on the fabric surface to penetrate it. The greater the required force, the more water-resistant the fabric. Differences in water resistance can be determined by sprinkling fabrics with water, under varying degrees of pressure, and noting the wetness of a blotter placed under them. Increase in weight of the blotter is usually used to determine degree of water resistance.

CONVENTIONAL. *Conventional waterproof fabrics* do not allow insensible perspiration (water vapor) to escape to the environment. These fabrics are usually coated fabrics (Chapter 29); fabrics in which a substance such as vinyl or synthetic rubber completely covers a base layer of fabric and/or completely fills the fabric interstices. A modest buildup of moisture inside these garments causes discomfort. Careful design of the garment (holes in the underarm area, a collar away from the neck) is often necessary to allow water vapor to escape. If the wearer

---

[6] A hydrostatic water-entry pressure of 25 pounds per square inch is required for an outerwear garment to prevent the penetration of liquid water under all conditions.

FIGURE 3.7 Conventional and breathable waterproof fabrics.

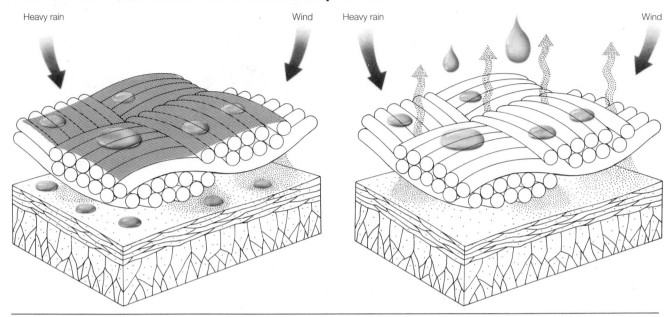

Conventional: A surface coating provides a complete barrier to the transport of water and prevents water vapor from dissipating from the skin surface to the environment so the skin surface becomes wet.

Breathable: The microporous nature of the fabric provides a complete barrier to the transport of water but allows water vapor to dissipate.

works or exercises arduously in extreme weather conditions, there is a serious threat of heat exhaustion or more commonly, in a cold, wet climate, severe body chill leading to hypothermia.

BREATHABLE. The need for waterproof fabrics with the ability to keep liquid water from penetrating (having holes <100 micrometers in diameter) but large enough to permit water vapor to pass through (having holes > 0.0003 micrometers in diameter) led to the development of *waterproof breathable* (WB) *fabrics.* There are over 200 fabrics of this type available today, offering a varied combination of waterproofness and water vapor permeability.

Maximum water vapor transmission without sacrificing waterproofness is accomplished in five ways: construction of fabric, fiber dimensions (microfibers), microporous membranes, microporous coatings, and monolithic films. The most familiar WB fabric is Goretex®, manufactured by Goretex Industries. It has a microporous membrane with a pore size ~ 0.25 μm. WB fabrics achieved by packing yarns tightly in a fabric have pore sizes of ~ 2–3 μm. The space through which water vapor is transmitted in monolithic films is the smallest of the WB fabrics.

TEXTILE PERFORMANCE PROPERTIES AND SENSORIAL (NEUROPHYSIOLOGICAL) COMFORT

Some people have such sensitive skins that contact with most fabrics causes them grave discomfort. They find few fabrics that they can wear and use. Fortunately, this situation rarely occurs, but (as anyone can readily appreciate) presents a major dilemma to those so afflicted.

More typically, people can tolerate the placement of fabric on their skin without experiencing unpleasant sensations. Sensitivity to fabric appears to differ widely, both within a population and between populations in different countries. Some unpleasant sensations, such as prickliness and roughness, are produced when fabric irritates sensory receptors and nerve fibers in the skin. Others, such as shock, are due to the electrical natures of the textile and the skin.

Feel of Fabric Against the Skin

The various sensations that result from the interaction of skin with fabric are triggered by sensory receptors in the skin. Researchers generally agree that three categories of sensory nerves cover all sensations: the pain group, the

FIGURE 3.8 Sensory nerves respond to fabric placed on or moved over the skin surface.

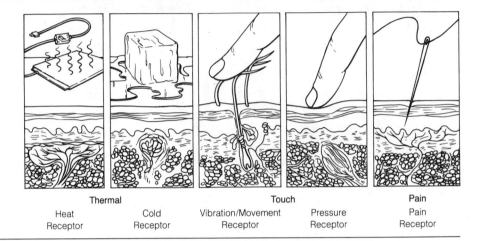

| Thermal | | Touch | | Pain |
| Heat Receptor | Cold Receptor | Vibration/Movement Receptor | Pressure Receptor | Pain Receptor |

touch group of pressure and vibration, and the thermal group of warmth and coolness (Figure 3.8). In each case, a receptor close to the surface of the skin is connected more or less directly to the brain by a nerve fiber. Which receptor is triggered depends on how the fabric interacts with the skin (for example, by downward pressure only or by downward pressure and movement across the skin) and on the surface features of the fabric (for example, fuzziness or smoothness).

Prickliness/Itchiness and Inflammation. Prickle from fabrics is often described as the sensation of many very gentle pinpricks. *Itch* is usually a component or resulting sensation of prickle. To relieve itch, people often scratch their skin, which can cause further irritation and, in time, exacerbate prickle. A few people experience *inflammation* from prickly fabrics, particularly after a long period of contact.

Prickle is an elusive sensation and may fluctuate in intensity over a period of seconds. It results from the stimulation of the pain group of sensory receptors. A delay of several seconds usually occurs between the time a fabric that can elicit a prickly sensation is placed on the skin and the time prickle is felt.

Prickliness is experienced when suitable fabric is gently patted or pressed[7] onto hairy skin, such as the forearm; it is not felt on the palms of the hands or on the fingers, which are hairless.[8] Prickle cannot be felt if the fabric is rubbed or wiped over the skin, if the skin is uncomfortably cold, or if the area of skin contact is smaller than ~ 0.16 square inches (1 square centimeter). Moisture on the skin greatly increases the magnitude of the sensation.

Inflammation results from the excitation of pain nerves. Chemicals released at or near the nerve endings dilate surface blood capillaries. Reddening first occurs in the vicinity of activated pain-nerve endings and then diffuses over larger areas. This is not an allergic response; it is an irritant response. Inflammation may appear rapidly (within one hour of skin contact) or more slowly (after several hours). It usually subsides quickly after the fabric is removed from the skin, unless skin contact over several days has produced a more severe reaction.

Roughness. The movement of a fabric across the skin stimulates the touch group of sensory receptors. Fabric roughness or surface contour may be felt quickly. Displacement of the skin takes place. As more skin is displaced under a fabric moving across it, the perception of fabric roughness becomes greater (the fabric creates an increasingly unpleasant sensation).

When fabric is in contact with skin, the force required to move it is opposed by the frictional force. Movement results when the applied force surpasses the frictional resistance. Frictional characteristics of sliding surfaces are

---

[7] A pressure of 4 grams per square centimeter (g/cm²) is considered to be near the upper limit of the typical clothing pressure at which prickle is sensed. R. K. Garnsworthy, et al., "Understanding the Causes of Prickle and Itch from the Skin Contact of Fabrics," Report No. G64 (Australia: CSIRO Division of Wool Technology, 1988).

[8] It is always advisable to try on next-to-skin garments prior to purchase instead of just feeling them with the hands, because prickliness can be detected in the former manner but not in the latter.

often described by the coefficient of friction, which is the ratio of the drag force parallel to the surface to the normal force pressing on the surface.

There is less friction between the skin and fabrics with smooth surfaces than there is between the skin and fabrics with rougher surfaces. For example, a filament silk blouse is judged to be smoother than a spun silk blouse when felt in the hands or when worn. Likewise, a percale cotton sheet is judged to be smoother than a muslin sheet.

Moisture at the fabric-skin interface alters the intensity of fabric roughness that is felt. Moisture increases friction; it causes larger amounts of skin to be displaced under a moving fabric and therefore triggers more touch receptors. Fabrics perceived to be tactually comfortable in low-humidity environments may not feel comfortable as humidity increases. Fabrics that are not sufficiently permeable to water vapor will be judged unpleasant to wear sooner than fabrics with acceptable levels of water vapor permeability because moisture increases at the fabric-skin interface.

Thermal Character (Warm/Cool Feeling). Textiles are warmer to the touch than common building materials. Think about getting out of bed in the morning and having your left foot fall on an area rug and your right fall onto the bare floor. It is more pleasant (warmer) to step onto a rug than onto a tile or wood floor. The rate of heat flow is greater from the right foot to the floor than from the left foot to the rug. The area of contact of the sole of the foot with the rug is less than that with the bare floor, so it feels warmer to step on the rug.

When fabric is placed on the skin surface, there is a momentary sensation of warmness or coolness. The *thermal character* of the fabric is the apparent difference between the temperature of the fiber and the temperature of the skin of the person touching or wearing it. Thermal character is believed to result from the rapid transfer of heat from the skin to the fabric surface immediately after the fabric is placed on the skin. The momentary flow of heat is sufficient to trigger the warm/cool receptors in the dermis (the layer of skin beneath the epidermis). The area of contact between skin and fabric seems to be responsible for the rate of heat flow. As the surface area of contact increases, the flow of heat from the skin also increases, so the fabric feels cooler. Cotton percale bedsheets, for example, feel cooler than cotton flannel bedsheets when you get into bed on a cold night, even when both fabrics are at the same temperature. In general, fabrics with fuzzy surfaces feel warmer than smooth-surfaced fabrics of the same fiber composition.

Electrical Conductivity/Electrical Resistivity

Charged fabrics cling to the body, resulting in an uncomfortable feeling. Garments look unsightly, and some restriction of body movement may occur. Charged fabrics may cause shocks when the wearer touches a metal object, such as a door knob or file cabinet, after walking over a carpeted floor, rising from a chair, or brushing against walls or furniture. The mild, tingling shock is generally considered a nuisance. If a spark of electricity is generated in a room where flammable gases are present (for example, in a hospital or a nursing home), an explosion—a more dangerous result—may occur.

Fabric Cling. *Fabric cling* results from the formation of an electrostatic charge on the fabric and the induction of this charge on the body. In normal use, adjacent layers of the apparel fabric and surrounding fabrics are pressed and rubbed together when the wearer is sitting down or walking about. During this contact, positive charges are produced on one surface; negative charges, on the other. As long as the fabrics remain together, no charge results. However, when the wearer moves or stands up after sitting in a chair, the fabrics separate and, depending on their natures, may become charged—one negatively, and one positively (Figure 3.9). Clothing may also become positively or negatively charged when it is removed from the body.

The electric field generated from the charged fabric can induce an opposite charge on the skin, causing fabric cling to occur. The degree of garment cling depends on the types of fabric worn next to each other and on both the charge and weight per unit area of fabric. When the electrostatic forces on the garment are greater than the gravitational forces that tend to make it hang vertically, it will cling. The surrounding humidity is also an important factor: the electrical conductivity of most textile fabrics increases as the moisture content of the atmosphere increases. Wet skin also helps to reduce fabric cling. Clinging behavior is the result of induction once the fabric is charged.

Static Shock. *Static shock* occurs when the human body becomes charged (either by induction or direct contact with a charged object) and the charge is not dissipated before the person touches a metal object. The shock may dissipate to the air or to the ground (if the soles of the shoes permit).

A person insulated from earth by shoes and standing near a charged fabric can become charged and may experience a shock on touching any metal. Hospital nurses

FIGURE 3.9   Charging of fabric and induction of charge.

(a)

(b)

(a) *Charging:* As a person rises from a chair, the separation of the garment fabric from the upholstery fabric results in a charge on both fabrics. In the diagram, the apparel fabric is positively charged and the upholstery fabric is negatively charged.

(b) *Induction:* Charge on the garment induces charge on the body. In the diagram, electrons are attracted to the concentration of positive charges on the fabric and are conducted along the skin to the back of the leg. Garment cling results.

frequently receive shocks when they touch metal bedsteads in warm, dry rooms while handling sheets that contain synthetic fibers. Such shocks can be avoided by ensuring that footwear and flooring are sufficiently conductive to allow the induced charge on the body to leak away quickly.

Static charge is produced each time a shoe makes contact with the carpet (Figure 3.10). While a shoe sole is in contact with the carpet surface, any charge that develops is equally and oppositely distributed on the contacting surfaces. Each time the shoe is lifted from the carpet, charge separation occurs. Charge on the shoe sole will usually pass quickly to the body. As a person walks over

FIGURE 3.10   Accumulation of static charge on the body while walking over a carpet.

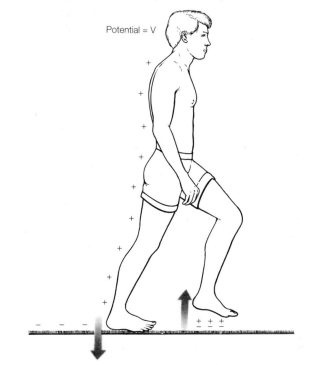

Potential = V

a carpet, charge accumulates on the body, raising its voltage.

During walking, charge may also leave the body via the shoe sole, which is in contact with the carpet. The rate of dissipation depends on the electrical resistivities of the shoe sole and the carpet. Rubber soles allow more charge to be dissipated than leather soles, because rubber has a higher electrical conductivity than leather. Therefore, milder shocks are felt in rubber-soled shoes than in leather-soled shoes.

TEXTILE PERFORMANCE PROPERTIES AND BODY-MOVEMENT COMFORT

People must be able to move around in the apparel items they wear. Fabrics are suitable apparel materials because they flex when only a small force is exerted on them. Discomfort may result, however, when a fabric restrains movement, creates a burden, or exerts pressure on the body.

Stretch

When people move, their skin stretches; it elongates and recovers. Skin is a highly elastic material; as it loses elasticity with age, it wrinkles and sags. Fabric placed close to the skin surface, as it is in tight-fitting garments, also must be elastic. It must elongate to accommodate body movement and then recover. As elasticity is lost in a fabric, it bags and sags.

Stretch is the ability of a textile to extend when a pulling force is applied and then to recover relatively quickly and fully to its original dimensions when that pulling force is removed. In other words, textiles that stretch have fairly high percentages of elongation and elastic recovery. Figure 3.11 shows the amount of extension generally needed for garment fabrics to be worn close to the skin. The amount of unrecovered extension, or fabric growth, is calculated as 100% minus elastic recovery.

Generally, fabrics with ≥15% elongation are referred to as *stretch fabrics;* fabrics with <15% elongation are *rigid fabrics.* Most woven fabrics are rigid fabrics because the interlacement of yarns allows little extension to occur under a tensile force. However, stretch woven fabrics can be structured from elastic fibers and yarns. Knit fabrics, due to the interlooping yarns, usually possess a minimum of 15% elongation, but they can be made into rigid fabrics.

Generally, stretch fabrics must have the following minimum percentages of elongation and recovery and maximum percentage of growth for comfort and appearance to be acceptable:

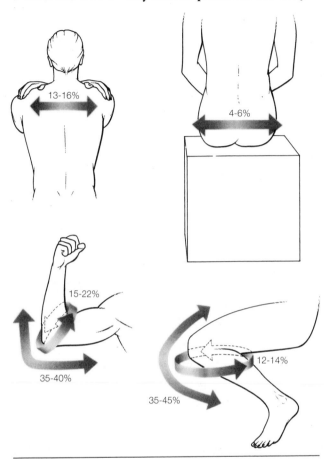

FIGURE 3.11   **Key stretch points on the body.**

	PERCENT MINIMUM ELONGATION	PERCENT MINIMUM RECOVERY	PERCENT MAXIMUM GROWTH
Tailored clothing	15–25	98	2
Spectator sportswear	20–35	95	5
Form-fit garments	30–40	95	5
Active wear	35–50	94	6

Comfort Stretch. *Comfort stretch fabrics* exhibit 15–30% elongation. These fabrics provide closer-fitting garments by reducing resistance to body movements, particularly around the elbows, knees, back, and seat. Woven slacks

and shirts are comfort stretch fabrics when 15% of the fiber is rubber, as little as 2–3% of the fiber is spandex, stretch yarns are used, or construction of the fabric allows for extension and recovery to occur.

Power Stretch. *Power stretch* ("action") *fabrics* have greater extensibility (30–200%) than comfort stretch fabrics plus the ability to firm and shape body flesh. These "action" fabrics rely as much or more on force of recovery as on percentage of elongation and degree of recovery for their utility. Body shaping results from compressive pressure of the fabric on the skin which is useful in swimwear, foundation garments, stretch ski pants, and active sportswear. Power stretch fabrics may also be used to support various parts of the body, such as

TABLE 3.2 Average Weight of Various Garments.

MEN'S GARMENTS	Pounds	Kilograms	WOMEN'S GARMENTS	Pounds	Kilograms
Jacket	2.43	1.10	Outerwear	1.06	0.48
Contents of pockets	0.79	0.36	(dress/skirt and blouse)		
Trouser	1.12	0.51	Underwear	0.68	0.31
Contents of pockets	0.37	0.17	Stockings or tights	0.09	0.04
Underwear	0.40	0.18			
Shirt and tie	0.64	0.29			
Sweater	0.66	0.30			
Total garments	6.41	2.91	Total garments	1.83	0.83
Socks and shoes	2.00	0.91	Socks and shoes	1.04	0.47

the bust when used in bras or the veins when used in support stockings.

It is a mistake to believe that power stretch fabrics can reduce the size of the figure. Flesh is practically incompressible. Total body volume is redistributed, not reduced (refer to the following discussion of pressure).

Stretch Direction. The direction of stretch in a fabric can be vertical, horizontal, or two-way. In *vertical stretch fabrics,* the length of the fabric stretches. Pants with stirrups are generally more comfortable when made of vertical stretch fabrics. *Horizontal stretch fabrics* stretch in the crosswise direction; most stretch fabrics are of this type. *Two-way stretch fabrics* stretch in both directions. All power stretch fabrics and some comfort stretch fabrics have two-way stretch.

Relationship to Other Fabric Properties. In addition to their contribution to comfort, stretch fabrics retain their shape well. Their ability to recover means reduced sagging and bagging of the fabric. Wrinkle resistance and resilience are inherent characteristics of stretch fabrics. Shape retention and resilience are aspects of the aesthetics of the fabric; these performance properties are discussed in Chapter 4.

Weight

Garment *weight* contributes to comfort or discomfort because it determines the burden the wearer must carry (Table 3.2). A heavy coat worn while shopping may well limit the length of time the shopper remains at the store. Marathon runners wear lightweight garments. Back-

packers and hikers carry lightweight tents and pack frames and wear lightweight garments to reduce their burdens as much as possible.

Garment weight depends on the amount of fiber in the garment. Weight may be expressed in terms of *specific gravity,* the ratio of the weight of a given volume of a substance to the weight of an equal volume of a reference substance. Water, the usual reference substance, weighs 1 gram per cubic centimeter.

It is a misnomer that heavier fabrics are warmer fabrics. Fabric with the greatest volume of dead air has the best insulative capability. Warmth without weight can be obtained from lightweight fibers capable of maintaining fabric thickness.

Pressure/Compression

Fabrics intended to shape body flesh (power stretch fabrics) exert pressure on the body surface. Other fabrics also may exert some surface pressure because they are supported by a relatively small body area. Garment design and fit are important in determining the amount of pressure exerted on the body.[9]

Pressure is a force per unit area; it is a ratio of the force acting on a surface to the area of that surface. Units of

---

[9]A pair of heavy trousers with keys and change in the pockets can weigh ~2.2 lb (1 kg). If the pants are held up with suspenders, two small areas on the shoulders must support the weight. If the pants are held up by the waistband or a separate belt, the weight is distributed over a somewhat larger area and the pressure is therefore lower. In a poorly fitting suit jacket, the weight of the jacket (~3.3 lb, or 1½ kg) is carried on the shoulder blades. The relatively comfortable feeling of a well-fitted jacket is substantially due to the more even distribution of weight on the body (less pressure at all points on the body surface).

pressure are frequently expressed as force divided by area unit—for example, pounds per square inch or newtons per square meter. Pressures of <60 grams per square meter exerted by fabric on the body are usually judged to be comfortable; pressures of 60–100 grams per square meter to be uncomfortable (the amount of discomfort depends mainly on the part of the body affected).[10] It may or may not be coincidental that this pressure is similar to the pressure in the capillary blood vessels near the skin surface. Surprisingly, the difference between what is acceptable and what is unacceptable pressure does not differ much from person to person.

The pressure exerted by fabric on the body becomes greater as the curvature of the body increases. For most females, the body curvature at the sides of the waistline is roughly $3\frac{1}{2}$ times greater than the curvature across the front of the body. Although the tension in a girdle fabric is the same, the pressure it exerts on the body is not con-

---

[10]M.J. Denton, "Fit, Stretch, and Comfort," *Textiles* 1/1 (1972): 14.

stant. The pressure on the sides of the waist is about $3\frac{1}{2}$ times greater than the desired figure-flattening pressure on the waist front! This often puts the side pressure into the discomfort range.

CHAPTER SUMMARY

Comfort is both *psychological* and *physiological*. In this chapter, we concentrated on the performance properties of fabric that contribute to physiological comfort. *Thermophysiological comfort* includes the attainment of a comfortable thermal state (not too hot or too cold) and the attainment of the appropriate skin and fabric moisture content (not too wet). *Sensorial (neurophysiological) comfort* includes the feel of the fabric against the skin and static cling and shock resulting from the electrical resistivity of fabric. *Body-movement comfort* includes considerations of stretch, weight, and pressure/compressibility. Detail View 3 provides definitions of each of the comfort performance properties.

Aesthetic Appeal Properties

Aesthetic appeal involves the degree of pleasantness of the textile to the eye, hand, ear, and nose (the sensory mechanisms of the human body).

PERFORMANCE PROPERTY	DEFINITION
Appearance	**Effects perceived by an observer and determined by the interaction of light source, object, and observer.**
Translucence/opacity (covering power)	The result of a textile transmitting, scattering, and absorbing incident light. (Ability of a textile to hide what is placed underneath it.)
Luster/dullness	The specular and diffuse reflection of incident light from a textile surface.
Pattern and texture	Discernible differences in surface features and/or contour due to differences in reflection and scatter of incident light from different locations on the textile surface.
Color	The result of colorants modifying light (selectively absorbing and scattering it).
Drapability	The manner in which a fabric hangs over a three-dimensional form; the flow of fabric into folds.
Appearance Retention	**No discernible difference in an observer's assessment of the original fabric appearance and the same fabric after use.**
Color Considerations	
Colorfastness	Resistance to color change under specified conditions, such as exposure to a bleach solution.
Crocking resistance	The ability of a textile to resist the transfer of colorant when rubbed.
Frosting resistance	The ability of a textile to resist a change in color over a limited area of its surface due to abrasive wear.
Bleeding resistance	The ability of a textile to retain colorant when placed in water or a drycleaning solvent.
Yellowing	An increase in the intensity of yellow light reflected from a textile.
Resilience	The ability of a textile to work against restraining forces as it returns from a deformed state.
Wrinkle resistance and recovery	The ability of a textile to resist bending and the formation of wrinkles and/or to return to a flat state.
Compressional resilience (loft)	The ability of a textile to spring back to its original thickness after a downward force is applied and removed.
Shape retention	The ability of a textile to retain its original dimensions (not to bag) while in use.
Crease retention	The ability of a textile to retain pleats and creases intentionally placed in the fabric.
Pilling Propensity	The likelihood that small balls of tangled fibers will form and adhere tenaciously on a fabric surface.
Snagging Propensity	The likelihood that parts of yarns will be pulled above a fabric surface.
Feel	**Effects perceived by an individual while manipulating an object in the fingers.**
Body	The lightness/heaviness, firmness/looseness, and springiness/limpness of a fabric.
Hand	The total sensation experienced when a textile is manipulated in the fingers.
Texture and Drapability	Defined above.
Smell and Sound	**Effects that an individual associates with a textile through the auditory and olfactory senses.**
Odor absorption/release	The ability of a textile to resist the absorption of objectionable odors and the ease with which these odors can be removed from a textile.

*A*esthetic Appeal

Fabrics that please the eye, hand, ear, and nose have aesthetic appeal. Evaluation begins as soon as the fabric can be seen and/or felt. Comments such as "This color of green reminds me of tree leaves in spring," "The subdued luster of this fabric complements skin tone," "This fabric feels so soft," or "The rustle of this fabric delights me" convey that certain aspects of fabric are pleasing.

In many consumer purchase decisions, aesthetic appeal is the priority consideration; if the aesthetic appeal of the textile is undesirable, it usually will not be purchased. Aesthetic appeal can be so powerful that the buyer forgets to consider other performance attributes. A fabric's softness, luxurious feel, subdued sheen, and magnificent colors can be so overwhelmingly influential that the consumer readily forgets to consider how durable the fabric will be or what type of care procedures are required. In contrast, aesthetic appeal is generally a low priority in the purchase of industrial textiles.

Aesthetic appeal includes the appearance of the fabric, the feel of the fabric in the hand, and the sound and smell of the fabric. The sensory mechanisms of sight, hearing, smell, and touch provide information concerning fabric aesthetics. Taste is the only human sense not involved. The performance properties that define fabric aesthetic appeal are organized into sections (appearance, appearance retention, feel, and smell and sound) by the primary sensory mechanism involved in their assessment. Generally, two senses interplay. The performance properties of aesthetic appeal are listed and defined in Detail View 4.

APPEARANCE

Appearance requires a light source, the object it illuminates (in our discussion, the textile), and an observer with an eye and brain to perceive the modified light. A photosensitive detector and auxiliary equipment can approximate the ability of the eye and brain to detect light.

Throughout this discussion of the performance properties of appearance, remember that the fabric must be seen. If a textile were placed in a box, so that you could touch it but could not look at it, you could not completely describe its appearance. In contrast, if you were allowed to view the fabric but not to touch it, you could provide a fairly complete description. Before we consider how textiles modify light, let's briefly review the principles of light.

Light

Visible light is the very small fraction of electromagnetic radiation that the eye can see (Figure 4.1). X-rays, radio waves, gamma rays, and infrared radiation all lie outside the range of visible light. Light can be described by its wavelength, which is stated in nanometers (nm); 1 nm = 10^{-9} meters. Wavelengths of ~380–750 nm can be detected by the human eye.

Many sources of light, such as the sun, hot metals like the filaments of light bulbs, and fluorescent lamps, emit light that is white or nearly white. *White light* is normally composed of all the visible wavelengths and can be

FIGURE 4.1 Wavelengths of electromagnetic radiation.

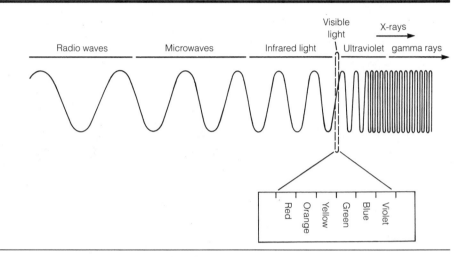

dispersed into a spectrum of colors or hues (Figure 4.2). Each hue of light lies within a narrow wavelength band. The hue we recognize as red lies between 630 nm and 750 nm and represents the longest wavelength of visible light. Green lies roughly between 480 nm and 560 nm.

Other light sources do not emit light of all wavelengths. Mercury, neon, carbon, and sodium light sources emit only a few specific wavelengths characteristic of these materials.

Light from any source can be described in terms of the relative power (amount of light) emitted at each wavelength. When this power is plotted as a function of wavelength, the spectral distribution curve results. All sources of white light have continuous curves. The amount of light at each wavelength will differ, however.

When light strikes an object, it may be transmitted, reflected, absorbed, or scattered. The object modifies the light that is incident on it. Light reflected by an object has changed its direction. Light absorbed by an object is lost as visible light. Light absorbed and re-emitted at the same wavelength, with part traveling in one direction and part in another, is scattered. Only light transmitted through an object remains unchanged. An object may cause all, only one, or any combination of these modifications to occur. The object can be selective about what wavelengths within the light source it transmits, reflects, absorbs, or scatters.

Translucence/Opacity (Cover Power)

Textiles are transparent, translucent, or opaque, depending on how much of the incident light on their surface is transmitted through them (Figure 4.3). When all light passes through a textile, it is *transparent.* When light scattering is so intense that no light passes through a textile, it is *opaque.* An opaque textile completely blocks an object from an observer's sight. When part of the light is absorbed or scattered and part is transmitted by the textile, it is *translucent.* An observer can see an object through a translucent textile, but not as clearly as when the textile is removed. Textiles range in degree of translucence; a highly translucent textile approaches being transparent; a textile with low translucence approaches being opaque. Adjectives used to describe degree of translucence include sheer, gauzy, gossamer, clear, filmy,

FIGURE 4.2 White light dispersed into a spectrum of colors.

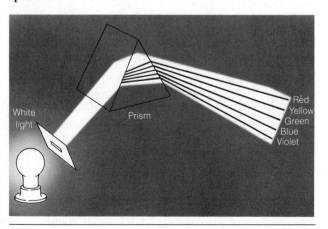

parchment-like, pale, and thin. Terms used to describe opacity include solid, cloudy, dark, and thick.

Translucence in End Use. Whether an opaque, translucent, or transparent textile is desired depends on end use and individual preference. For such end uses as sheer curtains, translucent fabrics are desirable. When privacy is needed, curtains and draperies made from opaque fabrics are a better choice. Bathing-suit manufacturers check the translucence of a potential fabric by pulling a prepared tube of it over a cylinder imprinted with letters that differ in degree of darkness. The size of the tube and cylinder approximate the amount of extension of the bathing-suit fabric on the human body. The manufacturer knows which letters should not be visible for the textile to be an acceptable bathing-suit fabric.

Covering Power. *Cover* or *covering power* indicates the translucence/opaqueness of a fabric. Technically, covering power is the ability of the fabric to hide what is placed under it. The cover factor is the ratio of fabric surface occupied by yarn to total fabric surface. A cover factor of 100% means that the fabric surface is covered completely with yarn (the yarns are packed densely, with no open spaces between them). Few fabrics can actually achieve such complete cover; generally, some space, however small, remains between the yarns.

Luster/Dullness

How lustrous a textile is depends on its surface contour (Figure 4.4). Highly lustrous fabrics reflect light specularly from their surfaces. In *specular reflection*, equal angles of light from the textile surface are made by incident and reflected light beams. The smoother and flatter the fiber, yarn, and fabric surface, the more lustrous the textile.

Conversely, as the fabric, fiber, or yarn surfaces become rougher, luster is reduced and *diffuse reflection* from the surface increases. Although all the incident light is reflected, the same as in specular reflection, it is scattered rather than concentrated.

The degree of *luster* of most textiles is a combination of specular and diffuse reflection at the same time. Luster is also a combination of diffuse reflection at the surface of fibers, yarns, and fabric and within fibers.

Luster is desirable in some end uses and undesirable in others. Lustrous fabrics are associated with formal apparel and furnishings. *Matte* or *dull* fabrics are associated with a less formal appearance in apparel and fur-

FIGURE 4.3 Modification of light by transparent, opaque, and translucent textiles.

Transparent textile: All light is transmitted through the textile.

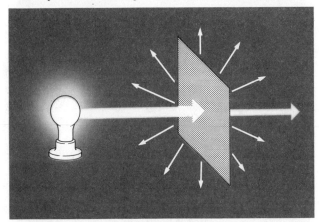

Translucent textile: Some light is transmitted and some is diffusely reflected by scattering.

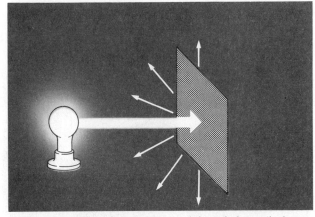

Opaque textile: No light is transmitted through the textile, but some is diffusely reflected by scattering; some reflection may occur at the surface.

FIGURE 4.4 Luster of textiles due to specular and diffuse reflection of light.

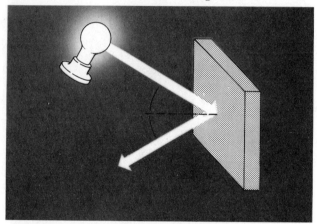

Specular reflection of light from a smooth surface.

Diffuse reflection of light from a rough surface.

Combination of diffuse and specular reflection due to scattering from beneath and reflection from a smooth surface.

nishings. Fashion trends alter consumer acceptance of bright or dull fabrics.

The luster of a fabric may be altered as the fabric is used. Water-soluble chemical finishes can wash off during laundering. Abrasion may roughen the surface of the fabric, so that it reflects less light, producing a worn, dull look.

Unwanted luster, or *sheen,* also can be introduced when a fabric becomes flattened during wear and use, as can occur at the elbows and seat of suitpants. Some suits are sold with two pairs of pants because manufacturers realize that the seat area is likely to look worn long before the jacket does.

Pattern and Texture

A *pattern* can be seen on white and solid-color fabrics when yarns are arranged in such a manner that the combination of specular and diffuse reflection differs from one area to another. The patterns on many dobby and Jacquard woven fabrics are solely due to differences in light reflection.

Texture is an interplay of surface appearance and feel— a sensory impression understood by sight and by touch. The *visual aspect* of texture is detected by the eye, which perceives intricate variations in the intensity of scattered light across a fabric surface. A texture appears rough or smooth due to the interplay of light. The feel aspect of texture, a component of fabric hand, is detected by the friction between fingers and fabric and by the surface contour of the fabric (how much it deviates from flatness). Adjectives such as soft, crisp, smooth, and rough describe different fabric textures.

Color

In many ways, the perception of color is the most pleasurable visual sensation. Coloring of textiles has been practiced ever since men of the New Stone Age discovered that the colored clays their Old Stone Age forebears used for cave decoration could also be applied to textiles. Color on modern textiles results from the use of synthetic *colorants* (dyes and pigments).

Color is "what we see—the result of the physical modification of light by colorants as observed by the human eye (called a perceptual process) and interpreted in the brain (which introduces psychology)."[1] Like other

---

[1] F.W. Billmeyer, Jr., and M. Saltzman, *Principles of Color Technology* 2d ed. (New York: John Wiley, 1981), p. 1.

aspects of appearance, color is governed primarily by the composition of the light reflected from the fabric, which initially depends on the composition of the light falling on it. Textiles appear to be colored because the colorant they contain selectively absorbs part of the wavelengths of incident light on them and reflects the other part[2] (Figure 4.5). A green colorant absorbs all wavelengths from white light except the green wavelength, which it reflects; a blue colorant absorbs all wavelengths except the blue wavelength; and so on. A black colorant absorbs the whole spectrum. White textiles are white because all of the spectrum incident on them is reflected. Blue-green is perceived when a colorant absorbs all other wavelengths except blue and green.

At least 1 million colors are visibly different from all other colors. Each color differs in *hue*, *value* or *shade*, or *intensity*. *Hue* is the name of the color, *value* is its whiteness to darkness, and *intensity* is its brightness to darkness. Many of these colors are acceptable matches—colors so close to each other that they are usually regarded as the same color. Coats and Clark, Inc., a thread manufacturer, may be asked to provide 3000 different colors of a particular hue in any 1 year. These are chosen from a library of 10,000 colors, and each is different in shade and intensity.

Color is determined largely by the type of colorant on or within fibers. The intensity of a color is decided by the amount of colorant and is modified by the scattering of light at the surfaces of fibers, yarns, and fabrics. The perception of color is a highly complex topic that always involves consideration of the light source, the colorant, and the observer. Color perception is not considered in this introductory text; further information about colorants and coloring (dyeing and printing) can be found in Chapters 34 and 35.

Drapability

Drape is the manner in which a fabric hangs (falls) over a three-dimensional form—the flow of fabric into folds. Drape occurs when only part of a fabric is directly supported and gravity produces deformation in the unsupported portion. Fabrics that fall in numerous "soft," vertical folds are highly drapable. The drape of a fabric is visible because light reflects differently at the tops of the folds than at the valleys of the folds.

FIGURE 4.5   Color: a change in the spectral reflection of incident light by a colorant as interpreted by an observer.

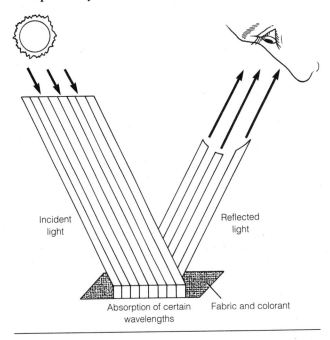

Incident light

Reflected light

Absorption of certain wavelengths

Fabric and colorant

Although the preferable way to determine drapability is to look at the fabric, feel alone also can tell us about drapability. If you place your hand inside a box and pick up a fabric, you can determine its drapability by feeling how the fabric falls around your hand.

Drapability is related to fabric weight, stiffness (flexural rigidity, ease of bending or flexing), and shear resistance. Weight and stiffness are the most important factors. The weight of a fabric tends to cause it to fall; the stiffness of a fabric opposes gravity. The greater the fabric weight, the more likely the fabric is to drape. The greater the fabric stiffness, the less likely the fabric is to drape.

Shear resistance relates to the friction between yarns and fibers within the fabric that must be overcome as the fabric assumes a nonplanar configuration. Fabrics with low shear resistance (low internal friction) fall into folds more readily than fabrics with high shear resistance (high internal friction). A textile scientist determines shear resistance by assessing the force required to pull a rectangular piece of fabric into a parallelogram.

A heavy, limp, less shear-resistant fabric will hang down in many small folds, following the form of the

---

[2]The chemical structure of dyestuffs is presented in Chapter 34. An explanation of how this structure permits selective absorption of incident light will also be found there.

body or object. A light, stiff, highly shear-resistant fabric will not follow the outline of the form supporting it and will form fewer, less sharp folds.

APPEARANCE RETENTION

Generally, fabrics should retain their original appearance for the life expectancy of the product. Notable exceptions to this are denim and Indian madras cloth. In the 1980s, the sooner a worn look was obtained, the more desirable a denim garment became. The beauty of Indian madras is that the dyes bleed and the colors "wash" together during laundering.

Appearance retention is a primary factor in determining the longevity or service life of apparel fabrics and interior and household textiles. Carpeting is so durable that it loses its aesthetic appeal well before it "wears out"; it may matt and fuzz before physical deterioration begins. Abrasive action on apparel fabrics may cause pilling (the development of unsightly balls of fuzz) long before durability is affected.

Although the appearance of a fabric is evident as soon as it is seen, the ability of the fabric to retain that appearance is much more difficult to ascertain. Little, if any, information is provided in the marketplace concerning colorfastness, wrinkle resistance, loft, crease retention, or the propensity to snag or pill. These potential changes in fabric appearance are considered in this section. Appearance changes resulting from soiling and staining are examined in Chapter 5.

Color Considerations

The retention of the original color by a textile during use is an important performance property. No textile, with the possible exception of synthetic fibers that have been pigmented with carbon black during spinning, has perfectly fast colors (is resistant to color change under any circumstance). The ability of the fabric to resist the transfer of its colorant to objects it contacts or to other areas of its surface during use is also critical.

Colorfastness. *Colorfastness* is the ability of the fabric to maintain its original color. A highly colorfast fabric retains its color; a fabric with poor colorfastness fades and/or changes color.

In general, a fabric exhibits good or acceptable colorfastness toward one destructive agent (for example, sunlight) but poor colorfastness toward another agent, such as perspiration or chlorine water (bleaches used in laundering or chlorine added to swimming-pool water). Fabrics usually are dyed or printed with colorants that are sufficiently fast for their intended end use, but trouble arises when fabrics are used for purposes the dyer or printer could not foresee. For example, it may not be wise to use apparel fabrics for window curtains because these textiles probably are not suitably colorfast to light. Conversely, a curtain fabric probably does not have sufficient colorfastness to perspiration to be used as a dress fabric. A manufacturer does not meet needlessly high dyeing standards because the faster dyes are to a wide variety of destructive agents, the more expensive they tend to be both in material and processing costs.

Many agents can cause color change, including light, chlorine water, perspiration, perfumes, ozone, and nitrogen oxides. Several of them also cause the fabric to disintegrate (lose its physical integrity). These agents are discussed in Chapter 5.

Crocking. *Crocking* is "the transfer of color (colorant) from the surface of a colored fabric to an adjacent area of the same fabric or to another surface principally by rubbing action." Fabrics that resist color transfer when rubbed have good crocking resistance. Usually, there is no visible color loss to the original fabric; the fabric that rubs against it becomes stained. Dark colors are most likely to crock, and crocking is more likely to occur when moisture is present in the fabric.

Frosting. *Frosting* is "a change in color in a limited area of a fabric caused by abrasive wear." It can result when fibers within a blend wear (abrade) away at different rates, if the fibers have been dyed different colors or shades. The degree of frosting is proportionate to the contrast in colors between the fibers.

Durable-press polyester/cotton blend fabrics are known to frost. The durable-press treatment greatly reduces the abrasion resistance of cotton fibers but not that of polyester fibers. Further, cotton fibers are likely to be a darker shade than polyester fibers; as the cotton fibers wear away, a light streak appears on the fabric surface.

Frosting also can occur on single-fiber composition fabrics as they become abraded if the colorant does not penetrate some fibers completely or evenly. Incomplete penetration may result when a thick, single-fiber composition fabric is dyed; the fibers near the fabric surface can become more completely penetrated than those near the center. During abrasion, the incompletely dyed fibers may be brought to the surface, resulting in a frosted effect.

Bleeding. *Bleeding* is "the loss of color from a dyed fabric when immersed in water, drycleaning solvent, or similar liquid medium, with consequent coloring of the liquid medium." Colorant is withdrawn from the interior as well as the surface of the fibers due to weak colorant-fiber bonding. Dark-colored fabrics are more likely to bleed than pastel fabrics. The original textile usually does not change color itself because excess colorant is lost.

Color staining—"the undesired pickup of color by a fabric"—may occur on other textiles in the solvent. Garments should therefore be sorted according to depth of color: whites, pastels, and dark colors should be laundered separately. When washing products such as dark towels, the manufacturer recommends laundering like colors together. Reputable drycleaners also carefully sort garments by color.

Yellowing. The yellow discoloration of textiles, particularly white ones, is an age-old color problem. Unlike the other color problems considered thus far, yellowing does not result from colorant transfer or loss. Instead, the textile appears yellow because the light reflected to the eye from the textile contains more yellow wavelength than the light incident on it. There are more than 20 different ways (several of the major ones are considered here) in which white or pale-colored textiles are altered, causing this undesired change in appearance.

Yellowing may occur due to the natural ageing of organic polymers, of which most fibers are composed. It is the result of oxidative or degradative processes. Manufactured fibers may contain stabilizers to reduce the effects of ageing.

The oxidation of built-up body oils on fabric also results in yellowing. Yellowed cotton and flax (linen) fabrics can usually be whitened with chlorine bleach (usually available in liquid form). Oxygen bleach, which is milder than chlorine bleach and usually available in powdered form, can remove some soil residues on synthetic fiber fabrics. Success varies. Prevention of soil buildup is a better approach to reduced yellowing. Generally, yellowed synthetic garments have been laundered too infrequently or under conditions too gentle to remove the oils. Laundering frequently in water of at least 100° F (37.8° C) and with a detergent is recommended. The longer oily deposits are left on a fabric, the more difficult they are to remove because they oxidize. Overuse of bleach can cause yellowing to occur.

Increases in the level of atmospheric pollution, particularly nitrogen oxides from high-density traffic and from gas and oil-fired heating systems, cause fabric yellowing. Oxides of nitrogen are almost always present in the atmosphere. Fabric yellowing is not a problem at low concentrations, but can be at high concentrations.

Certain fluorescent whitening agents[3] that are applied to fibers and fabrics also can cause fabric yellowing if they are present in too high concentrations and/or inadequately fixed to the fiber. Yellowing of fluorescent-brightened fabrics may be accelerated when oxides of nitrogen are also present.

Packaging materials can induce some yellow staining in alkali-finished or washed fabrics if BHT[4], nitrogen dioxide, and moisture are all present. Yellow stains caused by BHT during storage usually take the form of rings, spots, or streaks on areas near openings, perforations, or holes in the bag or packaging film.

Resilience

Resilience is that "property of a fabric, fiber, or yarn by virtue of which it is able to do work against restraining forces during return from a deformed state." As a fabric is worn or used, it is subjected to bending, twisting, compressional, and other distorting forces. These forces can cause wrinkles and creases; eventually, the fabric may bag or sag. Fabrics, fibers, and yarns differ in their abilities to resist distorting forces and to recover once these forces have been removed. Wrinkle resistance and wrinkle recovery, compressional resilience (loft), crease retention, and shape retention are important aspects of resilience.

Wrinkle Resistance and Recovery. *Wrinkles* (short, rounded folds) are undesirable fabric deformations. They are visible largely due to differences in the reflection of the light from the section of the fabric adjoining the wrinkle and the wrinkle itself. In other words, luster differs over the surface. Lustrous, smooth-surfaced fabrics, such as satin, show wrinkles more readily than matte, rough-surfaced fabrics, such as cotton flannel, because there is a larger contrast in the angles of light re-

---

[3] A fluorescent whitening agent, a type of colorant, enhances a white appearance by giving a blue fluorescence. It can change ultraviolet light, which is not visible, to blue. The amount of visible blue light reflected from the fabric is greater than that incident on it. The fabric appears whiter. Fluorescent whitening agents are yellow powders and liquids. When incident light is very low in ultraviolet wavelength, the yellow color of the fluorescent whitening agent can be seen.

[4] At one time, BHT, or butylated hydroxytoluene, was a component of some ethylene bags in which textiles were stored, but bag manufacturers have stopped adding this compound. BHT is found in foam shoulder pads, polyurethane furniture cushions, soaps, cardboard cartons, glue, and cosmetics.

FIGURE 4.6 Compressional resilience.

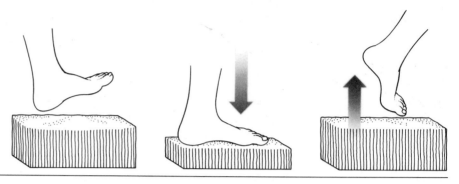

flected from the smooth and wrinkled portions on the satin than on the flannel. Printed or patterned fabrics mask or hide wrinkles.

Compressional Resilience (Loft). *Compressional resilience* or *loft* is the ability of a textile to spring back to its original thickness after a compressional force has been applied (Figure 4.6). Low loft is described as matted or flattened; high loft, as springy.

Compressional resilience is an important performance property of fiberfill products, socks, and pile fabrics, such as carpeting. High compressional resilience preserves the air space within fiberfill batts, maintaining their insulating ability. Sock fabrics with acceptable compressional resilience continue to allow water vapor and heat to flow through the fabric interstices. The soles of some socks now have exceptional compressional resilience to reduce shock and jar to the runner wearing them. Carpeting with excellent compressional resilience prevents matting in high-traffic areas. This ability extends the service life of the carpet because changes in surface appearance often occur before abrasive deterioration becomes severe.

Shape Retention. Garment fabrics that bag at the elbows and knees, skirts and pants that pouch in the seat area, hosiery that droops at the ankles, knitted neckbands, waistbands, and cuffs that increase in circumference during wear, fabrics that appear crinkly on molded seat cushions—all of these textiles have failed to resist distorting forces and to recover from them.

Some fabrics retain shape better than others. Woven fabrics retain shape better than knitted fabrics, because the yarns are less easily moved in weaves than in knits. In

general, felts and nonwoven fabrics have poor shape retention when distorting forces act on them. Spandex fibers are often combined with other fibers to improve shape retention. Yarn structures, such as core spun, incorporate a spandex fiber into the yarn, which provides quick, full recovery from extension.

Moldability and tailorability are related to shape retention. Moldability is the ability to curve a fabric and have it retain the curvature. Tailorability permits curvature to be added to certain fabrics at, for example, the lapels or collar.

Crease Retention. *Creases* are intentionally placed bends in a fabric, such as in a pleated skirt or trouser legs, that are intended to be permanent. Compared to wrinkles, creases are sharper bends: the fabric is bent over on itself and remains in a folded position. Fabrics that contain thermoplastic fibers with a heat set finish retain creases best during wear, laundering, and drycleaning (Chapter 33).

Pilling Propensity

Pilling is a fabric surface fault characterized by the accumulation of *pills*—"bunches or balls of tangled fibers which are held to the surface of a fabric by one or more fibers." Fabrics composed of staple fibers (short fibers) are subject to pilling.

Fabric pilling results from abrasive action, which causes fibers to migrate from the body of the fabric to protrude partially above its surface. Further abrasive action "twists" the protruding fiber ends into balls (pills); it also may loosen or break the anchor fibers from the fabrics, reducing the number of pills on its surface.

Whether pilling occurs to the extent that it causes an unacceptable change in surface appearance depends on three factors: (1) the rate of formation of surface fiber fuzz, (2) the rate of fuzz entanglement, and (3) the rate of pill wear-off.

Pills can be accentuated and aggravated by laundering and drycleaning. Accentuation occurs when lint collects on the pills and makes them much more visible, especially on dark-colored fabrics.

The reduction of pilling in fabrics is a complex technical problem. Fiber, yarn, and fabric alterations designed to increase the rate of pill break-off also can increase pill formation. Considerable advances have been made, but the problem has yet to be solved.

Snagging Propensity

A *snag* is a yarn or part of a yarn that is pulled or plucked from the surface of a fabric and protrudes above that surface. *Snagging resistance* is the ability of the fabric to resist this yarn displacement.

Snagging is probably the most serious problem of knit fabrics. Their relatively open, looped-yarn structure permits sharp objects to catch and displace the yarns. Protruding yarns as well as shiners (tight yarns that form on either side of the snag) contribute to an unattractive surface appearance. Snags may be worked back into the fabric, but shiners remain. Cutting off snags may cause the fabric to run, or ladder.

FEEL

The sense of touch is involved in the assessment of four performance properties of fabrics. Drape and texture have been previously considered, because sight is the primary sense used to interpret these performance properties. Here, we consider body, which is primarily a feel-related property, and hand, which can only be determined by the sense of touch.

Body

Body is related to the lightness or heaviness, firmness or looseness, and springiness or limpness of a fabric. Fabrics with "full" body are those that feel "substantive" in the hand; they are thick, firm, and springy. A full-bodied fabric could be compared to a person who heartily grabs another person's hand and shakes it vigorously. Fabrics with little body are lightweight, loose, and limp; they do not feel substantive. These fabrics can be com-

pared to a person who shakes hands as if their arm and hand were a wet dishtowel!

Some idea about the body of a fabric is revealed by looking at it. Thickness and how the fabric drapes are clues to body. The type of body required differs according to end use.

Hand

For nearly 60 years, textile scientists worldwide have tried to answer the questions, "What is fabric hand?" and "How can hand be measured or quantified?" Although there are many definitions of "hand," each stresses that *hand* involves the total sensations experienced when a fabric is touched or manipulated in the fingers (Table 4.1). It is a complex phenomenon of considerable interest; hand is often the fundamental aspect that determines the success or failure of a textile product.

When fabric is manipulated (felt) with the fingers, it is bent; sensations of stiffness or rigidity result. When the fabric is squeezed (compressed), sensations of softness or hardness, as well as thickness, occur. How easily fingers slide across the fabric surface elicits a sense of slipperiness or harshness. The evenness (smoothness or roughness) of the surface and a sense of the fabric's thermal character (warmth or coolness) also can be detected. Hand has at least eight different components and can be soft, hard, springy, limp, rough, smooth, mushy, sleasly, dead, clammy, or waxy.[5] Unfortunately, these words do not have the same meanings to everyone who uses them.

There is no reliable method for the quantitative evaluation of hand, but considerable progress is being made in this area. Most felt sensations arise from the exertion of low stress on the fabric by the fingers. Instruments can now simulate these actions. The force required to bend, compress, shear, and extend a textile are measured on separate instruments; surface contour and friction, on another instrument. The thermal character of a fabric also can be quantified.

SOUND AND SMELL

For the most part, fabrics make little discernible noise when used or worn. Occasionally, however, the *sound* that a fabric makes can be the reason it is selected or rejected by the consumer. Taffetas, the shiny relatively

---

[5]Prickliness is one sensation that is not felt to the same extent by nerves in the fingers as it is by nerves in other parts of the human body and is often missed in hand manipulation.

TABLE 4.1   Terms Related to Fabric Hand.

COMPONENT	EXPLANATORY PHRASE	TERMS TO DESCRIBE RANGE OF COMPONENT
Flexibility [flexural rigidity]	Ease of bending	Pliable (high) to stiff (low)
Compressibility	Ease of squeezing	Soft (high) to hard (low)
Extensibility	Ease of stretching [ease of elongation]	Stretchy (high) to nonstretchy (low)
Resilience*	Ability to recover from deformation	Springy (high) to limp (low)
Density	Mass per unit volume	Compact (high) to open (low)
Surface contour	Divergence of surface from planeness	Rough (high) to smooth (low)
Surface friction	Resistance to slipping offered by the surface	Harsh (high) to slippery (low)
Thermal character	Apparent difference between the temperatures of a fabric and the skin of the person touching it	Cool (high) to warm (low)

*Resilience may be flexural, compressional, extensional, or tortional.

stiff fabrics used extensively in evening wear and bridal gowns, have a characteristic rustle. This sound is acceptable to some people but not to others; acceptability may depend on the situation in which the fabric is to be worn as well as on fashion considerations. Many silk fabrics make a "dry," crunching sound. The friction of two fabrics as they move over each other may produce desired or undesired sounds; for example, consider the movement of pants fabric on the inside leg area.

The production of sound by a textile can be more than a mere annoyance; it can place a person in danger. The clothing worn by a combat soldier must be as quiet as possible to help in concealment. In winter combat environments, fabrics with good snow-shedding and waterproof properties are needed, but many of these fabrics rustle when worn. Research has been undertaken to develop "quiet polymers" for this application. The military also has requested the development of a hook-and-eye[6] tape that generates little or no noise.

Textiles also have the ability to absorb sound from the environment. We examine sound absorption in Chapter 6.

Most fabrics do not have any particular fragrance, but laundry products often contain perfume and may add fragrance to certain fabrics. One recent development in textiles is the incorporation of scented capsules into fabric, which are then activated by every movement of the wearer.[7]

Fiber content and chemical finishes may be sources of disagreeable fabric smells. Raw silk (silk fibers that are still coated with the gum deposited around them by the silkworm) may have an odor. Wool develops an odor when wet. At one time, fabrics finished with formaldehyde (for example, durable-press fabrics) could have a very pungent odor, but manufacturers now use low or nonformaldehyde finishes.

Fabrics differ in the degree to which they absorb and retain odors from the human body or the atmosphere. Synthetic fibers retain odors to a greater extent than natural fibers do. When perspiration and oils are not removed from fabrics, odor problems increase.

CHAPTER SUMMARY

All of the human body's senses except taste are involved in the assessment of the *aesthetic appeal* of textiles. *Sight and touch* are the most important senses; *smell and hearing* play more minor roles. Aesthetic appeal is often the most compelling reason for the selection of a textile. However, excellent aesthetics do not guarantee acceptable overall performance. The aesthetic condition of the fabric during use (color changes, pilling and snagging, resilience) as well as its initial aesthetic appeal (luster, color, translucence, pattern and texture, hand) have been examined here. Detail View 4 provides a definition for each of the properties of aesthetic appeal considered in this chapter.

[6]Hook-and-eye tape is made by Velcro Incorporated and is commonly called "Velcro® tape."
[7]"Sweet as a Rose," *First Magazine* (October 1989).

Maintenance Properties

Maintenance is the ability of a textile to remain in the same state of cleanliness, size, physical integrity and color as when purchased, following wear, use, and/or care procedures.[*]

PERFORMANCE PROPERTY	DEFINITION
Cleanliness (drycleanability, launderability, steam cleanability)	**The ability of a textile to resist soiling and staining; if soiled and/or stained, the ability to release oils, particulate matter (dirt particles), and staining substances during "normal" textile cleaning procedures.**
Soiling propensity	The adsorption, absorption, and entrapment of particulate and oily soils.
Soil release	The desorption of soil from fibers.
Stain resistance	The ability of a textile to resist discoloration by substances accidentally brought into contact with them.
Size (dimensional stability)	**The ability of a textile to retain its original dimensions after wetting, drying, or exposure to high humidity.**
Shrinkage	A reduction in length and/or width.
Growth	An increase in length and/or width.
Physical Integrity and Color (ageing, weathering, rot resistance, or environmental sensitivity)	**The ability of a textile to retain its original level of durability and color properties.**
Light resistance	The ability of a textile to withstand degradation by photo-oxidation and color change when exposed to light.
Biological resistance[†]	The ability of a textile to resist degradation or discoloration by microorganisms and insects.
Chemical resistance[**]	The ability of a textile to resist degradation on submersion or contact with various chemicals during use, storage, and cleaning.
Heat durability	The extent to which a textile retains its useful properties *after* being exposed to a certain temperature and environment for a specified time period and then being returned to ambient air conditions.
Heat resistance[††]	The extent to which a textile retains useful properties *during* exposure to a certain temperature and environment for a specified time period.

---

[*] Maintenance of appearance was considered as appearance retention in Detail View 4.

[†] Do not confuse with permeation resistance to biological organisms or with bacterial adherence (see Detail View 6).

[**] Do not confuse with permeation resistance to chemicals (see Detail View 6).

[††] Do not confuse with thermal resistance (see Detail View 6) or heat durability.

5

*M*aintenance

Usually, the purchaser wants a textile product to remain exactly the same over the entire period it is to be used. The textile is expected to remain clean, the same color, and the same size and to retain its physical integrity. A notable exception is denim; obtaining a worn, faded-look as quickly as possible is highly desirable to many consumers.

In this chapter, performance properties related to the maintenance of cleanliness, size, and physical integrity and color due to environmental factors are considered (Detail View 5). The focus is on maintaining the textile in its state at the time of purchase. Appearance retention (Chapter 4) is closely related to this chapter discussion.

CLEANLINESS

Unfortunately, all fabrics become dirty when they are used or stored. Some textiles soil and stain more rapidly than others; some are easier to return to their original state of cleanliness than others.

Carpeting is particularly susceptible to soiling. Dirt from the outdoors is constantly deposited and ground into it; beverages and other foods are often spilled on it. Most carpeting (73.4%, or ~1.8 billion pounds) is made from nylon[1], a fiber highly vulnerable to oily soiling and staining. Various modifications have been made to nylon

---

[1]Dalton, GA: Carpet and Rug Institute, (1990).

fiber and chemical finishes have been added in an attempt to decrease the rate of soiling.

Children's playclothing and clothing worn in certain occupations, such as road construction, agriculture, and automobile mechanics, may be exposed to extremely dirty conditions. Everyday clothing is primarily subjected to oils and perspiration from the body on which they are worn.

Soiling Propensity

Soil commonly found on textiles is a mixture of:

1. *Particulate soils* (clay, soot, and metal oxides of various sizes and shapes), which originate mostly from wind-blown topsoil but may be products of the combustion of fuel used in homes, industry, and transportation.

2. *Oily and fatty soils*, which come from sebum (secretion of the sebaceous glands) and sweat from the human body, oils and fats from food and cosmetics, and lubricating oils and grease from automobiles and machinery.

Usually, particulate soil is found in the open spaces between fibers and yarns, where it is mechanically entrapped or held by electrostatic forces. Shaking or vacuuming successfully removes mechanically held soil; placing the fabric in water neutralizes the electrostatic attraction.

Oily soils, with or without embedded particulate dirt are found in high concentrations in fabric interstices and

FIGURE 5.1   Location of soil in a polyester/cotton fabric.

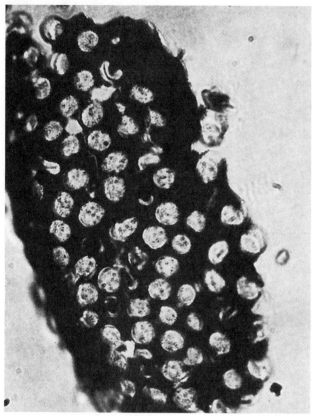

Soil is shown as black in both photographs, due to reaction with osmium tetroxide. Note the concentration of oil in the interfiber spaces of this cross section of a yarn.

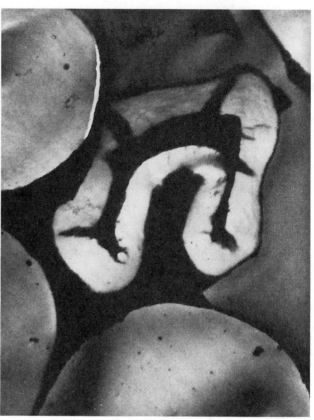

Note the oil on the polyester fiber surfaces (round fibers) and in the center of the cotton (kidney-bean shaped fiber).

on fiber surfaces. Oil is found in cotton fibers but not in synthetic fibers (Figure 5.1). During wear, cotton fabrics take up seven to ten times more oil than fabrics containing synthetic fibers. Among the synthetics, acrylic fabrics take up higher quantities of oil during use than polyester or nylon fabrics do.[2]

Soiling is primarily the adsorption of oily soil over the fabric surface. Removal of oily film from individual fiber surfaces presents the greatest challenge. Failure to remove this film in cleaning accelerates the deterioration of the fabric's appearance because particulate soils continue to accumulate in the retained oil layer.

[2]S.K. Obendorf, Y.M.N. Namesté, and D.J. Durnam, "A Microscopical Study of Residual Oily Soil Distribution on Fabrics of Varying Fiber Content," *Textile Research Journal* 53 (1983): 375.

Soil Release

Soil release is a desorption process in which oily soil is removed from the fiber surface and placed in suspension in a detergent solution. It involves the displacement of one interface (oil-fiber) and the formation of two new interfaces (oil-water and fiber-water). The *desorption process* (Figure 5.2) is the steady retraction of the oil film from a relatively flat configuration into a drop of oil. This type of soil release is referred to as a *roll-up process.*

Oily soil is easier to remove from a hydrophilic (water-loving) fiber or surface than from a hydrophobic (water-avoiding) fiber or surface. The forces of attraction between an oil film and a hydrophilic surface are considerably less than those between a hydrophobic surface and the same oil film. Also, hydrophilic fibers allow water to spread

FIGURE 5.2   The desorption (roll-up) process.

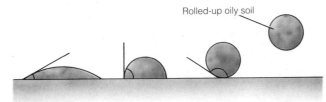

Water rolls up the oily soil and lifts it from the fiber surface.

Desorption is easier to achieve on a hydrophilic surface than on a hydrophobic one.

and wet their surfaces more readily than the hydrophobic fibers do. When a hydrophilic fiber is placed in water, the water wets the exposed fiber surface and is able to penetrate between the oil film and fiber surface. As penetration proceeds, the oil film is rolled up. Water does not spread as readily on a hydrophobic surface and penetration between oil and fiber surface is more difficult due to the greater attraction of oil for the hydrophobic surface.

The roll-up of oily soil is significantly enhanced by the presence of surfactant molecules in the water. Surfactants, one of several ingredients in detergents, are wetting agents. They lower the surface tension of the water, permitting it to spread over and penetrate the fabric more readily. This action brings the surfactant molecules into contact with the oily soil on the fibers, where the molecules anchor themselves. They loosen, surround, and, in effect, solublize or suspend the soil until it is rinsed away. Increased water temperature and agitation further facilitates soil removal. Other ingredients in a detergent formulation, such as builders and antiredeposition agents, also aid in soil removal.

Cotton and rayon fabrics are easier to clean than polyester, nylon, acrylic, and olefin fabrics under identical soiling and laundry conditions. Chemical finishes that decrease hydrophilicity also decrease the ease of soil removal; an example is cotton fabric that has been given a

durable-press finish. Finishes that increase hydrophilicity enhance ease of soil removal; an example is soil release finishes on 100% polyester fabrics and on durable-press polyester/cotton fabrics (Chapter 33).

Although hydrophilicity is the prime factor in soil release, other textile factors also play a role. They include a negative charge (which tends to repel most soils because they also are negatively charged), swelling in water, a smooth fiber surface, a hard fiber surface, and low surface energy in the dry state (to prevent the spreading of oily soils).

Oily soils generally become more difficult to remove with time. When soil ages, its melting point increases due to oxidation and polymerization. Oil secreted from sebaceous glands in the skin normally melts in washwater at temperatures of 68–122° F (20–50° C); aged soil may not melt until the washwater is 158° F (70° C), or above. Aged soil can sometimes be cleaned from fibers that can withstand high water temperatures, but usually not from other fibers.

Staining and Stain Removal

Staining is the undesired pickup of color by a fabric when it comes into contact with substances containing colorants. Staining substances may be water-borne (coffee, tea, catsup, and blood) or oil-borne (lipstick, margarine, shoe polish, and ballpoint pen ink). Special procedures are necessary to remove stains, because a stain is chemically attracted to the fibers in the fabric. Bleaches may be used to remove some types of stains; specialized solvents are necessary for others. Extreme caution should always be exercised, so that the stain is not set into the fabric and so that the chemical itself does not cause fiber and fabric damage.

Stain also may indicate a discolored area on the fabric caused by a difference in light reflection. For example, a stained or discolored area results when clear oil penetrates a fabric. This definition of stain is not used in the text.

Apparent Soil

Apparent soil is particulate soil that is magnified and seems to cover all surfaces. Round, smooth filament fibers, which are transparent, are particularly vulnerable to this type of soiling. Nylon fiber is the prime exhibitor of apparent soiling, and manufacturers of carpet nylon have been instrumental in solving the apparent soil effect. Textile scientists have successfully overcome the problem of soil magnification by adding delustrants to the fiber, but they introduce a somewhat chalky appearance to the nylon and eventual soil buildup makes the delustered fiber carpet look very dirty. Multilobal and trilobal modifications are very successful in combatting magnification, but the indentations in the fiber surface can be traps for soil. Round-cornered square fibers with a smooth surface and internal longitudinal tunnels do not trap soil and can avoid the apparent soil effect.

SIZE

Purchasers of cotton T-shirts usually know from past experience that the T-shirt is likely to become smaller when washed—sometimes decreasing 22% in length and enough in girth to cause discomfort after only five launderings and dryings.[3] Therefore, at the time of purchase, the consumer should select a shirt that is a size or two larger to allow for shrinkage. A similar decision may be made for polyester/cotton T-shirts, which can shrink as much as 11.3% in length after five wear and laundry cycles. Some jeans are made to "shrink to fit"; the purchaser buys a pair of these jeans that clearly does not fit and then washes it to produce the correct size. When buying most apparel items and interior textiles, the consumer makes little, if any, allowance for shrinkage. If shrinkage subsequently occurs, the textile item may not be usable.

Just as serious as a reduction in size is an increase in the size or dimensions of a textile when it is wetted, steamed, or exposed to an increase in atmospheric humidity. Drapery fabrics composed of certain fibers, such as rayon, may lengthen when the humidity is high and may or may not return to their original length when more normal levels of humidity are restored.

The retention of size or dimensions is called *dimensional stability.* A fabric may increase (grow) or decrease (shrink) in size. The potential for dimensional change often dictates care procedures: whether the textile can be laundered or must be drycleaned and what the maximum water temperature, agitation, and drying temperature can be.

Calculation of Dimensional Change

To determine the amount of shrinkage or growth of a fabric, both the lengthwise and crosswise directions are usually measured. The fabric is then laundered or dry-

cleaned, and the distances are measured again. The percentage of shrinkage or growth is calculated as

$$\frac{\text{Final Measurement} - \text{Initial Measurement}}{\text{Initial Measurement}} \times 100$$
$$= \% \text{ Dimensional Change}$$

A positive result is growth and a negative result is shrinkage.

Consider the following example. Before cleaning, the distance between marks placed on a fabric is 10 inches. After cleaning, the lengthwise distance is 9.8 inches, so that

$$\frac{9.8 - 10}{10} \times 100 = -2\% \text{ (2\% shrinkage)}$$

and the crosswise distance is 10.3 inches so that

$$\frac{10.3 - 10}{10} \times 100 = +3\% \text{ (3\% growth)}$$

Acceptable Values of Dimensional Change

A 5% shrinkage in a women's dress represents a reduction of one-half a dress size; that is, a size-11 dress would shrink to a point approximately midway between a size-9 and a size-11 dress, and the garment probably could no longer be worn by the purchaser. Most woven fabrics should have shrinkage values below 3% to retain the fit of the garment. For knit fabrics, shrinkage values of 5% can be tolerated, because knit fabrics have a greater potential to elongate than other fabric constructions.

Causes of Dimensional Change

Tension, swelling, and felting result in fabric shrinkage. Only one or all three may occur in a single fabric.

Tension. Tension introduced during processing may make a fabric shrink after purchase. When the stressed fabric is agitated in water or tumbled in humid air, the internal tension may be relieved and the fabric may relax, or shrink. A "structural readjustment" takes place. Shrinkage due to the relief of tension is called *relaxation shrinkage.*

In the case of woven fabrics, those fabrics in which yarns are interlaced at right angles to each other, the straightness or crimpiness of the yarns may indicate the degree of tension in the fabric (Figure 5.3). There is a degree of crimp in the crosswise and lengthwise yarns

---

[3]Sanforset® brochure from The Sanforized Company.

FIGURE 5.3 Different amounts of yarn crimp in a woven fabric.

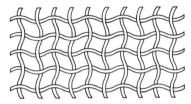

The most stable configuration: yarn crimp in both lengthwise and crosswise yarns.

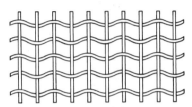

A typical yarn configuration after weaving: lengthwise yarns are taut.

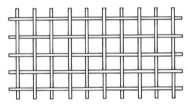

The least stable configuration: a typical yarn configuration after routine finishing: both lengthwise and crosswise yarns are taut.

that results in a fully relaxed fabric which is the most stable configuration.

Lesser degrees of crimp lead to shrinkage. During weaving, the lengthwise yarns are held very taut in a straight configuration. Fabric in this state will shrink mainly in the lengthwise direction as the warp yarns seek the most relaxed state, a more crimped configuration. During dyeing and finishing, the cloth is wet and hot and under tension in both the lengthwise and crosswise directions. The hot, wet fibers are readily molded to a new shape, and the fabric is commonly dried while under tension. A fabric also can be stressed in both directions, the least stable configuration; in this case, the potential for shrinkage in both length and width is high.

In knitted fabrics, the stable state is controlled by the interplay of forces required to shape the interlocking loops of yarn. The loops in knitted fabric can be elongated by 35% during manufacture, providing great potential for shrinkage.

When fabric is removed from manufacturing equipment, it usually cannot assume a balanced or most stable state because frictional forces between the yarns and fibers hinder movement. Wetting the fabric does not allow the fabric to fully relax (to assume the most stable state). Agitation in soap or detergent (which acts as a lubricant) decreases the frictional forces between yarns and fibers, and the fabric then begins to assume its most stable state. Usually, a single wash (no matter how long it continues) will not bring the cloth to its most stable state. Shrinkage may continue throughout several washes, but the amount lessens with each wash. This phenomenon is called *progressive shrinkage.*

Tension may also exist in the fibers themselves, and the polymers within fibers may need to assume a more stable configuration. Heat may allow molecular movement to occur. The polymers may fold up or be brought into better registration (Figure 5.4). In either case, the fiber contracts. Manufacturers of synthetic fiber fabrics usually heat set the fabric, so that it has little or no tendency to shrink when exposed to normally encountered temperatures. However, if the consumer exposes the fabric to temperatures higher than those for which the fabric has been heat set, shrinkage will occur. Generally, a clothes dryer would need to be malfunctioning badly for heat shrinkage to occur. For example, nylon and polyester fibers are heat set at temperatures of ~390° F (200° C), and dryer temperatures seldom exceed 158° F, or 70° C (measured in exhaust gases).

Swelling. In addition to relaxation shrinkage, some fabrics shrink during laundering because their fibers absorb water molecules and *swell* (increase in diameter). Hydrophilic fibers (cotton, flax, rayon, silk, and wool) can swell 14–26% in diameter; hydrophobic fibers do not swell much, if at all. Fabrics containing rayon fibers are most likely to exhibit the greatest swelling shrinkage or growth, because rayon fibers absorb the most water.

Fiber swelling leads to fabric shrinkage (Figure 5.5). A swelling in fibers is accompanied by a corresponding swell in the yarn because the fibers are held close to each other by the twist in the yarn. In other words, fiber swelling does not simply fill the interstices between the fibers in the yarn. The increase in yarn diameter requires an increase in yarn crimp, because each yarn must interlace with a larger yarn. An increase in crimp can occur only at the expense of a reduction in fabric length and

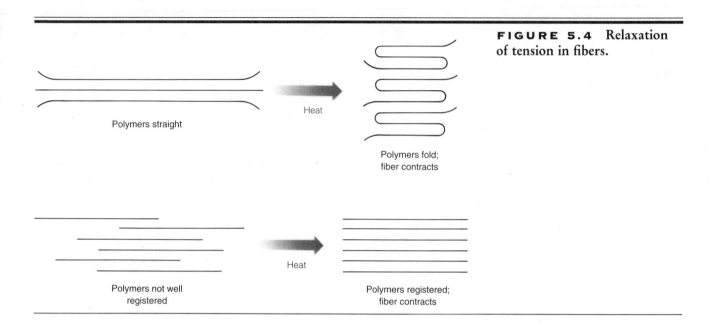

FIGURE 5.4 Relaxation of tension in fibers.

Polymers straight

Heat

Polymers fold;
fiber contracts

Polymers not well
registered

Heat

Polymers registered;
fiber contracts

width. When the fabric is dried, its reduced dimensions remain due to frictional forces between the fibers and yarns.

Fiber swelling also may lead to fabric growth. When the fiber is swollen, it may be in a weakened condition because normal polymer bonding within the fiber is lessened. If the weakened, wet textile is subjected to longitudinal forces, it lengthens. For example, conventional-rayon drapery fabrics lengthen under conditions of high humidity because the weight of the drapery exerts a longitudinal force on the weakened fibers.

Felting. If fabrics that are made from wool or that contain a significant percent of wool are washed energetically in hot water, they are likely to shrink excessively and become thick and stiff. Some of this shrinkage results from tension and fiber swelling. Additional shrinkage is due to the interlocking of fibers in a process called *felting.* Felting shrinkage is unique to fabrics that contain wool fibers.

Felting occurs because a wool fiber has overlapping scales from root to tip (Figure 5.6) that produce a directional frictional effect. The fiber feels smoother (less friction occurs) when it is rubbed from root to tip and coarser (more friction occurs) when it is rubbed from tip to root.

Wool fibers also move in only one direction due to the manner in which their scales overlap. If you hold a wool

fiber at its midpoint and move your thumb back and forth along its length, you will see the fiber travel toward the fiber root. (If the root end is to your left, the fiber travels toward the left; if the root is to your right, the fiber travels toward the right.)

When a mass of wool fibers is subjected to mechanical action, each fiber can only move in one direction. The fibers become entangled, and the cloth shrinks. This behavior is enhanced if the fibers are in a warm alkaline or acid bath. Using a drycleaning solvent and less mechanical action is the recommended way to clean most wool fabrics so that felting shrinkage does not occur. Some wool fabrics are given a special finish to reduce felting shrinkage and make them machine-washable (Chapter 33).

Relationship of Dimensional Stability to Other Performance Properties

Dimensional stability is closely related to shape retention. Both properties are related to the ability of a fabric to retain its original size or dimensions. The major difference between the terms lies in what causes the fabric to change dimensions. Dimensional stability generally refers to the dimensional changes that can occur when a fabric is exposed to wetting, steaming, or variations in humidity. Shape retention usually refers to the potential changes in the size (length or width) of a fabric that can be induced by a mechanical force.

FIGURE 5.5 Fabric shrinkage due to fiber swelling.

Dry fiber

Swelling of hydrophilic fibers as water is absorbed between the fiber polymers.

Wet fiber

Swelling of lengthwise and crosswise yarns leads to a decrease in fabric length and width:

Before washing: no fiber or yarn swelling.

After washing: fiber swelling and increased yarn crimp; shortening of fabric length and width.

After drying: no more swelling and fabric has shortened further.

PHYSICAL INTEGRITY AND COLOR

Textile fragments survive from the time of the Swiss Lake Dwellers, the Copts, and the Egyptian Pharaohs. The hot, dry and dark or cool and anerobic conditions under which these peoples stored their textiles helped to preserve them. Although these fragments have lost a considerable degree of their original levels of durability and color, the fact that they remain at all after such a time span is remarkable.

Museum textile curators and conservators consider how to display and store historic textiles to prevent further disintegration and color change. Most people are not concerned about preserving textiles for generations or ages, but they do expect them to maintain their physical integrity and original color over a "reasonable" time period. Replacement of textiles in too short a time span is a costly matter.

In this section, we consider the *age resistance* of a textile, or its ability to retain strength, abrasion resistance, and other durability properties. The effects of four environmental factors—ultraviolet radiation, chemicals, microorganisms and insects, and heat—on the textile during use and storage are paramount. Their influence on the whiteness or color of textiles during use and storage also is included here.

Closely related concepts to age resistance are weather resistance, rot resistance, and environmental sensitivity. Each is defined on the basis of the combination of environmental factors being considered. *Weather resistance* is generally limited to the effects of ultraviolet radiation in the presence of various amounts of moisture. *Rot resistance* refers to the interactive effects of biological degradation, moisture, and heat. *Environmental sensitivity* is usually discussed in terms of a specific factor, such as sensitivity to acid rain or ultraviolet radiation.

It is important to remember that high age resistance is not always desirable. When objects are discarded because they have served their purpose, the expectation is that "Nature" will clear away what has become refuse. Such degradation is an essential process in the maintenance of the world in which we live and a means of recycling many of the essential elements contained in these textiles and other materials. However, when degradation is an unwanted process, it can be a serious and costly problem.

Light Resistance

Exposure to intense outdoor sunlight for long periods of time causes most fabrics to break down physically. Ultraviolet light (the portion of sunlight that degrades textiles) will weaken most textiles to the point that they can no longer serve their purpose. The fabrics in tents, deck chairs, awnings, boat-cushion covers, and outdoor carpeting are regularly exposed to sunlight. Garments and household textiles that are frequently dried outdoors can also receive sufficient exposure to deteriorate. In some climates, clothing must be brought inside as soon as it is dry to preserve fabric integrity.

Behind glass, textiles degrade and fade at a much slower rate, because glass effectively filters out a considerable amount of ultraviolet light. Curtains and draperies, carpeting, and upholstered furniture near windows can be observed to fade. However, the degrading effect of sunlight may not be evident until the fabric is cleaned. The friction and stress on the textile is then sufficient to cause it to disintegrate. Drycleaners often warn customers that a drapery may not survive the drycleaning process due to "invisible" damage over time from ultraviolet-light exposure. Interior fabrics in automobiles receive considerable sunlight exposure under glass.

Fluorescent lighting is also a source of ultraviolet light. Interior textiles, such as carpeting and upholstered furniture, in rooms with such lighting may show fading.

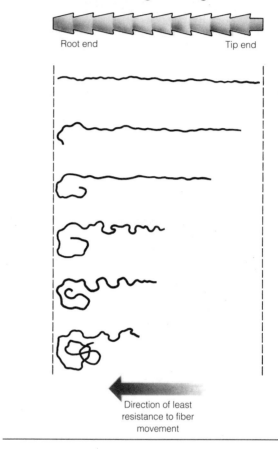

FIGURE 5.6   Felting shrinkage.

Root end   Tip end

Direction of least resistance to fiber movement

Garments displayed in retail stores with fluorescent lighting may show light streaks in the areas that receive the most direct exposure.

Light resistance is the ability of textile fibers to withstand degradation by photo-oxidation due to ultraviolet exposure. Viewing a fabric through an electron microscope reveals how ultraviolet light affects individual fibers (Figure 5.7). The amount of light resistance required depends on the end use of the textile.

How Light Resistant? Loss in breaking strength is often used as an indicator of the light resistance of a fiber, yarn, or fabric. The breaking strength of the textile is determined prior to and after exposure to ultraviolet light, and the percent of loss in strength is calculated. Comparisons are only meaningful when conditions of exposure are identical.

FIGURE 5.7 Degradation of nylon 6, 6 fibers due to exposure to ultraviolet radiation.

Original surface

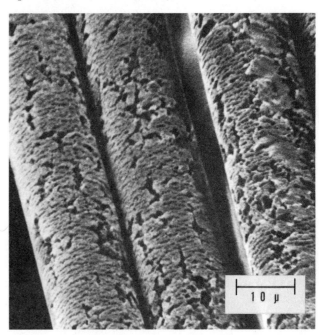

After 672 hours exposure to borosilicate filtered light

In view of the inherent sensitivity of textiles to ultraviolet light, they manage to provide a reasonable service life in many environments. Part of the reason for this is that even the brightest sunlight can only penetrate fabrics to a limited depth before it is scattered and absorbed. Damage may therefore be superficial, affecting only those fibers at the fabric surface. In temperate climates, the very slowness of the ultraviolet-light reaction may offset fabric breakdown.

Other Effects of Ultraviolet-Light Exposure. Both visible and ultraviolet wavelengths contribute to fading. The effect of light on certain colors outdoors differs from that on colors indoors behind glass.

Chemical finishes may be susceptible to photo-oxidation, reducing their effectiveness. For example, flame-retardant treatments on cotton can be degraded to water-soluble compounds by exposure to ultraviolet light; the degraded finish is then washed away in laundering or in rain. Some water-repellent treatments are rendered ineffective in a similar manner. Ultraviolet-light absorbers eventually become ineffective against ultraviolet radiation. Fabric coatings undergo the same oxidation processes and slowly become weak, embrittled, and stiff.

Sunlight also may decompose optical brighteners, which enhance the brilliance or whiteness of a fabric by converting ultraviolet wavelengths into visible wavelengths. When the optical brightener decomposes, a bright, white fabric is converted to an unsightly yellow, green, brown, grey, or (in some cases) pinkish color. Some brighteners may begin to decompose within an hour of exposure. Once the brightener has decomposed, it is not usually possible to restore the fabric.

Biological Resistance

The *biological resistance* of a textile is its ability to resist destruction or discoloration by microorganisms and insects.

Microorganisms. *Microorganisms* inhabit the soil, water, and air and can develop and proliferate on textiles. Species of microfungi, bacteria, actinomycites (filamentous bacteria), and algae can cause the biodeterioration or discoloration of a textile if they encounter favorable growth conditions: certain degrees of moisture and warmth and a substance from which they can assimilate carbon. Figure 5.8 shows mildew seen through an electron microscope.

BIODETERIORATION. *Biodeterioration* is the chemical alteration of a textile by the cellular enzymes that microorganisms excrete when they obtain food. When the fiber is attacked, the excreted enzyme breaks the chemical linkages in the molecular chains of the fiber. Sometimes a surface finish or dirt on the fabric may be attacked. Heavy growth of microorganisms leads to *rot*—the breakdown of fibers and the subsequent loss of such properties as strength and flexibility.

DISCOLORATION. The mild growth of some microorganisms can lead to fabric *discoloration*. Pigments excreted by microorganisms stain the textile. Many mildew-producing fungi stain fabrics. Once it is stained by mildew, returning the textile to its original condition may prove difficult, if not impossible.

MICROBIOLOGICAL RESISTANCE IN END USE. It is particularly important to consider the microbiological resistance of a textile to be used in the tropics and other humid climates. People who sprinkle their clothing before ironing it and then avoid the ironing task as long as possible should be aware of the potential danger of microorganism attack. When the following products are purchased, their microbiological resistance should be considered:

shoe and shoe linings	outdoor furniture fabric
military uniforms	boat covers
coated fabrics (rainwear)	tents
shower curtains	sails
carpet (backing)	awnings
mattress pads	tarpaulins
beach and table umbrellas	

Insects. Dozens of different species of insects are destructive to natural fibers (Figure 5.9). The *common clothes moth*, which is smaller than the ordinary house moth, is probably the most significant wool-fabric pest. At least seven types of *beetles* are also wool predators; the black carpet beetle and the furniture carpet beetle cause the most damage. *Silverfish* attack fabrics that contain cellulosic fibers (cotton, flax, rayon) and fabrics that are starched.

Female moths and beetles fasten their eggs to the wool fabric with an animal adhesive. A common clothes moth, for example, can lay over 250 eggs in two weeks.[4] The larvae, or grubs, from these eggs eat the fiber. The protein keratin, which is the polymer in wool, serves as

---

[4]M.W. Townsend, "Moths and Wool," *Textiles* 12/1 (1983): 8.

FIGURE 5.8 Mildew growth as seen under an electron microscope (~350×).

the food source. Each grub can consume 0.0014 ounces (40 milligrams) of wool in 30 days. The progeny from one moth alone can eat 93 pounds (42 kilograms) of wool in one year. Grubs that build protective cases can live for four years and may chew away at the wool all of that time.

The best way to prevent damage is to keep the fabric clean: brush, wash, or air it. Moth and beetle grubs do not survive on articles that are mobile, on clothes that are frequently washed, or on carpets that are regularly vacuumed and cleaned. Ironing also can be a deterrent if the heat is high enough (>130° F, or 55° C) to kill the grubs. A cedar chest or closet is recommended for long-term storage of wool fabrics; the use of mothballs is also effective. Both the cedar odor and the napthalene in mothballs are offensive to the female moth.

Carpets, billiard cloths, piano felts, and blankets containing wool fibers need to be protected from pests while in use. Chemical finishes can be applied that kill the lar-

FIGURE 5.9   Insects destructive to natural fibers.

Casemaking clothes moth

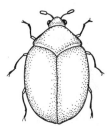

Variegated carpet beetle

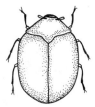

Furniture carpet beetle

Common clothes moth

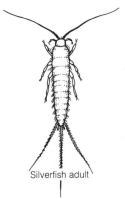

Silverfish adult

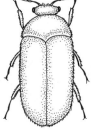

Black carpet beetle

vae as soon as they try to eat the wool or that prevent the larvae from eating the wool because they cannot digest it (Chapter 33).

Chemical Resistance

Most fibers are not inert substances; their polymers react with other chemicals. In the manufacture of fibers and fabrics, chemical reactivity often enhances product performance. (Unit V is devoted to this topic.) *Chemical resistance*—the ability to withstand deterioration and color change when in contact with environmental chemicals—is often desired in end use. Here, we focus on the resistance of the textile to chemicals during use.

In use, during cleaning, and in storage a textile comes into contact with many chemicals that can affect it adversely. A fabric may dissolve almost instantaneously, as happens when acetone (a component of fingernail polish remover) is spilled on an acetate fabric. Similarly, the concentration of sulfuric acid in the air of many metropolitan areas may be high enough to cause fiber breakage

in nylon hose. At the other extreme, fabric damage (weakening) may occur very slowly, as is the case when acids are released from certain papers wrapped around fabrics in storage.

Prolonged contact with food stains may result in disintegration of the fabric when it is finally laundered. Drycleaners often note that holes that develop in fabrics during drycleaning are actually due to prolonged exposure to stains. They recommend that customers bring stained garments in to be cleaned immediately, instead of collecting garments over a period of time. Chemicals also may cause color fading; chlorine bleach and perfumes are two examples. Household products and foods differ in alkalinity and acidity levels (Table 5.1). The sensitivity of protein fibers (wool and silk) to alkaline stains and of cellulosic fibers (cotton) to acidic stains has been demonstrated.[5] Each fabric was completely saturated, and the product remained on the fabric for one week at

[5] International Fabricare Institute, "Fabric Damage Caused by Stains," *IFI Fabricare News* (July 1989), pp. 7–8.

room temperature. It was found that a hair-coloring product could decrease the strength of cotton fabric by 11.1% and of silk by 1.4%. Bleach caused a 4.2% loss in strength in the cotton fabric and a 10.5% loss in the silk fabric. In the case of milk, which soured during the week, cotton lost 16.6% of its strength; silk, 15.2%. Cola, under accelerated ageing, yielded a strength loss of 40.5% on cotton but only losses of 20.8% on silk and of 1.6% on wool.

Other acidic and alkaline conditions encountered include perspiration, polluted air, acid rain, and chlorine in swimming pools, hot tubs, and most municipal water supplies. Detergent solutions and laundry bleach are usually alkaline. Drycleaning and stain-removal products contain organic solvents.

Sulfur dyes can degrade cellulosic fibers (cotton, flax, ramie, rayon). This fabric tendering results from the gradual buildup of sulfuric or sulfonic acids as loosely bound sulfur in the dye oxidizes. Heat and humidity accelerate the rate of tendering. Fabrics are gradually weakened during storage, and damage is aggravated by normal wear and abrasion. This damage often does not show up until the textile is laundered or drycleaned.

Heat Durability and Heat Resistance

Exposure to heat can shorten the service life of a textile. In a mildly heated environment, prolonged exposure may be necessary before the fabric degrades enough to be discarded. Intense heat may render the fabric unusable, even though it appears unaltered to the eye. Heat durability and heat resistance are performance properties that relate to the effect of heat on the mechanical nature of a textile.

Specifically, *heat durability* refers to "the extent to which a material retains useful properties at ambient air conditions, following exposure to a specified temperature and environment for a specified time and its return to the ambient air conditions." *Heat resistance* refers to "the extent to which a material retains useful properties as measured during exposure of the material to a specified temperature and environment for a specified time." Breaking strength is a useful indicator of both properties.

The definitions of heat durability and heat resistance are very similar. However, the breaking strength (or other selected property) of the textile is assessed while the fiber is heated to determine heat resistance but after the fiber has returned to ambient air conditions (cooled) to determine heat durability. In both cases, the initial strength (performance) of the textile is determined in ambient air conditions prior to heat exposure.

TABLE 5.1   Acidities and alkalinities (pH levels) of common household products and foods.

M O R E A L K A L I N E	——— 14	
	——— 13	Oven cleaner, household disinfectant
		Bleach
	——— 12	
	——— 11	
	——— 10	Hair color, merthiolate
	——— 9	Permanent-wave solution
	——— 8	Nail-polish remover, makeup
NEUTRAL	——— 7	Liquid laundry detergent, milk, chocolate ice cream, hair spray
M O R E A C I D I C	——— 6	
	——— 5	Tea, coffee, tomato juice, yogurt
	——— 4	Beer, catsup, after-shave lotion, benzyl peroxide, mayonnaise, fabric softener, orange juice, mustard, apple juice, wine, oil, vinegar, grape jellies, grape juice
	——— 3	
	——— 2	Cola
	——— 1	
	——— 0	

Heat durability is of more interest in most use situations. For example, it is important to assess the effect of heat (minus the effect of ultraviolet light) on awning, tent, and drapery fabrics. Apparel fabrics are subjected to heat during washing, drying, and ironing, and it is of interest to assess the effect of this heat on wearlife.

Fabrics used in protective garments, particularly clothes designed to protect firefighters or foundry workers from intense heat, usually are assessed for both heat durability and heat resistance. The level of heat resistance should ensure that the fabric will not fail during the interval and degree of heat exposure. The level of heat durability establishes the number of times a thermal protective garment can be worn and continue to provide the degree of safety required.

The distinction between heat resistance and heat durability has been made fairly recently, and these terms are still being used interchangeably. Other words used to indicate the effect of heat on the durability of textiles are thermal stability and thermal resistance. Thermal resistance has been given yet another meaning related to the ability of a fabric to protect the human from heat injury (Chapter 6).

CHAPTER SUMMARY

All textiles require maintenance to preserve and/or restore cleanliness. Textiles differ in their propensity to soil and in ease of soil removal. During cleaning, the dimensional stability of a textile is altered due to inherent stresses in the fabric, fibers that swell, and fibers that felt. Textiles differ in their resistance to degradation by biological organisms, ultraviolet radiation, chemicals, and heat. Ultraviolet light initiates a chain reaction that severs polymer bonds, microorganisms emit a substance that hydrolyzes (breaks) the polymer chains, insects literally eat certain fibers as a source of food. Heat also may initiate a chain reaction that leads to fiber degradation. Detail View 5 lists and defines the properties related to the maintenance of textiles.

Health/Safety/Protection Properties

Health/safety/protection performance properties include those which make textiles potentially hazardous substances as well as suitable for protecting the human body and the environment from a variety of harmful substances. It also includes properties that make textiles appropriate for use in diagnosis, prevention and treatment of medical problems.

PERFORMANCE PROPERTY	DEFINITION
As Potentially Hazardous Substances	
Allergens, irritants, and carcinogens	Role of textiles in causing classical eczematous dermatitis, in irritating the skin, or being cancer-causing substances.
Bacterial adherence and contamination	Role of textiles in tenaciously holding bacteria to their surfaces.
Incendiary spark generators	Role of textiles in igniting atmospheric gas due to static accumulation.
Combustability and flammability	Role of textiles in serving as a fuel source.
Protective Garment Fabrics in Hazardous Environments	
Thermal resistance	The ability of a textile to block sufficient amounts of heat from an external open heat source; for example, fire, to prevent injury to the human body.
Heat resistance and heat durability	Defined in Detail View 5.
Permeation resistance	The ability of a textile to prevent another substance; for example, microorganisms, chemicals, and hazardous minute particles, from reaching the skin.
Ultraviolet light penetration resistance	The ability of a textile to limit the amount of ultraviolet light reaching the skin.
Toxic gas adsorption ability	The ability of a textile to provide an impermeable barrier or to adsorb toxic gases, thereby limiting skin exposure to those gases.
High-energy impact penetration resistance	The ability of a textile to withstand the impact of bullets and knives due to a combination of high strength and high elongation at break.
Provision of Healthy, "Clean" Environments	
Filtration efficiency	The ability of a textile to remove solid substances (germs, skin particles, particulate matter, etc.) from liquids and air passing through it.
Absorption of air pollutants	The ability of a textile to reduce the degree of air pollution by absorption.
Sound absorption	The ability of a textile to absorb sound.
Diagnosis, Prevention, and Treatment of Medical Problems	
Biologic compatibility	The degree of inertness of a textile toward its biologic environment (blood and other body fluids) thereby preventing tissue irritation and tumor growth.
Absorbability (biodegradability)	The ability of a textile to be absorbed by the body once its function is complete.
Ultrafiltration	The ability of a textile to filter out extremely small particles.
Light transfer	The ability of a textile to transfer light around corners by retaining it inside specially designed fibers while they are bent and turned.

6

Health/Safety/
Protection

Most textiles serve to enhance health and safety and to provide protection in hazardous situations. However, textiles can produce deleterious rather than beneficial effects: they can be potentially hazardous materials and hold toxic chemicals at the skin surface.

Chapter 6 focuses on the performance properties of textiles that make them highly suitable materials for use in a variety of hazardous occupations (as protective garments) and in the diagnosis, prevention, and treatment of medical problems, as well as in providing healthy, "clean" environments. It also focuses on those properties of textiles that introduce an element of health and safety risk. Detail View 6 outlines the major health/safety/protection properties.

POTENTIALLY HAZARDOUS
SUBSTANCES

Most textiles are combustible materials. They can ignite, burn, and produce smoke; they may emit toxic fumes and/or give off sufficient heat to cause burn injury and even death. Textiles may irritate the skin, be the cause of classical eczematous dermatitis, and possibly contain cancer-causing substances. They also can generate sparks, which can lead to an explosion in the presence of ignitable gases. The tendency of bacteria to adhere tenaciously to fibers may lead to infection when they are used in medical products. The absorption and/or entrapment of hazardous chemicals in textiles may lead to health risk, especially if the fabrics are not or cannot be sterilized or decontaminated before and/or between use.

Allergens, Irritants, Carcinogens

Although wearing clothing is usually a necessary and pleasurable experience, the wearer can experience cutaneous intolerance (Figure 6.1). Dermatologists have been able to identify about 30 different colorants and 10 chemical finishes that are *contact allergens*. Allergic responses to fabric are rare, but they are significant to the affected individual.

Fabrics that contain free formaldehyde or that may release formaldehyde are of major concern today. Formaldehyde, a known contact allergen, is found in much higher concentrations in other consumer products. In fabric, it occurs as a component of resin finishes on flame-resistant and durable-press fabrics. Individuals who have problems wearing these fabrics have been sensitized (become allergic) to formaldehyde from other sources.

Carpets also can contain formaldehyde. When they do, the formaldehyde is released as a gas into the air. These trace amounts are not sufficient to pose a health hazard.

In all cases of allergic contact dermatitis, a chemical must be transferred from fabric to skin, be absorbed into the skin, and react with a protein. The individual must be sensitized to the chemical before a visible reaction occurs. Very weak contact allergens are found in fabrics; long exposure is necessary before a problem arises.

Textiles are much more likely to be *irritants* than to be contact allergens. Irritants are stiff fibers, fabrics, or labels that poke and abrade the skin. Intolerance to wool, long believed to be an allergic response, is now known to be an irritant response in which excitation of pain nerves in the skin causes a chemical to be released and the skin to redden (see Chapter 3). When there is considerable fabric movement over the skin surface (particularly when the skin is wet), layers of skin may be rubbed away; marathon runners experience such extreme skin irritation.

Carcinogens, substances known to cause cancer, may be inhaled, absorbed through the skin, or ingested. In 1977, Arlene Blum and Bruce N. Ames, biochemists at the University of California-Berkeley, discovered that the chemical TRIS (2, 3-dibromopropylphosphate), which was used extensively on children's polyester nightwear to make it flame-resistant, was a potential carcinogen. Great concern was expressed that children who sucked on their pajamas could ingest sufficient quantities of this compound to trigger cancer-cell production. Almost overnight, all children's sleepwear with any flame-retardant chemical applied was withdrawn from the marketplace, and such fabrics are no longer treated with chemicals to provide flame resistance.

Other suspected textile carcinogens are benzidene dyestuffs handled by textile artisans, dyestuff workers, and consumers who use home dye products. These dyes are now clearly labeled, and directions for handling them are given.

Bacterial Adherence and Contamination

Long before microorganisms were known to exist, people assumed that fabric could harbor the "seeds" of disease in some way. This idea can be traced at least to the sixteenth century. Today, using electron microscopy, bacteria and other microorganisms can be seen adhering to fibers (Figure 6.2).

Cotton and flax (linen) fibers are often considered purity fibers, because fabric made from them can be boiled. Women once boiled fabrics that had been used by an ill person in their home to sterilize them for future use. Hospital sheets and surgical gowns have been autoclaved for many years; disposable sheets and gowns are now used when it is economical to do so. Fabrics purchased with antimicrobial (antibacterial, bacteriostatic, or anti-

FIGURE 6.1 Allergic contact dermatitis due to either a colorant or chemical finish in a garment fabric.

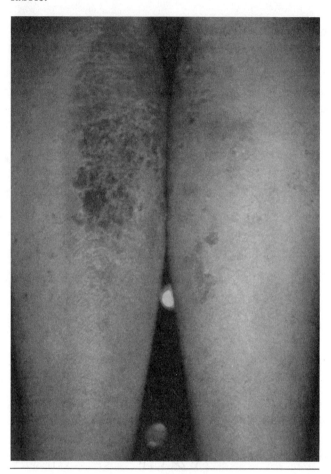

septic) finish provide an increased margin of safety by inhibiting bacterial growth. Hospital carpeting is often chemically treated to reduce the possible spread of infections (Chapter 31).

New research has been undertaken due to the increased use of synthetic fibers in sutures (nylon) and vascular prostheses (usually polyester) and the strict requirement to eliminate the incidence of pathogenesis introduced when bacteria adhere tenaciously to these fiber surfaces. Radioactive tracers and electron microscopy are revealing how fiber hydrophilicity, water absorbency, and surface roughness influence bacterial adherence when different cleaning and autoclaving methods are used. Some day, medical researchers hope to engineer a fiber that is easily and totally freed of bacteria.

FIGURE 6.2 *Staphylococcus epidermidis* **adhere in different amounts to various fibers.**

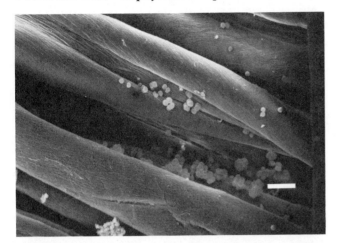

Cotton

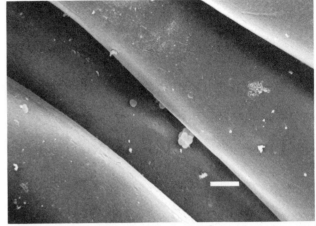

Nylon

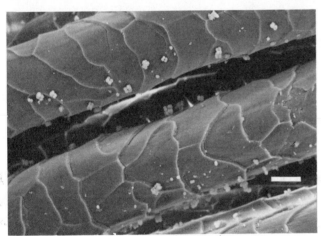

Wool

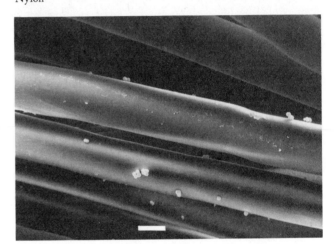

Polyester

Incendiary Spark Generation

Electrostatic shocks and spark discharges from the body, which arise from static electricity on clothing and carpeting, are a common but uncomfortable experience. When a spark is discharged in a flammable atmosphere, such as in an operating room, a hazardous fire situation may occur.

In Chapter 3, we learned how fabrics and the body can become charged and about shock and clinging that result. An important question in the current discussion is how much energy must be generated before an explosive situation actually occurs? We might think that an explosion results when the energy on the body is equal to the ignition energy of the flammable gas in the environment and a spark is produced. However, the energy on the body must be significantly greater than the minimum ignition energy of the atmosphere for a hazardous situation to arise. Two reasons have been found for this fortunate situation: (1) the discharge from the body is fragmented into discrete sparks (it is not one large discharge), and (2) part of this energy is absorbed as heat due to the resistance of electron flow along the body.

Textiles to be used in potentially explosive environments are carefully developed to reduce charge generation. For example, small metal fibers are incorporated into carpet pile and backing to aid electron flow.

Combustibility and Flammability

Burn injuries are excruciatingly painful from the moment they occur; serious burns can require a long series of reconstructive surgeries, followed by life with the physical and emotional scars. Death may even result, depending on what percentage of the body is burned and on the severity of these burns (first-, second-, or third-degree burns), on the degree of smoke inhalation, and/or on the off-gassing of toxic fumes by the burning textile.

All too often, burn injuries are inflicted on the elderly and the very young because they are least able to take quick action during a fire. Frequently, the burn injury is the outcome of a careless action, resulting in a fabric being the first material to be ignited. Playing with matches, standing too close to a trash fire, smoking in bed, and starting a fire with flammable liquids (such as charcoal lighter) are all potentially dangerous situations that could result in a burn injury. Apparel fabrics, upholstery textiles, bed linens, and fabrics and fibers used in mattresses are then first to burn. Carpeting and draperies may help to spread a fire but are usually not the first materials to ignite.

Describing the Burning Behavior of Textiles. Understanding the terms used to describe the combustible nature of textiles may be easier if we view a schematic that shows the major terms and their relationships (Figure 6.3). First, textiles are either noncombustible or combustible.

NONCOMBUSTIBLE. *Noncombustible fabrics* "neither ignite nor give off vapors that will ignite when subjected to external sources of ignition." Fabrics made from glass fibers or asbestos fibers are noncombustible. Noncombustible fabrics are not necessarily indestructible in a fire. At high temperatures, many fibers melt. Before melting, strength and other performance properties may be lessened; that is, heat resistance and heat durability may be affected. Noncombustible textiles that are "totally unaffected by fire" may be referred to as *fireproof.*[1]

COMBUSTIBLE (FLAMMABLE AND NONFLAMMABLE). Most fabrics are combustible materials. When exposed to an open flame (a lighted match, a lit cigarette), intense radiant heat from a portable room heater or an electric stove burner, or molten metal in a foundry, *combustible fabrics* "will ignite and burn or give off vapors that will ignite and burn." Combustible textiles that burn with a flame are referred to as *flammable;* those that burn without a flame, as *nonflammable.* Most textiles are flammable.

How easily the fabric ignites, how rapidly it burns, whether or not it melts and drips after ignition, how much heat and smoke it produces as it burns, how easily the fabric can be extinguished, and other observable or measurable burning behaviors vary widely among combustible textiles. The risk of burn injury or even suffocation from smoke differs dramatically, depending on what type of fabric is burning.

While never officially defined, the common interpretation is that *highly or dangerously flammable fabrics* ignite so easily and burn so rapidly that escape from the inferno-like environment they produce is unlikely. Such textiles pose an "unreasonable" health risk. The so-called "torch" sweaters of the late 1940s and early 1950s (sweaters that exploded into flame the instant an ignition source as small as a cigarette ash fell on them), provide an example of this degree of flammability and risk. Another example concerns the Coconut Grove Night Club fire in the 1940s. Carpeting used to cover the walls as well as the floor was instrumental in the rapid spread of the fire; people in the packed nightclub had little opportunity to escape. Such incidents provided the momentum for passage of the Flammable Fabrics Act (FFA) in 1953.

In *flame-resistant fabrics,* or *FR-fabrics,* "flaming combustion is prevented, terminated, or inhibited following application of a flaming or non-flaming source of ignition, with or without subsequent removal of the ignition source." In other words, FR-fabrics are flammable, but they are less flammable fabrics. They do not offer complete safety, and all of them do not offer the same degree of safety. They do not exhibit any one set of burning behaviors.

Consider the case of wool fabrics. Wool fiber is often described as inherently flame-resistant. Compared to most other fibers, a fairly high temperature is required to ignite wool. If a wool fabric does ignite, the flame spread usually is not sustained for a very long time after the ignition source is removed. The wool is said to "self-extinguish."[2] Even though wool is called a flame-resistant fiber, it is not sufficiently flame-resistant to provide protection, let's say, to a firefighter, unless a special chemical treatment is applied.

---

[1] M.L. Joseph, *Introductory Textile Science,* 5th ed. (New York: Holt, Rinehart and Winston, 1986), p. 310.

[2] ASTM states that "self-extinguishing" has no meaning except in association with a specific test method or specific conditions of burning.

FIGURE 6.3   Terms related to the burning behavior of textiles.

Noncombustible textile   OR   **Combustible textile**

"A textile that will neither ignite nor give off vapors that will   "A textile that will ignite and burn or that will give off vapors
ignite when subjected to external sources of ignition."   that will ignite and burn when subjected to external sources
                                                                                 of ignition."

Flammable textile   OR   **Nonflammable textile**

"Any combustible textile that burns with a flame."   "Any combustible textile that burns without a flame."

Flame-Resistant (FR)   **Normal Flammability**   **Highly or Dangerously Flammable**

A textile whose "flaming combustion is   Textiles in this category differ in: A textile that ignites so easily and burns
prevented, terminated, or inhibited   Ease of ignition   so rapidly that escape from burn injury or
following application of a flaming or   Ease of extinction   death is unlikely.
nonflaming source of ignition, with or   Rate of flame spread
without subsequent removal of the   Amount of heat generated
ignition source." A relative term used to   Density of smoke generated when
compare one fabric to another.   exposed to an open-flame source.
                                               During and after burning, these textiles
                                               differ in whether or not they melt, exhibit
                                               a melt-and-drip phenomena, char, have
                                               afterglow, or tend to smolder.

Fabrics that are marketed and labeled as flame-resistant have been tested under precise conditions in which the amount of moisture in the fabric, the type of ignition source, the flame impingement time (the length of time the flame is held on the fabric surface or cut edge), the position of the fabric during the test, and other factors known to influence ignition and flaming are controlled. These test conditions vary, depending on the end use of the fabric. The test for children's sleepwear differs from the test for protective clothing fabrics. The test for carpeting differs from the test for draperies; actually, there are many different tests for carpeting which differ in terms of treatment and exposure to flame. Agencies or industries establish the criterion or criteria that a fabric must meet to be declared flame-resistant or not flame-resistant.

Federal Textile Flammability Laws and Standards. In 1953, the U.S. government passed the Flammable Fabrics Act (FFA). The intent of the FFA was "to regulate the manufacture for sale in interstate commerce all highly flammable *wearing apparel fabrics.*" This act did not in-clude interior textiles. In 1954, the federal Flammability of Clothing Textiles Standard (Title 16 CFR 1610) was first implemented. This standard requires that a *45°-angle test* be performed to determine whether or not a fabric is "dangerously flammable."

In the 45°-angle test, a "bone-dry" fabric is placed in a holder at a 45° angle and a flame of specified size is impinged on the apparel fabric for 1 second. If the rate of flame spread up ~5 inches of fabric occurs in less than 3.5 seconds (4.0 seconds for a napped fabric), then that apparel fabric is banned from sale within the United States. To comprehend the burning rate that would be necessary for a fabric to "fail" this test, consider that dried newspaper would *not* fail. All apparel items and fabrics imported to the United States as well as fabrics made in the United States must pass the 45°-angle test.

The degree of safety that many legislators, consumer advocates, and consumers themselves thought should be afforded the American public was not achieved with the passage of the FFA and the Flammability of Clothing Standard. Data collected concerning numbers of burn injuries and deaths when textiles were the first item to ignite led to further legislation. Currently, federal flammability standards exist for children's sleepwear (sizes 0–6x and 7–14), large carpets and rugs, small carpets and rugs, and mattresses and mattress pads. A different test procedure and measures (criteria) for acceptable level of flammability have been established for each type of item. The Consumer Product Safety Commission ensures that manufacturers comply with these standards and that all apparel fabrics meet the Flammability of Clothing Standard.

Other Flammability Regulations. There are no clear national standards for the flammability of residential and contract furnishings. The standards in effect are a hodge-podge of documents issued by local agencies, federal agencies, individual associations, and voluntary standards writing organizations. More than 70 flammability tests devised by 20 different agencies apply to textiles, plastics, and other contract furnishing materials.[3] This number does not include tests for the combustion toxicity of interior fabrics. As of December 16, 1989, no drapery or wall fabric may be used in any installation in New York State unless fire-gas toxicity tests have been conducted and filed with the state government. This action is expected to trigger a similar regulation for draperies throughout the United States and to be expanded to carpeting. Upholstery fabric is not under consideration at the present time for toxicity regulation.

Achievement of Flame-resistant Fabrics. Flame resistance is achieved in a number of ways: using inherently flame-resistant fibers, modifying fibers for flame resistance, finishing the fabric to enhance flame-resistance, and modifying fabric structure. Specific information about each approach to flame resistance will be given when the various fibers are discussed in Unit II, when fabric structure is discussed in Unit IV, and when flame-retardant finishes are discussed in Unit V.

PROTECTIVE GARMENT FABRICS IN HAZARDOUS ENVIRONMENTS

The health and safety of hundreds of thousands of people who work in hazardous occupations are safeguarded by protective clothing. Fabrics used in these garments, as

well as the garments themselves, must be designed specifically to exclude the external hazard. In some cases, several different fabrics or layers of the same fabric are required to obtain protection. In all cases, the total protective system must allow for thermophysiological comfort and the ability to perform the task at hand. Protective clothing systems must maximize the protection required but minimize the unacceptability of the garment to the worker. Realizing that garment design is just as important as fabric design, we will discuss only fabric requirements in this section.

Thermal Resistance

Firefighters, foundry workers, welders, race-car drivers, and astronauts are all exposed to intense radiant heat, flames, or molten metal splashes in their work environments. The clothing they wear not only must be flame-resistant; it also must provide *thermal resistance*. The fabric must keep a sufficient amount of external heat from reaching the person inside the protective garment (Figure 6.4).

In essence, thermal resistance is the ability of the fabric to serve as a thermal insulator thus preventing a dangerous elevation of skin temperature. At an ambient temperature of 73.4° F (23° C), average skin temperature is about 86° F (30° C). If this temperature rises to 111° F (44° C), skin injury begins. The severity of the burn depends on how high the tissue temperature rises above 111° F and on how long it is sustained at the skin surface. Fabrics with high values of thermal resistance reduce the risk of burn injury.

Generally, thermal-resistant fabrics also need to be heat-resistant, and heat-durable—maintain their useful properties during and following exposure to high temperatures. Note the very similar terms (thermal-resistant, heat-resistant, and heat-durable). Some textile scientists use these terms interchangeably which means that careful interpretation is usually needed.

Permeation Resistance

In certain work situations, a fabric must resist the penetration of biological organisms, chemicals, and "intruding" particles (Figure 6.5). The porosity of the fabric is a highly important factor in achieving such *permeation resistance*.

To Biological Organisms. Medical and laboratory personnel who are exposed to biological agents, such as vi-

[3] *Govmark Book on Flammability Standards and Flammability: Test Methods of Textiles, Plastics, and Other Materials Used in Home and Contract Furnishings,* Book I: *Analysis of Codes;* Book II: *Reprints of Codes* (Bellmore, NY: Govmark Corporation, 1988).

FIGURE 6.4 Garments made from fabrics that provide high thermal resistance.

Typical firefighter's turnout gear. Kneelength coat covers bunker pants.

An aluminized suit planned for work close to flame or extreme high temperatures (based on a design by ILC Dover).

FIGURE 6.5 Garments made from fabrics that provide high permeation resistance.

A protective garment for pesticide spraying.

A biological-protective suit to be worn in a laboratory where infectious materials are present (design: U.S. Army Research and Development Command).

ruses and bacteria, must protect themselves against the fluids that transmit the organisms. Because of the current emphasis by the scientific community on biotechnology, which involves the handling of living organisms in the laboratory, the need for clothing that provides this type of protection is beginning to receive considerable attention. Protective clothing worn by professionals in the health-care and biotechnology industries includes latex and polymer gloves, gowns, and other emergency-response clothing items. Primary considerations are whether the pores of the fabric are sufficiently small to trap or be penetrated by the microorganisms and whether the protective garment fabric allows fluid migration. In these situations, protective items usually are disposable; no attempt is made to clean or decontaminate them.

To Chemicals. Pesticide applicators (agricultural workers, backyard farmers, commercial landscape and pest-control personnel, and aerial sprayers), chemical-spill cleaning crews, PCB-leak trouble shooters, chemical-waste handlers, and riot police are faced with potential exposure to a range of hazardous chemicals as they perform their essential tasks. Other workers who face chemical exposure include those who handle liquid chemicals during manufacture, those who work around acid baths and other such treatments in the electronics industry, and those who repair equipment leaks or failures.

A protective outfit for soldiers who dismantle chemical weapons (design: U.S. Army Research and Development Command).

Disposable coveralls for radiation protection.

Most workers who could experience skin contact while working with hazardous chemicals are protected by some form of chemically resistant clothing or gloves. They may wear anything from single latex gloves to totally encapsulating suits. Historically, most chemical-protective clothing fabrics were developed to be "impermeable"—to provide an absolute safeguard. However, new test procedures are showing that such complete protection is not actually realized. Research is currently underway to remedy this situation.

Another highly active area of chemical-protective fabric research focuses on fabrics that provide a barrier to pesticides. These fabrics and garments tend to be tightly woven cotton fabrics or disposable olefin nonwoven fabrics. Pesticide applicators may or may not take the precaution of wearing such garments over their regular workwear.

To Intruding Particles. Intruding particles include radioactive particulate matter, micrometeorites, X-rays, microwaves, electromagnetic rays, and atomic and other minute particles. Astronauts, workers in nuclear power plants, food-inspection personnel, uranium mine workers, medical X-ray technologists, and people who work in the area of transmitting power antennae and high-frequency generators all may encounter intruding particles in the workplace.

Whether or not garments or fabrics can provide the required degree of protection from particulate matter depends on the specific "impact intruder." In a nuclear power plant, for instance, protection from radiation requires lead or concrete shielding. Clothing can only protect workers from alpha and beta rays. Clothing plus respirators can keep the radioactive substances carried in dust, oil, and grease in repair and maintenance areas from being deposited on the skin surface or carried into the body through the lungs, where they would cause considerable destruction of body tissues.

To block X-rays, the protective fabric must be lead-impregnated vinyl, which is very heavy and awkward to wear. It is generally constructed as an apron-like garment and worn only for brief periods of time. In areas of high energy density, people can only spend long periods of time (more than 6 minutes) if suitably shielded rooms are used and metalized fabrics (generally nickel, at a thickness of 0.05–1.0 micrometers) are worn. Shielding reflects a high degree of the radiation away from the body. In fact, virtually all incident radiation can be reflected if all body parts are covered in a well-designed garment.

Ultraviolet Light Penetration Resistance

Ultraviolet radiation also can be considered an "impact intruder" because it too is in the electromagnetic spectrum. It is discussed in a separate section here because exposure to ultraviolet radiation is the direct cause of skin cancer, one of the leading causes of death in the United States. This exposure does not occur in a specific work environment but on a regular basis as people move outside on sunny as well as overcast days.

People have been made aware of the health risk associated with exposure to ultraviolet light, and many of them are limiting the amount of time they spend directly in the sun and using high protective factor (SPF) sunscreens to block as much of the harmful rays of the sun as possible. Recently, skin-cancer researchers have recommended that people in sunny climates use a sunscreen every day, because most exposure to ultraviolet radiation occurs from daily outdoor activities rather than from sunbathing.

One sunscreen-lotion manufacturer and one dermatologist[4] have investigated the role of fabric in blocking ultraviolet light radiation. They have found that fabrics do not provide very effective barriers to ultraviolet light penetration. Researchers at Plough, Inc., found that clothing probably blocks no more than 50–75% of all ultraviolet radiation. Terrycloth robes often worn at beaches and pools were found to be less protective than a sunscreen lotion rated SPF 15. Fabrics that provided the best protection tended to be those with the tightest constructions.

Toxic Gas Adsorption Ability

Fabrics that protect the wearer from toxic gases either form an impermeable barrier or incorporate some form of carbon to adsorb the toxic gas. Attempts to prevent toxic gases from passing through fabrics by reducing the size of the fabric pores to the smallest dimension possible have not been successful. Gases readily flow through because they do not form droplets or particles.

Coated fabrics may form an impermeable barrier to toxic gases, but they are not comfortable to wear. When carbon is used in fabrics, it adsorbs the toxin and still allows the fabric to "breathe," making the garment more comfortable to wear. Carbon powder can be placed in hollow, polypropylene fibers with microporous fiber walls, making it accessible to gases but protecting it from water.

High-Energy Impact Penetration Resistance

Since time immemorial, humans have fought each other with every imaginable weapon. Fragmenting munitions produced about 70% of all injuries and fatalities in the two World Wars. Today, terrorist activities involve handguns, bombs, and rifles. Every conceivable material and

---

[4]B. Berne and T. Fischer, "Protective Effects of Various Types of Clothes Against UV Radiation," *Acta Dermatovener* (Stockholm) 60/5 (1980): 458–59.

FIGURE 6.6 The effect of a bullet on the first, fourth, sixth, and ninth layers of nylon ballistic assembly.

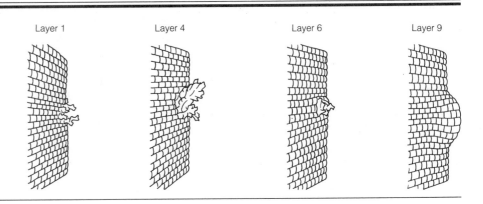

Layer 1   Layer 4   Layer 6   Layer 9

device has been developed to protect personnel who must deal with these threats from bullets and metal fragments.

During World War I, ballistics textiles were made of silk; modern ones consist primarily of nylon (Chapter 16) and Kevlar® aramid fiber, a trademark of the du Pont Company (Chapter 21). The most recent fiber to enter the ballistics-protective clothing market is Spectra® polyethylene olefin, a trademark of Allied Fibers (Chapter 21). These fibers, when properly constructed into fabrics that are then layered and fabricated into garments, can provide substantial protection at a fraction of the weight of their metal or ceramic counterparts (Figure 6.6).

PROVISION OF HEALTHY, "CLEAN" ENVIRONMENTS

For centuries, physicians stressed that the body must be kept warm by surrounding it with woolen garments to ward off diseases! As a result, the health of infants and children deteriorated the minute they encountered their first cold draft. At the turn of the twentieth century, several medical practitioners began to stress that a ventilated skin was healthier than one kept overly warm by clothing. After World War I, the English medical hygienist Leonard Hill showed that an overly warm "jungle-like" microclimate actually impairs the normal physiological responses of skin and predisposes it to sweat rash and fungal infection.

A great deal has been learned since the turn of the twentieth century about the influence of fabric on a healthy environment at the skin surface. The recent development of noninvasive methods of studying skin wetness and the consequences of skin wetness on bacterial counts, friction, and absorption of chemicals, has pro-

duced more information about this important relationship. For example, R. E. Zimmerer and his coresearchers[5] at the Proctor and Gamble Co. research laboratories established that a baby's skin remains drier when disposable diapers, rather than cloth diapers are worn. Bacterial counts, chemical absorption, and friction are all lower on drier skin than on wetter skin. With the current interest in health and exercise, future research should lead to more clothing recommendations to maintain a healthy skin and good health in general.

The larger environment is also influenced by how effectively textiles reduce human-generated contaminants as well as industrial effluents.

Filtration Efficiency

Millions of square yards of filtration fabric (~ 50% woven and 50% fiberwebs, or nonwovens) are manufactured each year. This fabric has significance for everyone's health and well-being. Almost all of the air we inhale inside modern buildings has been passed through one or more filters to remove particulate matter. All the drinks we consume have been filtered at some stage in their production. Vacuum cleaner filters collect dust. Large industrial filters greatly reduce smoke to the breathing atmosphere and effluents emitted into rivers, oceans, and streams.

Other textile "filters" are fabricated into garments that are generally intended to protect an object (sensitive equipment) or an ill person from contamination. Surgeons and nurses wear masks in the operating room. Tunnel suits, or "pseudopods," allow nurses and doctors

---

[5]R.E. Zimmerer, K.D. Lawson, and C.J. Calvert, "The Effects of Wearing Diapers on Skin," *Pediatric Dermatology* 3/2 (1986): 95–101.

to care for patients in germ-free isolation wards without introducing any foreign particles that might endanger them. Astronauts returning from their first voyage to the moon wore a biological isolation garment intended to protect others from potentially hazardous moon particles. Fabrics in these garments could entrap particles as small as 0.45 micrometers. Fabrics also have been developed for immune-deficient children. Well-designed filtration garments provide some degree of mobility so that these patients do not need to be confined to a hospital insulation chamber. Workers who manufacture microprocessors also must wear protective garments, so that their skin particles do not become lodged between microcircuit components, which are spaced only a few micrometers apart. These garments must also be nonlinting.

Fabrics are particularly useful as filters. Large apertures in fabrics allow the gas or liquid that is being filtered to flow relatively easily; that is, the flow is not too restricted. Due to the thickness of a textile filter and the random geometry of its fibrous structure, the gas or liquid does not follow a straight line through the textile filter. Thus, there is a high probability that a particle in the fluid stream will adhere to a fiber. This happens despite the fact that many particles are much smaller than the fibers and the spaces between them. The filtration action of fabrics has been compared to firing a gun into a forest: the bullet is very small compared to the trees and the gaps between the trees, but it is unlikely to penetrate the forest without hitting (adhering to) a tree. The *filtration efficiency*—the removal of whatever has to be removed to an acceptably low level of concentration at an economic cost—of textile filters is high, because textile filters are designed to achieve the type of filtration required.

Absorption of Air Pollutants

Most of the information concerning the absorption of air pollutants on textiles focuses on the detrimental effects to the textile itself. In this context, absorption is considered a negative process, because it decreases the useful life of the textile. Recently, however, it has been found that the absorptive property of textiles may effectively reduce indoor air pollution.

Air pollution has an adverse effect on health; episodes of unusually high air pollution are accompanied by a high incidence of sickness. Indoor air pollution can be greater than outdoor air pollution. A case in point is sulfur dioxide concentrations.

Indoor sulfur dioxide concentrations can be reduced below outdoor levels when effective absorptive materials are used in interior furnishings (primarily cellulosic wall-paper, cotton and rayon furnishing fabrics, and wool carpets). Wool carpeting prolongs this beneficial effect, undoubtedly due to the high acid-combining potential of wool.

Sound Absorption

As living spaces become smaller, population density increases, and more homes are under aircraft flight patterns or near freeways, a greater number of us are likely to suffer from the problem of unwanted noise. Open office designs have many positive attributes but irritation due to sound carried from one workspace into another is often a negative consequence. In recent years, attention has been paid to what role textiles can play in providing effective accoustics in interior spaces.

A good sound absorber—one that has just the right amount of resistance to the vibration of a sound wave—can be thought of as a maze. It is porous, so that sound waves can enter the material and continue to move through its channels, rather than be reflected from its surface. In addition, its pores must be limited in size and must be sufficiently mazelike to resist the direct passage of sound waves.

The greater the maze, the more sound energy it will convert. Thus, the thicker a specific material, the more sound it will absorb. For sound to become "exhausted," it must be allowed to continue to move through a maze until all of its energy is converted. As a general rule, rough, soft, porous, and light materials absorb more sound than smooth, hard, dense, and heavy materials.

Textiles may also reduce impact-generated sound by diminishing the energy of impact transmitted to the underlying building-structure materials. Carpeting is an excellent acoustical material for the reduction of impact sound transmission, particularly at high frequencies. However, differences between carpeting in reducing impact noise are small.

DIAGNOSIS, PREVENTION, AND TREATMENT OF MEDICAL PROBLEMS

The Egyptians are believed to have used flax (linen) fibers to draw the edges of separated tissue together so that wounds could heal properly. Through the centuries, various fibers and materials, including silk, catgut, leather, nylon, polyester, polypropylene, and stainless steel, have been used as surgical sutures. The most recent addition to this list is biodegradable polymers. Today surgeons can choose from well over 200 types of sutures, which can be broadly categorized as natural or manufactured, single- or multiple-strand, and absorbable or nonabsorbable, as well as by size. Interestingly, sutures remain a major use of textiles in modern surgical applications.

Since the early 1950s, the application of textiles in medicine and surgery has grown considerably due to the development of sophisticated surgical procedures requiring materials with very specific performance features, which can be met by engineered fibers and fabrics. These applications include: reconstruction of soft tissues, cardiovascular prostheses, orthopedic prostheses, kidney dialysis membranes, endoscopes (to view internal areas of the body without surgery), and wound repair. Fabric meshes assist in hernia repair, reconstruction of chest walls, and replacement of abdominal walls. The first cardiovascular prostheses were textile tubes (vascular grafts), which carried blood through the human body without adverse side reactions. The successful replacement of arteries and veins with grafts led to the experimental use of textiles as strut covers over sewing rings on replacement heart valves and as linings in heart-assist devices. Orthopedic surgeons are finding certain fibrous materials exceptionally useful in the repair of torn tendons and ligaments. Figure 6.7 shows some uses for textiles in medicine.

Many other textile applications in the prevention, diagnosis, and treatment of medical problems could be listed and discussed. Regardless of the biomedical application, each must meet a very specific performance criteria. Here, we will consider four performance properties: biologic compatibility, absorbability (biodegradability), ultrafiltration, and light transfer.

Biologic Compatibility

Biologic compatibility concerns the interaction of the textile with its biological environment. In general, all textile materials implanted in the body must be inert as well as compatible with blood and other body fluids. In addition, they must not cause tissue irritation, be toxic, release foreign material, or cause tumors over long-term use. In essence, these textiles have to be viewed as drugs.

Absorbability (Biodegradability)

Today textile sutures, fabric meshes, and cardiovascular prostheses are available in either absorbable or nonabsorbable materials. The surgeon decides whether or not the implanted suture, mesh, or cardiovascular device

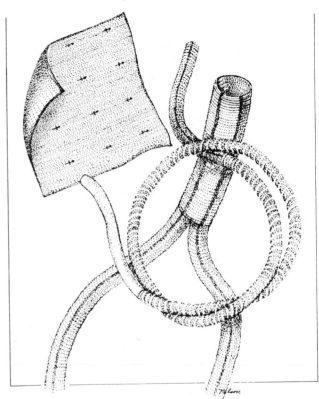

FIGURE 6.7 Textile vascular prostheses and fabric meshes for implantation.

should retain its mass and mechanical integrity at the implant site. If loss of mass and, consequently, physical presence at the implant site is desired within an arbitrary period of one year, then an *absorbable* polymeric material will be used. If the device must retain a significant fraction of its original mass and remain partially or fully functional beyond one year, then a *nonabsorbable* polymeric material will be implanted. Further, the surgeon must know exactly how rapidly an absorbable material will be depleted, because tissue healing must usually be complete at the time the textile implant is absorbed.

Ultrafiltration

When kidney failure occurs, metabolic products, such as urea, increase in concentration instead of being eliminated from the body. A buildup of these toxic substances can be prevented, even on a chronic basis, by the use of kidney dialysis, a membrane-separation process. Because urea molecules are much smaller than blood-plasma proteins, they can be separated from blood by using ultrafiltration membranes, with blood on one side and dialysis fluid on the other. Solutes diffuse between the blood and dialyzing fluid; those with elevated concentrations in the blood are transported to the dialyzing fluid and removed. To minimize blood volume, the rate of species transport must be high and the surface area of the membrane must be maximized.

Both of these conditions can be achieved by using hollow fibers with "skinned" surfaces made up of very fine pores. A bundle of these fibers (each being 50–200 micrometers in inside diameter) exhibits a very large surface-to-volume ratio, the logical geometry for use in an artificial kidney. Usually the fibers are made of regenerated cellulose (Chapter 14).

Light Transfer

Fiber optics is the field of physics that deals with the transfer of light from one place to another through long, thin, flexible fibers of glass or plastic. These *optical fibers* have the ability to transfer light around corners because the sides of each fiber reflect light and keep it inside as the fiber bends and turns. Optical fiber technology became important in the 1970s.

Many dental drills are fitted with optical fibers to concentrate light on the tooth being repaired. One of the most exciting medical events in the recent past has been the development of a fiber optic probe, which allows physicians to obtain a clear image of an organ inside the body. This feat is accomplished by using two fiber bundles: one illuminates the tissue, while the other one transmits the image back to the outside. The probe can be inserted through the mouth, rectum, or blood vessels. With the fiber optic probe, a surgeon can also insert biopsy forceps and withdraw tissue, using separate channels in the fiber scope. Surgeons also can measure the oxygen content of the blood, the velocity of red blood cells in an artery, and the pressure or temperature in tissue. This technology probably will replace heart-bypass surgery in the future.

There are many applications of fiber optics outside the medical field. The communications industry uses optical fibers to greatest advantage.

CHAPTER SUMMARY

In the 1970s and 1980s, tremendous strides were made in the development of fibers and fabrics with engineered performance to provide the degree of protection necessary in our health- and safety-conscious society. Flame-resistant textiles are now available for apparel and interior end uses. In the area of occupational safety clothing, the gains have been significant. Much of the research has led to rewarding and fruitful improvements in protection from intense radiant heat, molten metal splashes, bullets and other high-energy projectiles, biological and chemical exposure, and "impact intruders." Never before have so many different textiles been used in medical applications; fiber optics, solubility, ultrafiltration, and other performance features of textiles have been paramount to patient recovery. Much more progress is likely in the future.

II

Fiber Structure and Performance

Textile Fiber Classification

A *textile fiber* is a unit of matter, either natural or man-made [manufactured], which forms the basic element of fabrics and other textile structures.

NATURAL FIBERS

Any fiber that exists as such in the natural state.

PROTEIN				CELLULOSIC			MINERAL
Sheep's Wool	Specialty Wool		Silk	Cotton	Specialty Cellulosic		Asbestos
	Cashmere	Misti			Flax	Henquen	
	Mohair	Guanaco			Ramie	Abaca	
	Cashgora	Vicuna			Jute	Pina	
	Camel hair	Qiviut			Hemp	Sisal	
	Llama	Yak			Kenaf	Coir	
	Alpaca	Angora			Urena	Kapok	
	Huarizo	Mink					

MANUFACTURED OR MAN-MADE FIBERS

Any fiber derived by a process of manufacture from any substance which, at any point in the manufacturing process, is not a fiber.

CELLULOSIC	SYNTHETIC		INORGANIC	PROTEIN
	General-Use	**Special-Use**		
Rayon	Nylon	Vinyon*	Glass	Azlon*
Acetate	Polyester	Saran	Metallic	
Triacetate*	Olefin	Modacrylic	Silicon	
	Acrylic	Aramid	Tetrafluoroethylene	
	Spandex	Sulfar	Alumina	
	Rubber	PBI	Carbon	
		Anidex*		
		Lastrile*		
		Novoloid*		
		Nytril*		
		Vinal*		

*No longer produced in the United States.

Cotton, wool, silk, and flax fibers from both plants and animals have been used by humans for centuries. Although these fibers are among the oldest and most familiar materials, they remained chemical mysteries until the twentieth century. They are elaborately structured products of living things, and their very complexity endows them with wonderfully versatile and powerful properties. Unlocking nature's secret of making fibers presented a great challenge to scientists: their goal was not only to learn how natural fibers are constructed but also to devise new materials that nature had neglected to create. Today, there are more than 18 types of *manufactured* fibers in the U.S. marketplace; another six fibers have been developed but are not currently manufactured in this country. Take a moment to study Overview II, which provides a list of fibers; many of them are examined in Unit II.

WHAT IS THE NATURE OF TEXTILE FIBERS?

A fiber is a unit of matter with an extremely small diameter and a length at least 100 times longer than its width. The figure in Overview II shows the length-to-width ratio of a cotton fiber—one of the shortest textile fibers. Most fibers are several thousand times longer than they are wide. Each fiber is composed of long chain molecules called *polymers;* each polymer consists of small molecules, or *monomers.*

There are many different fibrous substances. The ones that can be used to make fabrics are classified as *textile fibers;* others are classified as *nontextile fibers.* Textile fibers have a minimum length (about $\frac{1}{2}$ inch, or 15 millimeters) and a minimum width (~0.0004 inch, or 10 micrometers[1]). Fibers shorter than $\frac{1}{2}$ inch (15 millimeters) are generally considered nontextile fibers because it is too difficult to commercially twist them into a yarn of adequate strength and uniform diameter. Fibers that are too fine and too delicate to process into yarn are also categorized as nontextile fibers. At the other size extreme, fibers exceeding ~0.002 inch (50 micrometers) in diameter are generally classified as nontextile fibers because they are too coarse and thick to be comfortable if worn next to the skin. Most of the "stringy" portions of plants cannot be used as textile fibers.

The length-to-width ratio of a fiber determines whether or not it is suitable for spinning into yarn, provided it meets the length and width requirements. The smallest suitable length-to-width ratio is ~350:1, but fibers with ratios of 1000:1 are more desirable.

A useful textile fiber must possess certain properties that make it suitable for textile applications. For example, melting temperature must be sufficiently high. Until recently, polyethylene fibers (a type of olefin fiber) were not useful in textile applications because their melting point was too low. Years of research were required to raise the melting point to a desirable level while preserving other fiber properties. Today, polyethylene fibers are used in sailcloth, marine ropes, and gloves designed to protect the wearer from injury by power tools.

HOW ARE TEXTILE FIBERS CLASSIFIED?

Overview II presents a classification scheme for textile fibers. Textile fibers are either natural or manufactured (man-made), depending on origin.[2] A *natural fiber* is "any fiber that exists as such in the natural state."[3] The fibers in this class occur in natural states in a form that can be readily converted to yarns and fabrics. A *manufactured fiber* is "any fiber derived by a process of manufacture from any substance which, at any point in the manufacturing process, is not a fiber.[4] The fibers in this class are produced from raw materials that may or may not have fibrous forms.

Fibers are either protein, cellulosic, mineral (inorganic), or synthetic.[5] These designations are determined by the chemical nature of a fiber. *Protein fibers* are composed of polymers of amino acids; *cellulosic fibers,* of polymers formed from glucose (sugar). *Mineral (inorganic) fibers* may be composed of silica obtained from rocks or sand; *synthetic fibers,* of polymers that originate from small, organic molecules (obtained from oil refineries) that combine with water and air.

Within each chemical group, fibers are called by a common or generic name. Natural fibers have *common names;* manufactured fibers have *generic names*. The fibers comprising each group have similar chemical natures and share a set of similar properties. A common or generic name applies to all members of a group and is not protected by trademark registration. The generic names to be used in the United States for manufactured

---

[1] 1 micrometer = 10^{-6} meter, or 1/25,400 of an inch.

[2] Until 1989, the preferred designation for fibers made from fiber-forming substances was "man-made." In 1989, the Man-Made Fiber Producers Association changed its name to the American Fiber Manufacturers Association, and the preferred name for this fiber classification changed with it.

[3] Definition from the Textile Fiber Products Identification Act.

[4] Definition from the Textile Fiber Products Identification Act.

[5] Sometimes the synthetic group is erroneously called the "thermoplastic group." Although many synthetic fibers are *thermoplastic* (they repeatedly soften when heated and harden when cooled), others do not melt when heated. This point is discussed further in Chapter 8.

fibers were established as part of the Textile Fiber Products Identification Act enacted by Congress in 1954.[6]

Common names of natural fibers were established centuries ago. Cotton, flax, and ramie are among the common names for natural cellulosic fibers. Cotton, for example, covers many different varieties of cotton fiber, including Pima and Egyptian. Wool, silk, mohair, and angora are among the common names for natural protein fibers. Wool fiber, as a common name, refers to many different types of wool, including Merino and Shetland.

Generic names for manufactured fibers include rayon, nylon, and polyester. Rayon, as a generic name, refers to several different types of fibers, including viscose and cuprammonium. Nylon, as a generic name, refers to fibers composed of polymers called polyamides.

Two groups of synthetic fibers are presented in Overview II. *General-use fibers* find application in a wide variety of end uses and are manufactured in the greatest quantities. *Special-use fibers* are developed for specific or limited applications and are produced in comparatively small quantities. Some special-use fibers are no longer manufactured.

UNIT ORGANIZATION

Overview II shows how the topics in Unit II are organized. Chapters 10 and 11 discuss the natural protein fibers; Chapters 12 and 13, the natural cellulosic fibers; and Chapters 14 and 15, the manufactured cellulosic fibers. Chapters 16–20 examine each of the general-use synthetic fibers in turn; Chapter 21 focuses on special-use synthetic and inorganic fibers.

Before we turn our attention to specific fiber groups, however, we will look into the microscopic world of fibers to learn about their structural features, chemical natures, and molecular arrangements and explain the synthesis of polymers by nature and by humans. Chapter 8 outlines the properties of fibers and their relationship to fiber structure. Chapter 9 discusses the required (federally mandated) components of correctly labeled textile products and considers relevant federal legislation; it also explains fiber trademarks, licensed and certification marks, and textile warranty programs.

The concepts presented in Unit II are the heart of textile science. After studying these chapters, you will understand how each type of fiber differs in its properties from other fibers. You also will recognize new innovations in fiber development, which occur continuously in today's world of textiles.

LEARNING THE PERFORMANCE OF EACH FIBER

Properties of each fiber are summarized in the first table of Chapters 10–19. For each of the 29 properties listed, a high, medium, or low ranking has been assigned based on the position of the fiber relative to other natural fibers, manufactured cellulosic fibers, and general-use synthetic fibers. Take a few minutes to find these tables and study their format. When studying each fiber, ask yourself how many high, medium, and low rankings the fiber has and in which of the property groups (mechanical, sorptive, thermal, chemical, and miscellaneous) the majority of these ranks occur. Then associate specific properties with the high and low ranks. A low rank does not mean poor performance, nor does a high rank indicate excellent performance. Low means that the quantitative data for that fiber placed it in the lower third of the range of data for that property; a high ranking in the upper third of the range.

In Chaper 8, a series of graphs and tables provides quantitative and descriptive data by property. Study of these graphs and tables establishes the range of values (or behaviors) and places each fiber within that range. Take a few more minutes and examine the tables and graphs in Chapter 8.

In learning the properties of fibers, it is also useful to realize that several fibers may share a similar set of properties. For example, the natural protein fibers, wool and silk, have a number of properties for which quantitative and descriptive data is similar. Properties which are similar for fibers in the natural protein, in the natural cellulosic, the manufactured cellulosic, and the synthetic classifications are provided below.

1. Natural protein fibers

■ Good to excellent resilience.
■ Highly hygroscopic and hydrophilic.
■ High heat of wetting.
■ Mechanical properties altered as fiber absorbs water. (Lower tenacity, modulus, stiffness, resilience, elastic recovery. Increased elongation.)
■ Harmed by alkalies (wool by weak alkalies; silk by concentrated ones).
■ Harmed by chlorine bleach and perspiration.
■ Weakened and yellowed by ultraviolet light.
■ Not readily flammable.

---

[6]Other countries refer to fibers by different common and generic names.

2. Natural cellulosic fibers

■ High moisture absorption that increases tenacity, modulus, and elongation at break and decreases fiber stiffness.
■ Swells in water; dimensionally stable because they return to original dimensions as they dry.
■ High resistance to degradation by alkaline solutions; can be changed structurally by submersion in concentrated alkalies, especially sodium hydroxide.
■ Low resilience.

3. Manufactured cellulosic fibers

■ Low tenacity.
■ Weaker wet than dry.
■ Low abrasion resistance.
■ Medium resistance to ultraviolet light.
■ Drycleaning or gentle laundry procedures recommended.

4. Synthetic fibers

■ Lowest moisture regains.
■ Lowest softening temperatures.
■ Highly oleophilic (most difficult removal of oily soil).
■ Highest electrical resistivity, leading to static buildup.
■ Highest toughness.

■ Medium to high resilience.
■ Highest resistance to moths, mildew, and fungi.

TERMINOLOGY

The common and generic names of fibers and the definitions of these terms are provided by the Textile Fiber Products Identification Act. Other terms related to the structure and manufacture of fibers are taken primarily from the *Hoechst Celanese Dictionary of Fiber and Textile Technology.* (Product/Technical Communications Services, 1990.)

OBJECTIVES

The objectives of Unit II are to:

■ Clarify the classification scheme for fibers.
■ Explain and describe the structure of fibers.
■ Outline the properties of fibers, and explain how each property is a result of fiber structure.
■ Show how fiber composition and care instructions are correctly (lawfully) conveyed in the marketplace to insure fair trade practices.
■ Examine the performance properties that are unique to each common and generic group of fibers.

Fiber Structure and Formation

OUTLINE	DEFINITION AND KEY WORDS
MORPHOLOGY	The study of the size, shape, and structure of a material.
Macrostructure	*Fiber features discernable to the eye.*
Length	Key words: staple and filament
Size	Key words: micrometers, denier, tex
Crimp	Key words: linear, 2- and 3-dimensional crimp
Color	Key words: shades from white to black
Microstructure	*Fiber features discernable under a light microscope.*
Longitudinal form	Key words: rod-shaped and ribbon-shaped even and uneven along the length
Surface contour	Key words: smooth, irregular
Cross sectional shape	Key words: round, oval, elliptical, serrated, kidney bean, dogbone, trilobal
Submicroscopic Structure	*Fiber features discernable under an electron microscope.*
	Key words: skin and core, fibrillar, medulla, scales, cortex, cuticle, primary wall, etc.
Fine structure	*Description of the polymers composing a fiber and their arrangement in the fiber.*
Polymers	Macromolecules in the form of hundreds or even thousands of individual chemical units called monomers covalently bonded together in a chain-like structure.
	Key words for types: homopolymers, copolymers, block
	Key word for length: degree of polymerization
	Key words for configuration: straight, helical, planar
	Key words for chemical makeup (monomers): cellulose, polypeptide, polyamide, polyester, polyhydrocarbon, etc.
	Key words for side (reactive) groups: polar and non-polar
Arrangement	Key words: degree of orientation and percent crystalline and amorphorous
Forces of Attraction (bonding of polymers)	Key words: van der Waals, dipole-dipole, hydrogen, ionic, covalent crosslinks
POLYMER SYNTHESIS AND FIBER FORMATION	Processes involved in reacting starting compounds to obtain monomers and the polymerization of the monomers to form a polymer as well as spinning the polymers into fibers.
Polymer synthesis for synthetic fibers	Key words: polymerization step-growth or step reaction chain-growth or chain reaction
Synthetic fiber formation (spinning or extrusion)	Key words: melt, dry (solvent), and wet spinning Drawing and heat setting
Biosynthesis of natural fiber polymers	
Manufactured cellulosic fiber formation	Key words: dry (solvent) and wet spinning Drawing and heat setting
VARIANT OR MODIFIED FIBER	A fiber that has a different feature or features than the regular fiber of its common or generic group.
Modifying natural fibers	
Modifying manufactured fibers	
Specialty fibers	
Bicomponent fibers	

Fiber Morphology and Formation

In the 1880s, organic chemists began the quest to understand natural fibers and other related materials they believed were composed of large molecules. Some scientists looked for solvents that would dissolve materials containing large molecules. Frederick Schoenbein discovered that cellulose (the material of trees, plants, and cotton fibers) would dissolve in a mixture of ether and alcohol if first treated with nitric acid. He formed a fiber from this dissolved cellulose, but the fiber (nitrocellulose) was highly explosive. Count Hilaire de Chardonnet improved on Schoenbein's work by discovering how to change the nitrocellulose back to cellulose. This work, and that of many other scientists, led to the production of 60,000 kilograms of rayon in 1896 and about 1000 tons by 1900. Commercial production of rayon fiber began in the United States in 1910.

Other chemists attempted to make large organic molecules in the laboratory. At first, all of their efforts resulted in waxy, gluey, or sticky messes. Around 1920, chemists began to call these giant molecules "poly"-something because they were now reasonably sure they were composed of many small molecules joined together. *Polymer chemistry,* a new branch of organic chemistry, was slowly emerging.

Soon after World War I, a number of far-seeing leaders in science and industry recognized that a systematic exploration of polymer chemistry could pay large returns, both industrially and in terms of basic knowledge. One of the most fruitful investigations was the memorable work of Wallace H. Carothers in the laboratories of E. I. du Pont de Nemours and Company. Supported by the vast resources of du Pont and a large group of brilliant collaborators, Carothers developed a systematic knowledge of the chemistry of polymerization and synthesized many hundreds of polymers. This campaign produced among other things, the fiber nylon in the 1940s, which was soon followed by the polyesters and polyacrylics and, in the 1950s, by the polyolefins and polyurethanes. Development efforts focused on producing fibers with suitable textile properties. Research during this period centered on the molecular structure of these fibers and the dependence of properties on structure.

By the 1960s, the accumulation of a large body of knowledge on structure-property relationships had led to a reverse approach to fiber development: the necessary properties were determined and the fiber was then tailor-made accordingly. Systematic macromolecular engineering led to a very large number of modified fibers within each generic class. Application of knowledge about structure-performance relationships literally has changed life in America and continues to provide enhancements today.

Detail View 7 lists the features comprising fiber structure and the methods of polymer synthesis and fiber formation (all major topics to be considered in this chapter) in its left-hand column. Definitions and key words are provided in the right-hand column.

MORPHOLOGY

Morphology is the study of the size, shape, and structure of a material. It is also the study of the relationships between aspects of structure: the morphology of fibers includes macrostructure, microstructure, submicroscopic structure, and fine structure.

Macrostructure

The features of a textile fiber that are discernible to the eye constitute its *macrostructure.* Observable features of fiber structure include length, width, crimp, and color.

Length. Textile fibers are either staple or filament length. *Staple textile fibers* range from ¾ to 18 inches (2–46 centimeters); *filament textile fibers* are of infinite length. All natural fibers except silk are staple length fibers. Silk and manufactured fibers may be staple or filament length.[1]

Size. *Fiber size* is usually specified in terms of diameter or linear density. Sometimes cross-sectional area and specific surface are used. Fibers are classified by size as coarse, medium, fine, microfiber, and ultrafine microfiber.

SPECIFICATION. The size of natural fibers is usually given as a diameter in micrometer units. It reflects the average width along the fiber's length (natural fibers are not uniform in width along their length). Cross-sectional area is useful for comparative purposes, because it takes into account the various fiber shapes.

The size of silk and manufactured fibers (except glass) are usually given in denier or tex units. Denier is used in the United States; in most other countries, denier has been replaced by tex. Denier and tex specify the linear density based on weight per unit length. By definition, denier is the weight in grams of 9000 meters of any linear material. Officially, it is the number of unit weights of 0.05 grams per 450-meter length. A 1-denier fiber would weigh 1 gram if 9000 meters of it were placed on a balance; a 2-denier fiber would weigh 2 grams if 9000 meters of it were weighed. Tex (a metric measure) is one-ninth of 1 denier; 1 tex is the weight in grams of 1000 meters of a linear material. As the denier or tex number

increases, the size of the fiber increases. A 1-denier polyester fiber is not equal in size to a 1-denier nylon fiber, however, because the fibers differ in density. Fiber size also may be given the unit decitex; 1 decitex is the number of grams that 10,000 meters of fiber weigh (1 decitex = 10 tex).

CLASSIFICATION. Textile fibers are available in a range of sizes (Figure 7.1). Natural fibers are 11–70 micrometers in diameter. Fine fibers have the smallest diameters and coarse fibers have the largest diameters for any fiber type. For example, sheep's wool is 17–40 micrometers in diameter. Fine wools are close to 17 micrometers in diameter; coarse wools, to 40 micrometers. The size range for cotton is 16–21 micrometers. Fine cotton fibers are close to 16 micrometers in size; coarse cotton fibers, to 21 micrometers. In general, the finer the natural fiber size, the higher the "quality" of the fiber. Natural fibers from the same plant or animal are subject to growth irregularities and usually are not all the same size. They also tend to vary in width along their length.

Manufactured fibers are available in a wide range of sizes. Until about five years ago, these fibers were classified as *fine* (<2.2 denier, 0.24 tex, or 2.4 decitex), *medium* or *normal* (6.3–2.2 denier, 0.70–0.24 tex, or 7.0–2.4 decitex), and *coarse* (>6.3–25 denier, 0.7–2.78 tex, or 7.0–27.8 decitex). Fiber manufacturers then began to produce *microfibers* (usually <1 denier, 0.11 tex, or 1.1 decitex in size) and, more recently, *ultrafine microfibers* (usually ≤0.3 denier, 0.033 tex, or 0.33 decitex in size).

Crimp. *Crimp* refers to waves, bends, twists, or curls along the fiber length (Figure 7.2). It is expressed as crimps per unit length.[2] Some natural fibers are linear; others are crimped. For example, silk is very linear: when it is laid on a flat surface, its entire length rests on that surface. In contrast, a wool fiber is kinky: only a small proportion of it rests on a flat surface.

Crimp may be two- or three-dimensional. *Three-dimensional crimp* occurs when a fiber waves above and below a surface as well as back and forth on a surface (for example, a wool fiber). *Two-dimensional crimp* occurs when a fiber waves in a single plane (for example, a mechanically crimped or textured manufactured fiber). Crimp also may be inherent or latent. *Inherent crimp*

---

[1] The influence of fiber length on yarn and fabric properties is discussed in Unit III.

[2] *Crimp* may also be the difference in distance between two points on an unstretched fiber and the same two points when the fiber is straightened under specified tension.

FIGURE 7.1 Fibers differ in size (fineness).

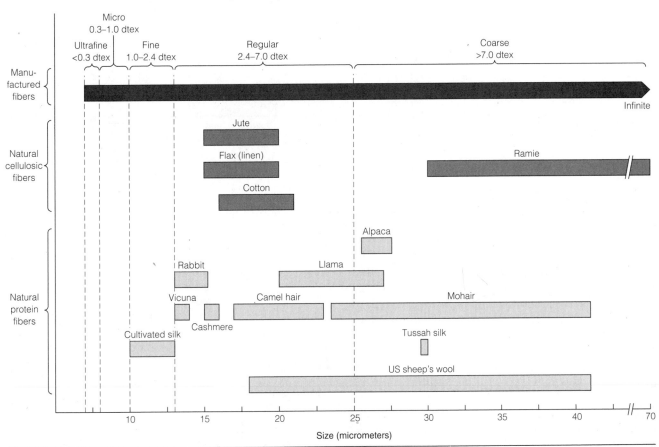

Microstructure

A light microscope is necessary to observe the *microstructure* of fibers, which includes their surface contour and cross-sectional shape.

Surface Contour or Longitudinal Form. Surface contour is a description of the surface of the fiber along its length. Surface contour may be smooth, serrated, lobed, striated, pitted, scaly, or convoluted. The photomicrographs (photographs taken through a microscope) in Unit II show the surface contours of various fibers.

Cross-sectional Shape. Cross-sectional shape refers to the shape of a horizontally cut fiber section (Figure 7.3). Shape may be round, triangular, dog-bone, kidney-

develops in the fiber as nature forms it or as it originally forms during spinning. *Latent crimp* is developed after fiber formation, often by exposing the fiber to heat and/or moisture. Crimped fibers tend to have higher elongation than linear fibers. A longitudinal force removes fiber crimp before stressing the internal structure of the fiber.

Color. White or colorless fibers can be dyed or printed to any hue and shade. Natural fibers may be white, off-white, some shade of tan or brown, or black. Some off-white fibers, such as cotton and sheep's wool, can be bleached white. The natural coloration of other fibers such as cashmere (which is tan) is retained. Manufactured fibers generally are white or off-white.

FIGURE 7.2 Fibers differ in degree and type of crimp.

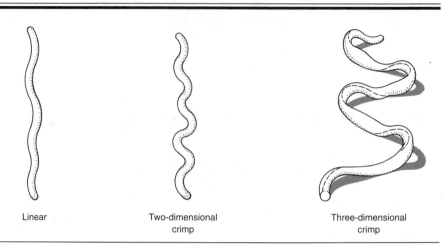

Linear

Two-dimensional crimp

Three-dimensional crimp

bean, flat, or multilobal, to cite only a few examples. The cross-sectional shape of natural fibers is determined by nature. There is a characteristic shape for each type of natural fiber. The typical cross-sectional shape of manufactured cellulosic fibers is serrated; of most regular or unmodified synthetic fibers, round.

Submicroscopic Structure

Submicroscopic structure becomes apparent when a cross section of a fiber is observed through an electron microscope (Figure 7.4). Most natural fibers have distinct submicroscopic features because nature builds intricate fibers with a number of distinct layers. For example, wool has a cuticle, a cortex, and a medulla. In contrast, manufactured fibers and silk tend to lack readily discernible submicroscopic features and to be uniform throughout. Often, the layer of material forming the outer surface of a manufactured fiber is denser than the material forming the center. The fiber is then said to have a *skin* and *core*.

Fine Structure

Fine structure is a description of the polymers that compose a fiber, including their length, width, shape, and chemical composition. It is also a depiction of the arrangement of the polymers and the bonds that hold them together.

Polymers. All fibers share one common structural feature: macromolecules, in the form of hundreds (even thousands) of individual chemical units, covalently bonded together one after the other. These macromolecules are called *polymers* (*poly* = "many"; *mer* = "unit"). An individual unit is a *monomer*. Polymers cannot be seen, even with the most sophisticated analytical instruments in use today. They are very long in relationship to their width. If a fiber polymer were $\frac{1}{8}$ inch (0.32 centimeters) in diameter, it would be 40 feet (12.2 meters) long.[3]

[3] Wunderlich, B. "The Solid State of Polyethylene," *Scientific American*, 211/5 (1964):81.

FIGURE 7.3 Fibers differ in cross-sectional shape.

Round   Oval   Kidney-bean   Dogbone   Trilobal

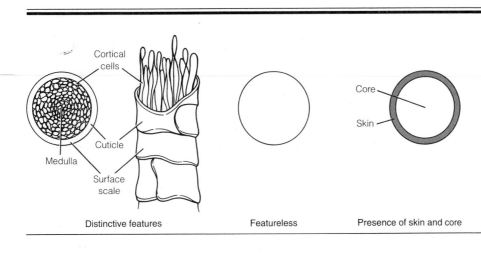

FIGURE 7.4 Fibers differ in submicroscopic structure.

Distinctive features   Featureless   Presence of skin and core

Polymers can be represented by "ball-and-string" structures. Each "ball" represents a monomer; each "string," a covalent bond between monomers.

TYPES. Three types of polymers—homopolymers, copolymers, and block polymers—comprise textile fibers. In *homopolymers,* the most common type, 1 monomer (one chemical compound) repeats itself along the polymer chain. The repeating monomer is represented by the identical balls in Figure 7.5. Cotton, the specialty cellulosic fibers rayon, acetate, triacetate, wool and silk, polyester, nylon, olefin, sulfar, aramid, and PBI fibers are composed of homopolymers. The monomers of cotton and olefin (see Figure 7.5) illustrate the diversity of monomers in terms of chemical composition, size, and shape.

In *copolymers,* two or more monomers comprise the polymer chain. Acrylic, modacrylic, vinyon, and saran fibers contain copolymers. The polymer in acrylic fiber generally contains two monomers, one of which is present in greater quantity than the other. The ball-and-string structure of a copolymer contains a lengthy series of white balls (the first monomer) and an occasional black ball (the second monomer), as shown in Figure 7.5.

In *block polymers,* blocks comprised of homopolymers are repeated along the polymer chain. The ball-and-string representation of a block polymer (Figure 7.5) alternates a block, or segment, of black monomers with one of white monomers. The number of monomers within a black block and a white block do not need to be the same. Spandex fiber is composed of block polymers.

LENGTH. Polymer length is specified as the number of times the monomer is repeated along the chain. This is called the *degree of polymerization.* In Figure 7.5, the degree of polymerization of each polymer shown is 12. Fibers contain polymers with high degrees of polymerization ranging from 500 to 10,000. The degree of polymerization of cotton is ~10,000, resulting in a polymer ~1/5080 inch (~1/200 millimeter) long at full extension.[4]

Polymer length plays a role in fiber tenacity, elongation, and modulus (Figure 7.6). If two fibers are alike except for polymer length, the fiber with the longer polymers generally is stronger, extends a shorter distance at a given load, and requires more force to cause elongation. Greater cohesive forces must be overcome to separate long polymers than to separate shorter polymers. Once polymer length has reached a stage at which the energy required to make a polymer slide over adjacent polymers is greater than the energy required to break the polymer itself, further increases in chain length do not affect fiber tenacity. The force then ruptures individual polymers.

CHEMISTRY. The backbone of most polymers is comprised of carbon atoms covalently bonded to each other (–C–C–) or to oxygen (–C–O–C–). These covalent bonds are strong and relatively stable; severe, prolonged exposure to chemicals and/or heat is usually required to break these covalent bonds. In other polymers, carbon atoms are covalently bonded to nitrogen atoms

[4]R.W. Moncrieff. *Man-Made Fibres,* 6th ed. New York: John Wiley, 1975).

FIGURE 7.5 Fibers differ in the types of polymers they contain.

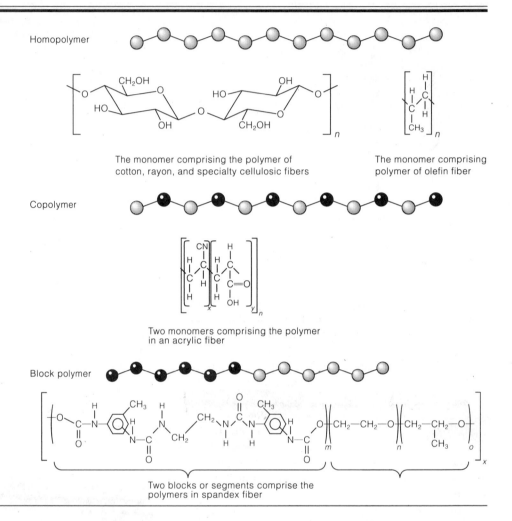

Homopolymer

The monomer comprising the polymer of cotton, rayon, and specialty cellulosic fibers

The monomer comprising polymer of olefin fiber

Copolymer

Two monomers comprising the polymer in an acrylic fiber

Block polymer

Two blocks or segments comprise the polymers in spandex fiber

(–C–N–C–); these polymers are more susceptible to degradation by chemicals and heat.

The backbone of most polymers is in a zig-zag configuration, created by the tetrahedral bonding of each carbon atom ($\overset{|}{\underset{|}{C}}$). When a fiber is stressed, the force may act to straighten the polymer backbone.

The backbone atoms are covalently bonded to a number of different types of atoms or chemical groups. They may be covalently bonded to hydrogen (–H) or to a methyl group (–CH₃). *Methyl groups* do not attract water or charged dye molecules; they are not reactive. In other polymers, polar groups are covalently bonded along the polymer chain. *Polar groups* such as hydroxyl (–OH) attract water, certain types of dye molecules, and charged staining substances; they may react with various chemicals applied to the fiber. Figure 7.7 shows some typical side groups on polymer chains.

The size of reactive groups influences fiber performance. In general, polymers with large reactive groups are less densely packed within the fiber, so that the fiber is less crystalline. Realistically, the balls in ball-and-chain polymer structures would not be the same size and shape for all fibers.

Orientation and Crystallinity. The thousands of polymers within a fiber lie more or less parallel to the longitudinal axis of the fiber itself (Figure 7.8). All polymers cannot lie randomly within a textile fiber; if they did, minimum property levels would not be achieved. When a relatively high proportion of polymers are aligned with the fiber axis, the fiber is said to be "highly oriented." Lesser proportions lead to lower degrees of orientation.

Within fibers, adjacent polymers are found tightly packed together in spacially ordered *crystalline regions*

FIGURE 7.6 Fibers differ in degree of polymerization (length of the polymer chains).

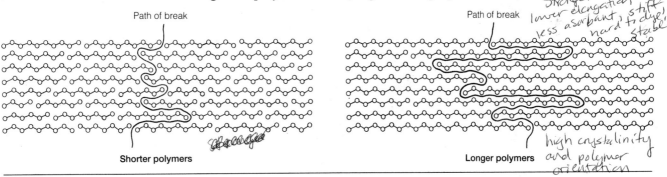

(handwritten notes:) Stronger, lower elongation, less absorbant, stiff, hard to dye, stable.

high crystalinity and polymer orientation

Path of break   Path of break

Shorter polymers   Longer polymers

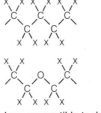

and further apart in *amorphous regions,* so that voids are formed within the fiber. Each polymer is so long that it runs through several amorphous and crystalline regions. The proportion of crystalline to amorphous regions varies for different fibers. The left-hand drawing in Figure 7.8 represents a fiber with a relatively low degree of polymer orientation and crystallinity; the right-hand drawing represents a fiber with a higher degree of orientation and crystallinity.

Orientation and crystallinity have a significant impact on many fiber properties. If two fibers are alike except for degree of orientation and crystallinity, the fiber that is more crystalline and oriented is stronger, has lower elongation at break, is less absorbent, stiffer, more difficult to dye, more resistant to deteriorating chemicals, and more stable (less susceptible to changes in temperature and moisture).

Intrafiber or Interpolymer Forces of Attraction. The integrity of a fiber is determined by the entanglement of the polymers and the forces of attraction between them (Figure 7.9). *Intrafiber* or *interpolymer* forces occur between

FIGURE 7.7 Fibers differ in the nature of the bonds along the polymer chain and type of reactive group, shown as X.

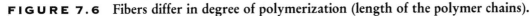

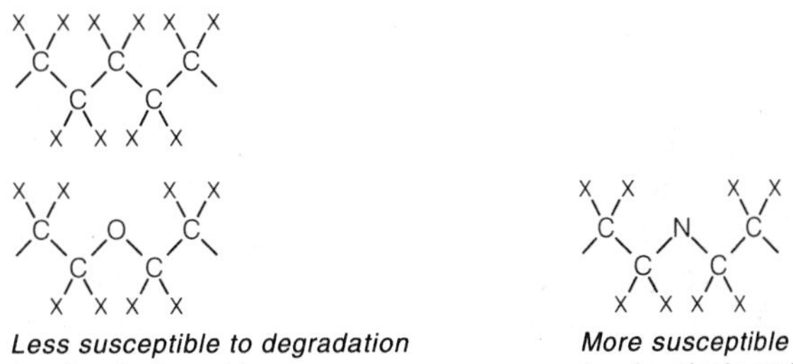

Less susceptible to degradation by chemicals and heat

More susceptible to degradation by chemicals and heat

X may be: Nonreactive groups such as hydrogen (—H) or
                                             methyl (—CH3).
    Reactive groups such as   hydroxyl (—OH),
                                             amino (—N—C=O),
                                             carboxyl (—C⟨=O/OH⟩),
                                             imido (—NH) not attached to any acid
                                                    group, and
                                             carbonyl (⟩C=O).

FIGURE 7.8 Fibers differ in orientation and crystallinity.

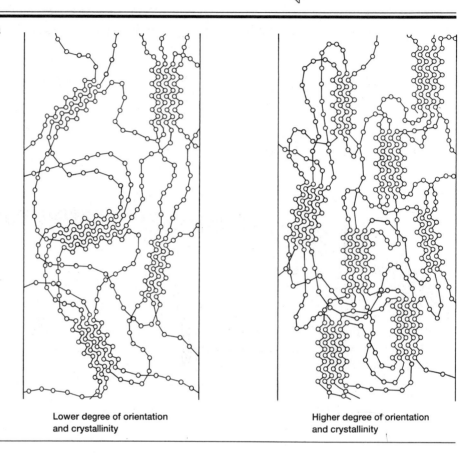

Lower degree of orientation and crystallinity

Higher degree of orientation and crystallinity

polymers within fibers. The forces of attraction that occur in fibers are: van der Waals forces, dipole-dipole interactions, hydrogen bonds, and/or ionic bonds. Polymers also may be crosslinked through covalent bonds.

Bonding is important in determining many fiber properties, including tenacity, elongation, elastic recovery, modulus, and resilience. Stronger and more numerous bonds strengthen the fiber, and lower its elongation. When bonds are broken under stress and reform while the fiber is bent, the fiber will remain in the deformed state.

VAN DER WAALS FORCES. *Van der Waals forces* are very weak electrostatic forces which attract neutral molecules to each other. They become an intrafiber force of attraction when any two or more polymers (or polymer segments) lie very close together, as occurs in the crystalline regions of any fiber. The diameter or size of the atoms that give rise to van der Waals forces influences the relative strength of this very weak, intrafiber attraction;

larger atoms give rise to stronger van der Waals forces than smaller atoms do.

DIPOLE-DIPOLE INTERACTIONS. *Dipole-dipole interaction* is the attraction of the positive end of one polar molecule for the negative end of another polar molecule. In hydrogen chloride, for example, the relatively positive hydrogen end of one molecule is attracted to the relatively negative chlorine end of another. In general, dipole-dipole interaction binds polar molecules together more strongly than it holds nonpolar molecules of comparable molecular weight. Dipole-dipole interaction is important in the intrafiber bonding of polyester and acrylic fibers.

HYDROGEN BONDS. Hydrogen bonding is the strongest type of dipole-dipole interaction, so is usually discussed separately. *Hydrogen bonds* occur between hydrogen atoms that are covalently bonded to strongly electronegative atoms, such as oxygen, nitrogen, and fluorine.

FIGURE 7.9 Fibers differ in types of bonding between polymers.

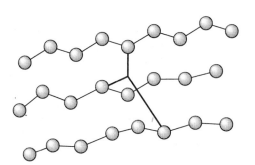

van der Waals forces: Attraction of neutral molecules to each other due to very weak electrostatic forces between them.

Dipole-dipole interactions: Attraction of the positive end of one polar molecule for the negative end of another polar molecule; polarity arising from the unequal sharing of electrons.

Hydrogen bonds: A strong dipole-dipole attraction occurring between hydrogen atoms covalently bonded to strongly electronegative atoms, such as oxygen, nitrogen, and fluorine.

Ionic or electrostatic bonds (salt links or bridges): Attraction between negatively and positively charged ions due to a transfer of electrons.

Covalent crosslinks: Attraction between an atom on one polymer chain and an atom on the adjacent polymer chain due to the sharing of electrons.

The hydrogen atoms assume a very slight positive charge or polarity; the oxygen, nitrogen, or fluorine atoms assume a very slight negative charge or polarity. Hydrogen bonds may form only when the distance is less than ~0.5 nanometer (the millionth part of a millimeter) between two very slightly polar but oppositely charged atoms.

The attraction of water molecules to each other is a simple example of hydrogen bonding. In each water molecule, the oxygen atom partially pulls electrons from the hydrogen atoms covalently bonded to it, causing a partial negative charge on the oxygen atom and a partial positive charge on the hydrogen atoms. Hydrogen bonds then form between two water molecules because the partial negative charge on the oxygen atom of one water molecule is attracted to the partial positive charge on the hydrogen of the second water molecule. The partial transfer of electrons is indicated by a delta sign (δ); the hydrogen bond, by a dotted line:

$$H^{\delta+}$$
$$\diagdown$$
$$O^{\delta-} \cdots H^{\delta+}$$
$$\diagup \qquad \diagdown$$
$$H^{\delta+} \qquad\qquad O^{\delta-}$$
$$\diagup$$
$$H^{\delta+}$$

Hydrogen bonding may occur between adjacent polymer chains at points where a slightly positively charged hydrogen atom and a slightly negatively charged atom, such as oxygen or nitrogen, are in close proximity—generally in the crystalline regions. The hydrogen bond is stronger when the polarities of the atoms on either side of it are greater. The polymers bond strongly to each other if they are close together and hydrogen bonds are numerous. Hydrogen bonding is particularly important in cellulosic fibers (cotton, flax, and rayon), in nylon, and in protein fibers (wool and silk).

IONIC BONDS. *Ionic* or *electrostatic bonds* (also called *salt links* or *bridges*) occur between negatively and positively charged radicals. Common table salt ($Na^+ Cl^-$) is an example of an ionic bond in a simple molecule. (A negatively charged radical forms when it gains one or more electrons over its normal electron complement.) Ionic bonds may occur between very closely adjacent fiber polymers. Reactive groups permit these bonds to form between the polymers of protein fibers (wool and silk) and at the ends of nylon polymers.

COVALENT CROSSLINKS. When single covalent bonds occur between polymers (in addition to those between monomers along the backbone of the polymer), the polymers are *crosslinked*. Reactive groups along each polymer chain are covalently bonded.

POLYMER SYNTHESIS AND FIBER FORMATION

The bonding together of monomers to form polymers is called *polymerization*. It is a fundamental process of nature and is of prime importance in the formation of manufactured fibers. The formation of natural polymers is however less fully understood then the formation of the polymers for manufactured fibers.

Polymerization involves a series of collisions between monomer molecules, which constantly move in random directions. Each monomer contains a site that is capable of reacting with a second monomer to form a covalent bond. A polymer chain lengthens only when two monomer molecules collide at their reactive sites. Some monomers are more reactive than others, so that a higher proportion of collisions cause the units to join (more collisions are successful).

Polymerization may occur spontaneously or at least very rapidly when monomers are mixed together. In many cases, however, the monomers react slowly under ambient conditions. Energy in the form of heat, light, or highly reactive initiator molecules is required to increase the incidence of bond-forming collisions and therefore chain lengthening.

Theoretically, chain lengthening can continue until all the monomer units and intermediate molecules have joined together to form one extremely long chain. In the synthesis of polymers for manufactured fibers, however, several termination mechanisms limit the degree of polymerization once the molecular chains reach an average length suitable for the intended application.

Polymer Synthesis for Synthetic Fibers

Polymerization is typically carried out in a closed chemical reactor equipped with stirring facilities as well as monomer inlets and a polymer outlet. The temperature and pressure inside these reactors are closely controlled. Polymerization is usually conducted at an elevated temperature and pressure in the presence of a catalyst, which increases the reaction rate. The reactions that build polymers for synthetic manufactured fibers occur by either a step-growth or a chain-growth mechanism,[5] depending on the type of monomers involved.

Step-Growth or Step Reaction. In *step-growth* or *step reaction* (Figure 7.10), the formation of each covalent bond in the polymer chain is accompanied by the liberation of a small byproduct molecule. Water is the byproduct of many reactions; other byproducts include hydrogen chloride, ammonia, and simple alcohols. The monomer units usually have a reactive site at each end (the darkened sides of the balls). If the molecules collide at their reaction sites, (1, 2, and 3), a bond forms and a small molecule is liberated. If collision does not occur at two reaction sites (4), no bond forms. Further reactions among intermediate molecules, which still have reactive sites at each end, eventually produce a long polymer chain.

Chain-Growth or Chain Reaction. In *chain-growth* or *chain reaction* (Figure 7.11), unreacted monomer molecules (shaded circles) are approached by a highly reactive

---

[5]The classical terms for these mechanisms are *condensation* and *addition*, respectively.

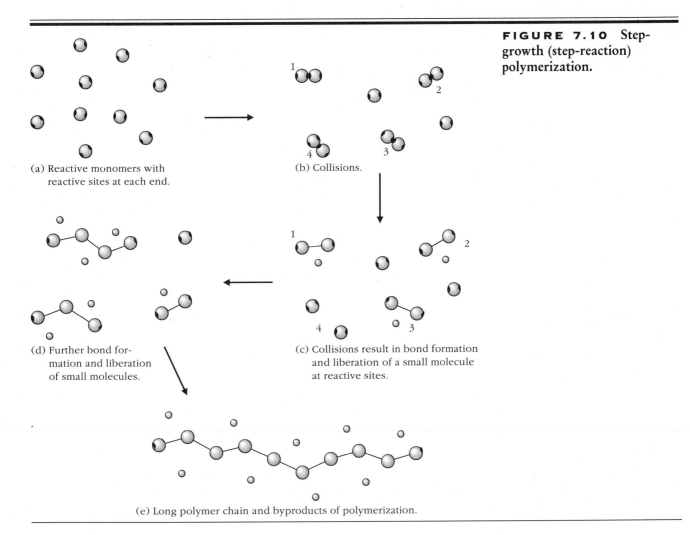

(a) Reactive monomers with reactive sites at each end.

(b) Collisions.

(c) Collisions result in bond formation and liberation of a small molecule at reactive sites.

(d) Further bond formation and liberation of small molecules.

(e) Long polymer chain and byproducts of polymerization.

FIGURE 7.10 Step-growth (step-reaction) polymerization.

initiator molecule (black circle). The monomer molecules generally contain a double bond between their two end carbon atoms (–C=C). When the initiator molecule collides with one of the monomers, the double bond between the two end carbons is broken, producing a free radical (an atom or group of atoms with an odd or unpaired electron, indicated by *). A free radical is extremely reactive: it is seeking an additional electron which it can gain by colliding with another molecule. Because monomers are present in the largest concentration, they are most likely to be struck by the free radical. Chain propagation continues as the growing free radical continues to collide with monomers.

Catalysts included in chain-growth polymerization reactions function by temporarily "holding" a monomer molecule so that collision with a second monomer unit

or growing chain is more likely to occur at a reactive site. Catalyst molecules also may have a "lock and key" facility; they may specifically bind one type and shape of monomer molecule to the exclusion of others.

Synthetic Fiber Formation. Synthetic fibers are formed by extruding (forcing) a liquid polymer solution through one to thousands of holes in a *spinneret* (Figure 7.12). This process of *extrusion* is often referred to as *spinning* or *fiber spinning*. It should not be confused with the process of converting fiber to yarn, which is also called "spinning."

CONVENTIONAL EXTRUSION PROCESSES. The polymeric material to be converted to fibers is often in the form of chips or powder that must be dissolved in a suitable solvent or melted to make the polymers "free flowing." The

FIGURE 7.11 Chain-growth (chain-reaction) polymerization.

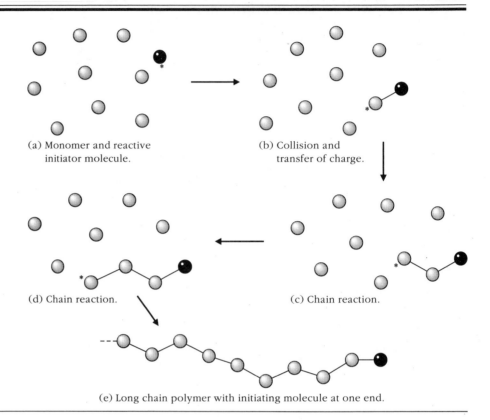

(a) Monomer and reactive initiator molecule.

(b) Collision and transfer of charge.

(d) Chain reaction.

(c) Chain reaction.

(e) Long chain polymer with initiating molecule at one end.

liquid polymeric material is then extruded and must harden. The three conventional processes involved in the conversion of polymers to manufactured fiber are melt spinning, dry (solvent) spinning, and wet spinning.

Melt spinning requires thermoplastic polymers. The polymer chips are heated until they melt. The molten polymer is forced through the holes in a spinneret, emerges in fibrous form, and solidifies on cooling in air.

Dry (solvent) spinning is used for polymers that are adversely affected by heat at or close to their melting temperatures. The polymer is dissolved in a solvent. The liquid polymer is extruded through a spinneret into a circulating current of hot gas, which evaporates the solvent from the polymers and causes the filament(s) to harden. The solvent is removed and recycled.

In *wet spinning*, the polymers also are dissolved in a suitable solvent. The liquid polymer is extruded through a jet into a liquid bath, where the filaments coagulate. The solvent is removed and recycled.

OTHER EXTRUSION PROCESSES. In *reaction spinning*, polymerization occurs during extrusion through the spinneret. Monomers are placed in solution and ex-

truded; heat then solidifies the filaments. Some spandex fiber is made by reaction spinning.

Gel spinning is used to form fibers that have ultra-high molecular weights (>500,000). A dilute but highly viscous polymer solution is prepared. It is fluid at the extrusion temperature but sets into a gel when cooled to ambient temperature. The gel fibers are mechanically stable and are processed further before use.

In *dispersion spinning*, fine particles of the polymer are dispersed in a carrier. Following extrusion through a spinneret, heat coalesces the polymer and removes the carrier.

Drawing and Heat Setting. After extrusion, the fiber is said to be "unoriented" or "undrawn." The polymers within the fiber have begun to orient themselves with the longitudinal axis of the fiber because the long polymers turned to flow through the spinneret hole. However, their degree of orientation and crystallinity is quite low. The filaments are therefore drawn (elongated) and heat is generally applied to cause the polymers to vibrate and move closer together. (Details of this process are provided in Chapter 24.)

FIGURE 7.12   Conversion of polymers to manufactured fibers.

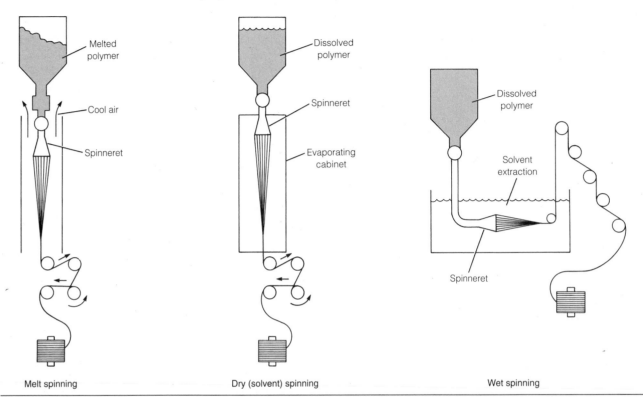

Melt spinning   Dry (solvent) spinning   Wet spinning

Biosynthesis of Natural Fiber Polymers

While synthetic polymers can be manufactured in a matter of hours, it takes weeks, months, or even years for plants and animals to form polymers. Moreover, natural polymers can be formed only within a restricted range of atmospheric temperatures and pressures.

The conversion of suitable chemical monomers into polymers occurs inside the cells of plants and animals. Polymerization requires a catalyst (an enzyme) and usually an input of energy to enable cell replication and growth of the organism to occur at an acceptable rate. The cell can be viewed as a microscopic vessel in which thousands of complex chemical reactions occur simultaneously. The supply of chemical raw materials to the cell and the disposal of waste products from it are carried out by the fluid (blood or sap) circulating through the organism.

Cellulose Polymers. The formation of cellulose polymers (*polysaccharides*) begins when cell components convert radiant energy from the sun to chemical energy.

With the aid of this chemical energy and enzymes within the cell, water and carbon dioxide molecules are converted to carbohydrates (sugars) and oxygen through a series of chemical transformations in which the number of carbon atoms increases progressively from one to six. This mechanism involves numerous chemical intermediates (containing two, three, four, or five carbon atoms and various combinations of oxygen and hydrogen atoms) that also can participate in biosynthetic pathways other than sugar production. A considerable input of light energy is required for step-growth carbohydrate synthesis.

Glucose—the sugar of importance in cellulose polymer formation—contains five carbon atoms and one oxygen atom, joined together to form a six-membered ring (Figure 7.13). Glucose rings are puckered and highly flexible; they can interconvert to several types of configurations, each with a different spatial arrangement of atoms. Only β-D-glucose can form a linear cellulose polymer. Step-growth polymerization occurs at the number 1 carbon atom of one glucose molecule and the number 4 carbon atom of a second glucose molecule. A

FIGURE 7.13 Formation of a cellulose polymer (polysaccharide) by the step growth of β-D-glucose.

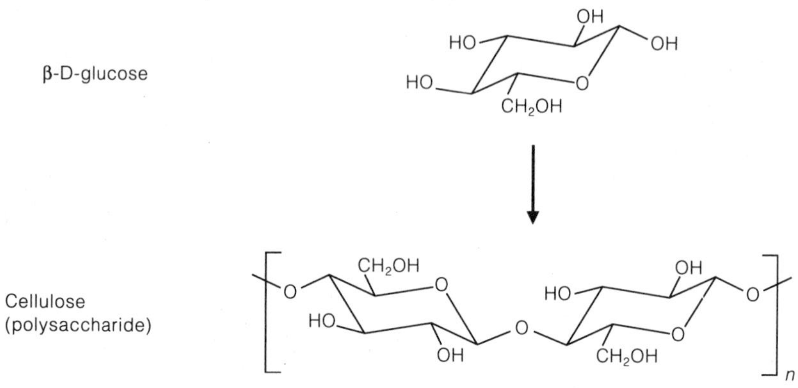

β-D-glucose

Cellulose
(polysaccharide)

molecule of water is eliminated in each reaction as the cellulose chain grows. Cellulose polymers have yet to be formed in the laboratory.

Protein Polymers. Protein polymers (*polypeptides*) are synthesized from amino acids as the monomer units (Figure 7.14). There are many different amino acids in nature; 18 types are contained in wool and silk fiber polymers.[6] The atoms composing "R" in the general formula differ for the various amino acids, making them different in shape and chemistry. Amino acids are given names such as cystine, glycine, aspartic acid, and lysine.

The amino acids are arranged in a precise fashion along the protein polymer chain. The genetic code for the arrangement is carried by the chromosomes inside the nucleus of the cell. Each chromosome consists of thousands of genes, each of which is responsible for synthesizing a particular polypeptide chain. Each gene essentially sends numerous template molecules out of the nucleus and into the cell, where they bind the amino acid monomers in the predetermined sequence.

Figure 7.14 presents a schematic representation of protein biosynthesis involving six amino acids. In the template, each amino acid has a different shape. Each binding location accepts only one amino acid monomer unit with the complementary structure; all other amino acids are rejected at that site. Once adjacent amino acids

are in position, a covalent bond (in this case, a peptide bond) forms between them. Amino acids are added sequentially until the template molecule is full; the polypeptide polymer then completely detaches.

Manufactured Cellulosic Fiber Formation

To manufacture cellulosic fibers, the cellulose made by plants is converted to fibrous form by wet or dry spinning (see Figure 7.12). The chemist dissolves the cellulose mass and extrudes it through a spinneret into a bath containing chemicals that coagulate the liquid cellulose into fiber strands.

VARIANTS OR MODIFIED FIBERS

A fiber that has a feature or features different from other fibers within its common or generic group is called a *fiber variant* or a *modified fiber*.[7] Principles of plant and animal genetics, as well as knowledge of chemical reactivity, are used to produce natural fiber variants. The structure-property relationships of textile fibers are applied to produce manufactured fiber variants.

Modifying Natural Fibers. A plant geneticist or animal scientist may use genetics or selective breeding to improve a natural fiber. For example, a variety of cotton,

---

[6]Some types of silk fiber contain 15 different amino acids; some references state that there are 19 amino acids in wool polymers.

[7]Some textile scientists limit the use of the term "fiber variant" to manufactured fibers.

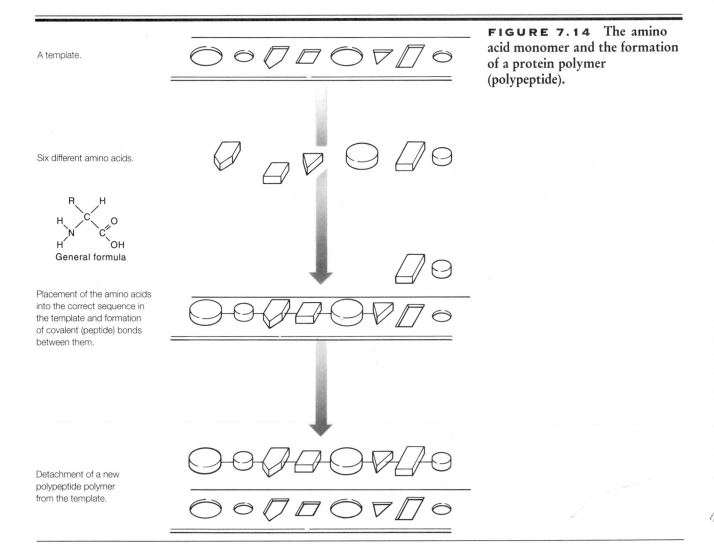

A template.

Six different amino acids.

General formula

Placement of the amino acids into the correct sequence in the template and formation of covalent (peptide) bonds between them.

Detachment of a new polypeptide polymer from the template.

FIGURE 7.14 The amino acid monomer and the formation of a protein polymer (polypeptide).

Pima cotton, was developed to produce a longer staple fiber than the one obtained from the Upland cotton plant, a source of commodity cotton fiber. Colored cotton can be grown by genetic manipulation. The Merino sheep, a result of crossbreeding, produces a fine-quality wool fiber.

The textile scientist also may modify the structure of a natural fiber by immersing it in or reacting it with certain chemicals.[8] For example, sodium hydroxide or liquid ammonia can be used to rearrange the polymers of cotton fiber but leave the fiber as pure cellulose. Other chemicals may build covalent crosslinks, as found in durable-press cotton.

A premium price is paid for modified natural fibers; the product label often indicates the variety (for example, Pima cotton), treatment (for example, mercerized), or breed of animal (for example, Merino). Modified natural fibers are usually used in the same applications as commodity fibers, but in goods of higher quality. Fewer modifications can be made to natural fibers than to manufactured fibers.

Modifying Manufactured Fibers. The performance properties of manufactured fiber variants are generally engineered to match special end-use applications. For

---

[8]This process generally occurs after the fabric has been formed. Natural fiber modifications are therefore discussed in Unit V.

FIGURE 7.15 Modifications to manufactured fiber to form variants.

1. Altering fine structure   Shown in Figures 7.6 and 7.8
   Polymer length
   Orientation and crystallinity

2. Changing cross-sectional   Shown in Figure 7.3
   shape

3. Incorporating a chemical
   between polymer chains

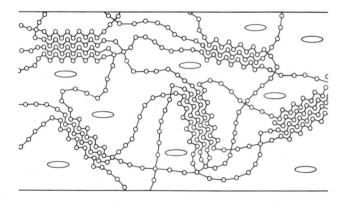

4. Incorporating a small
   proportion of a third monomer

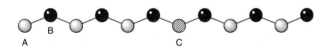

5. Grafting and incorporating
   bulky reactive groups

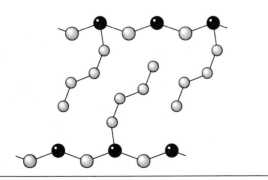

example, the comfort performance of polyester to be used in dresses is different than that required for exercise apparel.

SPECIALTY FIBERS. A *specialty fiber* can be created by modifying a first-generation fiber (the original fiber) in a number of ways (Figure 7.15). Cross-sectional shape and surface contour may be modified. The fiber manufacturer may alter the degree of polymerization, the degree of polymer orientation and crystallinity within the fiber, and other aspects of fiber fine structure.

A specialty fiber may have the same polymers as the first-generation fiber but a chemical may be found incorporated between polymers within the fiber. When a lower luster is required, titanium dioxide is added to the polymer solution prior to extrusion. Flame-retardant and antistatic chemicals also can be incorporated.

A specialty fiber may differ from other fibers in its generic group because a "unique" monomer is covalently bonded in its polymer chain. Depending on the chemistry of this monomer, which forms only a small proportion of the polymer chain, the specialty fiber may be easier to dye, be more receptive to different types of dyes, and so on.

When bulky chemical groups are introduced along a polymer chain, the orientation and crystallinity of the fiber are altered and the properties related to these structural features change. The nature of the fiber surface is also likely to change because the polymers there tend to orient with the bulky groups facing outward. Hydrophobic fiber surfaces can be made more hydrophilic, improving their ability to release soil and increasing water absorbency and wickability.

The specialty fibers discussed thus far are *homogeneous fibers:* all the polymers within the fiber are of like chemical composition. *Heterogeneous* specialty fibers, called *bicomponents,* contain two different polymers.

BICOMPONENT FIBERS. A *bicomponent fiber* consists of two polymers that are chemically and/or physically different (Figure 7.16). Wool fiber is the only natural fiber that is a bicomponent; all other bicomponents are manufactured.

To form a manufactured bicomponent fiber, the textile scientist may combine polymers from *within* a generic group that differ chemically or physically. On extrusion, a *side-by-side configuration* or a *sheath-core configuration* may result in which one type of polymer comprises one section of the fiber and a second type of polymer comprises the other section. The textile scien-

FIGURE 7.16   Bicomponent (heterogeneous) fibers contain two structurally and/or chemically different polymers.

Bicomponent configurations

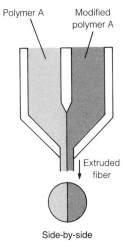

Side-by-side

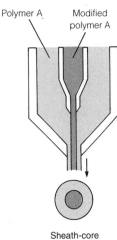

Sheath-core

Bicomponent bigeneric configurations

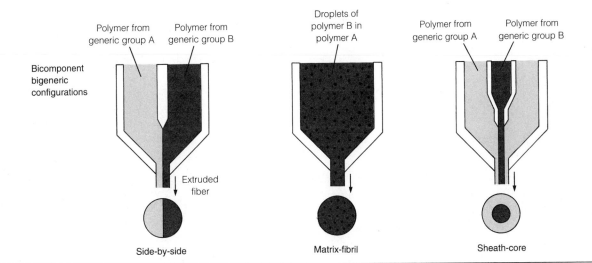

Side-by-side   Matrix-fibril   Sheath-core

tist also may select polymers from *different* generic groups to form the bicomponent fiber. This type of fiber may be called a *bigeneric* or a *bigeneric bicomponent.* On extrusion, the polymers may be arranged in a side-by-side, sheath-core, or *matrix-fibril configuration,* in which one polymer is distributed in discrete units (fibrils) throughout the other polymer system (the matrix).

Bicomponent fibers are usually marketed with fiber trademarks. A complete description of a bicomponent

includes the trademark, physical arrangement of components, number of components, number of generic classes, generic class names, makeup of generic classes, percentage of generic classes, and production form.[9] An example of a complete description of a bicomponent bi-

[9] American Society for Testing and Materials, "Terminology for Multicomponent Textile Fibers," *1988 Annual Book of ASTM Standards,* ASTM Standard D 4466 (Philadelphia, PA: ASTM, 1988).

FIGURE 7.17 Percentage distribution of fiber shipped to U.S. consumers in 1990.

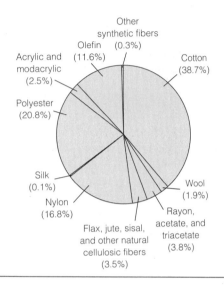

FIGURE 7.18 Primary market distribution of fiber shipped to U.S. consumers in 1989.

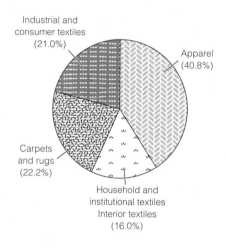

generic fiber is: Source®, matrix, bicomponent, bigeneric (nylon 6,6 [70%]/polyester [30%]).

Properties that cannot be attained with homogeneous fibers may be achieved with heterogeneous fibers. The set of properties depends on the polymers selected and the arrangement of those polymers within the fiber. Bicomponent fibers are expensive to produce.

FIBER UTILIZATION

In 1990, 15,525.7 million pounds of fiber were shipped to U.S. textile mills for conversion into textile products. As shown in Figure 7.17, the largest proportion of fiber shipped was cotton and polyester, making them the most used fibers in the United States. Four fibers—cotton, polyester, nylon, and olefin—accounted for almost 90% of all fiber shipped. About 44% of fiber utilized was natural fiber and about 56% manufactured fiber.

On a worldwide basis in 1989, 54.1% of fiber utilized was natural fiber (48.9% cotton, 5% wool, 0.2% silk). Manufactured fiber utilization was 45.9% (7.5% cellulosic; 38.4% synthetic).[10] As shown in Figure 7.18, most of the U.S. fiber was converted into fabrics to be used for apparel. Very little of it was exported.

CHAPTER SUMMARY

Textile fibers are long, linear materials composed of long, linear molecules called polymers. Because polymers lie more or less parallel to the fiber axis, fibers have various degrees of polymer orientation. The polymers also form crystalline and amorphous areas within the fiber, so that fibers differ in their degree of crystallinity. Generally, highly oriented fibers are also highly crystalline. A fiber derives its integrity from the forces of attraction between its polymers: van der Waals forces, dipole-dipole interactions, hydrogen bonds, ionic bonds, and covalent crosslinks. Which forces are operational depends on how closely the polymers are packed together and on whether or not polar groups are present. The strength of the bonds depends on the particular atoms involved.

The structure of a fiber also includes a description of its surface contour, cross-sectional shape, length, diameter, crimp, and color. Every aspect of structure influences the performance of the fiber in some way. Textile scientists use their knowledge of structure/performance relationships to alter the structure—and therefore the properties—of manufactured fibers. Fiber variants or modified fibers are made. The fibers may be homogeneous or heterogeneous (bicomponent) variants. Natural fibers can be modified genetically or chemically.

Polymers are synthesized by either step-growth or chain-growth mechanisms. The monomers for synthetic fiber polymerization are obtained from the products of oil refineries; for natural fibers from biosynthesis. Polymerization is not required for cellulosic manufac- tured fibers; the polymer is formed by nature. Manu- factured fibers are produced by extruding the liquid polymer through a spinneret. Conventional extrusion processes are wet, dry, and melt spinning.

Fiber Properties

KEY WORD	DEFINITION

MECHANICAL PROPERTIES

Stress — Resistance to deformation (a change in length) developed within a fiber being subjected to a pulling or tensile force.

Strain — Deformation (lengthening or extension) of a fiber caused by application of a pulling or tensile force.

Tenacity — Stress expressed as a force per linear density (grams-force per denier or newtons per tex).

Breaking tenacity — Tenacity of a fiber at rupture.

Elongation — Extension (lengthening) expressed as a percent of its original length.

Elongation at break — Elongation of a fiber at rupture.

Modulus — Ease of extending a fiber expressed as a ratio of change in stress to change in strain.

Toughness (work of rupture) — Ability of a fiber to absorb work (the force during extension); ability of a fiber to endure a large deformation (extension) without rupture.

Elastic recovery — Degree of return of a fiber to its initial length following its extension as the stress to which it has been subjected decreases with time.

Resilience (work recovery) — Ability of a fiber to spring back after extension expressed as the ratio of recoverable work to total work required to strain the fiber a specified amount.

Stiffness (flexural rigidity) — Resistance of a fiber to bending or ability to carry a load without deformation (lengthening).

Abrasion resistance — Ability of a fiber not to crack, break, or wear away under a rubbing force.

Flexibility — Number of times a fiber can be bent without rupture.

SORPTIVE PROPERTIES

Moisture regain — Percent of moisture in a fiber calculated on the basis of its dry weight.

Swelling and lengthening — Increase in a fiber's cross-sectional area or length when saturated with water.

Heat of wetting — Heat evolved when a fiber absorbs water.

Oil absorption — Amount of oil adsorbed and absorbed by a fiber.

Oil release (oleophilicity) — Ease with which a fiber releases oily soil when placed in detergent solution.

THERMAL PROPERTIES

Specific heat — Amount of heat required to change the temperature of a unit mass of fiber 1°.

Thermal conductivity — Rate of heat flow along a fiber.

Heat resistance (heat durability) — Temperature at which a fiber begins to degrade.

Softening and melting (thermoplasticity) — Temperatures at which a thermoplastic fiber softens and changes from a solid to a liquid.

Decomposition — Temperature at which a fiber's polymer structure looses identity.

Combustibility — Based on fiber ignition temperature, heat of combustion, limiting oxygen index, and other burning characteristics.

CHEMICAL PROPERTIES

Resistance to degradation — Reduction in breaking tenacity or another mechanical property due to exposure to acids, alkali, solvents, and other chemicals.

Reaction with chemicals — Discussed in Unit V.

MISCELLANEOUS PROPERTIES

Resistance to ultraviolet light — Weakening (degradation) or deterioration of a fiber caused by exposure to ultraviolet rays of sunlight or artificial light.

Resistance to biological organisms — Weakening (degradation) or decomposition of a fiber caused by mildew, fungi, moths, beetles, and silverfish.

Electrical resistivity — Difficulty of longitudinal electrical flow through a fiber of unit length and unit cross-sectional area.

Specific gravity — Ratio of a mass of fiber to the mass of an equal volume of water at 4°C.

8

Fiber Properties and Identification

Fibers of various types respond differently when they are exposed to mechanical forces, water or other solvents, dry and wet heat, ultraviolet radiation, chemical solutions, and biological organisms. Fiber properties are generally grouped as mechanical, sorptive, thermal, chemical, and miscellaneous (Detail View 8).

MECHANICAL PROPERTIES

The mechanical properties of fibers are their responses to applied forces and to recovery from those forces. The ability of a fiber to withstand and recover from mechanical forces is largely determined by its fine structure (degree of orientation, crystallinity, polymerization of polymers, and bonding between polymers). In the case of natural fibers, aspects of their macroscopic and microscopic structure also play a significant role.

Stress-Strain

Many of the mechanical properties of a fiber are determined by applying a gradually increasing force or *stress* along the fiber axis. This force elongates or *strains* the fiber. When the amount of strain (elongation) is plotted against the amount of stress (force), a *stress-strain curve* is created. Each fiber has a characteristic stress-strain curve (Figure 8.1).

In a stress-strain curve, stress is generally expressed as grams per denier (g/den) or as newtons per tex (N/tex)

on the vertical axis; the strain is expressed as a percent on the horizontal axis.[1] All stress-strain curves begin at zero stress and stop at the amount of force which ruptures the fiber. Studying the shapes, lengths, and heights of stress-strain curves and the size of certain areas under these curves tells us how well a fiber resists elongation, how far it will elongate before rupturing, how strong it is, how tough it is, and how much work it does against restraining forces. The curve also establishes the point at which a fiber will not recover fully from an applied stress. A fiber's stress-strain curve is generally determined when the fiber is in an environment maintained at 70°F (21°C) and 65% relative humidity.

A model stress-strain curve (Figure 8.2), the curve for a model fiber, is helpful in learning to interpret each fiber's stress-strain curve and to obtain quantitative data about its initial modulus, tenacity, elongation at break, and work of rupture. The curve for a model fiber begins with a straight line segment that rises as stress is increased (AB) and then it suddenly flattens and rises at a slower rate (BC). Close to the rupture point, the curve rises steeply for a short distance (CD). This characteristic shape reflects the stress acting to force the polymers to straighten and to slide by each other. Aspects of fiber structure that permit or resist polymer straightening and movement of the polymers relative to one another determine the exact shape of the stress-strain curve for each fiber.

---

[1]See page 19 for the equation for the determination of percent elongation.

FIGURE 8.1 The stress-strain curves of textile fibers at 70°F (21°C) and 65% relative humidity.

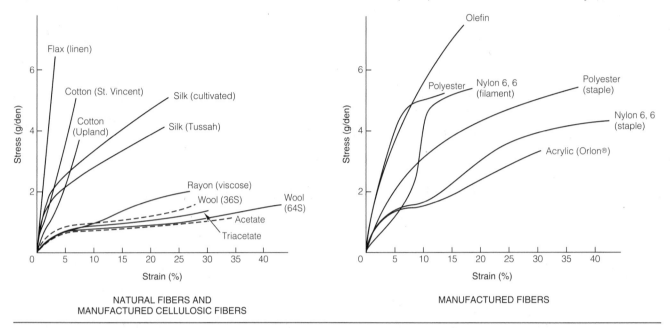

NATURAL FIBERS AND
MANUFACTURED CELLULOSIC FIBERS

MANUFACTURED FIBERS

Initial Modulus. Generally, the first segment of a stress-strain curve is a straight line which indicates that stress is proportional to strain. The slope of this line (the ratio of stress to strain) provides a measure of the fiber's *initial modulus,* also called Young's modulus. When this segment rises steeply, as AB does for the model fiber, a relatively large increase in stress produces a relatively small increase in strain. The model fiber is said to have high initial modulus. If the line slopes at a 45° angle, then there is a unit increase in strain for each unit increase in stress and the initial modulus of the fiber is average. As the slope decreases or the line becomes more horizontal, the initial modulus of the fiber becomes lower.

Fibers with low initial modulus are relatively easy to elongate; a slight force results in considerable fiber lengthening. In contrast, a large force must be applied to fibers with high initial modulus for small amounts of extension to occur. In Figure 8.1, flax, cotton, polyester, and olefin (polypropylene) fibers have high initial modulus; wool, acetate, triacetate, rayon, and nylon have low initial modulus.

Initial fiber modulus indicates how easily the fiber extends under small stress. In some applications (for example, women's sheer hosiery), it is desirable for the fiber to extend under low stress; in other applications, including most apparel fabrics, it is desirable that a fiber resist lengthening under small stress. Nylon fiber is widely used in women's sheer hosiery because it has lower modulus than polyester fiber. However, polyester fiber is used much more widely in apparel fabrics than nylon fiber partially due to its higher initial modulus. Of course, other fiber properties also play a role in fiber selection.

In this initial segment of the stress-strain curve, the lengthening of the fiber is (1) the result of the degree to which polymers lying at angles to the fiber axis can be moved into alignment with the axis and (2) polymers with a nonlinear configuration can be straightened. Therefore, low-modulus fibers tend to be less oriented and crystalline than high-modulus fibers. Polymer slippage does not occur within the fiber during this initial modulus segment of the stress-strain curve.

Yield Point. The point at which the stress-strain curve flattens, called the *yield point,* represents the point at which the internal fiber structure permanently changes. The polymers "yield;" they begin to slip by each other. The stress has become larger than the force of attraction between the polymers.

The point at which permanent deformation starts to take place can be just as important as the point at which breakage occurs. In such applications as ropes and automobile safety belts, it is important that fibers have yield points beyond the stress level to which they will be subjected. If fibers reach their yield points, their ability to withstand the next force will be significantly reduced.

Most fibers have a definite yield point as shown in Figure 8.1; their stress-strain curves bend in a manner similar to the model curve in Figure 8.2. However, flax and cotton fibers do not exhibit clear yield points. Moreover, fiber yield points occur after various amounts of elongation (strain). The yield point of polyester fiber occurs after the fiber has extended ~8% of its initial length; wool fiber yields when it has extended ~3% of its initial length.

Hardening Point. As the structure yields, it extends more easily under increasing stress and the stress-strain curve begins to flatten. Once the polymers begin sliding by one another, additional stress easily extends the fiber. The slope of this segment of the curve (BC) largely reflects the strength of intrafiber bonding. The greater the bonding strength, the greater the slope of this segment of the stress-strain curve.

The polymers also become more compact as stress increases. The fiber reaches a deformation limit or *hardening point.*

Tenacity. Following hardening, the internal structure of the fiber begins to give way catastrophically and the rupture point is reached. The polymers have either slipped by each other because the applied stress is greater than the intrafiber bonding force or the applied stress has surpassed the strength of the polymers themselves, causing them to rupture.

A fiber's breaking tenacity is obtained by drawing a horizontal line from the rupture point to the vertical axis of the stress-strain curve. Flax and olefin fibers have the highest breaking tenacities of the fibers shown in Figure 8.1; acetate and wool have the lowest tenacities. Differences in tenacities reflect the degree of polymerization, degree of orientation and crystallinity, and strength of intrafiber bonding. As the values of each of these aspects of fine structure increase, the tenacity of the fiber increases.

A fiber's tenacity is of significant interest when the textile in which it is to be used will be subjected to large, steady pulls. The force acting on the fiber must be lower than its breaking tenacity or the fiber will rupture.

Elongation at Break. The percent of elongation at break of a fiber is obtained by dropping a vertical line from the rupture point to the horizontal axis of the stress-

FIGURE 8.2   Stress-strain and elastic recovery curves for a model fiber.

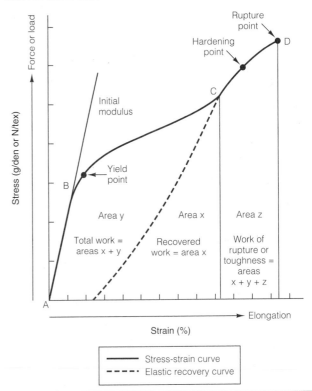

strain curve. Percent elongation just prior to rupture is of interest when the fiber is subjected to considerable stress such as when a snug-fitting garment is pulled over the head.

Fibers that are highly-oriented and crystalline and have strong intrafiber bonding and/or a straight polymer configuration tend to exhibit lower degrees of elongation at break. Conversely, fibers that are less oriented and crystalline and have weak intrafiber bonding tend to exhibit greater degrees of elongation at break.

The stress-strain curves in Figure 8.1 show a wide variation in amount of elongation at break. Wool and nylon fibers have comparatively high elongation at break with values greater than 40%. Cotton and flax fibers have low elongation at break with values lower than 7%.

Work of Rupture (Toughness). Work of rupture or toughness is a measure of the ability of a fiber to withstand sudden shocks of energy. The total amount of work (energy) required to deform a fiber up to the point of rupture is indicated by the area under its stress-strain

FIGURE 8.3 Elastic recovery curves of fibers at 70°F (21°C) and 65% relative humidity.

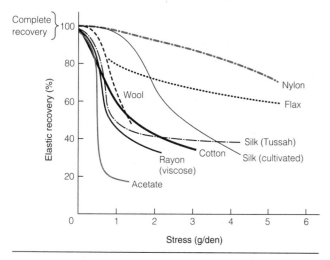

curve. It is a measure of fiber toughness, specified as grams per denier or newtons per tex.

A high work of rupture indicates that a fiber absorbs a considerable amount of energy, such as might be required in the shock-loading of a safety harness, in the opening of a parachute, or in stopping the fall of a climber tethered to a rope. A tough fiber tends to have moderately high tenacity as well as moderately high breaking extension because these two conditions tend to maximize the area under the stress-strain curve. Nylon and polyester are tough fibers; the areas under their stress-strain curves are considerably higher than those for other fibers shown in Figure 8.1.

Elastic Recovery. In the initial segment of the model stress-strain curve (AB), the fiber behaves like an elastic spring. Under the amount of stress applied here, the polymers are being straightened and perhaps becoming more oriented within the fiber. If the stress were removed at any point from A to B, the fiber would return to its original length because the polymers can revert to their initial positions. The elastic recovery of the fiber is therefore 100%.[2] If the fiber is stressed beyond the yield point, but not to its hardening point and the force is then removed, the fiber will partially recover; it will attempt to return to its original length.

A model *elastic recovery curve* can be added to the

model stress-strain curve by decreasing the force acting on the stressed model fiber and observing the amount of shortening of the fiber. This curve establishes how well a fiber can recover from different amounts of stress. The dashed line in Figure 8.2 represents the recovery of a fiber from varying degrees of stress. The fiber contracts but not as much or as quickly as it extended when stress was increased. The elastic recovery of the model fiber (of any fiber, for that matter) is not 100% because the recovery line does not return to the graph origin (0,0). The polymers are no longer able to cause the fiber to "spring" back to its original length.

The elastic recovery of various fibers from stress is shown in Figure 8.3. Here, units of stress are indicated on the horizontal axis and of elastic recovery on the vertical axis which is opposite to their location in Figure 8.2. All curves slope downward in Figure 8.3 because the amount of elastic recovery decreases as the amount of stress increases. The shape of the curves varies for the different fibers. Viscose rayon has low elastic recovery at low levels of stress which quickly worsens as greater amounts of stress are applied and removed. At the other extreme, nylon fiber almost completely recovers from low amounts of stress; it continues to recover about 75% even when the applied stress reaches 5 grams per denier.

Elastic recovery depends on the configuration of the polymer chains and on intrafiber bonding. Polymers that are spiraled and folded tend to act like springs; once stress is released they attempt to return to their original configuration. When polymers are covalently crosslinked, the crosslinks work to pull the polymers back to their original positions. When polymers are hydrogen or ionically bonded, however, elastic recovery tends to decrease because new bonds form as the polymers slide by each other.

Resilience (Work of Recovery)

The resilience of a fiber is the ratio of energy returned to energy absorbed when a fiber is deformed and then released. Fiber resilience may be extensional, flexural, compressional, or torsional. Resilience as a function of extension (elongation) can be determined from the fiber's stress-strain curve by measuring the area for extension (X + Y) and the area for retraction (X). In the model stress-strain curve in Figure 8.2, this would be the ratio of area X to area X + Y.[3]

---

[2]See page 20 for calculation of the percent of elastic recovery.

[3]L. Segal and P. J. Wakelyn. "Cotton," in M. Lewin and E. M. Pearce eds., *Fiber Chemistry: Handbook of Fiber Science and Technology*, vol. IV, Chapter 10 (New York: Marcel Dekker, 1983).

FIGURE 8.4   Flexural rigidity (stiffness) of fibers.

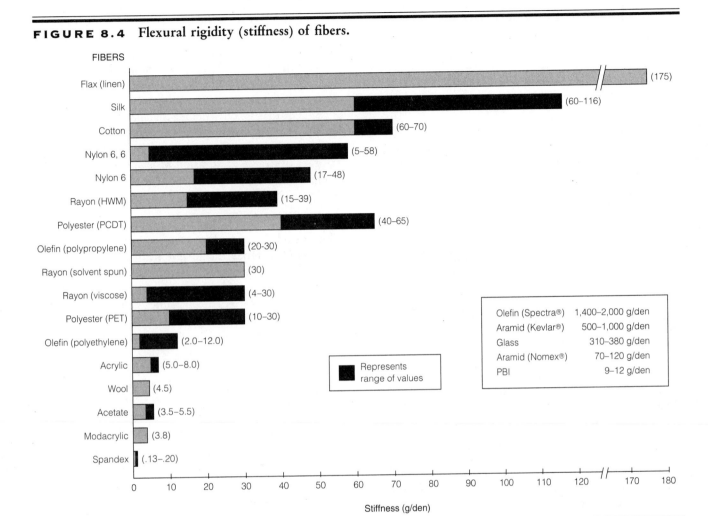

In general, crimped fibers are more resilient than smooth, straight fibers. The presence of hydrogen bonds lowers resilience. Considerable energy is required to break the hydrogen bonds so that polymers can slide by one another; little energy is expended when the stress is released because the polymers are "locked" into their new positions by newly formed hydrogen bonds.

Fibers are ranked according to degree of extensional resilience in Table 8.1.[4] Polyester fiber has the highest degree of resilience; whereas cotton and rayon have the lowest degree of resilience. Fabrics made from polyester fiber tend to be wrinkle-free; rayon and cotton fabrics tend to wrinkle badly.

[4]Detailed data concerning the resilience of fibers at various extensions can be found in "Tensile Recovery Properties of Fibers," duPont Technical Bulletin X-142 (September 1961).

Flexural Rigidity (Stiffness)

Fibers differ in flexural rigidity or stiffness. The flexural rigidities of fibers with identical size (denier) and cross sectional shape are given in Figure 8.4. Spectra® olefin fiber has the highest flexural rigidity of the fibers shown; it is difficult to bend. Spandex fiber has the lowest flexural rigidity of the fibers shown; it is easily bent. Most fibers of the same size have similar flexural rigidities. The major exception is the special-use synthetic fibers which have much higher flexural rigidities as shown in the insert to Figure 8.4.

When a fiber is bent, the polymers must extend and compress to accommodate the bending force. Think of bending a rubber hose. The rubber on the underside of the bend compresses; the rubber on the upperside of the bend extends. In a fiber, the polymers on the under cur-

TABLE 8.1 Resilience (Extensional) of Fibers.

FIBER	RATING
Polyester	Highest
Wool	
Nylon	
Modacrylic	
Acrylic	
Olefin	
Triacetate	
Silk	
Acetate	
Cotton	
Rayon	
Flax (linen)	Lowest

vature must compress; those on the upper curvature must extend to accommodate the bending force.

The flexural rigidity of a fiber depends partially on the stiffness of the polymers and their degree of orientation and crystallinity. As the proportion of amorphous area within a fiber becomes greater, the fiber tends to become less stiff. The more crystalline the fiber is, the stiffer it tends to be. Some polymer configurations are more easily bent than others.

Fiber diameter has a much greater influence than type of fiber on flexural rigidity. The physics involved in calculating bending resistance as diameter increases shows that doubling a fiber's diameter produces a 16–fold increase in resistance to bending. Likewise, a 2–fold reduction in fiber diameter decreases bending resistance 16–fold. In reality, fiber diameter cannot be varied at will. Mother nature determines the fiber diameter of the natural fibers; manufactured-fiber diameters are limited by production requirements and design specifications. Today's microdenier fibers (fibers with a denier of <1 or smaller than silk fiber) have low flexural rigidities.

Cross-sectional shape also influences the flexural rigidity of a fiber. Round fibers and fibers shaped like an "I" have high values of stiffness; flat fibers have relatively low values of stiffness. The flexural rigidities of fibers with other cross-sectional shapes lie between these extremes.

Abrasion Resistance

Textile scientists disagree about whether or not abrasion resistance is a fiber property, but the majority accept that it is. Quantitative data concerning the abrasion re-

sistance of fibers are difficult to obtain because it is difficult to rub individual fibers. When the fiber is formed into yarn and fabric, the yarn and fabric structure complicates the picture. Further, even when similar yarns or fabrics composed of different fibers are subjected to abrasion, resistance depends on how the abrading force is applied; that is, on whether the abrasion is flat, edge, or flex. Consequently, there are different estimates of the relative abrasion resistance of fibers. Fibers are ranked in order of degree of abrasion resistance in Table 8.2 by compiling quantitative data from a number of sources.[5]

Flexibility

The flexibilities of eight fibers are given in Figure 8.5. Triacetate fiber has the lowest flexibility of the fibers shown because the least number of bends are required to rupture it. Carbon fibers (data not shown) will rupture after being bent (folded) one time. Consequently, they must be embedded in resin so that they do not bend in use. Most fibers require a great number of 180° degree bends before rupture occurs. Triacetate fiber requires 900 bends and polyester fiber 437,000 bends.

Flexibility is related to the crystallinity of the fiber. As the degree of crystallinity increases, flexibility tends to decrease. Conversely, the more amorphous the fiber's fine structure, the more flexible it is.

Moreover, flexible fibers tend to have lower tenacities than inflexible fibers. This relationship exists because

---

[5] An excellent source for detailed data on the abrasion resistance of various fibers is W. E. Morton and J. W. S. Hearle *Physical Properties of Textile Fibres* (London: Heinemann, The Textile Institute, 1975), p. 436-37.

TABLE 8.2 Abrasion Resistance of Fibers.

FIBER	RATING
Nylon	Highest
Olefin	
Polyester	
Spandex	
Flax (linen)	
Acrylic	
Cotton	
Silk	
Wool	
Rayon	
Acetate	Lowest

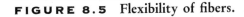

FIGURE 8.5 Flexibility of fibers.

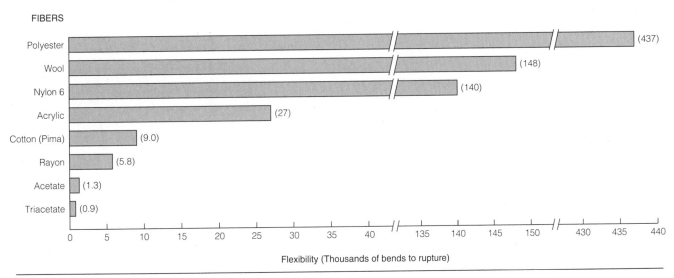

Flexibility (Thousands of bends to rupture)

both properties are linked to the degree of crystallinity. As crystallinity increases, tenacity increases and flexibility decreases. For example, carbon fibers are very strong (have high tenacity), but extremely low flexibility.

SORPTIVE PROPERTIES

Fibers vary significantly in quantity of water vapor, liquid water, and oils they absorb (take internally). *Hydrophilic* (water-loving) and *hydrophobic* (water-avoiding) are two categories into which fibers are placed depending on the amount of water they absorb. *Hygroscopic* fibers are hydrophilic fibers that can absorb significant amounts of moisture without feeling wet to the touch. *Oleophilic* (oil-loving) does *not* indicate the amount of oil absorbed by fibers; rather it describes how tenaciously fibers hold absorbed or adsorbed oil. *Oleophobic* describes a fiber that does not have a strong affinity for oil, a fiber that readily releases oil in a detergent solution.

Vaporous Water Absorption

Most textile fibers absorb moisture (water vapor) from the air. As the relative humidity of the air increases, the amount of moisture absorbed generally increases. The amount of moisture the fiber contains when placed in an environment at a certain temperature and relative humidity is called its *regain moisture* or its *moisture con-*

tent.[6] Of the fibers shown in Figure 8.6, polyester fiber absorbs the least and wool fiber absorbs the most moisture from the air.

The amount of moisture absorbed is of commercial interest because fibers are bought and sold on a weight basis. The more moisture the fiber contains, the less actual fiber a company may be buying. For example, 220 pounds (lb) or 100 kilograms (kg) of raw cotton can contain as much as 26.5 lb (12 kg) of water. For this reason, fiber weight is determined at an industry agreed on temperature of 70°F (21°C) and 65% relative humidity.[7]

The regain moisture content curves for fibers are S-shaped; the S becomes more distinct as the hydrophilicity of the fiber increases. In general, the amount of moisture absorbed increases rapidly as relative humidity increases from 0% to 10%, more slowly from 10% to 80%, and then more rapidly from 80% to 100%.

The extent to which fibers absorb moisture depends largely on the presence of polar groups and their availability in the amorphous areas and on the strength of hydrogen bonding. In segment A of the curves in Figure 8.6, moisture is absorbed by freely available polar groups in the amorphous areas. Wool fiber has numer-

---

[6]Technically, there is a difference between moisture regain and moisture content. Moisture regain is determined as a percent of the dry weight of the fiber, whereas moisture content is determined as a percent of conditioned weight. Refer to Chapter 3.
[7]Commercial regain values are given in Morton and Hearle, *Physical Properties of Textile Fibres*, p. 170.

FIGURE 8.6 Regain moisture content curves of fibers at various relative humidities.

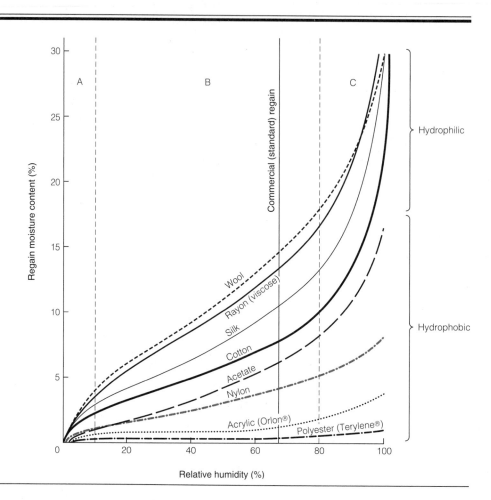

ous polar groups and is very amorphous; polyester has few polar groups and is highly crystalline. In segment B, a slower spreading apart of the polar groups in the amorphous areas occurs because saturation of all available polar groups is nearly complete. The greatest reduction in the rigidity of the fiber occurs in the region. This segment of the curve is flat for polyester fiber because additional moisture is not absorbed; segment B is quite steep for wool, rayon, silk, and cotton.

In both segments A and B, moisture is primarily bound to polar groups. The sharp increase in absorption that occurs in segment C results predominately from moisture accumulation between polar groups in the capillary pores of the fiber. This unbound moisture is held only loosely by the fiber.

The amount of moisture a fiber contains has a profound effect on the mechanical properties of the fiber and on its electrical resistivity. These effects are discussed later in the chapter.

Absorption of Liquid Water

When a fiber is immersed in liquid water, it will swell and lengthen to its greatest dimensions as the absorbed liquid forces the polymers apart. Because the majority of polymers lie parallel to the axis of a fiber, a fiber increases more in width than in length. (This phenomenon is one evidence that the polymers, which cannot be seen, must lie parallel to the fiber axis.)

Swelling, expressed as a percent increase in diameter,[8] can be as little as 0% or as much as or greater than 65% (Figure 8.7). The more hydrophilic the fiber, the greater the potential swelling. Rayon fiber increases the most in both diameter and length. Of the fibers shown, nylon is least altered in size when placed in liquid water. Swelling may lead to fabric shrinkage (Chapter 5).

---

[8] For percentage of transverse swelling based on area rather than diameter, as well as percent of volume swelling of fibers, refer to Morton and Hearle, p. 227.

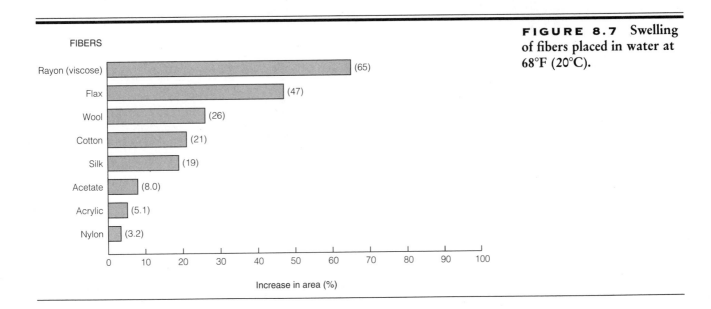

FIGURE 8.7 Swelling of fibers placed in water at 68°F (20°C).

The absorption of liquid water and subsequent swelling may effect the mechanical properties of a fiber. The influence of water absorption on fiber tenacity is indicated in Figure 8.8. Note that some hydrophilic fibers are stronger when wet than when dry (cotton and flax); others are weaker (for example, rayon, wool, and silk). Also, note that hydrophobic fibers are not affected or less affected by moisture than hydrophilic fibers. A fi-

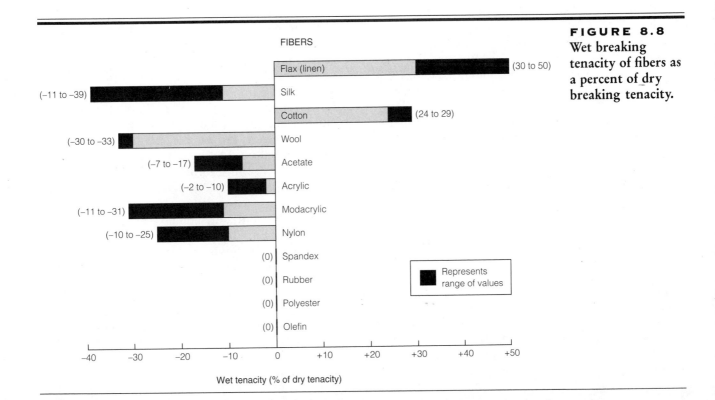

FIGURE 8.8 Wet breaking tenacity of fibers as a percent of dry breaking tenacity.

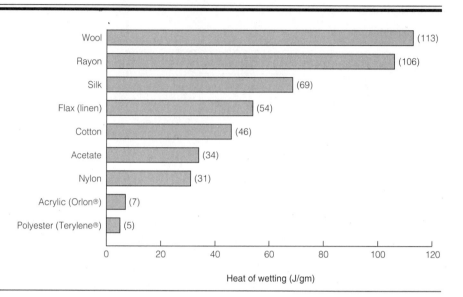

FIGURE 8.9 Heat of wetting of fibers from dry to saturation state.

ber's initial modulus may be affected by the amount of moisture it contains when stress is applied. If modulus is determined when the fiber has absorbed its maximum amount of water, the modulus is called *wet initial modulus* or *wet modulus.* Wet modulus may be the same, lower, or higher than "dry" modulus depending on the fiber. During laundering, when fibers are wet and agitation provides stress, fibers with low-wet-modulus lengthen and the fabric may "grow." Wet modulus is an important consideration in determining how successfully a fabric can be laundered, how vigorously it can be agitated, and how it can be dried. Fabrics containing low-wet-modulus fibers should not be hung to drip dry because the weight will elongate the fibers and therefore the fabric.

Amount of moisture absorbed may also alter a fiber's stiffness. As cotton fibers absorb water, they become less stiff. Consequently, fabric composed of cotton fiber collapses against the skin as perspiration is absorbed which may lead to chilling and greater skin water content.

Heat of Wetting

When a fiber absorbs vaporous and/or liquid water, heat is generated from the attractive force between the water molecules and the fiber polymer. The amount of heat that evolves is called the *heat of wetting* or the *heat of sorption.* Values for heat of wetting reflect the amount of

heat evolved when 1 gram of dry fiber is placed in water expressed as calories per gram (cal/g) or Joules per gram (J/g) of dry fiber.[9]

Heat of wetting is greatest for hydrophilic fibers and very small for hydrophobic fibers (Figure 8.9). Heat of wetting influences comfort, particularly when a person goes from an environment of low relative humidity into one of higher relative humidity.

Wool fiber has the highest heat of wetting and will be used to demonstrate the effect of heat of wetting on comfort. In a warm, dry room at 68°F (20°C) and 25% relative humidity, 2.2 pounds or 1 kilogram of wool clothing will contain 1.8 ounces (oz) or 50 grams (g) of absorbed moisture. If the wearer then goes outside into a cold, damp climate at 50°F (10°C) and 95% relative humidity, the wool will absorb 9.53 oz (270 g) of moisture and will emit heat of 10,000 calories (cal) or 42 kilojoules (kJ) slowly and evenly as water continues to be absorbed. This significant amount of heat gives the body time to adjust to the new environmental condition. Under similar conditions, nylon fiber emits only 2000 cal (8.4 kJ); polyester fiber and acrylic fiber < 500 cal (2.1 kJ).[10]

---

[9]Technically, heat of sorption is the heat that evolves when 1 gram of water is absorbed by an infinite mass of fiber at a given moisture regain and is expressed in Joules per gram of water absorbed.

[10]Example is from J. D. Leeder, *Wool: Nature's Wonder Fibre* (Victoria, Australia: The Australian Textile Publishers, 1984).

Oil Absorption and Oil Release (Oleophilicity)

Fibers absorb varying amounts of oil and differ in how tenaciously they hold oil during laundering (Table 8.3). The fibers that absorb the most oil are not necessarily those that hold it most tenaciously, however. In fact, fibers that tend to absorb the most oil are also those that more easily release it as indicated in Table 8.3. Oleophilic is the term used to describe fibers that hold oil tenaciously.

In general, natural fibers, rayon, and acetate absorb more oil and more readily release that oil in detergent solution than synthetic fibers do. Manufactured fibers, with the exception of rayon, are oleophilic. Removal of oily soil from these fibers is difficult because water (detergent solution) does not spread over the fiber surface and is not absorbed into the fiber so the oil cannot be dispersed.

Oleophilicity is related to the chemistry of the polymers. Polymers with polar groups tend to attract water which helps to release oily soil. Nylon fiber contains more polar groups than polyester fiber and, therefore, is less oleophilic than polyester fiber. Moreover, polyester fiber contains benzene rings which not only attract oils but hold it tightly.

THERMAL PROPERTIES

Table 8.4 shows five temperatures, heat resistant, softening, melting, decomposition, and ignition, that are of importance for fibers.

Specific Heat and Thermal Conductivity

The *specific heat* of a fiber is a measure of the amount of heat required to change the temperature of a unit mass of the fiber 1°. Fibers as well as other materials (water, silver, alcohol, etc.) have specific heat that are characteristic of the material. While values of fiber specific heats have been determined, they are not presented here because this fiber property does not have a major influence on fabric performance. The uptake and loss of heat from fabric which is actually dependent on fiber composition is due largely to heat of wetting rather than to the specific heat of the fibers.

The *thermal conductivity* of fibers is a measure of the rate of heat flow through them. Rather than measuring the heat flow along a single fiber, a mass of fibers are

TABLE 8.3 Oil Absorption and Ease of Oily Soil Release of Fibers.

FIBER	RATING FOR DEGREE OF ABSORPTION	RATING FOR EASE OF RELEASE
Cotton, other natural cellulosics, wool, silk, rayon, and acetate	Highest	Easiest
Nylon		
Acrylic		
Olefin		
Polyester	Lowest	Most difficult

used. The rate of heat flow may be given as calories of heat transferred through a square centimeter of a fibrous batt. (Relative rates of heat flow for various fibers are given in Figure 3.3.) Although fibers conduct heat or resist the flow of heat to varying degrees, these differences are not significant once the fibers are made into fabric. As discussed in Chapter 3, a large proportion of fabric is air which exhibits a substantially lower conductivity to heat flow than fibers do.

Heat Resistance (Heat Durability)

When a fiber is at a temperature less than its heat resistant temperature (generally <275°F or 135°C), it does not degrade; it shows no loss in tenacity or other mechanical properties over time. At the *heat resistant temperature*, it begins to degrade; the degradation is evident by decreases in its mechanical performance. The longer the fiber is exposed to its heat resistant temperature or to a temperature above the heat resistant temperature, the more rapidly the fiber degrades.

Softening and Melting (Thermoplasticity)

Certain fibers soften and melt when they are heated above their heat resistant temperature. Heat causes the polymers to vibrate which subsequently leads to the breaking of bonds between polymers, first in the amorphous areas and then in the crystalline areas of the fiber. The volume of a fiber slightly increases with increasing temperature. The temperature at which a fiber changes from a glassy state to a rubbery state is called its *glass transition temperature* (T_g). The temperature at which it

TABLE 8.4 Thermal Properties of Fibers.

FIBER	HEAT RESISTANT TEMPERATURE		SOFTENING TEMPERATURE		MELTING TEMPERATURE		DECOMPOSITION TEMPERATURE		IGNITION TEMPERATURE	
	F°	(C°)	F°	(C°)	F°	(C°)	F°	(C°)	F°	(C°)
Wool	275	(132)	—	—	—	—	446	(230)	1094	(590)
Silk	275	(135)	—	—	—	—	*	*	*	*
Cotton	300	(150)	—	—	—	—	581	(305)	752	(400)
Flax (linen)	500	(260)	—	—	—	—	581	(305)	*	*
Rayon	350	(177)	—	—	—	—	350–464	(177–240)	788	(420)
Acetate	350	(177)	364	(184)	500	(260)	572	(300)	842	(450)
Triacetate	450	(232)	482	(250)	550	(288)	*	*	*	*
Nylon	300	(150)	340	(171)	415–509	(213–265)	653	(345)	989	(532)
Polyester	250	(120)	445–490	(229–254)	450–500 or 540	(250–260 or 282)	734	(390)	1040	(560)
Olefin	165	(75)	260–320	(127–160)	275–338	(135–170)	*	*	*	*
Acrylic	300	(150)	473–490	(245–254)	—	—	549	(287)	986	(530)
Spandex	*	*	347	(175)	446	(175)	*	*	*	*
Rubber	*	*	*	*	*	*	*	*	*	*
Modacrylic	300	(150)	300	(149)	370 or 248	(188 or 120)	455	(235)	*	*
Saran	240	(115)	285	(141)	334	(168)	168	(76)	*	*
Vinyon	150	(65)	200	(93)	446 or 752	(230 or 400)	—	—	*	*
Aramid	*	*	—	—	—	—	<800	(>427)	*	*
PBI	*	*	*	*	*	*	840	(450)	*	*
Sulfar	*	*	*	*	545	(285)	*	*	*	*
Glass	600	(315)	1400	(760)	1472	(800)	1500	(815)	—	—
Metallic	variable		400–450	(204–232)	>572	(>300)	—	—	—	—
Asbestos	—	—	—	—	—	—	—	—	—	—
Polytetra-fluoro-ethylene	500	(260)	—	—	—	—	*	*	—	—

*indicates missing data.

—indicates does not melt, soften, decompose, or ignite.

softens or sticks is called its *softening or sticking temperature* and at which it melts (changes from a solid to a liquid) is called the *melting point temperature* (T$_m$).

The glass transition temperature is so named because the internal structure of the fiber is altered from that of glass to that of rubber at that temperature. Initially, the fiber is much like a glass rod (relatively difficult to bend and not easily extensible). Then all of a sudden, it takes on many of the characteristics of rubber; it becomes easy to bend and is easily extensible. In Figure 8.10, the dramatic change in the flexural rigidity (the ease of bending) of a model fiber at its glass transition temperature (T$_g$) is shown. This sudden change largely results when polymer chains in the amorphous areas of the fiber separate to a great enough distance that the bonding forces be-

tween these polymers are no longer effective. The model fiber has expanded in volume.

The strength of the intrafiber bonding and the rigidity of the polymers are the key determinants of how much heat is required for a fiber to reach the glass transition temperature. No molecular rearrangement has occurred in the amorphous or crystalline areas of the fiber. If the fiber is allowed to cool before or at its glass transition temperature with no distortive forces acting on it, the fiber will return to its initial state. Glass transition temperatures are difficult to determine and are dependent on the moisture content of the fiber.

When certain fibers are heated more, little change in flexural rigidity generally occurs immediately after the glass transition temperature as indicated by the horizon-

FIGURE 8.10 Effect of increasing temperature on the stiffness (flexural rigidity) of a model fiber.

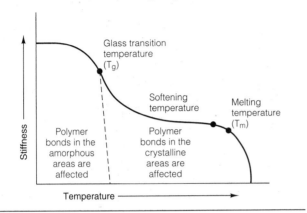

identity. The polymers fragment. The fiber in Table 8.4 with the lowest decomposition temperature (168°F or 76°C) is saran and with the highest is glass (1500°F or 815°C). Most fibers have decomposition temperatures in the range of 350°F–750°F (177°C–399°C).

Combustibility

Fibers differ as to whether or not they ignite (whether they are *combustible* or *noncombustible*) and as to the temperature at which ignition occurs (the *ignition temperature*). As shown in Table 8.4 and Table 8.5, natural fibers and most of the general-use manufactured fibers are combustible and ignite at temperatures between 780°F and 1,000°F. The special-use manufactured fibers do not ignite.

tal segment of the curve in Figure 8.10. In this region, the fiber may soften or become sticky. Softening may be sharp or occur over a range of temperatures.

The second transition temperature, the melting point temperature (T_m), is reached when the polymers in the crystalline areas of the fiber are converted to a liquid. In melting, there is a change from the regular order of a crystal to the disorder of a liquid. Note the rapid downturn in the temperature versus the flexural rigidity portion of the curve in Figure 8.10 as the melting temperature is approached.

As shown in Table 8.4, not all fibers have softening and melting temperatures. Those fibers that do soften when heated and harden when allowed to cool, such as nylon and polyester, are called *thermoplastic fibers*. Some fibers decompose before the heat can build to a sufficient temperature to cause their polymers to move far enough apart. For example, natural fibers and some synthetic fibers such as aramid, do not soften or melt before decomposition occurs.

Fiber manufacturers use transition temperatures to heat set fabrics containing thermoplastic fibers (Chapter 33). This treatment makes them dimensionally stable to temperatures below the one at which heat setting took place. Above the heat set temperature, thermoplastic fibers contract irreversibly. The softening temperature is important in determining wash water, dryer, and ironing temperatures.

Decomposition

Fibers have different *decomposition temperatures;* the temperature at which polymer structure looses chemical

TABLE 8.5 Classification of Fibers Based on Burning Behavior.

FIBER	CLASSIFICATION
Noncombustible	
Asbestos	
Glass	
Inorganic fibers	
carbon	
polytetrafluoroethylene	
silica	
Combustible	
Modacrylic	
Aramid	
PBI	Inherently Flame Resistant (FR)
Sulfar	
Wool	
Cotton	Flame Resistance Achieved by
Rayon	Chemical Modification
Nylon	(Additives or Finishes)
Polyester	
Wool	
Silk	
Cotton	
Specialty cellulosic	
Rayon	Normal (Regular)
Nylon	
Polyester	
Olefin	
Rubber	
Spandex	

TABLE 8.6   Burning Behavior of a Bundle of Combustible Fibers in Proximity to an Open Flame.

FIBER	MELTS NEAR FLAME	SHRINKS FROM FLAME	BURNS IN FLAME	CONTINUES TO BURN	APPEARANCE OF ASH
Wool	No	Yes	Yes	Yes (slowly)	Black soft flake
Silk	No	Yes	Yes	Yes (slowly)	Black soft bead
Cotton	No	No	Yes	Yes (rapidly)	Light-grey soft flake
Flax (linen)	No	No	Yes	Yes (rapidly)	Light-grey soft flake
Rayon	No	No	Yes	Yes (rapidly)	Light-grey soft flake
Acetate	Yes	Yes	Yes	Yes	Black hard irregular bead
Nylon	Yes	Yes	Yes	Yes	Grey hard round bead
Polyester	Yes	Yes	Yes	Yes	Black hard round bead
Olefin	Yes	Yes	Yes	Yes	Tan hard round bead
Acrylic	No	Yes	Yes	Yes	Black hard irregular bead
Modacrylic	Yes	Yes	Yes	No	Black hard irregular bead
Rubber	Yes	Yes	Yes	No	Black or grey fluffy irregular mass
Spandex	Yes	No	Yes	Yes	Black or grey fluffy irregular mass

Combustible fibers may be designated as *inherently flame-resistant* or as *flame-resistant* fibers. The burning behavior of an inherently flame-resistant fiber is derived from its polymeric nature. The burning behavior of flame-resistant fibers is derived from the addition of a flame-retardant chemical to the fiber. A flame-retardant chemical may be incorporated into a manufactured fiber at the time of its formation or added to fabric. In the latter case, the flame-retardant may be absorbed into the fiber or may coat the fiber surface.

Certain aspects of the burning behavior of combustible fibers is described in Table 8.6. The reaction of the fiber near a flame, in a flame, and immediately following removal from the flame are given as well as the type of ash formed. Combustible fibers also differ in the amount of smoke and heat they generate, called *heat of combustion,* and the amount of oxygen required for combustion to be sustained, called *limiting oxygen index.* Textile scientists can quantify these aspects of fiber combustibility.

CHEMICAL PROPERTIES

Fibers differ significantly in terms of their reactivity to chemicals and their resistance to degradation by chemicals. *Chemical reactivity* is of primary importance to textile manufacturers because it influences the type of chemical modifications that a fiber can undergo. A primary way in which natural fibers can be modified is through the use of chemicals. When chemicals are ap-plied to fabric, the reaction occurs within or at the surface of the fibers. Such chemical modifications are discussed in Chapters 30–33. Fiber dyeability is also de-pendent on the chemistry and structure of the fiber. The chemistry of dyestuffs and fiber dyeing are discussed in Chapter 34.

In end-use applications, *chemical resistance* is often of more interest than reactivity to various chemicals. Ex-posure to certain chemicals can break polymer chains and lead to degradation of the fiber. How rapidly a fiber degrades depends on the specific chemical to which it is exposed, the concentration of the chemical, the time of exposure, and the temperature. The chemical resistance of fibers is related to the type and strength of covalent bonds along a polymer backbone, the presence of reac-tive groups on the polymer, and the crystallinity of the fiber. Generally, the more crystalline a fiber is, the more difficult it is for the chemical to access the polymers. In highly crystalline fibers, degradation may be limited to the fiber surface.

Numerous graphs and tables would be necessary to depict the resistance of fibers to various chemicals. Table 8.7 describes the general resistance of fibers to chemicals to which they may be commonly exposed in end-use applications.[11]

---

[11] Detailed data are available in Du Pont Technical Bulletin X-48 "Comparative Chemical Resistance of Fibers," (March 1956).

TABLE 8.7 Chemical Resistance of Fibers.

FIBER	CHEMICAL AGENT				OXIDIZING AGENTS	REDUCING AGENTS
	INORGANIC ACIDS		ALKALIES			
	Dilute	Concentrated	Dilute	Concentrated		
Cotton	Hydrolyzed (hot)	Hydrolyzed (hot) Oxidized conc.	Resistant	Swells	Degrades[‡]	Degrades in conc. bleach
Flax (linen)	Hydrolized	Hydrolized	Resistant	Swells		
Wool	Resistant	Resistant[‖]	Degrades easily	Degrades easily	Degrades	Degrades
Silk	Fairly resistant	Dissolved	Attacked (hot)	Dissolved		
Rayon	Disintegrates (hot)	Disintegrates (cold)	Resistant	Swells (loses tenacity)	Attacked (strong agents)[#]	
Acetate	Resistant	Decomposed (conc.)	Resistant	Saponifies[§]		
Triacetate	Unaffected	Deteriorates	Resistant	Saponifies		
Nylon	Fair	Poor	Good	Good	Resistant	
Polyester	Resistant	Resistant[*]	Resistant	Degrades (hot)	Resistant	
Olefin	Resistant	Slowly oxidized	Resistant	Resistant	Moderate	
Acrylic	Resistant	Dissolves[†]	Resistant	Degrades (hot)	Resistant	Resistant (hot)
Spandex	Good to most acids		Good to most alkalies			

[*] Degrades in 96% sulfuric acid.
[†] In concentrated nitric and sulfuric acids.
[‡] In concentrated sulfuric acid.

[§] Reverts to cellulose.
[‖] Destroyed by hot sulfuric acid.
[#] Not damaged by hypochlorite or peroxide bleaches.

MISCELLANEOUS PROPERTIES

Miscellaneous properties includes resistance to ultraviolet light and biological organisms, electrical resistivity, specific gravity, and toxicity/contact allergens.

Resistance to Ultraviolet Light

The ultraviolet component—the range of short, high-energy wavelengths—in sunlight and fluorescent lights has a detrimental effect on fibers because it may break covalent bonds along the polymer backbone. Fibers differ in resistance to ultraviolet light (resistance to sunlight) as shown in Figure 8.11. Dull nylon fiber shows the most rapid degradation on exposure to sunlight; wool fiber is the least affected.

When ultraviolet radiation has sufficient energy to cause the rupture of a single bond in the polymer chain, a bewilderingly complex series of chemical reactions (a chain reaction) occurs. Oxygen is instrumental in breaking (oxidizing) additional bonds along the backbone of the polymer chain into small molecular fragments. The fiber eventually breaks down and its mechanical properties subsequently diminish.

Manufactured fibers may be enhanced to resist degradation by ultraviolet light by alterations in size, cross-sectional shape, and the addition of light stabilizers. Generally, the larger the size of the fiber, the greater its resistance because less radiation penetrates into the interior. Cross-sectional shape reduces degradation by altering the reflection, refraction, and transmission of ultraviolet radiation. Delustrants (a chemical added to fibers during spinning) decrease resistance to ultraviolet light by inducing scatter.

Resistance to Biological Organisms

Natural fibers and rayon are most susceptible and synthetic fibers are least susceptible to deterioration by biological organisms (Table 8.8). Insects, including moths, beetles, and silverfish, may eat away at the fibers. Microorganisms, including mildew, fungi, and bacteria, generally emit a substance that breaks fiber polymers which leads to deterioration of the fiber structure.

Electrical Resistivity

A fiber's electrical resistivity (ohms) is the voltage across the fiber divided by the current through it. Fibers ex-

FIGURE 8.11 Degradation due to sunlight (ultraviolet light resistance) curves of fibers.

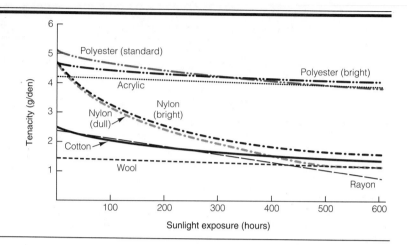

hibit different electrical resistivities as shown in Figure 8.12. Differences exist primarily because the fibers differ in moisture content at any given relative humidity. In general, fibers with higher moisture contents exhibit lower electrical resistivity. Therefore, hydrophilic fibers (water-loving) fibers do not tend to develop static charge but hydrophobic (water-avoiding) fibers do.

Further, the electrical resistivity of most fibers changes by 10 orders of magnitude as the relative humidity changes from 10% to 90%. When the relative humidity increases to 13%, many fibers exhibit a tenfold decrease in electrical resistivity.

In addition to moisture content, the strength with which electrons are held influences electrical resistivity. The tighter electrons are held, the less static charge generated. Olefin fibers, which are highly hydrophobic, do not build up static; their electrons are held tightly due to the small atoms (mostly hydrogen) composing the polymers.

Specific Gravity

The specific gravities of fibers, the ratio of fiber mass to the mass of an equal volume of water at 39.2°F (4°C), are shown in Figure 8.13. The range of values, 0.9 to 1.51, is narrow. The heaviest fibers shown are the cellulosic fibers and the lightest is olefin fiber. Olefin fibers are so lightweight they will float on water. Differences in the specific gravities of fibers influence the ultimate weight of a fabric.

Toxicity/Contact Allergens

Although fibers are sometimes marketed as hypoallergenic, there is no evidence that these fibers are safer to

TABLE 8.8 Biological Resistance of Fibers.

FIBER	MICRO-ORGANISMS	INSECTS		
		Moths	Beetles	Silver-fish
Wool	◐	●	●	○
Silk	◐	○	●	○
Cotton	●	○	○	●
Flax (linen)	◗	○	○	●
Rayon	●	○	○	●
Acetate	◐	○	○	○
Triacetate	◔	○	○	○
Nylon	◔	○	○	○
Polyester	◔	○	○	○
Olefin	○	○	○	○
Acrylic	○	○	○	○
Spandex	◔	○	○	○
Rubber	◔	○	○	○
Other synthetics	○	○	○	○

○ = Highest resistance

● = Lowest resistance

use than other fibers. Fibers are rarely the cause of allergic contact dermatitis and have not been linked to any toxic effects.[12]

FIBER IDENTIFICATION

Most textile products are labeled with fiber content information as required by law. When a label is missing, a purchaser may want to determine the fiber content. If a fabric fails to perform as expected and a complaint is made, the investigator usually wants to check the fiber composition. In criminal cases, textile fibers often become important pieces of evidence that can place a suspect at the crime scene if they can be matched to fibers from that person's clothing. Conversely, fibers in upholstery and carpets at the crime scene can be matched to fibers found on the suspect's clothing.

The fact that fibers are unique in structure and chemistry permits their identification. The precision of identification required (being able to state only the generic group to which a fiber belongs or being able to name a specific variant) and the amount of fiber available for test impact the selection of the test procedure. Which tests are appropriate also depends on whether the yarn and fabric are blends or are composed of only one fiber type. Tests generally include burning, chemical solubility, microscopic examination, staining, melting point determination, and instrumental analysis.

The Microscopic Test

In the microscopic identification test, several fibers are carefully placed on a microscope slide and their longitudinal (surface) features are observed. Magnification using a 10X eyepiece and a 40X objective is generally sufficient to observe differences in surface features. A cross section may also be made and observed. Photomicrographs of longitudinal and cross-sectional views of fibers are found in Chapters 12–21.

All natural cellulosic fibers, all natural protein fibers, rayon, and acetate can be identified positively by microscope because each of these fiber types has unique surface features. A novice would have difficulty distinguishing the specialty protein fibers from each other and from

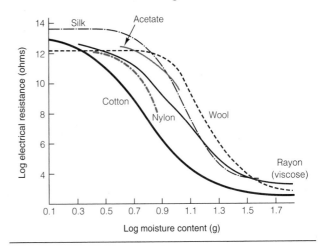

FIGURE 8.12 Electrical resistivity curves of fibers at various moisture regains.

sheep's wool, but an expert could accomplish positive identifications. Manufactured fibers (except rayon and acetate) are most difficult to distinguish from one another.

The Burning Test

In the burning test, a cluster of fibers or a yarn is held in tweezers and its reaction to an open flame (usually a lit candle, Bunsen burner, or alcohol lamp) is observed. Generally, the tester observes what happens as the fiber cluster or yarn is brought close to the flame, held in the flame, and removed from the flame and examines the residue.

A burning test can be used to categorize fibers as cellulosic, protein, thermoplastic (not as synthetic), and mineral or inorganic. It is difficult to differentiate fibers within the four categories because their burning behaviors are too similar.

The burning test should be used only when the yarn or fabric is composed of a single type of fiber. If a blend is tested, erroneous conclusions may be reached. The presence of one fiber type may go unnoticed because the behavior of the fiber that burns more easily is usually the only one observed.

The investigator should be aware that dyes and finishes may alter the burning behavior observed. Some finishes reduce or prevent flaming, whereas others may in-

---

[12] A review of the dermatological effects of fibers is provided in K. L. Hatch "Chemicals and Textiles; Part I Dermatological Problems Related to Fibers and Dyes," *Textile Research Journal* 54 (1984): 664–82.

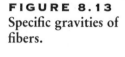

FIGURE 8.13
Specific gravities of
fibers.

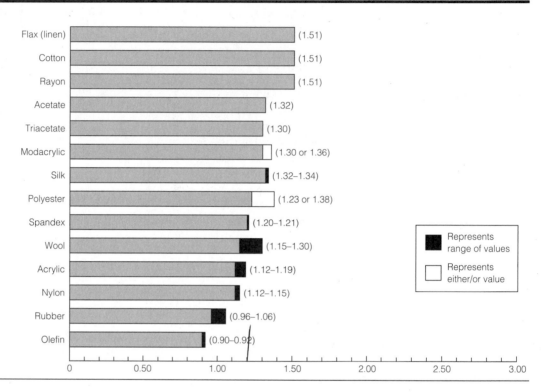

crease it. Both dyes and finishes can affect the color of the residue.

The Chemical Solubility Test

In a chemical solubility test, individual fibers are placed in a prepared chemical at a known concentration and temperature for a specific period of time, at the end of which, the experimenter observes whether or not the fibers have dissolved. Acetone, acetic acid, meta cresol, phenol, sodium hypochlorite, formic acid, hydrochloric acid, sulfuric acid, dimethyl formamide, xylene and some other reagents are used.

Most fibers can be identified from a chemical solubility test. These tests are particularly useful in distinguishing the synthetic fibers from each other. When a microscope is not available, cellulosic and protein fibers can be identified by solubility tests.

Chemical solubility tests are useful in determining if a yarn or fabric is a blend. The experimenter will observe that some test fibers dissolve in a given reagent but

others do not. Further solubility tests will determine the type of fibers in the blend fabric.

The Stain Test

A stain test involves placing white fabrics, yarns, or fibers into a bath containing many different types of dyes. Each type of dye has an affinity for selected fibers. After staining is attempted, the fiber, yarn, or fabric is dyed and its color compared to a known sample.

Melting Point Determination

One method of distinguishing among the various thermoplastic fibers (those that melt on exposure to heat) is to determine their melting temperatures. A fiber sample is placed on a plate that is heated slowly. This electrically heated device may be mounted on a microscope to permit easy viewing. The experimenter watches for the fiber sample to begin melting and at that point reads the temperature from the instrument dial. A comparison of this temperature with known melting temperatures of fibers determines which thermoplastic fiber is being examined. Melting point determinations are useful in distinguishing not only fibers of different generic groups but also fiber variants within a generic classification.

Instrumental Analysis

Positive identification of manufactured fibers, particularly the synthetics, may require the use of certain instrumental analyses. Analyses include determination of density, refractive index, index of birefringence, X-ray diffraction, infrared absorption, chromatographic separation, and appearance. These sophisticated techniques may lead to identification of specific fiber variants.

CHAPTER SUMMARY

Fiber properties are categorized as mechanical, sorptive, thermal, chemical, and miscellaneous. Mechanical properties largely result from the fine structure of fibers, particularly their degree of orientation and crystallinity.

Types and strength of bonding between polymers are also highly important in mechanical behavior.

The sorptive and thermal properties of fibers largely depend on whether they are classified as hydrophilic or thermoplastic. The mechanical performance of a hydrophilic fiber is highly dependent on the amount of moisture it contains. The mechanical performance of a thermoplastic fiber is highly dependent on the temperature of the fiber.

The chemical properties of fibers depend largely on the types of covalent bonds that form the polymer backbone and on the presence of reactive sites along the polymer chain. The accessibility of reactive groups to potential degrading or chemical-finishing agents is also important.

Because fibers cannot generally be identified by visual observation or by feel, a series of laboratory tests are usually performed to identify them. These tests include burning, microscopy, and solubility. One test may be fairly conclusive, but several tests are generally conducted to verify the identification.

Textile Labeling Topics

FEDERAL LAWS AND RULES GOVERNING LABELING

- Wool Products Labeling (WPL) Act
- Textile Fiber Products Identification Act (TFPIA)
- Care Labeling of Textile Wearing Apparel and Certain Piece Goods

FEDERALLY MANDATED ITEMS OF INFORMATION
Standard Terminology for Specifying Type of Fiber (Fiber Generic and Common Names)
Percent Composition
Manufacturer's Name
Country of Origin
   Made in X-Offshore Country
   Made in the U.S.A.
   Made in the U.S.A. of Imported Components
   Partially Manufactured in the U.S.A. and Partially Offshore
Care Instructions (Apparel Only)
   Standard Terminology
   Drycleaning Instructions
   Washing Instructions

TYPE AND PLACEMENT OF REQUIRED INFORMATION
Apparel Items with Necklines
Apparel Items without Necklines
Hosiery
Other Textile Products

PRESENCE OF NONREQUIRED INFORMATION
Care Symbols
Foreign Names of Fibers
Nondeceptive Fiber-Related Terms
Trademarks (Brandnames)
Licensed Trademarks and Certification Marks
Warranties

MAIL-ORDER AND ADVERTISEMENT PROVISIONS

RESPONSIBILITY AND ENFORCEMENT

PRODUCTS TO BE LABELED

Apparel items: suits, blouses, skirts, coats and jackets (except fur and leather ones), sweaters, hosiery and socks, sweatshirts, lingerie, underwear, etc.

Piece goods (over-the-counter fabrics)

Blankets sheets and pillowcases, comforters, bedspreads, towels, etc.

Carpets and rugs

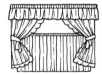

Draperies and curtains

9

*T*extile Labeling

Suppose that you are trying to decide whether or not to purchase a spectacular looking dress or shirt in a store full of textile items with no information attached to them. You know that the feel, color, and drape of the fabric are exquisite, but you do not know if the dress or shirt is machine-washable or if it was produced in the United States.

Knowing the fiber composition of the fabric would help you to determine care procedures. Is the shirt or dress made of silk, a silk-like polyester, or one of the washable silks lauded in the fashion magazines? The salesperson tells you that the fabric also could be made of rayon, acetate, or a rayon/acetate blend. After checking the purchase order, she discovers that the dress is 100% rayon but has no other information. Some rayons must be drycleaned, she tells you. Others can be hand-washed and require only touch-up pressing; still others are machine-washable. But what care instructions apply to this particular rayon fabric? You decide to leave the dress or shirt on the store hanger.

Consumers in the United States usually do not face such a dilemma because several federal trade laws protect them (as well as textile manufacturers and distributors) from unfair trade practices or economic loss arising from unlabeled as well as misleading or erroneously labeled textile products. Many textile manufacturers also provide consumers with additional information at point of purchase to help them make informed textile purchases.

Detail View 9 lists the three federal laws governing the labeling of textile products and outlines the topics to be considered in this chapter. Many of the products requiring labels are shown there.

FEDERALLY MANDATED ITEMS OF INFORMATION

Three major public laws and rules govern the labeling of textile products:

1. The Wool Products Labeling (WPL) Act of 1939 and its amendments.
2. The Textile Fiber Products Identification Act of 1960 (TFPIA) and its amendments.
3. The Federal Trade Commission Rule titled "Care Labeling of Textile Wearing Apparel and Certain Piece Goods" of 1972 and its 1984 amendment, the Care Label Rule.

All three laws and rules pertain to textile products produced domestically (U.S.-produced) as well as to those produced offshore (imported textile products).

In essence, the Wool Products Labeling Act governs the labeling of wool textile products (100% wool and wool blends); the Textile Fiber Products Identification Act, textile products composed of fibers other than wool. More specifically, apparel, household, interior, consumer and industrial textile products, as well as fabrics sold over-the-counter to the ultimate consumer (called piece goods or over-the-counter fabrics), must all be labeled.

A few textile products are exempt from labeling requirements. These products include upholstery stuffing; outer coverings of furniture; mattresses and box springs; linings, stiffenings, or apparel paddings incorporated for structural purposes (not for warmth); sewing and handicraft threads; and bandages and surgical dressings. It is interesting to note that the fiber content of the upholstery fabric covering a furniture frame at the point of sale does not need to be specified. Indeed, it is unusual to find information about fiber content attached to furniture in store displays. Fiber content information is required on upholstery fabrics sold over-the-counter and on swatches used to select a custom upholstered furniture fabric. However, state (rather than federal) statutory regulations do require upholstery stuffing and mattress fill materials to be identified on labels attached to furniture. Leather, suede, and fur apparel items are not considered textiles; furs are covered separately by the Fur Products Labeling Act of 1951.

The Care Label Rule is not as encompassing as the TFPIA or the WPL Act in terms of textile products covered. The Rule covers only textile apparel and certain piece goods. Therefore, the federal government does not require care procedures to be given for carpeting, draperies, sheets and pillowcases, upholstered furniture, and other interior, household, and consumer products. Further, leather, suede, and fur apparel items are not covered because they are not considered to be textiles. Additionally, certain textile apparel items are excluded from care labeling including: apparel sold to institutional buyers for commercial use (mechanic uniforms, police uniforms, etc.); shoes, gloves, and hats; nonwoven, one-time-use garments; and manufacturers' fabric remnants less than 10 yards (9.1 meters) in length when the fiber content is unknown and cannot be determined easily.

Collectively, the three federal laws require five items of information to appear on apparel and piece good labels: fiber content by name, fiber composition by percent of total fabric weight, manufacturer's name, country of origin, and care instructions. They require the first four of the named five items to appear on other textile products. Figures 9.1–9.3 show a variety of products labeled to conform to the requirements of the federal labeling laws. Use these labels to locate the required items of information, to study examples of how each required item is to be specified, and to appreciate the types of nonrequired information that is often included on product labels.

Standard Terminology for Specifying Type of Fiber (Fiber Generic and Common Names)

Only the generic and common names of fibers (see Overview II) are allowed to be used to designate the fiber content of a textile product. The WPL Act focuses on wool terminology; TFPIA, which focuses on all other fibers, provides the definitions of each generic group of fibers.

The Federal Trade Commission has established that the following criteria must be met before a new generic fiber name can be added to the TFPIA and therefore to textile product labels:

. . . the fiber must have a chemical composition "radically different" from other fibers or that chemical composition must give it significantly different physical properties; the fiber must currently be, or soon be, in active commercial use; and the granting of the generic name must be of importance to the consuming public "at large," rather than to a small group of knowledgeable professionals.

Further, all fiber contents must be given in letters of equal size and conspicuousness to eliminate the "promotion" of one fiber over another. For example, putting "SILK" and "polyester" on the same label would not be correct.

Also, no terms may appear on a label that imply the presence of a fiber that is not actually a part of the product. For example, it would be illegal to say "SILK-SHEEN blouses" when the fiber content is 100% polyester or to say "Wooly Warm Blankets" when the fiber content is 100% acrylic.

Percent Composition

Fiber names must appear in a vertical column in order of predominance by weight. The percent of the total fabric weight contributed by each fiber must precede the fiber name.

A type of fiber present in less than 5 percent of the weight of the fabric usually will not be listed by its common or generic name. Rather the designation "other fiber" or "other fibers" will appear because most fibers present in less than 5% of the weight of the fabric usually do not contribute to the overall performance of the fabric in use and are designated as "other fibers" on the label.

In essence, the 5% provision prevents a manufacturer from listing a premium fiber (such as silk or angora), which comprises a small percentage of the weight of the fabric, on the label in the hope that consumers will pay a

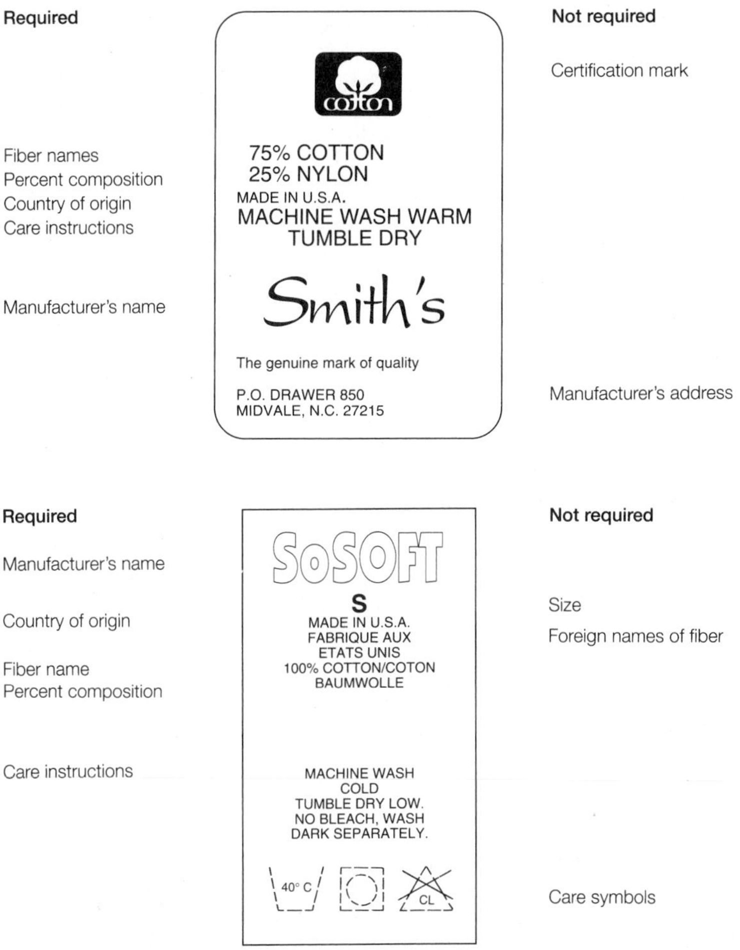

FIGURE 9.1 Labels for apparel items made from one fabric or several fabrics of the same fiber composition.

Required

Fiber names
Percent composition
Country of origin
Care instructions

Manufacturer's name

75% COTTON
25% NYLON
MADE IN U.S.A.
MACHINE WASH WARM
TUMBLE DRY

Smith's

The genuine mark of quality

P.O. DRAWER 850
MIDVALE, N.C. 27215

Not required

Certification mark

Manufacturer's address

Required

Manufacturer's name

Country of origin

Fiber name
Percent composition

Care instructions

S
MADE IN U.S.A.
FABRIQUE AUX
ETATS UNIS
100% COTTON/COTON
BAUMWOLLE

MACHINE WASH
COLD
TUMBLE DRY LOW.
NO BLEACH, WASH
DARK SEPARATELY.

Not required

Size
Foreign names of fiber

Care symbols

higher price for the product because they think that it has additional "performance value."

Sometimes a small percentage (less than 5 percent of the fabric weight) of a certain type of fiber does contribute significantly to fabric performance. In this case, the fiber is named, its percent by weight is given, and a statement specifying its performance contribution is provided. Examples include "1% spandex for elasticity," "2% nylon for strength," and "1% metallic to control static."

The percentage given may not be exact: a deviation of ± 3% percent is allowed. For example, a product label listing 40% of "X" fiber actually may contain anywhere from 37% to 43% of that fiber.

When a product is composed of more than one fabric, each of which has a different fiber content, the label must clearly state the fiber content for each *fabric* in the

product. A lined winter jacket is a good example of a textile product comprised of more than one fabric. The face and back fiber contents of pile fabrics, such as velvets, must be labeled.

Manufacturer's Name

A second important label requirement, federally mandated by TFPIA as well as the WPL Act, is that the name of the manufacturer, a RN (registered number), or a WPL number be given, so that consumers will know who to contact if the textile product fails to perform as expected and/or desired. Manufacturers can apply to the Federal Trade Commission (FTC) for a RN or WPL number if that is how they prefer to be identified. The FTC will provide the manufacturer's name when sent a

FIGURE 9.2 Labels for apparel items made from two or more fabrics with different fiber compositions.

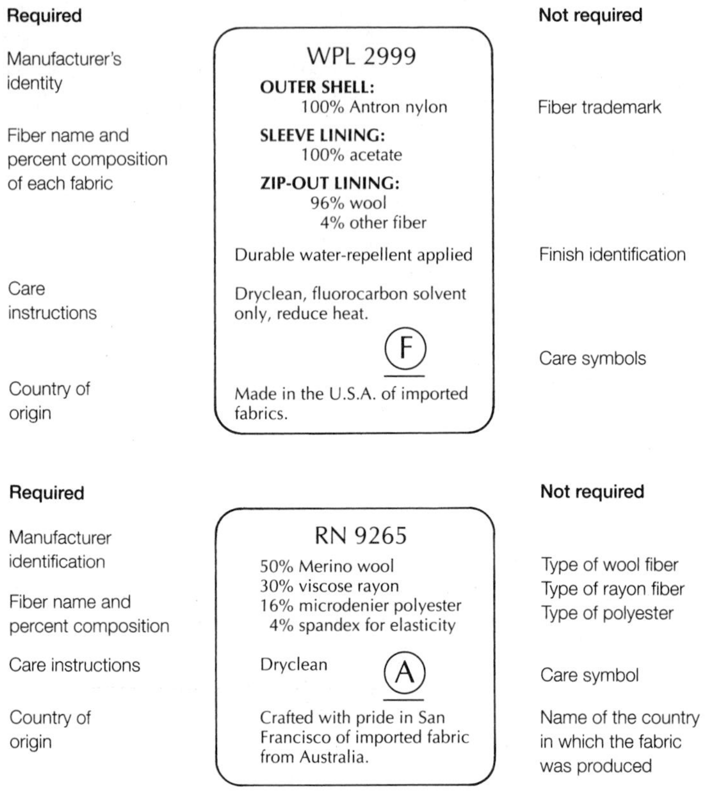

Required		Not required
Manufacturer's identity	**WPL 2999**	Fiber trademark
Fiber name and percent composition of each fabric	**OUTER SHELL:** 100% Antron nylon **SLEEVE LINING:** 100% acetate **ZIP-OUT LINING:** 96% wool 4% other fiber	
Care instructions	Durable water-repellent applied Dryclean, fluorocarbon solvent only, reduce heat. (F)	Finish identification Care symbols
Country of origin	Made in the U.S.A. of imported fabrics.	

Required		Not required
Manufacturer identification	**RN 9265**	Type of wool fiber Type of rayon fiber Type of polyester
Fiber name and percent composition	50% Merino wool 30% viscose rayon 16% microdenier polyester 4% spandex for elasticity	
Care instructions	Dryclean (A)	Care symbol
Country of origin	Crafted with pride in San Francisco of imported fabric from Australia.	Name of the country in which the fabric was produced

RN or WPL number by a consumer or retailer. These numbers also are published periodically.[1]

The manufacturer's name or number must be listed either first or last on the label, generally in larger lettering than the fiber-content information. It is common for a manufacturer to voluntarily include an additional label or hangtag with the company name printed boldly on it—a permissible practice if the company's identity also appears with the fiber-content information.

Country of Origin

In today's world market, the fiber in a textile product may be manufactured in one country, the yarn spun in another, the fabric made (woven, knitted, etc.) in still another; a fourth country may dye and/or finish the fabric, and a fifth country (and possibly a sixth) may fabricate the fabric into a garment or textile end-use product. However, only two countries, at most, are disclosed on a textile product label at the point of purchase—the last two in the manufacturing sequence, where a "significant transformation" of the product occurs. When two countries are named, one of the two is always the United States.

The country of origin must be designated on all textile fiber products (apparel, interior, household, etc.) currently sold at retail in the United States. This designation takes one of four typical forms.

Made in X-Offshore Country. Retail textile products labeled "Made in X-Offshore Country" indicate that the product was produced entirely offshore. The country named on the label is the last country involved in a "substantial" transformation of the product prior to its import to the United States. More than one offshore country may have been involved in the manufacture of the product, but this information is not required and usually is not provided.

[1] *RN and WPL Directory* (Washington, DC: Textile Publication Corporation, 1979.

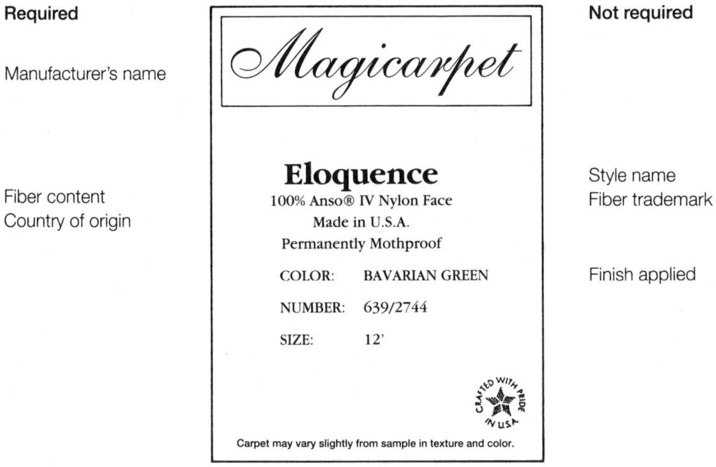

Required

Manufacturer's name

Fiber content
Country of origin

Not required

Style name
Fiber trademark

Finish applied

FIGURE 9.3 A minimally labeled carpet.

Magicarpet

Eloquence
100% Anso® IV Nylon Face
Made in U.S.A.
Permanently Mothproof

COLOR: BAVARIAN GREEN

NUMBER: 639/2744

SIZE: 12'

CRAFTED WITH PRIDE IN USA

Carpet may vary slightly from sample in texture and color.

The phrase "substantial transformation" is an important and controversial one. It helps to make quota restrictions work. The U.S. Customs Service needs to know in what country a textile product was last manufactured to prevent the country of manufacture from shipping goods through other offshore countries to circumvent its import quotas with the United States. Such shipments are called *transshipments.* For example, there may be an import quota of 100,000 pairs of cotton shirts from Bolivia. When 100,000 cotton shirts sewn in Bolivia have arrived in the United States, the U.S. Customs Service does not allow any more to be imported. The Bolivians cannot ship the shirts to Venezuela or some other country and then to the United States and claim that the shirts are imported from Venezuela. Venezuela may not have reached its quota of cotton shirts, but this country was not involved in the manufacture of the Bolivian shirts.

There is controversy about what constitutes a substantial transformation. At what point has a textile been altered so sufficiently by a country that it becomes the last country prior to import to the United States? When fabric parts cut in one country are sewn and assembled into finished apparel in another country, the country of origin is considered to be the one in which the textile is sewn and assembled.

In the case of knitwear, however, where parts are knit to shape in one country and assembled into finished garments in a second country, the country which produces the parts is considered the country of origin. In the case of fabric finishing, a substantial transformation requires a combination of dyeing and printing with at least two major finishing operations. Therefore, the country of

origin is most likely to be the country in which the fabric was made and not the country to which it was shipped to be finished. For example, China is the country of origin for a fabric woven in China and then sent to Hong Kong to be bleached and dyed before being imported to the United States.

Knowing the last country involved in the manufacture of a retail textile product is also useful to the consumer who wishes to purchase textile goods from certain countries and avoid purchasing goods from other countries. The label information is limited by the fact that not all countries are named.

Made in the U.S.A. Textile products made completely in the United States from materials made in the United States are labeled "Made in the U.S.A.," "Crafted with Pride in the U.S.A.," or "Made in [name of city], U.S.A." Other "clear and equivalent" terms also are allowed. Thus, a garment labeled "Made in the U.S.A." indicates that the garment was sewn in the United States of fabric, yarn, and fiber produced in the United States. An over-the-counter fabric bearing this label was woven, knitted, or otherwise formed in the United States of yarn and fiber manufactured in the United States.

Made in the U.S.A. of Imported Components. When a textile product (garment, over-the-counter fabric, craft yarn) is made in the United States from foreign components (fabric, yarn, fiber), the label must read "Made in the U.S.A. of imported fabric," "Made in the U.S.A. of imported yarn," "Made in the U.S.A. of imported fiber," or "Knit in the U.S.A. of imported yarn." The country that supplied the fiber, yarn, or fabric, may or may not be named.

A knit dress made of silk fiber imported from China which was spun into yarn, knitted into fabric, and then sewn in the United States would be correctly labeled if it read "Made in the U.S.A. of silk fiber imported from China" or "Made in the U.S.A. of imported fiber." The fact that the fiber is silk would be included in the fiber-content portion of the label in either case.

Partially Manufactured in the U.S.A. and Partially Off-shore.

When a textile product has been partially manufactured in the United States and partially manufactured in a foreign country, the label shows the manufacturing process performed in each country. The two countries named are the last two countries (one is the United States) involved in a substantial transformation of the product. Label examples include: "Imported Fabric, Finished in the U.S.A.," "Imported Fabric, Sewn in the United States," and "Made in [foreign country], finished in the U.S.A."

Care Instructions (Apparel Only)

Textile apparel items must have care instructions attached at the point of purchase. Bolts holding piece goods (over-the-counter fabrics) for home sewing must be labeled with care instructions and a separate label made available for the home sewer.

Care information must include instructions for "regular care for the ordinary use of the product." It does not need to instruct about care required in certain cases (for example, instructions for the removal of stains). Labels generally provide information about only one of three care methods: washing instructions, drycleaning instructions, or a statement that the product cannot be cleaned successfully. Only one method is required by the Care Label Rule, but a manufacturer may give both washing and drycleaning instructions. When only one care method is stated, the consumer does not know whether the alternative cleaning method is acceptable or whether it can cause fabric problems. The Care Label Rule does not require that a warning be given if the alternative method should not be used.

Care labels, then, do not indicate all the appropriate methods nor do they warn about a method that should not be used. The only way to insure that the product is not ruined in refurbishing is to follow the care instructions that are provided.

Standard Terminology.

The wording on care labels is carefully defined in the Care Label Rule. The more common phrases and their definitions are discussed here.

Drycleaning Instructions.

A label that reads "Dryclean" indicates that the textile apparel item can be taken to any commercial or self-serve drycleaner and successfully cleaned with any of the common organic solvents used to remove oily and particulate soils. If a certain drycleaning solvent should be used, the name of the solvent is specified. If, for example, the care label reads "Dryclean, fluorocarbon solvent only," the consumer must locate a drycleaner who uses the fluorocarbon solvent. This is the most expensive but mildest solvent, and only a small percentage of drycleaners use it. The most common drycleaning solvent is perchloroethylene (known as PERC).

Warning instructions appear when an aspect of the normal drycleaning routine will be harmful to the apparel item. For example, if steam should not be used, the label will read "Dryclean, no steam."

Washing Instructions.

For washable items, four specific procedures may need to be given:

1. A *wash procedure* is always given; it includes "Machine-washable" or "Hand-washable," as well as the water temperature if hot water will harm the apparel fabric.
2. A *bleach procedure* is given when all commercially common bleaches (chlorine and oxygen) cannot be used successfully. The phrase "No bleach" indicates that neither oxygen bleaches (such as Clorox II®)[2] nor chlorine bleaches (such as Clorox®)[2] should be used. The phrase "No chlorine bleach" eliminates the use of chlorine bleaches but permits the use of oxygen bleaches.
3. A *drying procedure* must indicate one appropriate method of drying ("Machine dry," "Line dry," "Lay flat to dry," etc.). When the instruction is "Machine dry," a temperature setting also must be given if too high a temperature will harm the apparel fabric.
4. An *ironing instruction* is given if ironing is needed on a regular basis. A safe ironing temperature also must be given if a hot iron will harm the apparel fabric.

In addition, a warning must be given if a regular procedure will harm a product being washed with the apparel item. For example, if the item is not colorfast to water, the label must state "Wash separately."

---

[2]Clorox II® and Clorox® are trademarks of The Clorox Company.

TYPE AND PLACEMENT OF REQUIRED INFORMATION

The type of label (sewn-in, hangtag, stamped-on, etc.) and its placement (location on the product) depend on the product being labeled:

1. Apparel Items with Necklines: A label containing information about country of origin must be sewn into the neckline area when a garment has a neckline. This label may be centered at the back of the neckline or located to one side of a brand label. Fiber content, manufacturer, and care instructions also may be included on this label. An apparel manufacturer may place country of origin, fiber content, and manufacturer identity on a hangtag or on a label attached to a conspicuous place on the inside or outside of the garment. In this case, the country of origin must be repeated in the neckline area, however. Care information must be placed on a label sewn into the garment. When apparel items (like T-shirts) are sold in packages, the fiber content, manufacturer, country of origin, and care instructions must appear on the package as well as on the product itself, so that the information is available at the point of purchase.

2. Apparel Items without Necklines: All of the required information must be disclosed in one place and located in a conspicuous spot on the inside or outside of the garment. A sewn-in label must give care instructions. Fiber content, manufacturer identity, and country of origin may appear on a sewn-in label or on a hangtag. If sold in a package, the package also must provide the required information, so that the consumer can read it at the point of purchase.

3. Hosiery: When hosiery is sold in packages, it does not need to have an individual label attached. The required fiber content, manufacturer, and country of origin information must be printed on the product package. Hosiery is exempt from the Care Label Rule; care instructions do not need to be given.

4. Other Textile Products: Fiber content, manufacturer, and country of origin must be conspicuously displayed in close proximity to each other at the point of purchase.

PRESENCE OF NONREQUIRED INFORMATION

Certain additional information may be included with the mandated information or on other labels and hangtags.

Care Symbols

Many times, care instructions are given in symbols in addition to the approved Care Label Rule phrases. The United States does not have an official set of care-labeling symbols, but many countries have adopted the International Care Label Symbols developed by the International Standards Organization (ISO). Some of the care symbols are shown in Figures 9.1 and 9.2.

Foreign Names of Fibers

When a manufacturer is making a textile product that is to be sold at retail in several countries, it is common practice to designate fiber content in the languages of the import countries on one label. Frequently seen foreign fiber designations are coton and baumwolle (cotton), soie (silk), wolle (wool), and polyamide (nylon).

Nondeceptive Fiber-Related Terms

Nondeceptive descriptions may be given in conjunction with a fiber name to clarify the type of fiber. For example, "Pima," and "Egyptian," which are different varieties of cotton, may appear in conjunction with the word "cotton." "Recycled," "Merino," and "Lamb's" are examples of adjectives that precede the word "wool" on many labels. "Spun" or "filament" may appear in conjunction with a manufactured fiber or silk to indicate the fiber form. "Viscose" and "cuprammonium" are descriptors of "rayon." These words and others are defined more precisely in the individual fiber chapters.

Trademarks (Brandnames)

By definition, a trademark is

a distinctive mark placed on or attached to goods by a manufacturer to identify them as made or sold by him. The use of a trademark indicates that the maker or dealer believes that the quality of the goods will enhance his standing or goodwill, and a known trademark indicates to the buyer the reputation that it staked on the goods. A trademark may be registered with the U.S. Patent Office, or sufficient use of it establishes the exclusive rights to it.[3]

Fiber manufacturers use trademarks to distinguish their fibers from those of other producers. Among nylon carpet fiber producers, Du Pont has trademarked its fiber

[3] W. H. Harris and J. S. Levey (eds.), *The New Columbia Encyclopedia* (New York: Columbia University Press, 1975).

FIGURE 9.4 Trademarks held by natural fiber producers' associations.

International Silk Association

Mohair Council of America

American Sheep Industry Association

Antron®; Allied Corporation, Anso®; and Monsanto, Cadon®. TFPIA states that fiber trademarks may appear in conjunction with the generic fiber name on textile product labels. Examples are "100% Dacron® polyester," "100% Antron® nylon," and "100% Avril® rayon."

Natural fiber producers' associations also use trademarks to identify products containing their members' fibers (Figure 9.4). Yarn manufacturers also use trademarks to distinguish the yarns they produce from other yarns. Helanca® and Superloft® are trademarks of the Heberlein and Lessona corporations, respectively, for filament yarns modified for enhanced stretch. Fabric manufacturers may trademark fabric they produce. Viyella® is a Williams Hollins and Company trademark of a cotton/ wool blend fabric; Ultrasuede® is a Springs Mills, Inc., trademark of a suede-like fabric. These trademarks may be used on labels giving the required information or used on separate labels.

When a trademark appears, it means that the company that holds the rights to the trademark assures consumers that the quality of *its* product is carefully controlled. When a company manufactures the final or ultimate product—the fabric, carpet, or constructed garment, it has full control of the quality.

In textiles, a problem arises in the use of trademarks to assure quality and confidence because the intrinsic properties of fibers and yarns do *not* automatically show up in the final product. Unfortunately, when a fabric carrying a fiber, yarn, or finish trademark fails to perform as the consumer expects, a negative image is created for the trademark and the company that holds it.

Licensed Trademarks and Certification Marks

Manufactured fiber producers, associations that represent natural fiber producers, yarn manufacturers, and companies that develop finishing processes have formulated licensed trademark and certification programs to assume greater control over the quality of the ultimate fabric in which their product or technology has been used (Figure 9.5). In these programs, companies that purchase fibers, yarns, or finishing technologies from a licensed trademark holder agree to use the licensed trademark only when their products pass performance tests established by the licensed trademark holder. It is the responsibility of the licensed trademark holder to establish the performance tests and to maintain a quality control laboratory in which to test fabrics sent by final-product manufacturers on a continuing basis. The trademark holder usually provides technical assistance to the final-product manufacturer.

The consumer is provided added assurance in the quality of the ultimate product because it has passed a series of performance tests determined by the licensed trademark holder. The consumer can tell if a product has been produced under one of these programs by carefully reading labels and advertisements. An asterisk (*) often will appear beside a trademark that references a note on the label or in the advertisement that "XX is a licensed trademark of the XX company" or that "XX is a certification mark of the XX company or association." A

FIGURE 9.5 Selected licensed trademarks and certification marks.

PURE WOOL

WOOL BLEND

100% wool fabric and wool blend fabric certification marks of The Wool Bureau, Inc./U.S. Division of the International Wool Secretariat.

Linen fabric certification mark of the International Confederation of the Flax and Hemp Industries (Official colors: gray (apparel); brown (interior furnishings); blue (household textiles).)

NATURAL BLEND

THE FABRIC OF OUR LIVES™

The Seal of Cotton is a registered trademark/service mark of Cotton Incorporated.

·SANFORIZED·
TRADE ® MARK

CRI

Certification mark of the Carpet and Rug Institute for carpet meeting its quality standards.

·SANFOR SET·
TRADEMARK OF THE SANFORIZED COMPANY

·SANFOR KNIT·
TRADEMARK OF THE SANFORIZED COMPANY

·SANFOR Knit-Fabric·
TRADEMARK OF THE SANFORIZED COMPANY

FLOOR TESTED℠ TREVIRA®
WITH BUILT-IN STAIN RESISTANCE

Floor-Tested is a certification mark of Hoechst Celanese Corporation for residential carpets meeting its quality standards.

Sanforized[R], Sanfor-Knit[R], Sanfor-Knit-Fabric[R] and Sanfor-Set[R] are registered trademarks of the Sanforized Company of Cluett, Peabody & Co., Inc. The Sanforized Company permits use by Licensees of the trademarks on fabrics which meet rigid requirements. Samples of fabric using these trademarks are regularly wash-tested and checked by The Sanforized Company.

superscripted "CM" by a trademark also indicates that it is a licensed trademark, a certification mark.

Licensed trademark and certification programs established by manufactured fiber producers are essentially alike. One major distinction is made in labeling, however. In certification programs, a manufactured fiber producer may hold the rights for two trademarks: a trademark that identifies the fiber, and a *certification mark* that identifies a product (not made by the fiber producer) that contains its fibers. Examples of this are

100% Orlon® Sayelle® acrylic

Sayelle®—a Monsanto[5] certification program for hand knitting yarn made of 100% bicomponent acrylic fiber. (Orlon is the tradename of the fiber).

100% Prima® Avril® rayon

Prima®—a Courtaulds North America certification program for rayon fabrics made of Avril® rayon fiber.

A manufactured fiber producer may trademark the yarn or fabric but not the fiber. Examples of this type of certification labeling are

Thermax®—a Du Pont certification program for fabric intended to provide thermal comfort in gloves, socks, and thermal underwear composed of a special Du Pont polyester fiber. (The fiber variant does not carry a registered trademark.)

Qiana®—a certification program for fabrics made of Du Pont nylon fiber.

ESP®—a Hoechst Celanese certification program for products produced with Fortrel® polyester type 661 fiber.

The tendency to trademark the fabric rather than the fiber is becoming more common among manufactured fiber producers. This approach reflects that fiber content is only one aspect of fabric performance and that fibers, yarns, and fabrics must be engineered to provide exacting performance in specific end-use situations.

Warranties

A textile manufacturer may indicate on a hangtag or label at the point of purchase that its product is covered by a *warranty* (Table 9.1). A warranty label will set forth the conditions under which the warranty applies and directions for receiving restitution.

TABLE 9.1   Selected Carpet Warranty Programs.

PROGRAM NAME	TRADEMARK HOLDER
XPS[CM] Carpet of Trevira®	Hoechst Celanese
Stainmaster[CM]	du Pont
WearDated®	Monsanto
Anso V Worry Free®	Allied Fibers
Genesis®	Hercules
Zeftron®	BASF
PermaColor®	Amoco Fabrics & Fibers Co. and 3M Co.

Many warranties are offered by manufactured fiber producers. Like licensed trademarks and certification marks, warranties provide assurance to consumers that the ultimate product has met minimum performance standards established by the trademark holder. Warranties offer consumers a replacement or a money refund—as provided in the Magnuson-Moss Warranty Act of 1975, which governs the offering and labeling of warranted items—within a stated time period if the textile article does not perform as claimed.

Interior textile products, especially carpeting, tend to be warranted. The assurance of product replacement or a money-back offer may be the deciding factor when a consumer makes such a major purchase.

MAIL-ORDER AND ADVERTISEMENT PROVISIONS

Consumers increasingly purchase textile products from mail-order catalogs and promotional materials—forms of advertising that solicit the buyer to make a purchase by telephone, mail, or some similar method without examining the product first. Under these circumstances, fiber content, manufacturer, country of origin, and care instructions must be given. The designation of the country of origin should be consistent with the wording found on the product itself. Mail-order companies often provide a legend explaining the meaning of their country of origin disclosures.

In advertisements intended to inform consumers about the availability of a new textile product, fiber content may or may not be given. In advertisements in which no reference is made to manufacturing methods or to fabric structure (woven, knitted, etc.), fiber-content information is not required. However, advertisements must

---

[5] Monsanto Co. purchased the Sayelle certification trademark and associated research and technology for the manufacture of bicomponent fiber from which these yarns are made in May 1991 from Du Pont.

carry all required information, including percentages of the component fibers, under certain circumstances:

1. When the terms in an advertisement describe a method of manufacture and/or a method of construction or weave.
2. When due to custom or usage, the terms are indicative of a textile fiber or fibers.
3. When using the terms constitutes or connotes the name or presence of a fiber or fibers.

RESPONSIBILITY AND ENFORCEMENT

It is the responsibility of the manufacturer to label retail textile products. If the last manufacturing process is completed in the United States, the U.S. manufacturer must follow the Textile Fiber Products Identification Act, the Wool Products Labeling Act, and the Care Labeling Rule. If the last manufacturing process is completed outside the United States, the foreign manufacturer must follow U.S. labeling regulations. In the case of care labeling, each apparel manufacturer is charged with determining the appropriate care procedures. Records must be kept of the tests performed to determine the appropriate procedures.

The Federal Trade Commission (FTC) enforces textile trade laws and rules and may levy fines. The FTC also is responsible for assessing the effectiveness of these rules and, when necessary, for instituting the process for change.

Labeling is ineffective if consumers do not use the label information to make the most appropriate selection and to care for the fabric as advised. Consumers must let legitimate dissatisfaction with a textile product be known to the store where the product was purchased and/or to the manufacturer. Only by conveying such problems can consumers expect to obtain redress and hopefully improve products in the future.

Home sewers need to consult care instructions to select fabrics that are compatible with each other. These consumers also should be sure the label they are given at the counter reads the same as the care instructions on the fabric bolt.

Retailers have a responsibility to make sure that textile products in their stores meet federal labeling requirements. Sales personnel should be trained to interpret these labels for customers who inquire about their meaning. Retailers, too, should work closely with textile manufacturers to alert them to performance and labeling problems.

CHAPTER SUMMARY

Labeling textile products for fiber composition and care instructions promotes fair trade practices. Without this information, consumers could not anticipate fabric performance.

The Wool Products Labeling (WPL) Act and the Textile Fiber Products Identification Act (TFPIA) present standard terminology that must be used to specify the fiber composition of a fabric, the percent composition of each fiber, and the manner in which country of origin and manufacturer are presented. Fiber composition, manufacturer, and country of origin must be specified for most textile products.

The Care Label Rule establishes the manner in which care instructions are conveyed on labels. It designates that only apparel items must carry care information using its standard terminology.

Textile product labels can carry other useful information about a product, including its registered trademark, licensed trademark, and certification mark. A product may be warranted and be so labeled. Labels may include descriptive terms, such as variety names of natural fibers, and information about whether the staple or filament form of a fiber has been used. The Textile Fiber Products Identification Act specifies how these items of nonrequired information may appear on the label to ensure fair trade practices.

It is the responsibility of the ultimate textile manufacturer to ensure appropriate labeling. The Federal Trade Commission (FTC) is charged with enforcing the mandated requirements.

Wool Fibers

Wool fibers are from the fleece of the sheep or lamb or hair of the Angora or Cashmere goat (and may include the so-called specialty fibers from the hair of the camel, alpaca, llama, and vicuna).

Cheviot
(medium)

Southdown
(medium)

Angora goat
(coarse)

Angora rabbit
(fine)

Cashgora
(medium)

Cashmere goat
(fine)

Fat-tailed
(coarse)

Lincoln
(coarse)

Romney
(coarse)

Corriedale
(medium)

Scottish Blackface
(coarse)

Llama
(coarse)

Alpaca
(coarse)

Guanaco
(fine)

Yak
(fine)

Merino
(fine)

Hampshire Down
(medium)

Bactrian camel
(medium)

SHEEP'S WOOL		Carpet Wools	SPECIALTY WOOLS
Garment Wools			
New wool	Worsted wool	Mothproofed wool*	Cashmere
Virgin wool	Oiled wool	Flame-retardant wool*	Mohair
Recycled wool	Washable wool*	Stain-resist wool*	Cashgora
Reprocessed wool	Mothproofed wool*		Camel Hair
Reused wool	Flame-retardant wool*		Llama
Lamb's wool	Permanent-set wool*		Alpaca
Merino wool	Sponged or London		Huarizo and Misti
Botany wool	Shrunk wool*		Guanaco
Shetland wool	Durable-press wool*		Vicuna
Saxony wool			Qiviut
			Angora
			Mink
			Etc.

*Discussed in Unit V.

Photo courtesy James M. Gurney. Copyright National Geographic Society.

C H A P T E R

10

$\mathcal{W}$ool Fibers

Wool fibers are made within an animal's skin follicles to protect that animal from heat, cold, sun, wind, and rain. The term "wool" refers to "the fiber from the fleece of the sheep or lamb or hair of the Angora or Cashmere goat (and may include the so-called specialty fibers from the hair of the camel, alpaca, llama, and vicuna)." Detail View 10 illustrates these animals and several others from which wool fibers are obtained; it also lists important terminology related to types of sheep's wool.

Sheep's wool is by far the more important type of wool fiber because it is the most plentiful. In 1989, 190 million pounds (86.2 kilograms) of scoured sheep's wool were converted to wool yarn and fabric in the United States (Figure 10.1). Most of this wool fiber (~73% of it) was used in apparel fabrics. However, this amount represents less than 2% of all apparel fiber processed in the United States that year. Another ~13% was used in carpeting: wool carpets are expensive and represent about 0.5% of the U.S. carpet market. The remaining ~15% of wool fiber was used in a wide variety of products, some of which are listed in Figure 10.1.

The production of specialty wool fibers per year on a worldwide basis amounts to approximately 70 million pounds of scoured fiber; this includes 50 million pounds of mohair, 10 million pounds of cashmere, 2 million pounds of alpaca, and 0.4 million pound of cashgora.[1] A few thousand pounds of vicuna may be available each year. Specialty wool fibers are more costly than sheep's wool and are used primarily in luxury sweaters, suits, and coats.

SHEEP'S WOOL

The modern sheep is a 24-hour-a-day fiber factory, with each fiber growing 0.008 inch a day. There can be 60,000 wool follicles per square inch of skin and 100 million fibers in one fine Merino fleece. One Merino can produce nearly 5500 miles of wool fiber in a year, at the rate of two-thirds of a mile per hour. The fibers of five Merinos, joined end to end, could tie a bow around the world.[2]

An average of 8 pounds (0.36 kilogram) of wool per year are clipped from a sheep. When this wool is cleaned, 3–5 pounds (1.36–2.27 kilograms) remain to be converted to yarns and fabrics.

Structure

The intricate physical and chemical structure of wool fiber has been extensively studied. Scientists studied wool protein before human protein because wool protein was simpler to understand. Ultimately, protein research led to the discovery of DNA, which is remarkably like wool protein.

---

[1] W. A. B. Davidson, "Mohair in Demand," *America's Textiles International* (1990) 1:62, 64; "Cashgora Yield Could Hit 300 Tons in 1990," *Textile World* 140 (1990): 38; "Natural Fibers: Wool, Camel, Cashmere, Angora, Mohair," *American Fabrics and Fashions* 124/125 [fall/winter] (1982–1983): 45–47.

[2] N. Hyde, "Fabric of History: Wool," *National Geographic Magazine* 173/5 (1988): 580.

FIGURE 10.1 Primary market distribution of 190 million pounds of wool fiber shipped to domestic consumers in 1989.

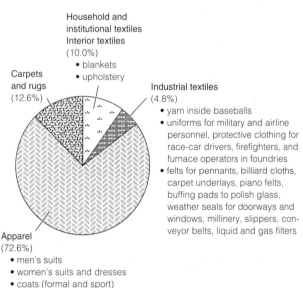

Household and institutional textiles
Interior textiles (10.0%)
• blankets
• upholstery

Carpets and rugs (12.6%)

Industrial textiles (4.8%)
• yarn inside baseballs
• uniforms for military and airline personnel, protective clothing for race-car drivers, firefighters, and furnace operators in foundries
• felts for pennants, billiard cloths, carpet underlays, piano felts, buffing pads to polish glass, weather seals for doorways and windows, millinery, slippers, conveyor belts, liquid and gas filters

Apparel (72.6%)
• men's suits
• women's suits and dresses
• coats (formal and sport)
• casual shirts
• scarves, hats, and gloves

Macrostructure. A wool fiber generally is *crimped three dimensionally.* A fine-diameter fiber has as many as 25 crimps per inch (10 crimps per centimeter); coarser wools, less than 1 crimp per inch (4 crimps per 10 centimeters).

Fiber length ranges from 1.5–15 inches (3.8–38 centimeters). In apparel, wool fibers of 2–5 inches (5–12 centimeters) generally are used because this length permits the most versatile and economical yarn manufacture.

Fiber size ranges from about 14 micrometers to more than 45 micrometers (Figure 10.2; see Figure 7.1). Kemp fibers, coarse guard-hairs grown by some sheep, have diameters of 70 micrometers. A premium price is paid for finer-diameter wools, particularly if they have an even diameter.

In general, fiber length-to-width ratios range from 2500:1 for the finer, shorter wools to about 7500:1 for the coarser, longer wools. For apparel, the longer fine-diameter wool fibers, called *tops,* are considered to be best. In carpeting, the longer and coarser fibers are considered to be the best quality.

The color of sheep's wool varies from *off-white to brown;* off-white to light cream is the more desired col-

oration. Darker fibers cannot be dyed successfully because the pigment cannot be removed and masks the dye.

Microstructure. The characteristic surface feature of a wool fiber, overlapping surface cells commonly called *scales,* are readily observed when the fiber is magnified (Figure 10.2). As many as 2000 scales may cover 1 inch of the fine sheep's wool (700 scales per centimeter); coarse wool may be covered by as few as 700 scales per inch (270 scales per centimeter).[3] All scales, which make up the *cuticle* of the wool fiber, point toward the fiber tip.

Wool fibers have a *medulla,* a hollow canal in the center. In coarse wool fibers, the medulla may occupy up to 90% of the cross-sectional area. In fine wool fibers, the medulla is small and may be intermittent along the length of the fiber. A dark central line observed in a longitudinal view of a wool fiber indicates the presence of a large medulla. Wool fiber usually has an *oval or elliptical cross-section.*

Submicroscopic structure. An *epicuticle,* a wax-like substance only a few molecules thick, covers the scales of a wool fiber (Figure 10.3). Its countless microscopic pores allow water vapor to be absorbed into the fiber interior but cause liquid water to be shed. The epicuticle is easily damaged during normal wear.

The *cortex* or *core* of the wool fiber, which forms about 90% of the fiber volume, consists of countless long, spindle-shaped cells. Each cell is wrapped in a cell membrane, and the cells are held together by a *intercellular cement.* The cement is weaker than the cells; stresses are dissipated in the weaker regions. The cement gives way under chemical or physical stresses, before the bulk of the fiber becomes damaged. The weak cement can be chemically modified to improve wear performance.

The cortex is divided into two distinct sections, the *orthocortex* and the *paracortex,* which spiral around each other along the fiber length. This aspect of wool structure partly explains the three-dimensional crimp. It makes wool a natural bicomponent fiber, because the polymers forming the orthocortex and the paracortex react differently to heat and moisture.

Each cortical cell is composed of a number of *macrofibrils,* each of which consists of hundreds of *microfibrils.* Each microfibril is made up of *protofibrils,* which spiral about each other; finally, each protofibril consists of three *keratin (polypeptide) polymers,* which also spiral around each other. This fibrillar, spiraling structure within the cortical cells contributes to the flexibility,

[3] M. L. Joseph, *Introductory Textile Science,* 5th ed. (New York: Holt, Rinehart, and Winston, 1986), p. 49.

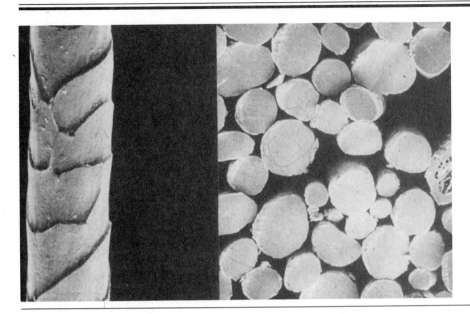

FIGURE 10.2 Photomicrograph of wool fiber showing the surface scales overlapping toward the tip of the fiber and an oval cross-section.

|———————| 50 μm (left)

|———————| 10 μm (right)

elongation, elastic recovery, and tenacity of the wool fiber.

The Keratin Polymer. The *keratin polymer* is a helix composed of amino acids joined end-to-end in a specific sequence. Figure 10.4 shows a segment of a keratin polymer and gives the general structure of an amino acid. The helical shape of the polymer is immediately evident. On closer inspection, amino acid monomers can be discerned by locating –N–C–C– groups in the polymer backbone. Several amino acids are shaded in Figure 10.4 to help you locate the monomer units. Note that there are approximately three amino acids per complete turn in the keratin polymer.

The keratin polymer contains 18 different amino acids. The "R" in the general structure of an amino acid and along the keratin polymer designates a hydrocarbon group but does not specify its exact nature. The natures of the "R" groups for the five major amino acids in the keratin polymer appear in Figure 10.5. No one amino acid constitutes more than 12% of a keratin polymer.

Because the amino acids are so diverse, many different colorants and chemicals can be used to impart color and improve specific fiber properties. The presence of polar groups in the amino acids accounts for the hydrophilicity of the wool fiber. The presence of cystine amino acid, which contains sulfur, is responsible for degradation by moths and beetles. The size of the "R" group, except for glycine, interferes with close packing of the polymer chains.

The keratin polymer is a right-handed or alpha(α)-helix that tends to straighten when a longitudinal force acts on the fiber. The new structure is called beta(β)-keratin. When stress is removed, the wool fiber and its polymers revert to the alpha or relaxed configuration.

The spiraling of the protofibrils, microfibrils and macrofibrils does not contribute to a well-aligned polymer system. In addition, the bulkiness of the "R" portion of many of the amino acids in keratin does not permit close packing to take place. In fact, the molecular arrangement within wool is unique, even among fibers, in its lack of systematic organization. The polymer system of wool is 25–30% crystalline and, correspondingly, 75–70% amorphous.

Intrafiber or Interpolymer Bonding. Several types of bonds form between adjacent polymers within a wool fiber and also within the helical structure. *Crosslinking* and *ionic bond formation* are shown in Figure 10.6. When two cystine amino acids—one on each of two adjacent chains—are in close proximity to each other, a cystine link forms. The link, a covalent bond between two sulfur atoms, is often called a *disulfide bond*. The cystine crosslink, like crosslinks in general, contributes to fiber strength. The sensitivity of a wool fiber to alkalies, bleaches, heat, and sunlight is related to the presence of the cystine linkage. Wool can be modified to have permanent set, to be nonfelting, and to be mothproof when this link is altered.

FIGURE 10.3 The submicroscopic structure of a wool fiber.

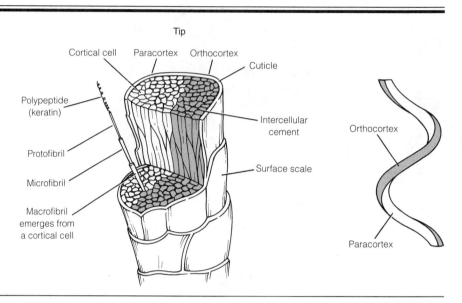

Properties

When two amino acids (for example, aspartic acid and arginine or glutamic acid and lysine) are in close proximity, they may form a *salt linkage* (an *ionic bond*). Fiber strength is reduced when the salt linkages are broken. It is the salt linkages in wool that react with acid dyes.

Hydrogen bonds also form between two polymers (when they are close enough together) or two amino acids in the helix. The dotted lines in Figure 10.4 indicate intrapolymer hydrogen bonding. Although individual hydrogen bonds are strong, relatively few form due to the amorphous nature of wool fibers. Hydrogen bonds contribute to the strength, elasticity, and temporary set of a wool fiber. Absorbed water can break these hydrogen bonds and push adjacent polymer chains further apart.

Properties

Table 10.1 provides a summary of the properties of wool fiber. To obtain numerical values for wool fiber properties and to compare the properties of wool to other fibers, refer to Figures 8.1–8.13 and to Tables 8.1–8.8.

Influencing Fabric Durability. Wool fibers are not very durable. Wool fabrics may be very durable, however, because the length, crimp, and scale structure of wool fibers increase cohesiveness within yarns and between yarns in fabrics.

Wool is a comparatively weak fiber. Its low tenacity is due to the low degree of orientation and crystallinity of its polymers and to the relatively few hydrogen bonds that form between them. Toughness is also low for wool.

This lack of tenacity is compensated for by the degree of elongation and elastic recovery in wool fibers, which is higher than it is for all other fibers except nylon and spandex. The 25–30% elongation of wool fiber, built in from the macroscopic, three-dimensional crimp to the helical polymer, allows sudden stresses or loads to be absorbed so that irreversible structural damage does not occur. The intercellular cement between cortical cells also absorbs stress. If the breaking tenacity of the wool fiber is not surpassed, it returns to its relaxed state when the cystine linkages, salt linkages, and hydrogen bonds pull the polymers back to their original positions. After 2% extension, the wool fiber has an immediate recovery of 99%; even at 10% extension, recovery is well over 50%. Permanent deformation generally occurs with repeated stresses.

A wool fiber can be bent 20,000 times without breaking if it contains sufficient moisture. When wool is dry, flexibility is low.

Abrasion resistance of wool apparel fabrics is fair to good; abrasion resistance of carpet wool is high. The intercellular cement absorbs initial stresses and then gives way, resulting in fibrillated fiber ends. Thus, wool fabrics do not wear out due to gradual fiber thinning. Instead, continual flexing and twisting movements during wear and use lead to individual fiber breakage and the continual loss of small portions of fiber. Eventually, holes or thin areas appear in the fabric.

FIGURE 10.4 The general structure of an amino acid and a segment of an alpha(α)-helix keratin polymer.

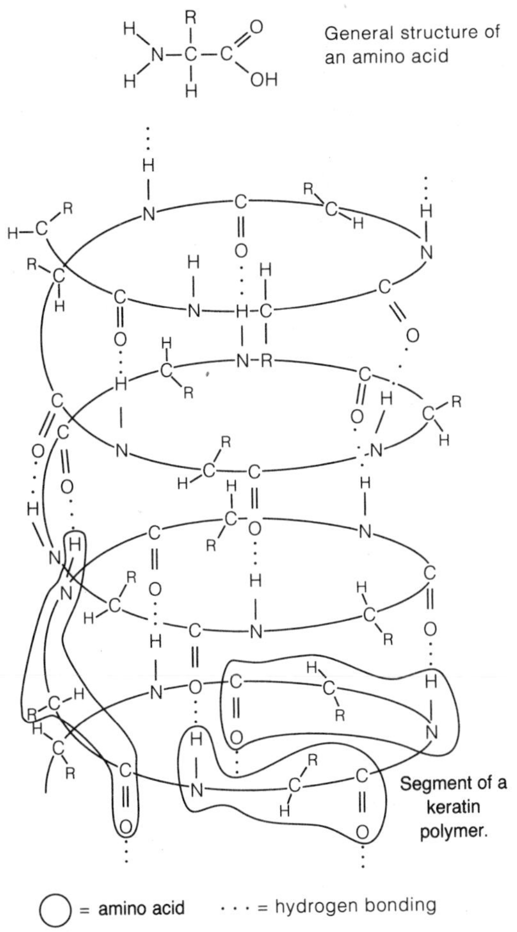

$\bigcirc$ = amino acid   · · · = hydrogen bonding

FIGURE 10.5 Structures of the five amino acids that occur most frequently along the keratin polymer in wool fiber.

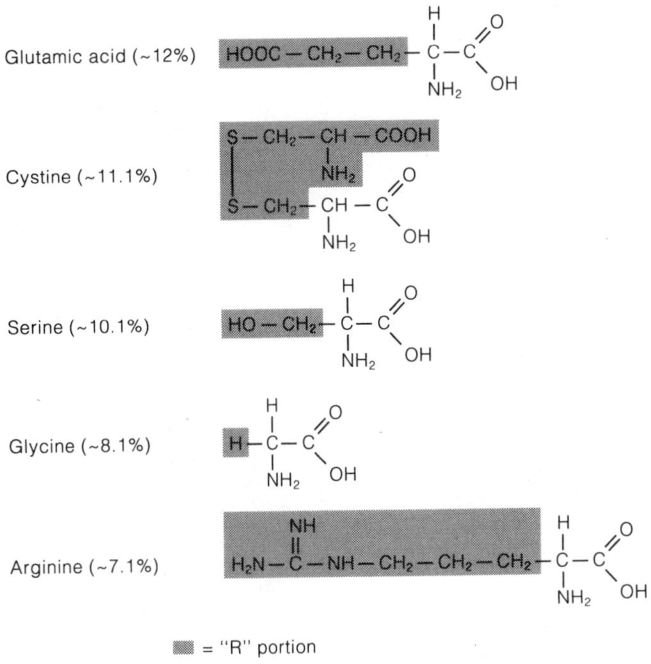

▨ = "R" portion

Influencing Fabric Comfort. Wool fiber structure and properties significantly influence thermophysiological, sensorial, and body-movement comfort.

THERMOPHYSIOLOGICAL COMFORT. Wool fibers can absorb large quantities of water. Water enters the amorphous areas and is attracted to the peptide and salt linkages. As absorption occurs, heat is liberated. Wool fiber has the highest heat of wetting of all fibers; it is of sufficient magnitude that a person wearing a wool garment can feel the heat being generated. Heat is liberated until the fiber becomes saturated, preventing the wearer from becoming chilled in cold, damp environments or when moving into and out of high and low humidities.

Wool fibers slow the rate of evaporation of body water because they hold large quantities of water vapor internally even when the external environment is hot and dry. Therefore, the relative humidity at the skin surface of a person wearing wool fibers is kept relatively high: the moisture vapor gradient from skin to external environment is kept to a minimum, lowering the rate of loss of body moisture. When it is critical to preserve body water, such as in a desert environment or in the summer sun, wearing thin wool fabrics is recommended.

Wool fibers have a natural water repellency. Their epicuticle does not permit ready saturation of liquid water, so it tends to bead up and roll off. Wool fabric, which generally has a discontinuous (fuzzy) surface, enhances water repellency. In gentle or misty rains, wool fabric sheds water. In a downpour, however, a wool fabric will not keep the wearer dry.

The thermal comfort (insulative ability) generally attributed to wool fabrics is not due to the thermal resistivity of the fibers. Rather, the three-dimensional crimp in wool fibers results in yarns and fabrics that are quite open: air space may occupy two-thirds of a wool

FIGURE 10.6 Ionic bonds and crosslinks occur when certain amino acids are in close proximity to each other.

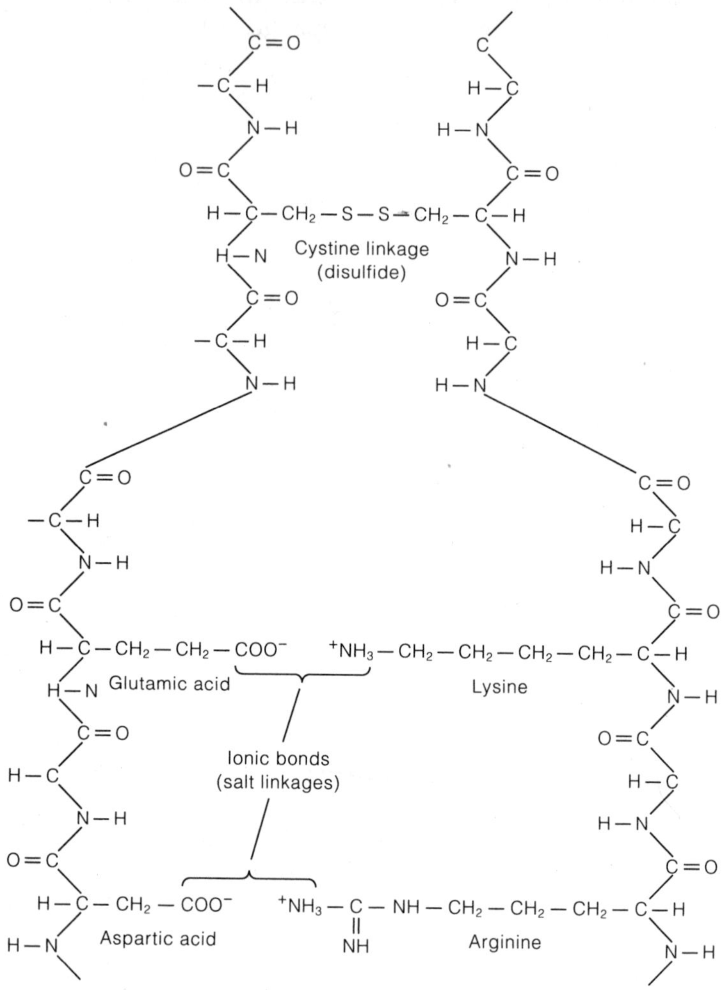

fabric by volume. During use, the air space in the fabric is maintained due to wool fiber crimp and resilience.

SENSORIAL COMFORT. A wool fiber is not very stiff compared to other fibers of equal diameter, possibly because its amorphous regions provide numerous spaces into which its polymers may be pushed when pressure is applied. In addition, the helical configuration of the fibers can give under pressure, allowing the fiber to bend.

When intolerance occurs from wearing wool fabric, it is usually a prickly or itchy sensation on the skin. Australian wool researchers have recently determined that the diameter of a wool fiber and the length of it that protrudes from the fabric surface are responsible for the un-

pleasant sensation.[4] Tests show that wool feels reasonably comfortable against the skin if the fiber diameter is less than 21 micrometers on average and if the proportion of fibers exceeding 30 micrometers is kept to a very low level. The use of 5% of coarse wool fiber in a fabric causes irritation problems.

The electrical resistivity of wool fiber is medium at its commercial moisture regain. As moisture content increases above this level, electrical resistivity decreases. When wool fiber is dry, as is the case in overheated rooms, wool garments may cling and shocks may result.

---

[4](CSIRO) Division of Wool Technology, "Understanding the Causes of Prickle and Itch from the Skin Contact of Fabrics," Report No. G64 (Geelong, Australia: Commonwealth Scientific and Industrial Organisation, February, 1988).

BODY-MOVEMENT COMFORT. Wool is a medium-weight fiber, but most wool fabrics are thick and bulky and weigh a considerable amount. Still, wool fabrics are relatively light compared to fabrics of equal thickness composed of other fibers because wool fibers have lower fiber density and pack more loosely within fabrics.

Influencing Fabric Aesthetics. The resilience, luster, odor absorption ability and low tenacity of wool fibers provide wrinkle-free, low pilling, and odorless fabrics.

RESILIENCE. The resilience of wool fiber is high. Many structural aspects of a wool fiber contribute to its resilience. The keratin polymer is helical and is crosslinked to other helical polymers, which spiral in protofibrils; protofibrils spiral in microfibrils, and microfibrils spiral in macrofibrils. The system is amorphous. The resulting orthocortex and paracortex cause three-dimensional crimp.

The resilience of wool fiber is diminished as its water content increases. Wet wool carpet should not be walked on, and wet wool garments should be carefully laid out to dry. Wool fabric that has been freshly steamed should not be worn immediately. Wool garments will be more wrinkle-free if hung for a few days after drycleaning. Wetting or steam-pressing tends to "jumble" the wool molecules, so that they pack less efficiently. Wool fiber that is allowed to dry and to rest, ages or *anneals*. During ageing, the wool molecules rearrange themselves into a more energy-efficient configuration.

Wool fabrics and carpets can be steamed to remove the wrinkles or loft the yarns. Steaming wool fabrics also permits the fabric to be tailored (molded to shape) and pleats and creases dulled by many wearings or drycleanings to be sharpened or reset. The breaking and reformation of hydrogen bonds along adjacent wool polymers accounts for this performance. The wool fibers are said to take "a temporary set." Pleats and creases also may be permanently set (Chapter 33).

LUSTER. Wool fibers have low luster. Coarser, longer wool fibers are more lustrous than fine wool fibers because they have less crimp.

PILLING PROPENSITY. Wool fabrics are subject to pilling because they generally have fuzzy surfaces. Pills do not tend to accumulate to distressing proportions because they break off due to the weakness of the wool fiber. More pilling occurs on fabrics composed of fine wool fi-

TABLE 10.1   Wool Fiber Property Summary

PROPERTY	RANK[a]
Mechanical[b]	
Tenacity	Low
Elongation	High
Elastic recovery	High
Flexibility	High
Abrasion resistance	Low to medium (apparel wool); high (carpet wool)
Stiffness (flexural rigidity)	Low
Resilience	High
Toughness (work of rupture)	Low
Initial modulus	Low
Sorptive	
Moisture regain/content	High
Cross-sectional swelling	Medium
Heat of wetting	High (highest of all fibers)
Effect on mechanical properties	High
Oil absorption	High
Ease of oil release	High
Thermal	
Heat resistance (durability)	High
Softening and melting	High (decomposes first)
Decomposition	High
Combustibility	Low
Chemical	
Alkali resistance	
Dilute	Low
Concentrated	Low
Acid resistance	
Dilute	High
Concentrated	Medium
Organic solvent resistance	High
Oxidizing agent resistance	Low
Miscellaneous	
Ultraviolet light resistance	Low
Microorganism resistance	Low
Moth and beetle resistance	Low
Silverfish resistance	High
Electrical resistivity	Medium (high when bone dry; static occurs)
Specific gravity	Medium

[a] Levels relative to other fibers except special-use synthetic fibers.

[b] At 70°F (21°C), 65% relative humidity.

bers than on fabrics composed of medium wool fibers, but the pills are easy to remove.

ABSORPTION OF ODORS. Wool fibers absorb unpleasant odors, such as the odor from perspiration, and deactivate them. Thus, significantly less underarm odor is generated when a wool fabric is worn than when a synthetic fabric is worn.

SMELL. Wet wool has a very definite animal odor that some consumers find objectionable. This limitation is more of a problem in humid than in dry environments.

Influencing Fabric Maintenance. Rate of soiling of wool fibers, release of that soil in detergent and soap solutions and in drycleaning solvents, potential degradation of wool fibers in alkaline solution, movement of wool fibers when agitated in water, and alteration of important mechanical properties all influence the establishment of wool *fabric* care procedures.

SOILING. Wool fibers may absorb large quantities of oily soil. In most use situations, the fiber's natural, waxy, water-repellent surface prevents oil absorption and permits spills to be wiped up before permanent staining occurs. Wool fibers are more resistant to oil-borne stains than to water-borne stains.[5]

Soil is readily released from wool fibers in both drycleaning solvent and in soap and detergent solutions. Steam cleaning releases soil from carpet wool.

WASHING AND DRYCLEANING. When wool fibers are placed in water, they swell and the bonds between their polymers are broken. The fiber's tenacity and modulus are reduced, and elongation is increased. The higher the water temperature, the greater the potential elongation when the fiber is pulled. A wool fabric therefore may increase in size if stressed while wet.

Wool fabric often shrinks when agitated in water. In this case, the fibers move out of relatively straight configurations and curl up on themselves. The fabric (not the fiber) shortens in length and width and becomes thicker. This action, called *felting shrinkage,* was discussed in Chapter 5.

Wool fibers are susceptible to degradation in mild alkaline solutions such as (detergent) solutions. Alkalinity weakens the keratin polymers at the salt and cystine

linkages in the fiber and increases felting. Due to this reaction to aklalies—as well as to the potential for wool fiber to elongate and for wool fabric to felt and the fiber's resistance to drycleaning solvents—it is often recommended that a wool fabric be drycleaned rather than laundered.

Wool fabrics can be hand laundered, but certain precautions are necessary. Low water temperatures are a must. Suds should be gently squeezed through the fabric. The wet article must not be wrung and should not be hung up to dry. A recommended procedure is to roll the hand-laundered wool item in a towel to remove excess moisture and then to lay this item flat to dry. Laundry products specifically formulated for hand laundering of wool fabrics are highly recommended. Bleach, particularly chlorine bleach, should not be used because it decomposes the fiber by breaking intrafiber bonds and also causes the fiber to yellow. It is recommended that a wool article remain immersed in water only for the time it takes to remove the soil to minimize fiber swelling and weakening.

POTENTIAL DEGRADATION IN STORAGE AND USE. The reaction of wool fibers to heat and ultraviolet light also influences aspects of care procedures recommended for wool fabrics. Dry heat causes the fiber to become brittle, to lose physical integrity due to breakage of the peptide and cystine linkages near its surface, and to yellow. It therefore is recommended that wool fabrics be pressed with moist heat. Wool fabrics should not be dried in sunlight, which accelerates yellowing and dulling when the wool is wet. Exposure of bleached wool to atmospheric oxygen, moisture, and pollutants tends to cause the wool to revert to its original off-white color and eventually to yellow.

Compared to other general-use fibers, wool fibers rank low in resistance to alkali and high in resistance to dilute acids but medium in resistance to concentrated acid. Its medium ranking is due to the potential degradation of the fiber in hot sulfuric acid. In the manufacture of wool fabrics, sulfuric acid is used under carefully controlled conditions in a finishing process called carbonization without degradation of the wool fiber (Chapter 30); the sulfuric acid carbonizes plant material (leaves, grass), which remains embedded in the wool fabric.

Decomposition of wool fiber is caused by bacteria and enzymes. When stored clean in a dry place, clean wool will not be attacked by bacteria and fungi. Compared to other natural fibers, wool fibers are more resistant to damage by mildew. Wool even can survive burial in soil

---

[5] Recently, a finish was developed to enhance the natural stain resistance of wool (Chapter 33).

under some conditions. Moths and beetles harm wool because it contains sulfur; stained wool is more readily attacked than unstained wool. Storage of wool garments in moth balls or in cedar chests is recommended. Chemical methods are available for mothproofing wool (Chapter 33).

Influencing Health/Safety/Protection. Wool fiber burns more slowly than most other general-use fibers, absorbs toxic odors, and fabric made from it has an outstanding ability to absorb noise.

FLAMMABILITY. A dramatic story, which illustrates wool's ability to protect the human body from burn injury, appeared in the *Australian and New Zealand Burns Association Journal.*[6] A New Zealand pilot was saved by a 100% wool pullover sweater. His plane crashed and he was thrown into a spreading pool of burning aviation fuel. The heat was so intense that it melted his metal watch strap to his skin. When the doctors cut the sweater away, they found that the skin under the wool sweater was in perfect condition. Surgeons spent a year rebuilding the pilot's badly damaged face, using skin tissue taken from his arms and chest—the parts of his body protected by the wool pullover.

Wool ranks among the least flammable of the combustible textile fibers. Dry wool burns slowly, emitting a sputtering, smoky flame. When the relative humidity is above 20%, wool fabric smolders rather than burns when a flame is held on its surface and self-extinguishes when the flame is removed. Wool is inherently self-extinguishing due to its high water content and its chemical composition. Much of the heat or kinetic energy released as wool burns is consumed in producing steam.

As it smolders or burns, wool gives off a warning smell similar to rotten eggs due to its sulfur content. A crisp, black, brittle, bead-shaped residue is formed.

The flame-resistance property of wool is adequate for most apparel purposes. However, in areas where public safety is involved and very stringent regulations are imposed, wool must be modified to improve its flame resistance (Chapter 31).

SOUND ABSORPTION. The three-dimensional crimp and felting of wool fibers contribute to an excellent sound-absorbing fabric structure. In carpeting, wool both deadens and absorbs sound. Special wool acoustic tiles may be used to reduce noise in enclosed areas. In music auditoriums, wool provides noise control. Wool felt is placed on machinery to deaden noise and is used to line high-fidelity speaker cabinets and piano hammers to attenuate the range of sound frequencies.

ENVIRONMENTAL CHEMICAL ABSORPTION. Wool fibers are extremely useful in removing toxic chemicals from the environment, particularly heavy metals. Wool has long been used to filter liquids and gases. The hydrophobic amino acids in the keratin polymer are believed to attract and hold oil. One application—an endless belt of wool fabric—dips into oil-contaminated water and picks up as much as 45 gallons (170 liters) of oil per minute; oil is continuously squeezed out of the belt.

HEALTH BENEFITS. It has been asserted that people clad in wool are better equipped to withstand stress, are less prone to respiratory diseases, have better body-temperature control, are more confident and self-reliant because they are comfortable and at ease, crave cigarettes less, suffer significantly less from rheumatic and arthritic conditions, and need less sugar to keep them warm and comfortable and therefore can slim more easily. These claims are unsubstantiated.[7]

Types of Wool Fiber

Wool fiber is often reclaimed for reuse due to its high cost and the fact that demand exceeds supply. In *reclaiming,* a manufacturer takes wool yarn or fabric (such as scraps left from garment cutting) and converts it back to a fibrous state during a process called *garnetting.* Wool fabrics that contain reclaimed wool fiber must be so labeled.[8] The correct term for reclaimed wool is "recycled"; prior to 1980, the words "reused" and "reprocessed" were used. "New wool" or "virgin wool" is wool fiber being used for the first time. If only the word "wool" appears, it is assumed to be new wool. "New or virgin wool" should not be inferred to be of superior quality to "recycled wool." Fiber damage does occur when wool fiber is reclaimed, but the "recycled" fiber still may be superior to a "new" wool fiber due to the wide range of fiber quality in new wools.

"Lamb's wool" indicates that the fiber was shorn from a sheep less than eight months old. This fiber is quite

---

[6]J. D. Leeder, *Wool: Nature's Wonder Fibre* (Victoria, Australia: Australian Textile Publishers, 1984).

[7]J. D. Leeder, *Wool: Nature's Wonder Fibre* (Victoria, Australia: Australian Textile Publishers, 1984).
[8]The Wool Products Labeling Act defines "recycled," "new," and "lamb's" wool.

fine and soft, due to the age of the animal, and because it still has a tapered rather than a blunt end.

The softest, warmest apparel fiber of the finest diameter is obtained from the Merino breed of sheep. However, Merino fiber is not the most durable wool fiber. More durable and resilient fibers come from Cheviot, Corriedale, Southdown, and Hampshire Down sheep, which produce medium-size fibers. The names of these breeds and the breeds that produce even coarser fibers usually do not appear on apparel or carpet labels.

Some proper nouns, such as "Botany" and "Shetland," convey the location where the sheep was raised. "Saxony wool" originally referred to wool fabric made from sheep raised in Saxony, Germany, but today indicates woolen fabrics similar in appearance to the original Saxony woolens.

"Worsted wool" indicates that the product contains long, staple-length wool fibers that are well oriented in the yarn (Chapter 22). "Oiled wool" has a greater percentage of lanolin left on the fiber than usual; these fibers are often used in yarns that are made into heavy sweaters, because the extra lanolin helps to shed water on drizzly days. Other words on wool-fiber product labels may give information about the finishes applied, such as "washable wool," "mothproofed wool," "flame-retardant wool," "permanent-set wool," "durable-press wool," "stain-resist wool," and "sponged" or "London shrunk wool" (Chapters 32 and 33.)

Production

About 55% of all wool fiber is produced in Australia, the Soviet Union, and New Zealand. Australia alone produces about one-half of that 55% or 25% of the world's total production. Another 30% is produced in China, Argentina, Eastern Europe, South Africa, Uruguay, Turkey, Britain, and the United States. Many other countries produce the remaining 15%.

Wool is either sheared from the sheep (*clipped* or *fleece wool*) or pulled from the hide after the sheep has been slaughtered for its meat (*pulled wool*). Clipped wool is considered to be superior in quality to pulled wool. A recent process for obtaining wool entails feeding the sheep a chemical that causes its hair to fall out within two weeks after ingestion. Fibers obtained in this way are slightly longer and less damaged than those sheared from the animal.

Most wool is clipped. An expert shearer can clip a sheep in less than a minute; sometimes it takes only 20 seconds. In the United States, shearing is done in the early spring. The fleece is removed in one piece, rolled, packed into bags, and shipped to the nearest marketing center.

Preliminary grading of wool fiber is done while the fibers are still in the fleece to establish the market value of the entire fleece. Factors used to determine the grade of the wool include fiber length and diameter, age of the animal, natural color, breed and living condition of the sheep. Usually grading is done by the wool grower prior to shipping to a marketing center. The marketer is responsible for purchasing the wool from the grower, grading the wool (if this has not been done), and selling it to a yarn or fabric manufacturer.

Fleeces are shipped in large bales to a scouring mill, where the fibers are first sorted. An expert sorter pulls each fleece apart, separating the fleece according to fiber fineness, color, and sometimes tenacity. As many as 13 different grades may be assigned. The grade of the fiber determines the type of product for which it will be used.

The sorted fibers are then *scoured* to remove wool grease (a waxy secretion of the sebaceous glands in the sheep's skin), suint (dried body excretions of the sheep), and sand, dirt, and some plant material (from the sheep's environment). *Raw wool* (uncleaned wool), may contain as much as 50% of these contaminants. The wool fibers are gently moved through a series of tubs containing a hot detergent solution, rinsed in clear water, and then dried. Lanolin, a component of wool grease, is recovered from the scouring bath, purified, and shipped to pharmaceutical or cosmetic companies. Scouring, no matter how carefully it is done, tends to tangle the fibers.

To insure product uniformity, wool fibers from different bales are blended before yarn formation begins. Often bales from different years are blended also, because fiber quality differs from year to year.

SPECIALTY WOOL

Specialty wool fibers are similar to sheep's wool in structure and properties (Figure 10.7). The specialty wools differ most from each other in fiber diameter (see Figure 7.1), length, and size, in number of fiber scales, and in natural coloration. With the exception of mohair, the specialty wool fibers are less durable than sheep's wool; fabrics made from these fibers require delicate treatment.

Cashmere. *Cashmere fibers* come from the Kashmir (Cashmere) goat; which has a long, thick, coarse outer fleece with cashmere fiber underneath. The Kashmir

wool. Guanacos, found in the Andes Mountains of South America, must be killed to obtain their pelts and fibers.

Vicuna. A vicuna is less than 3 feet (0.9 meters) high and weighs 75–100 pounds (34–45.4 kilograms). It has a distinctive apron of white hair on the neck between the front legs and white markings on its face and stomach area. A vicuna coat ranges in color from chestnut to fawn. An individual vicuna yields 4 ounces (114 grams) of very fine fiber and 10–12 ounces (284–340 grams) of shorter, less choice fiber. Vicuna are protected by the Peruvian government, which limits the number that can be taken each year. Vicuna fleece is sold exclusively under license.

Vicuna fibers are the softest, finest, rarest, and most expensive of all textile fibers. They are lustrous, silky, and delicate. The cost of a vicuna coat is comparable to a fur coat. A tailor pays $2000–$3000 for a meter of fabric that contains less than 30% vicuna fibers.[11]

Musk Ox. The musk ox, a domesticated animal in Alaska, is the source of Qiviut® (ki-vee-ute) fibers. ("Qiviut" means "down" or "underwool" in the Eskimo language.) The undercoat of the ox is combed out each spring during the shedding season; each musk ox sheds about 5 pounds (2268 grams) of the taupe-gray underwool each year. *Musk ox fibers* are as soft as cashmere. Only a ½ pound (226.8 grams) of fibers are needed to make a sweater due to the high resilience of the fiber. A Qiviut® fabric is eight times warmer than a sheep's wool fabric of identical weight.[12] Sweaters, scarves, gloves, and hats are made from Qiviut® fiber.

Yak. The yak, a bovine mammal with an oxlike build, lives in Tibet and adjacent regions. Wild yaks survive only in isolated highlands at elevations above 14,000 feet (4300 meters). The coat of the domestic yak, which is smaller than the wild yak, may be so long that it reaches the ground. *Yak fibers* can be black, brown, reddish, piebald, or albino.

Angora and Other Fur Fibers. Fiber may be clipped from animals that are usually prized for their furs or from their pelts. These fur-bearing animals include rabbit, mink, beaver, fox, chinchilla, muskrat, and raccoon.

Fur fibers usually are blended with other fibers and then spun. They add softness, color interest, and prestige value to fabrics.

One of the fur fibers often spun into yarn without being blended with other fibers is Angora. White, long haired rabbits, raised in the United States as well as in France, Italy, and Japan, are the source of these fibers. The rabbits are combed and clipped three or four times a year; each rabbit produces 12–14 ounces (340–397 grams) of fur fibers within the year.

Angora fibers are very soft, fine, and smooth, making them difficult to spin. They are silky and white but often are dyed pastel colors. Angora may be mixed with wool, staple silk, staple rayon, or staple nylon to make sweaters, scarves, and gloves.

CHAPTER SUMMARY

Wool refers to the fibers from sheep, goats, camels, oxen, and fur-bearing animals. The fibers are composed of a protein polymer called keratin. All wool fibers have scales on their external surface as well as a cortex and (often) a medulla. They are natural bicomponent fibers: protein in the orthocortex and paracortex differs slightly in its reaction to moisture.

Wool fibers are particularly unique in their ability to form fabrics with high thermal insulative capability: the three-dimensional crimp of the wool fiber reduces fiber packing and creates an air-filled fabric. Wool fibers also have the highest heat of wetting of the textile fibers. They are not strong fibers and become weaker when wet because water breaks the hydrogen bonds between their polymer chains. Drycleaning is the recommended care procedure for wool fabric due to its tendency to felt and be degraded by alkaline laundry detergents.

Sheep's wool is available in a much larger range of fiber sizes than specialty fibers, which generally have fine diameters. Sheep's wool also tends to be the more durable fiber. Most typically, sheep's wool is a white fiber that can be dyed to many beautiful colors; many specialty wool fibers contain a brown, black, or reddish pigment that is not removable.

---

[11] B. Lynn, "Politics Keeps Vicuna Off Market," *Women's Wear Daily* (October 9, 1990): 28.
[12] Data given by the Musk Ox Producers' Cooperative, Alaska.

Silk Fibers

Silk fibers are fine, strong, continuous filaments produced by the larva of certain insects, especially the silkworm, when constructing their cocoons.

Silkworm

Female silk moth

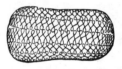

Cocoon

Chrysalis

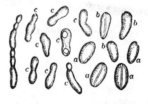

Eggs

CULTIVATED

Filament silk   Raw silk
Spun (waste) silk   Degummed silk

Duppioni
Weighted *
Pure dye *
Washable *
Scrooped *

WILD
Tussah

*Discussed in Unit V.

11

*S*ilk Fibers

Silk fiber is produced by the larva of certain insects for use in building their webs, climbing ropes, and cocoons. Spiders spin a silk filament so fine that attempts to commercially process it into yarns and fabric have not been successful. The commercial silk industry relies on the larva of one insect—the silkworm—to supply silk filament. Detail View 11 shows the silkworm at various stages in its life cycle and lists the various forms of silk fiber available.

Cultivated silk fiber is obtained from the cocoons of silkworms under the meticulous care of people called *sericulturists*. *Wild silk fiber* is obtained from the cocoons of silkworms left unattended in their natural habitat.

Today, most silk fibers are converted to apparel fabrics; minor amounts of silk fibers are used in upholstery, draperies, and bed linens.

STRUCTURE

Silk is the only natural *filament fiber*. It may be up to 656 yards (600 meters) in length, but generally averages 328 yards (300 meters). It has a very fine diameter of 12–30 micrometers, depending on the health, diet, and state under which the silkworm extruded the filament. A single silk filament is about $1\frac{1}{4}$ to $1\frac{1}{2}$ deniers in size.

Cultivated silk fiber, from which the gummy outer covering has been removed, is translucent and white. It has a soft, subdued luster. Wild silks may be tan.

Microstructure

A silk strand taken directly from a cocoon consists of two silk filaments. The strands are uneven in diameter: their irregular surfaces are marked by lumps, folds, and cracks. A coating of *sericin* (also called *gum* or *silk glue*) holds the filaments together.

Once the sericin is dissolved away, the filaments separate and, when viewed under a scanning electron microscope, appear as shown in Figure 11.1 and 11.2. Silk filaments are uneven in diameter along their length. Cultivated silk filaments have a triangular cross-sectional shape with rounded corners; wild silk filaments are almost rectangular (Figure 11.2). Wild silk is more ribbon-like in shape than cultivated silk.

Submicroscopic Structure

Cultivated silk fiber has no identifiable submicroscopic structure. It is a fine, coagulated stream of protein polymer solution. *Wild silk* or *Tussah silk*, has an internal fibrillar structure (Figure 11.3).

The Fibroin Protein Polymer

The silk polymer is a chain of amino acids forming a protein (polypeptide) called *fibroin*. The fibroin in silk is composed of 15–18 different amino acids, depending on the type of silk fiber.[1] Three amino acids—glycine, ala-

FIGURE 11.1 Photomicrographs of the longitudinal and cross-sectional views of cultivated, degummed silk.

├──────┤ 10 μm

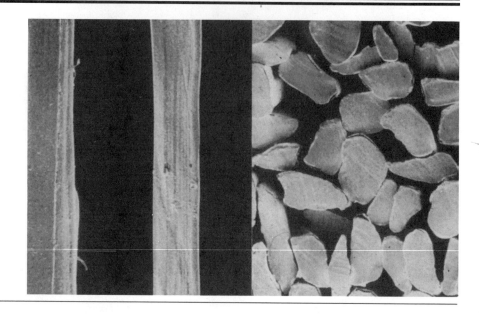

nine, and serine—make up about 86% of the fibroin polymer (Figure 11.4). These are not bulky amino acids because their "R" groups (—H, —CH₃, and —CH₂OH, respectively) are small. The relatively small size of these amino acids compared to those in keratin polymers

---

[1]The concept of protein synthesis, which involves the positioning of amino acids into a template by enzymes and the formation of bonds between amino acids, is discussed in Chapter 7 and illustrated in Figure 7.14.

(wool fiber) permits the fibroin polymers to crystallize readily. Silk fiber is estimated to be ~70–75% crystalline and, correspondingly ~30–25% amorphous. The chains lie close enough together that numerous hydrogen bonds are formed. Ionic bonds are formed also but are not the major force of attraction between fibroin chains.

Further, the fibroin protein occurs only in a pleated beta(β)-sheet configuration (Figure 11.5). The length of

FIGURE 11.2 Photomicrographs of the longitudinal and cross-sectional views of wild (Tussah) silk.

├──────┤ 25 μm

the polymer chain is slightly greater in silk fiber than in wool fiber. The differences in the number of types of amino acids, their relative sizes, and the configurations of the polymer chain account for many of the differences in the properties of silk and wool fibers.

PROPERTIES

For its producers—the silkworm and the spider—the major purposes of silk fiber are protection, transport, and food capture. Fiber durability is of the greatest significance to them. For humans, however, the luxurious aesthetics and supple feel of silk fabric against the skin are the major reasons for its use.

Silk fiber properties (summarized in Table 11.1) and the high cost of the fiber have limited the diversity of its applications in the late twentieth century. To obtain numerical values for silk fiber properties and to compare the properties of silk to other fibers, refer to Figures 8.1–8.13 and Tables 8.1–8.8.

Influencing Fabric Durability

Silk fiber has the highest tenacity of the protein fibers, but compared to all general-use fibers, its tenacity lies in the mid-range. The degree of orientation of its polymers, the degree of crystallinity, and the strength of hydrogen bonding account for its level of tenacity.

Silk has a medium elongation at break. When elongated 2%, its elastic recovery is 90%—high compared to other fibers. Its modulus lies in the mid-range.

Silk is moderately resistant to abrasion. In many of its end uses, this level of abrasion resistance does not present a problem. Silk upholstery fabrics may or may not be sufficiently abrasion resistant, depending on specific use and fabric construction.

Influencing Fabric Comfort

Thermophysiological Comfort. Silk fiber can absorb water up to one-third its weight without feeling wet to the touch (it is hydrophilic and hygroscopic). Water vapor that is emitted from the skin but is not able to diffuse through a silk fabric can be absorbed by the fiber, so that the skin remains dry. Heat of wetting is high, but it is not sufficient to be perceived by an individual wearing a silk fabric.

The greater crystallinity of the silk fiber polymer system compared to that of wool fiber limits the accessibil-

FIGURE 11.3 Longitudinally split filament of Tussah (wild) silk, showing its internal fibrillar structure.

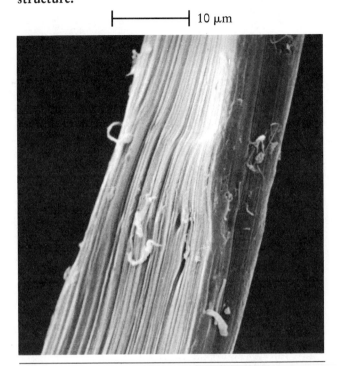

├──────────────┤ 10 μm

ity of sites that attract water. Absorbency and heat of wetting are therefore lower in silk than in wool fiber.

Silk fabrics are generally thought of as warm-weather fabrics. The smooth silk filaments lie against the skin

FIGURE 11.4 The three amino acids that occur most frequently along the fibroin polypeptide polymer in silk fiber.

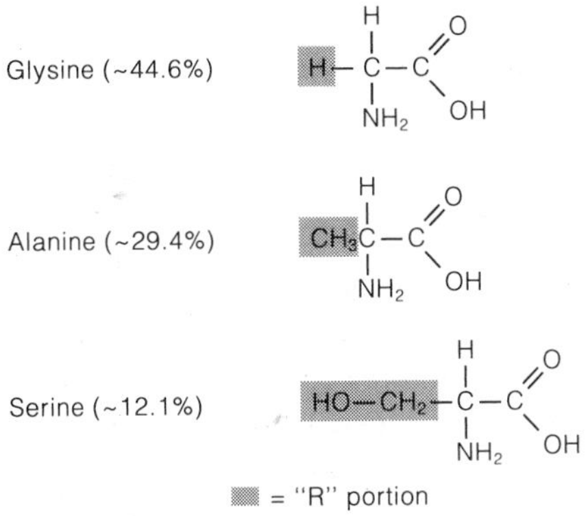

Glycine (~44.6%)

Alanine (~29.4%)

Serine (~12.1%)

▓ = ''R'' portion

FIGURE 11.5 The pleated (β)-sheet structure in the fibroin protein of silk fibers.

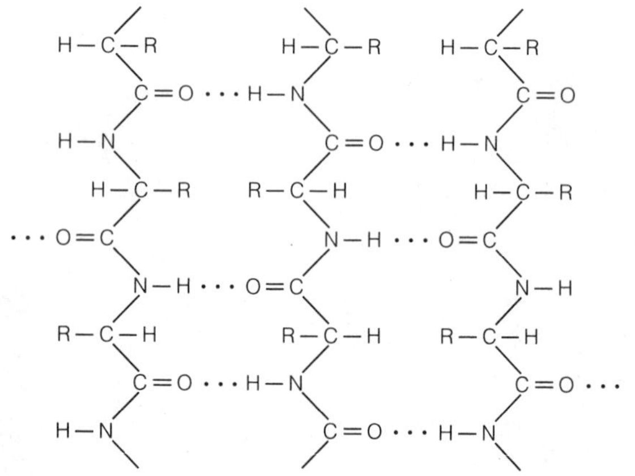

··· = hydrogen bonding

surface, creating a cool feeling. They pack tightly into yarns, but fabrics are generally open. When spun silk is used, sufficient air is incorporated into the fabric to provide some insulation.

Sensorial Comfort. Silk is sought for the sensorial comfort it provides. Filament silk fabrics are smooth and soft and feel cool. Spun silk fabrics feel warmer against the skin than filament silk fabrics. Static cling may result, particularly when the humidity is low.

Body-movement Comfort. The specific gravity of silk is medium. However, fabrics are usually thin, so the tendency is to think of silk as a low specific gravity fiber.

Influencing Fabric Aesthetics

The very word "silk" connotes softness, elegance, and luxury. Silk fiber is woven and knitted into a tremendous variety of fabrics.

Luster. The luster of silk fiber from which the gum has been removed is higher than that of gummed silk fiber. The luster of degummed silk fiber is soft with an occasional sparkle, due largely to the crystallinity of the fiber and its triangular cross section. Turning of the filament

along its length softens the luster by slightly scattering incident light. Luster is greater in filament form than in spun form, because there are few fiber ends to scatter the light randomly.

Resilience. Silk fiber has medium resilience. When a force pulls on a silk fiber, its polymers, which are already in an extended state (β configuration), cannot elongate so polymer slippage occurs. Hydrogen bonds are broken. When the force ceases, little work is done to return the polymers to their original positions. The polymers remain in their new positions, where new hydrogen bonds have been formed. This disorganizes the polymer system and results in wrinkling or bagging of the fabric.

Scroop. It is a mistaken claim that untreated silk fabric has *scroop* (makes a rustling sound). Some silk fabrics have scroop, but this is due to an acid treatment to silk fabric (Chapter 32). The acid causes the surface of the silk fiber to harden, which results in a dry, rustling sound when the treated fabric moves.

Influencing Fabric Maintenance

Drycleanable or Launderable. Silk fiber swells (~20% in cross-sectional area) because absorbed water breaks interpolymer hydrogen bonds and forces the polymers apart. The absorbed water causes silk fiber to lose up to 20% of its tenacity. Modulus is lowered, so the fiber is easier to elongate when wet than dry. Silk fiber is degraded by mild alkaline solutions and by oxidizing agents. Alkaline solutions cause yellowing, dulling, and degradation of silk due to rearrangement of and some shortening of polymers lying close to the fiber surface. Prolonged exposure leads to hydrolysis of the peptide chains; the polymer chains break, and a complete destruction of the silk fiber occurs. Silk fiber is stable in organic solvents. When exposed to high heat, silk fiber discolors and scorches. These properties suggest that silk fabric may be drycleaned and that, if laundered, special precautions need to be taken.

When silk fabric is hand-washed, a mild detergent or soap solution and gentle agitation are recommended. The fabric should not be left to soak for an extended period of time. Chlorine bleaches must never be used; bleaches of hydrogen peroxide and sodium perborate (powdered oxygen bleaches) are safe if the directions on the product are carefully followed. Water should be squeezed through wet silk (never wrung). The item should be rolled in a bath towel to remove excess water (never hung wet to dry) and then hung indoors, away from heat. Wild silk should be left to dry thoroughly. Other silks should be rolled in a towel when they are still damp to keep them damp until they are pressed. Using a press cloth and pressing on the wrong side of the fabric with the iron set at a moderate temperature are recommended.

Whether a silk fabric is labeled "dryclean" or "hand wash" depends more on the nature of the dyes and finishes or the yarn structure than on the fiber content. Some silks must be drycleaned because the dyes and sizings used are soluble in water; others must be hand-washed because the dyes and sizings are solvent-soluble. Silk fabrics containing crepe twisted yarns (highly twisted yarns, Chapter 24) must be drycleaned to prevent excessive fabric shrinkage: exposure to water can result in 50% or greater shrinkage of these silk fabrics. The new "washable silks" (Chapter 33) should not be drycleaned; care label directions must be followed.

Potential Degradation in Storage and Use. Silk is readily degraded by mineral acids, because it does not have covalent crosslinks between polymer chains. (Silk lacks the sulfur linkages found in wool.) Thus, perspiration, which is acidic, will cause the immediate breakdown of the silk polymer system—usually noticed as a distinct weakening of a silk fabric. Silk fabric manufacturers use the contraction of silk fiber that occurs during exposure to moderate concentration of mineral acids to produce crinkly, crepe surface effects in silk fabrics. Fabric manufacturers also use organic acids to harden the surface of silk filament, thereby producing scroop (Chapter 32).

Silk fiber is rated the lowest of all fibers in terms of resistance to the degrading effects of ultraviolet light. Compared to wool, silk is less resistant because it does not contain covalent sulfur crosslinks. Silk fabrics should be protected from exposure to direct sunlight and lighting that has an ultraviolet component.

Silk may be attacked by insects, especially carpet beetles. Silk is highly resistant to moths because the cystine amino acid, which contains sulfur, is not a component of the silk protein (fibroin). Care should be taken when storing silks to be sure they are clean: soil may attract insects that normally would not attack a silk fabric.

Silk is degraded by atmospheric oxygen. Textile curators in museums take special precautions in the storage and display of historic silk textiles to prevent further deterioration of fabric structures.

TABLE 11.1   Silk Fiber Property Summary

PROPERTY	RANK[a]
Mechanical[b]	
Breaking tenacity	Medium (strongest protein fiber)
Elongation	Medium
Elastic recovery	Medium
Flexibility	—
Abrasion resistance	Moderate
Stiffness (flexural rigidity)	Medium
Resilience	Medium
Toughness (work of rupture)	High
Initial modulus	Medium
Sorptive	
Moisture regain/content	High
Cross-sectional swelling	Medium
Heat of wetting	High but lower than wool
Effect on mechanical properties	High
Oil absorption	—
Ease of oil release	—
Thermal	
Heat resistance (durability)	Low
Softening and melting	High (decomposes first)
Decomposition	—
Combustibility	Low
Chemical	
Alkali resistance	
Dilute	Low
Concentrated	Low
Acid resistance	
Dilute	Medium
Concentrated	Low
Organic solvent resistance	High
Oxidizing agent resistance	Low
Miscellaneous	
Ultraviolet light resistance	Low
Microorganism resistance	Medium
Moth resistance	High
Beetle resistance	Low
Silverfish resistance	High
Electrical resistivity	Medium
Specific gravity	Medium

[a]Levels relative to other fibers except special-use synthetic fibers.

[b]At 70°F (21°C), 65% relative humidity.

Influencing Health/Safety/Protection

Silk fiber will ignite and burn. It will sometimes self-extinguish after removal of the flame. It leaves a crisp, brittle ash.

PRODUCTION

Most commercial silk is obtained from the cocoons of a species of moth known as *bombyx,* particularly from a variety called *bombyx mori.* The silkworms formed in the life cycle of this moth feed exclusively on the leaves of the mulberry tree (*morus*) and produce *cultivated* silk. The *bombyx mori* has lived as a domesticated species for thousands of years. Other species of moth (*Antheraea mylitta* and *Antheraea pernyi*) lay their eggs in the wild. The silkworms formed in their life cycle feed on oak and mulberry leaves and produce *wild* silk. Cultivated and wild silk differ in structure and performance.

The first step in the production of silk fiber is the raising of disease-free eggs. Each moth can lay a maximum of 700 eggs; about 50 moths will lay about 1 ounce (28.4 grams) of eggs. Each female moth is examined microscopically and, if disease is present, her eggs are destroyed. The disease-free eggs are placed in cold storage for about 10 months and then sold to the sericulture industry, which is responsible for raising the silkworms. Hatching, usually done in incubators, is timed with the emergence of new leaves on the mulberry trees. Cultivated silkworms eat only tender, slightly wilted mulberry leaves.

Silkworms eat almost continuously for 35 days, consuming prodigious quantities of leaves. The 36,000 silkworms that hatch from 1 ounce (28.4 grams) of eggs will eat 1 ton (907 kilograms) of mulberry leaves. After about 35 days and four moltings, one silkworm has consumed 50 times its weight in mulberry leaves (22 grams) and is approximately 10,000 times heavier than when it was born. At this point in the life cycle, the silkworms are huge and bloated—filled with synthesized protein, a liquid silk. Now they are ready to begin spinning a cocoon, or chrysalis case. The silkworms crawl onto straw frames and begin the spinning process by moving their heads in a figure eight.

The silkworm forces the liquid silk—the fibroin, contained in two glands inside the worm—through two openings in its head. The two streams of liquid harden on contact with the air. As the fibroin is extruded, the water-soluble gum (sericin) flows from two nearby glands. It keeps the two strands of silk joined and provides a glue to hold the cocoon together. In two or three days, the silkworm can completely surround itself with 1 mile (1.6 kilometers) of silk filament. At this time, the silkworm begins its transformation to a chrysalis and then into a moth. In its normal life sequence, the moth secretes a substance that dissolves the silk so it can emerge from the cocoon. The sericulturist prevents the emergence of the moth, so the silk filament remains one continuous length. The chrysalis is stifled (killed) with heat before it reaches the moth stage.

The 36,000 silkworms produce about 140 pounds (66.5 kilograms) of cocoons, or about 12 pounds (5.4 kilograms) of raw silk (fiber covered with sericin).[2] After the silk is unwound from the cocoon into skeins by a process called *reeling* and converted to suitable yarns by a process called *throwing,* about one-half of the silk fiber obtained is in filament form and one-half is staple length silk or spun silk.[3] When the sericin is removed, the weight of the fiber is reduced by as much as one-fourth.

Wild silkworms are easier to raise because they tend to their own needs, but the gathering of the cocoons from the oak trees takes time and patience. A considerable proportion of the cocoons are already pierced or damaged in some way, so that filament silk cannot be obtained.

In 1990, worldwide production of silk fiber was 145.5 million pounds (11.2 million pounds was imported to the United States).[4] About 95% was produced in five countries—Japan, China, the Soviet Union, India, and South Korea—where labor is cheap and climate permits the growing of mulberry trees.

For centuries, China was the sole producer of silk due to stringent laws (the penalty for exportation of moth eggs was death) and its isolation from the rest of the world. Chinese legend dates the beginning of silk sericulture as early as 2700 B.C., when the Empress was instructed by the Emperor to study the silkworm and learn whether its thread might contribute to the happiness of his people. Legend says she succeeded in obtaining sufficient silk fiber for a ceremonial garment for the Emperor.

TYPES OF SILK FIBER

The names of many forms of silk, some already introduced in this chapter, may appear on fabric labels in the consumer marketplace.

[2]J. G. Cook, *Handbook of Textile Fibres: Natural Fibres,* 5th ed. (Durham, England: Merrow Publishing, 1984), p. 149.
[3]More detail about the processes of reeling and throwing can be found in Chapter 24 where filament yarn formation is discussed.
[4]Data provided by the International Silk Association.

Raw silk is silk-in-the-gum (silk from which the sericin has not been removed). Many times the term "raw silk" is used incorrectly to describe wild silk. Wild silk may or may not have the gum removed.

The most important commercial type of wild silk is *Tussah*. Most wild silks are available only as staple length fiber, but Tussah silk may be in filament form because the Tussah silkworm leaves a hole covered with sericin at the end of the chrysalis to permit easy escape. Tussah silk is usually light brown but can be light shades of yellow, orange, or green. Fabrics made from Tussah silk are not available in white or light colors because the natural color cannot be bleached from the fiber. These fabrics have a rough linen appearance due to the unevenness of the fibers.

Duppioni silk results when two cultivated silkworms spin their cocoons together. The yarn is irregular in diameter; the fabric has a thick-and-thin appearance due to the fiber and yarn structure. The linen-look is much like Tussah silk fabric, but a Duppioni silk fabric may be brilliantly colored because the original fiber is white.

When a label states *"pure dye silk,"* this does not mean that the dye in the fabric is purer than it is in another fabric. It indicates that the silk contains less than 15% weighting for black and 10% weighting for all other colors. *Weighting*, a finish applied routinely to silk fabrics, adds back some of the weight lost when the gum is removed. Large percentages of weighting, which used to be frequently done, have a detrimental affect on silk fiber (Chapter 32). When silk fabric is heavily weighted, then by federal law, the label must specify the amount of weighting.

"Washable silk" is a recent technology. The finishing treatment used to produce washable silk is discussed in Chapter 33.

In the future, spider silk may be an important type of silk. In February 1990, a genetic scientist in the U.S. Army announced the discovery of a way to mass-produce tough spider silk.[5] J. E. Bishop extracted a gene from a

---

[5] J. E. Bishop, "Army Genetic Scientist Says He's Found Way to Mass-Produce Tough Spider Silk," *The Wall Street Journal* (February 26, 1990): A5A.

golden orb weaver spider and transferred it to a standard laboratory bacteria, which then produced the fibroin protein that comprises silk. Bishop also discovered a method of dissolving this protein and extruding it into a fiber. The spider silk produced has a tensile strength 5–10 times higher than a steel wire of similar diameter. It can be elongated by as much as 18% without breaking and is easily dyed. The Army intends to use the *genetically engineered spider silk* to make lighter and stronger bullet-proof vests and helmets. It also may be used in parachute cording, as well as lightweight tents, sleeping bags, and clothing.

CHAPTER SUMMARY

Silk is a fine, strong, continuous filament produced by the larva of certain insects, especially the silkworm, when constructing their cocoons. It is a natural protein fiber composed of fibroin. When extruded by the silkworm, two filaments are held together by a gum called sericin. The two main types of silk fiber—cultivated and wild—differ in diameter (cultivated is generally finer), evenness of diameter (cultivated is more even than wild); cross-sectional shape (cultivated is triangular; wild is rectangular), and submicroscopic structure (wild silk has a fibrillated structure; cultivated has no discernible structure). Further, cultivated silk is white and is dyed a wide range of colors; wild silks tend to be slightly yellow or brown. The most important commercial silk is cultivated.

Filament silk fibers are smooth and produce a cool sensation when placed on the skin. They are hydrophilic and hygroscopic and produce some heat as moisture is absorbed. Silk fibers are not affected by drycleaning solvents. In water, their strength is decreased. They are particularly susceptible to deterioration from mild alkalies, chlorine bleach, sunlight, perspiration, and heat.

Types of silk include filament or spun, cultivated or wild, and raw or degummed. Duppioni and Tussah are types of cultivated and wild silk, respectively. Silk fibers may be altered in finishing, resulting in weighted silk, scrooped silk, and washable silk.

Cotton Fibers

Cotton fibers are unicellular, natural fibers obtained from the boll of the cotton plant.

Flower   Boll   Open boll

COMMODITY VARIETIES   **LONG STAPLE VARIETIES**   **OTHER VARIETIES**
Upland   Pima-SuPima   Colored
                                   Sea Island
                                   Egyptian

CHEMICALLY MODIFIED*
Mercerized
Formaldehyde Treated
Liquid-Ammonia Treated
Flame-Retardant Treated
Durable-Press Treated
Water-Repellent Treated

*Discussed in Unit V.

12

*C*otton Fibers

Cotton is a seed hair obtained from the boll of the cotton plant. On average, 4000 fibers emerge from a single cotton seed; up to 20,000 fibers can be generated by one seed, or more than 250,000 fibers to the boll.[1] Detail View 12 shows an opened cotton boll, the flower of the cotton plant, and an unopened boll. Types of cotton fiber are also listed.

Cotton fiber provides a set of properties that leads to acceptable fabric performance in over 100 different textile end uses.[2] In the United States in 1990, 65% of all cotton fiber was made into apparel fabrics for men, women, boys, girls, and infants (Figure 12.1). More than half of all fiber used in the manufacture of apparel fabrics is cotton, making cotton the most used apparel fiber. The manufacture of household and institutional textiles, such as sheets and towels, consumed an additional 27% of cotton fiber, or about a fourth of the fiber used in that market. Industrial and consumer textile products accounted for more than 7% of cotton consumption.

STRUCTURE

The cotton fiber is a single plant cell. The structure of this cell is quite complex.

---

[1] J. G. Cook, *Handbook of Textile Fibres I. Natural Fibres* (Durham, England: Merrow Publishing Co. Ltd., 1984), p. 39.
[2] National Cotton Council of America, "Cotton: From Field to Fabric" (Memphis: NCCA, 1981).

Macrostructure

Cotton fibers are *staple length* fibers ranging from $\frac{1}{8}$ inch to $2\frac{1}{2}$ inches (0.32–6.35 centimeters) in length. Most cotton fibers used in the manufacture of yarns and fabrics are $\frac{7}{8}$ inch to $1\frac{1}{4}$ inches (2.22–3.18 centimeters) long.

Among textile fibers, a cotton fiber has one of the smallest diameters, ranging from 16 to 20 micrometers (Figure 7.1). As a cotton fiber becomes longer it usually becomes narrower. The fiber length-to-breadth ratio ranges from about 6000:1 for the longest and smallest diameter types to about 350:1 for the shortest and widest types. In general, the longer the length of the staple, the higher the fiber quality.

A cotton fiber is fairly uniform in width along much of its length; the central portion is wider than either end, however. Immature fibers are normally more irregular than mature fibers.

The color of the fiber is never truly white; it varies from creamy white to dirty grey. The whiter the fiber, the higher its quality. Off-white cotton can be bleached.

Microstructure

Mature cotton appears as a *flat, twisted ribbon* (Figure 12.2; see Detail View 12). The fiber tip, which is less than one-quarter of the fiber length, tapers to a cylindrical point. The seed end of the fiber is irregular, having been torn from the epidermis (skin) of the cotton seed.

FIGURE 12.1 Primary market distribution of
4448 million pounds of cotton fiber produced in the
United States and shipped to domestic consumers
in 1989.

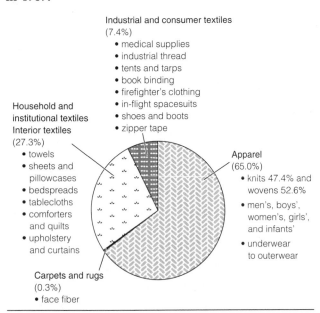

Industrial and consumer textiles
(7.4%)
- medical supplies
- industrial thread
- tents and tarps
- book binding
- firefighter's clothing
- in-flight spacesuits
- shoes and boots
- zipper tape

Household and
institutional textiles
Interior textiles
(27.3%)
- towels
- sheets and
  pillowcases
- bedspreads
- tablecloths
- comforters
  and quilts
- upholstery
  and curtains

Apparel
(65.0%)
- knits 47.4% and
  wovens 52.6%
- men's, boys',
  women's, girls',
  and infants'
- underwear
  to outerwear

Carpets and rugs
(0.3%)
- face fiber

A single fiber averages 125 twists, or *convolutions*, per inch (50 per centimeter) along its length (see Figure 12.2). The twists reverse in direction along the fiber length. No other fiber has a similar structure. Therefore, a microscope can be used to positively identify cotton fiber.

Mature cotton has a *kidney-bean, cross-sectional shape*. Some fibers are nearly circular; some are elliptical (Figure 12.2).

Submicroscopic Structure

The cotton fiber is composed of five distinct regions (Figure 12.3). The cuticle—the "skin" of the cotton fiber—is a waxy layer only a few molecules thick. The inert nature of the wax could protect the rest of the fiber against chemical and other degrading agents during consumer use, but scouring and bleaching (routine processes in cotton fabric manufacture) remove much of it. Laundering gradually removes most of the remaining cuticle.

The *primary cell wall* is composed of very fine structures called *fibrils*. The primary cell wall can be visualized as a sheath of spiraling fibrils; each layer spirals 20–30° to the fiber axis. Mature fibers have thick primary walls; immature fibers, thin primary walls. When the cell wall is too thin, the fiber bends and becomes entangled. In processing immature cotton fiber, clumps, called *neps*, are formed. The presence of neps in yarns and fabrics lowers the quality of the cotton textile: fabrics do not dye uniformly, and the fabric surface is irregular.

FIGURE 12.2 Photomicrograph showing the longitudinal and cross-sectional views of cotton fiber.

├─────┤ 25 μm

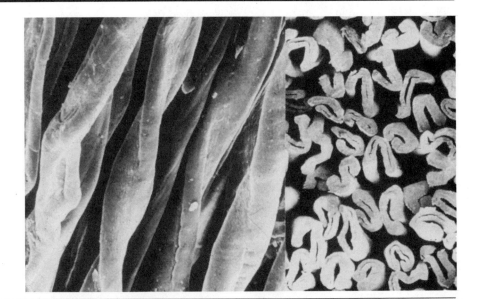

Beneath the primary cell wall lies the *secondary cell wall*, which forms the bulk of the fiber. Concentric layers of spiraling fibrils, not unlike the growth rings of trees, make up the secondary wall. Each of these 20 or so spiraling layers is formed during a single day's growth. The first layer of the secondary wall differs somewhat in structure from the remainder of this wall, so it is specifically named the *winding layer*. Whenever the fibrils change the direction of their spirals, a weak area exists in the secondary wall structure. At these weak areas, the fiber alters the direction of twist.

The hollow canal, running the length of the fiber, is the *lumen*. The lumen was once full of cell sap. As the sap evaporated, the fiber collapsed inward, accounting for the twisted-ribbon longitudinal form and kidney-shaped cross section of the cotton fiber. Immature cotton fibers have large lumens. Mature fibers have small lumens that may not be continuous because the wall closes the lumen in some sections.

Polymer System

The fibrils in the spiraling layers are composed of linear cellulose polymers. The degree of polymerization of cotton cellulose ranges from 6000 to 10,000. The most important chemical group on the cellulose polymer is the hydroxyl group (—OH).

Even though the cellulose polymer is composed of six-membered puckered rings, the polymers can pack closely together. About 65–70% of the cotton fiber is crystalline, and 35–30% is amorphous.

As shown in Figure 12.5, hydrogen bonding does *not* occur between polymers at every site where two hydroxyl groups lie opposite one another. (Actually, these groups are not close enough for hydrogen bonding to occur.) Rather, hydrogen bonding involves the oxygen atom located between rings and the hydroxyl group attached to the sixth carbon atom (see the dotted line in Figure 12.4). This bonding confers strength and additional rigidity to the fiber.

Hydroxyl groups will react with a variety of chemicals, which allows the textile chemist to modify cotton fiber by reacting chemical finishing resins with it. Hydroxyl groups also attract and hold water in the fiber.

The backbone of the polymer chain is made up of carbon-oxygen-carbon (—C—O—C—) bonds. These bonds are more subject to breaking by oxidation than carbon to carbon (—C—C—C—) bonds.

It has been estimated that as much as 20–41% of the volume of a cotton fiber consists of unoccupied space.

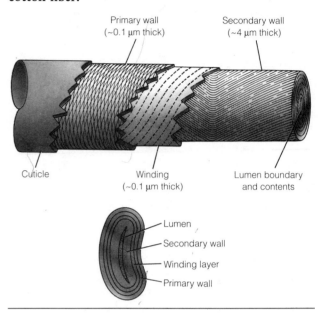

FIGURE 12.3   The submicroscopic structure of cotton fiber.

Primary wall (~0.1 µm thick)

Secondary wall (~4 µm thick)

Cuticle

Winding (~0.1 µm thick)

Lumen boundary and contents

Lumen

Secondary wall

Winding layer

Primary wall

One-third of this space is accounted for by the lumen; the rest, by the spaces among the fibrils in the fiber walls. In general, coarser varieties of cotton are more porous than finer cottons.[3]

PROPERTIES

The properties that make cotton fiber such a widely used fiber are summarized in Table 12.1. To obtain numerical values for cotton fiber properties and to compare the properties of cotton to other fibers, refer to Figures 8.1–8.13 and Tables 8.1–8.8.

Influencing Fabric Durability

The tenacity and initial modulus of cotton fiber are medium, and its elongation at break is low. When a longitudinal force acts on a cotton fiber, it is thought that the force first pulls the polymers that are spiraling around the fiber in the primary and secondary walls more into

---

[3] D. S. Hamby, ed., *The American Cotton Handbook*, 3d ed., Vols. 1 and 2 (New York: Wiley Interscience Publishers, 1965).

FIGURE 12.4 Hydrogen bonding occurs between adjacent polymer chains in the crystalline areas of a cotton fiber only between polar groups that are appropriately positioned in space. The positions are the oxygen linking two six-membered rings on one polymer and the hydroxyl group attached to carbon number six on the adjacent polymer.

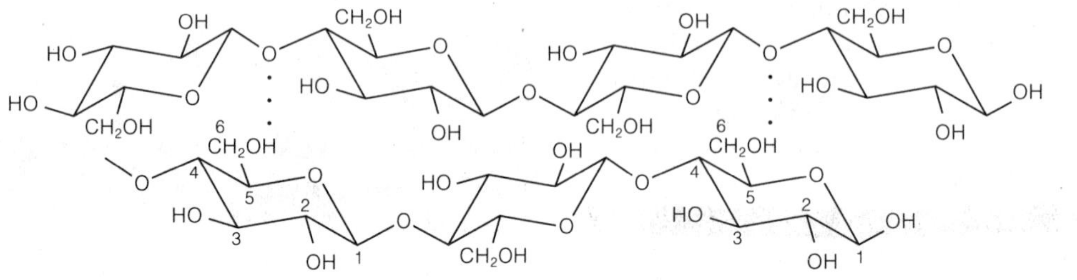

• • • = hydrogen bonding

alignment with the fiber axis. Some elongation of the fiber occurs because the polymers change from spiraling to being more in alignment with the fiber axis. Then the force begins to stress the polymers themselves. Numerous, strong hydrogen bonds work to prevent the polymers from slipping by one another as force is increased. The fiber elongates very little under increasing force due to the effectiveness of the hydrogen bonded system. In the highly crystalline cotton fiber, the strength of the covalent bonds along the polymer chain is lower than the strength of the hydrogen bonded network, so the cotton fiber breaks instead of elongating very much.

Elastic recovery of cotton fiber is low; its recovery is only 75% at 2% extension. At 5% extension, cotton exhibits less than 50% elastic recovery. When the fiber is elongated (although not very far), hydrogen bonds are broken. They reform as the polymers slide by one another. When the stress is removed, the polymers stay bonded in their new locations.

Abrasive action on a cotton fabric surface tears fiber cell walls, cracks fibers, and breaks fiber tips. This damage appears as a thinning of the cotton fabric.

Influencing Fabric Comfort

The cotton fiber is fairly rigid and stiff. Small variations in the diameters of cotton fibers make a considerable difference in fiber stiffness and in the next-to-skin comfort of fabric made from them. The larger the fiber diameter, the stiffer the cotton fiber and the more harsh the cotton

fabric feels. The naturally tapered ends of the cotton fiber yield pleasurably to the touch. The convolutions and kidney-shaped cross section of the cotton fiber permit it to contact the skin only at random, which is considered to be comfortable.

Cotton is a hydrophilic fiber. At 65% relative humidity and 70°F (21°C), its regain is 8.5%; at 95% relative humidity, 15%; and at 100% relative humidity, as high as 25–27%. The high degree of moisture content is partially due to water being attracted to the numerous hydroxyl groups. It also is due to the drawing up of water between the various layers or walls and the absorption of water between the many fibrils on the fiber surface. Water molecules enter the polymer system in its amorphous regions but not in its crystalline regions, because the interpolymer spaces in the crystalline regions are too small. As cotton fiber absorbs moisture, it becomes less rigid. Wet cotton fabric therefore collapses onto the skin surface, increasing its contact area with the skin. Wet cotton fabric is generally considered uncomfortable. Because cotton dries slowly (the water is tightly bound within the fiber), the wearer can become chilled rapidly.

Under drier conditions, cotton fabric is often considered comfortable. Cotton fiber absorbs water vapor emitted by the body, so the skin does not become wet. Considerable heat is given off as the fiber picks up moisture. This heat is usually not perceptible to the wearer of a cotton garment, however. In addition, the kidney-bean shape of the cotton fiber leads to yarn and fabric structures that are generally open enough to permit the passage of water vapor. The amount of moisture taken up by cotton fiber at low humidities also eliminates problems with static accumulation.

Water-resistant fabrics may be made from cotton fibers because they swell in water. Cotton fabric can be constructed closely enough so that when it becomes wet, the swelling of the fibers within it is sufficient to fill the fabric pores. A fabric results that is sufficiently compact to prevent liquid water from penetrating but open enough to permit water vapor to pass through. A water-repellent treatment is usually applied to the closely woven cotton fabric so that water will bead up on its surface (Chapter 31).

Cotton is used in greater quantities for hot-weather than for cold-weather apparel fabrics. The way in which the cotton fiber is constructed into yarns and fabric determines whether the cotton fabric is suitable for use in hot or cold weather. Smooth-surfaced and open-structured cotton fabrics are excellent for summer wear; fuzzy-surfaced and close-structured cotton fabrics are more suited for winter use. Consumers appreciate the cool feel of cotton percale sheets in the summer and the warm feel of cotton flannel sheets in the winter.

Cotton is one of the most dense (heaviest) of the commonly used fibers. However, the narrow diameter of the cotton fiber and the ability to make fine cotton yarns of adequate strength permit fine, lightweight cotton fabrics to be manufactured.

Influencing Fabric Maintenance

Soiling. Cotton fiber is susceptible to water-borne soiling due to its highly hydrophilic nature. It also absorbs large quantities of oil, which can fill the lumen and lie between the numerous internal layers. Solid dirt particles become lodged in the convolutions of the fiber. However, cotton fiber readily releases oily and particulate soil in laundry solution and drycleaning solvents. Graying and yellowing of cotton fiber can be avoided by following appropriate care procedures.

Launderability. Cotton fibers are dimensionally stable in water. They swell but then return to their original diameter as they dry. When wet and subject to agitation (stress), cotton fiber increases in tenacity. Its wet tenacity may be 10–20% greater than its dry tenacity. Cotton is one of the few fibers to gain tenacity when wet. The increase in tenacity is thought to be due to a temporary improvement in polymer alignment in the amorphous regions of the polymer system as a function of swelling.

TABLE 12.1 **Cotton Fiber Property Summary**

PROPERTY	RANK[a]
Mechanical[b]	
Tenacity	Medium
Elongation	Low
Elastic recovery	Low
Flexibility	Low
Abrasion resistance	Medium
Stiffness (flexural rigidity)	Medium
Resilience	Low
Toughness (work of rupture)	Low
Initial modulus	Medium
Sorptive	
Moisture regain/content	High
Cross-sectional swelling	Medium to High
Heat of wetting	Medium (not perceptible)
Effect on mechanical properties	High
Oil absorption	High
Ease of oil release	High
Thermal	
Heat resistance (durability)	Medium
Softening and melting	High (decomposes first)
Decomposition	High
Combustibility	High
Chemical	
Alkali resistance	
Dilute	High
Concentrated	High (swells)
Acid resistance	
Dilute	Low when hot
Concentrated	Low
Organic solvent resistance	High
Oxidizing agent resistance	Medium
Miscellaneous	
Ultraviolet light resistance	Medium
Microorganism resistance	Low
Moth and beetle resistance	High
Silverfish resistance	Low
Electrical resistivity	Low (static not a problem)
Specific gravity	High

[a]Levels relative to other fibers except special-use synthetic fibers.

[b]At 70°F (21°C), 65% relative humidity.

Further, the uptake of water in the lumen untwists the fiber, which improves tenacity.

These fiber properties may mean that no special precautions need to be taken when laundering cotton fabric to avoid vigorous agitation, wringing or twisting the fabric to remove water, or hanging it up wet to dry. Cotton fabric shrinks during laundering due to relaxation of yarn tension introduced during fabric manufacture rather than to fiber distortion.

Cotton fiber is highly resistant to degradation by alkalies, so all detergents on the market—including the non-phosphate detergents, which are the most alkaline—can be used. Although cotton fiber absorbs oil and water-based soils, it releases them during "normal" laundering. A detergent solution can wet the hydrophilic fiber surface and permeate the fiber structure to remove oils.

Both chlorine and oxygen bleaches can be used, although prolonged or overuse of bleach causes degradation of the cotton fiber. Careful bleaching leaves the fiber polymer system largely intact; the bleaching action is restricted to the polymers on the fiber surface.[4]

Potential Degradation in Storage and Use. Strong acids degrade cotton fiber. Hot, dilute acids cause the fiber to disintegrate. Cold, dilute acids cause gradual fiber degradation; the process is slow and may not be immediately evident. Air pollutants, which are usually acidic, lead to eventual fiber degradation. Curators usually store or display antique cotton articles in acid-free paper, because acids would act on the cellulose polymer. Mineral or inorganic acids, which are stronger than organic acids, will degrade (*hydrolyze*) the cotton polymer more rapidly. Acidic conditions break (hydrolyze) the cotton polymer at the glucoside oxygen atom, which links the glucose units forming the polymer chain.

Cotton is highly resistant to most organic solvents, including those used in normal care and stain removal. Cotton is soluble in cuprammonium hydroxide and cupriethylene diamine, but these chemicals are not encountered in everyday living and are relatively minor considerations.

Cotton fibers are damaged by fungi, such as mildew, and by bacteria. Damage is evident as a disagreeable odor and/or stains and as a weakening of the fiber. The odors and stains are difficult to remove, but the textile can be restored if stain-removal procedures are patiently

used. Degradation, on the other hand, is not reversible. Silverfish eat cotton cellulose, especially if it is heavily starched; cottons should be stored unstarched and un-ironed. Moths and beetles do not attack or damage cotton.

Prolonged exposure to sunlight causes cotton fiber to yellow and gradually degrade. Moisture and acidic air pollutants speed these reactions, as does the presence of some vat and sulfur dyes.

Cotton fibers conduct heat energy, therefore minimizing destructive heat accumulation. Cotton fabrics can withstand hot ironing temperatures.

Excessive application of heat energy causes the cotton fiber to scorch (char) without prior melting. Cotton is not thermoplastic, which may be attributed to its extremely long fiber polymers and numerous hydrogen bonds. Polymers are prevented from assuming new positions when heat is applied.

Influencing Fabric Aesthetics

The luster of cotton fiber is low. The convoluted fiber surface reflects light in a scattered pattern. The low luster of cotton fiber and the fuzziness of cotton yarns produced from this short fiber result in low-luster cotton fabrics.

The resilience of cotton fiber is low. Cotton fabrics wrinkle during use and laundering and must be ironed, unless they have a durable-press finish. Bending and crushing places considerable stress on the fiber polymer system. Bending is sufficient to cause the original hydrogen bonds to break. New hydrogen bonds form when the fiber is in the bent position and prevent the fiber from recovering after the bending force is removed. When cotton fabric is ironed, the hydrogen bonds within the fibers are broken and reformed, making the fibers straight and placing the fabric in a flat, smooth configuration.

Cotton fabrics have good bulk and cover, providing opacity for a reasonable weight of fiber. Pilling is not a problem when cotton fabrics are abraded. Cotton fibers come out of the fabric structure or are broken off by the abrasive action. Cotton fabrics therefore *lint* rather than pill.

Influencing Health/Safety/Protection

Cotton burns readily and quickly. It smells like burning paper, and leaves a fluffy, gray ash. Cotton fabrics exhibit afterglow: the edges around the burned area appear red for a brief time after the flame has disappeared. Cot-

---

[4]Reactions between the oxygen liberated by bleach and the molecules on the fiber surface that are responsible for discoloration are not known in any detail. In general, the oxygen forms water-soluble compounds when it reacts with contaminants on the fiber surface. These compounds can then be rinsed off the fiber.

ton also smolders, which is highly dangerous because a fire may not break out for hours after the cotton has been ignited. This property limits the use of cotton as a batting material in upholstered furniture and mattresses. Accidental ignition of the batting by a dropped cigarette or other heat source can and usually does result in a fire hours after ignition; the occupants of the dwelling often are sleeping at this point, unaware of the danger. Cotton can be chemically treated to reduce its flammability (Chapter 31).

Cotton is biodegradable, which makes it an ecologically sound fabric choice. Because cotton can be boiled and sterilized, it is applicable in many hospital uses where the spread of infection from one individual to another is of prime concern. There are no known cases of skin irritation or contact allergy caused by cotton fibers.

TYPES OF COTTON

Plant genetics can be used to produce different varieties of cotton with different fiber qualities. Cotton may be chemically modified following its formation by nature.

Varieties

The words "Pima," "Egyptian," and "Sea Island" may appear before the common name "cotton" on a label or in an advertisement. These words refer to the variety of the cotton plant from which the fiber was obtained and indicate long-staple, fine-diameter varieties.

The cotton grown in nearly all cotton-growing countries—a variety called American Upland—makes up more than 50% of the world crop. Upland is the major type of cotton grown in the southeastern United States and in California. This cotton fiber is white and $1\frac{13}{16}$ to $1\frac{1}{4}$ inches long (2.1–3.2 centimeters) on average, with a diameter of 18 micrometers. It would be unusual for a fabric label to specify "Upland cotton."

American Pima cotton fibers are longer than Upland fibers, varying from $1\frac{3}{8}$ to $1\frac{5}{8}$ inches (3.5–4.1 centimeters). Pima cotton, which is grown mostly in southern California, New Mexico, and Arizona, is more costly to process and produce. The extra cost is reflected in the premium price of textile products labeled Pima cotton.

Egyptian cotton is also a long-staple cotton ranging from $1\frac{1}{2}$ to $1\frac{3}{4}$ inches (3.8–4.4 centimeters). The fibers are yellowish-brown in color and are not as uniform as Pima fibers.

Sea Island cotton was first grown on islands off the coast of South Carolina and Georgia. Sea Island fiber is

the longest of all cotton fibers, averaging from $1\frac{3}{8}$ to $2\frac{1}{2}$ inches (3.5–6.4 centimeters), and the most expensive to produce. The fiber is yellowish. It is now grown in limited quantities.

Long-staple cotton is generally used to form *combed yarns* (Chapter 22). The longer the fiber, the higher the technical quality of the fabric.

Cotton also can be genetically modified so that it is colored.[5] Several attempts have been made to develop plants that consistently produce fibers of a predicted color in qualities suited for commercial markets. In 1985, a generation of plants produced fibers in a rainbow of colors, including pink; however, it proved difficult to breed plants that consistently produced pink. The colored cotton being offered today is either brown or green. Colored cotton is a way to avoid toxic waste produced with the use of dyes.

Chemically Modified Cotton

Cotton fiber may be altered by placing it in sodium hydroxide (a strong alkali) or in liquid ammonia, both of which cause the fiber polymers to realign and the cotton fiber to untwist. The sodium hydroxide or liquid ammonia is completely removed after mercerization or liquid-ammonia treatment, respectively. Both treatments occur after cotton yarn or fabric is made and, for this reason, are considered in Unit V (Chapter 32).

Many chemicals can be reacted with cotton to enhance its properties. In the case of durable-press finishing, crosslinks are formed between cellulose polymer chains to improve the resilience of the cotton fiber. Flame-retardant chemicals react with the hydroxyl groups along the polymer chain to reduce the combustible behavior of cotton fiber. Water-repellent treatments coat fiber surfaces. These modified forms of cotton fiber also are considered in Unit V.

PRODUCTION

Cotton is the food-and-fiber plant. Cotton seed is an important supply of vegetable oil for food. The meal obtained from grinding the seed is a valuable feed supplement, or fodder, for cattle and smaller animals. Efforts are presently underway to obtain vegetable protein suitable for human consumption from the cotton seed. Cotton fibers longer than $\frac{1}{2}$ inch (1.3 centimeters) are used

[5]T. Link, "Naturally Colored, Nonfading Brown Cotton to Hit Market Soon as Foxfibre." *Arizona Daily Star* (October 27, 1989), p. D6.

directly in the production of yarns and fabrics. Fibers shorter than $\frac{1}{2}$ inch, called *cotton linters*, provide cellulose for making plastics, explosives, and rayon (the manufactured cellulosic fiber).

Cultivation

The chief cotton-producing countries of the world are the United States, the Soviet Union, China, India, Brazil, and Egypt; other cotton producers are Pakistan, Turkey, Mexico, and the Sudan. In the United States, a 15-state "Cotton Belt" extends 3000 miles East to West and 700 miles North to South.

Cotton can be grown in these regions because they have six or seven frost-free months per year, during which the sun shines 12 hours per day. It rains 3–5 inches in each month the cotton plant is growing, or adequate irrigation can be supplied. The climate is dry when it is time for the fiber to mature.

Cotton seeds are planted in rows in well-tilled fertilized soil and, under normal climatic conditions, germinate in 7–10 days. Flower buds appear in 35–45 days; beautiful blossoms, 21–25 days later. The blossom initially is creamy white or light yellow in color, but has changed to pink, lavender, or red by the second morning. By the end of the third day, the flower falls, leaving a young green ovary attached to the plant. The ovary ripens, enlarges, and forms a pod—the *cotton boll*. Thousands of moist fibers from inside the boll punch through the coating of the newly formed seed.

The growth of the fiber is slow at first, then speeds up, and slows again until the lengthwise growth comes to a sudden stop. The fiber looks like a long, thin balloon distended with water. The primary cell wall of the fiber has been formed. The lengthwise growth lasts $4-4\frac{1}{2}$ weeks. The cotton fiber then begins the process of laying down layers of cellulose in growth rings. Each day, a new layer of cellulose is deposited (a new growth ring is added).[6] Each growth ring is composed of two layers: one solid and compact; the other porous. These rings (20–30 are formed) comprise the secondary cell wall.

As the fibers grow, the boll expands. A mature boll, shaped like a punching bag, is about $1\frac{1}{2}$ inches long (3.8 centimeters). The green, closed boll begins to open 45–90 days after flowering. Now the moisture evaporates from the fibers. The cell walls collapse, forming the flat, ribbon shape of the fibers, and the fibers twist

lengthwise, forming the convolutions. The boll also dries, splits apart, and the fluffy cotton bursts forth. The cotton boll is ready to be picked.

Harvest

Unfortunately, all cotton bolls do not open at the same time. This was not a problem when cotton was hand-picked, because the picker could pick the open bolls and leave the closed bolls for another day. Hand-picked cotton is the highest-quality cotton because only mature fibers are picked. In industrialized countries, hand picking is not feasible (50 people are needed to pick the same amount of cotton as one mechanical picker). Today, almost 99% of all cotton is machine-picked. The field is harvested once, perhaps twice; the optimum time must be selected so that the greatest proportion of the fiber is mature. The bolls cannot be left open to the environment for too long because sunlight degrades the fiber and dirt begins to discolor it. Before the field is picked, the plants are sprayed with a defoliant which causes the leaves to fall off.

The yield per acre for U.S. cotton is now about one bale, or 500 pounds (227 kilograms). The use of fertilizers, insecticides, and herbicides, as well as improved plant genetics, account for this high yield.

Ginning –Seperated

After cotton is picked, it is taken to the gin, where the fiber (cotton lint) is separated from the seed. Care must be taken or the fiber quality can be reduced during this process. The gin also removes some foreign matter, such as twigs, leaves, and parts of the bolls. The cotton lint is then packed into bales. The seed is sent to oil mills, where linters (the remaining fuzz) are removed from the seed.

Grading Value

Samples of fibers are removed from the bales and sent to be graded or classed to determine the value of the cotton. Structural features examined are length of staple, uniformity of length, and fiber diameter. Strength, maturity, color, and amount of foreign matter also are determined, and damage resulting from ginning is assessed.

There are 33 grades of American cotton, which are divided into six major color categories (extra white, white, spotted, tinged, yellow stained, and gray). The white grade represents the largest part of the American Upland crop. Within the white grade, as well as the other grades,

---

[6]The structure is similar to the growth rings of a tree, except the new layer of cellulose is added to the inside rather than to the outside of the structure.

the following terms are used to provide a scale from high to low for variation in ginning preparation: middling fair, strict good middling, good middling, strict low middling, low middling, strict good ordinary, and good ordinary.

The current trend is to grade cotton quality by high volume instrumentation (HVT) instead of by hand. New spinning systems require different properties (strength and fineness) than traditional spinning systems. Manufacturers of cotton fabrics combine grades of cotton in the preparation of yarn and fabric to maintain relatively even quality in cotton textiles.

CHAPTER SUMMARY

Cotton fiber is 100% cellulose; its polymers form a highly crystalline structure with numerous strong hydrogen bonds. The cellulose polymers are laid down in layers in the cotton fiber, forming a primary cell wall, a winding layer, and a 20–30-layer secondary cell wall. A waxy cuticle covers the fiber. The polymers spiral around the fiber rather than being oriented to the fiber axis.

The properties of cotton fiber that make it unique are hydrophilicity; medium tenacity, stiffness, and modulus; and low elongation and elastic recovery. As cotton fiber gets wet, it increases in tenacity and loses stiffness. Cotton fiber swells considerably in water but dries to its original dimensions. It can be cleaned by boiling and vigorous agitation; other mechanical stresses applied in laundering do not harm the fiber. It is highly resistant to mild alkalies (including detergent solutions) and fairly resistant to bleaching.

Cotton fiber can be genetically engineered and altered by the use of chemical treatments. In the marketplace, labels such as "mercerized," "Pima," and "Sea Island" denote modified cotton fibers.

Cotton fiber is the most used fiber in the world. It has more than 100 end-use applications, perhaps making it the most versatile fiber.

Specialty Cellulosic Fibers

Specialty fibers are obtained from the stems, leaves, and seed pods of plants.

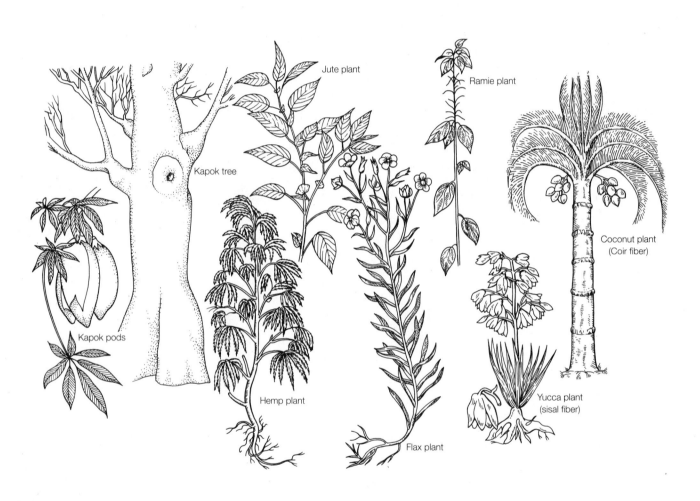

BAST FIBERS
Flax
Ramie
Jute
Hemp
Kenaf
Urena

LEAF FIBERS
Henequen
Abaca (Manila hemp)
Pina (pineapple)
Sisal

SEED FIBERS
Coir
Kapok

13

Specialty Cellulosic Fibers

Plants are the sources of at least 12 different fibers, excluding cotton, used in textile applications (Detail View 13). These specialty cellulosic fibers are obtained from plant stems, plant leaves, and plant seeds. *Bast fibers* comprise the most important group of specialty cellulosic fibers. Of these, flax has the greatest economic importance in the United States.

FLAX FIBERS

Flax was probably the first fiber to be used to make textiles in the Western Hemisphere. When Tutankhamen's tomb was opened in 1922, linen curtains, placed in the tomb about 1250 B.C. were still intact. Remnants of linen also have been found among the remains of the Swiss Lake Dwellers, who lived 10,000 years ago in 8000 B.C.

Flax fiber is obtained from the inner bark of the stem of a plant grown in temperate and subtropical regions of the world. Sometimes the flax fiber is referred to as *linen fiber,* but the term "linen" usually describes fabric composed of flax fibers. Linen fabric has a characteristic appearance and feel (a thick-and-thin irregular surface and crispness). When fabric made of other fibers has these features it may be labeled "X-fiber linen" (for example, rayon linen). In very fine flax linen fabrics, these features may be absent.

About 55% of flax fiber is processed into fabrics for apparel items and accessories (including dresses, skirts, blouses, suits, coats, ties, handbags, hats, shoes, and

handkerchiefs), and about 35% is used in interior textiles such as draperies, wallcoverings, slipcovers, and upholstery fabric. The remaining 10% is made into tablecloths and napkins, placemats and runners, towels, sheets and pillowcases, as well as altar cloths, religious vestments, interlinings, artist's canvas, and sutures for delicate surgical operations.[1] Leather working thread for boots and shoes is still produced from flax, because the fiber's tenacity combined with its ability to swell in water prevents water from penetrating through the needle holes in the leather.

Structure

The flax fiber is a natural, cellulosic, multicellular bast fiber. Flax fibers are 4–40 inches (10–100 centimeters) long, averaging ~19.5 inches (50 centimeters). A "good" fiber is 8–24 inches (45–60 centimeters) in length. Long fibers (47–59 inches, or 120–150 centimeters) are known as *line;* short fibers (4–6 inches, or 10–15 centimeters), as *tow.*

The diameter of flax fibers varies from 40 to 80 micrometers—two to four times the average diameter of cotton fibers. The economic value of flax is directly related to fiber length and diameter. For finer diameter flax, the length-to-width ratio is normally 15,000:1.

---

[1] Personal communication with International Linen Promotion Commission, New York.

FIGURE 13.1 Longitudinal view of two flax fibers showing their crossmarkings or nodes, and a cross-sectional view of several fibers showing their polygonal ultimate cells.

|———————| 25 μm

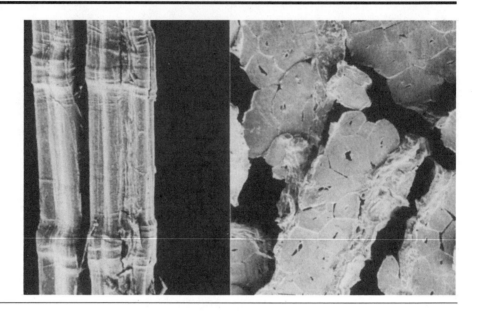

Coarse flax fibers may have a length-to-width ratio of 1500 : 1 or less.

The color of flax varies from light blond to gray blond, depending on the agricultural and climatic conditions under which the fiber was grown and the care taken in processing the fiber.

A cross section of several flax fibers under the microscope shows that they are composed of a number of cells, generally 10–40 cells per section, called *ultimates* or *ultimate cells.* Each ultimate cell is polygonal in shape and has a lumen (Figure 13.1). In a longitudinal view, cross markings, called *nodes*, can be seen on each fiber. The ultimates average about 33 millimeters in length and are tapered at their ends. They overlap each other and are held together with a waxy film to form a flax fiber. The width of a flax fiber therefore depends on how many ultimates are in a cross section; characteristically, the width of a flax fiber varies several times along its length. In fabric form, these differences in width along the flax fiber's length cause an uneven, thick and thin fabric.

At the submicroscopic level, the cell wall of each ultimate is constructed of fibrils composed of cellulose polymers, which spiral at approximately 6° in relation to the fiber axis. The walls are thicker than the cell walls in cotton fiber. The degree of polymerization of cellulose in flax fiber and the proportion of the fiber that is crystalline are slightly higher than in cotton fiber.

Properties

The properties of flax fiber are discussed in comparison to those of cotton. The reasons for the differences in level of performance are explained.

Influencing Fabric Durability. Flax is a stronger fiber than cotton. The difference in tenacity is not due to a difference in the degree of cellulose polymerization, because this is approximately the same in both fibers. The polymers in flax lie almost parallel to the fiber axis; when a pulling force is applied, each polymer takes its share of the stress. In cotton, some polymers lie parallel to the fiber axis, but many polymers lie at an appreciable angle to the axis; only the polymers that are parallel take a share of the stress. Flax is also slightly more crystalline than cotton, resulting in more and stronger hydrogen bonds.

The percent elongation at break for flax fiber is even lower than it is for cotton: only 1.8% when dry and 2.2% when wet. The cellulose polymers spiral at a 6° angle in flax and at a 20–30° angle in cotton. When a pulling force acts on the flax fiber, less alignment with the fiber axis therefore takes place. Within its degree of elongation, the flax fiber has good elastic recovery.

Flax fibers have lower flexibility than cotton fibers. Linen tablecloths that are ironed repeatedly with a crease exactly down the center eventually will split at that crease line after successive launderings. Cotton table-cloths will not split under the same conditions. The greater crystallinity of the flax fiber accounts for this difference.

Influencing Fabric Comfort. Linen fabric is noted for the very cool feeling that results when it is worn next to the skin. This feeling is partly attributed to the fact that the smoothness and length of flax fibers allow fabrics made with them to lie close to the skin surface, creating a large area of contact. In comparison, cotton fibers are considerably shorter and the surfaces of most cotton fabrics are fuzzier. Also, the absorption and desorption of water is believed to be more rapid between the skin and flax fiber than between cotton fiber and skin. Both cotton and flax fibers are hydrophilic. Flax dries quickly; cotton dries slowly.

Influencing Fabric Aesthetics. The luster of flax is subdued due to its long, regular fiber surface coated with wax. The luster improves as the flax is cleaned. Compared to cotton fiber, flax is more lustrous because it does not twist about itself and flax fibers are longer.

Flax fiber is considerably stiffer than cotton fiber. Most linen fabrics are not very drapable. Linen textile fabrics wrinkle and crease readily due to the highly crystalline polymer system within flax fibers.

Influencing Fabric Maintenance. Normal laundering of linen results in alkaline hydrolysis of the waxes and gums that bond the cells of the flax fiber together, leading to a condition called *cottonizing*. In cottonized linen, bundles of cells, separated into individual fibrils, project above the surface of the linen material and give it a fuzzy appearance. Severe cottonizing noticeably weakens linen. Cottonizing does not occur in cotton fabrics.

Flax fibers increase in tenacity when wet, suggesting that they can withstand vigorous laundering. However, gentle agitation is recommended for linen fabrics to minimize cottonizing.

In general, soil resistance is higher for linen fabrics than for cotton fabrics. Dirt does not adhere as readily to the surfaces of flax fibers. The higher crystallinity of flax prevents soil from penetrating into the interior of the fiber. Flax is more difficult to bleach than cotton, and bleaching causes flax to deteriorate. Flax fibers do not shrink or elongate to any marked degree.

Flax has the highest heat resistance of all commonly used textile fibers. It does not decompose until ~302°F (150°C), and prolonged exposure at this temperature is

necessary for degradation to begin. A safe ironing temperature is 500°F (260°C).

Flax fiber is slightly more resistant to rotting and weathering than cotton fiber, and dry flax is highly resistant to mildew. These resistances are thought to be due to the harder surface of the flax fiber. Under severe conditions of warm temperatures, dampness, and contamination, mildew may attack flax fiber.

Production

Flax crops are usually raised either for the linseed oil (from the seeds of the plant) or for the fiber (from the stem). Today, the Soviet Union and Eastern bloc countries grow the largest quantity of flax plants for fiber, accounting for 80% of world output. France, Belgium, and the Netherlands are the principal producers in Western Europe. Flax is not produced in abundance because the flax plant must be grown in areas of high rainfall. Flax farming is not readily mechanized, so fiber processing requires a good deal of hand labor.

Ideal conditions for the growth of the flax plant are homogenous soil, adequate daylight, cool and short nights, and weather that is both damp and warm. The time from sowing the seed to harvest is 100 days. Flax seeds are planted very close together to insure straight, tall plants and strong fiber. Flax plant grown for fiber reach heights of 3–4 feet (90–120 centimeters). The plant has a single stem. The fiber extends from the top of the stem to the root, forming between the bark or cuticle surrounding the outside of the plant and the woody inner portion of the plant stem. Flax fibers transport food and water in the living plant. Fibers occupy about one-quarter of the stem volume. The fibers which occur in bundles held together by resins, lie end to end or slightly overlap each other.

When the plant flowers, the seeds begin to ripen and the stem yellows. At this time, the plant is pulled up by the roots by hand or by mechanical pullers. Pulling rather than cutting the stem preserves the length of the fibers. The seeds are combed away from the stalk during a process called *rippling*.

A series of steps or operations must be followed to obtain the fiber from the plant stem. The most desirable processes preserve the length of the fiber and its color.

Retting, the first step, rots the woody matter and bark by bacterial action in the presence of moisture. In *dew retting*, the crop is laid out on the ground and left for several weeks. Rotting by molds is encouraged by dew and rain. The fiber darkens, which is undesirable, but

FIGURE 13.2   The length and color of flax fibers depend on the type of retting process.

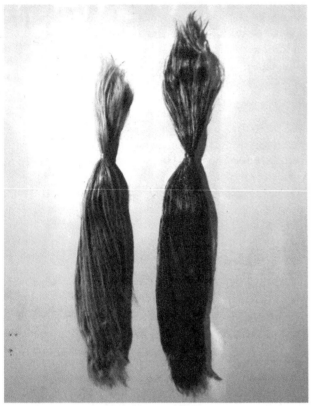

Water or tank-retted flax   Dew-retted flax

the method is economical. In *tank retting*, flax plant stems are placed in heated, water-filled tanks for three days. Some of the most uniform flax is produced this way, but the fiber length of tank-retted flax is shorter than that of dew-retted flax. Figure 13.2 shows the difference in length and color of flax resulting from these two most frequently used methods of retting.

Scutching breaks away the rotted bark and woody matter, freeing coarse bundles of fibers. The retted stems are passed between fluted rollers in a way that preserves fiber length without damaging the fibers.

In *hackling*, the coarse bundles of fiber are separated into finer bundles. The fibers are then arranged parallel to one another by drawing the bundles through sets of successively finer pins. This process does not separate flax fiber bundles into individual fiber cells. Typically, 67% of the fibers are line (long and fine) and 33% are

tow (short).[2] The fiber is now ready for yarn formation or spinning (see Unit III).

OTHER BAST CELLULOSIC FIBERS

Some bast fibers, such as jute and hemp, have been used since the dawn of civilization; others, such as ramie, for hundreds of years; and still others, more recently to fill special applications. All bast fibers must be removed from the stems of plants, and processing is similar to that of flax. These fibers are therefore labor-intensive commodities. The length of the fiber depends on the original length of the plant stem and on how much of that length is preserved in processing.

Ramie Fibers

Ramie fibers are currently found in the United States in a wide variety of imported apparel items, especially sweaters, shirts, blouses, and suitings. Ramie is often blended with cotton in these items. Ramie also is found in table linens, ropes, twines, nets, and other industrial textiles. Prior to the 1980s, little ramie was found in the United States. Unfortunately, the stem of the plant from which ramie is obtained grows with a gummy, pectinous bark. Further, the useful fiber cells are glued firmly together in a ribbon layer below the surface. The gum material is difficult to degrade by rotting; until recently, quality ramie fiber could be obtained only by hand stripping.

Two events led to increased quantities of ramie in the world textile marketplace. First, a mechanical method to remove the ramie fiber from the plant stem was developed that was not labor-intensive and controlled fiber quality. Second, the Multifiber Arrangement (MFA) limited the amount of certain fibers that could be imported. Of significance were import quotas placed on cotton goods but not on ramie goods. When quotas for cotton goods were filled, ramie items and ramie/cotton blends could still enter the United States to satisfy the consumer demand for fabrics made of natural fibers. A renegotiated Multifiber Arrangement included ramie in import quotas.

The plant from which ramie fiber is obtained is a tall shrub from the nettle family that requires a hot, humid climate for growth. It grows primarily in the People's Republic of China, the Philippines, and Brazil. Efforts

---

[2]Line fibers are generally used for apparel fabrics. Tow fibers are used in canvas, rope, warp-lay wallcovering, and upholstery fabrics. Waste flax fiber is made into high-grade banknotes, as well as writing and cigarette papers.

to grow ramie in the Everglades and Gulf Coast regions of the United States were not successful.

Like flax fiber, ramie fiber is composed of ultimate cells (Figure 13.3), but the cells in ramie are considerably longer (1.6–9.8 inches or 40–250 millimeters) than those in flax (0.2–3.0 inches or 4–77 millimeters). Ramie fiber is longer (59 inches or 150 centimeters or more) than flax fiber (3.9–39.4 inches or 10–100 centimeters). Ramie is more lustrous than flax fiber; it is pure white and silklike in appearance, compared to the grayish color of flax. However, ramie is a coarser fiber (4.6–6.4 deniers) than flax (1.7–17.8 deniers). Ramie does not have the fineness and softness sought in fabrics for apparel and interior uses. Although fabrics composed of 100% ramie are made (they have the characteristic appearance and hand of linen), ramie fabrics are usually blended with cotton, flax, silk, and some manufactured fibers.

Jute Fibers

The amount of *jute fiber* produced in the world ranks second to that of cotton when only the natural cellulosic fibers are considered. About seven times more jute is produced than flax on a worldwide basis. Jute is not considered to be as economically important as flax fiber, however. Jute plants grow throughout Asia, chiefly in Bangladesh, India, and Thailand. The greatest part of the production goes into making bagging, rope, cordage, and twine. Jute fiber is also used for carpet backing (where it reduces slippage and adds stability)[3] and in furniture construction (where it serves as a base fabric and webbing before surface fabrics are applied). In fabric form, jute is known as *burlap* or *hessian*. Jute is processed into fabrics in Asia, Scotland, and the United States.

The jute plant grows to a height of 8.2–11.5 feet (2.5–3.5 meters). Processed fibers range from 0.2 to 3 inches (5–800 millimeters) in length. Each fiber consists of up to 20 single cells (Figure 13.4), each cell being about the same size as a cotton fiber cell. On average, jute fibers are 10 times larger than cotton fibers. Jute is a creamy to brown color. It is pliable when first removed from the stalk but, on exposure to water, turns brown, weak, and brittle.

Jute is one of the weakest natural cellulosic fibers. It has low elastic recovery and elongation. It is stiff and has a natural odor. It absorbs moisture readily. Jute resists deterioration by sunlight, microorganisms, and insects well. Dry jute retains its tenacity for a long period of time, but deteriorates quickly when exposed to water.

Hemp Fibers

Today, *hemp fibers* are used primarily for twine, cordage, and thread and also as sacking and heavy-duty covering

---

[3] Most carpet backing in the United States is made from olefin fibers, however.

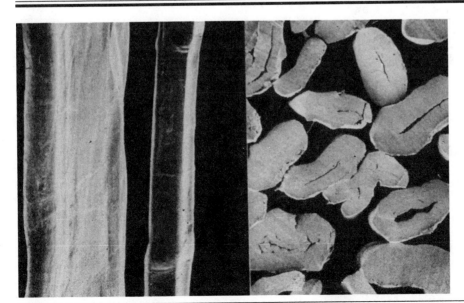

FIGURE 13.3 Longitudinal view of two ramie fibers showing their smooth surface and a cross-sectional view showing the ultimate cells.

├─────┤ 25 μm

FIGURE 13.4 Longitudinal view of a jute fiber and a cross-sectional view showing the shape of the ultimate cells.

|———————| 25 μm

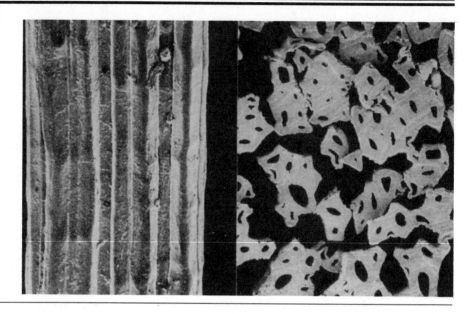

fabrics. Outside the United States, hemp is made into fine fabrics for use as wall coverings and draperies.

Hemp fibers come from a tall herb of the mulberry family. This hardy plant grows at altitudes up to 8000 feet (2440 meters), as well as in warm and hot climates. Hemp fibers are dark tan to brown in color and vary from ¾ inch to several inches in length. They are not as fine as flax fibers.

The tenacity of hemp (5.8–6.8 grams/denier) is comparable to that of flax. Hemp has low elongation and low elastic recovery. This high-tenacity fiber does not rot readily when exposed to water. Hemp is resistant to insects but is damaged by mildew. Sunlight affects hemp in the same way it affects cotton.

The chemical properties of hemp are similar to those of cotton and flax. Hot concentrated alkalies dissolve hemp, but hot or cold dilute alkalies or cold concentrated alkalies do not damage the fiber. With the exception of cool, weak acids, mineral acids reduce its tenacity and eventually destroy the fiber completely. Bleaches and organic cleaning solvents, if used properly, do not degrade hemp.

Hemp has good absorbency. Moisture regain is 12%, and it can absorb moisture up to 30% of its weight.

Hemp was commercially important until the end of World War II. Many of its uses are now assumed by synthetic fibers developed after that war.

Kenaf

During World War II, *kenaf* was used as a substitute for jute in twine and cordage and still can be found in those products. In Africa, the origin of the plant from which kenaf is obtained, the fiber is often made into clothing and cigarette paper. Investigations are currently underway in the United States to assess the usefulness of kenaf as a fiber for newsprint, for paper on which to print U.S. stamps and currency, and for cardboard. Other potential uses include carpet backing and padding, roofing felt, and fireplace logs.

Kenaf produces a paper product that is as tough as wood-pulp paper but generally is brighter and more appealing to the eye and doesn't yellow quickly. Less ink rub-off occurs with kenaf paper than with wood-pulp paper, and kenaf requires less energy to process than wood pulp.

Kenaf is grown mainly in India and Pakistan. It also can be grown successfully throughout the southern United States. If U.S. farmers see a demand for kenaf fiber, it could become a solid cash crop.

Urena Fibers

Urena fiber was developed to fill a shortage of jute during World War II. It is used primarily in Africa for low-cost apparel and decorating fabrics. Urena is white, soft, and has a natural luster.

LEAF AND SEED CELLULOSIC FIBERS

Leaf fibers are of limited use. They usually are made into cordage. The most widely used leaf fibers are from plants of the agave family (henequen and sisal), the banana family (abaca or Manila hemp), and the bromelaid family (pina or pineapple). The leaves are harvested, and the extraneous matter is mechanically scraped and broken away from the fiber.

Henequen and Sisal Fibers

Henequen and *sisal* are used for better grades of rope, twine, and brush bristles. Sisal is also important in the manufacture of matting, rough handbags, and carpeting. It sometimes replaces horsehair in upholstery. Sisal fiber is obtained from agave grown in Mexico (especially the Yucatan peninsula), Africa, Java, and some areas of South America. Both fibers are smooth, straight, and yellow and are degraded by saltwater.

Abaca Fibers

Abaca fibers are used for ropes, cordage, floor mats, table linens, and clothing. Abaca fabrics are typically lightweight and delicate in appearance. The banana-like tree from which abaca is obtained grows mainly in the Philippines.

Abaca fibers are coarse and very long: some reach 15 feet (4.6 meters). Good quality fibers are off-white; poor quality fibers are dark gray or brown. The abaca fiber is strong and flexible.

Pina Fibers

Pina or *pineapple fiber* is used to produce lightweight, sheer fabrics that are fairly stiff. Often the fabrics are embroidered and used for formal wear in the Philippines. Pina fiber also is used to make mats, bags, and table linens. The pina fiber is obtained from the leaves of the pineapple plant, which is grown primarily in the Philippines.

The white or light ivory pina fiber is soft, lustrous, and 2–4 inches (5–10 centimeters) in length. It is highly resistant to water but highly susceptible to deterioration by acids and enzymes. Any acid stains (fruit stains) should be rinsed out immediately, and enzymatic presoaks should be avoided. Hand washing is recommended.

Coir Fibers

Coir fiber is used for floor mats and outdoor carpeting. It is obtained from the fibrous mass between the outer shell and the actual nut of a coconut. Coir is a seed fiber. The fibers are removed by soaking the husk in saline water for several months. Sri Lanka is the major producer of coir fiber.

Coir is a very stiff, rich, cinnamon-brown fiber. Its resistance to abrasion, water, and weather is good. It is a practical fiber for outdoor use.

Kapok Fibers

Kapok fiber is used primarily as fiberfill for life preservers and as pillow and upholstery padding. A kapok life preserver can remain in water for hours without absorbing an appreciable amount of water, even while holding up considerable weight. Polyester fiberfill, rubber, and polyurethane foam are the major competing textiles.

Kapok is obtained from the seed pod of the Java kapok or silk cotton tree, which is native to the tropics. The hollow, air-filled fiber is extremely buoyant. Kapok is very lightweight and soft, with exceptional resilience. It resists wetting. The brittleness of kapok limits spinning it into a yarn and accounts for its breakdown into a powder with use.

CHAPTER SUMMARY

Of the specialty cellulosic fibers, jute is produced in the greatest quantities but flax is economically most important as an apparel, household, and interior textile fiber. Ramie recently has become an important apparel fiber in the United States. Most of the other specialty cellulosic fibers are used for rope, twine, and cordage. Many are grown primarily in the tropics.

Rayon Fibers

Rayon fibers are manufactured fibers "composed of [100%] regenerated cellulose, as well as manufactured fibers of regenerated cellulose in which substituents have replaced not more than 15% of the hydrogens of the hydroxyl groups."

VISCOSE RAYON

Regular (conventional)
High tenacity
High-Wet-Modulus (HWM)
  High-performance
  Modal
  Polynosic
Crimped high-performance
  Crimped HWM
Delustered
Optically brightened
Producer-dyed
Acid-dyeable
Self-crimped (regular)
Flame-resistant
Superabsorbent

CUPRAMMONIUM RAYON

SOLVENT-SPUN RAYON

Rayon Fibers

The development of rayon fiber can be traced back to 1664. That was the year English physicist Robert Hooke suggested it might be possible to spin artificial filaments from a gummy substance resembling the secretion of silkworms.

In the next two centuries, several inquisitive scientists tried numerous methods to produce an "artificial" silk. George Audemars, a Frenchman, made the most serious attempt. He was able to make a thread by dipping a needle into a thick solution of mulberry bark and a gummy rubber, but the process was painstaking slow. The first practical cellulose solution that could be spun into a fiber was an outgrowth of the invention of gun-cotton (nitrocellulose) by Swiss chemist Schoebein in 1864. When dissolved in alcohol and ether, nitrocellulose produced collodion (a thick viscous solution). The next breakthrough is attributed to the efforts of two great inventors, Englishman Sir Joseph Swan and American Thomas Edison, who were interested in making carbon filaments for light bulbs. They were able to force nitrocellulose dissolved in acetic acid through a small hole into alcohol and draw it out into a continuous filament. The fiber was denitrated (converted back to cellulose) to reduce its explosive property. Swan recognized that filaments could be used as textile fibers; his wife crocheted some doilies and table mats from the cellulose fiber.

The first practical commercial production of rayon fiber is credited to Count Hilaire Chardonnet, the Frenchman called the "father of rayon," who devoted 29 years to research on producing an "artificial" silk fiber and was awarded a patent in 1884. Chardonnet built a production plant, spun fibers, and displayed fabrics from the new fiber at the 1889 Paris Exhibition. The display was greeted with acclaim: "A Scientific Miracle," "A Feat of Alchemy," and "A Boon to Humanity" read the newspaper headlines of the day. The first rayon was produced in the United States in 1910.

Until 1926, rayon fiber had no official or generally accepted name. It was called artificial silk, Chardonnet's silk, Art silk (abbreviated from artificial), art SILK, A. silk, fiber silk, FLOS, GLOSS, GLISTRA, and KLIS (silk spelled backward), among other names. Manufacturers objected to the word "artificial" because they believed it created a stigma that prevented public confidence in the fiber. Consumers and retailers were confused about the identity of the fiber. Finally, a committee was formed at the American Viscose Company. A nationwide contest to name the fiber was held, with an incentive of $1000 for the person who suggested the best name. Although 10,000 suggestions were received, none of them met committee approval. At a last desperate meeting, one committee member reportedly said "Let's just see if we can shed a Ray of Light on this problem. Why not the word RAYON." All immediately agreed that this word—a derivation of a French word roughly translated as "rays of light"—was ideal. The word "rayon" was adopted, trademarked, and dedicated to public use.

FIGURE 14.1 Primary market distribution of 464.4 million pounds of rayon, acetate, and triacetate fiber produced in the United States and shipped to domestic consumers in 1990.

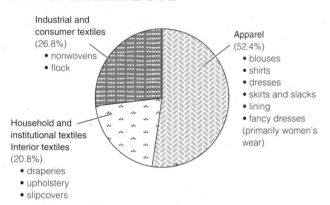

Note: An additional 135.8 million pounds of manufactured cellulosic fiber was imported. Reporting of primary market data for manufactured cellulosic fiber sold as staple and tow was discontinued in 1988; reporting for filament yarn was not. The percentages given here are estimates based on the assumption that the distribution of staple and tow is the same in 1990 as in 1988.

In 1954, the Federal Trade Commission accepted the name "rayon" for the generic group of fibers which are "composed of regenerated cellulose, as well as manufactured fibers of regenerated cellulose in which substituents have replaced not more than 15% of the hydrogens of the hydroxyl groups." The definition covers rayon made from four processes: nitrocellulose, viscose, cuprammonium, and solvent spun. Nitrocellulose rayon was manufactured in the United States from 1920 to about 1940, when it was replaced by the viscose and cuprammonium processes, which were developed simultaneously. In the 1980s, solvent-spun rayon was commercialized. Most of the rayon produced today (95% or more) is viscose rayon. Detail View 14 lists the three types of rayon fiber currently produced and the fiber variants for viscose rayon.

Rayon fiber represents less than 4% of total fiber consumed in the United States (see Figure 7.16) and finds its most important market in apparel fabrics (Figure 14.1), primarily woven women's wear. Nonwoven fabrics, intended for industrial wipes, medical supplies, diapers, sanitary napkins, and tampons, comprise a substantial portion of the industrial and consumer market. A considerable amount of rayon is used as flock in the production of flocked fabric. Rayon fiber is also used in draperies, upholstery, and slipcover fabrics.

REGULAR VISCOSE RAYON FIBERS

Labels on fabrics and garments containing viscose rayon identify the fiber content as "100% viscose," "100% viscose rayon," or "100% rayon." The first designation is not legally correct because it does not conform to the Textile Fiber Products Identification Act, but it does accurately convey that the fiber was manufactured by the viscose process of making rayon.

Structure

Rayon fiber is 100% cellulose (see Detail View 14). Its degree of polymerization is ~400, quite short in comparison to cotton fiber cellulose (6000–10,000). Rayon fibers are 35–40% amorphous and 60–65% crystalline. The short polymers make it difficult for a more crystalline polymer system to form. Further, the polymers are not well aligned with the fiber axis.

The surface of regular viscose rayon is characterized by tiny grooves, called *striations*, which appear as dark lines in a longitudinal view and by *serrations* in a cross-sectional view of the fiber (Figure 14.2). Rayon fiber is a fine, coagulated stream of regenerated cellulose solution, so it does not have a complex submicroscopic structure. When the fiber is stained, the outer surface layer, called the *skin*, appears darker than the *core*. The skin contains numerous, relatively small and imperfect crystals; the core has fewer, larger, more perfect crystals. The striations and accompanying serrated cross-sectional shape result from greater shrinkage of the skin compared to the core as the liquid polymer solution coagulates during fiber formation.

Rayon fibers are used in both filament and staple length. Most rayon is used in staple form. Filament is cut to the length of cotton, flax, or wool fibers. Normally, fibers range in denier from 1.5 (very fine) to 15 (quite coarse). In the 1980s, rayon microfibers (those with a denier <1.0) were introduced.

Properties

The properties of regular viscose rayon are summarized in Table 14.1. To obtain numerical values for rayon fiber properties and to compare the properties of rayon to other generic and common groups of fibers, refer to Figures 8.1–8.13 and Tables 8.1–8.8. To compare the mechanical properties of regular viscose rayon to cotton,

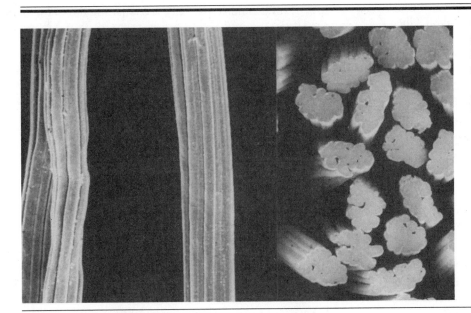

FIGURE 14.2 Photomicrograph of regular viscose rayon fiber showing the striated surface and serrated cross-section.

|———————| 25 μm

modified viscose fibers, and solvent spun rayon, refer to Figure 14.3 and 14.4.

Influencing Fabric Durability. Regular viscose rayon fiber has medium breaking tenacity, high elongation at break, and low modulus compared to other fibers (see Figure 8.1). The modulus of regular rayon is about one-half of that generally required, so fiber distortion may readily occur. The elastic recovery of rayon is low.

When a longitudinal force acts on a rayon fiber, relatively few polymers support the load because most polymers are poorly aligned with the fiber axis. There is a low proportion of crystalline areas and, consequently weak hydrogen bonding. A small, longitudinal force on the fiber is sufficient to begin polymer slippage, and the fiber begins to elongate. The slope of the initial segment of the rayon stress-strain curve is relatively low. In this polymer system, the path of break is short.

Influencing Fabric Comfort. Rayon fibers are hydrophilic, having a moisture regain of 13% at 70°F (21°C) and 65% relative humidity. Water molecules are attracted to the hydroxyl groups along the polymer chain. Rayon is much more absorbent than cotton and flax fibers because its higher proportion of amorphous area allows water molecules easier and greater access to the hydroxyl groups. Rayon fibers absorb insensible perspiration, maintaining "dry" skin.

In general, rayon fibers are easily bent (are soft); the term "limp" is sometimes used to describe them. The amorphous molecular system in which polymers are not sufficiently long to align satisfactorily or form numerous, strong hydrogen bonds results in limp rather than stiff performance. The irregular surface of the rayon fiber contributes to next-to-skin contact comfort.

Rayon fibers do not build up static electricity to cause the discomfort associated with clinging garments. The density of rayon fiber, rated high in comparison with other fibers, is similar to that of cotton fiber.

The heat of wetting of rayon fiber is high (comparable to wool fiber). However, rayon fiber absorbs water so much more quickly than wool and silk fibers that the heat of wetting is liberated quickly and the wearer does not notice the effect.

Influencing Fabric Aesthetics. The resilience of rayon is low. When rayon fibers are bent, the cellulose polymers are compressed and extended within the fiber as cellulose polymers are in cotton fiber. Hydrogen bonds between polymers are broken and reform at the new positions of the polymers.

Regular rayon is highly lustrous and translucent. Its ability to provide cover is therefore low. In the early days of its use, these properties restricted the use of regular viscose rayon to formal apparel fabrics.

Rayon fabrics are noted for their beautiful draping quality. The fact that rayon fibers are easily bent due to

TABLE 14.1   **Regular Viscose Rayon Fiber Property Summary**

PROPERTY	RANK[a]
Mechanical[*]	
Tenacity	Medium
Elongation	Medium
Elastic recovery	Low
Flexibility	—
Abrasion resistance	Low
Stiffness (flexural rigidity)	Low
Resilience	Low
Toughness (work of rupture)	Medium
Initial modulus	Low
Sorptive	
Moisture regain/content	High
Cross-sectional swelling	High (highest of general-use fibers)
Heat of wetting	Medium
Effect on mechanical properties	High
Oil absorption	High
Ease of oil release	High
Thermal	
Heat resistance (durability)	Medium
Softening and melting	High (decomposes first)
Decomposition	High
Combustibility	High
Chemical	
Alkali resistance	
Dilute	High
Concentrated	Medium (swells with loss of strength)
Acid resistance	
Dilute	Medium
Concentrated	Medium
Organic solvent resistance	High
Oxidizing agent resistance	Medium
Miscellaneous	
Ultraviolet light resistance	High
Microorganism resistance	Medium
Moth and beetle resistance	High
Silverfish resistance	Low
Electrical resistivity	Low (static is not a problem)
Specific gravity	High

[a] Levels relative to other fibers except special-use synthetic fibers.

[b] At 70°F (21°C), 65% relative humidity.

low flexural rigidity partially accounts for the drape of the fabric.

Influencing Fabric Maintenance. Rayon fibers swell to 50–113% of their original size (about four times more than cotton fibers) and lengthen considerably as water is absorbed. As water molecules are attracted to the easily accessible hydroxyl groups, they force the polymers apart. Because many of the polymers lie at angles to the fiber axis, rather than parallel to it, lengthening as well as swelling is observed.

Wet regular rayon fiber has lower breaking tenacity, higher elongation at break, and lower modulus than the dry fiber as shown by comparing the stress-strain curve in Figure 14.3 to that in Figure 14.4. Rayon loses about 50% of its tenacity when saturated with water. Elongation increases about 20%; it is almost twice as easy to elongate the saturated fiber.

It is difficult to launder regular rayon fabrics due to the behavior of rayon fibers in water and to the use of water-soluble sizings. Drycleaning is generally recommended.

In general, rayon fibers are more sensitive to acids, alkalies, bleaches, sunlight, and weathering than other cellulosic fibers. The very amorphous nature of rayon fibers offers greater access to chemicals; degradation of already short polymers leads to further disintegration of the fiber.

Influencing Health/Safety/Protection. Rayon is a highly flammable fiber. It burns rapidly and forms a fluffy ash. It cannot be distinguished from cotton on the basis of its flammability. Rayon was used in men's and women's sweaters and cowboy play costumes in 1948 and 1949. The combination of a flammable fiber and a bulky or fluffy fabric structure permitted a large oxygen supply within the structure, creating an ideal situation for a flash fire. Small ignition sources, such as a cigarette ash, were sufficient to start burning the fibers. Rayon can be made flame-resistant.

Production

The viscose process is largely the work of Charles F. Cross and Edward J. Bevan, two Englishmen who were awarded a patent in 1892. Many refinements have been made over the nearly 100 years this process has been used.

In the production of rayon, purified cellulose in sheet form is chemically converted to a viscous solution, which is pumped through spinnerets into a bath. There, the

FIGURE 14.3 Stress-strain curves for rayon and cotton fibers when dry (70°F, 65% relative humidity).

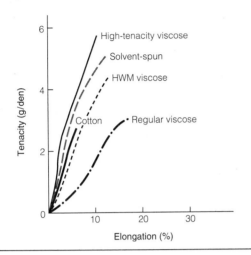

FIGURE 14.4 Stress-strain curves for rayon and cotton fibers when wet (saturated).

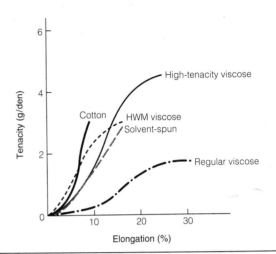

liquid is changed back to solid 100% cellulose in filament fiber form by *wet spinning* (see Figure 7.12). The name *viscose* is derived from the word "viscous," which means "thick as, and/or flows like, honey."

The preparation of the spinning solution begins at a pulp mill, where cellulose is extracted from wood and then purified and formed into sheets about 2 feet (0.61 meters) square. These cellulose sheets are steeped in sodium hydroxide, which causes the cellulose to swell and converts it to alkali cellulose. The alkalized pulp sheets are pressed and then shredded into crumbs to increase the surface area of the pulp.

The crumbs are aged. During ageing, a chemical reaction occurs between alkali cellulose and oxygen in the air. The oxygen acts as a chemical "scissors" to shorten the cellulose polymer chain from a higher to a lower degree of polymerization to permit a fiber to be spun. The alkali cellulose crumbs are then reacted with carbon disulfide, which changes the white crumbs to bright orange crumbs called cellulose xanthate. These crumbs are dissolved in dilute sodium hydroxide to form a honey-colored liquid—the viscose spinning solution. The solution is aged until it reaches the correct viscosity and filtered to remove remaining solid material that could clog the spinnerets. Any air present also is removed to prevent air bubbles from forming within the fiber. The viscous solution is then delivered to the spinning machines.

Pumps force the viscose solution through holes in a platinum spinneret into an acid bath. Coagulation of the filaments occurs almost immediately, followed by simultaneous controlled stretching and regeneration of the cellulose xanthate to cellulose. Each chemical in the bath has an important role: sodium sulfate primarily assists coagulation; sulfuric acid hydrolyzes the xanthate esters of the viscose and causes regeneration; zinc sulfate slows the rate of regeneration to allow the polymers to orient to some degree. The composition and temperature of the spin bath can be varied to change the rate of coagulation and conversion. These factors also influence type of cross section and whether or not latent crimp can be imparted to the final fiber.

Filaments are withdrawn continuously from the acid bath and treated with hot, dilute acid to complete regeneration of the cellulose xanthate to pure cellulose. The filaments are thoroughly washed to remove any impurities that might adhere.

When the filaments are withdrawn from the bath, they are either combined directly into yarns or cut into short lengths to be spun into yarns. Staple length fibers are usually mechanically crimped to facilitate spinning the fiber into yarn. This crimp is not permanent; it is lost as soon as the fiber becomes wet.

The rayon process is a complicated one with high energy and labor requirements. Pollution-control costs are high, but the technology has been developed to almost completely recover the chemicals used throughout the manufacturing process.

MODIFIED VISCOSE RAYON FIBERS

Rayon fiber can be infinitely engineered to provide optimum properties for a variety of end uses. Improved rayon fabric durability and maintenance performance are the results of alterations in the preparation of the viscose solution to produce high tenacity, high-wet-modulus, and crimped high-wet-modulus rayon. In these rayons, the degree of cellulose polymerization is greater than it is in regular viscose rayon. The longer chain length is achieved by shortening or eliminating the ageing of the white crumbs. Retarded coagulation rates tend to produce rayon with an all-core structure. Changes in spinneret design and the addition of various chemicals to the fiber spinning solution have improved the comfort, aesthetics, and safety of rayon fabrics. Major viscose fiber modifications for consumer markets are given in Detail View 14.

Improved Fabric Maintenance

The properties of regular viscose rayon remained about the same until 1940, when high-tenacity rayon was commercialized. Continued research led to what is now considered the greatest technological breakthrough in rayon fiber development—high-wet-modulus rayon, which was commercially available in 1955. Crimped high-performance rayon followed in 1977. Differences in the dry and wet stress-stain properties of these fibers make significant differences in the maintenance of fabrics made from them (Figure 14.3 and 14.4).

High-tenacity Rayon. *High-tenacity rayon* has greatly improved dry tenacity compared to that of regular viscose rayon (Figure 14.3). It loses tenacity when wet (compare Figure 14.4 to Figure 14.3). Its initial modulus in the dry state is higher than that of dry cotton but lower than that of cotton when wet. High-tenacity rayon fibers were developed for uses where dry tenacity was tantamount. High-tenacity rayons provide excellent performance when used in tire cord, conveyor belts, drive belts, and hoses—all uses where the fiber is embedded in rubber or plastic. Just as rayon replaced cotton in the tire-cord market, high-tenacity rayon has been replaced largely by nylon and polyester tire yarns. High-tenacity rayons are still used for industrial sewing threads, tent fabrics, and tarpaulins.

To produce high-tenacity rayon, the concentration of zinc sulfate in the spin bath is increased. This slows down the regeneration process, producing fibers that essentially are all "skin" (composed of highly oriented cellulose polymers), with round or nearly round cross sections.

High-Wet-Modulus Rayon. *High-wet-modulus rayon* is frequently abbreviated "HWM rayon." Other names for HWM rayon are high-performance (HP) rayon and polynosic rayon. Polynosic® has been adopted recently as a trademark by a U.S. rayon fiber producer; adding to the confusion, "polynosic" is a generic name for HWM rayon in Europe. (Another generic name, "modal," also may soon be in use in Europe.) In the United States, "rayon" is the only generic group name for these 100% manufactured cellulose fibers.

PERFORMANCE. HWM rayon fabrics are easier to launder than regular viscose rayon fabrics because they are machine-washable, rather than hand-washable or dry-cleanable. Improvement in the wet modulus of regular viscose fiber has stimulated a resurgence in the use of rayon in apparel fabrics.

The modulus of HWM rayon fiber is essentially the same as the modulus of cotton fiber. Its dry and wet tenacities are greater than those of regular viscose rayon. When wet, the tenacity of HWM rayon is equal to that of cotton fiber.

Swelling of HWM rayon fiber has been lowered relative to regular viscose rayon. Although absorbency remains high, it is slightly decreased relative to regular viscose rayon. HWM rayon is somewhat stiffer than regular viscose rayon but not as stiff as cotton. HWM rayon fabrics have a crisp, lofty hand and greatly improved dimensional stability.

Having a modulus like cotton fiber also means that HWM rayon can be successfully blended with cotton. HWM rayon fiber (either 100% or in blends with cotton) can be mercerized or given a durable-press finish or a finish to control relaxation shrinkage (Chapter 33). The modulus of HWM rayon also permits successful blending with nylon, polyester, and acrylic. These blend fabrics are strong due to the synthetic fiber component and readily absorbent due to the HWM rayon component.

PRODUCTION. A higher grade of cellulose is used to produce HWM rayon than is used to produce regular viscose rayon. Ageing and ripening are eliminated, and chemical concentrations are altered so the molecular chains are not shortened as much as they are in regular rayon fibers. The acid bath is less concentrated and at a lower temperature, slowing regeneration and coagulation. More time therefore exists to stretch the fiber and increase molecular orientation.

STRUCTURE. HWM rayons have a tough skin and a round cross section (Figure 14.5). The degree of polymerization is greater than that of regular rayon. HWM rayon has a microfibrillar structure; the word "polynosic" means many fibrils. HWM rayon has a more crystalline and oriented structure than regular rayon.

Crimped High-performance Rayon.

Although HWM rayon fabrics perform better than regular viscose rayon fabrics, they still do not have desirable levels of bulk and cover. Improving the bulk and cover of fabric required that a crimped fiber be produced. Inherent crimping of the HWM rayon fiber can be achieved by increasing the temperature of the spin bath, which ruptures the skin on the outer peripheries of the lobes (see Figure 14.5). The difference in the thickness of the skin causes the fiber to crimp permanently. Crimped high-performance rayon fibers are also called crimped HWM rayon fibers.

Improved Fabric Aesthetics

Regular viscose rayon can be modified to reduce luster, improve whiteness, and enhance the acceptance of different colorants.

Delustered Rayon.

If delustered (dull) rayon fibers are desired, a delustering agent (usually titanium dioxide) is added to the viscose solution. This agent breaks up the light rays and reduces the shine. The degree of brightness or dullness can be controlled by the amount of titanium dioxide added. In microphotographs of fibers, the delustering agent is visible as dark spots.

Optically Brightened Rayon.

Chemicals called optical brighteners may be added to the viscose solution before extrusion. Optically brightened rayon fibers are whiter and brighter than fibers without this chemical.

Producer-dyed Rayon.

Since the early 1950s, viscose rayon manufacturers have produced some fibers that have been dyed before extrusion. This process, called producer dyeing (Chapter 34), improves colorfastness. Usually, producer-dyed rayons are used in interior textiles but not in fashion apparel.

Acid-dyeable Rayon.

Acid-dyeable rayon has been developed so that, when blended with wool, the rayon fiber will accept the same dyes as wool fiber. In this case, proteins or polymers containing $-NH_2$ groups are included in the viscose solution prior to spinning.

Self-crimped Rayon.

Inherent crimp can be developed in regular viscose rayon as well as in HWM rayon. The latent crimp imparted at spinning is formed under wet, relaxed conditions. These self-crimped rayon fibers have an imbalance in the structure of the skin and core that is achieved by reducing the acid in the spin bath and increasing the bath temperature. Chemically crimped regular rayon is wool-like and is used alone or in blends with polyester, nylon, acetate or wool to make upholstery, bedspreads, and apparel fabrics. Fabrics made from these fibers have high bulk if dried in a relaxed state.

Enhanced Health / Safety / Protection

Flame-resistant (FR) Rayon.

An important modification of rayon has been the development of flame-resistant (FR) rayon. Flame resistance is achieved by introducing special chemicals into the viscose solution. FR rayon, which was developed in response to legislation for flame-resistant children's sleepwear, is rarely used in apparel fabrics today due to the general concern about the health effects of chemicals. FR-rayon can be found in institutional applications where the requirement to meet standards of flame-resistance is a prerequisite to use. The flame resistance of these fibers is permanent under normal use and care. Care instructions should be carefully followed.

Superabsorbent Rayons.

Although regular rayon, with water retention as high as 100% of its dry weight, is the most absorbent manufactured fiber, fibers have been made that will hold up to 380% of their dry weight in water. Superabsorbent rayon fibers are used in surgical, medical, and other nonwoven disposable products.

FIGURE 14.5 Photomicrographs of the cross sections of different viscose rayon fibers and drawings highlighting their skin and core structure.

├─────────┤ 10 µm

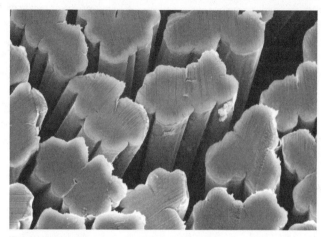
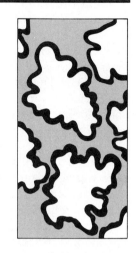

Regular viscose rayon

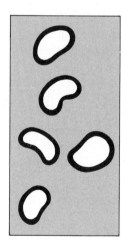

High-wet-modulus rayon

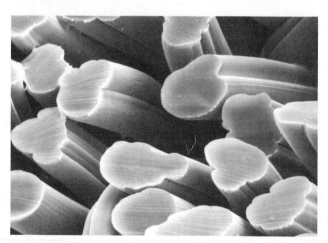
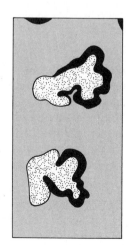

Crimped high-performance rayon

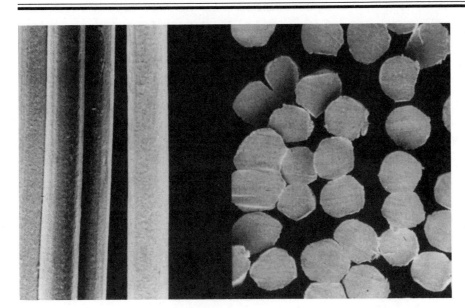

FIGURE 14.6 Photomicrograph of cuprammonium rayon showing its smooth surface and nearly round cross section.

├────┤ 10 μm

CUPRAMMONIUM RAYON FIBERS

Cuprammonium rayon is obtained by dissolving cellulose in aqueous cuprammonium hydroxide solvent to form the spinning solution. Cuprammonium rayon was produced in the United States from 1925 to 1975 by the American Bemberg Rayon Corporation; it is still manufactured in Japan and the Soviet Union. Products on the American market are labeled "Bemberg® rayon" or "cuprammonium rayon"; in Europe, the name "cupra rayon" may appear.

Structure

Cuprammonium rayon is used in filament form. It is smoother and can be made in finer deniers than viscose rayon. Cuprammonium rayon is a featureless cylinder with a round cross section (Figure 14.6). Its degree of polymerization (~1000) is higher than that of regular viscose rayon but less than that of HWM rayon. There is a greater degree of orientation of the molecules.

Performance

The performance of cuprammonium rayon is considered to be superior to that of regular viscose rayon. The fineness of the fiber denier (close to that of filament silk)

gives cuprammonium rayon fiber a silk-like character. This rayon has a high sheen. It is stronger than regular rayon but not as strong as the high-wet-modulus rayons. Most cuprammonium rayon is used in fabrics for scarves, ties, dresses, and linings.

A special hollow cuprammonium fiber has been developed for hemodialysis in artificial kidneys, a small but significant market. The pores in the fibers permit water to pass through but retain salts and other impurities with larger molecules, thereby assisting many people whose kidneys are no longer able to function properly.

Production

Henry Despeissis is credited with discovering the cuprammonium process. Cellulose from either wood pulp or cotton linters is purified, bleached to pure white, and then dissolved in a solution of ammonia, copper sulfate, and caustic soda, which is carefully controlled to maintain about 4% copper, 29% ammonia, and 10% cellulose. A clear, blue liquid is formed that requires no ageing before spinning. The blue cuprammonium solution is pumped from the spinneret into a funnel, through which soft water is running. The movement of the water stretches the newly formed filaments and introduces a small amount of molecular orientation. The fibers then move to the spinning machine, where they are washed, put through a mild acid bath to remove any adhering solution, rinsed, and twisted to form yarns.

SOLVENT-SPUN CELLULOSIC FIBERS

Solvent-spun cellulosic fibers were developed in the 1980s by Courtaulds Fibers of England and Lenzing AG of Austria. Their production is simpler and ecologically safer than the conventional process. Improved fiber performance results. One of these new fibers, trademarked Tencel®, has been manufactured in England since 1988; its production is expected to begin in mid-1992 in the United States. The Austrian manufacturer expects to begin fiber production in 1994.

Structure

Solvent-spun cellulosic fiber is 100% cellulose; it is free of contamination by processing chemicals. Solvent-spun fiber is more crystalline than viscose rayon and modified viscose rayons. The fibers have smooth surfaces and round cross sections (Figure 14.7). They are spun as 1.4, 1.5, and 2.7 denier fibers and are commonly cut to a staple length of 1.5 inches (38 millimeters).

Performance

The stress-strain curve for a dry 1.5-denier, solvent-spun cellulose fiber is shown in Figure 14.3; for a wet fiber in Figure 14.4. Solvent-spun cellulosic fibers have improved dry and wet tenacity and greater dimensional stability compared to regular viscose rayon. Dye absorption is optimal.

Influencing Fabric Durability. Solvent-spun cellulosic fiber at commercial regain moisture content is 82% stronger than U.S. middling cotton fiber, 67% stronger than viscose rayon, and ~14% stronger than HWM rayon. Elongation at break for solvent-spun fiber is similar to that of HWM rayon; it is 50% greater than that of cotton and 30% less than that of viscose rayon. Its initial modulus is higher than cotton, HWM and regular rayon fiber. The similarity of the initial moduli of solvent-spun fiber to that of cotton and polyester fiber means that it can add to the strength of yarns at most proportions of blending.[1]

---

[1] The discussion of blended yarns presented in Chapter 24 includes an explanation why fibers must be compatible so that each fiber adds to the performance of the blended yarn.

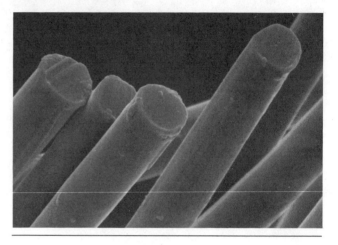

FIGURE 14.7 Photomicrograph of a solvent-spun rayon fiber showing its smooth surface and round cross section.

Information is not yet available concerning the abrasion resistance of fabrics composed of solvent-spun fiber.

Influencing Fabric Maintenance. When wet, the tensile strength of solvent-spun fiber decreases; the loss of tenacity is ~12.5%. Compared to wet cotton, the wet tenacity of solvent-spun fiber is 29% lower; compared to wet regular viscose rayon, it is 188% higher. It is 64% less than the wet tenacity of polyester, which is not affected by moisture. When solvent-spun fiber is wet, elongation at break increases 12.5%. There is a slight reduction in initial modulus, but the wet modulus remains greater than that of regular viscose rayon fibers.

Influencing Fabric Comfort. Solvent-spun fiber is denser than viscose rayon. It absorbs ~28% less water than viscose rayon and ~13% less than HWM rayon but ~30% more than cotton.

Production

In the manufacture of solvent-spun fiber, wood pulp is mixed with amine oxide (a chemical in the family of compounds used in the manufacture of hair shampoo) and then passed through a continuous dissolving unit. The clear, viscose solution that results is filtered and extruded through a spinneret immersed in a dilute aqueous bath of amine oxide. In the bath, the cellulose is precipitated out in filament form. After the filament is washed and dried, cut staple fiber is produced. The dilute amine oxide from fiber spinning and washing is purified and reconcentrated by removing it from the water. The concentrated, purified amine oxide is then fed back into the main process. Virtually all of the amine oxide is recovered; the major effluent from the manufacture of solvent-spun fiber is water.

End Uses

Four markets have been targeted for solvent-spun rayon fiber: woven apparel fabrics (particularly blouses and dresses), residential interior fabrics, technical fabrics, and specialty nonwoven fabrics. The fiber is used in 100% form, as well as in blends with viscose rayon, polyester, and cotton.

CHAPTER SUMMARY

Rayon fibers are "composed of [100%] regenerated cellulose, as well as manufactured fibers of regenerated cellulose in which substituents have replaced not more than 15% of the hydrogens of the hydroxyl groups." Currently, three processes are employed in the manufacture of rayon fibers: viscose, cuprammonium, and solvent-spun. Viscose rayon accounts for 95% of all rayon produced. Regular viscose rayon fiber is composed of short chains of cellulose that are poorly oriented and form a fiber with a low proportion of crystalline regions. The fiber is weak, with high elongation at break and a low modulus. It is not resilient but is a soft fiber. When wet, the fiber becomes weaker and has a higher elongation at break and an even lower modulus. Regular viscose rayon fibers swell considerably.

Viscose rayon can be modified to produce high-wet-modulus (HWM) rayon fibers and crimped high-performance rayon fibers, both of which have improved dimensional stability to the point that fabrics made from them are machine-washable. Crimped high-performance fibers add bulk to a fabric and provide better cover compared to HWM fibers. Viscose rayon can be modified in many ways, resulting in high-tenacity, delustered, optically brightened, producer-dyed, acid-dyeable, self-crimped, flame resistant, and superabsorbent fibers.

Acetate and Triacetate Fibers

Acetate and *triacetate fibers* are manufactured fibers "in which the fiber-forming substance is cellulose acetate. Where not less than 92% of the hydroxyl groups are acetylated, the term triacetate may be used as the generic description of the fiber."

ACETATE

TRIACETATE

Regular (Conventional)
Producer-dyed
Modified cross section
Textured or crimpable
Sunlight resistant

Acetate and Triacetate Fibers

Triacetate and acetate have been called "fiber siblings." The Textile Fiber Products Identification Act states that *acetate* is "a manufactured fiber in which the fiber-forming substance is cellulose acetate. Where not less than 92% of the hydroxyl groups are acetylated, the term *triacetate* may be used as the generic description of the fiber." In acetate fiber, 2 or 3 of the hydroxyl groups on each six-membered ring have been replaced by an acetyl group resulting in an average replacement of ~2.5 (Detail View 15). Sometimes acetate is called *diacetate*. Triacetate is so-named because nearly all three (2.91– 2.96) of the hydroxyl groups on the six-membered rings have been acetylated.

In both acetate and triacetate, few hydroxyl groups remain along the polymer chain. The difference in the number of hydroxyl groups remaining (or in the number of groups acetylated) causes fiber properties to vary. Detail View 15 shows the repeating unit for acetate and triacetate fibers and the types of acetate fiber.

Acetate fiber has been produced in the United States since 1924, 14 years less than rayon fiber. Triacetate was not commercialized until 1952 in the United States. In 1982, U.S. triacetate fiber production ceased. Triacetate fiber is still imported to this country, where it can be found in a variety of end-use products.

ACETATE FIBERS

The word "acetate" is derived from the name of the polymer solution, cellulose acetate, used to form the fiber. Cellulose acetate was first formed in 1869 by Paul Schutzenberger, but 35 years of additional experimentation were necessary to find a practical, safe, and relatively inexpensive method of producing a cellulose acetate solution. Henri and Camille Dreyfus utilized the new discovery to apply a "dope" of cellulose acetate dissolved in acetone to the wings of airplanes, which made them impervious to air and water. (Airplane wings were covered with fabric in the early 1900s.) The supply of cellulose acetate was inadequate to treat the airplanes of the Allies in World War I, so the Dreyfus brothers were asked to leave Switzerland and start a factory in England to manufacture the solution in large quantities. When the war ended in 1919, their factory had the capability to produce large quantities of cellulose acetate, but little demand for it existed. After an estimated 20,000 experiments under the inspiring leadership of Henri Dreyfus, a method of converting the cellulose acetate to fibrous form was discovered. Acetate fiber was first marketed in England in 1921 and in the United States in 1924.

Currently, the major use for acetate fibers is in lining fabrics for suits and coats, caskets, and draperies.[1] Acetate fiber also is used in lingerie and housecoats, as well as in fancy dresses and blouses. Tricot (a warp knit), brushed tricot, and fleece knits containing acetate abound in the lingerie / housecoat market; acetate taffetas, moiré

---

[1] Consumption figures for acetate fiber are no longer reported separately from those for rayon fiber. Figure 14.1 shows the consumption of both rayon and acetate.

taffetas, and brocades are popular formal apparel fabrics. Drapery fabrics also may contain acetate fiber (acetate/rayon blends are more common than 100% acetate drapery fabrics). In antique satin, acetate filament yarns are used in the warp and rayon staple slub yarns are used in the filling. The acetate then lies primarily on the back side of the fabric; the rayon, on the face or fashion side. Other uses for acetate fiber include bedspreads, quilts, fiberfill, satin sheets, and ribbons. Acetate in a taffeta construction is extensively used for choir and graduation robes. Labels consume a surprisingly large amount of acetate fiber.

Structure

Acetate fibers have a striated surface appearance (Figure 15.1) like viscose rayon fibers, except the striations are farther apart. The cross section shows that the acetate fiber is lobed. The lobes are rounder and have a columnar appearance, not the sharp points that sometimes appear in a cross section of viscose rayon fiber. Acetate fiber has a skin and a core.

The degree of polymerization of cellulose in acetate fiber is ~250–300, much lower than it is in cotton fiber (6000–10,000) and in regular rayon fiber (~400). In acetate, the heterogeneous hydroxyl and acetyl side groups, which occur randomly along the polymer chain, and the bulkiness of the acetyl groups do not allow the polymers to become oriented and crystallize. Hydrogen bonding is much less in acetate than in cotton, flax, and rayon.

Acetate fiber is usually used in filament form. The appearance of acetate fiber is very similar to filament silk: bright, shiny, and smooth to the eye and hand. Some acetate fiber is cut into staple length and mechanically crimped.

Properties

Acetate has been called the "beauty fiber" and the "gardenia fiber." Both of these descriptions emphasize its luxuriousness, softness, and fragility. If we imagine the moist skin of a physically beautiful person or dewdrops on a gardenia, the idea of "just right" absorbency also is conveyed by these phrases. Acetate fiber exhibits both hydrophilic and thermoplastic behavior. The properties of acetate fiber are summarized in Table 15.1. To obtain numerical values for acetate fiber properties and to compare the properties of acetate to other fibers, refer to Figures 8.1–8.13 and Tables 8.1–8.8.

Influencing Fabric Durability. Acetate is *not* noted for durability; it is noted for fragility. The fiber is not particularly strong or resistant to abrasion, and it is relatively easy to elongate. The short polymer length, low degree of orientation, and small extent of hydrogen bonding account for this mechanical performance. Elastic recovery is low. Like regular rayon, acetate fiber has a low modulus.

Influencing Fabric Comfort. An acetate fiber is easily bent and is noted for its silk-like softness. The feel of acetate fabric against the skin also is enhanced by the level of moisture absorbency of the fiber; moisture regain at different relative humidities is almost the same as for cotton. Acetate is classified as a hydrophobic fiber, but it is "the most hydrophilic of the hydrophobic fibers."

Acetate fiber has low electrical resistivity; it does not readily build up static. It is slightly less dense than cotton fiber.

Influencing Fabric Aesthetics. Acetate fabrics are luxurious. They are usually shiny due to the filament form of the fiber and its chemical composition. Many acetate fabrics make a slight rustling sound. White acetate fabrics keep their white color—an advantage over white silk fabrics, which yellow readily.

Acetate fiber is moderately resilient. It is thermoplastic but cannot be successfully heat-set. Permanent pleats and creases cannot be formed in acetate fabric.

Influencing Fabric Maintenance. Acetate fiber is thermoplastic: it softens and shrinks when the washwater, dryer, or ironing temperature is too high. Wrinkles, which prove to be difficult to remove, can result from improper laundry procedures. This temperature sensitivity is a major reason why drycleaning is recommended for all acetate fabrics.

Although acetate fiber is classified as hydrophobic, it absorbs water and swells. It increases in length more than it increases in diameter. It becomes weaker when wet and has a lower modulus, so the fiber elongates more easily when wet than dry. When acetate fabrics are handwashed, mild, lukewarm, sudsy water should be used, followed by lukewarm rinsewater. Twisting and wringing of the fabrics must be avoided. Blotting up excess water with a towel and drip-drying the article are recommended.

Acetate fiber is resistant to weak alkalies and acids. It can be bleached with chlorine or oxygen bleaches.

FIGURE 15.1 Photomicrograph of acetate fiber showing its columnar (striated) surface and lobed cross section.

⊢―――⊣ 10 μm

Acetate is soluble in acetone. Fingernail polish and polish remover, which contain acetone, should be used with great caution around acetate fabrics. An excellent way to tell whether a fabric contains acetate is to place a few yarns in a couple of drops of acetone. If they dissolve, the yarn is composed of acetate fibers; if the yarn does not disintegrate but feels sticky after being removed from the acetone and stiffens permanently when dry, then the yarn contains some acetate. Only a few seconds are necessary for the reaction to occur.

Most acetate fabrics should be pressed on the wrong side while slightly damp, with the iron at the lowest setting. If ironed on the right side, a press cloth should be used. Acetate softens and sticks at ~375–401°F (190–205°C). It is considered to have high resistance to degradation by heat.

Acetate fiber degrades on continuous exposure to ultraviolet light. It is more resistant to degradation by ultraviolet light than silk, polyester, and nylon but degrades faster than cotton, rayon, and acrylic.

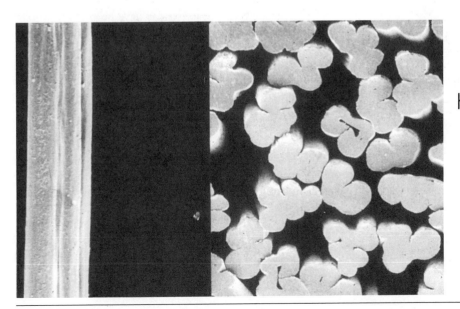

FIGURE 15.2 Photomicrograph of triacetate fiber showing its columnar (striated) surface and lobed cross section.

⊢―――⊣ 25 μm

TABLE 15.1   Acetate Fiber Property Summary

PROPERTY	RANK[a]
Mechanical[b]	
Tenacity	Low
Elongation	Medium
Elastic recovery	—
Flexibility	—
Abrasion resistance	Low
Stiffness (flexural rigidity)	Low
Resilience	Low
Toughness (work of rupture)	Medium
Initial modulus	Low
Sorptive	
Moisture regain/content	Medium (highest moisture regain of fibers classified as hydrophobic)
Cross sectional swelling	Low
Heat of wetting	Low
Effect on mechanical properties	Medium
Oil absorption	Medium
Ease of oil release	Medium
Thermal	
Heat resistance (durability)	High
Softening and melting	Medium
Decomposition	
Combustibility	Medium
Chemical	
Alkali resistance	
Dilute	High
Concentrated	Low
Acid resistance	
Dilute	High
Concentrated	Low
Organic solvent resistance	Low to acetone
Oxidizing agent resistance	Medium
Miscellaneous	
Ultraviolet light resistance	Medium
Microorganism resistance	High
Moth and beetle resistance	High
Silverfish resistance	Medium
Electrical resistivity	Medium
Specific gravity	Medium

[a] Levels relative to other fibers except special-use synthetic fibers.

[b] At 70°F (21°C), 65% relative humidity.

Acetate fibers are resistant to insects, but are slowly degraded by mildew and bacteria.

Influencing Health/Safety/Protection. Acetate fiber burns freely. It melts, forming a black, charred bead. As it burns, it gives off an acetic, vinegar-like odor. It is difficult to distinguish acetate from other thermoplastic fibers based on the results of a burning test.

Variants

Acetate fiber has been on the market for almost 70 years. During those years, research has been conducted to overcome its performance deficiencies: low tenacity, abrasion resistance, and dimensional stability.

For decades, acetate fiber has been produced in considerable quantity and in a variety of lusters, from bright to semi-matt to full-matt. Titanium dioxide (TiO_2) is usually added to the fiber spinning solution and becomes distributed between the fiber polymers. It dulls the fiber but it also acts as a photosensitizer, leading to more rapid degradation of dull acetate than lustrous acetate fiber. Such delustered acetate fibers are not the best choices for curtains and draperies.

A modified cross section—a Y-shape—provides sufficient loft to permit acetate to be used as a fiberfill. Flat acetate provides glitter in fabrics.

FR-acetate—a flame-resistant fiber was developed to be blended with polyester for children's sleepwear and for curtains and draperies. It is no longer produced for children's sleepwear.

In recent years, great strides have been made to produce fancy yarns from acetate fibers by using various texturing and blending processes. Acetate fibers are textured by means of air jets into spun-like yarns for knitwear (Chapter 24). Acetate often is blended with nylon to improve fabric strength.

Production

The acetate fiber producer purchases purified and bleached cellulose in the form of sheets and rolls. Sheet cellulose usually originates from pine and spruce trees, but also can come from cotton linters. The cellulose is shredded and placed in a specially built mixer. Acetic acid is added to open up the closely packed molecules of the pulp. Acetic anhydride and a sulfuric acid catalyst are then added, and a chemical reaction called *acetylation* takes place in which all the hydrogen atoms in the hydroxyl groups are replaced by acetyl groups. During acetylation, a competing reaction—*degradation*, or *depolymerization*—occurs, and the length of the cellulose chain is shortened. Precautions are taken to control the amount of degradation. When acetylation is complete, the huge mixer tips and pours out an entirely new substance: *cellulose triacetate*. This clear solution, called *acid dope*, is not yet ready for spinning. First, it must be aged or ripened by adding water. Hydrolysis occurs, which removes some of the acetyl groups from the cellulose molecule and replaces them with hydroxyl groups. Secondary cellulose acetate is formed and plunged from storage jars into cold water, where it precipitates into solid, white flakes. Washing the flakes in water frees them of acid. After drying, the flakes are dissolved in acetone and a clear solution, as thick as molasses, forms. This solution, called the *spinning dope*, is ready to be spun into fiber.

The molasses-like solution is forced through a spinneret and pulled in fine streams by gravity down a tall, spinning shaft. The solvent evaporates instantaneously from the surface of each fine dope filament, and a solid skin forms over its still plastic interior. As the filaments pass down the column, more and more solvent is removed from their interiors. The filaments are drawn out of the shaft at the bottom and twisted together to form a multifilament yarn. This method of spinning is called *dry spinning*.

Excess acetic acid and sulfuric acid are recovered from the washwater and rinsewater for reuse, which helps to reduce the cost of manufacture and prevent environmental pollution. The acetone is recovered from the spinning process for the same reasons.

TRIACETATE FIBERS

The longitudinal appearance and cross section of triacetate fibers are striated and lobed, respectively, like those of acetate (Figure 15.2). Triacetate fibers have very low crystallinity following extrusion. However, heat-setting the fibers causes the polymers to pack closely together and form a highly crystalline structure. Heat-setting is a routine process for triacetate fibers; without it, their optimum properties cannot be realized.

Triacetate fiber is used in 100% triacetate fabrics and also in mixture and blended fabrics (Chapter 23). In women's apparel, triacetate tricot knits and woven satins, taffetas, crepes, challis, and sharkskins are found. An

important application is velour and suede-like fabrics for dresses and robes.

Properties

Triacetate and acetate fibers share some of the same properties. They both are soft and silk-like. Both are highly resistant to molds, mildew, and insects. Their resistance to ultraviolet light and to most chemicals (except acetone) is similar; acetate dissolves in acetone, but triacetate does not. Neither is a particularly durable fiber.

Triacetate fiber differs significantly from acetate fiber in three major ways. Of particular note is that triacetate fibers are made into "wash-and-wear" and "ease-of-care" fabrics. Triacetate fabrics can be machine washed and tumble dried. They are dimensionally stable: they emerge from the drier relatively wrinkle-free. When pressing is necessary, the iron may be turned to the wool setting and a press cloth is not needed. Triacetate fabrics retain their whiteness during laundering; they do not pick up color or soil.

Second, the resilience of triacetate fabrics during wear is high. Triacetate fabrics can be worn without becoming wrinkled and mussed, even in high humidity. Permanent pleats or creases can be set into a triacetate fabric. To retain their sharpness, hand washing and drip-drying are preferred to machine washing and drying.

Third, triacetate fabric is considered to be intermediate in comfort. Triacetate fiber is classified as hydrophobic and is more similar to polyester fiber than acetate fiber in moisture regain.

These three major differences in performance are due to the fact that triacetate fiber has a higher softening and melting point than acetate fiber does due to a higher degree of crystallinity. Triacetate fiber can be heat set; acetate fiber cannot.

Production

Celanese (currently, Hoechst Celanese) Corporation produced a triacetate fiber and marketed it under the trademark Arnel® from 1952 until 1982, at which time the last plant was closed. Triacetate currently is produced in Japan and the Soviet Union, as well as in several other countries, and imported into the United States.

The initial steps in the production of triacetate fibers are the same as those for acetate fiber, because cellulose must be completely acetylated to make both acetate and triacetate. In acetate production, the cellulose is subsequently deacetylated, dissolved in a solution of 95% acetone and 5% water, and extruded. In triacetate production, the flake cellulose triacetate is dissolved in a solution of 90% methylene chloride and 10% methanol and dry spun. The warm air solidifies the filaments.

CHAPTER SUMMARY

Acetate and triacetate are cellulosic fibers in which a substantial proportion (83–98.7%) of the hydroxyl groups along the polymer chain have been acetylated. Acetylation produces fibers that are hydrophobic and thermoplastic. Acetate fiber has a higher moisture regain than triacetate fiber, resulting in more comfortable fabrics that require gentle laundering conditions. Triacetate fiber has higher softening and melting temperatures and can be heat-set. Triacetate fabrics retain permanent pleats and creases and have a wrinkle-free appearance.

Nylon Fibers

Nylon fibers are "manufactured fiber(s) in which the fiber-forming substance is any long-chain synthetic polyamide in which less than 85% of the amide linkages are attached to two aromatic rings."

NYLON 6,6
(Polyhexamethylene adipamide)

NYLON 6
(Polycaproamide)

NYLON 3
NYLON 4
NYLON 5
NYLON 7
NYLON 8
NYLON 12
NYLON 46
NYLON 6,10

Variants for Improved Fabric Comfort
Absorbent or hydrophilic fibers
Microfibers
Antistatic fibers

Variants for Improved Aesthetic Appeal of Fabric
Trilobal fibers
Delustered fibers
Flat cross-sectional fibers
Silk-like fibers
Microfibers
100%-nylon bicomponent fibers
Optically whitened fibers

Variants for Improved Carpet Maintenance
Delustered fibers
Trilobal fibers
Squared fibers
Nylon/fluorocarbon, matrix/fibril bicomponent fibers
Stain-resistant, topically treated fiber*

**Variants for Improved Fabric Durability and
   Resistance to Deterioration**
High-tenacity fibers
Ultraviolet-light-resistant fibers

*To be discussed in Chapter 33.

16

*N*ylon Fibers

Nylon fiber, the first manufactured synthetic fiber, marked its fiftieth anniversary in 1988. The word *nylon* was coined in October 1939, following 11 years of basic and applied experimentation with polymers. In 1940, hosiery made from the "miracle fiber" was sold to a waiting American public. This fiber captured public attention like no other fiber ever has!

Involved in the development of nylon were the creative and scientific minds of chemists guided by Wallace Carothers at the Du Pont Company. In the years 1928 to 1930, prior to the discovery of the polyamides—the polymer from which nylon is made—many disappointments occurred for this dedicated group of scientists. Then one day in April 1930, Julian Hill, a young research chemist, stuck a heated glass rod into a taffy-like substance in a laboratory vessel; when he withdrew the rod, several strands of the substance adhered to it. The strands were not as brittle as Hill had expected. He pulled on one of the strands. It stretched several times its original length and, in the process, seemed to become stronger. The strand stayed drawn out. Fortunately, Du Pont was in the rayon-fiber business, and so the significance of the strand was immediately recognized in the laboratory.

The fiber Hill pulled out of the vessel that day was a long way from being a nylon textile fiber, however. It softened in water, melted at a low temperature, and dissolved in common cleaning fluids. Further laboratory experimentation perfected the fiber. Another five years

of developmental work involving 230 chemists, engineers, and physicists and $27 million were required to commercially produce nylon fiber. Until 1969, nylon was produced in greater quantity than any of the other synthetic fibers; in that year, polyester fiber surpassed it. Today, nylon fiber is available as both homopolymer and copolymer and in numerous variations (Detail View 16).

In 1990, 2487.7 million pounds of nylon fiber were produced by U.S. fiber manufacturers and shipped to domestic customers. An additional 123.5 million pounds of nylon fiber was imported that year. As shown in Figure 16.1, the largest market for nylon fiber is carpet-face fiber. So much nylon fiber is used in carpeting that it has captured about 80% of that market, leaving the other 20% to be shared by olefin, polyester, wool, and acrylic. The industrial and consumer market is the second largest market, but only 14% of all nylon fiber produced is used in this market: slightly more than 40% in tire cord and fabric,[1] with 60% of the 14% used in a wide array of products (some of which are named in Figure 16.1). Apparel is the third largest market for nylon

---

[1] Nylon tire cord is used in replacement tires but not in original equipment tires because nylon tires tend to flat spot, which means the tire develops a flat area where it sits on the ground. Heavy cars that are not driven everyday are most likely to have flat spotting occur. The nylon cord elongates as it is held under tension for long periods of time. When the car is eventually driven, the stretched region causes the tire to bump. After the car travels a few miles, the tire heats up and the cords return to their original length.

FIGURE 16.1 Primary market distribution of nylon fiber produced in the United States and shipped to domestic customers in 1990.

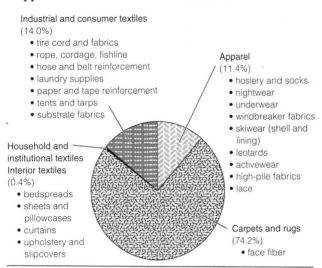

Industrial and consumer textiles
(14.0%)
- tire cord and fabrics
- rope, cordage, fishline
- hose and belt reinforcement
- laundry supplies
- paper and tape reinforcement
- tents and tarps
- substrate fabrics

Household and
institutional textiles
Interior textiles
(0.4%)
- bedspreads
- sheets and
  pillowcases
- curtains
- upholstery and
  slipcovers

Apparel
(11.4%)
- hosiery and socks
- nightwear
- underwear
- windbreaker fabrics
- skiwear (shell and
  lining)
- leotards
- activewear
- high-pile fabrics
- lace

Carpets and rugs
(74.2%)
- face fiber

fiber. Of the 11% of nylon fiber used for apparel, about 40% of it is used in hosiery of all styles for men, women, and children. Very little nylon is used in household or interior textiles (other than carpeting). Although nylon has the durability and ease-of-maintenance attributes needed in upholstery fabrics, it does not compete satisfactorily with other fibers because its appearance is not acceptable to consumers. Nylon fiber is widely used in upholstery fabric of automobiles, however.

In the apparel and industrial/consumer markets, most nylon is used in filament rather than staple form: 98.1% filament in apparel; 86.5% filament in consumer and industrial products. In the carpet market, about 50% is

filament and 50% is staple. Over all markets, 64.2% of all nylon fiber is used as filament; 35.8%, as staple fiber.

GENERIC GROUP MEMBERS

Initially, nylon was called "rayon 6,6" or "fiber 6,6." The 6,6 came from the fact that the two compounds used to form the polymerization monomers each have six carbon atoms (Figure 16.2). These names were not very appealing for use in marketing the fiber, and neither was polyhexamethylene adipamide—the chemical name of the polymer. So a committee was formed to find a name for the new fiber. Floods of suggestions were made. One was "Duparooh" for "du Pont pulls a rabbit out of hat." Another was "Delawear," because nylon fiber was first produced and sold in Delaware. About $2\frac{1}{2}$ years passed before the name "nylon" was agreed on. The word seems to have originated with the suggestion that the new fiber be called "no-run." However, stockings from the fiber, as good as they were, were not really runproof, so that name was vetoed. Then the word was turned around to "nuron," but that sounded like a nerve tonic. An "i" was substituted for the "u" and an "l" for the "r," giving "nilon," but some people pronounced it "nillon," so the "i" was made a "y" and everybody—well, almost everybody—liked it. Lengthy consideration was given to registering "nylon" as a trademark, but it was decided to dedicate the name as a generic.[2]

The Textile Fiber Products Identification Act definition of nylon is "a manufactured fiber in which the fiber-forming substance is any long-chain synthetic polyamide in which less than 85% of the amide linkages

[2]J.L. Meikle and S. Spivak, "Nylon: What's in a Name?," *Textile Chemist and Colorist* 20/6 (1988): 13–16.

FIGURE 16.2 The starting compounds for the formation of nylon 6,6 and nylon 6.

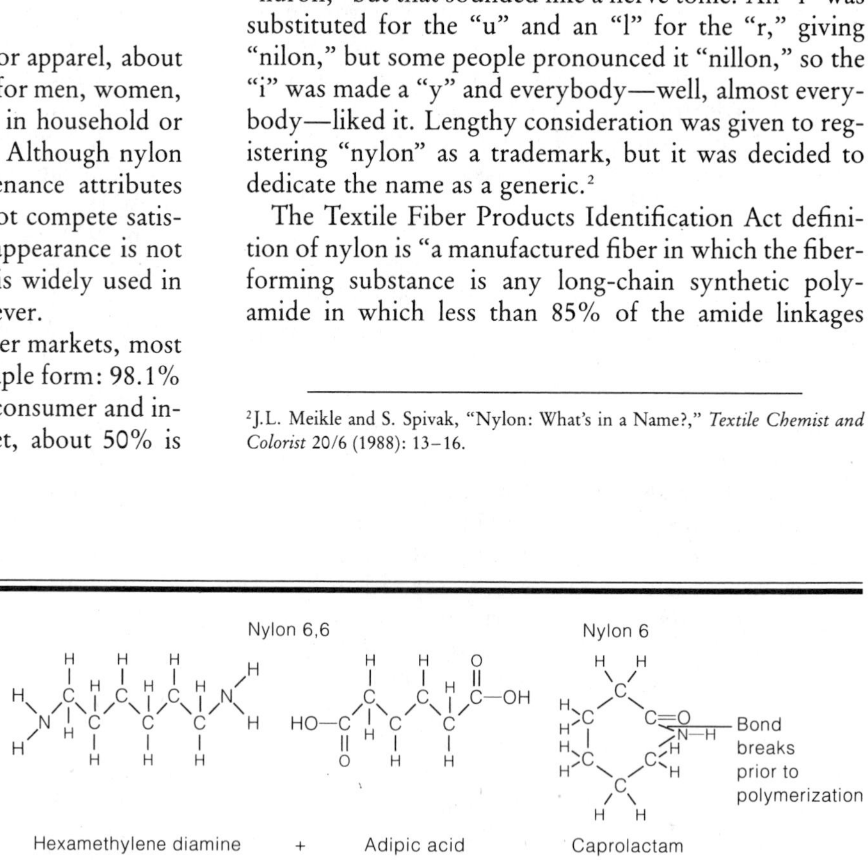

Nylon 6,6

Nylon 6

Hexamethylene diamine   +   Adipic acid

Caprolactam

Bond breaks prior to polymerization

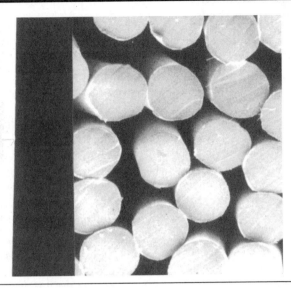

FIGURE 16.3
Photomicrograph of regular nylon fiber, showing its round cross section, rod shape, and smooth surface.

├───┤ 10 μm

are attached to two aromatic rings."[3] The monomers that form the polymers of the two major members of the nylon generic group are shown in Detail View 16. Nylon generic group members are named by number as well as by monomer unit (the number of carbon atoms in the chemicals reacted together). One major member is nylon 6,6—the nylon Carothers first made in his laboratory. The other important member is nylon 6. The starting compounds, hexamethylene diamine and adipic acid, used in the polymerization of nylon 6,6 and the starting compound, caprolactam, used in the polymerization of nylon 6 are shown in Figure 16.2. Caprolactam, a ring compound, opens up and reacts with another opened ring of caprolactam.

Other members of the polyamide family include nylon 3, nylon 4, nylon 5, nylon 7, nylon 8, nylon 12, and nylon 46, as well as nylon 6,10. These members are made in limited quantities for specific uses. Only nylon 6 and nylon 6,6 are considered in this chapter.

STRUCTURE

The cross-sectional shape of regular nylon (nylon 6 and nylon 6,6) fiber is round, reflecting its rod form; its sur-

face is smooth (Figure 16.3). The polymer of nylon is called a polyamide because many amide molecules are linked together. Organic chemists call the product of a reaction between a carboxylic acid and an amine an amide.

$$-C\!\!\begin{array}{c}O\\\\OH\end{array} + -C\!\!-N\!\!\begin{array}{c}H\\\\H\end{array} \rightarrow \text{amide}$$

acid   amine

The characteristic feature of an amide is the presence of the chemical grouping,

$$-C\!\!-N\!\!- \atop H$$

which is indicated in boldface in the monomers shown in Detail View 16. These amide linkages also occur in natural protein fibers (Chapters 10 and 11) and in aramid fibers (Chapter 21).

The degree of polymerization can be controlled but generally ranges between 50 and 80, depending on the specific end use of the nylon fiber. The molecular chains have a linear, zigzag configuration. These linear, zigzag polymers are well-aligned and pack closely together to form a highly crystalline fiber (Figure 16.4). It is esti-

---

[3]Those polyamides in which more than 85% of the amide linkages are attached to two aromatic rings are called aramids, another generic classification of synthetic fibers (Chapter 21).

FIGURE 16.4 The location of hydrogen bonds between polymers of a nylon 6,6 fiber.

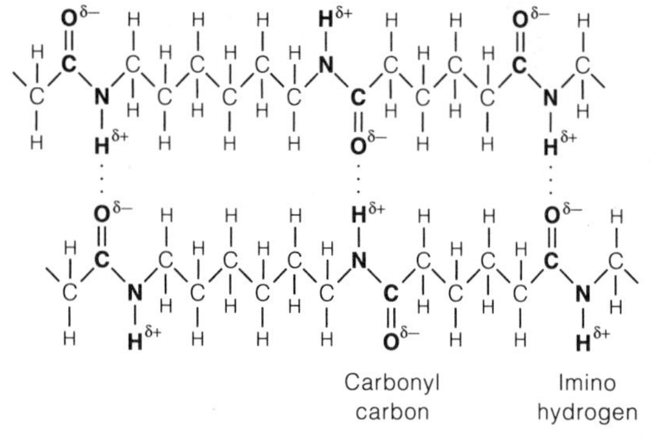

Carbonyl   Imino
carbon   hydrogen

. . . = hydrogen bonding

mated that nylon fiber is 65–85% crystalline and 15–35% amorphous.

The most important chemical group in the polyamide polymer is the polar amide group.

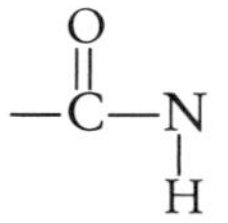

The carbonyl oxygen has a slightly negative charge and the imino hydrogen has a slightly positive charge, as shown in Figure 16.4. Hydrogen bonds form between the -C=O and -N-H groups along adjacent polymer chains in the amorphous as well as in the crystalline regions of the fiber. The hydrogen bonds form a regular "grid" or a "pleated sheet" structure much like that within the silk fiber. The other important group is the amino group

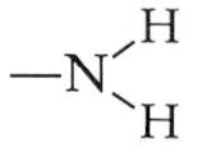

found at the end of the polyamide polymer. These groups provide the sites for attraction of dye molecules.

Comparing the polymer of nylon 6,6 with the polymer of nylon 6 reveals a difference in the spacing and orientation of the amide groups in the polymer chains, as shown in Detail View 16. In nylon 6, the amide groups all point in the same direction and are separated by five methylene

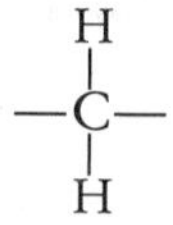

units. In nylon 6,6 the direction of the amide groups alternates along the polymer chain and the spacing exhibits a 6-4-6-4 repeat pattern. These differences in polymers should lead to differences in fiber properties. One of the major differences is that nylon 6 has a lower melting temperature than nylon 6,6. However, it has been questioned whether or not there are other real performance differences between nylon 6,6 and nylon 6, because the fibers made from each type of polymer usually differ in other aspects of structure as well.[4]

PROPERTIES

Nylon was heralded as the "miracle fiber" when its development was first announced in 1939. Rumors spread about its remarkable properties. Some were so exaggerated that Du Pont found itself in the unusual position of having to set the record straight about some of the "miracle" claims others made. The properties of nylon fiber are summarized in Table 16.1. To obtain numerical values for nylon fiber properties and to compare the properties of nylon to other fibers, refer to Figures 8.1–8.13 and Tables 8.1–8.8.

Influencing Fabric Durability

Nylon is known as the "strong man" fiber. The fiber has the human, muscle-like ability to elongate and recover and also the tenacity associated with strong individuals. Its combination of high tenacity with exceptional elongation and recovery is unique among the textile fibers.

Weight for weight, nylon filament is stronger than steel wire. Two tenacities are made: regular tenacity for the apparel market, and high tenacity for the industrial and carpet markets. Nylon fiber tenacity is due not to the degree of polymerization of its polymers but to the very crystalline polymer structure, which contains hydrogen bonds of the strongest kind. (The polarity of the amide groups is high, and the charges are very close to each other.) When nylon fiber is subjected to a longitudinal force, that force must be greater than the strength of the hydrogen bonds to cause the polymers to slide.

[4]R.A.F. Moore, "Nylon 6 and Nylon 66: How Different Are They?," *Textile Chemist and Colorist* 21/2 (1989): 19–22.

Under stress, nylon fiber elongates considerably more than the other "hard" fibers.[5] Nylon fiber then recovers so that it is prepared to withstand the next stress exerted on it. Nylon resembles the elastomeric fibers in this respect but does not snap back nearly as fast. Regular nylon filament recovers 100% up to 8% extension; high-tenacity fiber recovers 100% up to 4% extension.

Generally, high crystallinity and orientation, combined with strong interpolymer bonding, means low fiber elongation. In the case of nylon fiber, this is not the case. When nylon fiber is subjected to a longitudinal force, it is the zigzag polymers that are straightened. Further, because these polymers are bonded by a grid of hydrogen bonding, slippage of polymers relative to each other is prevented. When the longitudinal force is removed, the polymers return to their zigzag configuration and to their original position within the fiber. There is a limit to the extent of elongation and recovery, however. Severe stress causes the hydrogen bonds to break, resulting in polymer slippage and, ultimately, in fiber breakage.

Nylon fiber is one of the toughest fibers in common use. Its toughness is due to its elasticity and the grid of very strong hydrogen bonds, as well as the tenacity of the polymer itself.

Nylon is unsurpassed in abrasion resistance. It can take an enormous amount of rubbing, flexing, scraping, and similar forces without wearing away. Often, nylon is used in blends as a reinforcement fiber (for example, in cotton or acrylic socks). Nylon itself is an abrasive material. If staple nylon is not properly blended and formed into yarns, it can damage the other fiber in the blend by rubbing against it.

Nylon fiber has high flexibility—a flexibility equal to that of wool fiber. The flexibility of nylon fiber is largely due to the zigzag configuration of its polymers, whereas that of wool fiber is due to its high proportion of amorphous area.

Influencing Fabric Comfort

Nylon has the highest moisture regain of the synthetic fibers. There are no hydroxyl groups (-OH) along the polyamide polymer, but there are polar amide groups to attract water molecules. The accessibility of these groups

[5] All fibers except the elastomeric fibers (spandex, rubber, and anidex) are referred to as "hard." The elastomeric fibers that have considerable elongation and high recovery are "spongy" or "soft" by comparison. "Soft" here is used in the sense of compression of the fiber rather than bending ease.

TABLE 16.1 Nylon Fiber Property Summary.

PROPERTY	RANK*
Mechanical[†]	
Breaking tenacity	High
Elongation	High
Elastic recovery	High
Flexibility	High
Abrasion resistance	High
Stiffness (flexural rigidity)	Medium
Resilience	High
Toughness (work of rupture)	High
Initial modulus	Low
Sorptive	
Moisture regain/content	Medium (highest of *synthetic* fibers)
Cross-sectional swelling	Low
Heat of wetting	Medium
Effect on mechanical properties	Medium
Oil absorption	Medium (low compared to other hydrophobic fibers)
Ease of oil release	Medium
Thermal	
Heat resistance (durability)	Medium
Softening and melting	Medium
Decomposition	High
Combustibility	Medium
Chemical	
Alkali resistance	
Dilute	High
Concentrated	High
Acid resistance	
Dilute	Low
Concentrated	Low
Organic solvent resistance	High
Oxidizing agent resistance	Low (weakened by chlorine bleach)
Miscellaneous	
Ultraviolet light resistance	Low
Microorganism resistance	High
Moth and beetle resistance	High
Silverfish resistance	High
Electrical resistivity	High (static is a problem)
Specific gravity	Low

* Levels relative to other fibers except special-use synthetic fibers.

[†] At 70°F (21°C), 65% relative humidity.

is limited to the outer surface of the fiber, due to the very crystalline polymer system of nylon fiber. Water vapor emitted from the skin surface therefore can be absorbed partially by nylon fibers and diffused to the outer environment.

The round, smooth, rod shape of the nylon fiber permits close packing of the fibers in yarns and of the yarns in fabric. Water vapor as well as air permeability through nylon fabric interstices can be very low. Men who wore filament nylon shirts in the 1950s reported that they felt as if they were wearing plastic because water evaporating from their skin could not dissipate to the environment. The close packing of regular nylon fibers within yarns is an asset, however, when fabrics with low air permeability, such as those used in windbreaker jackets and outer shell fabrics for ski garments and other cold-weather clothing, are desired.

Fabrics containing regular nylon fibers tend to lack skin-contact comfort, inducing a feeling often described as "cold and clammy," because the smooth filaments lie flat on the skin surface. Nylon fiber may be crimped to provide a more pleasant sensation as well as to increase the porosity of the fabric to water-vapor diffusion (Chapter 24).

In comparison with other fibers of the same size, nylon fiber is about average in stiffness. The very crystalline polymer system and the grid of strong hydrogen bonds contribute stiffness, which is moderated by the zigzag configuration of the polymers. When warmed, nylon fiber becomes limper because heat breaks the hydrogen bonds.

Nylon fibers readily develop static electricity, because they do not absorb sufficient water to dissipate the accumulation of electrons. The problem is more acute when the air is dry than when it is humid. Nylon fibers tend to hold a static charge until it can be discharged to a good conductor, such as the human body.

Nylon fibers have low specific gravity; they are lightweight. A backpacker's burden is significantly lightened by use of nylon tents and backpacks. The combination of high tenacity and low specific gravity is unique to nylon fibers.

Influencing Fabric Aesthetics

Nylon fibers are highly resilient due to the zigzag configuration of the polyamide polymers and the grid of hydrogen bonding. When a nylon fiber is bent, the polymers lengthen on the outside of the curvature (the zigzag configuration becomes less pronounced) and are compressed at the inside of the curvature (the zigzag con-

figuration becomes more pronounced). The hydrogen bonds are stressed, but they hold the polymers in position relative to each other. When the fiber is released, it straightens (flattens). When the stress applied causes the hydrogen bonds to be broken, the fiber does not straighten.

Due to the resilience of nylon fiber, fabrics made from them tend to be wrinkle-free during wear and laundering and to retain their shape. Nylon carpet pile has high compressional resilience (maintains loft). Heat setting of the fabric enhances the resilience of the nylon fiber and therefore that of the fabric (Chapter 33).

Influencing Fabric Maintenance

Soiling and Staining. Nylon fiber attracts and holds soil primarily on its surface. It tends to attract dirt particles from the air due to its static nature. Further, it tends to attract charged particles (colorants and soils) from laundry water. These particles stain the fiber because they bond with the polar sites at the fiber surface. Staining of nylon carpeting, particularly oil-borne staining, occurs readily.

Soil Removal from Apparel Fabrics. If fabric-care procedures were based on fiber content alone, nylon fabrics could be drycleaned or laundered, because nylon fibers are not harmed by drycleaning solvents or by the alkalinity of detergent solutions. Generally, nylon fabrics are laundered.

The complete removal of soil from nylon fiber during laundering is difficult. White nylon fabrics are particularly challenging to keep white. Grayed, yellowed, or otherwise discolored nylon fabrics are almost, if not impossible, to restore to original appearance.

The partial attraction of water to the surface of nylon fiber is helpful in facilitating the removal of soil but not particularly helpful in removing stains. Water is attracted to the polar groups along the polymers, and the detergent solution spreads. The swelling of nylon fiber in water, its thermoplastic nature, and the effect of these responses on its mechanical properties limit the vigorousness of laundering conditions and therefore the completeness of soil removal. The thermoplastic nature of the fiber also must be taken into account in terms of limiting the degree of wrinkling and shrinkage during laundering. The yellowing of nylon fiber by bleaches also limits the use of bleach to remove soil.

Nylon fiber weakens slightly in water; it elongates more when wet than when dry and has a lower wet-than-dry modulus. These changes occur as a result of the breakage of hydrogen bonds in the amorphous regions of the fiber as water molecules are absorbed. As a result, more polymer slippage occurs as the fabric/fiber is agitated. Gentle agitation and spin cycles, rather than regular washing cycles, therefore, should be used.

Hot water should not be used because it softens nylon fiber too much.[6] At higher washwater temperatures, the fiber is distorted more easily (has a lower modulus) and the fabric is more likely to wrinkle. Although warm washwater also softens nylon fiber, it is needed because soil removal is not effective in cold water. Use of a permanent-press machine setting is desirable, because cool water is added to the warm washwater before the fabric is spun up against the interior of the washbasket. The fibers are thus cooled and become stiffer.

Low dryer temperatures are also necessary. Hot garments should not be allowed to lie in the bottom of the dryer. If laundry temperatures are too high, fabric wrinkling can be permanent. Ironing, which must be done at a low temperature setting, will not remove these wrinkles.

Oxygen bleaches may assist in soil and stain removal. Chlorine bleaches also work but they degrade and yellow the fiber as well and should not be used.

White nylon should be washed alone or with other white items, so that there is no colorant in the washwater. Nylon items should be rinsed thoroughly to prevent colorant in the detergent from being left on the fabric.

Soil Removal from Carpeting. Recommendations for cleaning nylon carpeting include vacuuming frequently, cleaning the most used areas periodically with a powdered carpet cleaner, and using an extraction or scrub-and-extract method to remove dulling film and deep-down soil. Dry powder cleaners work effectively; they are gently brushed into the surface of the carpet and only remove soil they touch. The most effective way to remove soil from carpeting throughout an entire house is by extraction cleaning. A moderately soiled carpet can be cleaned adequately with the extraction method alone; a heavily soiled carpet (one that looks dirty) will need the scrub-and-extract method.

Potential Degradation and Yellowing. Nylon fiber is vulnerable to degradation in acids because they hydrolyze the amide linkages along the polymer chain. Such fragmentation results in a loss of the effectiveness of in-

terpolymer hydrogen bonding, and the fiber is weakened. Nylon fiber dissolves almost immediately in hydrochloric, nitric, and sulfuric acids. The weak sulfuric acid formed from sulfur in soot plus atmospheric oxygen in large cities is of sufficient concentration to weaken the nylon filament in sheer hosiery and cause a "run." Acid hydrolysis on the surface of nylon fibers changes light reflection; white nylon becomes duller and assumes a yellow hue.

Phenols and organic solvents found in household disinfectants can damage nylon fiber. Alkalies, organic solvents used for stain removal, and perspiration have little effect on nylon fiber tenacity.

Nylon fiber has low resistance to sunlight. If left in direct sunlight for several weeks, nylon fibers may decompose. The ultraviolet light causes the imino hydrogen of the amide groups to react with the oxygen in the air, producing reactive groups that cause polymer fragmentation and breakage of interpolymer bonds. In a polluted (acidic) atmosphere, degradation from ultraviolet light is accelerated.

In cold environments $-40°$ F $(-40°$ C), nylon retains its tenacity well. Nylon can withstand temperatures up to 150°F (66°C) for hours. Prolonged exposure to heat encountered in normal consumer use leads to lowered tenacity and to yellowing.

The fiber is impervious to most biological organisms, even in hot, humid environments. This performance feature was particularly useful in World War II military applications in the Pacific theater. Moths, beetles, fungi, and even termites do not attack nylon fibers. Finishes on nylon fabric may allow mildew-producing organisms to grow, however.

Influencing Health/Safety/Protection

Nylon fabric fuses and draws away when exposed to an open flame. It melts and drips, and some flame is carried down with the drip. White smoke is given off. White nylon fabric forms a tan bead; dyed nylon, a black bead. Certain finishes on nylon fabric increase its flammability.

Nylon fiber received an undeserved bad reputation shortly after it was introduced on the market. The phrase "nylon dermatitis" was coined, due to an epidemic of allergic contact dermatitis occurring on the legs of women who wore the new nylon hosiery. When the cause was discovered for these skin eruptions, nylon fiber was exonerated. The culprit was, in most cases, a new resin finish. This finish was immediately removed from the market, and such an event has not recurred.

---

[6]Hot water can be used to remove oily soil from the oleophilic nylon fiber, but considerable caution is necessary.

PRODUCTION

Organic compounds obtained from refined crude oil are reacted with each other in a complex series of steps to yield the polymerization monomers. The polymerization reaction takes place in a stainless-steel pressure vessel; an inert atmosphere of nitrogen or hydrogen is used to ensure that oxygen is excluded, because the polyamide polymer is extremely susceptible to decomposition. In the preparation of nylon 6,6, a nylon salt is formed first. This does not occur in the production of nylon 6. Water, which is given off as the polymerization monomers join end-to-end to form the polymer, must be removed from the reaction mixture. When the desired degree of polymerization is reached, the polymer solution is extruded through a slit in the base of the reaction vessel. The ribbon of viscous material is cooled to solidify the solution and then chopped into tiny chips for convenient handling. These chips are washed and dried.

Next, the prepared polymeric chips are melt-spun. The denier of the fiber and its cross-sectional shape are controlled by the size and shape of the holes in the spinneret. Extrusion rates can be as high as 1200 meters per minute. The fiber at this stage of manufacture is called "undrawn polymer." *Drawing*—the process of stretching the solidified fiber to unfold the polymers within the fiber and arrange them in a more orderly fashion—then takes place (Chapter 24).

VARIANTS

About 200 variants of nylon 6,6 and nylon 6 are manufactured. Alterations of fiber denier, cross section, and crimp predominate.

Variants for Improved Fabric Comfort

For many years, the approach to improving the thermophysiological comfort of nylon fabrics was to crimp nylon yarn mechanically. Water vapor permeability of the fabric thus is significantly improved by decreasing the close packing of the fibers in yarns and of the yarns in fabric. In the late 1980s, nylon-fiber manufacturers began to work closely with yarn and fabric manufacturers to develop fabric systems with improved moisture transport, particularly for activewear (athletic) applications. They discovered that manufacturing block polymers and microfibers leads to improved fabric comfort.

Hydrofil® nylon fiber, a fiber trademark of Allied-Signal, Inc., is an example of an *absorbent* or *hydrophilic*

nylon fiber. It is a block copolymer of nylon 6 and polyethylene oxide diamine (PEOD). The ratio by molecular weight is ~85% nylon 6 and 15% PEOD. The copolymer maintains most of the desirable properties of nylon but adds moisture absorbency at a level generally found only in cellulosic fibers. Fabric composed of Hydrofil® nylon fiber pulls sensible perspiration (sweat) away from the skin, providing more effective evaporation.

Nylon microfibers permit a waterproof, breathable fabric to be made. Fiber manufacturers hold the following certification trademarks for fabrics made with their nylon microfibers:[7] Microfine® and Supplex® Microfiber® by Du Pont and Tactel® Micro® by ICI Fibers. The interstices formed in the yarns and fabric are large enough to permit water vapor to be diffused from the skin to the environment but small enough to prevent rainwater from penetrating, even when it forcefully hits the fabric. Waterproof, breathable, microfiber fabrics also provide superior wind protection and a soft feel.

Nylon fiber also may be modified in several ways to reduce the degree of static buildup. Antistatic chemicals—those that have the ability to absorb water or are conducting polymeric materials—may be added to the nylon polymer solution prior to extrusion. Another method is to graft the nylon polymer; the graft provides the antistatic improvement.

Variants for Improved Aesthetic Appeal of Fabric

Nylon fiber may be modified to improve the aesthetic appeal of the fabric by using additives, such as delustrants and optical brighteners, in the spinning melt, changing the cross-sectional shape, and making microfibers. Figure 16.5 shows examples of nylon fiber modified to improve fabric aesthetics. These fabrics therefore may have greater or lesser luster and sparkle, smoother feel, more silk-like aesthetics, and better shape retention than fabrics containing regular nylon fiber.

Nylon fibers may be modified to provide a subtle spark by making a trilobal cross section; this modified fiber reflects light in much the same way as a diamond prism. However, unlike diamonds, *trilobal fibers* do not separate light into colors. Instead, the reflection appears as a subtle sparkle that prevents even dark colors from appearing dull. Antron® nylon fiber by Du Pont is one example of a trilobal nylon fiber.

---

[7]Remember that fiber manufacturers produce fiber but not fabric. They may, however, hold a certification trademark for the fabric through licensed control or certification programs, a concept discussed in Chapter 9.

FIGURE 16.5 Nylon fiber variants to improve the aesthetic appeal of nylon fabric.

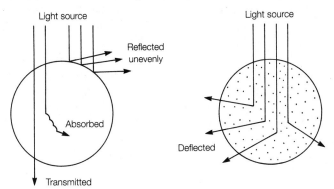

A comparison of the pattern of light absorption, transmission, and reflection from a regular nylon fiber and a delustered nylon fiber demonstrates the decrease in luster and improvement in opacity that can be achieved.

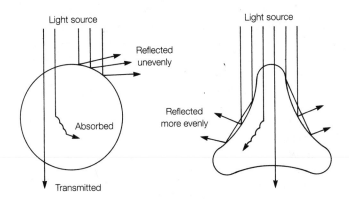

A comparison of the pattern of light reflection from the surface of round cross-sectional (regular) nylon fiber and trilobal cross-sectional (modified) nylon fiber demonstrates the improvement in luster achieved.

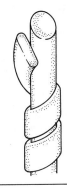

A comparison of the bending of round cross-sectional (regular) nylon fiber to the bending of a flattened cross-sectional (modified) nylon fiber around a center filament demonstrates the improvement in yarn smoothness that is achieved.

Delustered nylon fibers—fibers to which titanium dioxide has been added in the spinning melt—are duller than regular nylon fibers. A delustrant, a pigment added to the fiber melt, alters the reflection of light. More light is absorbed by the delustered fiber.

To make a more bendable nylon fiber to cover spandex filament in hosiery yarn, a flat cross-sectional nylon fiber has been made. The "flattened" cross section permits closer wrapping of the nylon filament around spandex fiber than that of round fiber. Improved smooth-

FIGURE 16.6 Nylon fiber variants for improved carpet maintenance.

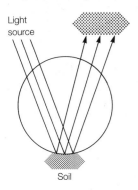

Round fiber

Most incident light is transmitted through the fiber, strikes dirt particles, and is reflected back to the eye. Soil is clearly seen and is magnified.

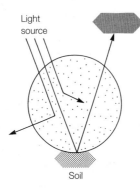

Delustered round fiber

Most of the incident light is deflected by the delustrant; some is transmitted, strikes the dirt particles, and is reflected to the eye, some is deflected but reflected to the eye. Soil is partially hidden; that seen appears hazy.

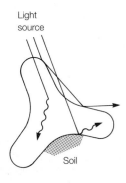

Trilobal fiber

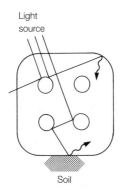

Squared fiber with voids

Most of the incident light is reflected from the fiber surface or deflected internally. Soil is hidden because little light is transmitted through the fiber to strike the soil particles. Of this transmitted light, little of it reaches the eye.

ness, sheerness, and better protection of the spandex filament result. The fiber is Du Pont type 782, and the yarn is trademarked Ribbonshear®.

Silk-like nylon fibers may be achieved by changing the chemistry of the polymers and by reducing the denier of the fiber to or below that of silk fiber. The first of the silk-like nylon fibers—Qiana® nylon fiber,[8] which was introduced by Du Pont in 1969 and discontinued in 1984—was chemically different than regular nylon. Its denier was similar to silk fiber, which was a technical breakthrough at that time. Trademarked fabrics on the market today that contain fine nylon fibers include Supplex® nylon (a fabric composed of yarns containing 66–196 nylon filaments, compared to the 36 filaments composing a regular nylon yarn) and Tactel® nylon 6,6 (a fabric containing fine nylon filaments with trilobal cross sections, which has been air-jet textured with the intent of producing a softer nylon fabric with a more "natural" hand). In the late 1980s, nylon microfibers were introduced and promoted as silk-like fibers. Fabrics include Tactel® Micro®, a trademark held by ICI Fibers, and Microfine®, a trademark held by Du Pont.

A *100%-nylon bicomponent fiber*, a fiber with a side-by-side arrangement of two types of amide polymers, has led to improved fabric shape retention. The fiber is said to be chemically crimped. The crimp is permanent. In hosiery, these bicomponent nylon fibers provide improved fit, because the fibers in the stocking as well as its knit structure can expand to fit the leg. The crimp of the bicomponent nylon fiber relaxes to help the stocking fit closely.

Optically whitened nylon fibers, those containing an optical brightener compound, offer improved whiteness and brightness retention. The optical brightener is usually added to the melt solution.

Variants for Improved Carpet Maintenance

Nylon carpet fiber may be modified to make soiling less noticeable or to reduce the degree of soiling (Figure 16.6). Round, transparent fibers show soil the most. In fact, a round shape actually magnifies the degree of soiling. *Delustered nylon fibers* hide soil but do little to enhance carpet beauty. *Trilobal nylon fibers* and *squared nylon fibers* with voids scatter or disperse light, effectively hiding soil that has accumulated in the carpet. Most major carpet producers today use the trilobal shape, because it also adds significant bulk and resilience to the fiber and allows brighter luster and clearer colors. Nylon fibers with modified cross sections reduce the frequency of carpet cleaning, not the amount of soil on the fiber.

[8]The Qiana® trademark presently is used by the Du Pont company for a certification program for apparel fabrics.

Stain resistance can be improved with the use of a *nylon/fluorocarbon, matrix/fibril bicomponent fiber.* A fluorocarbon, like Teflon ®, forms the fibril portion; the nylon polymers form the matrix portion of the fiber. The resulting reduction in surface energy provided by the fluorocarbon leads to resistance of water-based and oil-based soil. Carpets made from these matrix/fibril bicomponent fibers are not completely stain-proof, but resistance to staining tends to be better than topically applied treatments because the protection is built into every filament. The fluorocarbon remains an integral part of the nylon fiber for the life of the carpet. The licensed trademark for carpets made from the matrix/fibril bicomponent nylon fiber manufactured by Allied Fiber is Anso V Worry Free Carpet ®.

Nylon fiber also may be made stain resistant by the application of a topical finish to the carpeting. This modification is discussed in Chapter 33.

Variants for Improved Fabric Durability and Resistance to Deterioration

High-tenacity nylon fibers are made for use in many industrial applications. Increased degrees of polymerization and higher degrees of orientation and crystallinity are achieved. Stabilizers and antioxidants may be added to nylon polymers in the spinning melt to enhance resistance to heat, light, and oxidation (yellowing). Delustrants decrease resistance to ultraviolet radiation. Bright nylon, which is used in curtains, has better resistance to degradation than delustered or dull nylon.

CHAPTER SUMMARY

Nylon fiber is a polyamide fiber. Its polymers have a zigzag configuration with a partially positive polar site (imino hydrogen) and a partially negative polar site (carbonyl oxygen). It is highly crystalline, oriented, and strongly hydrogen bonded by the polar groups in both the crystalline and amorphous areas.

The unique set of properties of the nylon fiber include its high tenacity combined with high elongation and elastic recovery and its high tenacity combined with low specific gravity. It has the highest moisture regain, resilience, and flexibility of the synthetic fibers. It is susceptible to degradation by weak acids and sunlight.

Nylon fiber is often modified in cross-sectional shape, in diameter, and by the addition of chemicals to the fiber-spinning solution. Nylon fiber is melt-spun; its major end use is as carpet-pile fiber.

Polyester Fibers

Polyester fibers are "manufactured fiber(s) in which the fiber-forming substance is any long-chain polymer composed of at least 85% by weight of an ester of a substituted aromatic carboxylic acid, including but not restricted to substituted terephthalate units $\left[\rho(-R-O-\underset{O}{\overset{\|}{C}}-C_6H_4-\underset{O}{\overset{\|}{C}}-) \right]$ and

parasubstituted hydroxybenzoate units $\left[\rho(-R-O-C_6H_4-\underset{O}{\overset{\|}{C}}-O-) \right]$."

PET
(Polyethylene terephthalate)

PCDT
(Poly-1,4-cyclohexylene-
dimethylene terephthalate)

PEB
(Polyethylene oxybenzoate)

Variants for Improved Fabric Durability
High-tenacity fibers
Polyester core/low-melting-polymer sheath bicomponent fibers
Variants for Improved Fabric Comfort
Chemically modified surface fibers
Hydrophilic fibers
Tetra-channel fibers
Hollow-core fibers with convoluted surfaces
Microfibers
High-shrinkage fibers
Variants for Improved Aesthetic Appeal of Fabric
Silk-like fibers -star-shaped or pentalobal cross-sectional fibers
                 -trilobal cross-sectional fibers
                 -microfibers
                 -sodium-hydroxide-treated fibers*
Thick-and-thin fibers
Delustered fibers
Low-pill fibers
Cationic-dyeable fibers
Antistatic fibers
Better-blending fibers
Variants for Improved Safety/Protection
Inherently flame-resistant fibers
Topically treated, flame-retardant fibers*

*To be discussed in Chapter 31.

17

$\mathcal{P}$olyester Fibers

Polyester was introduced to Americans at a 1951 press conference. A suit that had been worn continuously for 67 days, with periodic machine washings but without pressing, was shown to reporters. Amazingly, the suit made from the new polyester fiber was still presentable! Other fibers then available (the natural fibers, rayon, acetate, acrylic, and nylon) would not have performed nearly this well. American consumers, hearing of the outstanding resilience and dimensional stability of this new fiber, were convinced that polyester had a place in their wardrobes.

A constant growth in the demand and use of polyester fiber continued for more than two decades. In the 1970s, a decline in the utilization of polyester fiber occurred. Apparel manufacturers had flooded the market with polyester double-knit fabrics, many having questionable design quality, aesthetics, and comfort. The American public attributed the shortcomings of the double knits to polyester fiber rather than to fabric and garment design. The demand for polyester fiber and garments declined as a result. Producers of polyester fiber are still attempting to correct the image problem associated with their fiber. A concerted public relations campaign has been directed at both consumers and retailers. Fashion garments of polyester fiber by major designers have been placed in the public eye. Emphasis on positive performance attributes of the fiber are expounded, as they rightly were in 1951.

Polyester-fiber manufacturers sell four major polyester products: filament fiber, staple and tow fiber, fi-

berfill,[1] and nonwoven fabric structures.[2] In 1990, 3061.6 million pounds of polyester fiber were produced by U.S. manufacturers and shipped to domestic customers (Figure 17.1). An additional 164.1 million pounds of fiber were imported. Polyester fiber ranks second to cotton fiber in the amount produced and shipped to domestic customers.

The primary market for polyester fiber is apparel; approximately 40% of all polyester fiber was used for men's, women's, children's, and infants' clothing in 1990. This amount of utilization represents ~35% of all fiber used in apparel annually. In comparison, ~40% of apparel fiber was cotton. The second largest market for polyester fiber is industrial and consumer textiles. Many different products are made, some of which are listed in Figure 17.1. Household textiles utilize ~17% of all polyester fiber. It is by far the most important fiber in lightweight curtain nets. Woven polyester and cellulosic blends (mainly polyester/cotton) occupy a very substan-

---

[1] Fiberfill is a synthetic batting produced to provide optimum thermal comfort and/or bulkiness. When used for thermal comfort, it is found in sleeping bags, comforters, and cold-weather outdoor clothing. When bulkiness is required, it is used in pillows and mattress pads. In both cases, fiberfill must provide a resilient structure. It also may need to be quick-drying, maintain its shape, and have uniform thickness.

[2] Spunbonded and spunlaced nonwoven fabrics are made as a continuous process with fiber production. Spunbonded fabrics contain filament polyester fibers; spunlaced fabrics, staple polyester fibers. The process and fabrics are discussed in Chapter 28.

FIGURE 17.1 Primary market distribution of polyester fiber produced in the United States and shipped to domestic customers in 1990.

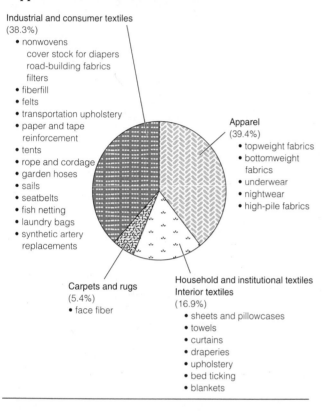

Industrial and consumer textiles (38.3%)
- nonwovens
  cover stock for diapers
  road-building fabrics
  filters
- fiberfill
- felts
- transportation upholstery
- paper and tape
  reinforcement
- tents
- rope and cordage
- garden hoses
- sails
- seatbelts
- fish netting
- laundry bags
- synthetic artery
  replacements

Apparel (39.4%)
- topweight fabrics
- bottomweight fabrics
- underwear
- nightwear
- high-pile fabrics

Carpets and rugs (5.4%)
- face fiber

Household and institutional textiles
Interior textiles (16.9%)
- sheets and pillowcases
- towels
- curtains
- draperies
- upholstery
- bed ticking
- blankets

tial place in the bedsheet and pillowcase markets. The use of polyester fiber as a carpet-face fiber is small but growing. Currently, polyester fiber has garnered ~7% of the carpet-fiber market.

Detail View 17 shows the various types of polyester fiber that are made today.

GENERIC GROUP MEMBERS

The generic group name "polyester" reflects the name given the chemical linkage of the monomers within the fiber (that is, ester). An *ester* is a chemical group with the general structure

$$R'\!-\!\overset{\displaystyle O}{\underset{\displaystyle \|}{C}}\!-\!OR,$$

where R and R′ can be any hydrocarbon chemical group.[3] In Detail View 17, the ester linkages are shown in boldface type. Esters are formed in a reaction between an alcohol and a carboxylic acid:

$$R\!-\!OH \;+\; R\!-\!C\!\!\overset{\displaystyle O}{\underset{\displaystyle OH}{\Big\langle}} \;\rightarrow\; ester$$

alcohol   carboxylic
             acid

To synthesize a polymer, the alcohol and the acid must have the reactive chemical group -OH and -COOH at each end of the molecule and therefore are called di-alcohols and dicarboxylic acids, respectively. Further, in polyester fiber, the carboxylic acid must be an aromatic one, which means that a benzene ring ⊚ is included.

By definition in the Textile Fiber Products Identification Act, polyester fibers are "manufactured fibers in which the fiber-forming substance is any long-chain polymer composed of at least 85% by weight of an ester of a substituted aromatic carboxylic acid, including but not restricted to substituted terephthalate units

$$\left[\rho(\!-\!R\!-\!O\!-\!\overset{\displaystyle C}{\underset{\displaystyle O}{\|}}\!-\!C_6H_4\!-\!\overset{\displaystyle C}{\underset{\displaystyle O}{\|}}\!-\!)\right]$$

parasubstituted hydroxybenzoate units

$$\left[\rho(\!-\!R\!-\!O\!-\!C_6H_4\!-\!\overset{\displaystyle C}{\underset{\displaystyle O}{\|}}\!-\!O\!-\!)\right]$$

Therefore, many possible members of the polyester generic group are possible, depending on which aromatic carboxylic acid or hydroxybenzoate unit is reacted with a dialcohol. Capital letters are used to name the members of the polyester generic group; the letters indicate the chemical nature of the polymer. Two members are commercially important; a third was recently withdrawn from production.

[3] "R" is a symbol used in chemistry to denote a general chemical group. For the alcohols and carboxylic acids, "R" stands for a hydrocarbon chain. As examples, methyl alcohol is CH_3-OH and ethyl alcohol (ethanol) is CH_3-CH_2-OH.

Polyethylene Terephthalate (PET)

The most important member of the polyester generic group of fibers is polyethylene terephthalate (PET), which was introduced on the U.S. market in 1951. The starting compounds used in the formation of PET are shown in Figure 17.2. J.T. Dickson and J.R. Whinfield, employed in the laboratories of the Calico Printers' Association in Lancashire, England, are credited with the pioneering work. They formed the first commercially feasible PET polyester textile fiber in 1941. A polyester polymer was previously formed by members of Wallace Carothers' research team at Du Pont, but development of polyester polymers was set aside and resources were directed to polyamide (nylon) research. Development of polyester was slowed by World War II, but the fiber had been investigated sufficiently by 1947 that ICI Fibers in England and Du Pont in the United States purchased the rights to manufacture polyester fiber from the Calico Printers' Association. The first fibers were marketed as Terylene® polyester in England and as Dacron® polyester in the United States. More than 95% of all polyester fiber manufactured today is PET.

Poly-1,4-cyclohexylenedimethylene Terephthalate (PCDT)

The second most important member of the polyester generic group is poly-1,4-cyclohexylenedimethylene terephthalate (PCDT). The Eastman Kodak Company is the only PCDT producer in the United States. This polyester was introduced in 1958; on consumer labels, PCDT is called Kodel II®. (Other Kodel® polyester fibers, marketed as Kodel IV®, are PET.) To market various PCDT fibers to yarn and fabric manufacturers, Eastman Kodak identifies the fibers by numbering them between 200 and 299. This polyester was developed for use as a blending fiber with cellulosics and wool, as a carpet fiber, and as a fiberfill (batting) fiber.

Polyethyleneoxybenzoate (PEB)

Polyethyleneoxybenzoate (PEB) was manufactured in Japan during the 1970s and early 1980s and marketed under the tradename A-Tell®. This member often is called benzoate polyester or benzoate fiber. The manufacturer requested a new generic classification because the Federal Trade Commission (FTC) definition of polyester at that time did not allow a carboxylic acid

FIGURE 17.2 **Starting compounds in the formation of polyethylene terephthalate (PET) polyester fiber.**

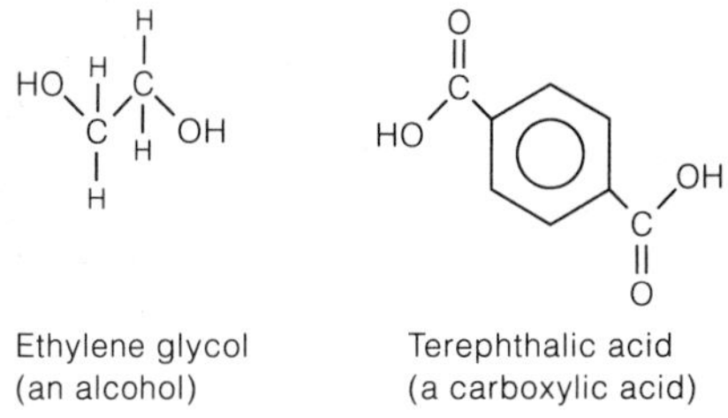

Ethylene glycol   Terephthalic acid
(an alcohol)   (a carboxylic acid)

other than terephthalate to be a starting compound. The FTC decided to modify the polyester definition in 1973 to include the benzoate polyester rather than form another generic group of fibers. Production of the PEB fiber has been discontinued because it did not offer sufficient performance advantages to retain a place in the textile market.

STRUCTURE

Polyester fiber is smooth and even in diameter (Figure 17.3). It has no identifiable microscopic features. The cross section is nearly circular. Fiber diameter generally varies from 12 to 25 micrometers (μm), or 1.5–10 denier, depending on end-use requirements. The fiber is white or slightly off-white in color and is partially transparent.

The important chemical groups in the polyester polymer are the methylene groups, the carbonyl groups, the ester links, and the benzene rings.

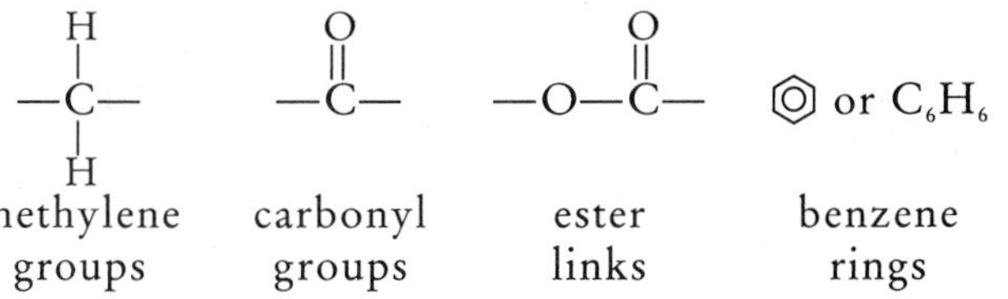

methylene   carbonyl   ester   benzene
groups   groups   links   rings

The polymer is linear, and the degree of polymerization ranges from 115 to 140.

Polyester fibers are composed of ~35% crystalline area and ~65% amorphous area. The polymers in the amorphous area are highly oriented to the fiber axis. The polymers can pack very tightly together (Figure 17.4).

FIGURE 17.3
Photomicrograph of regular
polyester fiber, showing its round
cross section, rod shape, and
smooth surface.

|————————| 25 μm

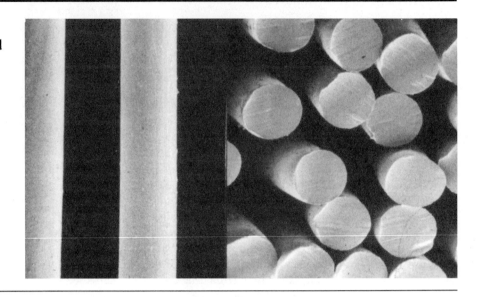

Hydrogen bonds are not formed in polyester fiber due to the low polarity of the carbonyl oxygen and the non-polarity of the methylene hydrogens. However, very effective forces of attraction between polymers occur because there is a cloud of electrons above and below each of the benzene rings, as shown in Figure 17.4. An induced dipole–dipole interaction is probable.

PROPERTIES

Polyester is known as the "workhorse" fiber, since it is the most-used fiber in the United States and the second most-used fiber in the world. Polyester also is known as the "big mixer" because it is blended with most other fibers. Polyester/cotton blends predominate in woven fabrics, but wool/polyester as well as rayon/polyester blends are readily found. Polyester is blended with acrylic in knits. In addition, polyester has been called the "jack-in-the-box" fiber, because polyester fabrics literally snap back to a flat configuration after the bending and crushing forces encountered in normal, everyday wearing situations have been applied and released. Table 17.1 summarizes the properties of polyester fiber. To obtain numerical values for polyester fiber properties and to compare the properties of polyester to other fibers, refer to Figures 8.1–8.13 and Tables 8.1–8.8.

Influencing Fabric Durability

The mechanical properties of polyester fibers are well suited to the durability requirements for apparel end use. These properties are adequate tenacity, excellent resistance to repeated small stresses, and low elongation of the fiber under small, repeated stresses.

Polyester fibers have high tenacity. In fact, their dry tenacity is approximately equal to that of nylon fiber. The high tenacity of polyester fiber is due to its highly crystalline polymer system, which allows the formation of very effective interpolymer interactions of the electrons of the benzene rings. The polymers are also well oriented within the fiber.

FIGURE 17.4 Dipole–dipole attraction is believed to occur in polyester fibers because the benzene (aromatic) rings can lie in close proximity to each other due to the planar nature of the polymers.

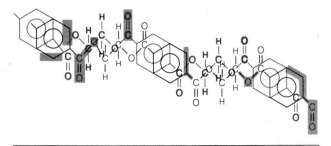

The elongation of polyester fibers at low stress levels is low. The extensive interpolymer interaction of benzene electrons along the oriented and crystalline polymers keep the polymers from slipping. Polyester fibers extend only 2–7% when subjected to forces that would break the natural cellulosic fibers.

Elastic recovery is high under low stress. Recovery is 97% at 2% elongation. Polyester fibers, however, do not exhibit high elastic recovery after subjection to high levels of stress. Under repeated high stresses, the van der Waals forces between polymer chains as well as the benzene electron clouds soon allow polymer slippage.

Polyester fibers perform best when small, repeated stresses rather than large stresses are placed on the fiber. The former types of stresses are those encountered while garments and household and interior textiles (except carpets) are used. The stiffness of the polymer chains resulting from the rigid benzene rings and the strength of the interactions provided by the electron clouds provide dimensional stability.

The abrasion resistance of polyester fiber is high. Polyester is not successful in the carpeting market, however, due to its low compressional resilience (loft).

Influencing Fabric Comfort

Polyester fibers are classified as hydrophobic. Their moisture regain is very low, even in an environment at 95–100% relative humidity. The insignificant amount of moisture in polyester fabric exists as a molecular film of water on the fiber surfaces. The lack of polarity to attract water, the presence of benzene rings, which are hydrophobic, and the fairly crystalline structure, which resists the entry of water molecules into the polymer system, account for the very low moisture regain of the polyester fiber.

Polyester fibers typically have a low level of wicking due to their round, smooth surfaces. The transport of vaporous and liquid water through polyester fabric relies on yarn and fabric constructions that create porosity.

Polyester fabrics do not retain water readily in the interfiber and yarn voids in the fabric (that is, the water of imbibition). After a standard spin cycle, polyester fabric retains only ~4% water. (For comparison, nylon retains ~15%; cotton, ~50%.) This performance is desirable in wet environments because the fabric or fiberfilled item will dry quickly, improving the level of comfort.

Polyester fiber has high electrical resistivity, which leads to surface charge and problems associated with electrostatic discharge under conditions of relatively low

TABLE 17.1 Polyester Fiber Property Summary.

PROPERTY	RANK*
Mechanical†	
Breaking tenacity	High
Elongation	High
Elastic recovery	High
Flexibility	—
Abrasion resistance	High
Stiffness (flexural rigidity)	Medium
Resilience	High
Toughness (work of rupture)	High
Initial modulus	High
Sorptive	
Moisture regain/content	Low
Cross-sectional swelling	Low
Heat of wetting	Low
Effect on mechanical properties	Low (none)
Oil absorption	Medium
Ease of oil release	Low
Thermal	
Heat resistance (durability)	High
Softening and melting	Medium
Decomposition	High
Combustibility	Medium
Chemical	
Alkali resistance	
Dilute	High
Concentrated	Low to hot
Acid resistance	
Dilute	High
Concentrated	High
Organic solvent resistance	High
Oxidizing agent resistance	High
Miscellaneous	
Ultraviolet light resistance	High
Microorganism resistance	High
Moth and beetle resistance	High
Silverfish resistance	High
Electrical resistivity	High (static is a problem)
Specific gravity	Medium

* Levels relative to other fibers except special-use synthetic fibers.

† At 70°F (21°C), 65% relative humidity.

humidity. The electrical resistivity is due in large measure to the hydrophobicity of the fiber. Polyester fiber also has a medium specific gravity.

Influencing Fabric Aesthetics

An outstanding property of polyester fiber is its resilience. Consequently, polyester fabrics rarely wrinkle during use. If laundered according to recommended procedures, polyester fabrics typically do not need to be ironed. The crystallinity of the polymer system is largely responsible for the exceptional resilient behavior.

Due to the thermoplasticity of the polyester fiber, pleats and creases can be set permanently into polyester fabrics; these pleats and creases remain sharp after repeated cleaning cycles. Polyester fabrics also can be permanently embossed. The fiber takes on the "permanent" set when shaped at high temperatures. Provided polyester fiber is present in sufficient proportion in a blended fabric, the polyester also can confer permanent set on the blended fabric.

Polyester fiber is described as having a "hard hand." The crystalline polymer system causes stiffness because polyester polymers resist being bent or flexed. The waxier hand of polyester fabrics, compared to that of nylon fabrics, is due to the presence of the methylene groups and benzene rings in the polyester polymer.

Polyester fabric, which is made entirely from staple-length fibers or from blending with other fibers, is particularly susceptible to pilling. The pills, once formed, do not break off, due to the high tenacity of the polyester fibers. Numerous pills therefore accumulate on the fabric surface, causing an unsightly appearance.

Influencing Fabric Maintenance

Polyester fabrics can be subjected to fairly vigorous laundering conditions to remove tenaciously held soils and emerge from this process virtually wrinkle-free. Polyester fibers have high all-around resistance to chemicals, light, and biological degradation.

Soiling and Staining. Polyester fiber attracts and holds oily soil, as well as the particulate particles it contains, tenaciously on its surface. Oil usually is not absorbed into the polyester fiber. The presence of the benzene rings in the polymer accounts for the adherence of the oil. Polyester fiber tends to resist water-borne staining, but oil-borne staining readily takes place. Particulate soils are attracted from the air due to easily developed static electricity. Polyester fiber is not a scavenger of soil particles or colorants suspended in laundry water.

Soil Removal from Apparel Fabrics. Soil removal from polyester fibers and fabrics can be difficult due to the hydrophobic nature of the fiber surface and to the nature of the fabric interstices. These aspects prevent water (detergent solution) from reaching the soiled fiber surface and then spreading to facilitate soil removal. This fact might lead you to conclude that it would be more difficult to remove soil successfully from polyester fiber/fabric than from nylon because polyester is more hydrophobic than nylon is. However, soil removal from polyester is more complete than from nylon because more vigorous laundering is possible in the case of polyester fabrics. Of considerable importance is the fact that polyester fibers do not swell in water, so their mechanical properties are not changed significantly. The hydrophobic and crystalline polyester polymer system resists the entry of water molecules to any great extent. Further, fairly warm washwater temperatures can be used, which facilitate soil removal. The mechanical properties of polyester fiber are affected by heat but not significantly so at the temperatures used in care procedures. The dimensional stability of polyester fibers is therefore high under normal laundering conditions.

Polyester fiber is resistant to degradation by alkaline detergent solutions. Polyester fiber also may be bleached with chlorine and oxygen bleaches. Normally, polyester fabrics do not need to be bleached because detergent alone can remove the soil.

Certain precautions are advised and certain measures are recommended to obtain maximum soil removal and prevent fabric wrinkling. Permanent-press cycles and cool-down cycles in the washer and dryer reduce wrinkling, which will occur if softened fabric is spun up against the sides of the washtub or allowed to lie at the bottom of the dryer. Applying a liquid laundry detergent directly to a heavily soiled area will facilitate soil removal during a single wash. Another method is the use of "pretreatment" products, which contain organic solvents. Selecting a detergent with a soil-release ingredient also helps.[4]

If exposed to temperatures >385° F (195° C), drawn and heat-set polyester fiber/fabric will shrink. When

---

[4]Detergent manufacturers began to include a soil-release agent in detergent formulations about 1988. Liquid Tide®, a product of the Proctor & Gamble Company, is one of these detergents. Information on detergent containers will indicate whether the product contains a soil-release agent.

ironing is needed, a low iron temperature must be used or the polyester fabric will melt and stick to the sole of the iron.

Potential Degradation in Storage and Use. Polyester fiber is resistant to acids because they cannot break (hydrolyze) the polymer chain at the ester linkages or elsewhere. This acid resistance helps to protect polyester fabrics from the slightly acidic conditions that occur in polluted atmospheres. Polyester fiber can be degraded partially by concentrated alkalies. The degradation (hydrolysis) usually is limited to those polymers that lie near the fiber surface.

Polyester withstands the detrimental effects of ultraviolet radiation from the sun. In comparison to other general-use, synthetic fibers, its radiation resistance is matched only by that of acrylic fibers. This resistance is due to the presence of benzene rings in the polyester polymers.

Weathering resistance, the combination of resistance to sunlight and to acidic conditions, is high: polyester fiber ranks second only to acrylic fiber. In addition, polyester retains 70–80% of its tenacity following prolonged exposure to temperatures <300° F (150° C). Polyester fiber is resistant to molds, fungus, moths, and beetles.

Influencing Health/Safety/Protection

Polyester fibers are flammable. Their resistance to combustion is not much greater than that of cotton fiber.

When polyester *fabrics* are ignited at an edge, they tend to self-extinguish. The reason is that the heat that evolved during initial combustion melts the fabric ahead of the flame front, causing the flaming portion to drop away from the rest of the fabric. Therefore, the rest of the fabric remains unconsumed. This is called a *melt-drip phenomenon*. Polyester fabrics also tend to withdraw (curl away) from an open flame. Such behavior tends to make the fabric a little more difficult to ignite than if the fabric remained over the heat source.

Polyester fiber generates a lot of dense black smoke as it burns. Suffocation due to the smoke can be a problem in certain fire situations.

Polyester/cotton fabrics do not self-extinguish or draw away from an open flame. In the blend, molten polyester is retained on a scaffold of unmelted fabric. The combustion of such blends often is more rapid than the combustion of fabrics made from either fiber alone.

Polyester fibers have the best thermal resistance of the general-use, synthetic fibers. For this reason, polyester products can be sterilized without any problem and used in medical applications. Polyester is used for artificial arteries and veins, as well as for sutures.

There are no known cases of polyester being linked to skin rashes. Dyestuffs used on polyester can be the cause of allergic contact dermatitis in some individuals, but this rarely occurs. Polyester does not cause physiological reactions.

Polyester apparel fabrics that have a buildup of soil exhibit bacterial odor. Use of hot washwater, laundry agents such as borax, which is an odor minimizer, or bleach, which removes soil buildup and kills bacteria, may solve the problem.

PCDT Performance

PCDT shares many of the same performance attributes as PET polyester. The differences that do exist exert an important influence on the end use of the fiber.

PCDT polyester fibers have lower tenacity and elongation than PET polyester fibers. However, PCDT has superior elastic recovery. PCDT polyester is more suited to end uses for which compressional resilience (loft) is of greater importance than high tenacity. These uses are in carpets, rugs, knitwear, and fiberfill. Further, the lower tenacity contributes to the reduction of pilling, because the weaker PCDT fiber will break off of the surface of the fabric more readily than the stronger PET polyester fibers will.

PCDT polyester fibers have a lower specific gravity than PET polyester fibers. Therefore, PCDT polyester fibers have greater covering power. Lighter weight is ideal in fiberfill because more warmth (thermal retention) is possible for the same weight of filling material.

PCDT polyester fibers have a higher softening point than PET polyester fibers, which means that fabrics composed of PCDT polyester fibers can be safely ironed at a higher temperature than fabrics containing PET polyester fibers. PCDT also blends better with wool fiber than PET does.

PCDT polyester should only be drycleaned in petroleum solvents. By comparison, any drycleaning solvent is acceptable for PET polyester. Directions on fiberfilled end-use products should be followed strictly.

PRODUCTION

The two starting compounds used in the synthesis of PET polyester—ethylene glycol[5] and terephthalic

---

[5] Ethylene glycol may be more familiar as antifreeze.

FIGURE 17.5 A bicomponent bigeneric fiber with a polyester core and a sheath of low-melting polymers.

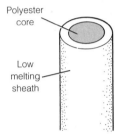

Polyester core

Low melting sheath

Celbond®, manufactured by Hoechst Celanese, is used to produce fiberwebs with softness, resilience, and sufficient strength for a variety of end-use applications.

acid—are obtained from naphtha, a component of crude oil. The synthesis of the polymer is carried out by heating the polymerization monomers and removing the water that forms as the reaction proceeds. When the desired degree of step-growth polymerization is reached, the clear, colorless polyester may be extruded through a slot onto a casting wheel, where the polymer solidifies into an endless ribbon. It is then cut into chips $\sim\frac{1}{8}-\frac{1}{4}$ inches (3–6 millimeters) on a side. Usually, however, the synthesized polymer is extruded through a spinneret.

Depending on the denier required, the spinneret may contain 100–3000 holes. Polyester fibers are melt-spun. The fibers solidify in the heated air they encounter as they emerge from the spinneret.

The filaments that emerge from the spinneret have low crystallinity and moderate orientation. They have high elongation (>200%) and shrink up to 70% in boiling water. The solidified fiber is drawn (Chapter 24). The drawing operation, followed by heat-setting, increases crystallinity and orientation and reduces elongation and shrinkage, thereby improving the polyester as a textile fiber.

VARIANTS

Many physical and chemical variations of polyester are available.

Variants for Improved Fabric Durability

High-tenacity filament and staple fibers are produced by increasing the degree of polymerization of the polymers and developing greater crystallinity (hot drawing process). High-tenacity staple (5.8–7.0 grams/denier) is used in durable-press apparel; high-tenacity filament (6.8–9.5 grams/denier), in tire cord and other industrial applications. Elongation of these high-tenacity fibers is lower than that of regular-tenacity fibers (24–28% for high-tenacity staple, compared to 40–45% for regular staple; 9–27% for high-tenacity filament, compared to 18–42% for regular filament).

Polyester core/low-melting-polymer sheath bicomponent fibers are being produced for use in the manufacture of nonwoven fabrics (Figure 17.5). The low-melting-polymer sheath permits a solid bond to form between fibers, adding strength to the final product. The nonwoven fabrics are used for diaper covers, high-loft batting for furniture, primary backing for automobile carpets and mats, which are molded, and structural reinforcement for automotive fabrics in door panels, headliners, and molded seat assemblies. Trademarked fabrics include Colback® (made by the Fibers Division of BASF), with polyester-core/nylon-sheath fibers, and Celbond® (made by Hoechst Celanese), with several different bicomponent fibers, all with a polyester core but with different sheath polymers.

Variants for Improved Fabric Comfort

Current research focuses on developing a more "natural" polyester fiber/fabric—a polyester with a better feel against the skin, increased absorbency, better insulative ability, and reduced static. Polyester fiber is modified in cross-sectional shape by the incorporation of voids within the fiber and by the use of antistats in the polymer melt to achieve these enhancements. Fiber modification along with carefully engineered yarn and fabric design are usually necessary.[6]

Trademarked Fibers. The introduction of voids within the polyester fiber helps to improve its ability to wick sweat and/or to insulate (Figure 17.6). Wellkey®, a fiber produced by Teijin Limited of Japan, is a polyester fiber having a hollow center and many minute holes 0.01–3.0 micrometers (μm) scattered throughout. Because some of the holes proceed to the hollow center, a capillary phenomenon occurs and the fiber wicks sweat from the skin surface. Wellkey® polyester fiber dries rapidly. It

---

[6]Chemical finishes that modify polyester fiber and therefore improve comfort when wearing polyester fabric are considered in Chapter 32; modifications to polyester filament yarn that also result in improved fabric comfort are considered in Chapter 24.

FIGURE 17.6
Polyester fibers modified by the
introduction of voids.

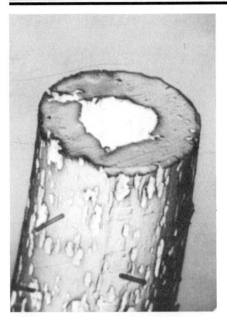 

Wellkey® polyester fiber, by Teijin Limited, wicks sweat through the fiber voids that transverse from one side of the fiber to the other.

Eizac® polyester microfiber, when made into a dense, fibrous webbing, provides better insulation than that composed of regular polyester fiber due to greater incorporation of dead air within the fiber voids.

contains ~15–20% dead air, so it adds to the heat-insulative ability of the fabric in which it is used. The fiber is primarily used in sportswear fabrics. Eizac®, a fiber also produced by Teijin Limited is a microfiber developed for use in dense, fibrous webbing that provides enhanced warmth by capturing more dead air. This microfiber contains microholes in addition to its small fiber size.

Polyester fiber also can be modified by altering the chemical nature of its surface. The chemically modified surface fibers will absorb and wick water. (The untreated fiber core repels water.) It is thought that Capilene®, a polyester fiber used exclusively by the sportswear manufacturer Patagonia for thermal underwear, is modified in this manner.

High Performance Dacron® (T90A for woven fabrics; T50A for knit fabrics) is composed of hydrophilic polyester, which is 12 times more absorbent than regular polyester. Hydrophilic fibers of different deniers (for example, 1.5 denier and 3.0 denier) are mixed to produce a more random packing of fibers in the yarn, allowing air and water vapor to diffuse through. Polyester fabric soaks up moisture and rapidly moves it through the fabric. Polyester fabric also may be finished with sodium hydroxide to achieve greater wettability (Chapter 31).

Polyester fiber also may be modified in fabric-finishing processes to improve comfort. These modifications are discussed in Chapter 31.

Trademarked Fabrics. Manufactured-fiber producers have developed several licensed trademark and certification programs for polyester fiber that has been modified to result in enhanced garment comfort.[7] Garment manufacturers, particularly of sportswear, also have taken the initiative to work with fiber producers to develop polyester-fabric systems engineered for specific sports activities.

Hoechst Celanese has developed a Comfort Fiber® certification program for fabrics containing its chemically modified polyester. The modified fiber is cut into a variable staple length with a length distribution similar

---

[7] Fiber producers produce and sell fiber only. They do not make fabric. Through certification programs, they work with mills to develop yarns and fabrics and may sell unbranded fiber under certification-program requirements. Certification programs are discussed more extensively in Chapter 9.

to that of combed cotton. The ultimate aim is to make the tactile sensation of the polyester fabric more like that of cotton.

The Du Pont company has developed Coolmax® fabric using a *tetra-channel polyester fiber* with a cross section like a double scallop (Figure 17.7). This shape gives the fiber 20% more surface area than regular fiber. Water thus is distributed over a greater area in the fabric, so it can evaporate faster. The fabric system is reported to provide superior wicking and evaporation of body-generated moisture. Fabrics are constructed into garments for bicyclists, joggers, tennis players, basketball players, and others engaged in sports activities in which maximum movement of sensible perspiration (sweat) through the fabric is desired. Coolmax® fabric also is used to line tennis shoes designed with side vents that continue the transport of water to the outside of the shoe. Drier feet are cooler and less likely to experience athlete's foot, friction-caused blisters, odor, and mildew.

For cold-weather wear, Du Pont has developed Thermax® fabric(s), which provide state-of-the-art thermal insulation. Thermax® is a certification program. Thermax® garments contain Du Pont T727 fiber—microsized (to one-sixth the size of a human hair) *hollow-core fiber* with a convoluted surface (Figure 17.7). The hollow center holds air, resulting in additional thermal insulation as well as a 20% reduction in fiber weight. The surface and convolutions provide for the wicking of moisture. Crimp creates interstices that entrap air effectively and resist its movement. This fiber is designed for use in thermal underwear, gloves, socks, and turtleneck T-shirts.

Polyester microfibers have been developed for use in sportswear items, including raincoats, anoraks, ski outfits, sailing outfits, track suits, jogging suits, and sweatsuits, as well as in fabric for sleeping bags and tents. Fabric can be structured with the microfibers so that there are as many as 6200 fibers per square inch (40,000 fibers per square centimeter). This fabric, with its fluorocarbon finish, has a high resistance to water penetration but is permeable to water vapor; it provides a lightweight, waterproof, breathable fabric. Wearer comfort is judged to be better than for coated or laminated waterproof, breathable fabrics. Microfiber fabrics are warmer than fabrics of similar weight due to the amount of dead air space they contain. Microfiber yarns have twice the bulk and surface area of normal fiber yarn. In addition, these sportwear fabrics can withstand extreme mechanical stress; they possess excellent abrasion and tear resistance. In the manufacture of polyester microfibers, a

FIGURE 17.7 Polyester fiber modified in cross section to improve fabric comfort.

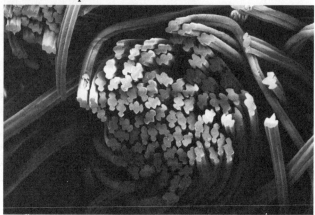

Polyester fiber used in Du Pont's Coolmax* certification-program fabrics to provide improved comfort under strenuous exercise conditions.

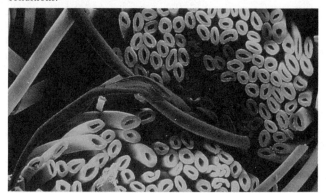

Polyester fiber used in Du Pont's Thermax* certification-program fabrics to provide thermal insulation.

higher proportion of the polymers are oriented along the fiber axis. The microfibers are distinguished by a higher crystalline order of the polymers. Trademarks of microfibers and fabrics include Trevira® Finesse® by Hoechst Celanese and Fortrel® MicroSpun® by Fiber Industries.

The use of high-shrinkage fibers can impart improved loft and warmth to polyester fibers to be used in knitwear and cold-weather clothing. These *high-shrinkage fibers*, when properly processed, result in high-bulk yarns and fabrics. When mixed with unmodified fibers, high-shrinkage fibers develop convolutions as they adjust to dimensional changes. This technology is used in both spun and filament yarns. In the latter case, it is incorporated into the production of yarns with simulated spun-yarn aesthetics.

Polyester fiber intended to be used for fiberfill has been improved in several ways. One way is to make the fibers hollow. Hollow fibers, such as Hollofill® manufactured by Du Pont, are not as compressible as regular fibers, so more dead air space is retained in the structure during use. Garments containing the hollow fibers are bulkier, but sleeping bags containing these fibers are warmer because the fiberfill between the ground and the individual allows less body heat to be conducted to the colder ground. Another way to improve polyester fiber is to incorporate air shafts in the fiber. Quallofil® pillows, sleeping bags, and hats contain such a fiber and are part of a Hoechst Celanese certification program.

Variants for Improved Aesthetic Appeal of Fabric

Polyester fibers are modified to provide silk-like aesthetics, a linen appearance, a low-pill fabric, and better cotton/polyester blends. Modifications include changing the cross-sectional shape, reducing the degree of polymerization, and introducing a copolymer.

Efforts to make more *silk-like polyester fibers* began with the introduction of the first nonround polyester fiber, Trevira® by Hystron Fibers (currently Hoechst Celanese). It was a *star-shaped* or *pentalobal cross-sectional fiber.* This modification to filament fiber resulted in an unusually silky appearance and texture in knit and woven fabrics composed of it. *Trilobal cross-sectional polyester fibers* are also more silk-like than regular polyester. The most recent development in silk-like polyesters has been in the production of microfibers and super, ultrafine microfibers. Polyester fabrics for fashionable women's and men's wear that contain the microfibers are supersoft, extremely drapable, and lightweight. Trademarked fabrics made from polyester microfibers include Mattique® and Micromattique® by Du Pont, MicroSpun® by Fiber Industries, Shingosen® by Toray Industries, and Trevira® Finesse® by Hoechst Celanese. This new polyester technology gave a fresh impetus to the use of polyester in everyday and formal wear. Polyester fiber, when subjected to a sodium hydroxide solution after fabric formation, can be modified to produce a silk-like polyester fabric. (This fiber modification is discussed in Chapter 33.)

A linen-like look is possible in a 100%-polyester fabric when thick-and-thin polyester fibers, which vary in diameter along their length, are used. Consequently, the yarns are thick and thin. The luster of polyester fiber can be decreased through the use of delustrants in round, cross-sectional fibers (delustered fibers) or the use of heptalobal and octalobal fibers. These shapes have little or none of the glitter characteristic of other cross-sectional shapes.

Low-pill polyester fibers contain polymers of lower degree of polymerization (lower molecular weight) than regular polyester fibers or contain a copolymer with sulfonate groups. These changes lower fiber tenacity, which means that the low-pill polyester fibers anchoring a ball of entangled fibers to a fabric surface will break. The pill is therefore removed from the fabric surface.

Dyeability is enhanced by the introduction of sulfonic groups to the polymer or by the substitution of isophthalic acid for a small portion of terephthalic acid. The fiber can then be dyed with cationic as well as disperse dyes. *Cationic-dyeable fibers* are important in the achievement of cross-dyed fabrics (Chapter 34).

Antistatic polyester fibers have been achieved by incorporating carbon particles into the surfaces of polyester fibers. These bicomponent bigeneric fibers provide a high level of protection against electrostatic charge, with little or no effect on color.

Better-blending polyester fibers are engineered to have elongation and elastic-recovery properties that closely match those of the fibers with which they will be blended. These fibers create the best-performing blended fabrics (Chapter 23).

Variants for Improved Soil Release

Research continues to find a means to modify polyester fiber to reduce its oleophilic nature. Certain finishes (discussed in Chapter 33) may be applied to polyester fabric/fiber to assist with oil release.

Variants for Improved Safety/Protection

One *inherently flame-resistant polyester fiber*—Trevira® type 271 by Hoechst Celanese—has been available from the U.S. manufacturer since 1984. Its manufacture involves copolymerization. Polyester fiber is generally treated topically with flame-retardant chemicals following fabric formation. (This topic is discussed in Chapter 31.)

CHAPTER SUMMARY

Polyester fibers are smooth rods by appearance. The two major forms of polyester are polyethylene terephthalate (PET) and poly-1,4-cyclohexylene-dimethylene terephthalate (PCDT), the latter being used primarily for fiberfill. Polyester is a highly crystalline and well-oriented fiber. Its polymers are weakly hydrogen bonded due to the slight polarity between the methylene hydrogen and the carbonyl oxygen. All polyester polymers, by definition, contain a benzene ring.

Polyester fibers are highly resilient. At low stress, they have high elastic recovery. At high stress, particularly repeated high stresses, they have low elastic recovery. They have low moisture regain and high melting points. Polyester fibers have high sunlight resistance and resistance to most chemicals. They are degraded by strong alkalies, however.

Polyester fiber/fabric systems have been developed to enhance thermal insulation, wicking, moisture regain/content, and water-vapor transport. Polyester fiber variants include those that exhibit higher tenacity and lower pilling, are more flame-retardant, more silk-like, and softer, and maintain better loft than the regular fiber. The polyester fiber has not been modified successfully to reduce its oleophilicity.

Olefin Fibers

Olefin fibers are "manufactured fiber(s) in which the fiber-forming substance is any long-chain synthetic polymer composed of at least 85% by weight of ethylene, propylene, or other olefin units except amorphous (noncrystalline) polyolefins qualifying under category (1) of paragraph (j) of Rule 7."

POLYETHYLENE

Variants
Ultra-high molecular weight, extended-chain fibers*

POLYPROPYLENE

Variants
Ultra-high-tenacity fibers
High ultraviolet-light-resistant fibers
High heat-resistant (heat-durable) fibers
Bacteriostatic fibers
Dyeable fibers

---

*To be discussed in Chapter 21.

18

*O*lefin Fibers

Olefin fibers, once regarded as having only limited industrial applications, became of significant importance in the 1960s—particularly for interior furnishing fabrics. In 1990, U.S. fiber manufacturers produced and shipped 1792.8 million pounds of olefin to domestic customers (Figure 18.1). An additional 1.6 million pounds of olefin fiber were imported. Of all U.S. manufactured olefin, ~52% was used in carpeting and rugs and an additional 4% was used in other interior textile products. In kitchen-style (indoor/outdoor) carpets, olefin is used as the face fiber; in other styles of carpets, it is used in the primary and secondary backing. Approximately 43% of all olefin fiber is used in industrial and consumer products, some of which are named in Figure 18.1. Recently, olefin fiber penetrated the activewear market, appearing in thermal underwear, socks, fiberfilled garments, sweatsuits, and knitted outerwear. Detail View 18 presents the types of olefin fiber discussed in this chapter.

GENERIC GROUP MEMBERS

Olefin fibers are "manufactured fibers in which the fiber-forming substance is any long-chain synthetic polymer composed of at least 85% by weight of ethylene, propylene, or other olefin units except amorphous (noncrystalline) polyolefins qualifying under category (1) of paragraph (j) of Rule 7," as defined in the Textile Fiber

Products Identification Act.[1] In Britain, olefin fibers are called polyalkenes.

The starting compounds used to polymerize polyolefins are saturated hydrocarbons (compounds with a double bond between two carbon atoms). Among the many potential saturated hydrocarbons that could be used, only two serve to synthesize polyolefin for fibers; these compounds are ethylene and propylene (Figure 18.2). The polymerization of ethylene and propylene yields polyethylene and polypropylene, respectively (Detail View 18).

Polyethylene

Attempts to polymerize ethylene, a hydrocarbon with two carbon atoms, began in earnest in the 1920s. The technical requirements were for the double bond to break and for the monomers to then add end-to-end, thereby forming a long-chain, unsaturated hydrocarbon (with no double bonds). This type of polymerization, called *chain growth* (Chapter 8), proved to be a difficult technical problem requiring ten years of work before success was achieved.

---

[1] Many textile products composed of olefin fibers are labeled as polypropylene, which is the major chemical type of olefin fiber. This deviation from the Textile Fiber Products Identification Act requirement that the generic group name be used is a widely accepted trade practice.

FIGURE 18.1 Primary market distribution of olefin fiber produced in the United States and shipped to domestic customers in 1990.

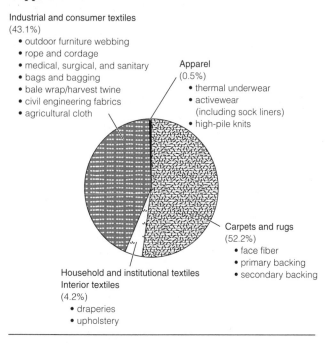

Industrial and consumer textiles
(43.1%)
- outdoor furniture webbing
- rope and cordage
- medical, surgical, and sanitary
- bags and bagging
- bale wrap/harvest twine
- civil engineering fabrics
- agricultural cloth

Apparel
(0.5%)
- thermal underwear
- activewear
  (including sock liners)
- high-pile knits

Carpets and rugs
(52.2%)
- face fiber
- primary backing
- secondary backing

Household and institutional textiles
Interior textiles
(4.2%)
- draperies
- upholstery

FIGURE 18.2 The starting compounds for the formation of polyethylene and polypropylene olefin fibers.

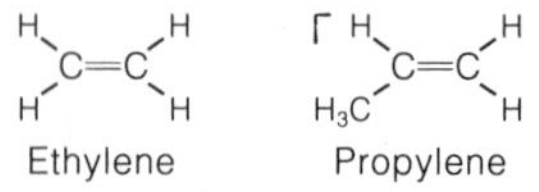

Ethylene   Propylene

Polypropylene

Propylene is a hydrocarbon with three carbon atoms (Figure 18.2). When it polymerizes in a step-chain reaction, it forms a polymer in which methyl groups ($-CH_3$) extend from the polymer backbone.

Three different polypropylene polymers—isotactic, syndiotactic, and atactic—are formed. These polymers differ in the position of the methyl groups in three-dimensional space. In the isotactic polypropylene, all the methyl groups are positioned on one side of the polymer. In the syndiotactic polypropylene, the methyl groups alternate from side to side; in the atactic polypropylene, they are in random positions (Figure 18.3).

Only the isotactic polypropylene is useful to form textile fibers, because it allows the polymers to pack closely enough for crystallization to occur. The other configurations result in viscous fluids or synthetic rubber due to a lack of crystallization.

Learning how to cause propylene molecules to position themselves consistently in three-dimensional space as they add to a growing polymer presented a tremendous challenge to polymer chemists. Giulio Natta is credited with the discovery of stereospecific polymerization (the positioning of monomers in space to add to a growing polymer). Simultaneously, Karl Ziegler worked with catalysts to obtain high molecular weight, crystalline polypropylene polymers. These two discoveries permitted the polymerization of isotactic polypropylene that could be formed into a textile fiber. Natta and Ziegler received the Nobel Prize in 1962 for these significant findings in polymer chemistry.

Further research was necessary because the polypropylene fibers formed from the 1960s to the mid-1970s were inherently prone to oxidation, which became progressively more serious when the fiber was exposed to rising temperatures and to ultraviolet light. In other words, the early olefin fibers were very heat- and light-

Filaments made with synthesized polyethylene in the size range for normal textile use, however, did not have sufficient tenacity or a high enough melting point. In 1954, Karl Ziegler, a German chemist, developed a process in which the melting point of polymerized ethylene was raised, but it was still too low for apparel fibers. Polyethylene fibers are chemically stable, very resistant to microbiological attack, and unaffected by water so they cannot be dyed.

Due to insufficient tenacity in fine deniers, polyethylene fibers usually are available as coarse monofilaments or multifilaments. They are used in blinds, awnings, car upholstery, curtains, tarpaulins, low-temperature filter applications, and protective clothing when contact with corrosive chemicals is likely.

Polyethylene fiber has been varied to produce an *ultra-high molecular weight, extended-chain fiber*. Because the performance of this fiber differs dramatically from that of other olefin fibers but is similar to that of the para-aramids, it is discussed in Chapter 21.

FIGURE 18.3   Positions of methyl groups along a polypropylene polymer.

Isotactic configuration

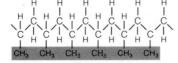

All methyl groups are on the same side.

Syndiotactic configuration

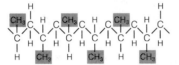

Methyl groups alternate from side to side.

Atatic configuration

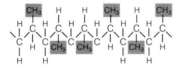

Methyl groups are randomly positioned.

sensitive. Their low melting point, in comparison with other synthetic fibers available, and almost zero absorbency were viewed as deficiencies.

By the 1980s, stabilizers were found and the limiting thermal- and light-stability problems were significantly improved. Further, it finally was recognized that some of the so-called performance deficiencies of olefin fibers were actually advantageous in certain products.

STRUCTURE OF POLYPROPYLENE OLEFIN FIBERS

Polypropylene olefin fibers are very regular rod-shaped, smooth-surfaced fibers with round cross sections (Figure 18.4). They are colorless.

The hydrocarbon polymer is composed entirely of carbon and hydrogen atoms. The backbone of the polymer is formed by carbon atoms lying in a plane in a zigzag pattern. Methyl groups ($-CH_3$) are present along the polymer chain. There are no polar groups. The proportion of crystalline area is usually 50–65%.

PROPERTIES OF POLYPROPYLENE OLEFIN FIBERS

The properties of polypropylene olefin are summarized in Table 18.1. To obtain numerical values for olefin fiber properties and to compare the properties of olefin to other fibers, refer to Figures 8.1–8.13 and Tables 8.1–8.8.

Influencing Fabric Durability

The abrasion resistance of olefin is high, and its tenacity is high. Elongation at break of olefin fibers varies 10–45%. They have high recovery when stress is released below breaking tenacity. These properties serve olefin well in carpeting and upholstery fabrics as well as in industrial end uses. The durability of olefin fiber is more than adequate for apparel end uses.

Influencing Fabric Comfort

Olefin fibers possess a unique combination of low moisture absorbency and exceptional wicking of water, which are advantages in providing comfortable apparel in certain circumstances. Olefin is the most hydrophobic of the general-use synthetic fibers. Its moisture regain is <0.1%, even at high relative humidities. Sensible and insensible perspiration generated by the body are not absorbed by the fiber. Sweat, however, is transported readily and rapidly away from the body by wicking of this moisture along the olefin fiber. Such moisture properties are sought for active sportswear fabrics, particularly sweatshirts, socks, and warm-up suits, because water is moved away from the skin. Olefin fabric does not become wet, so its thermal-insulating ability is retained.

Olefin is the lightest-weight fiber. The comfort of activewear garments is enhanced because lightweight fabrics that do not hinder body movement or provide an additional load or burden can be made with adequate cover. It takes 1.23 pounds (lbs) or 0.57 kilograms (kg) of nylon or 1.71 lb (0.78 kg) of cotton to provide the same cover as 1 lb (0.45 kg) of olefin fibers.

Comfort of carpeting and upholstery in part is due to the low static buildup on olefin fibers. Olefin fibers are unusual in that they are hydrophobic and yet do not exhibit major static problems. This phenomenon is due to

FIGURE 18.4
Photomicrograph of polypropylene olefin fiber, showing its round cross section, rod shape, and smooth surface.

|—————| 25 μm

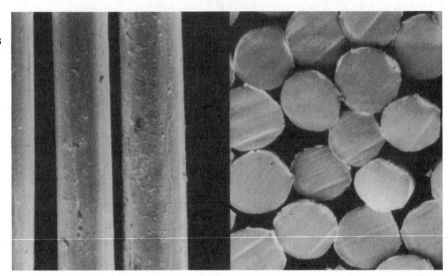

the fact that the fibers are nonpolar; electrons are not available to be brought to the surface of the fibers.

Influencing Fabric Aesthetics

Olefin fibers have a distinctive oily or waxy hand that some consumers find objectionable. This hand of the fabric is reflected in the generic group name; "olefin" is derived from the Latin word "oleum," which means oil.

Olefin fibers provide more cover per pound of fiber than other fibers due to their low specific gravity. This property is particularly important in the manufacture of carpets.

Olefin fibers have moderate resilience. Permanent pleats and creases inserted in olefin garments will be retained as long as low temperatures are maintained during care procedures.

Influencing Fabric Maintenance

The low melting point of olefin fibers compared to other synthetic fibers, its low moisture absorbency, and its heat- and light-sensitivity are key factors in the consideration of maintenance of olefin-fiber products during use.

Soiling and Staining. Olefin fibers exhibit exceptional resistance to water-borne stains due to their hydrophobicity and lack of chemical groups to which stains can bond. They are, however, subject to oily soiling.

Soil Removal from Apparel Fabrics. Drycleaning generally is not recommended because olefin is sensitive to perchloroethylene, the most frequently used drycleaning solvent. When drycleaning is indicated on a care label, petroleum solvent probably will be specified.

Soil removal during laundering is difficult. Olefin fibers hold soil tenaciously because the highly hydrophobic fiber surface is resistant to the spread of water (detergent solution). The laundering conditions that help to facilitate soil removal—high temperatures and vigorous agitation—should not be used, since the fiber softens at relatively low temperatures. Fiber swelling does not take place and therefore does not influence laundering factors.

The softening and melting points of polypropylene are low and are of concern in determining which washwater temperatures, dryer temperatures, and ironing temperatures to use. For most textile applications, a fiber should retain its dimensional stability on heating to at least 212° F (100° C). Polypropylene fibers meet this requirement, with melting points occurring at 325–333° F (165–170° C). Use of very hot water to launder olefin fibers may cause shrinkage. Warm or cool washwater is usually recommended. Polypropylene fabrics can be ironed, but a greater degree of caution is required than is necessary with most other established fibers. Generally, manufacturers recommend that olefin apparel items and blankets not be dried in an automatic dryer but rather be drip-dried to eliminate the possibility of shrinkage in an overheated dryer and the need for pressing.

The low melting point of olefin fiber tends to be a perceived limitation that weighs more heavily than it should in product use. Low melting is a serious disadvantage in finishing the fiber, however—a problem that fiber and fabric manufacturers have not completely solved.

Soil Removal from Interior Textiles. Olefin carpets and upholstery as well as apparel fabrics are relatively easy-care items. Many soils can be wiped off upholstery and carpets with a damp cloth.

Potential Degradation in Use. Polypropylene olefin fibers have a high resistance to most chemicals, including acids and alkalies. They are equally resistant to insects and microorganisms.

Pure polypropylene (propylene without chemical additives between the fiber polymers) degrades at room temperature, particularly in the presence of ultraviolet light. However, polypropylene fibers used in textile applications contain stabilizers to offset the effects of heat and ultraviolet light. These stabilizers are chosen so that more than adequate wearlife is provided for the intended end use. Care must be taken so that hot substances, such as hot bacon fat, are not dropped on olefin carpeting.

Polypropylene fibers are considered to be among the most resistant to loss of physical integrity during use. They rank with the acrylics and modacrylics in this respect. The fibers therefore are particularly suited to outdoor and industrial applications in which chemicals, insects, microorganisms, heat, sunlight, and/or moisture are present.

Influencing Health/Safety/Protection

Olefin fiber does not ignite readily. When exposed to flame, it shrinks, melts, and pulls away from the flame. A tan or off-white bead will result. The fiber may burn with a blue and yellow flame if the heat source is held in continued contact with it.

Olefin fiber may support the growth of bacteria. Olefin fibers do not cause any undesirable skin reactions.

PRODUCTION OF POLYPROPYLENE OLEFIN FIBERS

Olefin fibers (polypropylene) were first produced in Italy in 1957; U.S. production began in 1962. Polypropylene is made from a raw material, propylene, which is a by-product (in almost unlimited quantities at low cost) from the cracking process in the petroleum industry.

TABLE 18.1   Olefin (Polypropylene) Fiber Property Summary.

PROPERTY	RANK*
Mechanical†	
Breaking tenacity	High
Elongation	Medium
Elastic recovery	High
Flexibility	—
Abrasion resistance	High
Stiffness (flexural rigidity)	Medium
Resilience	Medium
Toughness (work of rupture)	High (highest of synthetic fibers)
Initial modulus	Medium
Sorptive	
Moisture regain/content	Low (lowest of synthetic fibers)
Cross-sectional swelling	Low (no swelling)
Heat of wetting	Low (no heat of wetting)
Effect on mechanical properties	Low (no effect)
Oil absorption	Medium
Ease of oil release	Low
Thermal	
Heat resistance (durability)	Low
Softening and melting	Low
Decomposition	—
Combustibility	Medium
Chemical	
Alkali resistance	
Dilute	High
Concentrated	High
Acid resistance	
Dilute	High
Concentrated	Medium (slowly oxidized)
Organic solvent resistance	Low (softens in perchloroethylene)
Oxidizing agent resistance	Low
Miscellaneous	
Ultraviolet light resistance	Low (lowest of all fibers)
Microorganism resistance	High
Moth and beetle resistance	High
Silverfish resistance	High
Electrical resistivity	Low (no static buildup)
Specific gravity	Low (lowest of all fibers)

*Levels relative to other fibers except special-use synthetic fibers.

†At 70°F (21°C), 65% relative humidity.

Propylene is polymerized at 10 atmospheres of pressure at <176° F (80° C). Oxygen must be excluded due to the sensitivity of the polymer to oxidative degradation. Low heat is necessary to permit maximum polymer length to be achieved. Special catalysts control the orientation of the monomers in space, so stereospecific polymerization takes place (in other words, so the methyl groups all end up on one side of the polymer backbone). Polypropylene generally leaves the reactor as a powder.

More than any other polymer used to prepare fibers, polypropylene owes its existence to fiber additives—stabilizers and pigments that help solve the performance deficiencies of pure polypropylene. Stabilizers are added to polypropylene to provide melt-extrusion stability, long-term thermal stability at normal-use temperatures, and stability to ultraviolet light. The degree to which stabilizers accomplish their objectives effectively without introducing other unwanted side-effects, such as yellowing, determines how useful the resultant fiber product will be. The specific additives selected and the amount of each must be determined by the fiber producer in consideration of the end use intended. The choice of additives is extensive. All additives are chosen at the same time because these chemicals interact with each other.

Olefin fibers are melt-spun. Filaments are cooled in air or water as they emerge from the spinneret. Unlike nylon and polyester, polypropylene crystallizes so rapidly that the undrawn filaments are highly crystalline.

Polypropylene fibers are cold-drawn to six times their spun length. Drawing orients the polymers and crystals in the filaments to increase tenacity and decrease elongation. There are many variations of the drawing process. Annealing or heat setting the filaments relaxes, at least partially, the stresses in the fiber and perfects the crystalline structure. Consequently, residual shrinkage is decreased.

Olefin-fiber producers also extrude fiber directly into spunbonded nonwoven fabric (Chapter 28) and as fibrillated yarn (Chapter 24). Spunbonded fabric is 50%, fibrillated yarn is 16%, and staple and filament fiber are each 17% of production.

VARIANTS OF POLYPROPYLENE OLEFIN FIBERS

The mechanical properties of polypropylene olefin fibers can be varied infinitely by altering the conditions of spinning and processing. *Ultra-high-tenacity fibers* are produced. Careful selection of stabilizers and pigment systems provide *ultraviolet-light-resistance* of olefin fibers. Polypropylene fibers are available that rival in heat stability all but the most expensive specialty synthetic fibers. Such *high heat-resistant* (heat-durable) olefin fibers retain their mechanical properties after exposure to air for extended periods at temperatures as high as 148° F (120° C). When the exposure temperature exceeds the melting point of olefin, the fiber degrades.

The observation that bacterial growth can occur within polypropylene fabric has led to the development of fibers containing bacteriostats. *Bacteriostatic olefin fibers* are being tested in carpets and in nonwoven fabric applications to determine whether there is greater permanence to reduced bacterial growth in them than in fibers simply finished with a bacteriostat.

Several modified polypropylene fibers currently on the market are dyeable, but dyeable fibers represent a very small part of total polypropylene production. Virtually all polypropylene fibers are colored with pigments. Attempts to modify polypropylene fibers for flame resistance have not been commercially successful.

CHAPTER SUMMARY

Polypropylene is available as monofilament, multifilament, and staple fibers, fibrillated or ribbon yarns, and spunbonded nonwoven fabric. Its major market is interior textiles, as primary backing for carpets, as pile fiber for low-loop style carpets, and as upholstery fabric. It is used widely in consumer, medical, and industrial applications. Little is used for apparel.

Olefin fibers usually are composed of isotactic polypropylene polymers. These polymers have methyl side groups positioned to allow the polymers to pack closely together, forming a highly crystalline fiber. The fiber is a smooth rod.

Olefin fibers marketed today possess a unique combination of properties: very low density, excellent wicking ability, excellent water-borne stain resistance, and outstanding resistance to degradation by chemicals, sunlight, and heat, as well as ample tenacity and abrasion resistance. Their extremely low absorbency and melting points are distinct performance advantages in certain end-uses.

Acrylic Fibers

Acrylic fibers are "manufactured fiber(s) in which the fiber-forming substance is any long-chain synthetic polymer composed of at least 85% by weight of acrylonitrile units $\left(-CH_2-CH-\right)$."
with CN below CH.

HOMOPOLYMER

COPOLYMER

GRAFT POLYMER

Variants for Improved Fabric Comfort
High-shrinkage (latent-shrinkage) fibers
Bicomponent fibers (100% acrylic fibers with a side-by-side
   arrangement of two types of acrylonitrile polymers)
Cotton-like, absorbent fibers
Antistatic fibers
Softer fibers

Variants for Improved Aesthetic Appeal of Fabric
No-pill or low-pill fibers
Controlled-shrinkage fibers
Basic- and acid dyeable fibers

Variants for Reduced Health Risk
Flame-resistant fibers
Molten-metal protective fibers
Antimicrobial fibers
Ion-exchange fibers

Acrylic Fibers

Acrylic fibers were named from the Latin word *acryl,* which means bitter, irritating, or pungent. These adjectives hardly apply to acrylic fibers but do describe a compound called acrylic acid. Acrylonitrile, which is chemically related to acrylic acid, is the compound from which acrylic fibers are polymerized. Acrylic is simply short for polyacrylonitrile.

In 1893, a French chemist, C. Moureu, synthesized acrylonitrile; a year later, he polymerized polyacrylonitrile. Almost until the outbreak of World War II, polyacrylonitrile was a laboratory curiosity. It decomposed before it reached its melting point, and no solvents were capable of dissolving it. These factors meant that the processing of the polymer was nearly impossible. But in 1930, acrylonitrile was a component in one of the important types of synthetic rubber being developed in Germany and the United States. During World War II, the synthetic rubber industry expanded rapidly in response to wartime needs. By the end of the war, acrylonitrile was readily available as a relatively inexpensive industrial chemical.

In 1943, Du Pont and I. G. Farbenindustrie, a German chemical company, simultaneously reported that they had discovered a solvent suitable for the spinning of an acrylic fiber. The Du Pont company developed a commercial process for the production of acrylic fiber and introduced Orlon® acrylic in 1944, with full-scale production beginning in 1950. Developments in this fledgling industry occurred rapidly from that time on. One of the most recent major developments has been the announcement in late 1990 by the Du Pont company, a major producer of acrylic fiber, that it was discontinuing production of its acrylic fibers.

In 1990, 352.2 million pounds of acrylic fiber were produced by U.S. fiber manufacturers and shipped to domestic customers (Figure 19.1). An additional 37.9 million pounds of acrylic fiber were imported. Most acrylic fiber (~80%) is used in apparel fabric; 99% of the 80% is knitted into high-pile fabrics, sweaters, socks, and other circular-knit products, and 1% of the apparel fiber is used in woven apparel fabrics. A major household textile product is blankets, with additional fiber being used in upholstery, drapery, and carpeting. Little acrylic fiber is used in industrial applications.

Today, there are many types of acrylic fibers. Several of these are presented in Detail View 19.

GENERIC GROUP MEMBERS

The Textile Fiber Products Identification Act defines acrylic fibers as "manufactured fiber(s) in which the fiber-forming substance is any long-chain synthetic polymer composed of at least 85% by weight of acrylonitrile units,"

$$-\underset{\underset{H}{|}}{\overset{\overset{H}{|}}{C}}-\underset{\underset{CN}{|}}{\overset{\overset{H}{|}}{C}}-$$

FIGURE 19.1 Primary market distribution of acrylic and modacrylic fiber produced in the United States and shipped to domestic customers in 1990.

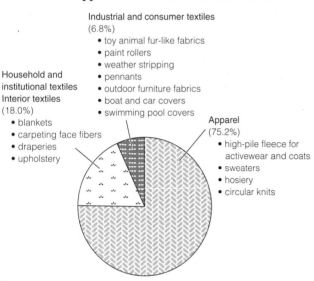

Industrial and consumer textiles
(6.8%)
- toy animal fur-like fabrics
- paint rollers
- weather stripping
- pennants
- outdoor furniture fabrics
- boat and car covers
- swimming pool covers

Household and
institutional textiles
Interior textiles
(18.0%)
- blankets
- carpeting face fibers
- draperies
- upholstery

Apparel
(75.2%)
- high-pile fleece for activewear and coats
- sweaters
- hosiery
- circular knits

Acrylonitrile monomer is, therefore, always the main component of acrylic fiber polymer. Other monomers also are used (Figure 19.2). The monomers that form the polymers of the generic group members are shown in Detail View 19.

Homopolymer

The first acrylic fiber produced, Fiber A, was 100% polyacrylonitrile, a homopolymer. In synthesis, the double bond of acrylonitrile is broken and then the chemical adds on end-to-end in a chain-growth polymerization. Fiber A was almost as strong as nylon and was highly resistant to chemicals (notably acids) and to sunlight. Fiber A was virtually undyeable, however, because the homopolymer acrylic had such a compact, highly oriented structure. Today, Mann Industries is the sole U.S. manufacturer of homopolymer acrylic fiber (Biokryl®).

Copolymers

When another monomer containing a double bond is reacted with the acrylonitrile monomer, a copolymer is formed. (Detail View 19 shows an example.) Usually,

FIGURE 19.2 Some compounds used in the formation of acrylic fibers.

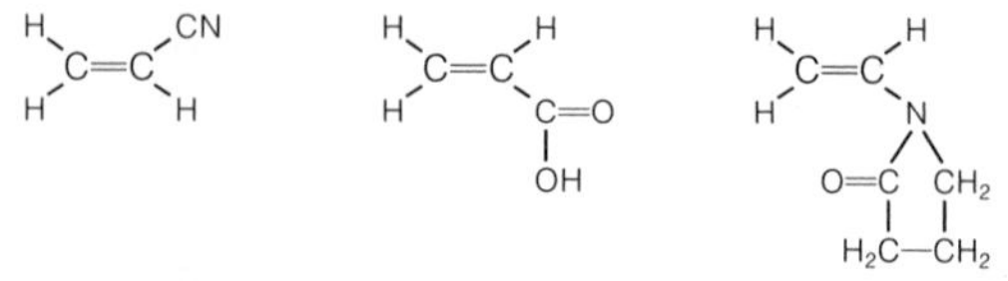

Acrylonitrile
(major component)   Acrylic acid   Vinylpyrrolidone

two comonomers are used in a particular fiber. The nature and proportion of each comonomer are rarely disclosed by manufacturers.

The purpose of one of the comonomers, such as methyacrylate or vinyl acetate, is to provide a more open fiber structure and increase the solubility of the polymer, so that it can be processed more easily. Fiber tenacity is reduced, but disperse dyestuffs are absorbed into the fiber more readily. The purpose of the second comonomer is to provide supplemental dye sites or to impart flame resistance. Ionic comonomers[1] are used in the first case; halogen-containing monomers[2] in the second case. Most acrylic fibers produced in the United States (for example, Acrilan® and Creslan®, which are manufactured by Monsanto and American Cyanamid, respectively) are copolymers.

Graft Polymers

Some acrylic fibers are *graft polymers.* The structure of the graft-polymer acrylic fiber is more open and less crystalline than that of the homopolymer or the copolymer. Dye receptivity is increased. The side groups may or may not be chemically reactive. The acrylic fiber trademarked Zefran® is a graft polymer.[3] It has been referred to as an "alloy" (a physical mixture of similar polymers).

STRUCTURE

Acrylic fibers produced in the United States are used as staple fiber. They are available in deniers of 1.2–15

---

[1] Ionic comonomers include sodium styrene sulfonate, sodium methallyl sulfonate, and sodium sulfophenyl methallyl ether.
[2] Halogen-containing compounds include vinylidene chloride, vinyl bromide, and vinyl chloride.
[3] BASF uses the trademark Zefran® for several generic fibers.

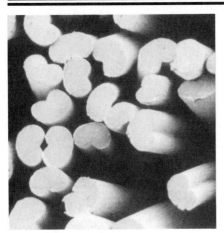
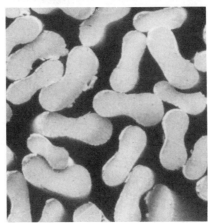

FIGURE 19.3
Photomicrographs of acrylic fibers showing their different cross-sectional shapes and surface appearances.

├─────┤ 25 μm (left)

├───┤ 10 μm (right)

Kidney-bean cross section of wet spinning (Acrilan®, manufactured by Monsanto)

Dogbone cross section of solvent or dry spinning (Orlon® acrylic, manufactured by Du Pont until 1991)

(0.13–1.7 tex, or 15–25 micrometers). Most apparel items contain fibers of ~3.0 denier; industrial and craft knitting yarns contain 5–6 denier fibers and carpet yarns contain ~15 denier fibers, so that the required stiffness and wear resistance are achieved. Fiber length-to-breadth ratio is usually in excess of 2000:1. The fiber is ivory or white and available in bright, semidull, and dull lusters. The fiber usually is crimped slightly.

Microscopic Structure

Acrylic fibers are dog-bone shaped, kidney-bean shaped, or round (Figure 19.3). When viewed longitudinally, their uniform diameter, rod-like shape, and some irregularly spaced striations or parallel lines are seen. In higher-magnification microphotographs, their grainy or pitted surfaces can be seen (Figure 19.4). Acrylic fibers do not have an identifiable submicroscopic structure.

Fine Structure

Acrylonitrile polymer is one of the longest manufactured fiber polymers, with a degree of polymerization of ~1000. The backbone of the polymer is all covalently bonded carbon atoms (that is, hydrocarbon linkages). The polyacrylonitrile polymer formed is rod-like, but it is a flexible rather than a rigid rod. Dipole–dipole interaction between the nitrile groups on adjacent polymers creates a fairly strong interaction between polymers.

There is also interaction between nitrile groups on the same polymer.

Textile scientists have not been as successful in developing a well-defined and easily understood structure for acrylic fibers as they have for other synthetic fibers. Acrylic fibers behave as though they contain a mixture of reasonably well-ordered crystalline areas and less well-ordered amorphous areas. The proportion of crystalline area to amorphous area has not been established for acrylic fibers.

PROPERTIES

Acrylic fibers are unusual in the scope of performance offered by the members of the group. The performance of acrylic fiber can be varied to almost an infinite degree by selection of the copolymer, spinning condition (dry or wet), and drawing process. Table 19.1 summarizes the performance properties of the acrylic fibers. To obtain numeric values for the properties of acrylic and to compare acrylic fiber properties to those of other fibers, refer to Figures 8.1–8.13 and Tables 8.1–8.8.

Influencing Fabric Durability

Overall, the durability of acrylic fiber is similar to that of wool fiber. It is relatively low compared to other synthetic fibers but is not of serious consequence, because acrylic fibers make their way in the textile market by virtue of their attractive hand, resilience, ease of care, and

FIGURE 19.4 Photomicrograph of acrylic fiber shows its pitted and irregular surface.

other properties. Durability is sufficient for the apparel and household textiles in which they are used.

The tenacity of acrylic fiber is medium. In general, graft polymers have a lower tenacity than copolymers. Acrylic fibers have a higher tenacity and toughness than wool fibers, which is significant because acrylics have replaced wool in many end uses.

Elongation at break of acrylic fiber is medium. Acrylic fibers have a high elastic recovery from small extensions (90–95% at 1% extension). The recovery from higher extensions is moderate (for example, 50–60% at 10% extension). In general, the recovery of acrylic resembles that of wool.

The abrasion resistance of acrylic fiber is moderate.

Influencing Fabric Comfort

Thermal comfort in cold-weather climates is provided by the bulky fabric structures made possible with acrylic fibers. The fibers tend to crimp, so they do not pack tightly in the yarn and fabric structure.

Acrylic fibers have a low moisture regain. Under exercise conditions, acrylic fibers will wick perspiration. It is thought that acrylic fibers wick due to their irregular surfaces.

Acrylic fibers have low specific gravity (slightly higher than nylon fiber) and therefore provide lightweight fabrics. The combination of wicking and low specific gravity make acrylic fibers desirable in athletic or activewear fabrics. Static electricity will build up on acrylics, particularly when the humidity is low.

Influencing Fabric Aesthetics.

Acrylic fibers and fabrics more successfully duplicate the positive aesthetic attributes of wool fibers and fabrics than any other manufactured fiber. As a generic group, acrylic fibers are among the softest. Within the generic classification, the bending stiffness of the dog-bone-shaped fibers is less than that of round or kidney-bean-shaped fibers of equal cross-sectional area. Dog-bone-shaped fibers are therefore the softest. Lower-denier acrylic fibers are softer than higher-denier fibers. In the case of acrylic fibers, softness is due to the flexibility of the polymers as well as to cross-sectional shape.

The excellent covering power and bulk of acrylic fabrics result from the low specific gravity and irregular cross-sectional shape of the fibers.

Acrylic fibers have moderate resilience. Fabrics resist wrinkling and undesirable creases hang out rather quickly. Bulky fabrics are especially resilient and lofty. Trouser creases and skirt pleats can be set in and remain unaffected by normal wear as well as laundering and drycleaning processes. Excessive heat and steam will remove "permanent" pleats and creases, however.

Influencing Fabric Maintenance

An outstanding feature of acrylic fibers is their exceptional resistance to degradation. A disadvantage of acrylic fibers is their lack of dimensional stability under hot-wet conditions (hot water and steam cleaning).

Soiling and Staining. Acrylic fiber is classified as oleophilic because it tenaciously holds oily soil. Removal of this soil generally is accomplished under mild laundering conditions.

Soil Removal from Apparel Fabrics. Acrylic fabrics may be laundered or drycleaned to remove soils. The fiber is not affected in any way by drycleaning solvents or by the alkalinity of detergent solutions. A direction on a care label to dryclean may be due to the presence of a water-soluble finish that will be removed if the fabric is laundered, resulting in a harsh feel. Drycleaning is usually the preferred cleaning method for pile fabrics composed of acrylic fibers.

Soil removal from acrylic fiber is accomplished in cool water with gentle agitation. Cool water brings about some fiber swelling, which decreases tenacity and increases elongation at break. The fiber and fabric can be stable dimensionally if care is taken during soil removal.

The dimensional stability of acrylic fibers is affected by increases in temperature (Figure 19.5). An increase in temperature when the fiber is wet can result in greater dimensional instability than occurs when the fiber is dry. Acrylic fibers are said to have poor hot-wet performance. In Figure 19.5, note the effect of temperature on the stress–strain curve for acrylic fiber in a dry medium (silicone oil) and in a wet medium (water). In the 77–86° F (25–30° C) range, the wet and dry curves are approximately the same in the two media. At 131° F (55° C), the curve for acrylic fiber in the wet medium is quite different than that for the fiber in a dry medium. The acrylic fiber in water has a lower modulus and a lower tenacity at break than the fiber in the dry medium. At 194° F (90° C) the acrylic fiber in the wet medium is very easily extensible (has a low modulus) and is considerably weaker than the fiber in the dry medium.

Hot *and* wet conditions must be avoided. Hot water must not be used to launder acrylic fabrics. Steam cleaning of acrylic carpeting is not desirable. The low hot-wet performance of acrylic fiber limits its use in woven fabrics and carpeting. To compensate for poor hot-wet performance, acrylic carpeting must be made in expensive, high-density constructions.

A dryer may be used for acrylic garments that are not pleated, provided the garments are quite cold when placed in the dryer. The majority of woven and firmly knitted garments may be drip-dried, but heavy knits should be dried flat. Tumble drying is not recommended unless the temperature can be maintained at <140° F (<60° C) and cold tumbling follows. Cool ironing can be done.

TABLE 19.1 **Acrylic Fiber Property Summary.**

PROPERTY	RANK*
Mechanical[†]	
Breaking tenacity	Medium
Elongation	Medium
Elastic recovery	Medium
Flexibility	—
Abrasion resistance	Medium
Stiffness (flexural rigidity)	Low
Resilience	Medium
Toughness (work of rupture)	Medium
Initial modulus	High
Sorptive	
Moisture regain/content	Low
Cross-sectional swelling	Low
Heat of wetting	Low
Effect on mechanical properties	Medium
Oil absorption	Medium
Ease of oil release	Medium
Thermal	
Heat resistance (durability)	High
Softening and melting	High (softens at 190°C; does not melt)
Decomposition	Medium
Combustibility	Medium
Chemical	
Alkali resistance	
Dilute	High
Concentrated	Low (dissolved by hot)
Acid resistance	
Dilute	High
Concentrated	Low (dissolves)
Organic solvent resistance	High
Oxidizing agent resistance	High
Miscellaneous	
Ultraviolet light resistance	High
Microorganism resistance	High
Moth and beetle resistance	High
Silverfish resistance	High
Electrical resistivity	High (static is a problem)
Specific gravity	Medium

*Levels relative to other fibers except special-use synthetic fibers.

[†]At 70°F (21°C), 65% relative humidity.

FIGURE 19.5   Stress–strain curves of acrylic fiber in a dry medium and a wet medium show the poor hot-wet stability of the fiber.

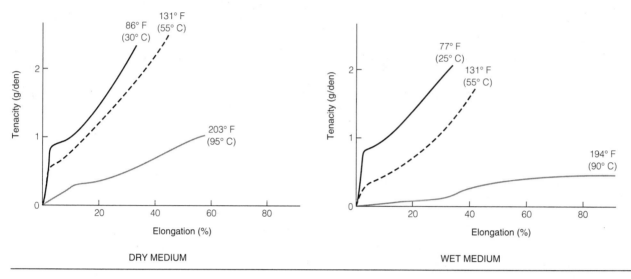

DRY MEDIUM   WET MEDIUM

Potential Degradation in Use. Acrylic fibers have good resistance to most chemicals. The polymers are attacked on prolonged immersion in concentrated solutions of acids and alkalies. Some uncommon chemicals will dissolve the fiber.

Acrylic fibers are resistant to insects and mildew. Acrylic fabric buried in soil containing a variety of microorganisms retains its original bursting strength after six months. Cotton fabric, under similar conditions, completely loses its strength after two weeks.

Resistance to sunlight is also high. Acrylic fibers are known to resist degradation from ultraviolet light eight times longer than olefin fibers, more than five times longer than either cotton or wool fibers, and almost four times longer than nylon fibers.[4] This remarkable resistance to degradation by sunlight makes acrylic fibers particularly useful for such outdoor applications as awning, lawn-furniture webbing, tents, and sandbags. Acrylic automobile upholstery is desirable in sunny climates.

As they are heated, acrylic fibers soften and get sticky. Their tenacity decreases but is not seriously impaired by

exposure to heat normally encountered in use and maintenance procedures. As heating intensifies, the fibers progressively discolor. At high temperatures, the fibers decompose rather than melt. The temperatures at which melting occurs are sufficiently high that no practical difficulties are encountered in normal textile use.

Influencing Health/Safety/Protection

Once ignited, acrylic fibers soften and then burst into flame and burn freely. The flame is yellow, and the odor is chemical. A gummy, hot residue is formed that drips away from the burning fiber. It is hot enough to ignite combustible substances on which it may fall. Acrylics exhibit a tendency to char while burning. Smoke generation is moderate—about the same as cotton fabric. The residue is hard, black, irregular, and crumbly.

Acrylic fabrics have reasonably good flame resistance. They are more flame-resistant than cotton or rayon. Additional flame resistance is required for certain end uses (blankets, carpets, drapery fabrics, and children's sleepwear).

Acrylic fibers applied to human skin for long periods have shown no dermatological or other ill effects. The fibers have no known toxicological effects.

[4]H.G. Fremon in *Fibers from Synthetic Polymers*, R. Hill, ed. (New York: Elsevier, 1953), Chapter 19.

PRODUCTION

Five steps are necessary to produce acrylic fibers: synthesis; extrusion; washing and drawing; drying; and crimping and relaxing.

The polymerization of acrylonitrile and its comonomer commonly is carried out by stirring the monomers with water in the presence of a catalyst and surfactants. As polymerization proceeds, the polymer, which is insoluble in water, is precipitated to form a slurry.

The polymer is dissolved with a solvent (usually N, N-dimethylformamide), forming a dope solution. Most often, this dope solution is wet-spun into acrylic fiber (78% on a worldwide basis), but it can be dry- or solvent-spun. Melt spinning cannot be used because the polymer decomposes when heated.

The acrylic filaments that emerge from the dry or wet spinning are unoriented and have little strength. They have large, tear-like voids, known as *macrovoids*, that begin near the outer edge of the filament and extend to the center. Drawing, which takes place in water at or close to the boiling point, is done to improve the orientation of the polymers within the fibers. However, drawing does not improve the crystallinity of acrylic fibers, as it does that of other synthetic fibers. As the acrylic fiber is drawn, the macrovoids become numerous *microvoids* within the fiber. Sufficient tenacity for use as a textile fiber has been developed at this point, but the fiber is dull and lacks other necessary properties.

During the initial stage of drying, water trapped within the filaments is evaporated. The filaments begin to collapse as the water leaves the microvoids and diffuses to the surface. The fiber becomes lustrous and changes cross-sectional shape. Although other fibers also are dried during processing, their structures and ultimate performances are not affected as dramatically as those of the acrylic fibers.

At this stage, the acrylic fiber has a tenacity that is more than sufficient for most textile applications, but its breaking elongation is low. The fiber is not very abrasion-resistant; it tends to fibrillate readily under abrasive action. The fibers are difficult to dye. Crimping is done to impart bulk and cover to the spun yarn. Crimp also provides the necessary cohesion between the staple fibers so that they can be spun into a yarn. Acrylic fibers are crimped mechanically by passing the *tow* (a loose, rope-like strand of filament fibers) through heated gears or by placing the tow in a stuffer box (Chapter 24). This crimp may not be permanent. In fact, it may not last through the dyeing and finishing processes, which must be completed at higher temperatures than the crimping process.[5]

A relaxation or annealing treatment makes the fibers more extensible. Usually this involves some type of heat treatment in the presence of moisture, which causes the fiber to shrink. Molecular disorientation lowers tenacity, but this effect is more than offset by an increase in breaking elongation and resistance to fibrillation. Tow is then boxed or cut and baled for shipment to a yarn or fabric manufacturer.

VARIANTS

Acrylic fiber is modified in a number of ways to enhance performance.

Variants for Improved Fabric Comfort

Acrylic fibers are wavy because an acrylic-fiber manufacturer routinely crimps the fiber mechanically. This crimp is not permanent, and since crimp is important in the success of many acrylic fiber end-use products, the fiber is modified to achieve a permanent crimp. High-shrinkage fibers or bicomponent fibers are made to achieve a permanent crimp.

Acrylic fibers manufactured with built-in shrinkages of 20–23% are referred to as *high-shrinkage* or *latent-shrinkage fibers;* yarns and fabrics made from these fibers are said to be *high-bulk (hibulk)*. High-shrinkage fibers are found in sweaters and knit goods. High-bulk yarns are made by spinning together high-shrinkage acrylic fibers and regular fibers. After the yarn is spun, it is heated under conditions that bring about relaxation of the high-shrinkage fibers. The regular fibers buckle and crimp and are forced to the outside of the yarn as the high-shrinkage fibers shrink (Figure 19.6).

High-shrinkage fibers can be produced because acrylic fibers are unusual in their ability to attain a metastable (temporary) state on hot drawing. When hot-drawn acrylic fibers are cooled, they remain in their elongated (stretched) state. This is a metastable state; when they are subsequently heated, they revert to their unstretched length. This behavior is reflected in the name "latent shrinkage." An alteration in the drawing process of

---

[5] Consumers also can decrease the loft and shape-retention of fabrics made with mechanically crimped fibers by using too hot washwater or dryer temperatures.

FIGURE 19.6 Use of latent- and regular-shrinkage acrylic fibers to prepare a bulk yarn.

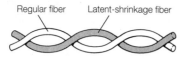

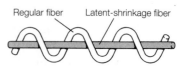

acrylic fibers produces the high-shrinkage fibers. The fiber is heated, stretched, and then cooled while in the stretched condition. High-shrinkage staple of uneven cut lengths may be produced by stretch-breaking tow; this is called the Turbo process.

Bicomponent acrylic fibers are three-dimensional crimped fibers (Figure 19.7). The acrylic polymers on each side of the fiber reacted differently to water. The bicomponent fiber loses much of its crimp when wet but regains it on drying. What is important from a consumer's point of view is that textile items made from this type of bicomponent fiber need to be tumble-dried, because drying without tension provides an opportunity for the fibers to crimp. Sweaters made from these fibers should not be blocked, as a wool sweater would be.

Cotton-like, absorbent acrylic fibers are being produced because manufacturers see the potential for their use in traditional cotton markets, particularly in activewear items. Kanebo Limited, a Japanese fiber manufacturer, has changed the basic structure of acrylic fibers to make them more water-absorbent (Figure 19.8). The system of adding spaces and micropores makes the fiber more quick-drying and also soil-resistant. The fiber is

used in jogging wear, sweatshirts, beachwear, socks, and towels. Other comfort modifications for specific end-use applications are *antistatic* and *softer fibers.*

Variants for Improved Aesthetic Appeal of Fabric

No-pill or low-pill acrylic fabrics can be engineered from modified acrylic fiber. The Monsanto Company, for example, offers *no-pill* or *low-pill* performance in knit garments purchased under its marketing program called HP Apparel®. No-pill performance requires the use of modified acrylic fiber, engineered yarn, and engineered fabric.

Natural fur aesthetics can be achieved by modifying acrylic fibers. The softness and loft of natural fur was readily achieved, but simulating the undercoat and guard hairs present on real furs was more challenging for acrylic-fiber manufacturers.[6] Since *controlled-shrinkage fibers* were developed (acrylic fibers with controlled de-

---

[6] In natural furs, soft, fluffy fibers form an undercoat and stiffer, longer fibers are guard hairs.

FIGURE 19.7 Effect of wetting and drying on the crimp of bicomponent acrylic fibers.

A moderate amount of random crimp exists following manufacture

The crimp relaxes when the fiber is wet

A full reversible crimp develops following drying

grees of shrinkage on exposure to heat), simulated furs became possible. Acrylic fibers with shrinkages of 30–45% are combined with nonshrinking, larger-denier acrylic fibers. The latent-shrinkage fibers become the dense, soft, inner layer of the fabric; the nonshrinking heavier-denier fibers become the guard hairs.

Basic-dyeable acrylic are fibers that can be dyed using a group of dyes called basic dyes. A comonomer with a cationic group (a group of negative charge) is used in forming the acrylic polymer. The negative charge along the polymer attracts the positively charged basic dye. *Acid-dyeable acrylics* contain a comonomer with an anionic group (a group of positive charge), which will attract an acid dye (a dye with a negative charge). The blending of acid-dyeable fibers with basic-dyeable fibers to produce cross-dyed fabrics (Chapter 34) has found wide acceptance.

Variants for Reduced Health Risk

Flame-resistant acrylic fibers are made for use in carpeting and in drapery fabrics. At one time, they also were used in children's sleepwear. The flame resistance of acrylic fibers may be improved by copolymerizing a halogen-containing monomer or by using dope additives.

Molten-metal protective fibers and fabrics are available that are composed of new high-temperature, heat-resistant acrylic polymers. The fabric, trademarked Celiox®, is said to provide protection equal to or better than asbestos and leather for welders and steel-mill foundry workers.

Antimicrobial acrylic fibers have been developed to control a broad spectrum of bacteria, fungi, viruses, and yeasts. A consequence of this control is inhibition of odor, contamination, and product breakdown. One example of an antimicrobial fiber is Biokryl®, a trademark of Mann Industries, Inc. Biokryl® is a homopolymer acrylic with an Environmental Protection Agency (EPA)-registered, antimicrobial agent called Microban® well-distributed throughout the body of the fiber. As the surface layer of the antimicrobial agent is removed by rubbing or washing, the antimicrobial agent within the fiber diffuses to the surface to provide permanent pro-

FIGURE 19.8 A water-absorbent acrylic fiber.

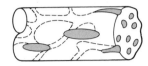

Water absorbent acrylic fiber

Lumize® acrylic fiber, manufactured by Kanebo Limited. (The tradename on the Japanese market is Aqualon®.)

tection from microorganisms. Antimicrobial fibers find applications in hospital textile products, such as surgical gowns, lab coats, bed linens, blankets, and mattress pads; in sports and outdoor products, such as socks, sweatshirts, shoe liners, and marine fabrics; and in household products, such as bathroom mats, shower curtains, and carpeting.

Ion-exchange acrylic fiber—a tubular fiber with ion-exchange ability for use in kidney dialysis—is a significant new application of acrylic fibers.

CHAPTER SUMMARY

Acrylic fibers are used in staple rather than filament form mainly in knit apparel items. Members of the acrylic generic group include homopolymers, copolymers, and graft polymers. All polymers contain acrylonitrile monomer. The fiber is not as crystalline as the other general-use synthetic fibers. Bonding between the polymers is weak.

Acrylic fibers are medium in tenacity, toughness, and abrasion resistance. Their mechanical properties are affected by both temperature and moisture. Acrylic fibers have poor hot-wet performance. They are soft fibers with low moisture regain. They exhibit high resistance to ultraviolet light and to most chemicals to which they commonly are exposed during use.

Acrylic fibers are extensively modified to enhance the warmth of fabrics made from them and to reduce the health risk from outside influences.

Elastomeric Fibers

An *elastomer* is "a material which at room temperature can be stretched repeatedly to at least twice its original length, and upon immediate release of the stretch, will return with force to approximate original length." Hundreds of materials meet this definition but fail as textile fibers.

RUBBER FIBERS

Rubber fibers are "manufactured fiber(s) in which the fiber-forming substance is comprised of natural or synthetic rubber. . . ." Generic group members are

SATURATED HYDROCARBONS
LASTRILE
CHLOROPRENES

SPANDEX FIBERS

Spandex fibers are "manufactured fiber(s) in which the fiber-forming substance is a long-chain synthetic polymer of at least 85% of a segmented polyurethane." Generic group members are

Hard segment
(polyurethane)

Soft segment
(polyether)

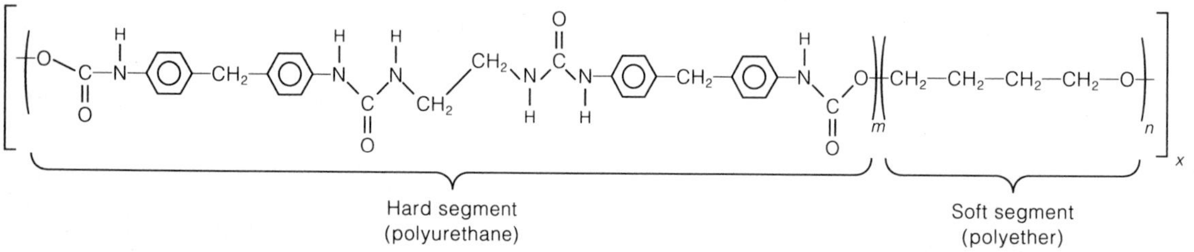

POLYETHER SEGMENTED POLYURETHANE

Hard segment
(polyurethane)

Soft segment
(polyester)

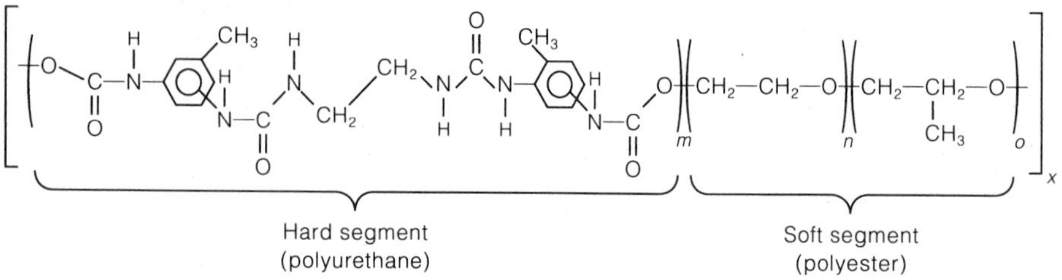

POLYESTER SEGMENTED POLYURETHANE

20

Rubber and Spandex Fibers

When clothing conforms to, extends with, and physically supports the human body, rubber or spandex fibers—the *elastomeric fibers*—generally will be found hidden within the woven or knit garment fabric. The amount of elastomeric fiber depends on the type of control and comfort levels required; it is never present as the sole fiber. In constraint-type garments, such as girdles, foundations, and swimsuits, 15–40% of the fabric may be elastomeric fiber. Sportswear knits may contain as much as 10% or as little as 3% elastomeric fiber. Surgical support hose contains more elastomeric fiber than sheer support hose.

By ASTM definition, an elastomer is "a material which at room temperature can be stretched repeatedly to at least twice its original length, and upon immediate release of the stretch, will return with force to [its] approximate original length." Hundreds of materials meet this definition but fail as textile fibers. Rubber and spandex, the generic group names of two elastomeric fibers, are commercially important textile elastomeric fibers. Anidex, the generic group name of an elastomeric fiber produced in limited quantities in the 1970s, is no longer marketed. Both rubber and spandex fibers are considered in this chapter because they directly compete for end-use applications. The structure and manufacture of rubber and spandex are considered separately before their properties are compared. The FTC definitions for rubber and spandex fibers as well as the generic group members are given in Detail View 20.

Today, ~25–30 million pounds of rubber fibers are produced annually in the United States. U.S. production of spandex fiber is approximately the same; worldwide production of spandex is ~70 million pounds. Considerably more fabric yardage is made from spandex than from rubber fibers, however, because spandex is used in smaller deniers and is more light weight than rubber.[1] Table 20.1 summarizes the uses of elastomeric fibers.

Rubber fibers predominate in narrow fabrics applications where large-denier fibers are common. Rubber has an economic advantage in heavy-denier applications. Heavy foundation garments (girdles and corsets), surgical support hose, and elastic bands used in the waist and hems in underwear usually contain rubber fibers. The major market for spandex fibers is apparel items; leotard fabric, running- and biking-shorts fabric, and swim suit fabric. It also is used in surgical and sheer support hose, bandages, and surgical wraps. Its value in improving the performance of outerwear fabric is just now being recognized.

Rubber fibers are made into single- or double-covered yarns before being incorporated into elasticized fabrics. Spandex filaments are used in three forms: bare filament, covered yarns, and core-spun yarns. Most of the spandex used is bare filament. These types of yarns are discussed in Chapter 25.

---

[1] M. Couper, "Polyurethane Elastomeric Fibers," *High Technology Fibers*, Part A, M. Lewin and J. Preston, eds. (New York: Marcel Dekker, 1985), Chapter 2.

TABLE 20.1   Uses of Rubber and Spandex Fibers.

FIBER	YARN FORM	FABRIC TYPES	APPAREL ITEMS
Rubber	Single- and double-covered	Power-net warp knits and narrow fabrics, especially elastic bands	Elastic bands on outerwear, underwear, bra straps, etc.; foundation garments
Spandex	Bare	Warp knits, circular knits, narrow fabrics, hosiery	Foundation garments, swimwear, control tops of panty hose, elastic gloves, waist and leg bands, upholstery
	Covered	Warp knits, circular knits, hosiery	Support hose, foundation garments, elastic bandages, sportswear, upholstery
	Core-spun	Wovens, circular knits, socks	Shirting, bras, sportswear

RUBBER

Rubber fibers, prepared by cutting rubber sheets, have been used in fabrics for more than a century. The polymeric material is obtained from the *hevea* tree in South America by cutting the bark and letting a thick, milky-white liquid drain into collecting containers. In air, this natural rubber material becomes a solid substance that elongates and quickly recovers. Thomas Jefferson is credited with naming this substance. The story is that he was sent a sample of the material and told that he could "rub" away writing errors made with his ink pen, so he called the material a "rubber"—the name retained today.

Natural rubber fibers are quite weak and have low melting points. The discovery of vulcanization (cross-linking the hydrocarbon polymers within rubber with sulfur) by Charles Goodyear in 1839 led to rubber fibers with improved tenacity, raised melting points, and enhanced dimensional stability that still retained high elongation and recovery. Round rubber monofilaments were produced in the 1920s by the U.S. Rubber Company. These natural rubber fibers were vulcanized after shaping.

Synthetic rubber fibers were developed in the early 1930s. During the next two decades, they were improved in fineness, uniformity, durability, and whiteness.

Generic Group Members

By definition in the Textile Fiber Products Identification Act, rubber fibers are "manufactured fiber(s) in which the fiber-forming substance is comprised of natural or synthetic rubber . . ." There are three major groups of rubber fibers. The *saturated hydrocarbons*—natural rubber, polyisoprene, polybutadiene, copolymers of dienes and hydrocarbons, or amorphous (noncrystalline) polyolefins—are one type. A second group, composed of copolymers of acrylonitrile and dienes, sometimes is referred to as *lastrile*. There is no commercial production or development of fibers in this group at the present time. The third group of rubber fibers is comprised of the *chloroprenes*.

Structure

Rubber fibers are monofilaments that are round or rectangular in cross section and usually white (Figure 20.1). The smallest-denier rubber fiber with sufficient performance levels for textile applications (~140 denier) is a large-diameter fiber.

In textile products, rubber will not be found as bare filament. Rather, it is generally the core in a covered yarn (Chapter 25). The manner in which the covering is wound controls the degree of extension and recovery of the rubber monofilament.

SPANDEX

Rearrange the syllables of the word "expand" and add an "s" and the name of the generic group of fibers with the greatest elongation—spandex—is derived. By definition in the Textile Fiber Products Identification Act, spandex fibers are "manufactured fiber(s) in which the fiber-forming substance is a long-chain synthetic polymer of at least 85% of a segmented polyurethane." In Europe, "elastane" is the generic fiber name. The birth and growth of spandex fibers is a story of high-technology polymer invention and development aimed at obtaining a fiber with substantially improved properties over natural and synthetic rubbers.

Structure

Spandex fiber is available as filament in a variety of deniers ranging from 20–5400 denier. Of particular note is the fine denier that is possible. Deniers of 20–210 denier are used in lightweight support hosiery; of 140–560 denier, in men's hosiery. Coarser deniers of 70–2240 denier are used in pantyhose tops, swimwear, and foundation garments. Spandex fibers are usually delustered and white.

Under the microscope, a monofilament spandex fiber may appear either round or square in cross section. A group of coalesced filaments (filaments partly fused together) or individual filaments (monofilaments) may be seen in Figure 20.2. When filaments are coalesced, fusion is intermittent along the length of the filaments (that is, two adjacent filaments are not joined down their entire length); 2–132 elements can be coalesced. This structure helps to eliminate needle cutting of the spandex fiber because the needle can slide between the filaments without severing a monofilament.

The molecular framework of spandex fiber is unique and remarkable. Very special structural geometry is required to cause molecules to recover well after being deformed several times their initial length. Research on elastomeric fibers from the 1940s showed that two types of segments—one soft and deformable, the other hard and crystallizable—alternating along the same chain were necessary. The polymers in spandex fibers therefore are made up of rigid and soft segments (Figure 20.3). The soft segments provide stretch (elongation and elastic recovery), because the polymers in these segments are capable of uncoiling and straightening when a pulling stress is applied. They also recoil rapidly and with force when the extension force is removed. The hard segments, composed of straight molecules, function to hold adjacent polymers together by forming hydrogen bonds between polymer chains. The proportion of soft-to-hard segments controls the amount of stretch in an elastomeric fiber. Soft segments comprise 65–90% of the weight of the fiber.

The tenacity of a spandex fiber is well maintained; as the fiber elongates and becomes thinner, the polymers in the soft segments become more aligned, producing more crystalline regions. The hard segments can be softened thermally when the fiber is in extended form. This property is useful in fabric manufacture because the width, weight, shape, and residual stretch of fabric containing spandex fibers can be engineered by proper heat setting. Spandex fibers are not heat-set until they are in a fabric.

FIGURE 20.1 Photomicrograph of rubber fiber.

├──────────┤ 250 μm

Generic Group Members

Fibers in the spandex generic group have hard segments that are chemically alike, but they differ in the chemical composition of the soft polymer segment, as shown in Detail View 20. Two members of the spandex group—the *polyester segmented polyurethanes* and the *polyether segmented polyurethanes*—result from this difference. Polyester members are spandex fibers in which the soft segment has ester groups; polyether members are spandex fibers in which the soft segment has ether groups.

The two spandex members differ in reaction to degradation by detergents and mildew, which is of considerable importance in certain end-use applications. Polyether spandex fibers are more resistant in this regard than polyester spandex fibers. On the other hand, polyester spandex fibers are more resistant to oxidation and oil absorption. When unsaturated body oils and suntan oils are absorbed, oxidative attack is accelerated. The in-use performance difference between the two members can be dramatic. Both members are produced in consid-

FIGURE 20.2 Photomicrographs of individual spandex filaments and coalesced spandex filaments.

|―――――| 50 μm (right)

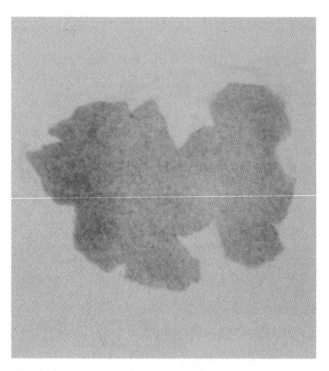

Individual spandex filament (monofilament), represented by Glospan® and Cleerspan® spandex manufactured by the Globe Manufacturing Company.

Coalesced spandex filament, represented by Lycra® spandex manufactured by the Du Pont company.

erable varieties, providing a range of spandex fibers to meet many different end-use requirements. Manufacturers of spandex fiber identify which type is being offered in their technical and sales literature, but no distinction is made on the consumer market. Lycra® spandex T-127, T-146, and T-141 are polyether-based spandex fibers. Lycra® T-128, Glospan®, and Cleerspan® are polyester-based spandex fibers. Lycra® spandex is manufactured by the Du Pont company; Glospan® and Cleerspan® are manufactured by the Globe Manufacturing Company.

Synthesis and Extrusion

Complex chemistry is necessary to synthesize a polymer with alternating hard and soft segments. The first step is to create the soft segment. Polyester or polyether chains, called macroglycols, with molecular weights of 1000–3000, are formed that have reactive hydroxyl groups ($HO\text{-}P_n\text{-}OH$) at each end. The second step is to react the

macroglycol with diisocyanate to form a macrodiisocyanate. The final step involves the creation of the hard segment during a process called *chain extension.*

The method used to spin the synthesized polymer into spandex fiber depends on the type of hard segment in the polymer. Although dry, wet, melt, or reaction spinning may be used, dry spinning is the most common procedure.

PROPERTY COMPARISON

The properties of rubber and spandex fibers are summarized in Table 20.2. To obtain numerical values for spandex and rubber fiber properties and to compare the properties of spandex and rubber to other fibers, refer to Figures 8.1–8.13 and Tables 8.1–8.8.

Influencing Fabric Durability

The durability of the elastomeric fibers is adequate, with spandex being considerably more durable than rubber.

FIGURE 20.3   The arrangement of polymers and hydrogen bonds in a relaxed and extended spandex fiber.

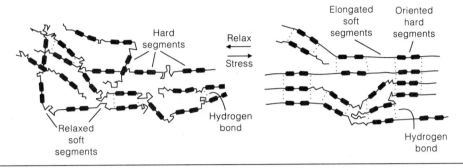

The breaking tenacity of spandex is low compared to other general-use fibers, but it is two or three times that of rubber of the same denier. The excellent elastic-recovery properties of spandex fibers give the impression that they are stronger than they actually are. Tenacity is affected only slightly by water. The flex life of spandex is considered to be excellent; that of rubber, only fair. Both fibers have poor abrasion resistance, but spandex is considered to have higher abrasion resistance than rubber.

Influencing Fabric Comfort

Spandex and rubber fibers are noted for their exceptional extensibility (at least 400%) and for their rapid and nearly complete recovery at high initial elongation levels (~97–99% at repeated 50% elongation). Both fibers are easy to extend (have a low modulus). Spandex fibers have a modulus twice that of rubber: it takes twice as much force to elongate a spandex fiber as it does to elongate a rubber fiber of the same denier.

Both spandex and rubber fibers possess high retractive power compared to other fibers. The higher its retractive power is, the better able the fiber is to hold and firm the human body. Spandex fibers have twice the retractive power of rubber fibers of the same fiber size. The higher retractive power of spandex fibers and their one-third lower specific gravity permit the manufacture of power-stretch fabrics significantly lighter in weight than rubber power-stretch fabrics that provide equal holding power.

Neither rubber nor spandex fiber is hydrophilic or possesses next-to-skin comfort. Usually these fibers are incorporated into yarns and fabrics so that they do not contact the skin. Thermophysiological and next-to-skin comfort therefore are determined by the other fiber(s) in the fabric.

Influencing Fabric Aesthetics

Rubber and spandex fibers are soft, pliable, and supple, with a hand much like that of a rubber band. Although pilling is not a problem with either elastomeric fiber, the fact that spandex fibers can pull away from seams and protrude above the fabric surface is aesthetically unpleasing. This is not a fiber fault but one that occurs during makeup of the final fabric and product. Rubber fibers are not dyeable; spandex fibers have an affinity for a wide range of different types of dye. Dyeing eliminates "show through" of the elastomer when the fabric is extended.

Rubber yellows with age. Spandex is subject to yellowing on exposure to atmospheric fumes, body oils, perspiration, chlorine bleach, and sunlight. A major aesthetic difference between rubber and spandex fabrics is in terms of shapability. Fabrics containing spandex can be molded because the fiber can be heat-set; rubber cannot be heat-set.

Influencing Fabric Maintenance

Rubber and spandex fibers tend to be affected by exposure to a variety of chemicals, to high and low temperatures, and to ultraviolet light. Because their initial levels of durability are not high, use/exposure conditions are particularly important.

Rubber and spandex fibers differ significantly in their ability to maintain extensibility and recovery performance on exposure to chemicals and ultraviolet light. Their resistance to biological organisms and heat is similar. In general, spandex is more resistant to perspiration, body oils, detergents, and drycleaning solvents than rubber. Rubber and spandex fibers are not resistant to chlorine bleach; however, spandex is resistant to the

TABLE 20.2 Comparison of Properties of Rubber and Spandex Fibers to Each Other and to General-use Fibers.

PROPERTY	ELASTOMER WITH HIGHER VALUE	RANKING RELATIVE TO GENERAL-USE FIBERS
Mechanical†		
Breaking tenacity	Spandex (twice rubber)	Low
Elongation at break	Spandex	High
Elastic recovery at 50% elongation	Rubber	High
Retractive power (recovery force/holding power)	Spandex (twice rubber)	High
Modulus of elasticity	Rubber (twice spandex)	High
Permanent set	Spandex	—
Abrasion resistance	Spandex	Medium
Flexibility	Spandex	High
Sorptive		
Moisture regain/content	Spandex	Low
Effect of moisture on mechanical properties	Spandex	Low
Oil absorption	Rubber	High
Effect of oil on mechanical properties	Rubber	High (rubber)
		Low (spandex)
Ease of oil release	Spandex	High
Thermal		
Heat resistance		
At high temperatures	Spandex	Low
At low temperatures	Spandex	Low
Softening and melting	Rubber	High (rubber does not melt)
		Medium (spandex)
Decomposition	—	—
Combustibility	Spandex	Medium
Chemical		
Alkali resistance	Rubber	—
Acid resistance	Spandex	Medium
Organic solvent resistance	Spandex	High (spandex); low (rubber)
Oxidizing agent resistance		
Ozone	Spandex	Low
Chlorine	Rubber	Low
Miscellaneous		
Ultraviolet light resistance	Spandex	High (spandex); low (rubber)
Microorganism resistance	Rubber and polyether-based spandex are equal; polyester-based spandex is less resistant	
Moth and beetle resistance	No difference	High
Silverfish resistance	No difference	High
Electrical resistivity	Rubber	High
Specific gravity	About equal	Medium

†At 70°F (21°C), 65% relative humidity.

concentration of chlorine in swimming pools. Spandex is not degraded by sunlight or by ozone. Spandex is considered to have a good shelf life; rubber, a poor shelf life.

Rubber and spandex fibers should not be exposed to high temperatures. Spandex is thermoplastic, with a melting point of 446–518° F (230–290° C). Spandex-containing fabrics can be dried automatically with caution. Ironing may be done on a low-temperature setting. It is best not to dry garments containing rubber fibers automatically. Both rubber and spandex fibers perform poorly at low temperatures.

Recommendations for the care of fabrics containing spandex fibers include hand or machine washing in lukewarm water with household laundry detergent and sodium perborate bleach. The fabric should be rinsed thoroughly and drip- or machine-dried at a low-temperature setting. If ironing is necessary, this should be done at the lowest setting and care should be taken to continuously move the iron. Spandex can be drycleaned. Rubber is severely affected by drycleaning solvents, so products containing rubber fibers must be hand-washed.

Influencing Health/Safety/Protection

The tremendous degree of extension and retractive force of both rubber and spandex fibers makes them quite useful in a number of medical applications, including support bandages for sprained ankles, wrists, and rib cages and surgical support hose worn to assist blood movement through varicose veins.

Rubber fibers may cause allergic contact dermatitis for some individuals. In the 1960s, an epidemic of allergic contact dermatitis was traced to spandex fiber. Investigation revealed that a chemical additive in the fiber-spinning formulation caused the skin rash. This chemical was immediately eliminated from production, and no further cases of allergic contact dermatitis from spandex have been reported.

CHAPTER SUMMARY

Rubber and spandex are elastomeric fibers. They can be stretched repeatedly to at least twice their original length at room temperature; when the extending force is removed, they immediately return with force to their approximate original length. Rubber and spandex are the commercially important elastomeric fibers.

The polymers in spandex fibers contain soft and hard segments. The soft segments extend and retract under a pulling force; hydrogen bonds form between the hard segments of adjacent polymers. Spandex fibers are available in smaller deniers than rubber fibers are.

Spandex fiber is considered superior to rubber fiber in terms of comfort afforded the wearer of elasticized garments. Spandex generally is less susceptible to deterioration by chemicals and light, is aesthetically more pleasing, and is easier to care for because it is machine-washable and drycleanable. However, spandex is not always the fiber of choice because the cost of various deniers plays an important role in fiber selection. Rubber fiber has an economic advantage in larger-denier sizes.

Special-use Manufactured and Asbestos Fibers

Special-use manufactured fibers and *asbestos fibers* find applications in industrial and consumer textile products where their high-decomposition temperature, high-ignition temperature, high resistance to degradation by concentrated chemicals, or high tenacity/high modulus is required.

INHERENTLY FLAME-RESISTANT FIBERS WITH LOW MELTING TEMPERATURES

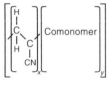

Modacrylic
(Acrylonitrile)

Saran
(Vinylidene chloride)

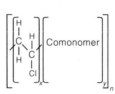

Vinyon
(Vinyl chloride)

Vinal
(Vinyl alcohol)

HEAT-RESISTANT (HEAT-DURABLE), CHEMICALLY RESISTANT ORGANIC FIBERS

Aramid
(Meta-aromatic amide)

PBI
(Imidazole)

Sulfar
(Phenylene sulfide)

HIGH-TENACITY, HIGH-MODULUS ORGANIC FIBERS

Aramid
(Para-aromatic amide)

Ultra-high molecular weight polyethylene

HEAT-RESISTANT, HIGH-MODULUS INORGANIC FIBERS

Asbestos   Silica   Alumino-silicate   Silicon carbide   Polytetrafluoroethylene (PTFE)
Metallic   Alumina   Alumino-boro-silicate   Boron
Carbon
Glass

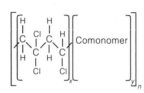

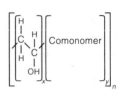

21

Special-use Manufactured Fibers and Asbestos

Special-use manufactured fibers also may be called *engineered fibers* or *specialty fibers*. They were developed to provide inherent flame resistance, heat resistance (heat durability), chemical resistance, and/or high breaking tenacity in combination with high modulus. General-use manufactured fibers may be modified to increase their levels of flame resistance, heat resistance, and breaking tenacity, but performance levels achieved do not approach those of the special-use fibers. The fibers considered in this chapter, with the exception of the inherently flame resistant fibers that melt on heating, perform in very extreme (highly hot, acidic, alkaline, mechanically rigorous) environments. Due to high developmental costs and small market potentials, special-use manufactured fibers are expensive compared to general-use manufactured fibers.

Detail View 21 presents the special-use manufactured fibers in four performance-property groupings. Generic group names or commonly accepted names are given, and chemical compositions and structures are provided. Table 8.4 (page 120) gives the heat-resistant, softening, melting, decomposition, and ignition temperatures of the fibers discussed here.

INHERENTLY FLAME-RESISTANT FIBERS WITH LOW MELTING TEMPERATURES

Modacrylic, saran, vinyon, vinal, and nytril are inherently flame-resistant fibers that melt when heated. Modacrylic and saran fibers are produced in the United States. Vinal and vinyon fibers are imported. Nytril is not produced anywhere in the world at this time.

This group of fibers is sometimes referred to as the *vinyl fibers* because the polymer in each is synthesized using a vinyl radical ($H_2C=CH-$). The Textile Fiber Products Identification Act definition for each of these fibers begins with "a manufactured fiber in which the fiber-forming substance is any long-chain synthetic polymer" and ends with the specific type and quantity of the vinyl radical, as follows:

- Modacrylic fiber "composed of less than 85% but at least 35% by weight acrylonitrile units."
- Saran fiber "composed of at least 80% vinylidene chloride units."
- Vinyon fiber "composed of at least 85% vinyl chloride units."
- Vinal fiber "composed of at least 50% by weight of vinyl alcohol units."

The vinyl fibers are chemically similar to olefin fibers and to acrylic fibers, discussed in Chapters 18 and 19, respectively. Photomicrographs of special-use vinyl fibers are shown in Figure 21.1.

Modacrylic Fibers

The first *modacrylic fiber* was developed by Union Carbide in 1948 under the trademark Vinyon N®. The modacrylic fiber presently produced in the United States

FIGURE 21.1 Photo-micrographs of inherently flame-resistant fibers with low melting points.

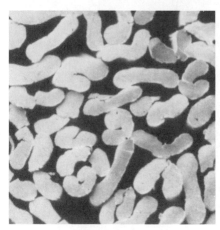

Modacrylic fiber

Saran fiber

is SEF®, which stands for self-extinguishing fiber. These fibers, manufactured by Monsanto Chemical Company, are used for children's sleepwear, draperies for public buildings, fleece-style pile fabrics, carpet-face fiber, transportation fabrics (airplane-seat upholstery, etc.) and wigs.

Modacrylic fiber is similar to acrylic fiber in most properties. A major distinction between the two is in reaction to heat. Modacrylic fiber has a lower softening temperature than acrylic fiber; modacrylic fiber melts, but acrylic fiber does not. Modacrylic fiber also has a lower decomposition temperature but a higher ignition temperature. Modacrylic fibers do not support combustion (they self-extinguish) due to their chemistry; acrylic fibers do.

Modacrylic fibers can be engineered so that there is little or no fiber shrinkage when exposed to hot water and temperatures <375° F (<170° C). They may be designed to shrink a predetermined amount when treated with boiling water or steam.

Saran Fibers

Saran fiber is used in the innersoles of military boots, cubicle cloth (the curtains that separate beds in hospital and nursing-home rooms), doll hair and wigs, and environmentally protective fabric (the material that shades delicate plants, such as tobacco and ginseng). In addition to its use as a fiber, saran has wide use as plastic sheeting.

The properties of saran fiber are more similar to those of olefin fiber than any other fiber generic group. The development of olefin resulted in the loss of markets for saran fiber, because olefin fiber is lower in cost and has some property advantages.

Saran fiber softens at a low temperature. When held in a direct flame, it burns very slowly but does not support combustion after the flame is removed.

It is an unusually tough, highly abrasion-resistant fiber. Saran fiber has a moisture content/regain of <0.1% but develops no static charge. Its mechanical properties are unaffected by water. Saran has an elongation at break of 15–30%, with excellent recovery; fabrics made from saran fiber therefore usually have excellent shape-retention. The fiber is stiff and resilient, so fabrics made from it are nondrapable but do not wrinkle. Saran fiber has good weathering properties and chemical resistance to acids, alkalies, and organic solvents. Exposure to sunlight causes the fiber to darken, but no tenacity loss occurs. Saran is also immune to biological attack. It is a heavy fiber.

Vinyon Fibers

Vinyon fiber was developed to obtain a fiber with a low softening temperature. Vinyon fiber does not withstand boiling water or normal pressing and ironing temperatures. Its thermoplastic nature makes it particularly suitable for use in heat-sealable paper, fulled and needled felts, and bonded fabrics. Its ability to shrink on exposure to heat (either alone or in combination with other fibers and yarns) has been utilized in molding, embossing, and bulking fabrics.

FIGURE 21.2 Photomicrographs of highly heat-resistant (heat-durable) organic fibers.

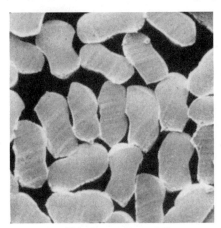

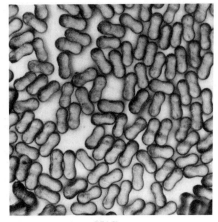

Aramid (meta-aromatic type) fiber   PBI fiber   Sulfar fiber

Vinyon fiber is inherently flame-resistant and, consequently, is used in protective clothing and flame-resistant synthetic Christmas trees. Vinyon comprises 50% of the bicomponent bigeneric fiber trademarked Cordelan®; vinal, the other 50%. Cordelan®, produced by Kohjin in Japan, is used in flame-resistant children's sleepwear, airplane blankets, and home furnishings.

Vinyon fiber is used to make tea bags. Vinyon polymer blended into a substrate results in a vinyl upholstery fabric that holds its shape longer.

Properties of note include imperviousness to moisture, and high electrical resistivity, chemical resistance, and resistance to insects and microorganisms.

Vinal Fibers

The major uses of vinal fiber are in fishing nets, filter fabrics, tarpaulins, and brush bristles. In water-soluble form, vinal is used to create lace-like and sheer fabrics by blending it with another fiber. Once the blended fabric has been produced, the vinal portion is dissolved and a sheer or lace-like fabric remains. Children's flame-resistant sleepwear may be made from vinal fibers. (Refer to the preceding discussion of the bicomponent bigeneric fiber Cordelan®.) Vinal is considered to have good resistance to alkalies and to common solvents; concentrated acids, however, harm it. Vinal fiber has excellent resistance to insects and microorganisms.

HEAT-RESISTANT (HEAT-DURABLE) ORGANIC FIBERS

Until the 1970s, *asbestos fiber* (a natural inorganic or mineral fiber) was chosen when fabrics were needed to protect workers under unusually hazardous conditions of exposure to fire, radiant heat, and molten metal. Unfortunately, asbestos fiber creates health hazards, so it is no longer used extensively in protective garment fabrics. New polymer and fiber research, largely initiated by specific fabric performance needs in the space program, led to the development and introduction of aramid, PBI, sulfar, and novoloid fibers. *Heat-resistant (heat-durable) organic fibers* exhibit exceptionally high heat resistance and high melting and ignition temperatures. (Novoloid fiber is no longer produced and is therefore not discussed in this chapter.) Photomicrographs of heat-resistant, special-use organic fibers are shown in Figure 21.2.

Applications include fire-department turnout coats, pants, and shirts; jumpsuits for forest-fire fighters; clothing and protective shields for welders; flightsuits for pilots of the Armed Services; suits for race-car drivers; pajamas and robes, particularly for nonambulatory persons; mailbags, carpets, upholstery, and drapes (required on some aircraft and on all U.S. Navy ships); cargo covers, boat covers, and tents; and industrial protective clothing (pants, shirts, coats, and smocks for workers in laboratories, chemical plants, and petroleum refineries). Flame-retardant cotton fibers/fabrics compete with these synthetic organic fibers in many of these applications. The fiber of choice depends on the degree of flame resistance needed and on other textile properties. For example, in protective clothing, the comfort-related properties of the fiber are highly important. When caustic chemicals also are included in a high-temperature environment, the fiber's chemical resistance is influential. Other applications for these synthetic organic fibers include filter bags for hot stack gases, press-cloths for industrial presses (for example, the application of durable-press finishes to cotton and cotton/polyester garments), ironing-board covers, sewing thread for high-speed machines, insulation paper for electrical motors and transformers, braided tubing for insulation of wires, and dryer belts for papermakers.

Aramid Fibers (Meta-aromatic Type)

Aramid fibers are "manufactured fiber(s) in which the fiber-forming substance is any long-chain synthetic polyamide in which at least 85% of the amide linkages

$$(-\overset{\text{O}}{\underset{}{\text{C}}}-NH-)$$

are attached directly to two aromatic rings."

In Detail View 21, the monomers for two types of aramid fiber are presented; one monomer appears under heat-resistant organic fibers; the other, under high-tenacity, high-modulus fibers. In both monomers, the aromatic (benzene) rings are the hexagons. The amide linkage is the same as that in the polymers comprising nylon fiber.[1]

The monomers differ only in the location of the two amide linkages on an aromatic ring. When the linkages are located directly across from each other on the aromatic ring, in what an organic chemist calls the "para" position, a rod-like or straight polymer is formed. This type of aramid is a *para-aromatic amide*. When the amide linkages are located in a "meta" position (not across from each other or adjacent on the aromatic ring),

a zigzag polymer backbone is formed. This type of aramid is a *meta-aromatic amide*. The type of monomer present is an important determinant of the properties of an aramid fiber. Meta-aramids are noted for their heat resistance and chemical resistance. Para-aramids are noted for their high tenacity and high modulus; they are discussed later in this chapter.

The first meta-aromatic aramid fiber was trademarked Nomex® by the Du Pont company, which developed and introduced it in 1963.[2] A similar fiber, developed by Teijin Limited of Japan and trademarked Conex®, was originally developed as a tire-cord fiber for jet aircraft to meet the need for a fiber with a melting point high enough to withstand the heat created by friction during landing. The nylon 6,6 fiber tire-cord was melting; the problem was solved by the use of aramid fibers, which do not melt.

Meta-aromatic aramid fiber has a high decomposition temperature and a high ignition temperature. It burns only with difficulty, and little smoke is generated. Fabric composed of meta-aromatic aramid fibers tends to shrink away from a flame or a high heat source. The force required to break meta-aromatic aramid fibers at 482° F (250° C) is similar to the force required to break conventional textile fibers at room temperature. It has useful tenacities to approximately 572° F (300° C). In contrast, nylon 6,6 fiber loses almost all of its tenacity at 572–662° F (300–350° C). Aramid fibers produce a thick char, which acts as a thermal barrier and prevents serious burns to the skin.

PBI Fibers

PBI, a generic group designation established in 1986 by the Federal Trade Commission, is an acronym for the polybenzimidazole polymer, of which the fiber is composed. The Textile Fiber Products Identification Act defines *PBI fibers* as "manufactured fiber(s) in which the fiber-forming substance is a long-chain aromatic polymer having recurring imidazole groups as an integral part of the polymer chain." The monomer comprising the polymer in PBI fibers is shown in Detail View 21.

PBI fiber was developed to increase the degree of safety under the most extreme fire conditions. The fiber

[1] Nylon fibers also contain polymers characterized by the presence of an amide linkage. However, according to the Textile Fiber Products Identification Act definition of nylon fiber, amide linkages must not occur between two aromatic rings. Most polymers in nylon fiber do not contain any aromatic rings (see Detail View 16).

[2] Nomex® fiber was assigned to the nylon generic group when introduced by Du Pont because chemically it is a polyamide. Because the polyamide polymer contains aromatic rings, the properties of Nomex® fibers are significantly different than those of other nylon fibers. A new generic group, aramid, was formed to accommodate Nomex® and other fibers composed of like polymers.

will not burn in air; charring eventually occurs if the fiber is exposed to high temperatures at high heat flux for prolonged periods of time. Even after a char has formed, however, a charred fabric still retains its integrity and flexibility and shows little shrinkage.

PBI fiber has excellent thermal stability and tenacity retention over a wide range of temperatures and environments. PBI performance is affected by temperature, duration of exposure, and availability of oxygen.

PBI fiber releases little or no smoke or offgasses up to its decomposition temperature. PBI generates less smoke than other flame-resistant fibers.

PBI protective fabrics have been rated comparable to cotton fabrics in tactile comfort. It is thought that the fiber's cross section, which approximates that of cotton, and low fiber stiffness contribute to PBI fabric softness. PBI fiber also has a high moisture regain (15% at 70° F and 65% relative humidity) for a synthetic fiber—actually two times higher than cotton fiber.[3]

Sulfar Fibers

In 1986, the Federal Trade Commission added the sulfar generic classification and defined *sulfar fibers*. The Textile Fiber Products Identification Act defines *sulfar fibers* as "manufactured fiber(s) in which the fiber-forming substance is a long-chain synthetic polysulfide in which at least 85% of the sulfide (-S-) linkages are attached directly to two aromatic rings." The monomer comprising the polymer in sulfar fibers is shown in Detail View 21.

The Phillips Fibers Corporation developed and currently markets Ryton® sulfar fiber. Sulfar fiber does not support combustion under normal atmospheric conditions. In a NASA study to rank 12 thermoplastic fibers in terms of fire safety in aircraft interiors, sulfar fiber was ranked as the most flame resistant. Sulfar fiber retains 40% of its breaking tenacity at 482° F (250° C), and its elongation at break remains unchanged at that temperature. Its stress–strain curve is much like that of polyester fiber.

CHEMICALLY RESISTANT ORGANIC FIBERS

Aramid, PBI, and sulfar fibers are *chemically resistant organic fibers* as well as heat-resistant fibers. They are slower to degrade or dissolve than other fibers when hot, concentrated chemicals are poured on them. The chemical resistance of cotton and wool fibers treated with flame retardants may rival that of the synthetic organic fibers considered here. Chemically resistant fibers are not resistant to degradation by all types of chemicals, however. In fact, the resistance of aramid, PBI, or sulfar fibers to degradation by a specific chemical may not be greater than that of a conventional general-use synthetic fiber.

PBI fibers have excellent chemical resistance to inorganic acids and alkalies, even at elevated temperatures. For example, PBI maintains 90% of its breaking tenacity with up to 24 hours exposure to 50% sulfuric acid vapors at temperatures as high as 160° F (71° C). PBI fiber maintains its tenacity when exposed to a broad range of organic chemicals and solvents. In addition, PBI fiber offers excellent resistance to steam hydrolysis.

When sulfar fibers are exposed to inorganic chemicals at elevated temperatures for a week, tensile retention is exceptional. They also are highly resistant to attack by organic chemicals. Only strong oxidizing agents, such as concentrated nitric, sulfuric, and chromic acids, can cause severe degradation. Sulfar fibers have proved to be outstanding in industrial-flue, gas-filtration applications, where they compete with PBI fibers.

Aramid fibers are much more resistant to acid than nylon 6,6 fibers but are not as acid-resistant as polyester fibers, except at elevated temperatures (particularly in the range of 4–8 pH). Their resistance to strong alkalies is comparable to that of nylon 6,6 fibers. Hydrolytic stability is superior to that of polyester and comparable to that of nylon 6,6.

HIGH-TENACITY, HIGH-MODULUS ORGANIC FIBERS

Traditional *high-tenacity, high-modulus fibers* include asbestos, carbon, steel, and glass, which are inorganic fibers. Newly developed fibers are organic and include the para-aromatic aramids and a ultra-high molecular weight, extended-chain polyethylene fiber trademarked Spectra®, both shown in Figure 21.3. These two fibers differ substantially in specific gravity, which is often the determining factor in selecting a fiber for a particular application.

High-tenacity, high-modulus organic fibers may be used in one or more of three types of applications: (1) tire cord in tire carcasses and belts in bias-belted and radial-belted tires, V-belts and cables; (2) parachutes and body

---

[3] The high moisture regain of PBI has prompted investigation of the potential use of this fiber as reverse-osmosis membrane material. Such membranes can desalinate brackish water and seawater.

FIGURE 21.3   Photomicrographs of high-tenacity, high-modulus organic fibers.

Aramid (para-aromatic type) fiber

Ultra-high molecular weight,
extended-chain polyethylene fiber

armor (bullet-proof vests, ballistic protective fabric, cut-resistant fabric); and (3) rigid, reinforced plastics in general; more specifically, high-performance boats and aircraft and other transportation vehicles, fan blades, and sporting goods (golf-club shafts, tennis rackets, skis, crossbow shafts, surfboards, fishing poles). In the third application, called a *composite application*, an assembly of fibers is prepared and impregnated with a liquid resin, which then is cured to form a rigid material.

Aramid Fibers (Para-aromatic Type)

Kevlar® aramid fiber, a product of the Du Pont company, was first manufactured in 1965 but was not introduced to consumers until 1973. Initial developmental efforts were directed toward tire reinforcement in the form of a replacement product for steel bracings in radial-belted type tires. Technora®, developed by Teijin Limited of Japan, is a more recent high-modulus, organic aramid fiber. Three types of Kevlar® aramid fiber are made; T-950 for use in tire reinforcement; T-29 for

industrial uses (ropes and woven fabrics); and T-49, a very high-modulus fiber, for use in plastics reinforcement. Teijin manufactures 13 different types of Technora® for the same and related applications.

On an equal-weight basis, the *para-aromatic aramid fibers* are two to three times stronger than high-tenacity nylon or polyester fibers and five to eight times stronger than steel wire. Their breaking elongation is ~4%; their modulus is approximately four times that of nylon and 50% higher than that of glass. Compared to the other types of Kevlar® aramid fiber, Kevlar T-49® has a slightly higher tenacity but, more importantly, more than twice the modulus. The specific gravity of the para-aramid fibers is lower than that of glass or steel.

Ultra-high Molecular Weight Polyethylene Fibers

A technical breakthrough by Allied-Signal Inc., in 1985, in an effort to improve the properties of polyethylene fiber, led to an *ultra-high molecular weight, extended-*

FIGURE 21.4 Photomicrographs of heat-resistant, high-modulus inorganic fibers.

Asbestos fiber

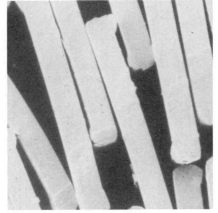

Metallic fiber

Glass fiber

Carbon fiber

Polytetrafluoroethylene fiber

chain polyethylene fiber, trademarked Spectra®. As the fiber name implies, the polymers are longer than those in regular polyethylene fiber and lie in a straighter configuration within the fiber. When a regular polyethylene fiber is made by melt spinning, it is thought that the polymers in it partly fold back on themselves as the fiber cools and crystallizes. The use of a longer polymer and solution spinning instead of melt spinning "stretches out" the polymers.

Spectra® fiber has a very high breaking tenacity and modulus and requires the greatest amount of force of any fiber to achieve breakage. It has the same low specific gravity, low moisture absorption, and low melting-point temperature of other olefin fibers.

The fiber is used in ballistic vests, riot shields, sailcloth, artificial ligaments and tendons, ropes and cordage, and gloves and other protective garments designed to prevent injury from cuts.

HEAT-RESISTANT, HIGH-MODULUS INORGANIC FIBERS

Heat-resistant, high-modulus inorganic fibers include metallic, carbon, and glass fibers. These three fibers represent the traditional high-temperature-resistant fibers. A recently developed fiber is polytetrafluoroethylene

(Teflon® by the Du Pont company).[4] Silica, alumina, alumino-silicate, alumino-boro-silicate, silicon carbide, and boron are capable of withstanding temperatures in excess of 1832° F (1000° C) in continuous use. This group of fibers, some of which are still experimental, are used for or have potential as lightweight materials for use in furnace linings and in insulation in the tail-cones and pipes of jet engines. They also find application as re-inforcement fiber in composite materials. Photomicro-graphs of heat-resistant, high-modulus inorganic fibers are shown in Figure 21.4.

Steel fibers are the cheapest and most common high-modulus fibers used in tires and composite materials. Typically, steel fibers have moduli ~2.5 times greater than glass fibers and five times greater than Kevlar® ara-mid fibers. Steel fibers are, however, very dense and are not suitable in applications in which light weight is also a critical factor.

Carbon fibers are composed of carbon. They have a tenacity unequaled by any other commercially available fiber. Their modulus is equivalent to steel, but their spe-cific gravity is only 1.8–2.0. Elongation and flexibil-ity are low. Most carbon fiber is used in composite applications.

Glass fibers soften and melt when heated to extremely high temperatures, such as those produced by the oxy-acetylene torch of the glassblower. These fibers do not burn at any temperature. Glass fibers are not used in fire-protective garments but have wide industrial ap-plication where noncombustibility is a primary asset. Fiberglass batts are used as insulation materials in build-ings and vehicles because the fiber does not burn. Glass mattress covers are produced for hotels, dormitories, and hospitals to reduce the risk of fires started by care-less smokers who fall asleep with lit cigarettes. Further, fire blankets and heat- and electrical-resistant tapes and braids are made of glass fibers. A silica-glass quilt was used on several space-shuttle missions. Glass fiber also is used in curtains and draperies. In the past five years or so, the amount of glass fiber used in these applications has, however, declined dramatically.

Glass fibers are not used in apparel applications for several reasons. One of the primary reasons is that glass fibers break easily due to their low flexibility. Glass fi-bers are also skin irritants. Glass fibers not only cause itching but can inflame the skin if they become im-bedded in fabric, as the result of either working with fiberglass insulation material or laundering garments after washing glass curtains without thoroughly rinsing the machine first.

Polytetrafluoroethylene fibers, also known as PTFE fi-bers, were introduced in 1954. The fiber is soft and very flexible and yet has a high melting point. It has the best thermal stability of the tough, flexible fibers. Its thermal stability is less than that of some inorganic fibers, such as glass or asbestos, but PTFE is tougher and more chemi-cally resistant than either of these fibers. When heated, it shrinks slightly. The fiber remains useful when exposed to temperatures of 401–527° F (205–275° C). It melts with decomposition. It does not burn; it is noncom-bustible. PTFE fiber is extraordinarily resistant to chemical degradation. In addition, the fiber has an un-pleasant, greasy hand, no moisture regain, and high spe-cific gravity. It has low modulus (even though it is grouped with the high-tenacity, high-modulus fibers). PTFE fibers are used in industrial specialty products, such as braids inside chemical pump shafts, gaskets for pipe flanges exposed to corrosive liquids, and filters for hot, corrosive liquids. These fibers also are used in laun-dry pads and roll covers and in protective clothing.

CHAPTER SUMMARY

The names of 22 special-use fibers are given in this chap-ter. Aramid, glass, modacrylic, novoloid, nytril, PBI, saran, sulfar, vinal, and vinyon fibers are the generic names established in the Textile Fiber Products Identifi-cation Act for ten of the special-use fibers. Two of these fibers, nytril and novoloid, are no longer manufactured. Asbestos is the common name for a natural mineral (in-organic) fiber. Four other fibers—boron, polytetra-fluoroethylene, steel, and carbon/graphite—are the most important inorganic fibers. No Federal Trade Commission definitions are available for these fibers.

In general, the special-use fibers find applications where their high-decomposition temperature, high-ignition temperature, high resistance to degradation by concentrated chemicals, or high tenacity/high modu-lus is of primary importance. They usually are used in industrial and consumer applications, including protec-tive clothing. Modacrylic fiber is used primarily in ap-parel and interior textile applications, however.

---

[4]Polytetrafluoroethylene polymers also are extruded into films, which can be used to make waterproof, breathable, laminated fabrics, such as Goretex®, manufactured by Goretex Incorporated. This polymer also forms the nonstick polymer coating on Teflon® cooking utensils.

$\mathcal{Y}$arn Structure and Performance

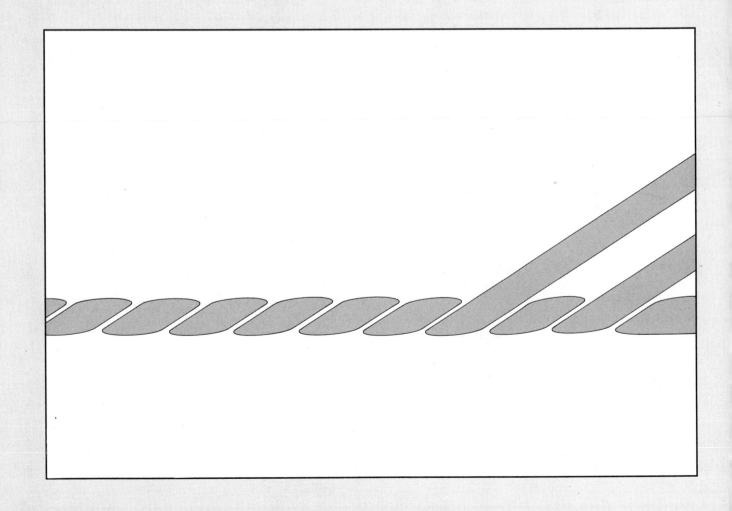

Yarn Structures

Yarn is "a generic term for a continuous strand of textile [staple] fibers, filaments or [other] material in a form suitable for knitting, weaving, or otherwise intertwining to form a textile fabric."

SPUN YARNS

Spun yarns are composed of [staple] fibers held together by some binding mechanism.

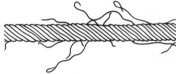

FILAMENT YARNS

Filament yarns are composed of a single filament or multiple filaments.

COMPOUND YARNS (COVERED AND CORE-SPUN)

Compound yarns are composed of at least two strands, one that forms the center or core and one that forms the covering or wrap.

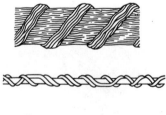

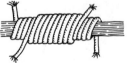

FANCY YARNS (NOVELTY OR EFFECT YARNS)

Fancy yarns differ significantly from the normal appearance of single or plied yarns due to the presence of irregularities deliberately produced during their formation.

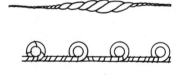

APPROXIMATELY 2½ YARDS of fine broadcloth fabric are required to make a shirt. In this fabric, there are approximately 22,500 yards, or 13 miles, of yarn. About 16 million twists lie along that yarn, holding the staple fibers and composing them into one continuous strand. Although the yarn in the shirting fabric is structurally simple, a tremendous amount of technology is involved in its production. The yarn plays a significant role in the performance of the shirt fabric.

WHAT ARE THE MAJOR TYPES OF YARNS?

This unit is about yarns, those "continuous strands of textile [staple] fibers, filaments or [other] material in a form suitable for knitting, weaving, or otherwise intertwining to form a textile fabric".[1] Fibers are assembled or arranged within yarns in many ways. All yarns are, however, conveniently classified into four groups: spun, filament, compound, and fancy (Overview III).

A spun yarn "is a continuous strand of fibers held together by some binding mechanism." The fibers are staple length, and binding is usually performed by twisting the strand of fibers. A filament yarn "is composed of (continuous) filaments assembled with or without twist." The difference in the lengths of the fibers in these two types of yarns makes the structure of each distinctive and the performance of each quite different. A compound yarn is composed of at least two strands, one of which forms the center or core of the yarn and one that forms the covering or wrap.[2] One strand is usually composed of staple fibers; the other of filament fibers. This type of yarn is even in diameter. A fancy yarn is "a yarn that differs significantly from the normal appearance of single or plied yarn due to the presence of irregularities deliberately produced during its formation." Fancy yarns usually consist of several preformed yarns, one of which is usually wrapped, looped, or twisted about a center yarn to achieve irregularity. Overview III shows diagrams of typical yarns in each of these four major categories.

A skill that you will want to develop is the ability to determine the type of yarn that a fabric contains. This skill begins with the ability to place a yarn into one of the four major categories: spun, filament, compound, and fancy. To determine the type of yarn that a fabric contains, it is necessary to remove a yarn from the fabric. A magnifying glass is helpful in making the determination.

Identification is not difficult when the yarn is fancy because this yarn is noticeably uneven in diameter along its length. The spun, filament, and compound yarns are all even in diameter. Because a compound yarn has visually different strands, it may be fairly readily identified if the observer dismantles or tears down the yarn. This strategy is effective because one strand is hidden in the center of the yarn.

Usually, distinguishing a spun yarn from a filament yarn is not difficult because spun yarns contain staple fibers and filament yarns contain filament fibers. The important step in the determination is to cut a short length of the yarn (2–3 inches for ease of manipulation) and separate it into fibers. In many cases, the yarn must be untwisted to observe the fibers composing it. If the fibers span the entire length of the section being examined, then the yarn is a filament yarn. If the fibers are too short to span the length of the section, then the yarn is a spun yarn.

An indication, though not always reliable, as to whether the yarn is spun or filament lies in the distinctness of the yarn edge or perimeter, the evenness of the yarn diameter, and the degree of packing of the fibers. Spun yarns are usually fuzzier than filament yarns, so spun yarns have more blurred or indistinct edges than filament yarns. However, some spun yarns appear so smooth that they can be mistaken for filament yarns, and some filament yarns have fuzzy edges. In addition, spun yarns are usually less even in diameter along their length than filament yarns. Some filament yarns, though, are sufficiently uneven that they might be mistaken for spun yarns. The fibers in spun yarns are usually less packed than the fibers in filament yarns.

UNIT ORGANIZATION

Between 90% and 95% of all yarns produced in the United States are spun or filament yarns. About 60% of the 90–95% are spun yarns; 40% are filament yarns.[3]

---

[1] *ASTM Annual Book of Standards*, Volume 7.01 (Philadelphia: American Society for Testing and Materials, 1990), p. 54. All other quoted definitions in this section are also taken from this source.
[2] Compound yarn is not defined by ASTM, but the term *compound* is used by ASTM to characterize the two types of yarns that have been grouped under this heading for discussion in this textbook.

[3] "Spun Yarn Production and Textured Yarn Production," *Current Industrial Reports*, U.S. Department of Commerce Bureau of Statistics, 1988.

The other 5–10% of yarns manufactured are compound or fancy yarns. Spun yarns are considered in Chapter 22, filament yarns in Chapter 23, and the construction of spun and filament yarns in Chapter 24. Compound and fancy yarns are considered in Chapter 25. The Detail Views provide diagrams and definitions of the types of yarns to be discussed in each chapter.

TERMINOLOGY

The American Society for Testing and Materials, Standard D 4849–88 "Standard Terminology Relating to Yarn" serves as the source of the definitions for the spun, filament, and compound yarns. When the ASTM defined a yarn only in terms of the method of its manufacture, descriptions of the arrangements of the fibers within the yarn and of other distinguishing features of the yarn were added in this textbook. Descriptions of the fancy yarns are from I. B. Wingate, *Fairchild's Dictionary of Textiles* (New York: Fairchild Publications, 1979) and S. R. Beech, (ed.), *Textile Terms and Definitions,* 8th ed. (Manchester, England: The Textile Institute, 1986). Precise naming of fancy yarns is not always possible due to the great variety of yarns; many do not fit one description precisely but have features of two closely related fancy yarns. Terminology related to the construction of yarns is from Standard D 4849–88.

It should be clarified here that the words *yarn* and *thread* should not be used interchangeably. Thread refers to the product used to join pieces of fabric together, usually by sewing. Yarn is the product used to make fabric.

LEARNING THE PERFORMANCE OF YARNS

In the discussions of yarn performance, two considerations should be kept in mind. The first consideration is that performance is discussed in a comparative way; quantitative values are not given. For example, the text will read "the strength of spun yarns is *lower* than that of filament yarns," or "monofilament yarns are *stiffer* than multifilament yarns." With very few exceptions, the two yarns whose performance is being compared are assumed to differ only in one structural feature. Usually the features that are similar will be stated in the comparison statement. To continue the above example, the text would include ". . . of the same fiber composition and the same size."

Secondly, *yarn* performance differences may be stated in terms of *fabric* performance differences. This approach is always taken when the yarn must be made into fabric before an assessment of the relevant performance properties can be made. For example, yarn structure can make a significant difference in pilling and tearing strength but this difference will not be known until fabric made from this yarn is evaluated. For ease of discussion, a yarn structure name will be given prior to the word *fabric:* for example, "open-end fabric" or "filament-yarn fabric" will be stated rather than "a fabric composed of open-end yarns" or "a fabric composed of filament yarns."

Performance differences between spun yarns and filament yarns and fabric made of them are considerable. Spun yarns are weaker than filament yarns of the same size and fiber type because spun yarns achieve their strength primarily from the ability of the fibers to adhere to each other. As spun yarns are stressed, the force causes the staple fibers to slide by each other. If the fibers do not slide, the force breaks individual fibers. Rarely are all fibers in a spun yarn cross section broken, however. In contrast, filament yarns achieve their strength from their filaments, because each filament spans the length of the yarn. All filaments, therefore, share equally in the stress upon the yarn, making it necessary to break all of the filaments in order to break the yarn.

Comfort differs in fabrics made from spun and filament yarns.[4] Spun-yarn fabrics are more adsorbent than filament-yarn fabrics of the same fiber content and yarn size because the fibers are less packed in spun than in filament yarns. More surface area is available for water adsorption in spun yarns. Spun-yarn fabrics also have higher water vapor permeability because the staple fibers in spun yarns do not lie as closely together as the filaments in filament yarns. Spun-yarn fabrics provide higher insulative capability because there is more air space in between the fibers in the yarn. Spun-yarn fabrics feel warmer than filament-yarn fabrics because the protruding fibers of spun-yarn fabrics hold the body of the fabric above the surface of the skin, minimizing the contact between the two. Additionally, the protruding fiber ends establish a thin air layer between the skin surface and the inner fabric surface.

---

[4] Filament yarns that are textured (Chapter 23) are very similar to spun yarns of like fiber composition in performance related to comfort.

Maintenance is affected in the sense that spun yarns do not shed soil as well as filament yarns do because dirt particles are more easily trapped within the spun yarn structure. Spun yarns lint more than filament yarns due to the shorter fiber length in spun yarns.

Aesthetics of spun-yarn fabric and filament-yarn fabric are greatly different. Spun-yarn fabrics are usually softer, less lustrous, and have higher covering power than filament-yarn fabrics. Even when delustered filaments are used, the yarns tend to have more sheen than comparable spun yarns. Spun-yarn fabrics pill more than filament-yarn fabrics because there are more fiber ends to ball up. When filament-yarn fabrics do pill, however, the pilling is a greater problem because the pills cannot be pulled off without destroying the fabric's integrity. Spun yarns tend to slip less in fabric because they are not as slick as filament yarns. Spun yarns snag less in fabrics; in contrast, a major drawback of filament yarns is their tendency to snag. In many end uses, the hand of spun-yarn fabrics is preferred to that of filament-yarn fabrics. As a fabric is used and worn, initial levels of performance are maintained better in spun-yarn fabrics because spun yarns tend to retain their cross-sectional shape better than filament yarns do under various compressional and bending deformations.

Due to the differences in performance of spun and filament yarns, more spun yarn than filament yarn is used in apparel. Consumers usually prefer the properties provided by spun yarns for their apparel items. Notable exceptions are lingerie, women's sheer hosiery, windbreaker jackets, and the shell and lining fabrics of ski wear. Likewise in carpeting, more filament yarn is used than spun yarn. Filament yarn is also used extensively in consumer and industrial textile products.

OBJECTIVES

The objectives of this unit are to

1. Describe the types of yarn available, name them, and provide instruction about their identification.

2. Consider how the structure of yarns relates to their performance as well as the performance of the fabrics in which they are used.

3. Develop an appreciation for the technology involved in the manufacture of yarns.

It is also hoped that an appreciation will be developed for the fact that although differences in yarn structure may appear subtle to the eye or even under a microscope, they can and do lead to substantial differences in yarn and fabric performance.

Spun Yarns

Spun yarns are composed of "[staple] fibers held together by some binding mechanism."

RING-SPUN YARNS

Ring-spun yarns are composed of fibers that are fairly well aligned with the yarn axis; they are the yarns against which other spun yarns are compared.

Carded yarns are ring-spun yarns composed of fibers that are less well aligned with the yarn axis and whose average length is lower than fibers in a combed yarn.

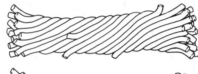

Combed yarns are ring-spun yarns composed of fibers that are better aligned with the yarn axis and whose average length is higher than fibers in a carded yarn.

Woolen yarns are ring-spun yarns composed of short wool fibers that are not as well aligned with the yarn axis as fibers in a worsted yarn.

Worsted yarns are ring-spun yarns composed of long wool fibers that are well aligned with the yarn axis. They are also composed of manufactured fibers whose length is similar to long-length wool fibers.

OPEN-END SPUN-YARNS

Open-end spun-yarns are composed of fibers that are less aligned with the yarn axis and do not lie as straight within the yarn as those fibers in a ring-spun yarn.

Rotor yarns are open-end yarns characterized as being more similar to cotton ring-spun yarns, with regard to relative fiber positioning, bulk, and surface texture, than to other types of spun yarns.

Friction yarns are open-end yarns characterized as being more similar to woolen ring-spun yarns, with regard to relative fiber positioning, bulk, and surface texture, than to other types of ring-spun yarns.

AIR-JET SPUN-YARNS

Air-jet spun-yarns are composed of a comparatively straight, central core of staple fibers, held together by taut surface staple fibers that are helically wound onto the central core.

Spun Yarns

Spun yarns, those "composed of staple fibers held together by some binding mechanism," are of three types: ring-spun, open-end, and air-jet (Detail View 22). Both the geometrical arrangement, or the positioning of the staple fibers within the yarns, and the binding mechanism make the three types structurally distinctive. In two types, the entire fibrous strand is twisted; in one, only the surface fibers twist around the fibrous strand. The two twisted yarns differ in the straightness of the staple fibers composing them and in the proportion of fibers that lie parallel to the yarn axis.

Also shown in Detail View 22 are four types of ring-spun yarns and two types of open-end spun-yarns. These types also differ in the positioning of the fibers. Their structural differences, however, are more subtle than those between ring-spun, open-end, and air-jet spun-yarns.

RING-SPUN YARNS

Ring-spun yarns are composed of fibers that are fairly well aligned with the yarn axis (Detail View 22 and Figure 22.1). Of the three major types of spun yarns, ring-spun yarns have the greatest proportion of fibers aligned parallel to the yarn axis and have the straightest fibers. Also, fibers throughout the yarn (fibers at the center and the surface) twist about the yarn axis.

Ring-spun yarns have been manufactured for over 150 years and comprise the greatest share of yarn manufactured today. Consequently, they are the yarns against which the structures and properties of other spun yarns are usually compared.

Ring-spun yarns may be cotton, wool, flax, staple-length manufactured fibers, or blends of these fibers. They are available in the widest range of sizes (Figure 22.2) and are found in every application in which spun yarns are used, including most apparel items, carpet face pile, carpet backing, upholstery, drapery and curtain fabrics, tents, and awnings.

In the case of ring-spun yarns, the degree to which the fibers lie parallel to the axis of the yarn is reflected by the words *carded, combed, woolen, worsted, tow,* and *line* (Figure 22.3). *Carded* and *combed* yarns are cotton or cotton blend yarns. Carded yarns contain fewer aligned fibers than combed yarns contain. Combed yarns contain longer fibers.[1] *Woolen* and *worsted* are terms used for wool yarns. Woolen yarns contain shorter fibers that are less aligned than the longer fibers in worsted yarns. *Tow* and *line* are the equivalent terms for flax fibers. Spun-silk yarns do not have names to indicate fiber length and alignment.

Sometimes the word *worsted* is used to describe 100% manufactured-fiber spun-yarns. For example, the label on an acrylic-knitting-yarn package often reads "100% worsted acrylic," indicating that the acrylic fibers are approximately the same length as wool fibers in worsted

---

[1] Research currently underway with open-end yarns includes the formation of a combed open-end yarn. In the future, a discussion of carded and combed open-end yarns may be appropriate.

FIGURE 22.1   Ring-spun, open-end, and air-jet spun-yarns.

Ring-spun   Open-end   Air-jet

wool yarns and have excellent alignment within the yarn. The presence of combed or worsted yarns in a product will often be indicated by the label. Textiles containing these yarns usually cost more than comparable products made from carded or woolen yarns.

Carded/woolen/tow yarns have more protruding fiber ends (are fuzzier), have less even diameters, and are usually larger (coarser or bulkier) than combed/worsted/line yarns. These structural differences, however, are small and relative. In general, differences are easiest to observe between woolen and worsted yarns and most difficult between carded and combed yarns (Figure 22.3).

Although examination of the yarn itself is always essential, the type of fabric may provide clues to the type of ring-spun yarn that composes it. Very high-count fabrics (those with numerous yarns/inch²) usually contain combed/worsted/line ring-spun yarns. Fuzzy, napped fabric surfaces are indicative of carded/woolen/tow yarns, whereas hard, glossy, smooth fabric surfaces are indicative of combed/worsted/line yarns.

Properties of ring-spun yarns and their resultant fabrics differ with the fiber length and alignment in the yarn. Strength is higher in longer-fiber/better-aligned yarns than in shorter-fiber/less well aligned yarns. Insulative capability is lower in yarns containing short, poorly aligned fibers because there is more dead air

space. Crease retention is higher for those fabrics containing longer-fiber/better-aligned fiber yarns. Worsted fabrics tend to have better crease retention than woolen fabrics. Resilience is higher in woolen fabrics than worsted ones because the fibers in woolen yarns are better able to slip by each other. Shape retention is usually higher in worsted/combed fabrics. Fabric luster increases with fiber length and alignment. Combed/worsted fabrics are said to have hard, smooth surfaces and low pilling propensity.

OPEN-END YARNS

In the 1970s, open-end spun-yarns became available (Detail View 22 and Figure 22.1). *Open-end spun-yarns* are those in which the fibers tend to be less well aligned with the yarn axis than those in ring-spun yarns. In addition, the fibers tend to have more bends; they do not lie as straight as those in ring-spun yarns.

Most open-end yarns are cotton or cotton blends and are rotor open-end yarns. Open-end spun-yarns are not available in sizes as fine as ring-spun yarns.[2] Open-end spun-yarns are, however, more even in diameter than ring-spun yarns. In the United States, about 35–40% of

---

[2] Open-end yarns as fine as a 60s cotton count ring-spun yarn are currently being made in research laboratories.

FIGURE 22.2   The sizes in which spun yarns are manufactured.

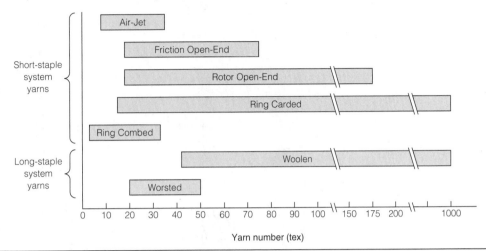

cotton spun-yarn is open-end with the remaining 60–65% ring-spun.[3]

Open-end yarns may be *rotor open-end* or *friction open-end*. Friction open-end yarns are also known as DREF-2® yarns, reflecting the name of the equipment on which they are produced.[4] Currently, by far the greater quantity of open-end yarn is rotor open-end.

Rotor open-end yarns are most similar to cotton ring-spun yarns and friction open-end yarns are most similar to woolen ring-spun yarns with regard to relative fiber positioning, bulk, and surface texture. Open-end yarns, whether rotor or friction, are produced in either coarse or medium diameters. Friction yarns have stronger interfiber binding, which results from the superimposition of single fibers on one another and the twisting of the fibers as the yarn is formed. Rotor open-end yarns are usually composed of cotton fibers. Friction open-end yarns may be composed of wool, but often they are composed of cotton and manufactured fibers. Fibers too short to process on other yarn-forming machinery, called waste, may be processed into friction open-end yarns. Both rotor and friction yarns have greater regularity and uniformity than ring-spun yarns; friction yarns rank the highest in this regard.

Rotor open-end yarns are well suited for denims, terry toweling, and heavier weights of bed sheeting. Their smooth, even surface makes them desirable as base fabrics for plastic-coated fabrics. Friction open-end yarns are currently found in blankets, tablecloths, and bedspreads. Interior uses include upholstery fabrics, rugs, and wallcoverings. Dust cloths, cleaning cloths, and dust mops are made from friction open-end yarns. Coat fabrics and denim fabric can be made from friction yarns.

Friction open-end yarns are the lowest in strength and ring-spun yarns are the highest in strength when friction, ring, and rotor yarns are compared. About 20% more twist is required to produce a friction yarn equal in strength to a woolen ring-spun yarn. In a study in which male college students wore jeans made from rotor open-end denim and ring-spun denim, the rotor open-end denim was less durable.[5] However, the differences were small and the durability of both fabrics was acceptable. The students judged the hand of rotor open-end fabric as "harsh." Friction open-end fabric tends to be softer than both ring-spun fabric and rotor open-end fabric. Fabrics containing friction open-end yarns tend to bag more than those containing ring-spun yarn due to the higher elongation in the friction yarn.

[3] Personal communication with James Parker, Director of the Textile Research Laboratory at Texas Tech University.
[4] The DREF-2 friction open-end yarn spinning equipment is manufactured by an Austrian company, Textilmaschinefabrik Dr. Ernst Fehrer AG.

[5] M.A. Morris, and H.H. Prato, "End-Use Performance and Consumer Acceptance of Denim Fabrics Woven from Open-End and Ring-Spun Yarns," *Textile Research Journal* 48 (1978): 177–183.

FIGURE 22.3 Carded and combed cotton ring-spun yarns and woolen and worsted wool ring-spun yarns.

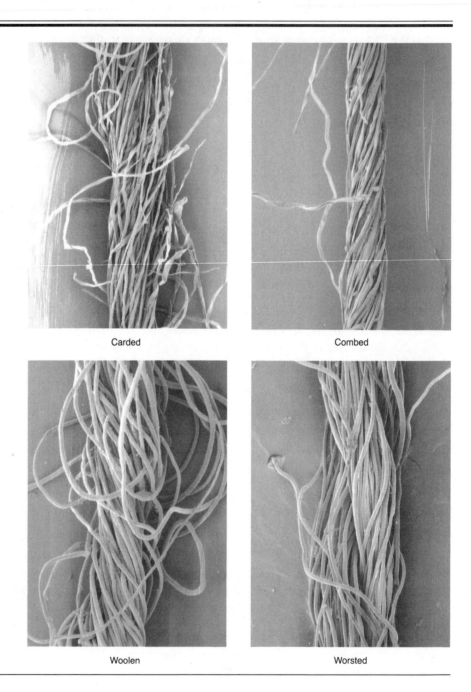

Carded

Combed

Woolen

Worsted

In general, open-end spun-yarns are more absorbent and less variable in strength along their length than ring-spun yarns. Fabrics composed of open-end yarns, compared to those composed of ring-spun yarns, are said to be more uniform and more opaque, lower in strength, less likely to pill, and inferior in crease recovery. Open-end fabrics are more subject to abrasion.

AIR-JET SPUN-YARNS

The most recent addition to types of spun yarns is *air-jet*.[6] The structure of air-jet spun-yarns is essentially that

---

[6] The development of air-jet yarn production is an extension of fasciated yarn production. Fasciated yarns are no longer manufactured.

of a comparatively straight, central core of fibers, held together by taut surface fibers that are helically wound onto the central core. Air-jet yarns are manufactured on air-jet spinning equipment. The uniformity of air-jet spun-yarns is high; it is comparable or slightly higher than that of ring-spun yarns. Air-jet spun-yarns are less fuzzy or hairy.

Initially, air-jet spun-yarns were composed of manufactured fibers, primarily polyester, about 1.5–2.0 inches (3.8–5.1 centimeters) in length. Now air-jet yarns of acrylic, cotton, and rayon, in addition to polyester, are produced.

Compared with ring-spun yarn of similar fiber composition, air-jet yarns are weaker and have lower elongation. Compared to ring-spun fabric, air-jet fabric has lower breaking and tearing strength, but its air permeability is increased and its pilling propensity, shrinkage, and drying time are reduced. There is no difference in the wrinkling of the two fabrics. Air-jet spun-yarn fabrics are neither as soft nor as smooth as comparable ring-spun yarn fabrics, but they are crisper.

The hand of fabrics made from air-jet spun-yarns is being improved by blending, using fiber variants, varying spinning conditions, and altering finishing processes. Due to their unsatisfactory hand in apparel fabrics, air-jet spun-yarns are used primarily in sheet and pillowcase fabrics. In these fabrics, the air-jet yarn is used in the crosswise direction and ring-spun yarns in the lengthwise direction.

FORMATION OF SPUN YARNS

The evolution of processes to convert bundles of fibers into suitable yarns has spanned centuries. The earliest technology dates back to 15,000 years ago in Asia or 12,000 years ago in North Africa. Today, engineers apply the latest technology to ensure rates of productivity and levels of yarn quality that meet the clothing and textile product needs of an expanding world population.

An important aspect of spun-yarn quality is evenness of diameter along the yarn length. Spun yarns are inherently uneven in diameter. The yarn manufacturer is concerned about this unevenness, including that which is not visible to the eye, because subsequent processing efficiency and fabric appearance are affected. When two yarns are identical in size, twist, and fiber composition but different in evenness, the more uneven one will contain more weak places as well as places of greater weakness. Such a yarn will suffer more breakages in spinning, winding, warping, weaving, and knitting. Production efficiency will be reduced and the cost of all subsequent

processes will be increased. In knit fabrics, weakness in the yarn structure detracts from fabric performance because holes can develop when yarns break. Yarns used in the lengthwise direction of woven fabric must be strong. Once a woven fabric is made, the presence of weak places in a yarn is not as critical because any variation is counteracted by the interlacing of the yarns. Small variations in yarn evenness will give a fabric surface an uneven appearance. When an uneven surface is desired, this is acceptable, but in the majority of cases, a flat fabric surface is required. Color problems may result when a fabric containing poorly manufactured yarns is dyed.

To be competitive, the spun-yarn manufacturer must also produce the even, strong yarn to the size, number of plies, softness, and other specifications as economically as possible. Minimizing fiber waste, fiber damage incurred during processing, items of equipment, floor space required for machinery, energy required for running the equipment, and human labor, and maximizing the speed of the process allows spun yarn to be produced at the lowest possible cost.

The three major processes for converting staple fiber to yarn are ring spinning, open-end spinning, and air-jet spinning. Ring spinning is the oldest of the processes and is the one that currently is used to convert the greatest quantity of fiber to yarn.

Production of Ring-Spun Yarns

The production of ring-spun yarn involves a series of operations in which a mass of entangled fibers is transformed into a rope-like structure in which the fibers are more aligned than in the entangled mass; the rope-like structure is twisted to bind the fibers.[7]

Processing Systems. There are three major systems used to produce ring-spun yarns: the cotton system, the worsted system, and the woolen system. The *cotton system* is "a spinning system adapted to fibers less than 2.5 inches (65 millimeters) in length"; the *worsted system* is "a spinning system adapted to fibers 2–9 inches (50–225

---

[7]Spinning, in its most general sense, refers to that series of operations required to form a single yarn from fiber. The trend today is to refer to the entire process of forming a yarn as "yarn manufacturing." Spinning, in a more limited sense, describes a single step in the entire yarn manufacturing procedure, that of preparing *spun* yarns. This operation is the one in which sufficient strength is given (usually by inserting twist) to a strand of aligned staple fibers. Additionally, the word *spinning* is often substituted for the word *extrusion* to describe the formation of filament *fibers*. A silkworm spins the silk fiber. Wet spinning, dry spinning, and melt spinning, therefore, are extrusion procedures for manufactured fibers. Once aware of the uses of the term *spinning*, the reader will not have difficulty because the meaning of the term will be clear from the context in which it is used.

millimeters) in length"; and the *woolen system* is "a spinning system employing a minimum of draft and producing yarns of low bulk density."

The three systems accommodate differences in fiber physical structure (length, diameter, crimp, etc.) and in fiber strength, elongation, and elastic recovery, all of which impact a fiber's processability and spinnability. The machinery of each system looks quite different.

Although the systems and machinery to convert staple fiber to yarn vary, all are designed to arrange an entangled mass of fibers into a parallel configuration in the direction of the axis of the yarn to be formed. The cotton system is used to illustrate the sequence of steps necessary to convert fibers shorter than 2.5 inches (65 millimeters) to a ring-spun yarn.

Making a Cotton Ring-Spun Yarn.

Numerous processes are required to produce a carded ring-spun yarn, with an additional one needed to produce a combed ring-spun yarn.

First, the fibers are prepared. The processes of opening, cleaning, and mixing or blending occur simultaneously. *Opening* refers to separating small clumps of fibers within a mass of fibers, *cleaning* to trash removal, and *mixing* or *blending* to combining fibers from different bales to achieve a homogeneous starting material. These functions are not completed, however, during fiber preparation; they continue during subsequent processes.

To prepare cotton fibers, they are removed from bales and placed onto a blending feeder, where they pass through rollers with sharp spikes. The fibers then fall onto a conveyor belt and proceed to an opener, where rapidly whirling beater blades take off small tufts of fiber, knock out the trash, and loosen up the mass. Cotton in a loose mass enters the picker, which is a series of beaters and screen rolls. It emerges as a sheet of fibers, or *picker lap*, and is wound onto rolls. In these operations, large lumps of cotton are reduced to smaller lumps and about one-third of the trash is eliminated.

The second step in the cotton system is to begin to align the fibers and form a continuous strand. To accomplish this task, the fibers must be separated almost to a single-fiber state so they can be reassembled. This very complete separation also results in very efficient cleaning. The process of fiber-to-fiber separation is called *carding*.[8]

---

[8] For short wool fibers, waste silk, and baled manufactured fibers, this process is also called carding. For flax fibers, this process is called hackling; and for long wool and manufactured fibers (3–5 inches) it is gilling. Manufactured fibers that have been converted from tow-to-top are already aligned.

Carding involves passing the picker lap through hundreds of fine wires on a card machine. One set of wires is usually mounted on revolving surface flats. The picker lap is pulled through a small gap (0.01 inches or 0.25 millimeters) between these two surfaces by the rotation of the cylinder. The teasing action of the wires completes fiber separation, removes extremely short fibers and more debris, and mixes fibers while aligning them roughly parallel to each other. A thin web of fiber is formed. Because a web is difficult to handle in further processing, it is shaped into a rope-like strand of partially aligned fibers. Cotton webs move through a funnel-shaped device. The rope-like strand formed is the *card sliver* (sly-ver), "a continuous strand of loosely assembled fibers that is approximately uniform in cross-sectional area and without twist." It is about the size of a person's thumb and is not very uniform in diameter.

The third step (necessary only when combed yarns are being manufactured) is to extract the shorter fibers and continue to align the longer fibers. The card sliver is formed into a *combed sliver*. In this process, 10–15% of the shortest fibers in the card sliver may be removed; this portion becomes waste. In combing, the card sliver is drawn and formed into a lap, which is then combed. The lap is literally torn to pieces in successive tufts. Both ends of each tuft are combed with metal combs, and the tufts are subsequently reassembled into a combed sliver.

The fourth step in the cotton system is to make a more uniform sliver and continue to align the fibers. To produce a yarn that is as even in diameter as possible, the sliver (either the card or the combed sliver) to be used in the final step of manufacturing must have a uniform diameter. To achieve this uniformity, six slivers are combined into an assemblage that is then reduced to the diameter of one of the original six slivers, with a length six times longer. This process is called *drawing* and the product is a *drawn sliver*. In drawing, the card sliver is passed between a series of paired rollers, each successive pair rotating at a faster speed than the previous pair. This operation may be repeated several times.

In the fifth step, the size of the drawn sliver is further reduced and the fibers are made nearly parallel. A single drawn sliver is converted to a *roving* by drawing it on a roving frame. The size of the roving relative to the drawn sliver depends on the draw ratio, or the ratio of the speeds of the feed and delivery rollers. For example, a draw ratio of 6 means the roving is 6 times smaller than the sliver. Because fiber-to-fiber cohesion is so slight at this stage, the roving is given a slight amount of twist to avoid damage. The amount of twisting must be sufficient

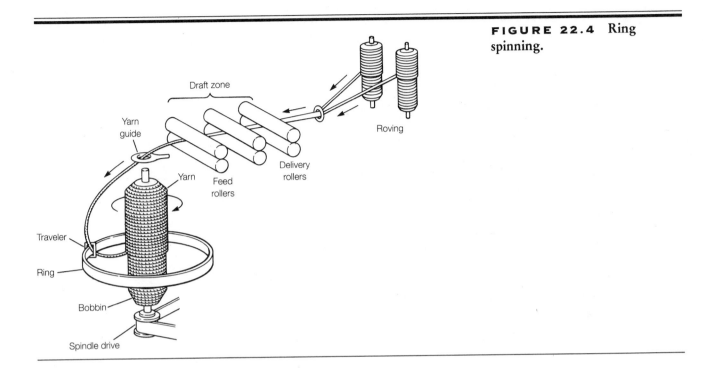

FIGURE 22.4 Ring spinning.

for the roving to be wound onto a package and unwound from that package without being damaged.

In the last step, the binding of the fibers occurs; the roving is converted to *yarn.* Sufficient strength must be imparted to the strand of prepared fibers so it can be converted into fabric. This has traditionally been accomplished by twisting the roving on a ring spinner. On the ring spinner (Figure 22.4), the roving is further reduced in size by passing it between rollers rotating at different speeds. The reduced roving passes through an eyelet and down and through a traveler. The traveler moves freely around a stationary ring. The spindle turns the bobbin at a constant speed in the range of 10,000–12,000 revolutions per minute. The traveler moves around the ring at speeds close to 2 miles per minute (3.2 kilometers per minute). The number of twists per inch along the yarn length is controlled by the rate at which the fibrous strand emerges from the front draft rollers. The yarn is twisted and wound onto a bobbin in a single operation.

In ring spinning, the bobbin can only hold a limited length (weight) of yarn because the bobbin mass must be rotated as twist is inserted. Doffing, the removal of full bobbins from the ring frame and replacement with empty bobbins, must be done fairly frequently due to the limited capacity of the bobbins. In a process called *winding,* yarn from these bobbins will be rewound onto larger packages, and in the process, knots will be tied to form a longer continuous yarn. Yarn quality is affected by the number of knots in the package. These packages are delivered to the fabric manufacturer.

Engineers have developed the ring spinner to the peak of its production capability. Maximum yarn-delivery rates on the order of 100 feet per minute (30 meters per minute) have been achieved. But the ring spinner remains expensive to operate; in fact, about half of the cost of fiber-to-yarn conversion is due to the cost of inserting twist. Efforts to further increase ring spinner efficiency and reduce its cost of operation have been precluded by the requirement that a heavy bobbin be rotated to insert the twist. As the bobbin's size and speed of rotation are increased (thereby improving productivity), the power—and hence the cost—required to drive the spindles increases at an even higher rate. Spinning is interrupted each time that the relatively small bobbins are filled with yarn, a factor that also contributes to the cost of ring-spun yarn. Ring-spun yarn costs are further increased by the necessity of winding yarn from several bobbins onto larger packages to obtain the continuous length of yarn needed in the subsequent manufacture of fabric. To reduce production costs and increase the rate of productivity of spun-yarn manufacture, open-end spinning was developed.

FIGURE 22.5 Open-end spinning.

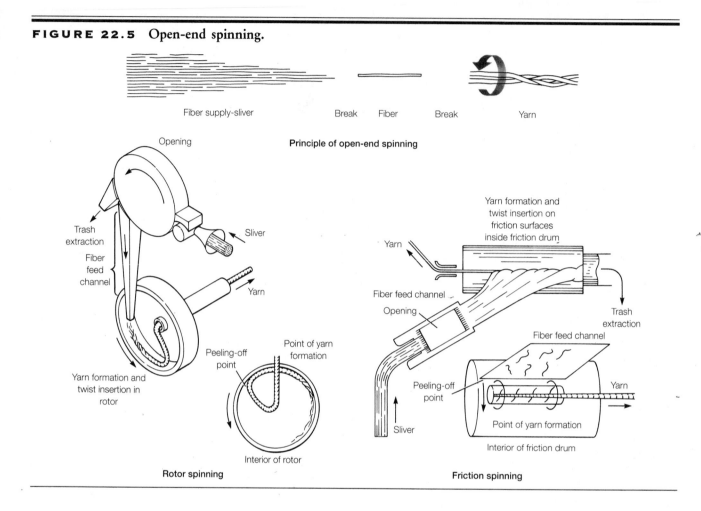

Fiber supply-sliver   Break   Fiber   Break   Yarn

Principle of open-end spinning

Opening

Trash
extraction   Sliver

Fiber
feed
channel   Yarn

Yarn formation and
twist insertion in   Peeling-off   Point of yarn
rotor   point   formation

Interior of rotor

Rotor spinning

Yarn formation and
twist insertion on
friction surfaces
inside friction drum

Yarn

Fiber feed channel

Opening   Trash
                                                        extraction

                                    Fiber feed channel

Peeling-off   Yarn
point

Sliver   Point of yarn formation

Interior of friction drum

Friction spinning

Production of Open-End Yarns

In open-end spinning, a gap or break is introduced in the flow of fibers between the delivery system and the yarn package (Figure 22.5). Twist is inserted by rotating the yarn end at the break; that is, the *yarn* at the point of yarn formation is rotated. The joining of fibers at an "open end" of yarn is the source of the name for this spinning operation. The mass of material to be rotated is, therefore, a minute fraction of that on the ring spinner. Further, the fibers in the supply can be aligned to a lesser degree than is necessary for ring spinning.

Fifty years of development preceded the introduction of machinery to bring the concept of open-end spinning to commercial reality. Open-end spinning is at least three times faster than ring spinning, with yarn delivery rates as high as 830 feet per minute (250 meters per minute). Yarns up to about 30 cotton-count (20 tex and coarser) can be spun more economically using open-end technology than ring spinning technology, though open-end spun-yarns require more twist than ring-spun yarns for satisfactory performance.

Several different systems have been developed to form the open-end yarn and insert the twist. The most successful of these methods are rotor spinning and friction spinning. Other approaches include electrostatic and fluid spinning.

In *rotor spinning*, fibers are prepared in the same manner as for ring spinning except that a card sliver rather than a roving is used for the prepared fiber supply. Fibers are taken from this card sliver by means of a small feed roller to a rapidly rotating beater that is covered with wire points. This beater detaches fibers individually from the sliver and projects them into the airstream flowing down the delivery duct. The fibers are deposited in a V-shaped groove along the sides of a lightweight rotor. Fibers from the side of the rotor are "peeled off" to join the "open end" of a previously formed yarn. As the fibers join the yarn, twist is conveyed to the fibers from the movement of the rotor. A constant stream of individual fibers enters the rotor, is distributed in the groove, and is removed after becoming part of the yarn itself. The formed yarn is continuously pulled from the delivery tube. Yarn from open-end spinning is wound directly onto fairly large packages during spinning, but it may also be rewound onto even larger packages so it can be stored and transported conveniently.

Friction open-end spinning is receiving considerable attention because it attains rates of yarn production that are substantially higher than those of rotor open-end spinning. Yarn delivery speeds are in the range of 830 feet per minute (250 meters per minute) as compared to rotor open-end at 400 feet per minute (120 meters per minute) in the medium-count range. The rate of yarn formation is not dependent on moving a rotor. Rate is limited only by the time that the yarn remains in the yarn formation zone.

In friction open-end spinning, a rotating carding drum opens a sliver to a web so that single fibers can be stripped from it and transported by air to the friction zone. The fibers are deposited into the nip between two cylinders (spinning drums) that are rotating in opposite directions. One cylinder is perforated to allow air passage; the other is covered with a solid substance having a high coefficient of friction. The fibers are twisted by the friction on the surface of these drums. The yarn is formed from the inside outward by superimposing individual fibers to create strong interfiber bonding. The cylinder speeds in relation to the delivery speed govern the degree of yarn twist. The friction open-end spun-yarn is drawn off and wound onto bobbins.

Production of Air-Jet Yarns

Figure 22.6 shows an air-jet spinner and the action of the air-jets on a fiber strand. A sliver is drafted to a predetermined size in the draft zone and then passes into a nozzle box. Within the nozzle box, air at high pressure is released from jets set in the walls. The direction of the air current swirling in the first nozzle is opposite to that swirling in the second nozzle. Fibers protruding from the main fiber strand are made to wind around the strand by the swirling air currents in the first nozzle, giving the strand cohesion and strength. The second nozzle en-

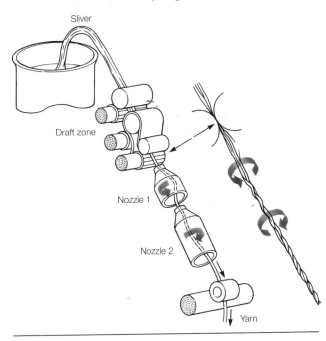

FIGURE 22.6 Air-jet spinning.

hances the cohesion of the strand to give the yarn its final strength.

The air-jet spinner can be used to spin a variety of fibers into yarn, including 100% cotton and synthetic fibers that are 2 inches (5 centimeters) or shorter. Cotton blended with polyester or 100% polyester short-staple fibers can be processed at delivery speeds ranging from 110–220 yards per minute (100–200 meters per minute) in yarn sizes ranging from 7.5–30 tex ($Ne_c10–Ne_c80$). This rate of productivity is as high as 10 times that of ring spinning and twice that of open-end-spinning.

CHAPTER SUMMARY

Three types of spun yarns—ring-spun, open-end, and air-jet—were described and compared in terms of the distribution of fibers within them and in terms of expected properties. Also introduced were carded and combed ring-spun yarns, woolen and worsted ring-spun yarns, tow and line ring-spun yarns, and rotor and friction open-end spun yarns. The manufacture of each of these yarns was described.

Filament Yarns

Filament yarns are "composed of (continuous) filaments assembled with or without twist." Filament yarns composed of a single filament are called mono-filament and those of many filaments are called multifilament.

FLAT YARNS

Flat yarns are filament yarns in which each filament lies straight and smooth within the yarn to achieve close packing and a smooth surface. Flat yarns are also called conventional yarns.

BULK YARNS

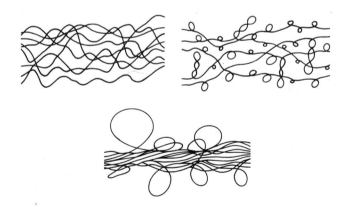

Bulk yarns are yarns "prepared in such a way as to have greater covering power, or apparent volume, than that of conventional yarn of equal linear density and of the same basic material with normal twist." The three types of bulk yarns are textured, stretch, and bulky.

Textured yarns are "filament or spun yarns that have been given notably greater apparent volume than conventional yarn of similar fiber (filament) count and linear density. The yarns have a relatively low elastic stretch. They are sufficiently stable to withstand normal yarn and fabric processing, including wet finishing and dyeing treatments, and conditions of use by the ultimate consumer. The apparent increased volume is achieved through physical, chemical, or heat treatments, or a combination of these."

Stretch yarns are "thermoplastic filament or spun yarns having a high degree of potential elastic stretch and rapid recovery, and characterized by a high degree of yarn curl. These yarns have been produced by an appropriate combination of deforming, heat setting, and developing treatments to attain elastic properties."

Bulky yarns are yarns that are "essentially free from stretch [and] in which a fraction of the fibers (in any cross section) has been forced to assume a relatively high random crimp by shrinkage of the remaining fibers which, in general, have very low crimp. (This effect is produced by heating or steaming a yarn containing a proportion of thermally unstable fibers so that the latter shrink, producing a permanent crimp in the other fibers.)"

*F*ilament Yarns

From the discovery of silk in about 2600 B.C. until Chardonnet made the first rayon fiber in the 1890s, silk was the only filament fiber. Today, all manufactured fibers may be used as filaments in filament yarns. Acrylic and modacrylic, however, are rarely used in filament form. *Filament yarns* are "composed of one or many (continuous) filaments assembled with or without twist."

Those yarns composed of one filament are called *monofilament yarns* and those with many filaments are called *multifilament yarns.* Multifilament yarns used in apparel fabric may contain as few as 2–3 filaments, as is the case in women's nylon hosiery, or as many as 50 filaments, a number not uncommon in filament yarns in apparel fabrics. In carpeting, a multifilament yarn may contain hundreds of filaments.

Most filament-yarn fabrics are made with multifilament yarns. Monofilament yarns are found in invisible sewing thread, fishing line, sheer nylon evening hosiery, saran webbing used in some lightweight beach and casual furniture as well as in industry, and knit fabrics with openwork effects. The major reason for the use of multifilament rather than monofilament yarns relates to the comparative strength and stiffness (flexural rigidity) of the yarns. A multifilament yarn that has the same size and fiber composition as a monofilament yarn will usually be stronger. If one filament in a multifilament yarn has a weak point, the remaining filaments can continue to resist mechanical forces exerted on them. Once the weak point in a monofilament yarn is reached, the yarn

structure fails. Multifilament yarns are much less stiff than monofilament yarns of the same size and fiber composition. Therefore, fabrics made from multifilament yarns are more drapable and softer than fabrics made from monofilament yarns.

In 1989, approximately 42.6% of filament yarn produced in the United States and shipped to domestic textile companies was used in the manufacture of carpet, 31.2% in the manufacture of industrial textile products, 19.4% in apparel fabrics, 3.9% in interior textile fabrics, and 2.9% in household textiles.[1] About 30% of the carpet filament was used to form carpet backing and 70% for face pile. The largest single use for filament yarn in industrial applications was tire cord and tire fabric. Other industrial uses include seat belts, industrial webbing and tape, tents, fishing line and net, rope, and tape reinforcement. Approximately 12.5% of apparel filament yarn was used for women's sheer hosiery, 10.0% for underwear and nightwear, 6.6% for anklets and socks, and the remaining 71% in a variety of apparel fabrics. The primary uses of the limited amount of filament yarns employed in interior and household products are bed ticking, curtains, bedspreads, sheets, and draperies, in descending order of utilization.

---

[1] Manufactured Fiber Producers Association, *Man-Made Fiber Fact Book,* Table 12 1986–1989, "Synthetic (Noncellulosic) Yarn + Monofilament Shipments by Secondary Trade or End Use."

FIGURE 23.1 Photomicrographs of flat filament-yarns.

Yarn to be used in the manufacture of seat belts

Yarn to be used in the manufacture of tire cord and fabric

The classification scheme for filament yarns is shown in Detail View 23. Filament yarns are either flat or bulk. In flat filament-yarns, each filament is almost perfectly straight, so that it lies flat and smooth in the yarn. In bulk filament-yarns, each filament is looped, crimped, curled, or otherwise configured. Also considered in this chapter are tape and network yarns. They are ribbon-like strands.

FLAT MULTIFILAMENT-YARNS

Flat multifilament-yarns are yarns in which the filaments are straight and well-aligned with the yarn axis (Figure 23.1). Filaments in multifilament yarns, particularly if they have a smooth surface, have a round, cross-sectional shape, and are even in diameter, pack closely together to form a yarn that is itself smooth, round, and even in diameter. Flat multifilament-yarns tend to be the smoothest of all types of yarns.

Flat multifilament-yarns are used extensively in the manufacture of seat belts and in tire cord and fabric, as shown in Figure 23.1. Flat multifilament-yarns are used to make apparel fabrics that require closely packed yarns, such as fabrics for windbreaker jackets. Apparel fabrics made with these yarns tend to be warm because of reduced air and water vapor permeability through fabric interstices.

Flat multifilament-yarns have little elongation when stressed because little straightening of filaments is possible. Elongation is determined by the type of filament: for example, nylon filaments elongate further than polyester filaments.

BULK MULTIFILAMENT AND SPUN YARNS

Bulk yarns are yarns that have "been prepared in such a way as to have greater covering power, or apparent volume, than that of conventional yarn of equal linear density and of the same basic material with normal twist." The filaments or fibers in bulk yarns tend to lie greater distances apart and be more randomly distributed than in flat or conventional yarns (Figure 23.2). Many bulk yarns are made from multifilaments, but they may also be made from staple fiber. If a bulk yarn and a flat filament-yarn of the same linear density (the same mass per

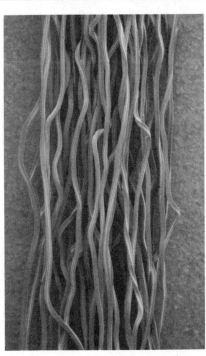

FIGURE 23.2 Photo-micrographs of bulk yarns.

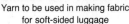

Yarn to be used in making fabric
for soft-sided luggage

Yarn to be used in the manufacture of carpet

unit length) were woven or knitted in the same manner, the fabric containing the bulk yarn would have greater covering power.

Bulk yarns are larger in diameter than the yarns from which they are prepared. Bulk yarns, however, are not necessarily large-diameter yarns. Three types of bulk yarns are textured, stretch, and bulky.

Textured Yarns

Textured is a generic term "given to filament or spun yarns with noticeably greater apparent volume than conventional yarn of similar fiber (filament) count and linear density. The yarns have a relatively low elastic stretch. They are sufficiently stable to withstand normal yarn and fabric processing, including wet finishing and dyeing treatments, and conditions of use by the ultimate consumer. The apparent volume is achieved through physical, chemical, or heat treatments, or a combination of these."

Influence of Texturing on Yarn and Fabrics Properties. Fabric comfort and aesthetics are improved, mainte-

nance of cleanliness is decreased, and durability is unaffected when textured multifilament-yarns are used instead of flat multifilament-yarns.

The wearers of the first nylon shirt fabrics complained that they felt like they were wearing a sheet of plastic. Moisture transport was poor due to the close packing of the round, straight, nylon fibers and the close packing of the yarns in the fabric. The introduction of textured yarns in the 1960s altered the comfort of multifilament-yarn fabrics dramatically. Today most apparel fabrics made from multifilament yarns contain textured rather than flat yarns due to the improved comfort performance that results.

Air and moisture-vapor permeability of fabric made from textured multifilament-yarns is greater than from flat multifilament-yarns due to the amount of air space between filaments. In the absence of wind, air is trapped within the textured yarns, enhancing the thermal insulative ability of the fabric. In a breeze, the open fabric permits the movement of body-heated air away from the body surface, and cooling results. Adsorbency is enhanced due to the greater surface available. The overall effect of use of textured rather than flat is to make fabric warmer in winter and cooler in summer. In windbreaker fabrics, flat multifilament-yarns closely packed together are desired because low air permeability is needed.

The feel of textured-yarn fabric against the skin is considerably different than that of flat-yarn fabric. Textured-yarn fabrics feel more like spun-yarn fabrics due to the hairiness of the textured yarn. Textured-yarn fabrics do not lay against the skin surface like flat-yarn fabrics do. The spun-like feel is preferred by consumers in numerous end uses. Body-movement comfort is also enhanced by texturing. Fabric made from these yarns elongates more, thereby allowing the wearer greater freedom of motion.

In terms of aesthetics, textured yarns give a fabric firmer body and a more pleasant hand (warmer, softer, and less synthetic feeling). Light reflection is more diffuse, granting the fabric a muted luster. Wrinkle resistance, however, is only slightly improved over that provided in flat-multifilament-yarn fabric because this property is more influenced by fiber composition than by whether the filaments are flat or textured yarn. Textured-yarn fabrics may pill more than flat-yarn fabrics because the surface of textured-fabrics contains small loops and curls that may ball up after breaking due to abrasion. In addition, snagging is more likely to occur in fabrics containing textured yarns than flat yarns. Finally, textured yarns provide more cover for the same amount of fiber used, and textured-yarn fabrics have better shape retention than flat-yarn fabrics.

Considering aspects of fabric maintenance, textured-yarn fabrics tend to soil more readily than flat-yarn fabrics because they are more open, allowing soil to penetrate more easily. The soil is then held within the fabric, making soil removal more difficult. Increased imbibition of water increases the drying time of textured-yarn fabrics.

Types. Textured yarns are classified as crimp, loopy or high-bulk yarns.

Crimp-textured yarns are usually composed of thermoplastic filaments. They have "relatively low elastic stretch (usually under 20%) and [are] frequently characterized by high saw-tooth type crimp or curl." A variety of mechanical crimping methods may be used, but the most prevalent one in the United States today is false-twist texturing.

The major use of crimp-textured yarn is in apparel fabrics. Nylon crimp-textured yarn is used in sheer hosiery, anklets and socks, and topweight fabrics. Polyester crimp-textured yarn is used in both top- and bottom-weight fabrics.

Loopy-textured yarns are yarns that are "essentially free from stretch [and] are characterized by a relatively large number of randomly spaced and randomly sized loops along the fibers of filaments." Because a concentrated stream of air directed at a flat yarn that is not held under tension may be used to displace the filaments and entangle them into the loopy yarn structure, this type of textured yarn is also referred to as air-textured, air-jet textured, or air-entangled. Loopy yarns range in size from 50–10,000 dtex. Loopy-textured yarn may contain nylon, polyester, or polypropylene olefin filaments.[2]

Loopy-textured yarns are used in apparel, soft-sided luggage, and automobile upholstery fabrics, as well as for reinforcement in V-belts and hoses. They represent a small proportion of textured apparel yarns, however. Currently, about 18,000 tons/year of flat yarn is air-textured to form loopy yarns for apparel uses, whereas 2.5 million tons/year is false-twisted to form high-bulk and crimp-textured yarn for apparel.[3] Two factors that account for the lower production of loopy-textured yarns are their high cost and high level of product shrinkage. Loopy yarns are not used in knitwear because of their inherently high level of yarn shrinkage in boiling water.

High-bulk yarns are yarns that are "essentially free from stretch [and] in which a fraction of the fibers (in any cross section) have been forced to assume a relatively high random crimp by shrinkage of the remaining fibers which, in general, have [a] very low crimp. This effect is produced by heating or steaming a yarn containing a proportion of thermally unstable fibers so that the latter shrink, producing a permanent crimp in the other fibers." High-bulk yarns have an unusually high degree of loft, or fullness.

Stretch Yarns

Stretch yarns are yarns composed of thermoplastic filaments and "having a high degree of potential elastic stretch and rapid recovery, and characterized by a high degree of yarn curl." A combination of deforming, heat-setting, and developing treatments are necessary to achieve these yarn characteristics.

A stretch multifilament-yarn has a tremendous amount of filament nonlinearity with minimal, if any, entangle-

---

[2] Some loopy-textured yarns may have a core, which also makes them a type of core-spun yarn (Chapter 25).
[3] Rieter-Scragg Ltd., "Reiter-Scragg: Jetex High-Performance Air Texturing," *Textile World* 140/4 (1990): 54.

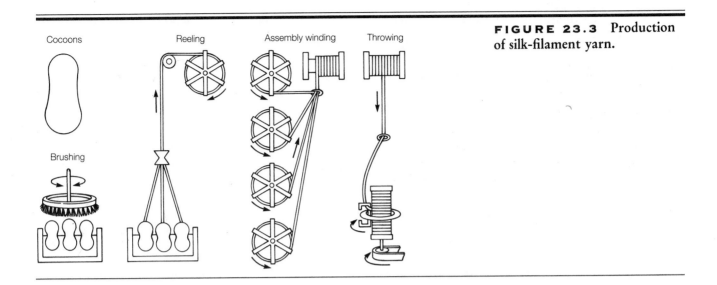

Cocoons   Reeling   Assembly winding   Throwing

Brushing

FIGURE 23.3 Production of silk-filament yarn.

ment of the filaments. This geometric configuration allows extraordinary extension and quick recovery. Elongation may be enhanced as much as 300–500% with complete and rapid recovery.

The first stretch multifilament-yarn was made of nylon and used in stretch ski pants. Introduction of stretch multifilament-yarns freed men from wearing garters to hold up their socks. Agilon®, the trademark of a nylon stretch multifilament-yarn by Hoechst Celanese, is used for women's nylon hosiery. The shape retention of the hosiery is enhanced by the elongation and recovery capabilities of the yarn. Nylon and polyester are the fibers most often used for stretch yarns. Other trademarks include Fluflon® and Superloft® of the Leesona Corporation.

Bulky Yarns

Bulky yarns are yarns "formed from inherently bulky fibers such as man-made [manufactured] fibers that are hollow along part or all of their length, or . . . yarns formed from fibers that cannot be closely packed because of their cross-sectional shapes, fiber alignment, stiffness, resilience, or natural crimp." *Bulked continuous filament* (*BCF*) yarns, composed of nylon and olefin filaments and used for carpet-pile, and a type of bulky yarn. Most carpet filaments have a "Y" cross-sectional shape because this shape does not allow close packing of the fibers. Usually 68 filaments are extruded at one time, forming one 1300-denier yarn. These strands are then plied with $3\frac{1}{2}$ turns/inch, forming a two-ply carpet yarn.

The bulk of the yarn is enhanced when the yarn is heat-set or autoclaved. The majority of the bulk of the yarn is actually achieved when the carpet made from it is dyed and finished.

FORMATION OF FILAMENT YARNS

Although the number of steps required to form a filament yarn, whether from silk or from manufactured fibers, is significantly fewer than for a spun yarn, the technology and skill involved are equivalent if not more complex.

Formation of Silk-Filament Yarns

Reeling, the process of unwinding silk from a cocoon and combining strands, involves immersing cocoons in hot water to soften the sericin holding the silk filaments to each cocoon, brushing the outside of the cocoons so that the end of the filament on each can be detected, then picking up the filaments from several cocoons and combining them (Figure 23.3). Although the principle is simple, a great amount of skill and labor are required. Reeling may be done entirely by hand, but in a modern filature (the name of the establishment in which reeling is done) steam power is used to rotate the reels onto which the silk is wound and automatic brushes brush the outside of the cocoons. Picking up the end of the filament from each cocoon, however, must still be done by hand by a highly skilled operator. The end of the filament must be picked up, threaded through a guide, and joined with other filaments so that a uniform-diameter yarn is formed. Two to twelve filaments will be combined. The reeling operator must be very quick to detect diameter changes and then add or take away one or more filaments. The reel cannot be stopped as this task is accomplished. One operator works two reels.

Raw-silk yarn from the filatures is wound into skeins. At this point in manufacture, the silk yarn is graded. The grade of the yarn depends on its evenness, size, color, cleanliness, and boil-off (the percentage of sericin remaining on the silk). The strength and elasticity of the fiber also play a role in the quality assessment. The silk yarn, too delicate to be woven or knitted into cloth is sold by weight to a throwster.

Throwing, or processing the silk into a form suitable for weaving or knitting, is the operation in which the required amount of twist is inserted. In throwing, several silk yarns may be plied to form filament yarns with names such as tram, organzine, crepe, and grenadine. Throwing, like reeling, is very simple in principle but requires highly specialized, complicated machinery and expert supervision. Tremendous numbers of spindles are needed to insert the twist and ply the yarns.

Formation of Flat Filament-Yarns

In Chapter 7, the extrusion of polymer melt or solution through a spinneret, its solidification into a fiber, and placement of the filaments onto a tube was discussed.[4] In the traditional sequence of discontinuous operations, the extruded and solidified multifilament yarn is wound up on a package running at about the same speed as the extrusion speed. Under these conditions, the polymers within each filament are "unoriented"; they are not well-aligned with the filament axis. The flat multifilament-yarn produced in the extrusion process is described as "unoriented" or "undrawn."

In the drawing process, an undrawn multifilament yarn from the extrusion package is elongated to approximately four times its original length. As the yarn is lengthened, the polymers substantially straighten within the filaments, reach their full load-bearing capacity, and become linked by bonds. At this point, the force needed to elongate the filaments and yarn suddenly increases, signaling that the yarn is "fully drawn."

Filament drawing has traditionally been carried out on *draw-twist* or *draw-wind machines.* "Unoriented" multifilament yarn from the extrusion package is gripped by two pairs of rollers, the second pair of which forwards the yarn at roughly four times the speed of the first. The point in the yarn path at which elongation and, hence, diameter reduction take place is called the draw zone. This zone contains either a cold "snubbing" pin or a heated plate, depending on the particular fiber processed. The fully drawn flat multifilament-yarn is either wound onto draw-twist bobbin or a draw-wind package. In the former case, a small amount of twist, usually about 1 turn for every 2 inches (5 centimeters) of yarn, is inserted by the ring-and-traveler arrangement of the wind-up. The speed of the draw-twist wind-up is roughly 875 yards per minute (800 meters per minute). In the latter case (the draw-wind process), no twist is inserted. The arrangement of the package allows for windup speeds as high as 4375 yards per minute (4000 meters per minute).

Texturing Processes

In most texturing processes, thermoplastic filament yarns are used. Intrafiber bonds break and reform during texturing processes. The use of twisting or other means to distort the fibers strains the bonds within them. Heating, while the yarn is distorted, breaks bonds between polymers. Cooling the yarn in the distorted state allows new bonds to form. When the yarn is untwisted or otherwise released from its distorted state, the filaments remain in a coiled or bent condition.

A large number of texturing processes have been developed over the years, but only one is prominent in the United States. The false-twist method holds about 90% of the textured-yarn market.[5] The remaining 10% is held primarily by air-texturing. Other methods of texturing include knit-de-knit, stuffer box, and gear crimp, but they are not discussed here due to their very limited use in the United States today.

False-Twist Texturing Process. False-twist texturing was developed from a three-stage discontinuous process in which filament yarns were highly twisted, set by steaming in an autoclave and cooling, and then untwisted. In this twist-set-untwist process, true twist was inserted;

---

[4]The word *spinning* may be used to denote both the formation of manufactured *fibers* and the formation of *yarns* from those fibers. A more definitive word for the former process is *extrusion* and for the latter process is *drawing.*

[5]Personal communication with James Connor of the American Textured Yarn Association.

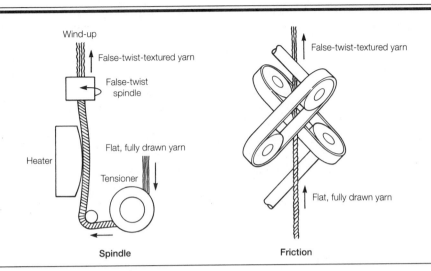

FIGURE 23.4 Production of textured yarn by false-twist texturing on spindle and friction devices.

the direction of twist was the same along the whole length of the yarn. The process could only be done discontinuously, resulting in low production rates. False twisting yields higher production rates than are achievable with true twisting. In false twisting, a spindle, belt, or other device rotates the yarn (Figure 23.4). A "false" twist is said to be inserted because the twist above the spindle is different than the twist below it.

In *spindle false-twist texturing*, flat, fully drawn multifilament yarn is supplied and tensioned. A spindle inserts false twist into the moving yarn. The twisted portion of the yarn passes over a heater maintained at a temperature somewhat below the melting temperature of the filament. The yarn untwists as it passes through the spindle and is finally wound up on the take-up package. Altering the amount of false twist and the degree of tension on the feed roll produces a range of properties in the yarn. Spindles swirl at about 600,000 revolutions per minute, generating a sound comparable to a jet engine.

In *friction false-twist texturing*, the spindle is replaced by a friction device. Frictional contact of the yarn with the device is used to impart the false twist. Approaches to friction twisting include passing a multifilament yarn run through a series of belts, a series of stacked disks or over the moving inner surface of a hollow tube of plastic or rubber. Friction false-twist texturing should not be confused with friction open-end spinning, a method of producing spun yarns.

Air-Texturing Process. In the *air- or air-jet texturing process*, flat, fully drawn multifilament yarns are fed

slack into a stream of air (Figure 23.5). The air stream creates a turbulence in which random loops are formed. The overfeeding of yarn is essential so that an excess of yarn length is available within the air-jet texturizer. The turbulent air flow disrupts and rearranges the filaments so that the loops formed are interlocked with sufficient interfiber friction to make a stable yarn. In the early stages of the development of this process, yarns had to be post-twisted to help lock in the entanglement of the fibers, but this is no longer necessary. Modifications to the air stream, combined with pulling the yarn out of the tube at right angles, cause sufficient locking.

Air-texturing is a common process because a fibrous strand of any type fiber can be used. Styling possibilities are unlimited; silk-like, worsted, heather, slub, and blends with spun and textured yarns can be produced. Air-jet texturing should not be confused with the production of air-jet spun-yarns or with air-jet methods to produce some compound yarns.

Continuous Processes

Until recently, the processing sequence for the production of most textured yarns consisted of three stages: (1) extrusion and wind, (2) draw-twist or draw-wind, and (3) texturing. The possibility of combining the processes had been considered but was not believed to be feasible due to the great differences in the speeds of the processes. These speeds were typically as follows: (1) extrusion and wind at 1093 yards per minute (1000 meters per minute), (2) draw-twist input at 219 yards per

FIGURE 23.5   Production of textured yarn by air-jet texturing.

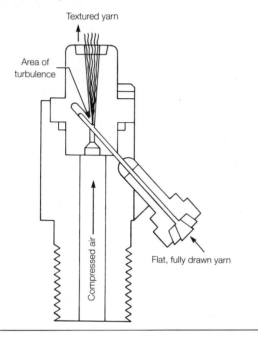

minute (200 meters per minute) and output at 875 yards per minute (800 meters per minute), and (3) false twist at 164 yards per minute (150 meters per minute) and stuffer box at 328–437 yards per minute (300–400 meters per minute).

The first development toward a continuous process was in combining extrusion and drawing for melt-spun fibers. This was possible with the development of high winding speeds of up to 4375 yards per minute (4000 meters per minute). Extrusion continued to take place at 1093 yards per minute (1000 meters per minute), and yarn then ran directly into a 1:4 draw zone with the fully drawn output wound at 4375 yards per minute (4000 meters per minute). This yarn was then conventionally textured by one of the methods presented earlier.

Two processes, *sequential draw-texturing* and *simultaneous draw-texturing,* were developed to eliminate the costly draw-twist stage. In the sequential process, the yarn is first passed through a draw zone and then into a separate conventional texturing zone. Any of the texturing methods work. In the simultaneous process, the yarn is drawn as it is twisted in the heater zone of the texturing machine. The simultaneous method can only be employed when texturing occurs while the yarn is under tension. Both of these processes are economically superior to the earlier discontinuous draw-twist and texturing process. In addition, both yield yarns of significantly higher quality and regularity. However, because undrawn yarn cannot be stored for any length of time without changes in its properties, draw-texturing of undrawn yarn can only be carried out by the fiber producer who has full control of the undrawn yarn, its storage time, and conditions between extrusion and texturing.

The next stage toward increased productivity was the introduction of high-speed extrusion (melt-spinning) processes. Polymer solution is extruded at speeds somewhat higher than those used in traditional processes, and the fibers formed are wound up at much higher speeds, up to about 11,500 feet per minute (3500 meters per minute). *Partially drawn or partially oriented yarns (POY)* are thus produced. The POY yarns have a much longer shelf life than undrawn yarns; their storage life is measured in months rather than days. They require a further partial draw in texturing.

The possibility of extrusion-draw-texture in a continuous operation has not yet become a commercial reality. Bicomponent fibers, in which texture is introduced at the spinneret, appear not to be a viable alternative to texturing, which suggests that further development of extrusion-draw-texture processes will proceed. Yet, the heavy investment that fiber producers and textured-yarn manufacturers have made in draw-texturing equipment suggests that a fully integrated continuous method will not quickly replace established methods.

TAPE AND NETWORK YARNS

Tape yarns are "ribbon-like structures."[6] They are wide in comparison to their thickness. They may be 0.003 inches (0.008 centimeters) thick and about 0.25 inches (0.6 centimeters) wide. Usually, they do not have the cylindrical shape typical of yarns that are composed of "regular" fibers (either filament or staple). When twisted, however, tape yarns do take on a cylindrical shape and have the appearance of filament yarns. Polypropylene olefin is most often used. Tape yarns have good strength, good abrasion resistance, and good stability.

The high width/thickness ratio dictates the end-use applications of tape yarn. Interior-furnishing applications include upholstery fabrics, wall covering, and primary backing for tufted carpets. In the latter use, tape

---

[6]D. C. Hossack, "Tape Yarns," in *Spinning in the '70s,* P. R. Lord, ed. (England: Merrow Publishing, 1970).

yarns compete with jute yarns and with a nonwoven structure called spunbonded.[7] Tape yarns are also used in packaging, bags, sacks, and bale wrappers, as well as in artificial turf. Horticultural uses include vegetable bags, greenhouse shades, and protective covering for growing bulbs. The end uses for twisted tape yarns are twine, cords, and ropes. Tape yarns are inexpensive to make and will probably increase in importance.

Tape yarns are manufactured by either split-film or slit-film techniques. The split-film yarn-formation technique, called fibrillation, consists of forming a sheet of polymer and drawing it in the lengthwise direction. This action orients the polymer molecules in the direction of the draw; the film is thus strengthened in the direction of the draw and weakened in the crosswise direction. The film breaks down into a mass of interconnected fibers, most of which are aligned in the direction of draw, although some are connected in the crosswise direction. Once split, the film can be twisted. In the slit-film yarn-formation technique, a film of polymeric material is formed. It is then cut into narrow, ribbon-like sections.

Network yarns "resemble a three-dimensional version of wire netting" (Figure 23.6).[8] They are made up of networks of small, interconnected fibers and may be twisted or untwisted. Network yarns resemble tape yarns (when the network yarn is not extended in its width direction) and they have bulk.

The strength of a network yarn cannot equal that of a corresponding multifilament yarn. In the network yarn, a higher proportion of the material does not resist forces applied. A range of strengths can be made, and any level of strength can be increased with the addition of twist. The drape and hand of fabrics made on an experimental basis from network yarns was very good but crease recovery was poor.

In the formation of network yarns, air is added to a polymer to create a foam structure. The foamed polymer is fed into a buffer zone or area where the quantity of material can be regulated. Foamed polymer is fed from the buffer zone into a draw chamber, where it is stretched. Small cells or bubbles of polymer that were created during the foaming process crack as the material is drawn, forming individual, interconnected fibers. The resultant yarn is made up of a network of small, interconnected fibers.

---

[7]Spunbonded fabrics are considered in Chapter 29.
[8]P. Volans, "Network Yarns," in *Spinning in the '70s*, P. R. Lord, ed. (England: Merrow Publishing, 1970).

FIGURE 23.6 Network yarns.

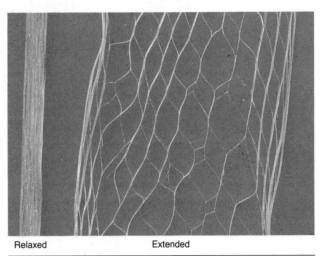

Relaxed   Extended

CHAPTER SUMMARY

Filament yarns are composed of filament fibers; when composed of one filament they are called monofilament yarns and when of many filaments, they are called multifilament yarns. Most filament yarns are multifilament, which are classified as either flat—those containing straight filaments—or bulk—those in which less weight of bulk yarn than conventional yarn is needed to make a fabric with the same covering power. Bulk yarns may also be composed of staple fibers. Textured, stretch, and bulky yarns are three types of bulk yarns. More flat multifilament-yarn is used than textured, stretch, and bulky yarn combined. In apparel, however, more bulk yarn than flat yarn is used. The properties of multifilament yarns and fabrics made from them depend largely on differences in the packing of the filaments and the ability of the filaments to be straightened within the yarn or fabric when it is stressed.

The processes necessary to convert silk filaments to yarn are reeling (removing filaments from the cocoon) and throwing (twisting). To form flat filament-yarns, manufactured filaments are either (a) extruded and wound and subsequently drawn and wound or (b) extruded, drawn, and wound as a continuous process. False-twist and air-jet texturing processes are used to form textured and stretch yarns. Processes in which draw-texturing occurs sequentially or simultaneously result in increased production rates.

Yarn Construction

Construction features of spun and filament yarns include degree and angle of twist, a yarn number, number of strands, and fiber composition. Number of filaments is a construction feature of filament yarns.

ASPECT OF STRUCTURE	TERM AND DEFINITION
Degree of twist	**negligible twist**-1–4 turns/inch (1–10 turns/centimeter). **low (napping) twist**-6–12 turns/inch (15–30 turns/centimeter). **moderate (average) twist**-20–25 turns/inch (50–65 turns/centimeter). **high (hard or crepe) twist**-40–80 turns/inch (100–200 turns/centimeter).
Direction of twist	**S and Z**-depending on whether the diagonal twist line follows the center portion of the letter *S* or the letter *Z*.
Yarn number	A measure of the fineness or size of a yarn expressed as mass per unit length or as length per unit mass, depending on the yarn numbering system. **count**-an indirect yarn numbering system in which the unit of mass is usually one pound. **denier**-a direct yarn numbering system in which the standard length is 9000 meters; units are given as the mass (in grams) of the 9000 meters of yarn. **tex**-a direct yarn numbering system in which the standard length is 1000 meters; units are given as the mass (in grams) of the 1000 meters of yarn.
Number of filament	**standard denier-per-filament yarns**-yarns in which the fibers are 7.0–2.4 dtex. **fine denier-per-filament yarns**-yarns in which the fibers are 2.4–1.0 dtex. **microfiber yarns**-yarns in which the filament are 1.0 dtex or less.
Number of strands	**single yarns**-"the simplest strands of textile material suitable for operations such as weaving, knitting, etc." **plied yarns**-yarns composed of two or more like strands of yarn that separate on the first untwisting; "a yarn formed by twisting together two or more single yarns in one operation." **cabled yarns**-yarns composed of plied yarns twisted together; "a yarn formed by twisting together two or more plied yarns."
Fiber composition	**self-blended or 100% yarns**-yarns containing only one species of fiber. **blended yarns**-"single yarns spun from a blend or mixture of different fiber species." **combination yarns**-plied yarns "twisted from single yarns of different fibers, for example, silk and rayon, or rayon and acetate."

Yarn Construction

Descriptions of the construction of yarns include details about their degree of twist, direction of twist, size (number), number of identical strands, and fiber composition. The relevance of each detail depends on the type of yarn. For example, twist information is applicable to ring-spun and open-end spun-yarns but not to air-jet spun-yarns, which are not twisted. Detail View 23 lists key words and definitions used to describe various aspects of yarn construction.

DEGREE OF TWIST

Twist in a yarn is "the number of turns about its axis per unit length." *Degree of twist* is expressed as turns per inch (tpi), turns per meter (tpm), or turns per centimeter (tpcm). Theoretically, the degree of twist could be determined by laying a ruler beside the yarn and counting the number of diagonal lines that lie across the yarn in one inch. This approach, however, is rarely taken because it would be tedious and inaccurate. The normal method is to secure the yarn in two clamps, one that rotates and one that does not. The clamp that rotates is turned until the fibers separate; that is, the twist is removed. The number of turns required is the twist per unit distance. The four levels of twist in yarns are negligible, low (napping), moderate (average), and high (hard or crepe), as shown in Figure 24.1.

Spun yarns are usually given *moderate twist* (20–25 tpi or 50–65 tpc) to produce a relatively smooth and firm yarn that, when constructed into fabric, creates a surface that can be printed and finished in a variety of ways. Moderate twist usually provides the best all-purpose combination of performance properties for spun yarns.

Multifilament yarns are usually given *negligible twist* (1–4 tpi or 1–10 tpc), just enough to facilitate the process of weaving and knitting them into fabric. Strands of filaments do not need to be twisted to form an integral structure because they are endless or continuous structures themselves. Yet, negligible-twist filament yarns are difficult to process into fabric, so they are rarely produced. When negligible-twist yarns are removed from fabric for examination, they appear to have no twist.

High-twist yarns (40–80 tpi or 100–200 tpc) are crimp-lively yarns. Filament and spun yarns are given high twist. A crepe (pebbly) texture results when they are made into fabric.[1]

Low-twist yarns (6–12 tpi or 15–30 tpc) are soft yarns usually composed of staple fibers. Knitting yarns, particularly bulky ones, are low-twist yarns. Napped fabrics, such as wool and cotton flannels or blends of wool or cotton with synthetic fibers, contain low-twist yarns in the crosswise direction. The low twist allows the fiber ends in those yarns to be gently raised by wire brushes to create a fuzzy fabric surface.

---

[1] Not all crepe-surfaced fabrics contain high-twist yarns. A crepe surface can be made with moderate-twist yarns when they are interlaced using the crepe pattern as discussed in Chapter 26. Crepe-surfaced fabrics differ substantially in performance depending on what gives them their crepe texture.

FIGURE 24.1
Degree of twist.

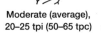

| Negligible, | Low (napping), | Moderate (average), | High (hard, crepe), |
| 1–4 tpi (1–10 tpc) | 6–12 tpi (15–30 tpc) | 20–25 tpi (50–65 tpc) | 40–80 tpi (100–200 tpc) |

Identification

Although the ultimate criterion for determining the twist in a yarn is to count the number of turns per inch, the feel of the yarn and careful observation may be sufficient. High-twist yarn feels wiry or hard. It kinks up as it is removed from a fabric, and it twists around itself when looped. At the other extreme, a low-twist yarn is soft, compressible, and often quite fuzzy. Gently tugging on a low-twist yarn is often sufficient to break it. Low-twist yarns tend to have larger diameters than more highly twisted yarns.

Influence on Yarn and Fabric Properties

Properties of yarns and of fabric made from them are influenced by the degree of twist in the yarn. As twist is inserted, the fibers or filaments become closer (they pack), yarn size is reduced, and an internal force called torque builds up. The influence of twist on yarn and fabric properties differs in many cases for spun and filament yarns.

Fabric durability is affected by the degree of twist in the yarns. Spun yarns with negligible twist have no strength unless they contain a bonding resin; a pulling force simply causes the fibers to slide past one another. As twist is inserted, fiber-to-fiber friction increases, thereby causing yarn strength to increase, up to a level of 20 tpi. After this point, the insertion of additional twist has no effect on yarn strength. At about 40 tpi, yarn strength rapidly decreases as the twisting begins shearing action; the fibers crush one another. Greatest strength occurs for moderate-twist spun yarns. High-twist spun yarns may become brittle and weak.

The strength of multifilament yarns, in contrast, is due mainly to the tenacity of the individual filaments. In filament yarns with negligible twist, all of the filaments lie parallel to the yarn axis and, therefore, each filament must bear the stress of the immediate force. Each filament breaks at its weakest point once the force becomes sufficient. The insertion of 3–6 turns per inch of twist increases the yarn strength because the filaments no longer lie parallel to the axis of the yarn. Thus, the filaments must first be straightened before they must withstand the applied force. Moreover, in a negligible-twist filament yarn, the filaments are better able to remain close enough together to absorb the force as a unit. As more twist is inserted, the filament-yarn strength remains constant, but at high levels of twist, strength decreases because shearing forces begin to weaken the filaments. Other durability performance properties are not significantly affected by changes in twist in multifilament yarns.

The abrasion resistance of a fabric increases as twist in spun yarns is increased. In a more tightly twisted spun yarn, many fibers are positioned in such a way that they appear on the surface, pass into the center of the yarn, and then return to the surface. As a result, it is relatively difficult for abrasive action to pull fibers from tightly twisted spun yarns. In low-twist spun yarns, fibers more readily pull out during rubbing action. As they pull out, the structural integrity of the yarn is decreased leading to greater fiber loss as abrasion continues. In sum, the durability of spun yarns is greatest for a moderate degree of twist. If the twist is too low, the yarn easily falls apart; when the twist is too high, internal forces cause the yarn to be weakened.

Fabric comfort properties also vary with the twist level of yarns. The lower the twist, the more adsorbent the yarn is, all other structural features being the same. In yarns made of absorbent fibers, the absorbency decreases as the amount of twist increases. The insertion of twist compacts the fibers together, decreasing the amount of surface area available to absorb water and the ability of the water to be absorbed internally into the fiber. The more a yarn is twisted, the less water can be held in between the fibers in the yarn. The less a yarn is twisted, the higher is water vapor permeability through the yarn structure.

The thermal insulation of fabric containing low-twist yarns is usually greater than that of fabric containing high-twist yarns because low-twist yarns contain more dead air space. They also have more protruding ends to provide an insulating layer of air between the skin surface and the fabric.

Comfort in low-twist multifilament-yarn fabrics is less than in high-twist multifilament-yarn fabrics. In negligible-twist-yarn fabrics, the yarns tend to flatten out when the fabric is worn, resulting in a tremendous increase in the area of contact between the fabric and the skin surface. This situation is not desirable in most apparel applications because the fabric feels cool and slick. Abrasive action on the skin is potentially greater with fabrics containing negligible-twist multifilament yarns than for those containing high-twist multifilament yarns. The flattening of the yarns decreases the permeability of the fabric to air and moisture, resulting in a wetter skin surface under certain environmental conditions.

Fabric maintenance is greatly affected by the amount of twist in yarns. Both low-twist and high-twist yarns (composed of natural fibers) are subject to excessive shrinkage. Low-twist yarns are subject to compaction by the mechanical action of laundering; thus, cotton flannels shrink excessively when laundered. Wool and rayon crepe fabrics, which have high twist, must be drycleaned because they are dimensionally unstable in water.

High-twist silk yarns are not dimensionally stable, and fabric made from them (called true crepe) shrinks excessively when cleaned in water. The water removes the sizing, which keeps the yarn lying flat in the fabric, and the yarn kinks up on itself due to its internal stresses. A true-crepe silk fabric can shrink to 50% of its original size. Dimensional stability of fabrics made from thermoplastic filaments given high twist is high if a heatsetting treatment has removed many of the internal stresses. Such true-crepe fabrics are labeled as hand or machine washable.

Yarns with high twist are better able to shed soil; they have lower soiling propensity because their surfaces are smoother and they contain less space between fibers for soil particles to lodge. Fewer fiber ends protrude from high-twist spun yarns to attract and hold soil.

Fabric aesthetics are also affected by the degree of twist in yarns. In most low-twist spun yarns, luster is low because incident light is randomly reflected. As twist is inserted into spun yarn, luster is increased, reaching a maximum at about 20 tpi. Luster remains unchanged from 20–40 tpi because light is reflected from a relatively smooth surface. Above 40 tpi, luster decreases because the twist produces deeper ridges in the yarn surface. High-twist yarns (both filament and spun) are, therefore, dull. It should be noted that when the fibers are well-aligned in a low-twist yarn, a soft luster is produced because the light is reflected in a regular pattern. In fabrics called sateen, such yarn is used to form filling floats over the fabric surface, thereby creating the soft, luster of sateen. (Chapter 26).

Pilling can be minimized by increased amount of twist in spun yarns. Fibers are held more tenaciously and resist being brought to the fabric surface by abrasive action. Fabric with high-twist yarns are among the most drapable and resilient fabrics because the increase in yarn twist lowers the bending (flexural) rigidity of the yarn. Fabric hand is said to be crepe-like and springy at high levels of twist compared to soft at lower levels of twist.

The surface character of the fabric may alter as yarn twist in a multifilament yarn is changed. Fabrics containing low-twist multifilament yarns are shinier and smoother than fabrics containing high-twist multifilament yarns. In a low-twist yarn, the filaments are aligned, so that the yarn acts as a smooth reflecting surface. Insertion of twist decreases the luster because the reflected light becomes more scattered. High-twist multifilament yarns produce a crinkly (crepe) surface.

Other aesthetic properties altered by the twist of multifilament yarns include snagging propensity and hand. Snagging is more of a problem in negligible twist as compared to high-twist multifilament yarns because individual filaments can be pulled from the main yarn more easily the lower the twist. Multifilament yarns with high twist are hard or wiry in hand, whereas those at negligible twist levels are softer, because increased twist gives greater bending stiffness (higher flexural rigidity).

DIRECTION OF TWIST

The direction in which twist is inserted into the yarn is denoted as S or Z (Figure 24.2). By definition, a Z-twist yarn is one in which the center of the letter Z matches

FIGURE 24.2   Direction of twist.

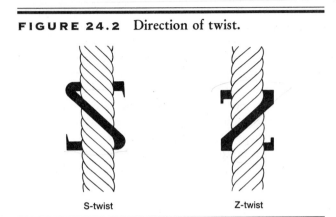

S-twist   Z-twist

the twist line on the yarn when the yarn is held in a vertical position. Similarly, an S-twist yarn is one in which the center of the letter *S* matches the twist line of the yarn when the yarn is held in a vertical position. The direction of twist is not dependent on the direction the yarn is held. That is, the direction of twist remains the same when the yarn is rotated 180 degrees.

Some yarns are large enough that the direction of twist is discernable to the naked eye. Many yarns, however, are too small to see the direction of twist. In such cases, a magnifying glass or microscope may prove helpful. The direction of the twist may also be established by denoting the direction (clockwise or counterclockwise) in which the yarn must be rotated to remove its twist.

The direction of twist does not influence the properties of single-strand spun and filament yarns.[2] By tradition, most cotton and flax spun yarns are Z-twist; woolen and worsted yarns are S-twist. This convention is rooted in medieval consumer protection laws; the buyer of fabric could determine whether the cloth was wool or cotton by the direction of the yarn twist. However, one cannot rely on this practice today.

YARN NUMBER

Yarns vary greatly in size, or diameter, from bulky ones used in sweater knits to extremely fine ones used in sheer fabrics. The size of a yarn is given as a *yarn number;* it is expressed as mass per unit length or as length per unit mass.

---

[2]Direction of twist does influence the properties of piled and cabled yarns, which are discussed later in this chapter.

Yarn Numbering Systems

A yarn's size could be specified as its diameter; for example 0.0004 inches (0.001 centimeters), but such values are rarely given. Two major problems arise in obtaining an accurate value for the measurement of yarn diameter. First, determining where the edges of yarns are is difficult because the edges of most spun yarns are not sharp. In fact, they are often quite fuzzy and indistinct. Second, many yarns are soft, so that almost any instrument used to measure the diameter would compress the yarn and distort it.

To circumvent these problems, the size or fineness of a yarn is expressed as linear density or the reciprocal of linear density. *Linear density* is "mass per unit length; the quotient obtained by dividing the mass of a fiber or yarn by its length." The reciprocal of linear density is length per unit mass; the quotient obtained by dividing length by mass. The length and mass of a yarn, unlike the diameter, can be accurately measured.

To comprehend how linear density and its reciprocal can be used to indicate yarn size, consider the following example. To determine the linear density of a yarn, a length of yarn needs to be measured and then that length needs to be weighed. If 1 kilometer of yarn is measured and the weight of that 1 kilometer is 10 grams, then the linear density is 10 grams per kilometer. If 1 kilometer of a second yarn has a mass of 20 grams, then its linear density is 20 grams per kilometer. The first yarn, with a linear density of 10 grams per kilometer, is smaller in diameter than the second yarn with a linear density of 20 grams per kilometer. Assuming that the two yarns have identical fiber composition, the second yarn can only weigh more than the first yarn if the second yarn is larger in diameter than the first because the two yarns are the same length. In using linear density, the larger the quotient, the larger the yarn.

The reciprocal of linear density is length per unit mass. To determine the reciprocal of linear density, the weight of the yarn is the first determination and is usually specified. Using the same two yarns in the preceding paragraph and keeping 10 grams as the standard or constant weight, the reciprocal of linear density of the first yarn would be 0.1 kilometers/gram. The reciprocal of linear density of the second yarn would be 0.05 kilometers/gram because a half of a kilometer would weigh the 10 grams. The first yarn is still the smaller yarn because a greater length of it is required to weigh the 10 grams. When the reciprocal of linear density is used to indicate yarn size, the larger the stated value, the smaller the diameter of the yarn.

To make the use of the concept of linear density and its reciprocal manageable, units of length and units of mass have been standardized. Depending on the standard lengths or masses, various yarn numbering systems have been established (Table 24.1). These systems are conveniently grouped into two major systems, a direct system based on linear density and an indirect system based on the reciprocal of linear density. In the case of spun yarns, either the direct or the indirect system may be used. In the United States, an indirect system is usually used; internationally, the direct system is preferred. In the case of filament yarns, the direct system is always used.

Indirect Systems. Indirect systems are systems "that express yarn number in length per unit mass, or as a reciprocal of linear density." Cotton count, worsted count, metric count, cut, run, and lea comprise the currently used indirect yarn numbering systems. Most of these systems use one pound as the standard weight. Each system uses a different unit for the length of yarn. *Cotton count* is "the number of 840-yard lengths of yarn per pound"; *worsted count* is "the number of 560-yard lengths of yarn per pound"; *run* is "the number of 1600-yard lengths of yarn per pound"; *cut* is "the number of 300-yard lengths of yarn per pound"; *lea* is "the number of 300-yard lengths of yarn per pound." *Metric count* is "the number of meters of yarn per gram." The standard lengths were chosen during the Middle Ages, the time at which the yarn numbering system was devised.

By convention, the cotton-count numbering system is used to specify the size of spun yarns composed of cotton fibers, cotton fiber blended with other fibers, or manufactured fibers whose length is 2.5 inches (65 milli-

---

TABLE 24.1   Systems Used to Specify Yarn Number in the United States.

Yarn number is "a measure of the fineness or size of a yarn expressed as 'mass per unit length' or 'length per unit mass,' depending on the yarn numbering system."

INDIRECT SYSTEM

"A system that expresses yarn number in length per unit mass, or the reciprocal of linear density." Linear density is "mass per unit length, or the quotient obtained by dividing the mass of a fiber or yarn by its length."

YARN COUNT SYSTEM	UNIT OF LENGTH	UNIT OF MASS	YARN COUNT (RECIPROCAL OF LINEAR DENSITY)	SYMBOLIC ABBREVIATION
Cotton count	840 yd	1 lb	840-yd lengths/lb	c.c Ne_c
Glass (U.K. and U.S.)	100 yd	1 lb	100-yd lengths/lb	g. N_g
Linen/Flax lea	300 yd	1 lb	300-yd lengths/lb	l.l. NE_l
Woolen (American cut)	300 yd	1 lb	300-yd lengths/lb	w/c Na_c
Woolen (American run)	100 yd	1 oz	100-yd lengths/oz	w.r. Na_r
Worsted count	560 yd	1 lb	560-yd lengths/lb	w.c. Ne_w
Metric count	1 km	1 kg	1-km length/kg	m.c. N_m

DIRECT SYSTEM

"A system that expresses yarn number in mass per unit length, or linear density." Linear density is "mass per unit length, or the quotient obtained by dividing the mass of a fiber or yarn by its length."

YARN NUMBER SYSTEM	UNIT OF LENGTH	UNIT OF MASS	YARN NUMBER (LINEAR DENSITY)	SYMBOLIC ABBREVIATION
Tex	1 km	1 g	g/km	tex T_t
Decitex	10 km	1 g	g/10 km	dtex
Denier	9000 m	1 g	g/9000 m	denier T_d

meters) or less. It is these fibers that can be processed on machinery usually used for the conversion of cotton fibers into yarn (the cotton system). The worsted-count numbering system is used for yarns composed of long wool fibers (2–9 inches or 50–225 millimeters), manufactured fibers of similar length, and blends of these manufactured fibers with long wool fibers. These fibers can be processed on machinery usually used for processing this length of fiber (the worsted system). Woolen run is used primarily for numbering yarns of low bulk density (yarns processed on the woolen system).

The number of lengths is the yarn number. Thus, when one 840-yard length of cotton yarn weighs one pound, the yarn number is 1. Because the cotton-count system was used, the yarn is a 1 cotton count (c.c.). When two 840-yard lengths of cotton yarn weigh one pound, the yarn number is 2 c.c. When three 840-yard lengths of cotton yarn weigh one pound, the yarn number is 3 c.c. Again, the larger the yarn number, the smaller the diameter of the yarn in an indirect system for determining yarn number.

Continuing with the example illustrating the use of yarn numbering systems, when one 560-yard length of a yarn containing wool fibers longer than 2 inches weighs 1 pound, the yarn number is 1 worsted count (1 w.c.). When two 560-yard lengths of this same type of yarn weigh one pound, the yarn number is 2 w.c.

Individuals who work continuously with yarn numbers can visualize the size of a yarn when they read the yarn number. For cotton yarns, coarse yarns are 12 count or less, medium-size yarns range from 12 to about 40 count, and fine yarns have counts greater than 40. The finest cotton yarn produced in the United States is about 80 count.

In technical literature, the yarn number may be preceded by the abbreviation *Ne*, which stands for "number in the English system," that is, standard lengths per pound. A subscript *c* then designates cotton count, and a subscript *w*, worsted count. Other designations are given in Table 24.1. Metric yarn numbers are designated by the abbreviation *Nm*.

Yarn numbers in one system can be converted to those in any of the other systems. Tables giving equivalent yarn numbers are available.[3]

Direct Systems. The *direct systems*, denier and tex, "express yarn number in mass per unit length; linear density."

The *denier* of a yarn is equal to the mass in grams of 9000 meters (9 kilometers) of that yarn.[4] Therefore, when the weight of 9000 meters of yarn is 1 gram, that filament yarn is a 1-denier yarn. When the weight is 10 grams, the yarn is a 10-denier yarn. In practice, much shorter lengths of yarn are used in the determination of denier because 9000 meters is over 5 miles of yarn.

The *tex* of a yarn is equal to the mass in grams of 1 kilometer of that yarn, or the number of grams that 1000 meters of it weigh. A 1-tex yarn is therefore a 1000-meter length of yarn weighing 1 gram. A 2-tex yarn is a 1000-meter length of yarn weighing 2 grams. The larger the yarn number when given in tex, the larger the size of the yarn. Tex is the universal system; it can be used to specify the size of any yarn.

Yarn numbers given as tex and denier are easily converted because the yarn number expressed in denier divided by nine gives the yarn number in tex. Conversely, tex multiplied by nine gives the yarn number in denier. When yarns are fine, decitex (dtex) may be used. *Decitex* is tex multiplied by 10, or the weight in grams of 10,000 meters (10 kilometers) of yarn. A yarn number in decitex is, therefore, almost equal to the denier designation.

Influence of Yarn Number on Yarn and Fabric Properties

As yarn diameters increase, the thickness of fabric in which they are used increases. Greater numbers of fine yarns than thick yarns are required to provide the same cover in a fabric.

The size of a filament yarn influences the properties of the yarn and the fabric made from it. The larger the size of the filament yarn, the greater the strength when other structural features are the same. The higher the denier of the yarn, the heavier the fabric becomes. In knits, snagging is reduced by using smaller denier yarns, which permit a more compact knit structure if knitting tension is high. Finer-denier yarns result in stronger, softer, and more drapable fabrics.

---

[3] American Society for Testing and Materials, *1991 Annual Book of Standards*, Method D2260–89 Standard Tables of Conversion Factors and Equivalent Yarn Numbers Measured in Various Numbering Systems (Philadelphia, PA: ASTM, 1991), pp. 634–646.

[4] Denier is also used to specify the size of individual filaments and staple fiber, as well as other textile strands.

FIGURE 24.3 Number of filaments.

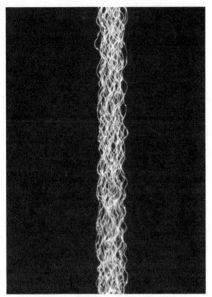
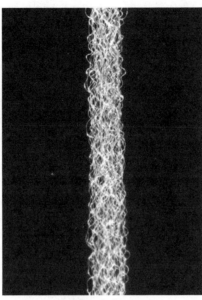
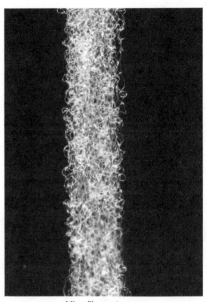

Standard denier-
per-filament yarn,
100/36 dtex

Fine denier-
per-filament yarn,
100/72 dtex

Microfilament yarn,
100/144 dtex

NUMBER OF FILAMENTS

In descriptions of filament yarns, the *number of filaments* is usually given in conjunction with the yarn number. For example, in the designation "100/36 dtex" the yarn number is 100 dtex and 36 filaments compose the yarn. The dtex of each filament can be calculated by dividing the yarn dtex by the number of filaments. The dtex of each filament in the 100/36 dtex yarn is, therefore, 2.8.

On the basis of the linear density of the filaments, multifilament yarns may be called *standard denier-per-filament, fine denier-per-filament,* or *microfilament (microfiber)* yarns (Figure 24.3). In 100-dtex apparel yarns, standard yarns usually contain 7.0–2.4 dtex filaments, fine denier-per-filament yarns contain 2.4–1.0 dtex filaments, and microfilament yarns contain filaments of less than 1.0 dtex. The dtex of the filaments in the standard yarn shown in Figure 24.3 is 2.8 dtex; in the fine denier-per-filament yarn, 1.4; and in the microfilament yarn, 0.7.

Comparing the photographs of the three yarns with identical linear densities and fiber compositions in Figure 24.3, it is apparent that as the number of filaments increases, the yarn diameter increases. The microfilament yarn has about twice the bulk and surface area of the standard filament yarn because the microfilament yarn contains about four times as many single filaments as the standard yarn.

The use of fine denier-per-filament and microfilament yarns alters the performance and aesthetics of the fabric in which they are used relative to the use of standard multifilament yarn. The greater the number of filaments in yarns of identical linear density, the softer and more easily bent the yarn becomes. Consequently, fabric drape is improved. In fabrics containing microfilament yarns, water repellency superior to that of polyester/cotton or 100% cotton fabrics can be achieved. The addition of a fluorocarbon finish increases water repellency while preserving water vapor permeability to the extent that microfilament-yarn fabrics can be used for skiwear and ordinary rainwear. Such treated microfilament fabrics are waterproof and breathable. Fine denier-per-filament and microfilament yarns and fabrics are stronger than standard-denier yarns and fabrics. However, the abrasion resistance of a filament yarn decreases as the fineness of the filaments increases.

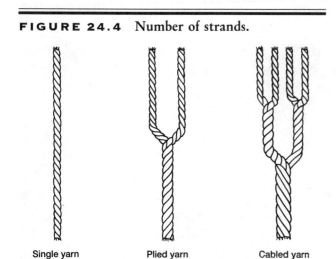

FIGURE 24.4 Number of strands.

Single yarn   Plied yarn   Cabled yarn

NUMBER OF STRANDS

The yarns described so far have been *single yarns,* "the simplest strand of textile material suitable for operations such as weaving, knitting, etc." When a single yarn is untwisted, the staple fibers slip by one another and the yarn or the filaments separate. Single yarns that are identical—except for fiber composition or color—may be combined to form plied and cabled yarns (Figure 24.4).

Plied yarns are composed of two or more single yarns that are twisted together. They are yarns "formed by twisting together two or more single yarns in one operation." When untwisted, the separate strands can be counted. Plied yarns are identified as 2-, 3-, 4-, etc. plied yarns; the number indicates how many single yarns make up the plied yarn. *Cabled or cord yarns* are composed of two or more plied yarns twisted together. They are yarns "formed by twisting together two or more plied yarns." The structure of a cabled yarn is indicated by the number of single yarns that make up each ply, followed by the number of plies in the cable.

The direction of twist usually alternates with each successive step in forming the ultimate yarn. In other words, the single yarns will be formed with an S-twist, the single yarns will be plied with a Z-twist, and when a cabled yarn is to be formed, the plies with be combined with an S-twist.

Balanced twist in a plied and cabled yarn "is that arrangement of twist which will not cause twisting on it-self when the yarn or cord is held in the form of an open loop." Yarn balance can be determined by taking a one-yard length of yarn and bringing the ends together between the thumb and forefinger. If the yarn hangs in a loop without rotating about itself, it is balanced. If it rotates about itself, then it is unbalanced.

Plied Spun Yarns

Plying single spun yarns produces yarns that (a) are more even, (b) have higher resistance to abrasion due to a more effective binding of the surface fibers into the bulk mass of the yarn, (c) are stronger because any weak spot in one of the strands is supported by the other strand, (d) result in improving fabric cover because the modified fiber arrangement gives the yarn a higher volume, and (e) result in fabrics with modified hand and appearance, including an increase in flexural rigidity or stiffness, a reduction in drapability but an increase in softness, and a potential reduction in pilling.

Between 20–25% of spun yarns are plied before use.[5] Woolen and worsted yarns—yarns composed of wool or manufactured fibers or blends of the two—are often plied. Many knitting yarns, especially bulky worsted yarns made of acrylic fiber, are plied. Therefore, plied yarns are found extensively in acrylic as well as wool sweaters. Some natural-fiber/synthetic-fiber blended yarns are plied yarns. These yarns, as well as 100% cotton plied yarns, are favored in shirting fabric (good quality broadcloth for men's shirts), premium denim fabrics, fabrics for work clothes, sportswear fabrics, sheeting fabrics, velvet fabrics, terry toweling, and upholstery fabrics.

Saxony-style, cut-pile carpet face yarns are normally plied to produce the required appearance and loft. Velour-style carpets do not require ply yarns and, therefore, rarely contain them. Most sewing thread has a plied-yarn construction. Here the need for a plied structure is undisputed. Only nylon and polyester sewing threads have sufficient strength to be used as single yarns.

Cabled spun yarns are rarely found in fabric but are found in ropes, some sewing thread, and tires.

Plied Filament Yarns

A single strand of silk yarn is usually composed of 2–6 silk filaments that are twisted together. These single

[5]R.R.C. Lorenz, "Yarn-Twisting," *Textile Progress* 16/1–2 (1987): 2.

strands have names, such as tram or georgette, that indicate the number of filaments and the degree of twist. These single yarns are very fragile and are used in the finest, sheerest silk fabrics. To improve the durability of silk yarn, single strands are plied. Silk plied yarns also have specific names that depend on the number of filaments in the single strands, the number of strands plied together, the degree of twist, and the direction of twist. Silk-plied-yarn names include two-by-two, organzine, and grenadine.

About 25% of manufactured-fiber multifilament yarns have a ply structure.[6] The single strands in these yarns usually contain many filaments and have low twist. Usually two single strands are plied with a negligible degree of twist. Plied yarns from manufactured filaments do not have specific names.

Carpet-pile yarns made of synthetic fibers are the largest end-use application of plied yarns made from manufactured filaments. Nylon- and polyester-filament sewing threads are plied structures because a torqueless structure is needed or else the yarn will kink. Some industrial filament yarns are also ply structures.

The main reason for plying multifilament yarns is to protect them against the stresses of weaving and knitting. Apparel filament yarns are usually *not* of a ply structure because the yarn volume decreases, thereby decreasing the cover of the fabric made with these yarns. Manufactured-filament carpet-pile yarns are extensively plied in order to produce a bulky yarn that retains softness. Also in carpeting, a plied yarn maintains the loft of the carpet better than a single yarn because it has improved mechanical and recovery abilities.

FIBER COMPOSITION

Fabrics of 100% fiber composition were long thought to be the most desirable. Competition was intense between producers of manufactured fibers and producers of natural fibers. In 1963, however, producers suddenly recognized that much could be gained by using two or more types or species of fibers in the same yarn and fabric because no fiber is perfect. After all, plants had been improved through hybridization, animals had been improved by crossbreeding, and construction materials had been improved by combining metals to form alloys. So why not blend fibers?

Self-Blended Yarns

Self-blended yarns are "single yarns spun from a blend or mixture of the same fiber species." A cone of such yarn would be labeled 100% cotton, 100% nylon, or 100% polyester. All natural-fiber yarns are self-blended for uniformity. A manufacturer of cotton or wool yarns, for example, will mix bales of fiber produced in different years or bales containing different grades of the same species fiber. Manufactured-fiber yarns are self-blended when fiber variants from the same generic group comprise one yarn. The use of acid- and basic-dyeable nylon fiber within one yarn constitutes a self-blended yarn. The use of acrylic fibers with different shrinkage potentials is another example of a self-blended yarn, in this case a self-blended bulk spun yarn. Ring-spun, open-end, air-jet, and multifilament yarns can all be self-blended.

Blended Yarns

Blended yarns[7] are "single yarns spun from a blend or mixture of different fiber species." Blending of staple fibers is widely practiced, but blending of filament yarns is not.[8] The type of blended yarn, intimate or nonintimate, depends on the pattern of distribution of the fiber species within the yarn (Figure 24.5).

Fiber Type and Distribution. In many blended yarns, the fibers of each species are fairly uniformly distributed throughout the yarn. Although ASTM definitions do not provide a specific name for this form of blended yarn, it is often referred to as an *intimate-blended yarn* or a conventional-blended yarn. All three types of spun yarn—ring, open-end, and air-jet—can be intimate blends. Intimate-blended yarns may be composed of (a) natural fibers combined with manufactured fibers, such as cotton with polyester or wool with acrylic, (b) manufactured fibers combined with manufactured fibers, such as acrylic with rayon or acrylic with polyester, or (c) natural fibers combined with natural fibers, such as wool

---

[7]In England, this type of yarn is referred to as a mixture yarn. In the United States, mixture is sometimes used as a synonym for blend, but such usage should be avoided because mixture has a different meaning that is given later in this chapter.

[8]Names of some blended filament yarns include: Monese®, which is composed of Dacron® polyester and Antron III® nylon that have been air-entangled; Lanese®, which is polyester and acetate with the polyester at the center of yarn with the acetate bulked at the exterior; and Bytrese®, which is polyester and nylon. Monese® and Bytrese® are trademarks on the Du Pont company and Lanese® of the Hoechst Celanese company.

---

[6]R.R.C. Lorenz, "Yarn-Twisting," *Textile Progress* 16/1–2 (1987): 1–93.

FIGURE 24.5 Types of blended yarns.

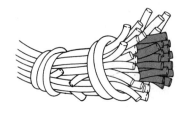

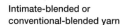

Intimate-blended or
conventional-blended yarn

Nonintimate-blended yarn
(Air-jet only)

with cotton or cotton with silk. The majority of intimate-blended yarns are composed of natural fibers mixed with manufactured fibers. The most commonly blended fiber is undoubtedly polyester, in combination with cotton, rayon, acrylic, and/or wool. An intimate-blended yarn may contain two, three or more fiber species. Apparel fabrics usually contain two species. In upholstery and draperies applications, it is not uncommon to find blends of three or more fiber species.

In air-jet spun-yarns, one fiber species may form the core and the other species the sheath, including the wrap fibers. Such blended air-jet spun-yarns are referred to as *nonintimate-blended yarns.*

Properties. Intimate blending provides an effective means of minimizing the negative properties and enhancing the outstanding positive properties of each fiber species. Skillful blending leads to a successful alliance of properties that fulfill performance needs. Blending will not increase or intensify a fabric property above the level found in a similarly constructed fabric containing only one of the fibers in the blend. Thus, a polyester/cotton intimate blend is not stronger than a similar fabric of 100% polyester, which is the stronger fiber in the blend. The polyester/cotton blend can, however, be stronger than a similarly constructed fabric of 100% cotton when properly blended. Improperly blended fabrics can be weaker than similarly constructed fabrics made entirely from the weaker fiber species.

The primary reason for intimate blends is a successful combination of performance properties. Many synthetic fibers are blended with natural fibers, such that sorptive properties of cotton, rayon, or wool are joined with the

high tenacity, toughness, abrasion resistance, resilience, and low shrinkage of polyester or nylon. In the process of intimate blending, however, performance disadvantages may be introduced. Two properties of note are increased pilling propensity and increased flammability. Fabrics that are blends of polyester and cotton have not been as successful in work clothing as should be expected because their flammability is higher than that of 100% cotton fabrics of similar weight. The safety of polyester/cotton garments can be less than that of similarly constructed cotton fabrics.[9] Pilling is almost absent in cotton fabrics but may be introduced when cotton fiber is intimately blended with polyester fiber.

Interesting color effects are another reason for intimate blends. White blended fabrics, placed in dye solutions containing dyes from different dye classes, will emerge from this cross-dyeing with a muted two-tone effect because the fibers have taken up different colorants from the dye bath (Chapter 34).

Costs can be reduced by mixing one relatively inexpensive fiber with a more expensive fiber. Reduction in cost is usually not a motivating factor for blending, however. Improvement in performance and unique coloration take precedence.

In the case of air-jet spun-yarns, there are several additional reasons for nonintimate blending. Nonintimate-blended air-jet spun-yarns are softer, less crisp, and more easily bent (have lower flexural rigidity) than either an air-jet yarn composed of only one of the fibers in

[9]C. Walker and H.L. Needles, "Flammability Characteristics of Lightweight Cellulosic and Polyester-Cellulosic Blend Fabrics," *Journal of Fire Sciences* 3 (1985): 461–471.

FIGURE 24.6   The effect on abrasion resistance and resilience as the proportion of polyester in a polyester/cotton intimate-blended fabric is increased.

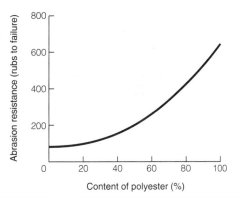 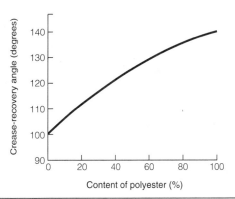

the blend or an intimate-blended yarn of similar fiber composition.

Blend Levels and Fiber Variants. In the marketplace, certain blend levels tend to dominate end-use applications. Taking polyester and cotton in apparel as an example, dominant blend levels are 80/20, 75/25, and 65/35 polyester/cotton, 60/40 cotton/polyester (reverse blends), and 50/50 polyester/cotton. In most cases, the manufactured fiber in the blend is a variant prepared specifically to achieve blending compatibility. Optimally blended yarns, therefore, are those containing the percentages of compatible fibers necessary to achieve the best results in the designated end use. Great technical knowledge is necessary to correctly blend fibers.

Figure 24.6 illustrates that only certain blend levels lead to improved performance in intimate-blended yarns or fabrics. In a polyester/cotton fabric, abrasion resistance does not begin to show improvement until over 20% of the fiber composition is polyester. Significant improvement is not reached until at least 50% of the fiber composition is polyester. Wrinkle resistance improves steadily with the addition of polyester fiber, with a noticeable improvement occurring at the 50% blend level. A 50/50 rayon/polyester blend, however, is not marketable as a wrinkle-free fabric without the addition of a resin treatment. For any fiber, increasing the polyester content to 67% is usually necessary to obtain a wrinkle-resistant fabric without a resin treatment.

The fibers in a blend must behave similarly when under stress if they are to be processed into blended yarns and if the yarns are to perform successfully in use. In particular, the fibers must have similar initial modulus and elongation at break. The Pima cotton curve in Figure 24.7 shows that considerable force is required to elongate the fiber (indicating a fiber that has a high initial modulus and is difficult to elongate). It shows that cotton breaks when a force of 3.5 grams per denier is reached at an elongation of 10%. The regular-tenacity polyester fiber shown is typical of polyester used in heavyweight fabrics. This fiber elongates 45–55% before it breaks at 4.8 grams per denier. Though stronger than cotton, regular-tenacity polyester does not contribute its full strength to a blend with cotton because it will still be elongating when cotton fibers are already breaking. The high-tenacity, high-modulus polyester, however, contributes to the strength of the intimate-blended yarn. At 10% elongation, when cotton fiber is beginning to break, this polyester is sharing the burden with cotton, increasing the strength of the intimate-blended yarns and fabrics.

End Uses. Blended yarns and fabrics share the marketplace with yarns and fabrics of 100% fiber composition. Several end uses—the pile of carpeting and the legs of pantyhose, for example—remain almost exclusively the domain of yarns of 100% fiber composition. At the other extreme are those market areas where it is more difficult to find fabrics of 100% fiber composition. A prime example is men's shirts: In the United States, 10–15% are all cotton and 5–10% are all polyester, with the remainder composed of various blend levels of polyester and cotton.

FIGURE 24.7 Stress-strain curves of several fibers used in blended yarns.

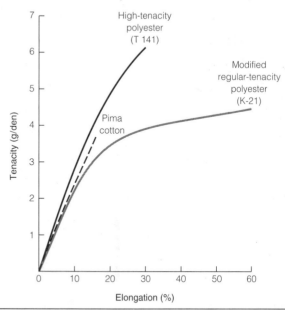

standard-denier and microdenier fibers or filaments. Although fiber companies classify microfibers as 1.0 denier or less, the microfibers used in microfiber blends may be less fine. The standard-denier polyester used in blends with wool fiber to make a worsted suiting is 3.5. In the microfiber blends currently being produced, the polyester ranges from 1.5–1.9 denier. The polyester fiber may be finer than the wool fiber, depending on the quality of wool fiber used.

Interest in microfiber blends has focused on polyester/worsted blends for tailored clothing fabrics. Polyester/worsted blends range from 5–65% by weight of polyester composing the yarn. The fabrics made from these microfiber blends have a finer, richer look without a synthetic shine and are softer, more supple, and more drapable than a blend comprised of 3.5 denier polyester.

Combination Yarns and Mixture Fabrics

Combination yarns (Figure 24.8) are plied yarns "twisted from single yarns of different fibers, for example, silk and rayon, or rayon and acetate." Each ply in the yarn is composed of a different species fiber, so blending is less thorough than in intimate blends. Combination yarns are not widely used.

Mixture fabrics, also called union fabrics, are more common. These fabrics are composed of various yarns that differ from each other in fiber composition. The usual arrangement is for the lengthwise yarns of mixture fabrics to be of one fiber composition (for example,

Microfiber Blends

Microfiber blends, introduced in Italy and Germany in 1989–1990, are fabrics in which the yarn contains

FIGURE 24.8 Combination yarns and mixture fabrics.

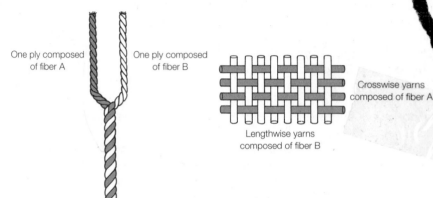

nylon) and the crosswise yarns of another fiber composition (for example, polyester). It is possible to find mixture fabrics with yarns of different fiber composition interlaced side by side.

Mixture fabrics with flax lengthwise yarns and cotton crosswise yarns were made as early as 150 B.C. In the 15th and 16th centuries, a union cloth called linsey-woolsey had flax lengthwise yarns and wool crosswise yarns. Interest in mixture fabrics continued in the 18th and 19th centuries. The original intent was to reduce costs by combining an inexpensive fiber with a more costly one. Today, many mixture fabrics are made to be cross-dyed in the piece, enabling yarn dye effects to be produced more quickly and often less expensively than through yarn dyeing (Chapter 34). Stretch denim, in which polyester textured yarns is used in the crosswise direction and cotton yarn is used in the lengthwise direction, is an example of a mixture fabric formed to provide comfort stretch.

CHAPTER SUMMARY

The construction features of spun and filament yarns and the effect of altering these features on yarn and fabric performance were considered in this chapter. Features that can be described for all types of yarns are linear density (yarn number), number of strands, and fiber composition. Degree and direction of twist are usually applied to ring-spun, open-end, and multifilament yarns but never to air-jet spun-yarns, which are not twisted. The number of filaments is usually given for multifilament yarns in conjunction with the yarn number.

Alterations in each of these features affect durability, comfort, aesthetic appeal, and health/safety/protection properties of the yarns and, consequently, of the fabric into which they are formed. In this chapter, we considered only the change in performance as a single structural feature was altered.

Compound and Fancy Yarns

COMPOUND YARNS

Compound yarns are composed of two or more strands, one forming the center, or core, and the other forming the wrap or covering.

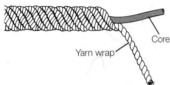

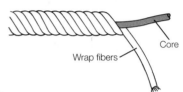

Covered Yarns

"Covered yarns consist of a readily separable core surrounded by a wrap or cover formed by one or more spun or filament yarns."

Core-Spun Yarns

"Core-spun yarns consist of a readily separable core surrounded by fiber and suitable for use as a yarn." The three types are filament core/staple-fiber wrap yarns, staple-fiber core/filament wrap yarns, and staple-fiber core/ staple-fiber wrap yarns.

FANCY YARNS

Fancy yarns are yarns that "differ significantly from the normal appearance of single or plied yarns due to the presence of irregularities deliberately produced during their formation."

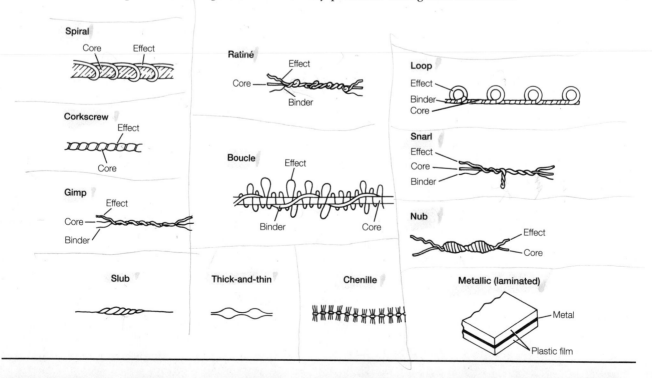

25

Compound and Fancy Yarns

Fancy yarns have been available for centuries, providing textural richness and beauty to fabrics. In sharp contrast, most compound yarns are a development of the late 20th century, and the appearance of fabric containing them emulates that of spun or filament fabrics. The beauty of compound yarns lies in their combination of desirable performance properties of spun and filament yarns into one structure.

Detail View 25 illustrates the major types of compound and fancy yarns. The structural similarity of the two groups is the presence of a core strand.

COMPOUND YARNS

Compound yarns, also called *composite yarns*, are structures consisting of at least two strands, one forming the center axis, or core, of the yarn, and the other forming the covering or wrap. One strand is usually composed of staple fibers; the other, of filaments. Compound yarns are even in diameter, relatively smooth, and available in the same size ranges as spun and filament yarns.

There are two types of compound yarns, covered and core-spun. The major difference between the two is the nature of the cover: In covered yarns, the wrap is a *yarn*, whereas in core-spun yarns, the wrap is a strand of *fibers*.

Covered Yarns

Covered yarns "consist of a readily separable core surrounded by a wrap or cover formed by one or more spun or filament *yarns.*" The core might be an elastomeric fiber, such as rubber or spandex, or a hard fiber, such as polyester or nylon (Figure 25.1). Covered yarns may have either a single covering or a double covering. The second covering is usually twisted in the direction opposite from the first covering.

Elastomeric filaments (rubber and spandex) are often covered to protect the elastomer from direct exposure to degrading agents such as ultraviolet light, fats, and oils (Chapter 20). In addition, rubber fiber cannot easily be dyed, so it is often covered with another yarn that can be dyed, thereby enhancing fabric appearance.

Another important reason for covering elastomeric fibers is to restrict or control their total elongation when they are used in support or power stretch fabrics, in waistband elastics, and in surgical and sheer-support hosiery. When elastomeric fibers are used without covering, they may elongate nine to ten times their original length. The covering yarn holds the elastomeric filament in a partially elongated state. In yarn to be used in fabric for support garments, the elastomer may be held at about 300% extension. The covered yarn itself will be held at 100–200% extension within the fabric. This combination of controlled extensions produces a fabric with a high initial resistance to elongation (high modulus). When a stretch garment is put on, it must first extend and then contract onto the body, exerting sufficient force to achieve the control that is desired. As the garment is worn, the covered yarns and the fabric in which they are used will repeatedly extend and return to the position of controlled extension. At some point, how-

FIGURE 25.1 Covered yarns.

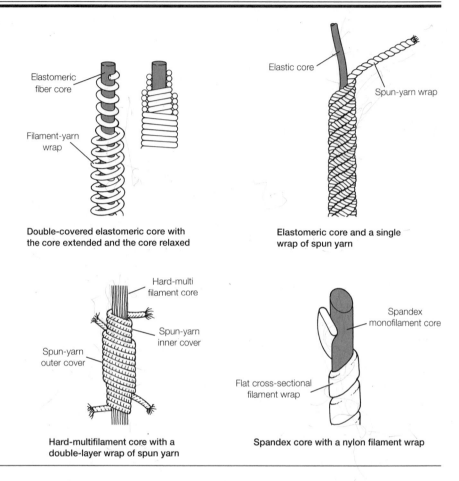

Double-covered elastomeric core with
the core extended and the core relaxed

Elastomeric core and a single
wrap of spun yarn

Hard-multifilament core with a
double-layer wrap of spun yarn

Spandex core with a nylon filament wrap

ever, the degree of extension increases and the degree of recovery decreases, largely due to the core filament properties.

In a covering machine, the elastomeric fiber passes through the center of a hollow spindle that rotates at high speed. As it rotates, the spindle wraps the covering yarn spirally onto the elastomeric fiber, which is held under a controlled degree of elongation.

Covered yarns with a hard fiber core are not as prevalent as those with an elastomeric core. When made, the hard fiber core usually improves the strength of the yarn over what it would be if only the covering yarn were used.

Core-Spun Yarns

Core-spun yarns "consist of a readily separable core surrounded by *fiber* and suitable for use as a yarn" (Fig-

ure 25.2). The fibers comprising the core and wrap are usually of different species. There are three types of core-spun yarns; filament core/staple-fiber wrap, staple-fiber core/filament wrap, and staple-fiber core/staple-fiber wrap (staple-core).

Filament Core/Staple-Fiber Wrap. *Filament core/staple-fiber wrap core-spun yarns* are characterized by the presence of filaments laying in the center of the yarn completely surrounded by a wrap of staple fibers. The wrap is often referred to as a sheath because it is composed of untwisted staple-length fibers. These yarns find application in apparel, household, and technical fields.

Core-spun yarns with a polyester-filament core and a sheath of combed cotton fibers are used in bedsheets and knit fabrics. The polyester-filament core provides strength and the cotton sheath, which contacts the skin, provides comfort. Core-spun-yarn fabrics have

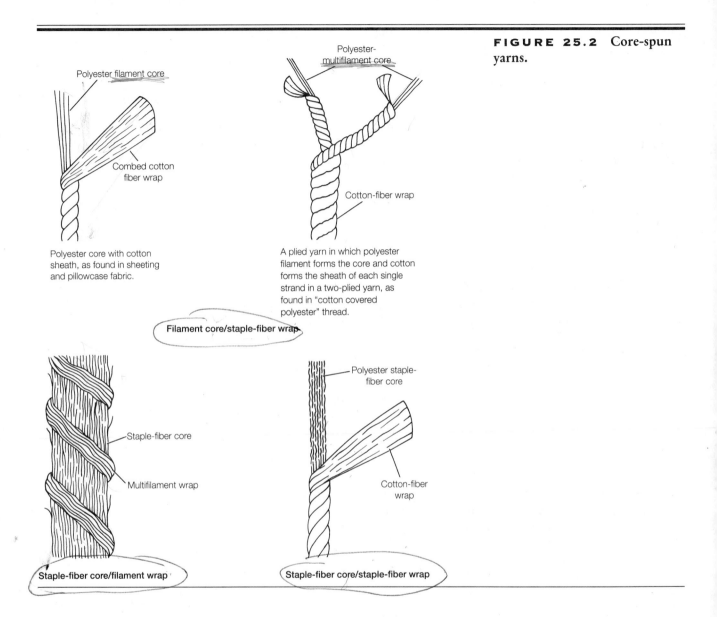

FIGURE 25.2 Core-spun yarns.

Polyester filament core

Combed cotton fiber wrap

Polyester core with cotton sheath, as found in sheeting and pillowcase fabric.

Polyester-multifilament core

Cotton-fiber wrap

A plied yarn in which polyester filament forms the core and cotton forms the sheath of each single strand in a two-plied yarn, as found in "cotton covered polyester" thread.

Filament core/staple-fiber wrap

Staple-fiber core

Multifilament wrap

Staple-fiber core/filament wrap

Polyester staple-fiber core

Cotton-fiber wrap

Staple-fiber core/staple-fiber wrap

better cover and pilling resistance than fabrics that contain intimate-blended polyester and cotton fibers or 100% cotton fabrics with comparable yarn size. The hand of a core-spun-yarn fabric is also fuller.

When plied, polyester core/cotton wrap yarns make sewing threads marketed as "cotton covered polyester". The core of each strand in the thread is polyester filament with a cotton-fiber sheath. Two single strands of core-spun construction are then twisted together to form the thread. The polyester core provides high strength, resistance to abrasion, perspiration resistance, and high resistance to chemical and bacteriological attack. The cot-

ton sheath gives extra grip to prevent slippage of seams and protects the polyester core from melting at high sewing speeds.

Core-spun yarns that have a core of elastomeric fiber (usually spandex) and a sheath of cotton fibers are used to make woven corduroy fabric and denim that stretch. When the spandex core is surrounded by cotton or acrylic fibers, the core-spun yarn is often incorporated into ribbing on knit garments to improve elastic recovery. In cotton-knit swimsuits, core-spun yarns are used to provide form-fit. The amount of spandex in the swimsuit may be as little as 1% in the core-spun yarn;

thus the resultant fabric has all the characteristics of the predominant staple fiber together with the advantages of excellent elongation and recovery. The staple-fiber sheath provides protection to the elastomeric core as well as contributing its fiber properties to fabric performance. Fabrics containing core-spun yarns with a spandex core are usually heat-set to adjust the elastic properties of the fabric to the application.

Secondary carpet backing is currently produced using polypropylene split or tape filaments for the core and polypropylene fiber for the wrap. Yarns for protective clothing and for flame-resistant curtains are composed of fiberglass-filament core surrounded with aramid fiber, aramid blends, or PBI fiber. Other yarns for these two uses have a carbon core surrounded with aramid fiber, flame-retardant blends, or PBI fiber. Protective gloves are made with steel wire surrounded by aramid-fiber blends. Sewing threads for the construction of flame-resistant products can also be core-spun yarns. For example, a spun-glass-fiber core may be wrapped with vinyon fiber to achieve slow burning.

The three major methods of producing core-spun yarns with a filament core/staple-fiber sheath are modified ring spinning, modified friction open-end spinning, and modified air-jet spinning. Each of these spinning technologies was previously discussed in Chapter 22. In each method, provision has been made for the "laying in" of the filament core.

Staple-Fiber Core/Filament Wrap. *Staple-fiber core/ filament wrap core-spun yarns* are characterized by the presence of an untwisted, parallel staple-fiber strand in the center of the yarn and a filament wrapped around this center strand. Yarns trademarked Coverspun® and Wonderspun® were developed and introduced into the market, but they were not commercially successful. Suessen PL® yarn, also called parafil or parallel yarn, is being produced worldwide.

The staple-fiber content in a typical staple-fiber core/ filament wrap yarn is 80–95% by weight, with the remainder being filament. All known textile fibers can be processed to make this type of yarn, and a wide range of counts, including fine, can be made. These yarns are particularly even in diameter.

Staple-fiber core/filament wrap yarns combine spun-yarn aesthetics with filament-yarn durability. They can be 100% stronger than spun yarns of the same size because more of the load-bearing capacity of each individual fiber is utilized. The fibers in these core-spun yarns are parallel and are in contact with each other along a greater percentage of their length than when twisted, as

is the case in spun yarns. These core-spun yarns can have greatly increased abrasion resistance.

Fabric aesthetics result, for the most part, from the properties of the staple fiber rather than the filament component. Since the staple core is not twisted, the fabrics tend to be soft and supple. The resistance to air permeability of fabrics made with staple-fiber core/filament wrap yarns is greater than that of fabrics made with twisted yarns. Some fiber combinations result in increased resistance to pilling compared to spun yarns; for others, the pilling is comparable to that of spun yarns. These core-spun yarns have superior covering power and excellent hand.

Staple-fiber core/filament wrap yarn production may increase because waste fibers, which may be obtained by shredding garment waste, may be used for the core. Less fiber is required to provide necessary cover because twist is not needed and the fibers are therefore not packed. Further, the most expensive aspect of producing a spun yarn, the insertion of the twist, is eliminated.

Staple-Fiber Core/Staple-Fiber Wrap. *Staple-fiber core/ staple-fiber wrap yarns* have a strand of parallel, untwisted staple fibers forming the center, which is completely wrapped with another staple-fiber strand.[1] This structure of core-spun yarns is referred to as staple-core yarns in textile literature. There are two forms of staple-core yarns: air-jet staple-core yarn and ringframe staple-core yarn, both named on the basis of the spinning system modified to produce them.

The development of staple-core yarns grew out of a effort to overcome the performance problems manifested in hard-filament core/staple-fiber wrap yarns. These problems included fairly easy stripping of the staple wrap, incomplete coverage of the core, and extraordinarily high yarn stiffness. By replacing the filament core with a staple-fiber core, it was thought that these problems could be minimized or eliminated. The majority of the development and production of staple-core yarns has focused on the use of polyester staple for the core and cotton fiber for the wrap.

The structure and properties of polyester/cotton core-spun yarns are most often compared to staple-fiber core/ filament wrap yarns and intimate-blended spun yarns. Figure 25.3 shows the cross-sectional shapes and distri-

---

[1]The type of yarn being considered here, that is, yarn composed entirely of staple fibers, could be considered to be a spun yarn. However, because the staple-fiber core/staple-fiber wrap yarns are an outgrowth of core-spun yarn research and structurally consist of a core and wrap that are separable, they are classed as core-spun yarns.

FIGURE 25.3   Cross sections of different types of blended yarns.

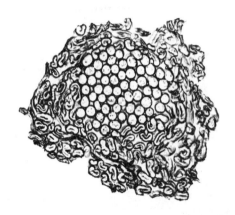

Staple-polyester core/
cotton wrap core-spun
yarn

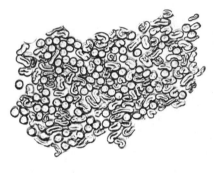

Polyester and cotton
intimate-blended
spun yarn

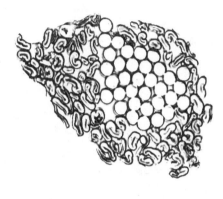

Filament-polyester core/
cotton wrap core-spun
yarn

bution of polyester and cotton fibers in a staple-core yarn, an intimate-blended polyester/cotton yarn, and a filament core/cotton wrap yarn. The staple-core and intimate-blended yarns are fairly round in cross section, but the filament core/cotton wrap yarn is not. Polyester fiber or filament is concentrated in the core of the core-spun yarns but is distributed throughout the intimate-blended yarn. As a consequence of these differences, the yarns differ in performance.

Modified ring-spun staple-core yarns in coarse, medium, and medium-fine counts have been produced which are stronger than equivalent intimate-blended (ring-spun) or 100% cotton yarns. The core provides high strength, easy care, and other functional properties of polyester, while the outer wrap provides the traditional appearance, feel, and comfort of cotton. When staple-core yarns, which were only modestly stronger than equivalent 100% cotton yarns, were woven into fabrics, the core-yarn fabric had remarkably improved performance compared to the fabrics made with ring-spun 100% cotton yarns. The core-spun fabric was stronger and more abrasion resistant, had improved dimensional stability that increased the ease of care, and was more comfortable.

Air-jet core-spun yarns with a 70% cotton-fiber wrap and 30% polyester-fiber core composition are more uniform in diameter and have higher elongation compared to 100% cotton ring-spun yarns. There is no difference in the breaking strength of the two yarns. When the yarns are knitted, the air-jet core-yarn knit has higher tearing strength, breaking strength, water vapor permeability, and water adsorption. It tends to dry more quickly and is judged less crisp than the ring-spun cotton fabric. Air-jet core-yarns are softer and less rigid than air-jet spun-yarns of 100% fiber content. Thus, blending is one way in which the objectional stiffness and hard hand of air-jet yarns can be reduced.

FANCY YARNS

The number of different fancy yarns equals the number of creative ideas in the minds of yarn designers. *Fancy yarns*, those that "differ significantly from the normal appearance of single or plied yarn due to the presence of irregularies deliberately introduced during their formation," are available in an almost bewildering variety. As the definition of fancy yarn suggests, random variation, irregularities, abrupt variations in width, as well as modulation between low and high twist along the yarn, are the inherent nature of these yarns. Fancy yarns, therefore, represent a dramatic departure from the uniformity of spun, filament, and compound yarns.

Fancy yarns are also known as novelty or effect yarns. They are usually composed of two or three strands (Detail View 25). All fancy yarns have a fancy, or effect, strand. Some have a core strand in addition to the effect strand. The core strand lies at the center of the fancy

FIGURE 25.4 Fancy yarns with effect and core strands with and without a binder strand.

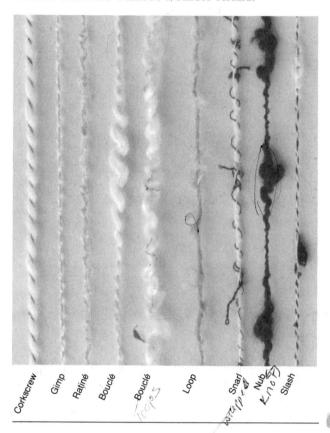

Corkscrew Gimp Ratiné Bouclé Bouclé Loop Snarl Nub Slash

yarn and serves as a base around which the effect strand is twisted. Other fancy yarns have a binder strand that serves to secure the effect strand to the core strand. The binder strand is usually small and is often not readily visible.

The history and development of the fancy yarn twisting industry can be traced to master craftsmen in Europe in the latter part of the 19th century. Ingenious devices were built for the production of fancy yarns, both those consisting of effect and core strands and those having a binder strand as well. The principles used in these devices are still used today. Woolen and worsted spun-yarn processes were modified for the random insertion of effect fibers. Friction open-end spinning machinery and air-jet spinning machinery have recently been modified to produce fancy yarns.

Effect and Core Strands With or Without a Binder Strand

Figure 25.4 shows a variety of fancy yarns composed of an effect strand and a core strand. Some of these fancy yarns also have a binder strand.

The differences in the appearance of the various yarns are largely a matter of the degree of prominence of the effect strand (the size of the effect strand) and the configuration assumed by the effect strand (wavy, looped, snarled, etc.). The yarns in Figure 25.4 are arranged in order from most subtle effect strand at the left-hand to most prominent effect strand at the right-hand. Fancy yarns also differ in how regularly or uniformly the "irregularity" occurs along the length of the yarn.

Spiral and *corkscrew yarns* both have one strand that spirals around the other strand. Usually one strand is a soft and bulky yarn, and the other strand is a fine yarn. In a spiral yarn, the thicker strand is usually wound around the finer strand. In the corkscrew yarn, the finer strand is wound around the thicker strand.

Gimp and *ratiné yarns* have a slightly wavy appearance. In both yarns, the effect strand is twisted around the core strand. Ratiné yarns are usually larger and more wavy than gimp yarns due to a larger effect strand. Ratiné and gimp yarns have an effect strand that lies closer to the core strand than is typical in bouclé and loop yarns.

Bouclé, loop, and *snarl yarns* have a dramatic effect strand. The effect strand in bouclé yarns is usually the softest and bulkiest of this group, and typically, does not lie near the core strand. In loop yarns, the effect strand is usually made of long, rigid fibers that may also be lustrous, such as mohair or wool, or untwisted thick filament strand. In both bouclé and loop yarns, the binder strand is necessary to hold the loops in place. The core strand in loop yarns is usually coarser and heavier than in bouclé yarns.

Bouclé yarns are found in both woven and knit fabrics that are often called bouclé fabrics. Loop yarns are frequently used in coating and suiting fabrics, for interior furnishings, and for specialty fabrics, either knit or woven.

A snarl yarn uses a twist-lively strand to form the projecting snarls. The twist of the effect strand is usually in the same direction as the twist that holds the effect and core strands; the binder strand is usually twisted in the opposite direction.

Nub and *slash yarns* have the effect strand twisted around the core strand a number of times in a small area to form an enlarged bump or "nub." A binder strand may or may not be used; a binder strand is not usually necessary to hold the nub in place. The nubs may be at regular or irregular intervals. The differences between the yarns lie in the size and shape of the bump. In a nub yarn, the bump is the largest in size and shortest in length, making it the roundest irregularity found in this type of fancy yarn. In a slash yarn, the enlarged area is longer and thinner than in a nub yarn. There are other yarns in this group, such as seed yarns, that have a similar appearance but differ in the size and spacing of the nubs.

Other Fancy Yarns

Other types of fancy yarns are shown in Figure 25.5.

Slub yarns are a variation of spun yarns in which dramatic changes in width occur along the length of the yarn, creating slubs, or short thick places. The changes in width are due to differences in the amount of twist, with areas of lower twist being thicker than areas of higher twist. The slubs may be dramatically larger or only subtly larger than the remaining yarn width, and they may be regularly or irregularly spaced. Equally spaced slubs are usually avoided because they tend to concentrate in certain areas, leaving other areas without slubs, when the yarn is woven or knit into fabric. Most slub yarns are single yarns, although there are some plied slub yarns. Slub yarns can be made from manufactured fibers, often rayon, to imitate the surface interest created in fabrics made from irregular-diameter silk and flax fibers. Such slub yarns are relatively small and have little variation in width. Large slub yarns are usually not used alone in fabric. Rather, they are combined with simple yarns to achieve adequate fabric strength. A variety of surface effects can be realized with large slub yarns.

Thick-and-thin yarns are a variation of multifilament yarns in which irregular-diameter filaments cause width variation along the yarn length. Some filament silk is of this type; likewise, manufactured fibers can be extruded from the spinneret so that their diameter varies along their length. When these filament yarns are used in fabric, the fabric surface generally has the appearance or texture that is characteristic of linen fabric.

Color-irregularity fancy yarns are fancy yarns in which the deliberately introduced irregularity is a color variation along the length of the yarn. This color irregularity may be accompanied by a subtle difference in yarn diam-

FIGURE 25.5 Other fancy yarns.

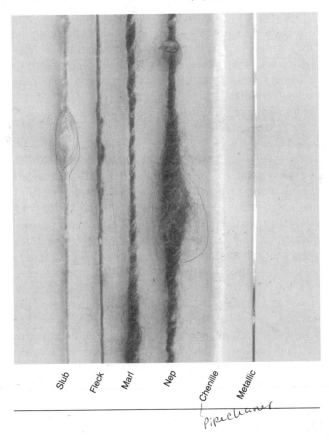

Slub   Fleck   Marl   Nep   Chenille   Metallic

eter at the location of the "inserted" colored fibers. *Nep yarns* show contrasting colored spots or neps (small balls of colored fibers) on the yarn surface. Nep yarns are relatively uniform along their length, with the small variation in size occurring at the site of the colored nep. Nep yarns must contain cohesive fibers such as wool so that the neps remain on the yarn surface as the fabric containing the nep yarns is used or worn. Nep yarns are often used in tweed fabrics. *Fleck yarns* have a more streaky appearance than nep yarns because the contrasting color fibers are more clustered together in the yarn. *Marl* and *marl-effect yarns*, the former composed of staple fibers and the latter composed of filament fibers, are characterized by a mottled (spotted or dappled) appearance created by twisting together two strands of different colors or shades.

Traditionally, these color-irregularity fancy yarns were mostly woolen and worsted single yarns manufactured on modified woolen and worsted machinery, so the contrasting color fibers introduced during the process of converting the fiber to yarn were not uniformly distributed throughout the yarn. Today, color-irregularity fancy yarns are also the result of modifications to friction open-end spinning machinery and air-jet spinning machinery and consequently many different fiber compositions result.

Chenille yarns resemble a caterpillar, hence the derivation of their name from the French word *chenille,* which means caterpillar. The effect is composed of tufts of yarn held between plied yarns that form the core of the chenille yarn. Chenille yarns are usually made from cotton, wool, rayon, or polyester and are used in fabrics that are soft, velvety, and drape well. The softness of chenille yarns makes them vulnerable to rubbing; consequently, fabrics containing them do not wear well because of a low abrasion resistance.

Chenille yarns are used as crosswise yarns in a woven fabric to create a velvet-like surface or occasionally placed in the filling to add surface interest. In woven fabrics, the yarns may be laid so that all the tufts lie on one side of the fabric or so that some tufts appear on both the face and the back. These fabrics are used for such varied purposes as dresses, draperies, and bedspreads. Chenille yarns are used in knit fabrics, often in bulky sweater knits. Some fabric is called "chenille" even though it does not contain chenille yarns. These fabrics, often used for bathrobes and bedspreads, have closely spaced tufts in continuous lines. They are actually tufted fabrics (Chapter 29).

Chenille yarns are manufactured by two different methods. The most common method is to construct a woven fabric in a leno weave using soft-twisted yarn in the crosswise direction. The warp yarns are usually about $\frac{1}{8}$ to $\frac{1}{4}$ inch (3 to 7 millimeters) apart. The fabric is then split into strips between the lengthwise yarns, and the soft-crosswise yarns held within the twists of the lengthwise yarns form the fuzzy pile surface of the chenille yarn.

In 1977, a machine was specifically designed for the manufacture of upholstery chenille. The core and effect yarns are fed from a creel to the chenille machine, where the effect yarn is cut into predetermined lengths and is twisted into the core yarn. The chenille yarn is then wound onto spools at the bottom of the machine. Modifications have resulted in the production of finer chenille yarns for other end uses, such as knitwear.

Metallic or *laminated yarns* have a central core of metal and a coating that is usually a plastic film but is sometimes a metallized film. They are produced in a flat, ribbon-like form to achieve maximum light reflectance. High-gloss, metallic sparkle is added to fabrics.

Early metallic yarns based on precious metals, mainly gold and silver, had disadvantages in addition to their high cost. They tended to tarnish during use and gave fabrics a harsh surface, and most had a metallic odor. Today, laminating helps to eliminate tarnishing, but even so, care must be taken in the maintenance of fabrics containing laminated yarns because the plastic film can melt during ironing or dissolve in drycleaning solvents. Mylar®-laminated yarns, however, are machine-washable, can withstand dryer temperatures, and can be ironed safely with a steam or dry iron.

Metallic-core yarns are used in carpeting to reduce the buildup of static charge because the central core will conduct electricity. When the coating is nylon, these yarns are identical in appearance to the rest of the fibers of the carpet yarn. These metallic-core carpet yarns perform in the same manner as the rest of the carpet and do not require special care.

Metallic yarns are formed by applying plastic film on both sides of a metallic sheet material. The three layers pass through rollers that bind the layers together. Strips of yarn are then cut and wound onto bobbins.

Performance Considerations

A fabric is seldom composed entirely of fancy yarns, except possibly in drapery applications and sweaters. The performance of all types of yarn in the fabric must be given consideration when fabric performance is being evaluated.

Fancy yarns are valued for the aesthetics that they contribute to fabrics. Use of these yarns in the plainest woven and knit fabrics creates interesting surface design and texture. Texture may vary from soft and pleasing to harsh and rough. The latter fabrics find limited use in apparel but wider use in interior furnishings.

Fancy yarns may detract from the performance of the fabric because they alter the evenness of the fabric surface. Abrasion resistance may be lowered: the fancier the yarn, the lower the abrasion resistance usually becomes because the frictional force is applied to the tops of the highest yarns rather than distributed over a wider surface area. In addition, the size and frequency of loops influences the snagging propensity: the more pronounced the loop, the greater the likelihood of snagging and ultimately damaging the fabric. In selecting fabrics containing fancy yarns, it is wise to consider durability and maintenance as well as fabric aesthetics.

CHAPTER SUMMARY

Compound yarns are yarns that look similar to spun and filament yarns but differ because they usually contain both spun and filament strands. The two main types of compound yarns are covered and core-spun. Compound yarns usually combine the durability of filament yarns with the comfort and aesthetics of spun yarns. Performance depends on the specific structure of the compound yarn as well as the fiber composition of the core and the cover or wrap. When the core is an elastomeric fiber (rubber or spandex), a stretch yarn results. Covered yarns are those in which the core strand is completely covered by a yarn strand. Core-spun yarns also contain a core but they are wrapped, completely or partially, by filament yarns or a sheath of staple fibers. The processes used to manufacture compound yarns are as varied as the yarns themselves. Most methods are designed to bring the core strand together with the covering yarn or the wrapping fibers.

Fancy yarns, also known as novelty and effect yarns, are yarns that differ from the normal construction of single and plied yarns by way of deliberately produced irregularities. All fancy yarns have an effect strand that introduces knops, curls, loops, slubs, and the like. The yarn may also have a core and a binder strand. Slub, thick-and-thin, gimp, and bouclé are names of some of the fancy yarns. Not everyone agrees on what the name of every fancy yarn produced should be because of the great diversity of forms that each yarn may assume. Fancy yarns add surface interest to fabric. Care should be taken in selecting fabrics containing them because other desired performance properties, such as high abrasion resistance, may be compromised.

*F*abric Structures
and Performance

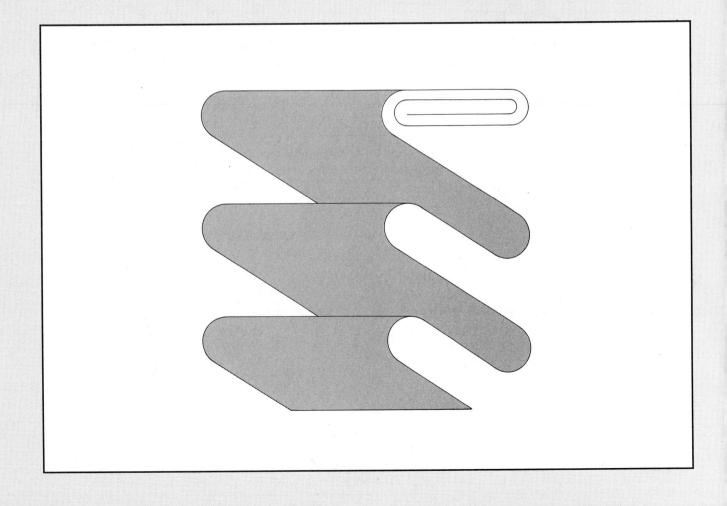

Fabric Structures

Fabrics are "manufactured assemblages of fibers and/or yarns that have substantial surface area in relation to thickness and sufficient mechanical strength to give this assembly inherent cohesion." The nature of the yarn or fiber arrangements determines the type of fabric structure.

WOVEN FABRICS

Woven fabrics have two or more sets of yarns *interlaced* at right angles to each other.

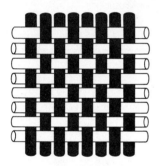

TWISTED AND KNOTTED FABRICS

Twisted and knotted fabrics have yarns that *intertwine* with each other at right or other angles.

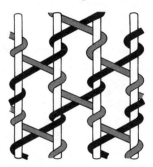

KNIT FABRICS

Knit fabrics are composed of *intermeshing* loops of yarn.

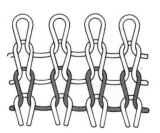

NONWOVEN FABRICS

Nonwoven fabrics are composed of webs (batts) of fibers (filament or staple-length) that are entangled or layered. The fibers are often bonded with adhesives, thread stitching, or other means.

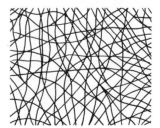

COMPOUND FABRICS

Compound fabrics are composed of two or more layers of fabric or of a fabric and another component (yarn, fiber, vinyl, film, etc.) held together by stitching, fusing, adhesive bonding, and other means.

*F*ABRICS ARE "manufactured assemblages of fibers and/or yarns that have substantial surface area in relation to thickness and sufficient mechanical strength to give the assembly inherent cohesion." The nature of the yarn or fiber arrangements determines the type of fabric structure or construction.

WHAT ARE THE MAJOR TYPES OF FABRICS?

Overview IV presents the major types of fabric structures or constructions: woven fabrics, twisted and knotted fabrics, knit fabrics, nonwoven fabrics, and compound fabrics. Three types—woven, knit, and twisted and knotted—contain yarns. One type, nonwoven, is comprised of webs or batts of fibers. Compound fabrics are layered fabrics in which the layers are usually dissimilar.[1]

Each fabric definition states the manner in which the fibers or yarns are assembled to form a coherent structure (a fabric). In the woven definition, the key word is *interlace*—meaning to cross one another, typically passing alternately over and under. In the definition for knit fabrics, the key word is *intermesh*—meaning to form a yarn into a loop and pull that loop through another loop. A synonym for intermesh is interloop. In the definition of twisted and knotted fabrics, the key word is *intertwine*, meaning twisting and winding. The nonwoven definition emphasizes *entanglement, layering, and bonding*, techniques for positioning and holding the fibers together. Lastly, the compound fabric definition specifies *stitching, fusing, and adhesive bonding* as techniques for holding component layers together.

UNIT ORGANIZATION

Chapter 26 focuses on woven fabrics. Chapter 27 discusses knit fabrics, Chapter 28 nonwoven fabrics, and Chapter 29 the compound fabrics. The major twisted and knotted fabric, Leavers lace, is included in the knit fabric chapter. This organization, centered on the basic types of structures, works well except when one wants to consider certain categories of fabrics—such as crepe fabrics, pile fabrics, nets and laces, and stretch fabrics—as a group or subject. These particular fabrics are not of

a singular structure or construction; they cannot be classified under just one of the major structural types presented in this unit. Pile fabrics, for example, can be woven, knit, tufted (a type of compound fabric), or stitchbonded (a type of nonwoven fabric). In the case of pile fabrics, the defining characteristic of the group is a fabric surface formed by tufts or loops of yarn or fibers that stand up from the base or ground of the fabric. In this text, pile knit fabrics will be discussed in the knit-fabric chapter, pile woven fabrics in the woven-fabric chapter, and other pile fabrics in the compound-fabric chapter.[2] Should you want to study pile fabrics, crepe fabrics, and so on, the index will assist you in locating the various fabrics belonging to the category of interest.

TERMINOLOGY

The definitions placed in quotes are those of the Textile Institute of Manchester, England, unless otherwise noted. The reference is S.R. Beech, (ed.), *Textile Terms and Definitions*, 8th ed. (Manchester, England: The Textile Institute, 1986).

LEARNING HOW PERFORMANCE IS ALTERED BY FABRIC STRUCTURE

The discussions of how fabric performance is altered as fabric structure or construction changes are comparative; for example, the performance of woven fabrics is compared to that of knit fabrics or the performance of plain woven fabrics is compared to that of twill woven fabrics. One difficulty encountered in comparing the performance of fabrics is that fabrics of various structures (even fairly similar ones) contain different types of yarns. For example, it is difficult to compare satin to twill woven-fabrics because satin fabrics usually are composed of multifilament yarns and twill fabrics are usually composed of spun yarns. Therefore, it is not just the interlacing pattern of the yarns that varies as one finds these fabrics in the marketplace. The fiber composition may also vary, confounding the comparison.

Another complication in performance comparisons in this unit is that some performance properties differ by fabric direction. For example, in woven fabrics, strength usually differs depending on whether the fabric is stressed lengthwise, crosswise, or diagonally (on the bias). The same is true for many nonwoven fabrics. Such

---

[1] The phrase *compound fabrics* is used here in order to conveniently incorporate a number of important fabric structures into one chapter. Textile dictionaries do not define compound fabrics or multicomponent fabrics, another phrase used to define a category of fabrics.

[2] If another organizational plan is used, these fabrics can be referred to as knit pile fabrics and woven pile fabrics.

structures are called anisotropic (those with different levels of performance in different directions). Other fabrics, such as triaxials and some nonwovens, are isotropic, having the same level of performance regardless of direction.

OBJECTIVES

The first objective of Unit IV is to provide the reader with the knowledge necessary to identify major types of fabrics and correctly use terminology related to their structures. It is expected that the reader will be able to make distinctions between woven fabrics, twisted and knotted fabrics, knit fabrics, nonwoven fabrics, and compound fabrics. Further, it is expected that the reader will also be able to identify various types of woven fabrics (plain, twill, satin, dobby, etc.), knit fabrics (weft and warp), and compound fabrics. The second objective is to emphasize the relationship of fabric structure to performance and continue to develop an appreciation of the complexity of determining fabric performance. The third objective is to develop an understanding of the technology involved in the production of fabric.

Woven Fabric Structures

Woven fabrics have two or more sets of yarns that are interlaced at right angles to each other.

BASIC STRUCTURES

Basic woven structures are those in which two sets of yarns interlace to create surfaces that can appear flat, as a series of crosswise ribs, as a series of diagonal ribs, or smooth and lustrous.

Plain-woven fabrics are fabrics in which "the odd warp yarns operate over one and under one filling yarn throughout the fabric with the even warp yarns reversing this order to under one, over one, throughout."

Twill fabrics are fabrics in which the "weave repeats on three or more warp and filling yarns and diagonal lines are produced on the face of the fabric."

Satin fabrics are fabrics "in which the binding [interlacing] places are arranged with a view to producing a smooth fabric surface, free from twill."

COMPLEX STRUCTURES

Complex structures are those in which two or more sets of yarns interlace to create texture, to form a woven-in design, or to develop two inseparable layers.

Leno fabrics are fabrics in which "warp yarns have been made to cross one another, between fillings, during leno weaving."

Crepe woven fabrics "have a random distribution of floats so as to produce an 'all-over' effect in the fabric to disguise the repeat."

Dobby fabrics are fabrics with a small woven-in design.

Jacquard fabrics are fabrics with intricate, detailed, woven-in motifs.

Piqué fabrics "show rounded cords [wales or ribs] in the filling direction, with pronounced sunken lines between them that are produced by the nature of the weave."

Surface-figure fabrics are characterized by design motifs formed with yarns other than those used in the base of the fabric.

Pile woven fabrics have yarns that stand vertically from a woven ground, resulting in fabrics approximately $\frac{1}{4}$ to $\frac{1}{2}$ inches thick, with looped or cut-looped surfaces.

Double-woven fabrics are "layered fabrics in which the separate layers or plies, each with its own warp and filling, are produced simultaneously and stitched together in one weaving process."

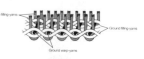

*W*oven Fabrics

Some authorities maintain that woven objects were in use as early as 6000 B.C. Others set the date at about 5000 B.C.[1] Regardless of the exact date, woven objects were made during the Stone Age. The early objects were composed not of yarn, but of reeds, grasses, saplings, and the like. These materials were passed one across the other, over and under, to form a coherent mass.

Bits of woven cloth of flax fiber and wool fiber were found during the excavation of the site where the Swiss Lake Dwellers lived. Many cloths of exquisitely fine linen with 540 warp yarns per inch unearthed in Egypt show the skill that early people had developed. It was almost 1950 before industrial machinery could duplicate the quality of the Egyptian fabric.

Woven fabrics are "fabrics in which two or more sets of yarns are interlaced at right angles to each other." This definition specifies three requirements for a fabric to be classified as woven: two or more sets of yarns (always one set lengthwise and one set crosswise), yarns that interlace (change position from the surface of the fabric to the underside and vice versa), and interlace at a right (90°) angle. There are eleven structures or types of fabrics—plain-woven, twill, satin, leno, crepe woven, dobby, Jacquard, piqué, surface-figure, pile woven, and double-woven—that fit into the woven category. They are divided into two groups, basic and complex, and are

listed and defined in Detail View 26, where a weave diagram for each type of woven fabric is also provided. By convention, the lengthwise yarns in weave diagrams are black and the crosswise yarns are white. Note that at least two sets of yarns interlace at right angles to each other in each diagram.

The performance of woven fabrics differs from those of other fabrics containing yarns. Usually, woven fabrics are firmer and more rigid due to the right-angle position of the interlacing yarns. Therefore, they are less drapable (have a higher resistance to shearing) and are not very extensible. The strength of woven fabrics cannot be directly compared to that of other fabrics containing yarns (particularly knits) because breaking strength is the appropriate measure for woven fabrics whereas bursting strength is appropriate for knits. It can be noted, however, that breaking strength in woven fabrics is usually greater in the lengthwise than crosswise direction. Relaxation shrinkage in woven fabrics is usually greater in the lengthwise than the crosswise direction due to the greater stress placed on the warp yarns during fabric manufacture and finishing.

GENERAL TERMINOLOGY

Terms used to describe woven fabrics are discussed in this section. These terms are used to identify specific woven fabrics.

---

[1] Z. Bendure and G. Pfeiffer, *America's Fabrics* (New York: Macmillan, 1947), p. 306.

Weave Descriptors

Figure 26.1 shows a small section of a woven fabric in a weave diagram. A surface view is presented along with two cross-sectional views, one lengthwise and one crosswise. The cross-sectional views represent how the yarn positions appear when the fabric is viewed at its cut edge. They are not necessary when the fabric has a simple structure, but they become useful as the number of sets of yarns increases. The weave diagram in Figure 26.1 is labeled with many of the terms discussed in this section.

The terms *warp, filling*, and *bias* specify direction. The crosswise direction of woven fabrics is called the *filling* direction, and the lengthwise direction is called the *warp* direction. The yarns that transverse crosswise are filling yarns and those in the lengthwise direction are warp yarns. Other terms used for filling are weft, woof, and picks. Warp yarns may be referred to as ends. In this textbook, the warp yarns are depicted in black and the filling yarns in white. The *bias* direction is any direction other than lengthwise and crosswise. A bias is either a true bias, meaning a direction at a 45° angle to the lengthwise edge, or a garment bias, meaning a direction at any angle other than 45° to the lengthwise edge.

Usually, the lengthwise edge of a woven fabric has a *selvage* to ensure that the fabric edge will not tear when it is subjected to the stresses of the finishing and dyeing processes. It is usually ¼ to ½ inches wide, is more closely woven (denser), and exists on both lengthwise edges of the fabric.

Woven fabrics have a *face* and *back*. The side called the face usually has the more attractive appearance and is the side viewed during use or wear, as with the outer surface of a garment. Some fabrics, such as plain-woven and leno, are structurally identical on the face and the back due to the interlacing pattern used. Others, such as warp-faced twills and satin, differ in appearance on the face and the back.

All fabrics have a *top* and a *bottom*. Usually these dimensions are not important because fabric appearance is the same regardless of which end is viewed. In other words, when a fabric is rotated 180°, its appearance is the same. However, pile woven fabrics—such as velvet, velveteen, and corduroy—exhibit different depths of color shade depending on the position in which they are viewed. This variation in appearance must be taken into account when fabricated products are made.

An *interlacing pattern* is a description of the *movement* of either the warp or the filling yarns from the surface to the back of the fabric and vice versa and of the manner in which adjacent yarns complete the movement relative to one another. The latter is called the *move number* or the *progression of interlacing* and is defined as "the number of filling yarns by which the interlacing of a warp yarn in a weave moves upwards relative to the warp yarn on its immediate left."

The weave diagram in Figure 26.1 is just sufficient to show one pattern or *weave repeat*, the smallest number of warp and filling yarns on which an interlacing pattern can be represented. In this case, five warp and five filling yarns are just sufficient (the three warp yarns in the salvage are excluded). The movement of each filling yarn is over four warp yarns and under one warp yarn. This pattern is best observed with the filling yarn at the bottom of the diagram. The movement of each warp yarn is under four filling yarns and over one filling yarn. This movement is most easily observed by viewing the first warp yarn at the left-hand edge of the body of the fabric. The progression of interlacing in the weave diagram is 2. To obtain this result, we first determine that the far right-hand warp yarn passes over the third filling yarn from the bottom. We then determine that the second warp yarn from the right passes over the fifth filling yarn from the bottom. Therefore, it is necessary to move up two filling yarns before reaching an identical interlacing point.

A *float* is "a length of yarn on the surface of a fabric between adjacent intersections. This corresponds to the number of yarns over or under which the intersecting yarn passes in a woven structure." In the weave diagram in Figure 26.1, the filling yarns form floats on the fabric face and the warp yarns form floats on the fabric back. The length of the floats is four. Floats can make a fabric surface flat and increase its luster. They can also be used

FIGURE 26.1   **Structural elements of woven fabrics.**

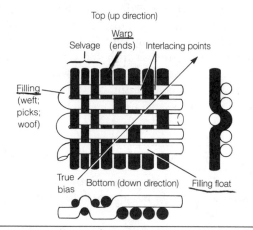

Top (up direction)
Warp
Selvage (ends)   Interlacing points
Filling (weft; picks; woof)
True bias   Bottom (down direction)   Filling float

to achieve design in fabrics such as dobby and Jacquard. Snagging is a problem when the float is relatively long because the float yarn can be caught on broken fingernails or other rough surfaces. Floats weaken the fabric by reducing the frequency with which yarns pass from one side of the fabric to the other. They enable yarns to slide under each other in the fabric and are used to make fabrics with high fabric counts (many yarns per square inch).

Interlacing patterns determine the number of *interlacing points* in each square inch of fabric and the spacing of the interlacing points. The interlacing pattern has a significant influence on appearance and performance. Fabrics with fewer interlacings per unit area and more space between yarns usually are softer (and more supple) and drape better than fabrics with more interlacing and less space between yarns. When a fabric having a high number of interlacing points per unit area is pulled or torn, the warp and filling yarns dig into one another at their points of interlacing and the yarns are weakened. However, at these same points, stresses are transferred from warp to filling and vice versa, helping the fabric to maintain integrity. When the points of interlacings are too widely spaced, the transfer of stresses is reduced, so the yarns break under stress.

The terms *on-grain* and *off-grain* denote whether or not the yarns in the woven fabric are at right angles to each other at the time the fabric is to be made into an end-use item. Off-grain alignment of the yarns yields a defective fabric. Fabrics may be pulled off-grain during dyeing, printing, and finishing operations. Usually, it is the filling yarns that are distorted. Failure to straighten the fabric—to return it to its on-grain position—results in poor drape in the end-use product.

Fabric Count

Fabric count is "the number of warp and filling yarns per inch of fabric."[2] It may be written as the number of the warp and the number of the filling ($W \times F$) or as the sum of the warp and filling counts. For example, the fabric count of a fabric with 80 warp yarns per inch and 80 filling yarns per inch can be given as either 80×80, 160, or 80 square. The fabric count of a fabric with 180 warp yarns per inch and 90 filling yarns per inch can be stated as 180×90 or as 270. Usually, the count is that of the fabric when removed from the loom, or the greige fabric. This count may change in subsequent processing.

In the consumer marketplace, fabric count is usually given on sheets and pillowcases. A common count is 80×80, or 160. In finer sheets, the fabric count is between 200 and 310. The more useful information is provided from the reporting of warp and filling separately because then one knows whether the fabric is balanced or unbalanced in its construction (discussed in a later section of this chapter). In mail-order catalogs, the fabric count may be printed to assist the consumer in knowing the construction of the fabric being sold.

Various adjectives are often used instead of precise counts to indicate the relative closeness of yarns in woven fabrics. These adjectives include: tight (tightly woven), close (closely woven), and dense (densely woven), as well as loose and open.

Fabric count is an important determinant of the quality of fabric. It is accepted that the higher the fabric count, the better the technological quality of the fabric. High fabric counts require the use of the finest of yarns. High fabric count is also facilitated by a low number of interlacings per square inch of fabric. If two fabrics are woven with yarns of the same size, the fabric with the fewer interlacings per inch is the higher-count fabric because yarns can be packed more closely together. High-fabric-count fabrics, although containing fine yarns, have close or dense structures that permit little yarn movement. On the other hand, yarns in low-fabric-count fabrics have some freedom of movement, enabling the fabric to better withstand the stresses of crushing and bending. Performance properties significantly affected by the fabric count appear in each of the five performance attribute categories.

Breaking strength increases as fabric count increases because more yarns are available to share the pulling force on the fabric. Tearing strength, however, decreases as fabric count increases. A tightly woven fabric allows only one yarn at a time to break as a tear propagates, but a loosely woven fabric allows more yarns to carry the load at any one time. Thus, a loosely woven fabric has a higher tear strength than a tightly woven one made of the same yarn.

Comfort is altered as fabric count increases: air permeability decreases, water resistance increases, and weight increases. The amount of fabric shrinkage decreases as the fabric count increases. Flammability is lowered as fabric count increases because less air remains within the fabric. Fabric aesthetics altered include cover, resilience, body, hand, and drape. Cover increases as fabric count increases; resiliency decreases. In a fabricated product, the higher the fabric count, the less raveling there is at the seams.

---

[2]The outdated term for fabric count is thread count. Fabric or thread count should not be confused with yarn number. Yarn number specifies the size (diameter) of spun yarns (Chapter 24).

Balance

Balanced woven fabrics are fabrics that have the same number of warp yarns and filling yarns per inch and contain yarns of equal size and character. The term _unbalanced_ is not defined but is commonly used to indicate that the ratio of the number of warp to filling yarns (or filling to warp yarns) in a fabric is two or greater. For example, cotton broadcloth with a fabric count of 144 × 76 and nylon satin with a count of 210 × 80 are unbalanced, with ratios of 2:1 and 3:1, respectively.

Balance is helpful in determining the warp direction of fabrics, which usually have more warp yarns than filling yarns. Some fabrics contain two or three times as many warp as filling yarns, but some contain twice as many filling as warp yarns. Balance is also helpful in determining the name of some specific fabrics that differ mainly in the balance of yarns, such as percale and broadcloth.

Raveling a fabric on two adjacent edges and looking at the density of the fringe provides a quick means of determining whether or not a woven fabric is balanced. The comparison of a balanced plain-woven fabric with two unbalanced plain-woven fabrics in Figure 26.2 is a case in point. When there is a distinct visual difference in the density of the fringe, the fabric is unbalanced. A count of the yarns is the more accurate method of determining whether or not the fabric is balanced.

Balanced fabrics are usually more durable than unbalanced ones. The yarns in a balanced fabric share the stresses placed on the fabric; hence the fabric wears more evenly. Unbalanced fabrics differ significantly in certain aspects of performance in warp and filling directions. For example, unbalanced fabrics have far greater shrinkage in the warp direction than in the filling direction. In a balanced fabric, the amount of shrinkage will differ between warp and filling directions, but the difference is smaller.

Width

Woven fabrics vary substantially in width. Hand-woven fabrics are usually 27–36 inches (69–91 centimeters) wide, a distance that represents the width through which a weaver can insert a filling yarn while sitting at the loom. Wool fabrics are traditionally 54–60 inches (137–152 centimeters) wide. Before the 1950s, cotton fabrics were limited by loom technology to a maximum width of 36 inches. Wider fabrics are more economical to cut and weave, however, so new technology was developed. Most cotton and cotton blend fabrics are now 45 inches (114 centimeters) wide. Silk and silk-like fabrics are also 40–45 inches (101–114 centimeters) wide. Some 156-inch (396-centimeter) fabrics are available.

Narrow fabrics are defined as fabrics up to 12 inches (30 centimeters) wide. These include ribbons, elastics, zipper tapes, venetian-blind tapes, couturiers' labels, hook and loop tapes such as Velcro® (a trademark of Velcro Incorporated), piping, carpet-edge tapes, trims, safety belts, and harnesses. Webbing is a particularly important group of narrow fabrics.[3]

Weight

Woven fabrics differ in weight. In the apparel trade, the terms _top weight_ and _bottom weight_ are frequently used. _Top-weight_ fabrics are those suitable for fabrication into shirts, blouses, and dresses. _Bottom-weight_ fabrics are those suitable for fabrication into pants, slacks, and skirts. Weight might also be conveyed as _very light_ (less than one ounce per yard^2), _light_ (2–3 ounces per yard^2), _medium_ (5–7 ounces per yard^2), _heavy_ (more than 7 ounces per yard^2), or _very heavy_.

When fabric weight is given in ounces per yard^2, the area of fabric is a constant, making it convenient to compare the weights of fabrics that differ in width. Fabric weight may also be given in ounces per linear yard. The comparison of the weight of fabrics with different widths therefore requires that weight/linear yard be converted to weight/yard^2.

The heavier a fabric is, the more load that is placed on the human body wearing or carrying it. In certain end uses, such as tents for backpacking, consideration of fabric weight is paramount. The weight of a fabric influences its body; usually, the greater the weight, the greater the body. Weight is not a determinant of thermal insulation: heavy fabrics are not necessarily warmer fabrics than lighter fabrics. Thermal insulation is determined primarily by the amount of dead air space incorporated into the fabric structure.

BASIC STRUCTURES

The simplest woven fabrics are plain, twill, and satin. Each structure contains one set of filling yarns and one set of warp yarns. The repeat pattern of these fabrics is determined with as few as two yarns and with rarely more than eight yarns. The surface can appear flat (featureless), as a series of crosswise ribs, as a series of diagonal ribs, or smooth and lustrous. For each structure, a weave diagram is provided together with a photograph

---

[3] Narrow fabrics may also have knit or braid structures.

of the face and back of a typical fabric. The fabric face is always on the left-hand side of the photograph and the fabric back on the right-hand side.

Plain-Woven Fabrics

In plain-woven fabrics "the odd warp yarns operate over one and under one filling yarn throughout the fabric with the even warp yarns reversing this order to under one, over one, throughout." All three weave diagrams in Figure 26.2 show the 1/1 pattern, or interlacing with a progression of one. Any two adjacent filling or warp yarns establish the pattern repeat.

The appearance of the face and back of plain-woven fabrics is always identical, due to weave interlacing. The face and back of each of the fabrics shown in Figure 26.2

FIGURE 26.2   Plain-woven fabrics.

Plain-woven fabrics are fabrics in which "the odd warp yarns operate over one and under one filling yarn throughout the fabric with the even warp yarns reversing this order to under one, over one, throughout."

BALANCED
Those plain-woven fabrics that contain the same number of warp and filling yarns per inch, with all the yarns about the same size.

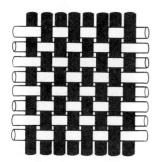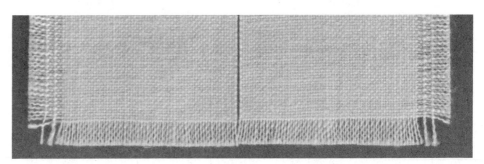

UNBALANCED (RIB)
Those plain-woven fabrics in which the ratio of the number of warp yarns to filling yarns is two or greater.

Regular
The size of warp and filling yarns is about the same.

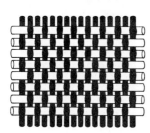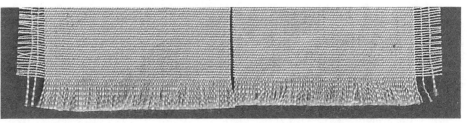

Prominent
The filling yarns are larger than the warp yarns.

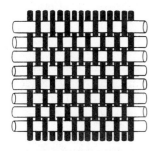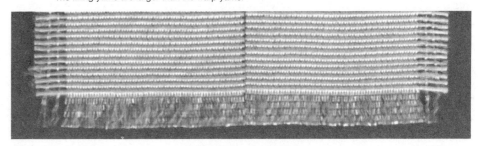

are therefore identical. Many of the plain-woven fabrics have a plain or flat surface, as shown in the top photograph in Figure 26.2. This surface serves well for printing designs, embossing, glazing, napping, and other surface finishes. Other plain-woven fabrics have crosswise ribs, as shown in the middle and bottom photographs in Figure 26.2. Color patterning of the warp and/or filling results in color-and-weave effects. Use of fancy and textured yarns as well as varying the twist and size of spun and filament yarns adds interest to the fabric.

More yardage of plain-woven fabric is available than all other types of woven fabric. Plain-woven fabrics can be found in almost any end use.

Performance. The high number of interlacings per square inch in plain-woven fabrics significantly influences their performance in comparison to the performance of twill and satin woven fabrics with identical types of yarns and fabric counts. Plain-woven fabrics wrinkle more, and the wrinkles are more visible, ravel less, have lower tearing strength, and are less absorbent.

Balanced Plain-Woven Fabrics. The largest group of plain-woven fabrics are balanced. In these fabrics, fabric count is essentially equal in the warp and filling directions, and the sizes of the yarns are approximately identical. When fringed on adjacent edges, the fringes appear to be about the same density. The fabric photographed in Figure 26.2, a typical sheeting fabric called percale, illustrates these features.

Balanced plain-woven fabrics vary in weight from very light to very heavy. They may be open or dense, depending on the fabric count, and they may contain any type of yarn. Yarns of different fiber compositions may be used in the warp direction than in the filling direction, resulting in mixture or union fabrics (Figure 24.8). When colored yarns comprise the fabric, checks and plaids may result. Fabrics are given specific names depending on weight, yarn structure, color-and-weave effect, and finishes. Names include batiste, buckram, calico, cambric, canvas, challis, chambray, cheesecloth, crash, crepe de chine, cretonne, crinoline, duck, flannel, gauze, georgette, gingham, lawn, muslin, organdy, percale, plissé, seersucker, sheeting, and voile.

Unbalanced Plain-Woven Fabrics. Unbalanced plain-woven fabrics, often called rib fabrics, are characterized by the presence of ribs (ridges) running crosswise on both the face and back of the fabric (Figure 26.2 middle and bottom). The ribs, equally prominent on face and

back, are due to the use of at least twice as many warp yarns as filling yarns interlacing in the over-one-and-under-one pattern of all plain-woven fabrics. A warp surface is created on both the face and back of the fabric. When the warp and filling yarns are different colors, the only color that shows is that of the warp yarns.

There are two types of these rib fabrics, regular and prominent. In *regular rib fabrics,* the warp and filling yarns are the same size, or nearly so, and are usually small; consequently, the crosswise ribs they form are almost indistinct. The photograph of broadcloth fabric in Figure 26.2 (middle) illustrates this characteristic. Note the difference in the density of the fringe at the two adjacent edges. *Prominent rib fabrics* are those unbalanced plain-woven fabrics in which the filling yarns are larger than the warp yarns. The greater the difference in the size of the warp and filling yarns, the larger and more prominent the ribs. The photograph of a fabric called faille in Figure 26.2 (bottom) illustrates a prominent rib fabric.

The prominence of the crosswise rib influences the ability of the unbalanced fabric to withstand abrasion. The larger the rib, the lower the abrasion resistance of the fabric because the yarn at the top of the ribs must absorb all of the abrasive force. In many rib fabrics, the warp yarns tend to be small. The warp yarns are damaged first, creating splits in the fabric. The filling yarns, covered by the warp, are protected from wear.

Slippage is a problem in unbalanced plain-woven fabrics made with filament yarns, especially in fabrics with low fabric counts. In garments, yarn slippage in the fabric occurs where abrasion and tension are greatest; for example, at seams and buttonholes. Unbalanced plain-woven fabrics with fine ribs are softer and more drapable than comparable balanced plain-woven fabrics. Those with large ribs have more body and less drape. Names of specific unbalanced plain-woven fabrics, given according to increasing prominence of the crosswise rib, are broadcloth, poplin, taffeta, faille, repp, grosgrain, bengaline, and ottoman.

Basket Fabrics. Basket fabrics are those in which two warp yarns interlace with one or more filling yarns (Figure 26.3). The most common basket fabrics have two warp yarns floating over two filling yarns, as shown in the diagram at the top of Figure 26.3, or four warp yarns floating over four filling yarns as shown in the fabric photographed at the top of Figure 26.3. *Half-basket fabrics* are those in which two warp yarns float over one filling yarn, as shown in the diagram and oxford cloth at the bottom of Figure 26.3.

FIGURE 26.3   Plain-weave variations.

Plain-weave variations include those fabrics in which two warp yarns interlace with one or more filling yarns.

BASKET FABRICS
Those plain-woven fabrics in which two or more yarns interlace "as one," usually in a 2/2 or 4/4 interlacing pattern.

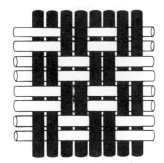

HALF-BASKET FABRICS
Those plain-woven fabrics in which two or more yarns interlace "as one," usually in a 2/1 or 3/1 interlacing pattern.

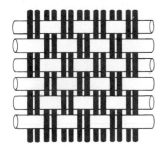
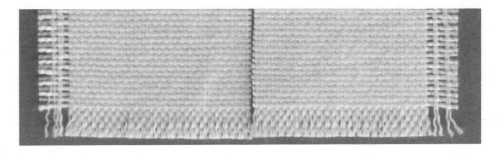

Although strictly speaking, basket fabrics and half-basket fabrics do not have an interlacing of over one yarn and under one yarn, they can be said to have this pattern if pairs of yarns are considered as one unit. The interlacing then progresses by one. Further, basket fabrics have the "flat" surface of plain-woven fabrics.

Basket fabrics have better wrinkle resistance than the balanced and unbalanced plain-woven fabrics because they have fewer interlacings per inch. For the same reason, they are more flexible. The floats, which are rather long because large spun yarns are widely used, cause basket fabrics to snag more easily and to be less durable than other plain-woven fabrics. The floats, however, do increase adsorbency. Due to the traditional low fabric counts, shrinkage is high.

In apparel, many basket fabrics are used for suits (hopsacking), sportswear (sailcloth), and shirts (oxford cloth and oxford chambray). Slipcovers for furniture, house awnings, and boat covers are often basket fabrics

that are sold under the names canvas and duck. Monk's cloth is also used in home furnishings.

Twill Fabrics

Twill fabrics are fabrics in which the "weave repeats on three or more warp and filling yarns and diagonal lines are produced on the face of the fabric." Therefore, the interlacing pattern is over more than one yarn and then under one or more yarns. The progression of interlacing is by one, thereby producing the diagonal line (Figure 26.4).

All twill fabrics have a series of diagonal lines, or twill lines, on at least one side of the fabric due to the interlacing of the yarns. When the twill lines appear more prominently on one side, that side is the face. When the lines are equally prominent, a convention related to the direction of twill line is used to establish the face side. The diagonal lines on the face of twill fabrics may run

FIGURE 26.4 Twill fabrics.

Twill fabrics are fabrics in which the "weave repeats on three or more warp and filling yarns and diagonal lines are produced on the face of the fabric."

WARP-FACED

Those twill fabrics in which the warp yarns pass over more filling yarns than they pass under, creating interlacing patterns of, for example, 2/1, 3/1, or 3/2.

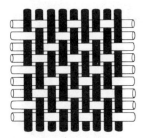

Right-handed

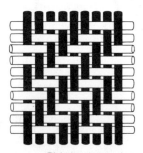

Left-handed

EVEN-SIDED

Those twill fabrics in which the warp yarns pass over the same number of filling yarns as they pass under, creating interlacing patterns of, for example, 2/2, 3/3, or 4/4.

Right-handed

Left-handed

from the lower left corner of the fabric to the upper right corner, creating *a right-handed twill*, or from the lower right corner to the upper left corner, creating *a left-handed twill*. The diagrams in Figure 26.4 show two left-handed twill fabrics and two right-handed twill fabrics. Both photographed fabrics have left-handed twill lines. The direction of the diagonal lines has no relation to the quality of a twill fabric. However, by tradition, cotton and cotton-like twill fabrics are left-handed and wool and wool-like twill fabrics are right-handed.

Twill fabrics do not have an up or a down (top or bottom) direction. This can be confirmed by noting the direction in which the diagonal line runs in the diagrams and fabrics shown in Figure 26.4 and then rotating the book until the text is upside down. The direction of the twill line in each diagram and fabric remains in the same direction. The twill line may lie at different angles. Twill lines near a 45° angle are called *regular;* those about 15° to 27° are *reclining;* and those from 63° to 75° are *steep*. The angle of the twill line in both photographed fabrics is close to 45°.

Twill fabrics are seldom printed due to their ridged surface. One exception is a fabric called surah.

End Uses. Twill fabrics are used in apparel for which a long wear life is important and for which the fabric will receive significant hard wear. Twill fabrics are used extensively in suits, sportswear, outdoor clothing, jackets and raincoats, work clothing, scarves, and neckties.

Performance. Twill fabrics are noted for their durability. Twill fabrics may have higher strength than is possible in comparable plain-woven fabrics because the use of fewer interlacings per inch in twill weaves allows higher fabric counts. Twill fabrics with steep twill lines tend to be considerably stronger than those with reclining twill lines. Twill fabrics with a regular line are intermediate in strength compared to steep and reclining twills. Fabrics with steeper twill lines are more unbalanced in construction (they have a higher proportion of warp yarns than filling yarns per inch) than those with regular or reclining twill lines.

Greater packing of the yarns (fewer interlacings) leads to increased wind resistance (lower air permeability) but reduced wrinkle resistance. When the packing of the yarns becomes too high, breaking and tearing strength are reduced.

Twill fabrics are more likely to develop shine or unwanted luster at points where abrasion is greatest. Abrasion flattens the diagonal ridge, causing light reflection to increase. The more prominent the twill line, the more

likely luster will develop. Twill fabrics are usually softer than comparable plain-woven fabrics due to the lower number of interlacing per square inch. Twill fabrics have greater wrinkle resistance than balanced plain-woven fabric. Durability must be sacrificed to achieve wrinkle resistance equal to that of rib (unbalanced plain-woven) or basket fabrics. Soil is less noticeable on twill fabrics than on plain-woven or satin fabrics because the surface is not smooth.

Twill fabrics have torque due to the "directionality" of the structure. Torque is a force or combination of forces that produces or tends to produce a twisting or rotating motion. This directionality can lead to problems in fabricated garments because seams may twist when the garment is washed, that is, as it relaxes.

Warp-Faced Twill Fabrics. *Warp-faced twills* are those twill fabrics in which the warp yarn lies predominately on the face of the fabric. Note in the warp-faced twill diagram in Figure 26.4 that the amount of black (warp) yarns visible is greater than the amount of white (filling) yarns. The warp yarns must always float over more filling yarns than they pass under, creating an uneven interlacing pattern of, for example, 2/1, 3/1, or 3/2. The diagram and fabric pictured contain a 2/1 pattern. The diagonal lines in warp-faced twill fabrics are always more prominent on the face than on the back of the fabrics, as can be observed in the photographed fabric. Sometimes, the diagonal lines cannot be seen on the fabric back. Names of specific warp-faced twill fabrics are calvary twill, covert cloth, denim, drill, dungaree, gabardine (photographed), jean, and whipcord.

Even-Sided Twill Fabrics. *Even-sided (regular) twills* are those twill fabrics in which the warp yarn floats over the same number of filling yarns that it floats under. In the lower diagram in Figure 26.4, the amounts of warp (black) and filling (white) yarns showing on the surface are about equal or even. The diagonal line in even-sided twills appears equally prominent on both sides of the fabric, as shown in the photographed fabric. The direction of the twill line, however, reverses. In the photographed fabric, it is left-handed on the face and right-handed on the back. Names of even-sided twill fabrics are foulard, herringbone, houndstooth, melton, and serge (photographed).

Satin Fabrics

Satin fabrics are fabrics "in which the binding [interlacing] places are arranged with a view to producing a

FIGURE 26.5 Satin fabrics.

Satin fabrics are fabrics "in which the binding [interlacing] places are arranged with a view to producing a smooth fabric surface, free from twill."

WARP-FACED

Those satin fabrics in which the warp yarns lie predominately on the fabric face.

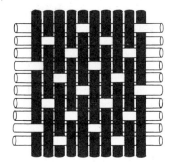
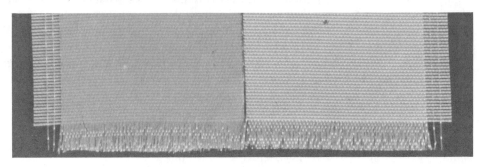

FILLING-FACED

Those satin fabrics in which the filling yarns lie predominately on the fabric face.

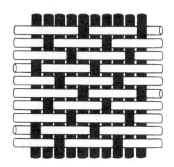
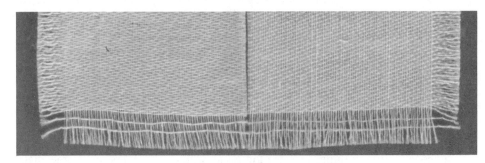

smooth fabric surface, free from twill." Either a warp or a filling yarn floats over 4 to 12 yarns before it passes to the back of the fabric and floats under one or two yarns in order for the smooth surface to result (Figure 26.5). The progression of interlacing must be greater than one so that the surface is free of the twill line. In satin fabrics, the interlacing points also tend to be covered by the floats of neighboring yarns, thus contributing to the formation of a smooth fabric surface. The face of a satin fabric is more lustrous and smoother than the back.

In comparison with plain-woven and twill fabrics, satin fabrics have fewer interlacings per square inch. Very high fabric counts are possible in satin fabrics because more yarns can be packed together. Satin fabrics are usually unbalanced, as can be seen by comparing the density of the fringe at adjacent edges of the two photographed fabrics in Figure 26.5.

Satin fabrics are lustrous on their face side. Those made with filament yarns are highly lustrous; those made with spun yarns are not so lustrous, but a higher sheen is achieved in the satin interlacing than in plain-woven or twill interlacings using the same yarns.

Performance. Satin fabrics are noted for their aesthetics. They are the most lustrous of the basic fabrics and are noted for their full body and beautiful drape. Some satin fabrics have such high fabric counts that they have exceptional wind resistance.

Satin fabrics are not noted for their durability, even though the interlacing pattern allows many yarns to be packed into each inch of fabric. Usually, very fine filament yarns are found in satin fabrics. In some cases, fine, low-twist spun yarns are used. The combination of fine yarns and long floats that are subject to damage by abrasion and snagging compromise the durability that might be achieved by the high fabric count.

Satin fabrics should be pressed on the back side, and the movement of the iron should be in the direction of the floats. Soil resistance is lower than in the other basic fabrics.

Warp-Faced Satin Fabrics. In *warp-faced satins,* the warp yarns lie predominantly on the face, as shown by the amount of black (warp) yarns lying on the surface of the upper weave diagram in Figure 26.5. Filament yarns are usually used in both warp and filling directions. Names of fabrics that have a warp-faced satin structure often include the word *satin,* as in slipper satin and bridal satin. Other fabric names are peau de soie and doeskin.

Satin fabrics are luxurious, formal fabrics. They are most frequently used in evening apparel, bridal wear, and as upholstery fabrics for elegant settings. Satin fabrics designed for windproofness are found in windbreaker jackets and coats. Satin is a suitable structure for linings because its smooth surface permits the garment to be slipped on and off with ease and has sufficient durability. It is more flexible than taffeta (an unbalanced plain-woven fabric with filament yarns); therefore, it does not split as readily at the hem and sleeve edges. More draperies are made of antique satin than any other fabric.

Filling-Faced Satin Fabrics. In *filling-faced satins* (sateens), it is the filling yarns that float on the fabric face, as shown in the lower weave diagram in Figure 26.5 and in the photographed fabric. Such fabrics are usually made from spun yarns and called sateen. Sometimes the weave is called sateen weave.

Sateens are used for draperies, drapery linings, and dress fabrics. Warp sateens are used where durability is important. Sateen fabrics are often used in slacks, shirts, pillow and bed tickings, draperies, and upholstery.

COMPLEX STRUCTURES

Complex structures are those woven fabrics in which texture or a design is woven in and/or those with more than two sets of yarns. The fabrics listed in the left-hand column of Detail View 26 represent an increasing complexity of texture and woven-in design (leno, crepe woven, dobby, Jacquard), and those listed in the right-hand column represent an increase in the number of sets of yarns used (piqué, surface-figure, pile woven, and double-woven). Weave diagrams are provided of each of the fabrics in this section. A photograph of the face and back of at least one typical fabric accompanies each weave diagram. The fabric face is always on the left-hand side and the fabric back on the right-hand side of the photograph. The diagram and fabric photographed do not always strictly correspond.

Leno Fabrics

Leno fabrics are fabrics in which "warp yarns have been made to cross one another, between fillings, during leno weaving." The crossing of the warp yarns may be the sole feature of leno fabrics, as shown in Figure 26.6, or may be used in combination with other weaves. At first glance, it appears that the yarns are twisted fully about each other, but that is not the case. One yarn of the pair is always above the other.

Leno fabrics are characterized by an open structure. They may be light and translucent or heavy and opaque,

FIGURE 26.6 Leno fabrics.

Leno fabrics are fabrics in which "warp yarns have been made to cross one another, between fillings, during leno weaving."

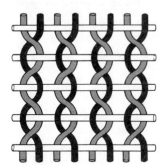
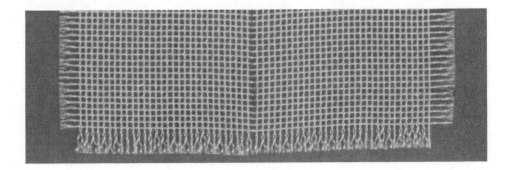

depending on the yarns. All pairs of warp yarns in the fabric may be crossed over each other, or other weaves may be combined with the leno weave.

A leno fabric called marquisette is used extensively for sheer curtains. Another leno fabric, mosquito netting, forms windows in tents or may be draped over a bed to provide protection from insects. It is also used to cover the faces of beekeepers. Other leno fabrics are used for laundry, fruit, and vegetable sacks. Some thermal blankets are made from leno fabrics.

Leno fabrics may be preferable to plain-woven fabrics having the same fabric count. Slippage of filling yarns, a common occurrence in plain-woven fabrics, is eliminated with the crossing over of the warp yarns in leno fabrics. Further, fabric distortion is considerably reduced because the crossed warp yarns provide additional strength. Leno fabrics are, however, subject to snagging in use.

Crepe Woven Fabrics

Crepe woven fabrics "have a random distribution of floats so as to produce an 'all-over' effect in the fabric to disguise the repeat" (Figure 26.7). A crinkly, pebbly, or sandy surface characterizes these fabrics. Crepe woven fabrics, however, are not unique in having a crinkly surface. Plain-woven fabrics containing high-twist yarns or textured yarns also have crinkly surfaces. Some fabrics are embossed to produce a crepe-surface appearance. All fabrics with this surface character are called crepe fabrics.

An advantage of crepe woven fabrics compared to other crepe fabrics is that the crinkle is permanent and does not flatten in use. Further, they tend to bag less (maintain their shape better) in use than most other crepe fabrics. They have the ability to hide wrinkles, as do other crepe fabrics, because the irregular surface hides unwanted bends and folds. Whether woven or otherwise constructed, crepe fabrics that contain crepe (high-twist) yarns are the most wrinkle-free fabrics in this category. Crepe woven fabrics are usually less drapable than crepe fabrics containing crepe yarns. Crepe woven fabrics are used in dress and blouse fabrics and for institutional table linens.

Dobby Fabrics

Dobby fabrics are fabrics with a small woven-in design (Figure 26.8). Geometric motifs are characteristic of dobby fabrics, although small floral motifs are also made. The number of filling yarns in one pattern repeat is greater than that required for any of the basic weaves but less than that of the Jacquard fabrics (to be discussed next). Usually, the maximum number of filling yarns in a repeat is 25. Two sets of yarns are used, one set of warp and one set of filling.

In dobby fabrics in which all the yarns are the same color, the design is visible due to the differences in the reflection of light off the weave in various areas of the fabric. The fabric shown in Figure 26.8, a birdseye, is white.

Yarn-dyed yarns, discussed in Chapter 34, are also used in dobby fabrics to extend the range of fabrics available. The color enhances the prominence of the design.

FIGURE 26.7 Crepe woven fabrics.

Crepe woven fabrics "have a random distribution of floats so as to produce an 'all-over' effect in the fabric to disguise the repeat."

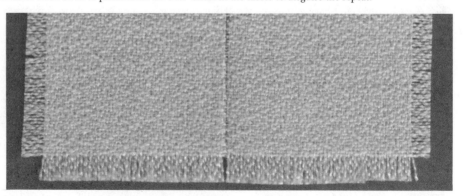

FIGURE 26.8 Dobby fabrics.

Dobby fabrics are fabrics with a small woven-in design.

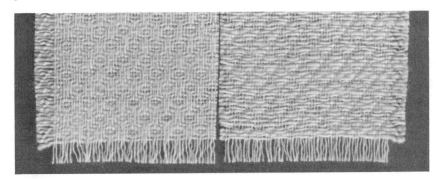

Jacquard Fabrics

Jacquard fabrics are fabrics with intricate, detailed, woven-in motifs. Patterns depicting paintings of photographs are possible. The designs involve at least two of the basic weaves in various arrangements.

The Jacquard fabric shown in Figure 26.9 is a white fabric; the design appears because light is reflected differently from various areas of the fabric surface. Yarn-dyed yarns are often used in Jacquard fabrics, extending the range of fabrics available. Jacquard weaving is also combined with pile weaving and double-fabric weaving.

Jacquard fabrics are noted for their beautiful design motifs and colors. Any fabric, from the most fragile (silk brocades) to the most rugged (tapestries), may have the Jacquard structure. Fiber composition and yarn structure play a more dominant role than structure in determining the performance of these fabrics. The length of the floats on the face of Jacquard fabrics is important in those end uses where the fabric will be subjected to abrasion. Jacquard fabrics are expensive compared to basic woven fabrics and the complex structures considered thus far.

FIGURE 26.9 Jacquard fabrics.

Jacquard fabrics are fabrics with intricate, detailed, woven-in motifs.

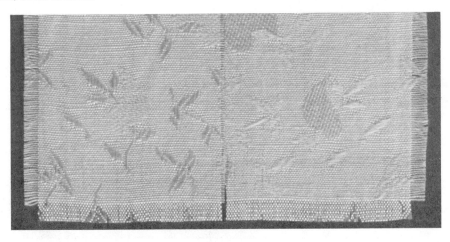

Piqué Fabrics

In French, the word *piqué* means quilted. *Piqué fabrics* share the characteristic of a soft, raised-surface effect with fabrics that are called quilted (Chapter 29). Technically, piqué fabrics "show rounded cords [wales or ribs] in the filling direction, with pronounced sunken lines between them that are produced by the nature of the weave." The weave on the face of the cords is often plain-woven. Warp floats that are the width of the cords appear on the fabric back. Stuffer yarns, additional warp or filling used in a fabric for the purpose of increasing its weight, bulk, firmness, or the prominence of the design, are part of the structure. These yarns are visible on the fabric back. Stuffer yarns may be easily removed because they are not interlaced into the main structure of the fabric.

Figure 26.10 shows a typical piqué fabric. The wales on the fabric face are crosswise, the stuffer yarns—seen on the back—traverse crosswise, but the floats, which are warp yarns, are vertical. Some piqué fabrics have wales that are lengthwise. In these fabrics, the stuffer yarns run lengthwise and the floats, which are filling yarns, run crosswise. Piqué fabrics thus vary by the direction of the wales and also the width of the wales. Usually, wales vary in width from 0.05–0.25 inches. Most piqués are white or a solid color. Piqué fabrics called birdseye piqué (photographed), bullseye piqué, and pinwale piqué are used for apparel and interior furnishing fabrics. Bedford cord, which is heavier, is used for bedspreads, upholstery, pants, and uniforms.

Piqué fabrics are more resistant to wrinkling, have more body, but have less drapability than flat-surfaced fabrics. Body increases and drape decreases as the wale and stuffer yarns become larger. Durability and aesthetics are linked to the longevity of the floats on the back of the fabric. When these are broken, the wales flatten in the area of the breakage. The fabric is resistant to tearing across the stuffer yarns. Tearing is more likely to occur in the direction of the wales because the weakest part of piqué is between the wales. The larger and more rounded the wale, the lower the abrasion resistance of the fabric. As with other uneven-surfaced fabrics, the tops of the ridges must withstand the total abrasive force.

The presence and absence of stuffer yarns is one criteria by which the quality of piqué fabrics is judged. It is generally accepted that the better-quality piqués have stuffer yarns and that each stuffer yarn is one large spun yarn rather than numerous small yarns laid next to each other. Better-quality piqués are made with long-staple, combed, mercerized yarns (Chapters 22 and 32). Carded-yarn piqués usually lack stuffer yarns and are printed.

It is advisable to iron piqué fabrics on the back. Ironing on the face tends to flatten the wales and thus diminish the beauty of the fabric.

Surface-Figure Fabrics

Surface-figure fabrics are characterized by design motifs formed with yarns other than those used in the base of the fabric (Figure 26.11). The figuring yarns may be the

---

FIGURE 26.10 Piqué fabrics.

Piqué fabrics "show rounded cords [wales or ribs] in the filling direction, with pronounced sunken lines between them that are produced by the nature of the weave."

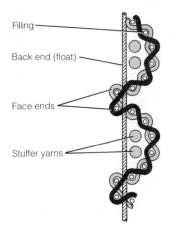
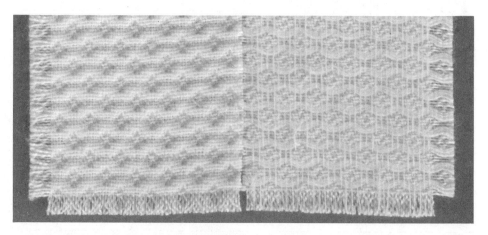

Filling

Back end (float)

Face ends

Stuffer yarns

FIGURE 26.11 Surface-figure fabrics.

Surface-figure fabrics are characterized by design motifs formed with yarns other than those used in the base of the fabric.

LAPPET FABRICS

Those surface-figure fabrics "in which figure is achieved by introducing extra warp yarns into a base fabric that is normally plain [-woven]."

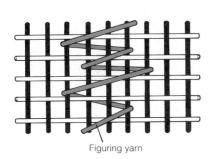

Figuring yarn

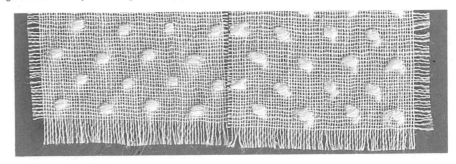

SWIVEL FABRICS

Those surface-figure fabrics "in which a figure is achieved by the introduction of additional filling yarns into a base fabric to produce spot effects."

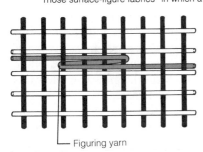

Figuring yarn

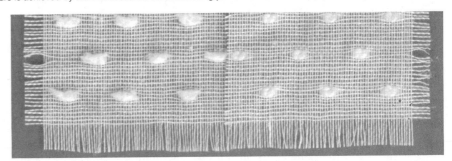

SPOT FABRICS

Those surface-figure fabrics in which a motif formed by figuring yarns repeats across the entire width or down the entire length of the fabric.

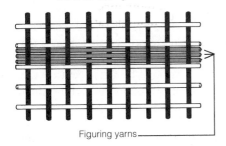

Figuring yarns

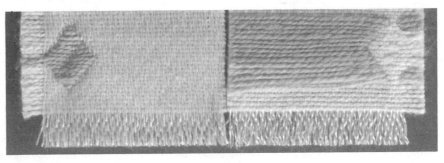

same structure as those in the base fabric but of a different color, or they may differ in size and/or structure. The design motif is usually small and the weave of the base fabric is often plain-woven. Almost without exception, the figuring yarns can be removed without affecting the integrity of the base fabric. This group of fabrics is also called extra-yarn (or figure) fabrics. The three main types of surface-figure fabrics are lappet, swivel, and spot or dot.

Lappet Fabrics. Lappet fabrics are fabrics "in which figure is achieved by introducing extra warp yarns into a base fabric that is normally plain[-woven]." In the dotted swiss fabric photographed in Figure 26.11, the pattern of the figuring yarn can be seen most clearly on the back of the fabric. On more complex lappet fabrics, the design motif appears as if it were hand-embroidered. The design motifs, if close together, are connected by a float on the back of the fabric. When the design motifs are widely spaced, the float is usually cut. The complexity of the design, however, is limited.

The design motifs on lappet fabrics is considered to be comparatively long-lasting. The design motifs usually remain in place longer if floats are left on the back of the fabric than if they are not. However, long floats are more subject to breakage during use. Lappet fabrics are comparatively expensive.

The complexity of the design motif determines whether a dobby or Jacquard loom is required. In all cases, a special rack is added to the loom. Lappet fabrics are not currently produced in the United States; rather, they are imported, primarily from European countries.

Swivel Fabrics. Swivel fabrics are fabrics "in which a figure is achieved by the introduction of additional filling yarns into a base fabric to produce spot effects." Decorative dots, circles, or squares formed by the figuring yarns are prominently raised above the base fabric. The figuring yarn is wound around a group of warp yarns. It is, therefore, fastened securely and usually cannot be removed without damaging the base fabric. Swivel fabrics may have different colored yarns in the same horizontal row. The color will, however, be the same in each vertical row on the fabric. Additionally, swivel fabrics can be recognized by the fact that the figuring yarn creates the same effect on both the face and back of the fabric.

Few, if any, swivel-figure fabrics are currently made in the United States. Limited amounts are imported. Some dotted swiss is a swivel fabric, as shown in the middle photograph in Figure 26.11.

Spot or Dot Fabrics. Spot or *dot fabrics* have a design motif that repeats across the entire width or down the entire length of the fabric. Warp or filling figuring yarns interlace with the warp or filling yarns that form the base fabric. Motifs appear where the figuring yarn lies on the fabric face. Floats appear on the fabric back between the motifs. A wide range of motifs are possible. The color incorporated into the design motif remains the same across a row if extra filling interlaces, as is the case in the fabric photographed in Figure 26.11. The color in the design motif will be the same in any column of figures when additional warp forms the design motif. Some fabrics may be reversible.

Unclipped spot fabrics are those in which the floats of the figuring yarns still traverse the entire length or width of the fabric on the back of the fabric. *Clipped* spot fabrics are those in which the floats of the figuring yarn have been cut. Such cutting is usually done when the de-

sign motifs are small and widely spaced. A short fringe of figuring yarn is usually left.

The longevity of the design motif depends on the compactness of the base fabric and the smoothness of the yarns forming the base fabric and the design motif. Spots in compact weaves are quite stable; those in loose weaves pull out of the fabric rather easily. The strength of the fabric depends solely on the base weave; it is independent of the clipped or unclipped spot design. There are many different clip spot patterns. One fabric is called eyelash.

Pile Woven Fabrics

Pile woven fabrics have yarns that stand vertically from a woven ground, resulting in fabrics approximately $\frac{1}{4}$ to $\frac{1}{2}$ inches thick, with looped or tufted surfaces (Figure 26.12).[4] One set of filling and one set of warp yarns—referred to as the ground filling yarns and ground warp yarns, respectively—comprise the ground, or base structure. Another set of yarns—referred to as pile filling yarns or pile warp yarns—form the pile. The pile yarns are interlaced into the ground or base.

The face of pile fabrics is that side where the yarns stand vertically. Pile fabrics have an up and a down direction because most are brushed during finishing, resulting in pile loops or tufts slanting toward one of the fabric ends. Consequently, pile fabrics appear darker in shade when viewed into the pile and lighter when viewed the other direction. The direction of the pile can be determined by running one's hand up and down the fabric in the lengthwise direction. The smoothest direction is that in which the pile lays down. Care must be taken during fabrication of products from pile fabrics to ensure that all the pile lies in the same direction in the final product.

In apparel, pile woven fabrics are found in coats, jackets, gloves, and boots. They may be the outer fabric, lining, and/or interlining. Many upholstery fabrics and some bedspreads are pile woven fabrics. Terry towels are almost exclusively pile woven fabrics. About 5% of carpets are pile woven fabrics.

Performance. Pile fabrics provide exceptional thermal retention due to the incorporation of dead air spaces within their structure, excellent absorbency/adsorbency

---

[4]Other types of pile fabrics are certain knits (for example, sliver pile knits and tricot variations discussed in Chapter 27), and Schusspol, Liropol, tufted, and fusion bonded carpets discussed in Chapter 29. Pile fabrics should not be confused with napped or sanded and sueded fabrics, that is, those with raised fiber surfaces (Unit V).

FIGURE 26.12 Pile woven fabrics.

Pile woven fabrics have yarns that stand vertically from a woven ground, resulting in fabrics approximately $\frac{1}{4}$ to $\frac{1}{2}$ inches thick, with looped or tufted surfaces.

FILLING-PILE FABRICS

Those pile woven fabrics in which tufts float over warp yarns prior to being cut and, consequently, are wrapped around warp yarns in the finished fabric.

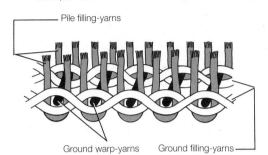

Pile filling-yarns

Ground warp-yarns   Ground filling-yarns

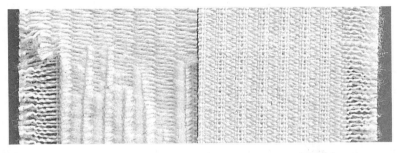

WARP-PILE FABRICS

Those pile woven fabrics in which loops or tufts lie between two ground warp yarns (they wrap around filling yarns).

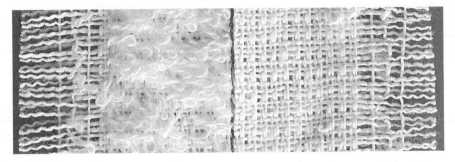

due to the increased amount of surface area available for liquids, and enjoyment of use due to their unique aesthetics.

Evaluating the performance of pile woven fabrics involves an assessment of both the pile and the ground. The pile receives surface abrasion and compressional or crushing forces. A dense pile will stand erect, resist crushing (have good compressional resiliency), and provide cover. A pile surface formed with a "W" rather than a "V" interlacing configuration is less likely to be pulled out of the fabric during use. A denser pile is possible with the "W" interlacing. "W" interlacing yields higher durability. Usually, uncut-pile woven fabrics retain height better than cut-pile woven fabrics. When fibers lack resilience, they are made into ply yarns that are used in an uncut-loop fabric. When insulative ability is a primary consideration, pile height becomes important. In such a case, the higher the pile, the greater the insulative effect, provided that other structural features are comparable.

The ground structure receives pulling stresses; it provides the strength. The tightness of the ground weave is important in holding the pile yarns. A tight weave prevents looped pile yarns from being pulled out if snagged and prevents cut pile from shedding and pulling out. The ground is usually a plain-woven or twill interlacing pattern. Higher counts, and therefore denser pile, are possible with a twill ground.

Pile woven apparel fabrics can be either washed or drycleaned. Care procedures that keep the pile erect should be used. Cut pile usually looks better when drycleaned. Pile woven fabrics are softer and less wrinkled when tumble dried rather than line dried. Pressing should be done with a minimum of pressure, in the direction of the pile, and on the back of the fabric. Special needle boards are available for pressing velvets and velveteens at home. A terry towel may be placed under the fabric instead of a needle board, but the result is not as satisfactory.

Pile woven upholstery fabrics are best cleaned by an

experienced upholstery cleaner. Although a considerable number of consumers believe that zippers are used in cushions so that the covers can be removed and laundered, in fact, laundering could be disastrous. Zippers are actually used to facilitate the construction of the cushion covers.

Filling-Pile Woven Fabrics. Filling-pile woven fabrics are fabrics in which a set of filling yarns form the pile surface; that is, the yarn that stands vertical is a filling yarn. Filling-pile woven fabrics are always cut-pile fabrics, with the pile height limited to $\frac{1}{8}$ inch. These features can be observed in the weave diagram and the photographed fabric at the top of Figure 26.12.

Filling-pile woven fabrics are made by cutting floats of yarn, which are created by floating some of the filling yarns. The lower portion of the _corduroy fabric_ photographed shows the fabric's appearance before the floats were cut; the upper portion shows the fabric after the floats were cut. Three yarns have been pulled into the fringe of the fabric; the lower two float over four warp yarns (they will become the pile), and the upper one interlaces frequently with the warp (it is a ground filling yarn). In corduroy fabric, the floats are arranged in columns. When they are cut, a lengthwise wale appears. If a warp yarn were pulled over into the fringe at the left edge of this fabric, it would look like a caterpillar because tufts of yarn would be observed wrapping around it, a condition that is characteristic of filling-pile woven fabrics.

Warp-Pile Woven Fabrics. Warp-pile woven fabrics are formed with an extra set of warp yarns; pile warp yarns are used. The pile may be cut or uncut. The photograph of single-sided *terry cloth* in Figure 26.12 illustrates the yarn systems in warp-pile woven fabrics. Three warp yarns are pulled over into the left-hand fringe to demonstrate that the loops are formed from pile warp yarns. The middle yarn of the group is one of a set of pile warp yarns. The other two are ground warp yarns. Note that the warp pile yarn interlaces with (wraps around) filling yarns. Warp-pile woven fabrics with cut loops are identified by the fact that the tufts of yarn forming the pile are wrapped around filling yarns. A filling yarn that is removed from warp-pile woven fabrics looks like a caterpillar.

Terry cloth, used for bath towels, beach robes, and sportswear, is usually characterized by long uncut loops. The loops may form one or both sides of the fabric. The loops may be cut to form a velour terry, but this fabric has decreased adsorbency because the amount of surface area is greatly reduced. In towels, therefore, only one side of the fabric has cut loops.

Velvet, velour, plush, and fur-like fabrics—other types of warp-pile woven fabrics—all have a cut, deep pile. Structurally, they are identical except that the depth of the pile varies. They are manufactured by a double-cloth or over-the-wire method. Frieze, an upholstery fabric, is a low-loop warp-pile woven fabric.

Woven carpets are either Axminster, Wilton, or velvet constructions (Figure 26.13). Prior to the mid-1960s, these three carpet structures dominated the market. Now about 5% of carpets are woven and 95% are tufted (Chapter 29). Axminster carpets are characterized by a heavy ribbed back and an even, cut pile that normally

FIGURE 26.13   Woven carpet constructions.

AXMINSTER CARPET
A machine-woven carpet in which successive weft-wise rows of pile are inserted during weaving according to a predetermined arrangement of colors.

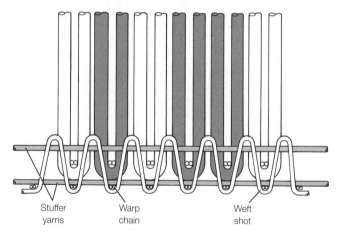

Stuffer yarns   Warp chain   Weft shot

WILTON CARPET
A machine-woven carpet in which the pile yarns run continuously into the carpet and are raised above the surface of the backing to form a pile.

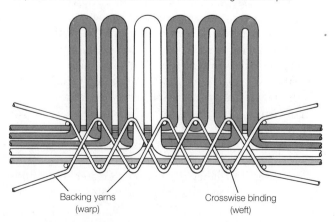

Backing yarns (warp)   Crosswise binding (weft)

FIGURE 26.13 (continued)

VELVET CARPET

A machine-woven carpet in which the pile yarns lie predominately above the surface of the backing.

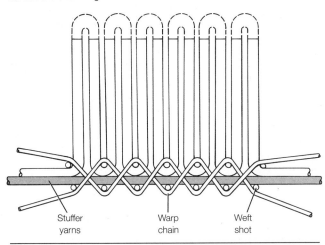

Stuffer
yarns

Warp
chain

Weft
shot

contains a pattern of many colors. Wilton carpets can be either cut or loop pile. Wilton patterns are limited to five colors. All of the colors contained in a pattern are carried along the base of the carpet; they are drawn to the surface only when the color is to be used in the design. This structure adds strength and resilience to the carpet. Velvet-woven carpets are usually a solid color in either a plush (even-surface cut-pile) or low-loop style. Combinations of loop and cut pile are possible, as well as combinations of high and low loops within a carpet.

Double-Woven Fabrics

Double-woven fabrics are "layered fabrics in which the separate layers or plies, each with its own warp and filling, are produced simultaneously and stitched together in one weaving process" (Figure 26.14). Double-woven fabrics may look the same on the face and back but often the face and the back are distinctly different in appearance. Double-woven fabrics may be reversible, or one layer may serve primarily as a supporting layer (back layer) for a face layer.

Double-woven fabrics tend to be heavier and have more body than single-layer fabrics. They are more flexible than single-layer fabrics of equal thickness. Beautiful effects that cannot be achieved in other fabrics are possible. All double-woven fabrics have more than two sets of yarns. The number of sets determines the specific type. The names are very similar: double-faced, double-weave or pocket, and double-cloth fabrics.

Double-faced fabrics have three sets of yarns, two warp and one filling or two filling and one warp. Blankets, satin ribbons, interlinings, and silence cloth may be double-faced. Blankets with one color on one side and another color on the other side usually have a double-

FIGURE 26.14 **Double-woven fabrics.**

Double-woven fabrics are "layered fabrics in which the separate layers or plies, each with its own warp and filling, are produced simultaneously and stitched together in one weaving process."

DOUBLE-FACED FABRICS

Those double-woven fabrics that are composed of three yarn sets, two filling sets and one warp set.

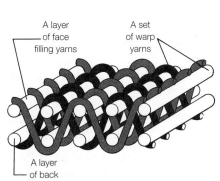

A layer
of face
filling yarns

A set
of warp
yarns

A layer
of back
filling yarns

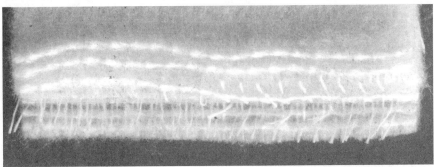

FIGURE 26.14 (continued)

DOUBLE-WEAVE OR POCKET FABRICS
Those double-woven fabrics that are composed of four yarn sets, two warp sets and two filling sets.

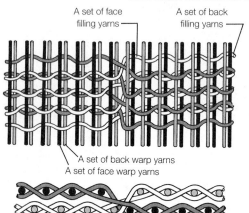
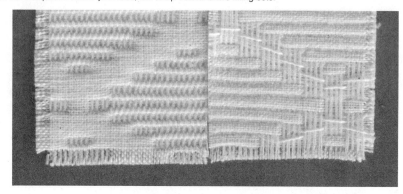

A set of face filling yarns

A set of back filling yarns

A set of back warp yarns
A set of face warp yarns

DOUBLE-CLOTH FABRICS
Those double-woven fabrics that are composed of five sets of yarn: two warp sets, two filling sets, and one set binding the two layers.

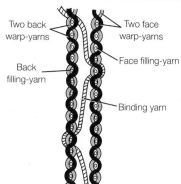
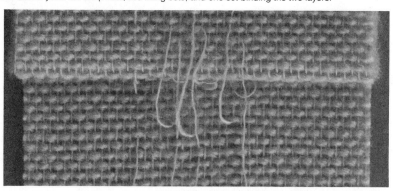

Two back warp-yarns

Two face warp-yarns

Face filling-yarn

Back filling-yarn

Binding yarn

faced structure containing one set of warp yarns and two sets of different colored filling yarns. The filling yarns are large with low twist; the warp yarns are small spun yarns with medium twist for strength. Satin ribbons, used in designer lingerie and evening wear, may be double-faced. They are lustrous on both sides. (Remember that satin fabrics are lustrous on one side only.) Two sets of warp yarns and one set of filling yarns are used.

Double-weave fabrics are composed of four sets of yarns, two warp sets and two filling sets. They have two layers that periodically reverse themselves from top to bottom. "Pockets" are found throughout these fabrics, so they are sometimes called pocket fabrics. They may or may not be reversible.

Double-cloth fabrics are composed of five sets of yarns: two warp sets, two filling sets, and one set that joins the two layers by interlacing between them. The two layers are "separable" when the yarns connecting the layers are cut. The two layers may be identical, but it is more usual for the two sides to be different. Most double-cloth fabrics are reversible. Double cloth is more pliable than the same weight of single-layer fabric because finer yarns can be used. Double cloth provides more insulation than a single layer of the same thickness due to the incorporation of an air layer at its center. Designers use double cloth for coats and capes. Double cloth is also used for military uniforms. It is an expensive fabric.

WEAVING TECHNOLOGY

Seven thousand years ago, weaving was already established as a domestic enterprise. At that time and until the early Middle Ages, it was a slow and tedious task accomplished by hand. Yet, the weaving process was considerably faster than the process of making yarn. For example, 3 days of labor were needed to weave 10 yards of the finest muslin fabric, whereas two months of toil spinning superfine cotton preceded the weaving operation.

The mechanization of the hand loom in the 18th century and subsequent improvements to it have increased production rates, so that today a yard of fine fabric can be produced in a matter of minutes. Still, even though production rates have increased dramatically, the basic technological principles of weaving have not been significantly altered.

Weaving Principles

A basic loom consists of a *warp beam*, a *cloth beam*, *heddles*, at least two *harnesses*, a *reed*, and a *shuttle* (Figure 26.15). The purpose of the warp and cloth beams is to hold the warp yarns tautly during the weaving operation. The warp beam serves as the supply of warp yarns and the cloth beam as storage for the fabric as it is formed. The heddle and harness arrangement provides a means to separate the warp yarns into a configuration called a shed. To accomplish this, each warp yarn passes through a hole in the wire heddle and the heddles are held in a harness frame. The harnesses are capable of moving up, and as they do so, they raise those warp yarns passing through the heddles. The reed, a set of flat wires in a frame, moves forward and backward and pushes an inserted filling yarn to the edge of previously formed fabric. The shuttle carries the filling yarn contained on its bobbin (technically a pirn) across the warp yarns through the shed.

The motions of weaving are: (a) *shedding,* the raising of one or more harnesses to separate the warp yarns to form a shed; (b) *picking,* the passing of a filling yarn through the shed; (c) *beating up,* pushing a filling yarn into place with the reed; and (d) *letting off* and *taking up,* unwinding additional warp yarns from the warp beam and winding finished fabric onto the cloth beam. These four motions are synchronized and are repeated over and over to weave a fabric.

Prior to weaving, a warp beam is prepared. Packages of warp yarn, each containing thousands of yards of yarn, are mounted on a creel (a frame) and carefully wound onto an initial warp beam. The warp yarns on the beam must lie side by side without entanglement. These warp yarns usually need to be strengthened temporarily so they can withstand the stresses of weaving. In a process called sizing or slashing, water-soluble starch, resins, or gums are added to the yarns to provide the strength and abrasion resistance required. The unsized yarns on the initial warp beam are run through a size bath and carefully rewound onto a final warp beam.

The final warp beam is then mounted on the loom and each warp yarn is threaded through its own drop wire, heddle eye, and reed dent. (The drop wire is a device that will stop the loom if a warp yarn should break.) Drawing in the warp yarns is time-consuming when done by hand. Machines have been developed for accomplishing this delicate task.

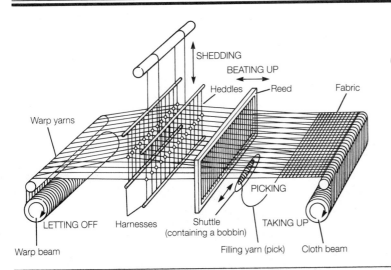

FIGURE 26.15 Essential loom parts and the formation of a plain woven fabric by the four basic loom motions.

Conventional Automatic Power Loom

John Kay is credited with inventing the flying shuttle in 1733, thereby paving the way for development of mechanically powered weaving. Instead of a person inserting the shuttle into the shed and pulling it through, the shuttle was hit by a mallet-like device at one edge of the loom with sufficient force to send it through the shed to the other side of the fabric. There, as soon as the shed had changed, it was hit again and sent back through the shed. John Kay's invention was not successful until the turn of the century because there was insufficient yarn to support "faster" weaving. Edmund Cartwright made the first practical power loom in 1787 but was not able to solve many operational problems. Richard Roberts, an exceptional machinery maker, used patented ideas of William Horrocks and others to produce a power loom so outstanding that it became the prototype of all fly-shuttle power looms subsequently built. Before the end of the 18th century, patterning devices (dobbies, Jacquard, and drop boxes) were added, and the power loom became as versatile as the most elaborate hand loom.

Just prior to the turn of the century, automatic devices were added to stop the loom when the supply of filling yarn contained on the bobbin (pirn) within the shuttle was about to be depleted. Thereafter, automatic shuttle-replenishment was accomplished. The most successful method was to drive the bobbin out the end of the shuttle and replace it with a fresh bobbin (pirn) in a single action performed so quickly that the loom did not need to be stopped. The rate of production of fabric was thus substantially increased, the cost of production decreased because the amount of labor was reduced, and the quality of fabric was not diminished. By 1850, 90% of all looms in North America were automatic looms.

No significant improvements were made in weaving for the next 100 years. However, increasing concern for a safer work environment as well as developments in fiber and yarn technology demanded changes in weaving technology. The shuttle was the target of modification efforts. The excruciating noise produced when the fly shuttle, an object weighing several pounds, was hit for each insertion of a filling yarn needed to be dramatically reduced. Moreover, the abrasion of the shuttle on the warp yarns prevented the formation of finer fabrics from new fibers and yarns. Finally, the speed with which the shuttle was sent back and forth was limited to about 200 picks per minute. (Weaving rates are usually specified as picks per minute. A pick is a filling yarn.) The greatest advantage of conventional looms is their ability to weave the widest variety of woven-fabric structures with the widest variety of yarns.

Shuttleless Looms

In shuttleless weaving, the continuous supply of filling yarn in a shuttle is replaced by a discrete length of yarn taken from an external supply package. The discrete length of yarn is passed through the shed at the appropriate time in the weaving cycle (Figure 26.16).

For many years, weavers refused to entertain the idea of shuttleless weaving. They objected to the "new" selvage edge, a fringed edge that puckered more than conventional selvages, which they thought consumers would not accept. In the 1950s, Sulzer Brothers in Switzerland made a major breakthrough by showing

FIGURE 26.16   Types of shuttleless weaving.

PROJECTILE
A small metal projectile carries the pick through the shed.

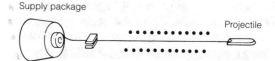

Supply package

Projectile

RAPIER
Long thin rod(s) carry the pick through the shed.

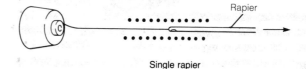

Rapier

Single rapier

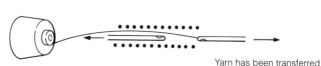

Yarn has been transferred

Double rigid rapier

Gripper heads

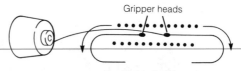

Double flexible rapiers

AIR- OR WATER-JET
A jet of air or water carries the pick through the shed.

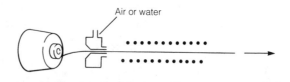

Air or water

that for many fabrics shuttleless (projectile) weaving yielded higher quality at a lower cost due to lower power requirements, less space required, and higher speed of production. Furthermore, noise levels were significantly reduced. In the United States today, the number of shuttleless looms is almost the same as the number of fly-shuttle (conventional) looms.[5]

Projectile or *gripper looms* use a small hook-like device to grip the end of a filling yarn. As this device accelerates, it pulls a filling yarn directly from a prepared yarn package and carries it through the shed (illustrated by the series of staggered dots in Figure 26.16). A stationary yarn package is positioned at one or both sides of the loom. As many as 420 picks can be inserted per minute or 1203 yards (1100 meters) of yarn per minute.[6]

Projectile looms are particularly important in the weaving of wide fabrics. The projectile can travel farther, more easily, and faster than the shuttle, with less power consumption. Two widths of sheeting may be woven side by side. Narrow fabrics, however, are not economical to produce due to the time spent on periods of acceleration of the projectile.

Rapier looms use a rapier, a rod or a steel tape, to carry filling yarns through the shed from a stationary yarn package at one end of the loom. When one rapier is used, it is the width of the fabric to be woven. After moving through the shed, it is retracted, leaving the filling yarn in place. When two rapiers are used, they are each half the width of the fabric to be woven. They meet in the center of the fabric and the yarn carried by one of them is transferred to the other. A mechanism measures and cuts the correct length of yarn. After each insertion, the filling yarns are cut near the edge and tucked back into the fabric to reinforce the edge. Rapier looms have found wide acceptance for weaving basic cotton, woolen, and worsted fabrics. They are considered to be more versatile than air-jet looms.

Speeds of 475–524 picks per minute or the insertion of 930–1404 yards (850–1285 meters) of yarn per minute are possible on rigid and flexible rapier looms, respectively.[7] One problem with rapier looms is the space they require. The housing for a rigid rapier must be equal to the width of the loom itself. A flexible rapier can be coiled as it is withdrawn. However, if the rapier is too stiff, it will not coil, and if too flexible, it will buckle.

Air-jet looms use a jet of air to carry the filling through the shed. The initial propulsive force is provided by a main nozzle. Electronically controlled relay nozzles provide additional booster jets to carry the yarn farther. The filling is premeasured and guided to the air nozzle. Production rates of 1200 picks per minute or the insertion of 2145 yards (1960 meters) of yarn per minute are possible.[8]

Air-jet looms can weave a variety of fabrics up to 157 inches (400 centimeters) in width. It is considered the most cost-effective shuttleless loom. There are, however, limitations in the type of filling yarns that can be carried successfully in the air stream.

Water-jet looms use a high-pressure jet of water to carry the filling yarns through the shed. The filling yarn is drawn from a stationary package at the side of the loom, enters a measuring drum, and continues through a guide to a water nozzle, where a jet of water carries it through the shed. After the filling is beaten, it is cut. When the fibers are thermoplastic, a hot wire is used to cut the yarn, fusing the ends to serve as a selvage.

The water-jet loom has proven ideal for fashion fabrics for men's slacks and shirtings, in which textured or flat multifilament-yarns are used. Almost every natural and synthetic fiber can be woven on the water-jet loom. Barré, or filling streaks in fabrics, rarely result because of the minimal tension on the filling yarn during insertion.

Filling yarn can be inserted at 1500 picks per minute or 2360 yards (2160 meters) of yarn per minute, which is the fastest of all the looms.[9] Production costs are relatively high because the fabrics produced are wet and therefore must be dried. Water from the jet dissolves regular warp sizings, resulting in increased warp yarn breakage. Water-resistant sizings are being developed to reduce the wettability of the yarns. The loom is more compact than conventional looms and far less noisy. Water-jet looms, however, have even more limited fabric capabilities than air-jet looms.

Multiple-Shed (Multiple-Phase) Loom

In each of the looms discussed so far, only one shed is formed at a time. The filling yarn is inserted through this shed. Multiple-shed or multiple-phase looms are capable

[5] M. Isaacs III, "Air-Jets Blow Hot in the U.S. Weaving Market," *Textile World* 139/11 (1989): 42.

[6] M. Isaacs III, "Air-Jets Blow Hot in the U.S. Weaving Market," *Textile World* 139/11 (1989): 43.

[7] M. Isaacs III, "Air-Jets Blow Hot in the U.S. Weaving Market," *Textile World* 139/11 (1989): 42.

[8] M. Isaacs III, "Air-Jets Blow Hot in the U.S. Weaving Market," *Textile World* 139/11 (1989): 43.

[9] M. Isaacs III, "Air-Jets Blow Hot in the U.S. Weaving Market," *Textile World* 139/11 (1989): 42.

of forming more than one shed at a time. The principle involved is for shedding, picking, and beating to occur continuously and successively across the width of the loom. A wave of shed opening starts at one edge of the warp yarns, permitting the passage of a tiny shuttle carrying just enough yarn for one complete pick. This shuttle is followed by a wave of shed closing and beating-up before the next wave of shed opening is initiated. At any one time, 8, 10, or more "waves of weaving" are traversing the width of the fabric at a steady speed. Consequently, very high weaving speeds are achieved. Additionally, the weaving is quiet, and the stresses imposed on the warp and filling yarns are low.

Patterning (Warp-Shedding) Devices or Controls

A conventional loom equipped with two harnesses is all that is required to produce plain-woven fabrics. Every other warp yarn is passed through the hole of a heddle on the first harness. The remaining warp yarns are passed through heddles on the second harness. When the first harness is lifted to form the shed, half of the warp yarns are above the filling yarn being inserted and half are below it. The interlacing pattern formed by the filling is over one warp and under one warp. In the next cycle, the second harness is raised. The interlacing pattern formed by the filling is again over one warp and under one warp.

Twill weaves require at least three harnesses. A 2/1 twill indicates that two harnesses are up and one down when a filling yarn is inserted, and the sum of the two numbers indicates the number of harnesses required, in this case three. The minimum number of harnesses necessary to weave satin fabrics is five. When woven-in designs are required, special mechanisms are added to the loom.

Box looms weave plaids and checks into a basic fabric by supplying different colored filling yarns to the shuttle as required. A mechanism at the side of the loom holds bobbins (pirns) of different colored yarns. A device removes a bobbin from the shuttle and replaces it with the bobbin containing the color of yarn that is to be inserted in the next pick(s).

Dobby looms are used to weave small-figure designs into a fabric. Thirty-two harnesses may be necessary to control the shedding operation. The mechanism that is attached to the loom to control which harnesses are raised to form a shed is called the dobby attachment. A pattern roll, similar to that for a player piano, is pre-

pared. Each row of holes in the roll controls a row of pattern and mechanically determines which warp yarns (harnesses) will be raised for each pass of the filling yarn.

Recent developments in dobby controls, such as double-cylinder and electronic controls, approximately doubles the size of the repeat that can be woven, thereby expanding design capabilities. Dobby looms may operate with or without a shuttle.

Jacquard looms, developed by Joseph-Marie Jacquard, automatically provide an infinite combination of unique sheds by incorporating a Jacquard, or patterning, head to a conventional loom. The heddles are removed from the harnesses, so that each warp yarn is controlled independently. Punched cards are prepared, one for each filling yarn in the design, and laced together into a continuous strip. The strip may contain as many as 7000 cards. The cards are mounted on the Jacquard head. Each card moves sequentially into position over a cylinder. The wires that control the heddle strings are engaged by the cards. The warp yarns that are to appear on the surface of the fabric are raised; those not wanted at that point are suppressed to be concealed on the back of the fabric. The filling yarn is then inserted through the shed and beaten up. The next card moves into position and the next shed is formed. This sequence is repeated until the design is complete.

In the past, sketching of the design, scaling it to square paper, cutting a set of cards, planning the warp colors, and preparing the loom required months of painstaking work. The use of computers, however, reduces the tediousness of the manufacture of Jacquard fabrics. Today, many Jacquard attachments are controlled by computer tapes rather than cards. The computer identifies which warp yarns are to be raised to form the shed. Graphics software permits designs to be drawn directly onto monitors and then converted into the pattern tape for controlling the shedding of the warp yarns.

Jacquard fabrics and some piqué fabrics are produced on the Jacquard loom. Warp-pile fabrics with woven-in designs are made on Jacquard looms equipped with the mechanisms to accommodate additional sets of yarns. Wilton rugs are also made on Jacquard looms.

OTHER INTERLACED FABRICS

In both braid and triaxial fabrics, yarns interlace but not at right angles to each other with one yarn perpendicular to the fabric edge (Figure 26.17).

Braid fabrics are fabrics in which "three or more yarns interlace in such a way that they cross one another in

FIGURE 26.17 Braid and triaxial fabrics.

BRAID FABRICS

Fabrics in which "three or more yarns interlace in such a way that they cross one another in diagonal formation."

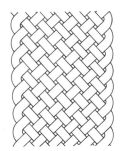

TRIAXIAL FABRICS

Fabrics in which "yarns are interlaced at 60° angles to each other."

diagonal formation." Braid fabrics are usually narrow. They possess excellent lengthwise elongation and are easily shaped. Braids are used as garment trims, especially at the neck and arm holes. They are also made into shoe laces.

Triaxial fabrics derive their name from "tri," meaning "three," and "axial," meaning "of or pertaining to the axis or center line." Thus, triaxial fabrics have three axes, or centerlines. Yarns are interlaced at 60° angles to each other. In essence, a series of equilateral triangles are formed.

The triaxial structure is not new, but the development of a commercial method to make fabrics with the triaxial structure did not occur until the late 1960s. A need for a dimensionally stable, lightweight fabric for a parachute-glider to bring space capsules back into dry-land recovery areas provided the impetus for their development.

Triaxial fabrics are noted for high bursting strength due to the superior load distribution provided by the three yarn sets. Tear resistance is also superior because tearing is always opposed by two yarn sets. As tear ten-

sion is imposed, the yarns reinforce each other, making tearing very difficult. Further, shear resistance can be maintained even when lightweight yarns are used. The strength is uniform in all directions, and the fabric has ravel resistance. Open structures are dimensionally stable, and yarn slippage is minimized.

Triaxial fabrics are used mostly in aerospace and industrial applications. Apparel, interior, and geotextile uses are being explored. In apparel, athletic and foundation garments are of interest because stretch in all directions may be incorporated into the structure with the appropriate selection of yarns. Close fit and strength are also possible. Upholstery fabrics are a likely application because the fabric structure would permit neat corners to be formed and provide the necessary bursting, tearing, and breaking strength. Sail cloth, tarpaulins, filter fabrics, air structures, and truck covers are being developed because these end-use products require many of the performance advantages offered by triaxial fabrics.

CHAPTER SUMMARY

Woven fabrics are fabrics in which two or more sets of yarns interlace at right angles to each other. The majority of woven fabrics are plain-woven, twill, or satin by construction. The surface can appear flat, as a series of crosswise ribs, as a series of diagonal lines or ridges, or smooth and lustrous. Other woven fabrics are more complex in construction due to the interlacing of two sets of yarns to create texture or form woven-in designs and/or to the use of more than two sets of yarns. Detail View 26 lists and defines the types of woven fabrics.

In comparison with other fabrics formed from yarns, woven fabrics are the least flexible and least extensible. Shape retention is excellent. Interlacing pattern and fabric count alter the performance of the various types of woven fabrics.

Woven fabrics are made on looms by a process called weaving. All looms operate via the same four fundamental weaving motions: shedding, picking, beating up, and simultaneous letting-off and taking-up. Conventional or automatic power looms are capable of weaving the widest range of fabrics. They use a shuttle to insert the filling yarn. Modifications to the automatic power loom include looms that increase the speed and ease of insertion of the filling yarn (projectile, rapier, air-jet, water-jet, and multiple-phase) and devices to shed the warp yarns to form complicated patterns (dobby and Jacquard).

Knit Fabric Structures

Knit fabrics are "composed of intermeshing loops of yarn."

WEFT KNITS

Weft knits are "characterized by the fact that each weft yarn lies more or less at right angles
to the direction in which the fabric is produced"; the yarns lie crosswise.

Single Knits
Jersey
Purl
Rib

Double Knits
Rib double
Interlock double

Shaped Fabrics and Integrally Knitted Products

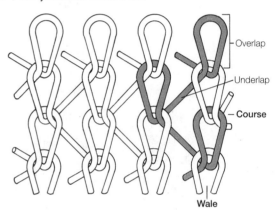

WARP KNITS

Warp knits are "characterized by the fact that each warp yarn is more or less in line
with the direction in which the fabric is produced"; the yarns lie lengthwise.

Tricots
One-bar
Two-bar
Three- and four-bar

Raschels
Basic
Fall-plate
Pile

Nets (Meshes) and Laces
Elasticized Fabrics and Bands
Insertion Knits
Double-Face Warp-Knits

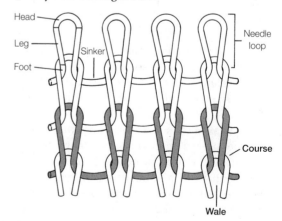

*K*nit Fabrics and Products

The quantity and diversity of knit fabrics available today is unprecedented. A revolution occurred between 1962 and 1972, when the quantity of fiber used to form apparel knits increased from 24% to 44%. Although predictions that more knit than woven fabrics would be used for apparel by the 1980s have not materialized, the amount of knit apparel fabric continues to rise.

Today about half of apparel fabrics are knit. Several apparel items—sweaters, hosiery, T-shirts and golf shirts, sweat and exercise suits, lingerie, swimming suits, gloves and mittens, and figure-shaping undergarments—are almost exclusively made from knit fabrics. Greater percentages of women's, infants' and children's wear than men's wear are knit. Much of the elastic banding used in garments contains knitted structures as well. In the interior furnishings market, lacy casement fabrics are the domain of knit fabrics. In fact, lace and net fabrics—regardless of their specific use—are usually knits. Knit upholstery fabrics and carpets are also available, though in limited quantity. Household textiles that may be knits are tablecloths, blankets, and sheets. Although only 3% of the industrial and consumer textile market is knit fabric, knit products in that market fill significant needs. In the medical and health care field alone, knit products include splints, antithrombosis stockings, bandages, ointment pads, flat and tubular dressings, dialysis filters, incontinence pads and underwear, hospital cellular blankets and stretch terry sheets, band-aid fabrics, hospital privacy curtains, nets for handling burn victims, fabric for artificial heart valves, and nets for blood filtration, abdominal surgery, and reconstructions.

William Lee of England is credited with starting the knit-fabric industry because he invented the first commercial knitting machine in 1775. His machine was capable of knitting a crude fabric for stockings. He knit a pair of silk hose for Queen Elizabeth. Although they were inferior to the hand-knitted silk hose of the day, the process was recognized as viable. In fact, hand knitters, who primarily made stockings and gloves, reacted by destroying knitting machines, which they felt threatened their means of livelihood. The knit technique in use prior to Lee's invention was believed to have originated in the Middle East and to have arrived in Europe during the medieval period, probably imported by Arab conquerors of Spain. The earliest known fragment of knit fabric dates from the first century A.D.

Knit fabrics are "composed of intermeshing loops of yarn." Detail View 27 presents the simplest structure for the two major types of knits. *Weft knits* are "characterized by the fact that each weft yarn lies more or less at right angles to the direction in which the fabric is produced." The intermeshing yarn traverses the fabric crosswise. *Warp knits* "are those characterized by the fact that each warp yarn is more or less in line with the direction in which the fabric is produced." The intermeshing yarn traverses the fabric lengthwise. The diagrams and photos of knit fabrics in this chapter convey the diversity of knits having one of these two basic structures.

Knitting machines are used to produce knit fabrics. Their rate of production is comparatively high, with the linear amount of fabric produced per unit of time about four times that of looms. In addition, the wider the knitting machine, the faster it produces fabric. For weaving, by contrast, the wider the woven fabric to be formed, the slower is its production. A comparison of square-yardage rates for producing knit and woven fabric, therefore, results in a greater difference than when linear-yardage rates are compared.

Such a high production rate does not mean that knit fabrics are less expensive to produce than woven fabrics. Knit fabrics require higher-quality yarn than do woven fabrics. Yarns must have even diameters because thick-and-thin places show more readily in knit than woven fabric. Also, smaller-size yarns—more expensive yarns—are necessary in knit fabrics to achieve the same cover as in a woven fabric. The economics realized by a high production rate are, therefore, offset by the need for more expensive yarns.

GENERAL CONSIDERATIONS

The language involved in describing the structure and technology of knit fabrics is unique. An understanding of the basic terms is an important tool for those interested in the design, sale, and/or merchandising of knits, as well as in their manufacture.

Terminology

The basic structural components of weft and warp knits are identified on the two diagrams in Detail View 27.

Courses and Wales. The width and length of knit fabrics are referred to as crosswise and lengthwise, respectively. A *course* is "a row of loops across the width of a fabric." A *wale* is "a column of loops along the length of the fabric." Courses, therefore, lie in the crosswise direction and wales in the lengthwise direction. Unlike woven fabrics, courses and wales are not composed of different sets of yarns. Rather, courses and wales are formed by a single yarn.

In some knit fabrics—for example, the 1 × 1 rib fabric in Figure 27.2 and the double weft knits in Figure 27.8—both the face and the back show colums of wales. Other knit fabrics—for example, the jersey knit in Figure 27.2 and the tricot knit in Figure 27.10—show vertical columns of loops on one side and horizontal rows of loops

on the other side. The first group of fabrics may be described as having wales on both sides and the second group as having wales on one side and courses on the other. Yet other knit fabrics, such as the purl fabric shown in Figure 27.2, show horizontal rows of loops on both sides. Such fabrics may be described as having courses on both sides.

All knit fabrics have both wales and courses. In some knits, however, the vertical appearance of wales predominates on one or both sides; in other knits, the horizontal feature of courses predominates.

Loops and Loop Elements. The basic unit of knit fabric is the *loop*. In weft knits, loops are called *needle loops*. A needle loop has a head and two legs. It also has a foot that meshes with the head of the needle loop in the course below it. The feet are usually open in weft knits; the yarn does not cross over itself. The section of yarn connecting two adjacent needle loops is called the *sinker*.

In warp knits, the needle loop is referred to as an *overlap* due to the type of motion taking place to form it. The length of yarn between overlaps, "the connection between stitches in consecutive courses," is called an *underlap*. The length and the direction of the underlaps are quite important in the design of warp knits. The feet of the overlaps may be open or closed, depending on whether the yarn forming the underlaps continues in the same or opposite direction from that followed during formation of the overlap.

Stitches. Each loop in a knit fabric is a *stitch*. A loop is always drawn through a previously formed loop. In Detail View 27, each stitch meshes through the previously formed loop toward the viewer, in what is called a *knit stitch*. Other types of stitches are discussed later.

Stitches, as well as structures of knit fabrics, will be illustrated in this text by diagrams that are magnified views of the intermeshed structure itself. The technical face of the fabric is toward the reader unless noted otherwise. The end of the fabric knitted first has been placed at the bottom of the page, and the next row of loops would be added to the diagrammed fabric at its top. Within the knit industry, different stitch notations are used. These are symbolic representations of the knit structure and are particularly useful as the complexity of the structure increases. There are two symbolic notation systems for weft knits and one for warp knits. Instruction in these notation systems, however, is beyond the scope of this text.

Cut or Gauge and Stitch Density. The openness or closeness of the intermeshing loops is indicated by the *cut* or *gauge*. Technically, cut or gauge "gives an indication of the number of knitting needles per unit length, along a needle bed or needle bar, of the knitting machine." The greater the number of needles in the specified length, the higher the cut or gauge number and, therefore, the closer together the loops are to each other. Usually, as the cut or gauge is increased, finer-size yarn is used. There is no universally accepted standard unit of length. Consequently, several different gauging systems exist. For example, a 21-gauge full-fashioned knit would be knitted on a machine having 14 needles/inch because the gauge is based on the number of needles in $1\frac{1}{2}$ inches on the machine used. However, a 21-gauge circular jersey knit would be knitted on a circular machine having 21 needles/inch. The approximate cut or gauge can be determined by counting the number of wales in a given distance on the knit fabric.

Stitch density is "the number of stitches per unit area in a knit fabric." It is obtained by multiplying the number of courses per inch by the number of wales per inch.

Technical Sides, Effect Sides, and Reverse Sides. When a knit fabric differs in appearance on each side, one side is the technical face and the other the technical back. The *technical face* is that side where the loops are pulled toward the viewer. The *technical back* is, therefore, the side in which the loops are pulled away from the viewer. In Detail View 27, the technical face is seen for both the weft and warp knit.

The *effect side* is that face intended to be used outermost on a garment or other textile product. In some cases, the technical face and the effect side are the same; in others, they are opposite. The term *reverse side* is used to indicate "the surface opposite to the effect side."

Flat, Tubular, and Shaped Fabrics. Knit fabrics are available as *flat*, *tubular*, and *shaped*. Knits are unique in their ability to be shaped into the size and shape of a garment or garment part as the fabric is being formed. Garments made from such shaped pieces are called full-fashioned garments. When knit fabric is flat or tubular, the textile product to be made must first be cut and then assembled. Some tubular knits are used to eliminate side seams in garments, as is often done in T-shirts. The products from flat and tubular knits are referred to as cut-and-sewn. Shaping is more expensive, but the product retains its shape better and cannot unravel at the fabric edges. Weft knits are widely available in all three forms; warp knits are usually flat.

Performance

Even though many different knit structures are available and their performance differs, some generalizations can be made about the unique set of performance attributes offered by the intermeshed structure that all knits have. Knit apparel fabrics are noted for freedom of body movement in form-fitting garments, ease of care, resilience, soft draping quality, and providing warmth in still air environments. Limitations of knit apparel performance include high potential relaxation shrinkage, tendency to snag and pill extensively, poor shape retention, and coolness in breezy weather. Many apparel knits will also run or ladder, causing holes to form and ending the wear life of the garment.

In upholstery applications, the extension and recovery performance of knit fabrics renders them easy to form to cushions. Abrasion resistance and strength of the fabrics are deemed adequate. When buttoning and sewing are required, however, their use is severely restricted. The asesthetics and economics of knitted-lace curtain fabrics account for their substantial production and use.

The text that immediately follows compares only knits to wovens and warp knits to weft knits in performance. These differences are explained in terms of differences in fabric structure. The performance and structure of specific weft and warp knits are given in the weft and warp knit sections that follow.

Elongation (Extendibility) and Form-Fitting Capability. Knit fabrics will extend in all directions because the loops that they contain widen or lengthen to accommodate any stress applied. Because simultaneous stress applied to both the length and the width of a knit increases the surface area that the knit fabric covers, form-fitting garments are feasible. Body movement is accommodated without binding or inhibiting, and furniture cushion covers fit snugly.

In comparison, woven fabrics have little elongation unless special finishing treatments or stretch yarns are used, and even then, the degree of extension is less than that of the majority of knit fabrics. In stretch woven fabrics, the extendibility is usually limited to either the lengthwise or crosswise direction; rarely is extension in both directions.

Comparing the two major types of knits, because weft

knits have greater freedom for yarn slippage, they have more elongation potential in both the lengthwise and crosswise directions than do warp knits. An examination of the structural diagram of a simple warp knit reveals the presence of short lengths of yarn (the underlaps) running crosswise, thereby limiting crosswise extension, and closed loops, which inhibit yarn slippage. Lengthwise extension is limited in warp knits due to the fact that the yarns forming them lie primarily lengthwise.

Elastic Recovery. Knit fabrics recover well from deformation because the loops attempt to return to their original positions. The looped configuration of the yarns accommodates this recovery more readily than does the interlaced configuration found in woven fabrics. The ease and quickness with which elastic recovery takes place is dependent on the structure and the fiber composition of the yarn. Usually, the smoother the yarn, the easier it is for the distorted yarn to return to its original looped configuration. Also, the more resilient the fibers in the yarn, the better the elastic recovery. Wool jersey knits, therefore, usually recover more fully from deformation than cotton jersey knits.

Shape Retention. Knits whose loops do not recover from deformation become "stretched out of shape" or they bag. In most cases, washing and drying the knit fabric assists the loops in returning to their original configuration. Weft knits usually have poorer shape retention than warp knits due to the manner of loop formation. Fiber content and yarn structure also play significant roles in both cases.

Growth of knit fabrics may occur during use. The weight of the fabric may be sufficient stress to cause an increase in length with a concomitant decrease in width.

Relaxation Shrinkage. Relaxation shrinkage of knit fabrics can be very high, especially when the fiber composition is hydrophilic fibers. In the case of wool fibers, the effect can be magnified by felting shrinkage. Such changes in dimensions after knitting can create major problems. Consumers often anticipate the amount of relaxation shrinkage and purchase a larger-size knit garment to compensate for potential shrinkage. Articles knitted from thermoplastic fibers can be heat-set to a dimension that is retained unless the setting conditions are exceeded during washing and drying.

The distortion and tension placed on the loops during a knit's manufacture result in poor dimensional stability.

During knitting, the loop structure is subjected to tension from sources such as the take-down mechanism. The extent of potential shrinkage of knit fabrics is usually higher than that of woven fabrics composed of the same type of yarn. Further, weft knits have higher potential shrinkage than warp knits.

Potential relaxation shrinkage can be reduced during finishing, but usually not to the extent that it can be in woven fabrics. Three percent shrinkage is considered acceptable in knit fabrics; only 2% shrinkage is tolerated in woven fabrics. Knit fabrics must be properly engineered during formation to minimize shrinkage.

Strength and Abrasion Resistance. The intermeshing of yarns allows knit fabrics to absorb the forces applied to them rather than break or be rubbed away. Most knit fabrics have so much extension that the resistance of the yarns to extension is rarely of consequence. In other words, the yarns within a knit fabric are rarely stressed (pulled) to the extent that they will be broken. For this reason, the yarns in knit fabrics do not need to be as strong as those in woven fabrics. Low-twist spun yarns are often used, contributing to the softness, bulkiness, and warmth of knit fabrics.

The strength of knit fabrics is difficult to compare directly to that of woven fabrics. A meaningful breaking strength can be determined for woven fabrics but not for knit fabrics. When a strip of knit fabric is pulled at both ends, it distorts; the fabric curls about itself to form a "structure" quite different from that of the fabric in use. The strength of knit fabrics is, therefore, commonly determined by a bursting test (Chapter 2). A circular swatch is mounted over a rubber diaphragm, to which air or hydraulic pressure is applied until the swatch bursts. The force in a bursting test is not comparable to that in a pulling strength test.

Knit fabrics compare well to woven fabrics that would reasonably be selected for the same purpose in terms of the degree of deterioration due to rubbing. A firm, closely woven fabric might appear more resistant to abrasion than a knit fabric, but in use, the knit, due to its pliability, might be subject to less rubbing pressure than the stiff woven fabric. On the other hand, appearance changes, particularly pilling and snagging, are far more likely to occur on a knit fabric than on a woven fabric as abrasion takes place.

Wrinkle Resistance and Recovery. Knit fabrics are considered to be ideal travel fabrics. They do not wrinkle to the extent that woven fabrics do because the yarns are freer to slip through the loop structure. This sliding ability prevents the formation of sharp folds and allows the yarn to move back to its original position when the constraining force is removed (when the suitcase lid is opened, the person stands up, or the hand crushing the fabric is opened).

Pilling and Snagging. The propensity of knit fabrics to snag is related to (a) the relative ease of catching a loop due to the amount of space between loops and (b) the ease of pulling a length of yarn to the fabric surface once a loop is caught. Sometimes the yarn length can be worked back into the loop structure of the fabric. When it cannot, the yarn length may be drawn to the back of the fabric but the row of stitches that remains is tighter than in the surrounding areas, detracting from the appearance of the fabric.

Knit fabrics are also noted for their propensity to pill. Staple fibers in the knit fabric are not bound as securely into the structure as in a woven fabric. This performance limitation arises more from the fact that low-twist yarns are often used. Fibers are easily pulled to the fabric surface and entangled by abrasive forces.

Insulative Ability and Air Permeability. The ability of a fabric to retain heat near the body surface is dependent on the amount of dead air space in the fabric. Thus, knit fabrics, which are open structures with a relatively great amount of space between yarns, are ideally suited for providing thermal insulation in still air conditions. Moreover, large bulky yarns can be used in knit fabric, further increasing the amount of air space between the fibers within the yarns. For a given weight per unit area, knit fabrics are usually thicker than woven fabrics. The thickness, of course, means more dead air space.

Better protection from the cold can be obtained by wearing a knit rather than a woven fabric of the same weight when there is either no wind or a light wind. The chilling effect of wind is, however, an important consideration in many use conditions. Combining an outer garment made of a closely woven fabric and an inner garment made of a knit fabric yields an ideal complementary system. Even very close constructions of warp knits are much more permeable to air than closely woven fabrics of similar weight.

The ability to make knit garments fit closely to the skin surface adds to the insulative capacity of the fabric. The layer of dead air that forms between the skin and the fabric surface adds to the amount of heat retained near the body surface, providing warmth to the garment wearer. On warm, humid days, knits may be too warm because they tend to fit snugly.

Weft knits are usually thicker, bulkier structures than warp knits. This characteristic is due primarily to the different yarns that are used in each structure rather than to the structure itself. Weft knits are more often made with spun yarns and warp knits more often with filament yarns.

Running or Laddering. Unlike other types of fabrics, knit fabrics may run or ladder when a yarn in the structure is broken, resulting in a hole or a vertical flaw. Most weft knits run; most warp knits do not.

WEFT KNITS

In *weft knits,* the yarn forming the fabric traverses the fabric crosswise. The structure of weft knits can be destroyed by pulling the yarn at a cut edge from the loops immediately below it. This reduction back to yarn is called unraveling or raveling.

The fundamental stitches that form the diversity of weft knits are illustrated in Figure 27.1. The *knit stitch,* also called a face loop, is one in which "the yarn meshes through the previous loop towards the viewer." The head of the knit loop lies on the technical back of the fabric and its legs on the technical face. The *purl stitch,* also called a back loop, is a mirror image of the knit stitch. The yarn forming the purl stitch "meshes through the previous loop away from the viewer." The head of the loop lies on the technical face and the legs on the technical back. A *float stitch* "connects two loops of the same course that are not in adjacent wales." It is identified by the occurrence of a length of yarn that lies behind a column of loops (a wale or wales). One could argue that a float stitch is not a stitch at all because a loop is not formed. (In single knits, the length of yarn lies on the back of the fabric but in double knits it usually lies between the two layers of loops.) The incorporation of float stitches usually makes a basic knit fabric narrower, thinner, and much less extensible. Floats are useful for hiding colored yarns when they are not required to be knitted into particular loops, as in Jacquard colored-stitch designs. A *tuck stitch* is "a stitch consisting of a held loop and one or more tuck loops, all of which are intermeshed in the same course." The length of yarn in the legs of the tuck stitch forms an inverted "V" on the

FIGURE 27.1 Fundamental stitches in weft knits.

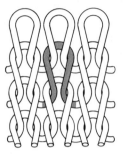
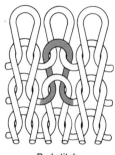
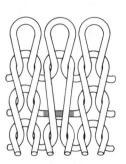
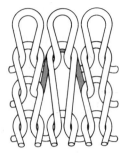

Knit stitch
(Face loop)

Purl stitch
(Back loop)

Float stitch
(Miss stitch)

Tuck stitch
with held loop

technical back. Tuck loops spread outward and are more open than knit loops because their feet are not held together by the loop below them. Usually, the use of tuck stitches in a basic knit structure makes the fabric wider, thicker, and slightly less extensible. They make vertical stripes possible.

Single Weft Knits

Single weft knits have one layer of loops formed with one yarn system. The three basic single weft knits are *jersey, rib,* and *purl* (Figure 27.2). Although the sections of the fabric in Figure 27.2 are different sizes and shapes, each section contains 10 wales and 15 courses. The types of stitches and their sequence in the three knit fabrics cause these structural differences as well as performance variations.

Jersey (Plain, Stockinette) Knits. Jersey (plain, stockinette) knits are those single weft knits "in which all of the component knitted loops are of the same sort and meshed in the same manner." They are composed solely

FIGURE 27.2 Three basic single weft knits.

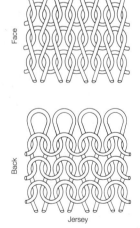
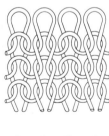
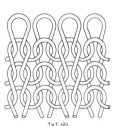

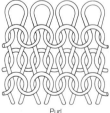

Jersey

1x1 rib

Purl

Jersey
fabric

1 × 1 rib
fabric

Purl
fabric

of knit stitches. Therefore, they have a different appearance on each side; wales show on the technical face and courses on the technical back. Jersey fabrics will unravel from both ends.

Jersey fabrics obtained their name from Lily Langtry, a lady who popularized their use in ladies' suiting in the late 1800s. Lily Langtry was also known as the "Jersey Lilly," a name that reflected her island birthplace. Jersey fabric is used extensively in hosiery, the foot section of socks, cotton underwear, golf and T-shirts, and sweater bodies.

Jersey knits curl to the technical face in the crosswise direction and to the technical back in the lengthwise direction. This curling is due to the fact that all the loops lie in the same direction; the top of each loop is always on the technical back. Torque is incorporated into the fabric during formation.[1] This curling feature is bothersome in the cutting and sewing of jersey knits. Jersey knits are also prone to running or laddering. How easily and quickly this occurs once a yarn is broken depends mostly on the fiber content. Wool jersey knits do not run readily because the wool fibers are cohesive enough to prevent the yarns from slipping out of the intermeshing loop structure. The nylon filament yarn used in hosiery, however, permits rapid slippage of the broken yarn ends. Jersey knits have good crosswise and lengthwise elongation, with crosswise elongation about twice as much as lengthwise elongation. Their elongation is considerably less than that of the rib single-knits. The degree of elastic recovery varies with the fiber content and yarn structure. Jersey knits are flatter than purl and rib single-knits made with the same type of yarn and with the same gauge. Their thickness is approximately twice the diameter of the yarn used. They are the most drapable of the three basic weft knits.

Jersey fabrics are made on the least complicated of all the knitting machines, a circular jersey knitting machine (Figure 27.3). The yarn is supplied from cones over the needle bed. The fabric formed by the needles falls into the center of the knitting machine and is collected on a roller at the bottom center. Because only knit stitches need to be made, the knitting element consists of only one needle bed. Latch needles are arranged vertically in a circular needle bed, in indentations called tricks, with the hooks facing outward. At any moment in a knitting cycle, adjacent needles are at various heights, as shown in the figure. As each needle rises and falls in its location

---

[1]Torque is a force or a combination of forces that produces or tends to produce a twisting or rotating motion.

in the trick, a new loop—a knit stitch—can be pulled through the previously formed loop that it holds, with the intermeshing occurring from the back to the face of the fabric being formed.

Figure 27.3 also illustrates how one knit stitch is formed, showing one needle making one complete cycle, starting at the right. At the starting position, an old loop is held securely in the hook of the needle because the latch is closed. As the cam rotates, the needle rises in the trick because its butt follows the incline of the cam. The old loop, held down by the fabric already formed, slides down the needle, contacting the latch and causing it to pivot open. At position 3, the cam has raised the needle to its highest position. Here, the old loop is "cleared" from the open latch spoon onto the needle stem. A yarn guide plate or other device prevents the latch from closing. Next, the needle starts to descend. Yarn is fed into the hook of the descending needle, almost at the same time that the old loop contacts the underside of the latch spoon, causing the latch to close and retain the new loop inside the needle hook. Lastly, as the needle continues to descend, the old loop is knocked over, it slides off the needle head, and a new loop is drawn through the old loop. The old loop becomes a previously formed loop and the new loop becomes the old loop for the next cycle. The setting of the stitch cam determines the distance the needle descends, which in turn, determines the size of the loop or the stitch length.

Rib Single-Knits. Rib single-knits are those weft knits "in which both back and face loops [knit and purl stitches] occur along the course, but in which all the loops contained within any single wale are of the same sort, i.e., back or face loops." In the simplest rib fabric, a 1 × 1, the knit and purl stitches alternate every other stitch. In other rib single-knits, several knit stitches may occur in any course followed by one or more purl stitches. The rib knit is named by the number of knit and purl stitches; for example, a fabric composed of two knit stitches followed by three purl stitches is a 2 × 3 knit.

Rib single-knits have a characteristic vertical "stripe," or rib. Whether or not the face and the back look identical depends on whether adjacent wales are composed of the same number of knit and purl stitches. Rib single-knits are used extensively for neck, waist, and cuff bands on garments. The fabrics are ideal for close-fitting sweaters, pants, and dresses.

Rib single-knits are noted for their excellent crosswise elongation and recovery. The alternation of knit and purl stitches allows the fabric "to collapse" upon itself, which

FIGURE 27.3 A circular jersey knitting machine with an enlarged view of the action of the knitting needles.

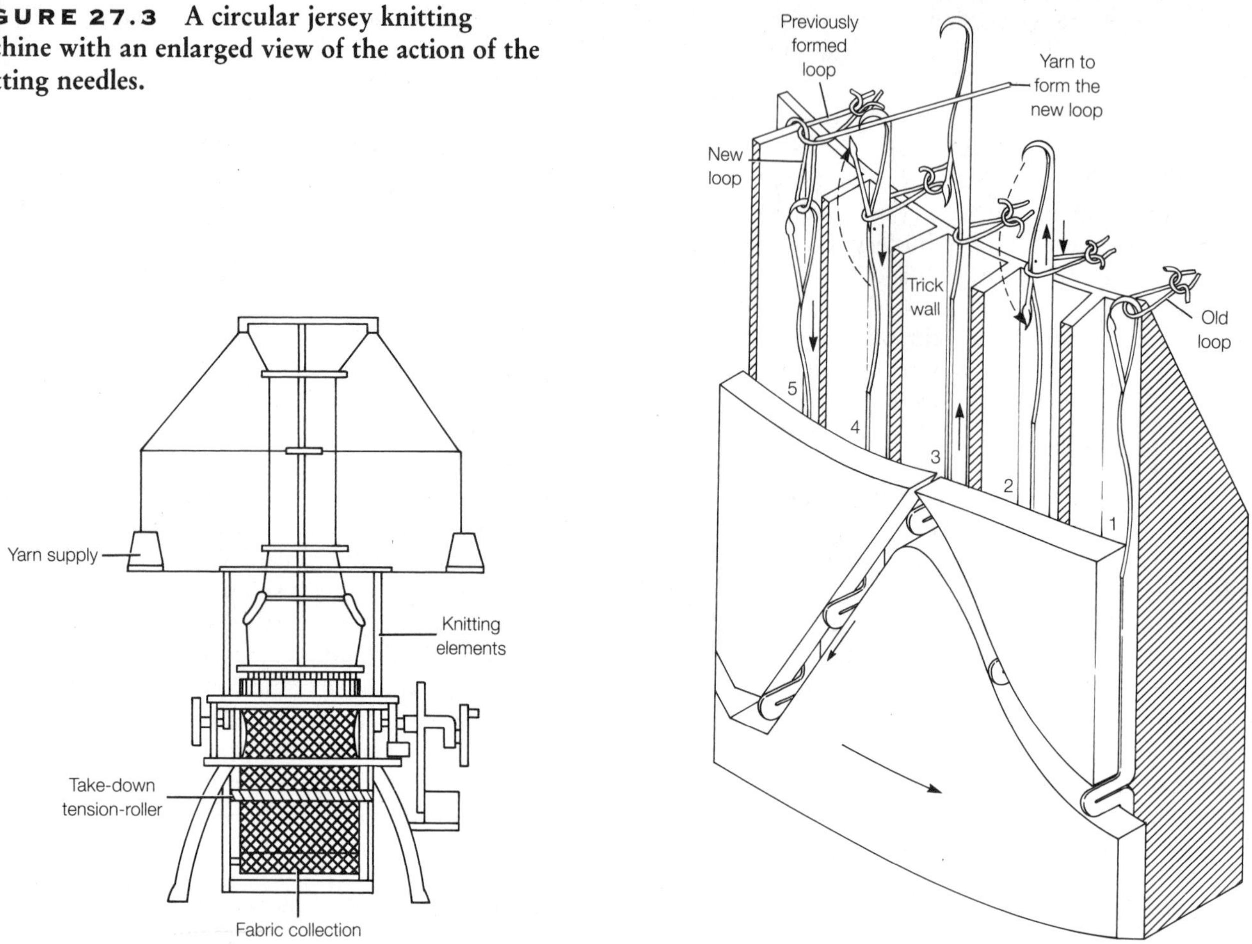

leads to the excellent extension and the ability of the fabric to pull itself back to its original dimension. Rib knits do not curl because the loops are pulled both to the face and to the back of the fabric. They lack the drapability of jersey knits.

Rib knits are made on rib knitting machines. One set of needles arranged in two needle beds is required (Figure 27.4). The latch needles in one needle bed, called cylinder needles, form the knit stitches, and the latch needles in the other bed, called dial needles, form the purl stitches. Laying the needles in the second bed in a horizontal position with their hooks facing upward allows loops to be pulled in the opposite direction to the vertical needles. Yarn is fed to consecutive needles in the same manner as on the jersey machine, and the action of the needles to form the knit and purl stitches is the same as previously described. The needle beds may be straight (V-bed rib knitting machines) or circular. The former arrangement results in flat fabrics and the latter in tubular fabrics. The needles are staggered in the two beds, an arrangement called rib gating.

Purl (Links-Links) Knits. Purl (links-links) knits are those single weft knits "in which both back and face loops are used in some or all of the wales." In the simplest purl fabric, a single course of back loops alternates with a single course of face loops. Each wale, therefore, contains alternating knit and purl stitches, as shown in Figure 27.2, and courses appear on both sides. At one time, purl was spelled "pearl" to convey that the appearance of the fabric was similar to that of pearl droplets.

Purl knits are used when both lengthwise and crosswise extension are desired. Two principle uses are golf sweaters and infants' and children's wear. The ability of the garment to "grow" lengthwise is a definite advantage

FIGURE 27.4 **Knitting elements on a rib knitting machine.**

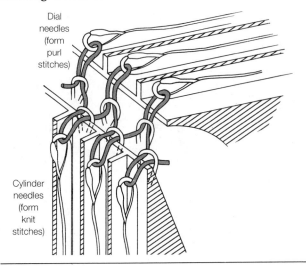

Dial
needles
(form
purl
stitches)

Cylinder
needles
(form
knit
stitches)

in infants' wear. The purl structure is found at the shoulder seam in some sweaters, where its function is to provide some stabilization.

Purl fabrics are about the same thickness as rib single-knits but considerably thicker (2–3 times) than jersey knits of the same type of yarn and cut. They are wider but shorter than a jersey knit containing the same length of yarn. Purl knits lack the draping quality of jersey, but they do not curl because the loops lie in opposite directions on alternate courses. Purl knits can be unraveled from both ends and will run. Purl fabrics are highly extensible in all directions. In particular, they are approximately twice as extensible as jersey knit in the length direction because of the lengthwise contraction of the fabric that occurs to form the coursewise ribs.

In knitting the simplest purl fabric, a knit stitch must be made in each previously formed loop across the width of the fabric. On the next course, a purl stitch must be made in each of the previously formed loops. One set of

latch needles with hooks at each end (double-ended needles) are arranged in two needle beds directly across from one another to achieve this knitting capability (Figure 27.5). In the manufacture of the simplest purl fabric, the needles all form stitches from one bed during the first course and then transfer over to the other bed to form the purl stitches in the next course. The machines are called purl or links-links. Purl knitting machines are capable of producing shaped garment pieces and other articles in addition to purl fabric.

Jersey Variations. The appearance of jersey knit is quite plain. To add interest, jersey knit is often printed. Horizontal stripes can be incorporated by using different colors of yarn in the courses. Fancy yarns create surface interest because they tend to hide the basic jersey structure. Modifications to the circular jersey knitting machine permit an even broader range of jersey fabrics to be produced. These modifications include mechanisms for incorporating another yarn as well as the formation of patterns. Many modified jersey structures are diagramed in Figure 27.6.

Plated jersey knits are "knitted from two yarns of different properties, both of which are used in the same loop whilst [while] positioned one behind the other. The special feature of the fabric is that each loop exhibits the characteristics of one yarn on the face side and the characteristics of the other yarn on the reverse side." Plating a cotton and a polyester yarn can provide the next-to-skin comfort and smooth shiny fabric surface desired by causing the cotton yarn to lie predominantly on one face and the polyester yarn on the other. However, perfect plating, in which the underneath yarn does not show in the surface, is rarely achieved.

In *pile jersey knits,* an extra yarn or sliver of fibers is incorporated into the jersey structure. The effect side, comprised of cut or uncut loops, resembles the appearance of woven pile fabrics. The pile is usually on the technical back, which therefore becomes the effect side.

Knitted terry cloth, velour, plush, and sliver-pile are specific pile jersey knits. In knitted terry cloth, the pile

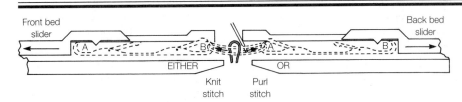

Front bed
slider

Back bed
slider

A   B   A   B

EITHER   OR

Knit
stitch

Purl
stitch

FIGURE 27.5 **Knitting elements on a purl or links-links knitting machine.**
The same needle has been drawn twice to show its two possible positions in the knitting bed.

FIGURE 27.6 Types of jersey knits.

All diagrams are of the technical back (the effect side).

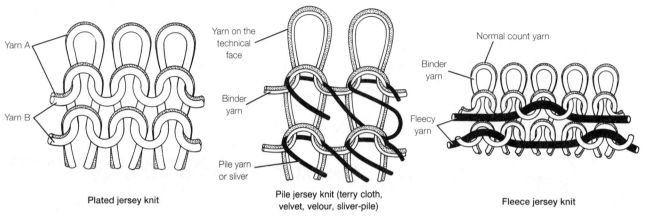

Plated jersey knit

Pile jersey knit (terry cloth, velvet, velour, sliver-pile)

Fleece jersey knit

The stippled yarn lies on the technical face and the white yarn on the technical back.

The shaded yarn emphasizes the pattern of stitches.

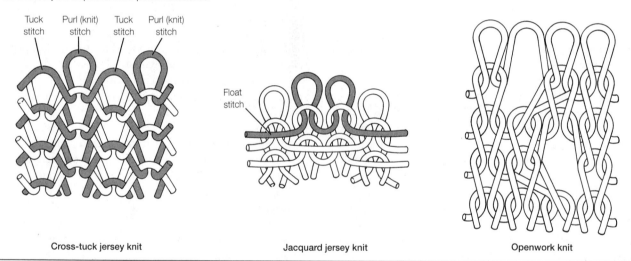

Cross-tuck jersey knit

Jacquard jersey knit

Openwork knit

yarn is looped; in velour and plush, it is cut, with plush having the deeper pile. Knitted terry cloth is most often used in baby and infant towels, washcloths, and sleepers. In these uses, softness, drape, and comfort of body movement are desired. On the other hand, knitted terry cloth lacks the dimensional stability and slight coarseness required in adult towels and washcloths. Knit velours and plushes are popular in pullover tops and loungewear. In sliver-pile jersey knits, also called high-pile and fake-fur fabrics, the pile is comprised of long fluffy fibers rather than a yarn. When properly finished, sliver-pile jersey knits can resemble real fur, particularly when they are made of acrylic and modacrylic fibers. Coat shells and lining are made of such sliver-pile fabrics. The stuffed toy industry also uses large quantities.

Sliver-pile jersey knits usually require drycleaning in which the procedure includes a cold tumble dry. The pile is combed rather than steam-pressed.

Fleece jersey knits are used extensively in sweat and exercise shirts and pants. Fleece jerseys "are composed of three separate yarns: a ground yarn of normal count, a finer binding yarn, and a thicker fleecy yarn that is held into the fabric at close intervals by the binding yarn. The fleecy yarn appears on the back of plain [jersey] knit fabric and presents an ideal surface for brushing or raising." The technical back is very soft and provides additional capability for holding heat at the body surface.

Cross-tuck jersey knits are popular for golf shirts. The knit construction "repeats on a minimum of two courses and tuck loops [stitches] alternate with knitted loops [stitches] within a course and between one course and another." In other words, each yarn knits and tucks at adjacent wales. In the next course, the stitch that was tucked previously is knitted; that which was knitted is tucked. The result is a fabric that does not roll at the edges and is more stable than a jersey knit. The technical face is identical to that of jersey. The technical back has a honeycomb effect.

Jacquard jersey knits are usually composed of "two or more yarns of differing color or texture to give a construction that consists essentially of knit and float loops but may incorporate tuck loops. The surface pattern is derived from the chosen arrangement of the yarns and of the knit and float loops. The inclusion of tuck loops into the construction eliminates long lengths of floating yarns from laying on the back of the fabric."[2] Where the design requires yarn of a certain color to appear on the fabric face, that yarn is knitted as a loop; elsewhere it lies on the technical back. Jacquard jersey knits are noted for stitch uniformity and clear definition of color. Even though the fabric has two layers of yarn it does not have two layers of loops, so it is a single rather than a double weft knit structure.

Intarsia knits are those "containing designs in two or more colors. Each area of color is knitted from a separate yarn, which is contained within that area." Intarsia jersey knits differ from Jacquard jersey knits in that no floats occur on the back of the fabric, fabric extendibility is not impaired, and unequaled color definition is achieved. Intarsia designs are usually large motifs and may contain a large number of colors.

---

[2] Patterned single-jersey *tuck* Jacquard fabrics are also made.

Openwork weft knits, those that are lace-like in appearance, are used for dresswear, underwear, nightwear, lingerie, sportswear, linings, blouses, shirts, as well as drapes and curtaining and industrial fabrics. One method of forming these fabrics is by transferring or spreading knit loops.

Rib Variations. Single-rib knits may also incorporate the tuck stitch (Figure 27.7). Tuck-rib knitwear structures are widely used in the body sections of heavyweight stitch-shaped sweaters. The tuck stitches cause the rib wales to stand apart. In a sweater with a border of rib stitches and a body of tuck and rib stitches, the body width is wider than the ribbing. The tuck stitches make the fabric thicker and heavier.

Half-cardigan knits are "1 × 1 rib fabrics in which each of the stitches intermeshed in one direction consists of a held loop and a tuck loop, and stitches intermeshed in the other direction consist of normal knitted loops." Half-cardigan fabrics differ in appearance on the two sides.

Full cardigan knits have the same appearance, that of wales, on both sides. They are 1 × 1 rib knits, every stitch of which consists of a held loop and a tuck loop. Full-cardigan knits are less extensible than 1 × 1 rib knits but more extensible than half-cardigan knits.

Double Weft Knits

Double knit is "a generic name applied to a range of knit fabrics made on a rib or interlock basis, the construction of which is often designed to reduce the natural extendibility of the structure." Double knits have two insep-

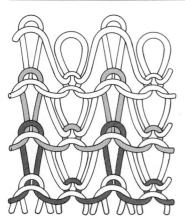
Half-cardigan knit

Full-cardigan knit

FIGURE 27.7 Tuck-rib knits.

The diagrams show the technical face.

arable layers of loops. Each yarn forms loops that appear on both faces of the fabric (Figure 27.8). Double knits are rib structures because knit and purl stitches alternate across the fabrics. The major difference in structure between the two types of double knits is the position of the wales on the face relative to the back. In rib double-knits, the wales are staggered, whereas in interlock double-knits, they are on top of one another. The position of the wales determines the performance characteristics.

Rib Double-Knits. In *rib double-knits,* the two layers of loops are staggered. This arrangement is most easily seen when a rib double-knit is viewed from a cut crosswise edge. At the height of their popularity, in 1973, rib double-knits were used extensively in women's outerwear. The polyester fabrics provided a crisp, resilient handle but were prone to snagging. The fabrics were in keeping with the garment styles of the day, but the trend in women's wear gradually turned to natural fibers and woven fabrics. Attempts to use the fabrics in men's leisurewear with finer gauges than in women's wear were not successful. The overexpanded rib double-knit industry failed to find new markets or fabric improvements, so the amount of rib double-knit produced today is far less than that in 1973.

Even though there is considerable diversity in the structures and appearances of rib double-knits, they share the characteristics of not running and being rather stiff structures with low elongation. They tend to bag, snag, shrink (to what extent depends on the fiber composition), and have high air permeability. They are usually judged to be too warm in still air and too cool in a breeze.

Rib double-knits are produced on knitting machines with two needle beds. The needles are arranged with rib gating, that is, staggered.

Interlock Double-Knits. Originally, interlock was knitted almost solely in cotton for underwear. From about 1950, finer-gauge machines (18 needles/inch) permitted semi-tailored suiting to be manufactured. *Interlock double-knits* consist of "two 1 × 1 rib fabrics joined by interlocking sinker loops. [They are] made on machines equipped with two sets of opposed needles (interlock gating)." Consequently, the loops on the fabric face lie directly over the loops on the fabric back. The appearance on both sides is that of the face of jersey knit. In the simplest structure, one yarn alternately forms a knit stitch on the fabric face and a purl stitch on the fabric back. The other yarn in the row knits and purls the alternate wales.

Interlock fabrics will elongate about 30–40% in the crosswise direction. They are smooth and stable structures that do not curl. Interlock double-knits run, but only from the end of the fabric that was knitted last. In comparison to jersey knits, yarn slippage is more difficult (runs are slower to form). Interlock is firmer and more rigid than jersey knit. The thickness is approximately twice that of jersey knit when the same yarns are used. Like 1 × 1 rib, interlock will not unravel from the end knitted first. It is thicker, heavier, and narrower than single rib of equivalent gauge. It requires a finer, better, and more expensive yarn.

In comparison to rib double-knits, interlock knits tend to have higher gauges: gauges as fine as 40 are possible in interlock double-knits, compared to 28 for rib double-knits. Interlock double-knits have better drape

---

FIGURE 27.8 Double weft knits.

The diagrams show the technical face.

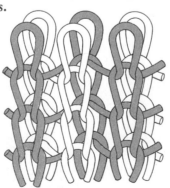

Rib double-knit

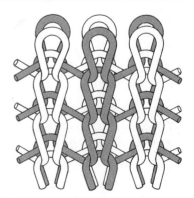

Interlock double-knit

and are softer, lighter, and thinner. Jacquard patterns are rarely produced.

Interlock double-knits are manufactured on knitting machines with interlock gating. Interlock gating is an arrangement where two needles lie directly opposite to each other in the two needle beds. Usually, both long and short needles are required. This type of gating, in comparison with rib gating, reduces productivity by half and causes finer tolerances in the knitting process—so the needles do not accidentally clash—but it permits finer gauges.

SHAPED FABRICS AND INTEGRALLY KNITTED PRODUCTS

Two unique products of knit technology are shaped fabrics and integrally knitted garments, which are complete as manufactured on the knitting machine. Sweater panels and certain types of long underwear exemplify shaped fabrics that are joined together to form a completed garment. Socks, ladies' hosiery, gloves, ties, and some baby apparel items are examples of garments that are structurally complete as they are taken from a knitting machine. Costs associated with cutting, as well as fabric waste, are thus eliminated. The cost of assembling garment pieces is also eliminated in the case of integral knitting. No other fabric-forming method duplicates these capabilities.

Much of the shaping of garments is the result of either stitch shaping, full-fashioning, altering stitch length or a combination of these techniques. In *stitch-shaped garments*, the widening and narrowing of the garment piece is accomplished by varying the stitch structures in the length of the panel and/or varying the stitch length. The number of wales (stitches across each course) remains the same throughout the entire length of the panel. Recall the discussion in the previous section about changes in fabric width as tuck stitches were added to a basic rib structure. Considerable quantities of knitwear, jerseywear, and underwear are knit to size and dimension by stitch shaping.

Full-fashioned garments are "shaped wholly or in part by widening and/or narrowing by loop transference to increase or decrease the number of wales." The addition or deletion of a stitch occurs near but not at the selvage of the shaped piece. Where a stitch is added/decreased, a fashion mark occurs. The fashion mark is created by the sinker loop of the fashion course and the needle loop of the previous course. Full-fashioned garments have clearly visible fashion marks that are the hallmark of classic full-fashioned garments. Full fashioning is usually limited to jersey fabric structures, which have selvage edges that are firm and can be joined together without cutting or seaming. The knitting machines used are designed so that the number of needles in action in the knitting width can vary.

In some garments, *mock-fashioning* marks result when "loop formation is different from that of the main body of the fabric in order to imitate the mark caused by fashioning." No narrowing or widening of the fabric occurs.

Highly sophisticated knitting machines are required for the production of shaped fabrics and fully integrated garments. All machines are classified as garment-length machines rather than fabric machines. The technology of stitch formation is the same, however.

WARP KNITS

Warp knitting began in the late 1700s. At that time, warp knitters had a virtual monopoly supplying lace, tatting, nets, and tulles for the opulent fashions of the day. The inventions of the bobbinet machine and the Leavers machine in 1803 and 1813, respectively, reduced the production of warp-knit laces dramatically. These machines were capable of providing lace with more intricate designs and finer yarns faster and less expensively than the warp knitting machines of the day. Today, however, the majority of nets and laces are the products of warp knitting, which is once again the most economical way to produce them. The highest price laces today are usually products of the Leavers machine.

Lace and net fabrics are one of the three structures produced in large volume by warp knitters; the other two are tricot and Raschel fabrics. Other warp knits are elasticized fabrics and bands, double-face knits, and warp-insertion knits. Development has occurred in the production of completed garments and tubular products.

Warp Knit Technology

To form warp knits, warp knitting machinery supplies each needle with a yarn (or yarns) and all needles knit at the same time, producing a complete course (row) at once. The overall view of a warp knitting machine in Figure 27.9 shows the location of the *yarn supply*, the *knitting elements*, the *fabric take-down*, and *fabric collection* areas. Most warp knitting machines are rectangular (rather than circular) because the needle bed(s) is (are) straight. Flat rather than tubular fabrics are usually produced. Fabric shaping is not possible. The warp yarns are held on warp beams that are usually divided into sections for engineering reasons.

Figure 27.9 also shows the knitting elements of the simplest warp knitting machine. One *guide bar,* one set of *warp yarns,* and one *needle bed* are shown. The guide bar and needle bed extend the complete width of the warp knitting machine. The guide bar contains individual guides through which one yarn from the warp beam is threaded. *Latch needles* are shown, but many machines use *spring-beard needles.*

The function of the guide bar is to wrap the yarns around the needles, or to feed yarn to the needles. The bar swings backward, shogs left or right, swings forward, and finally shogs left or right to form one course of stitches. In the first three movements, the yarn is moved into position for formation of the stitch overlap and in the last movement, the underlap is made. In Figure 27.9, the underlap motion is to the adjacent needle.

The function of the needles is to form the intermeshing loops from the yarn fed to them by the guide bars. The needles move up and down as in weft knitting. However, in warp knitting all needles along the needle bar are at the same height (position) at any one time. The three motions of the guide bar forming the overlap occur when the needles have risen to clearing height (the previously formed loop has cleared the needle hook). The underlap motion may occur anytime after the hook has been closed. The underlap movement may be left or right regardless of the direction in overlap movement. When the underlap and overlap shog direction are the same, an open loop is formed; when they are opposite, a closed loop is formed.

About 95% of warp knits are made on either tricot or Raschel machines. The major differences between these machines are the type of needle (and hence the types of yarn accommodated) and number of guide bars. Tricot machines are used in the production of tricot fabrics, which include some of the lace, net, and elastic fabrics, and a few warp- and weft-insertion fabrics. Raschel machines are used in the production of Raschel fabrics, elastic fabrics, and nets and laces, as well as insertion fabrics. The remaining 5% of warp knits (pile, double-face, and tubular) are made on the two double-needle-bed machines called Simplex and double-needle Raschel.

FIGURE 27.9   A warp knitting machine with an inset of the knitting elements and the motion of the guide bar.

The latch needles shown are typically found on Raschel warp machines. Tricot warp knitting machines would most likely have spring-beard needles.

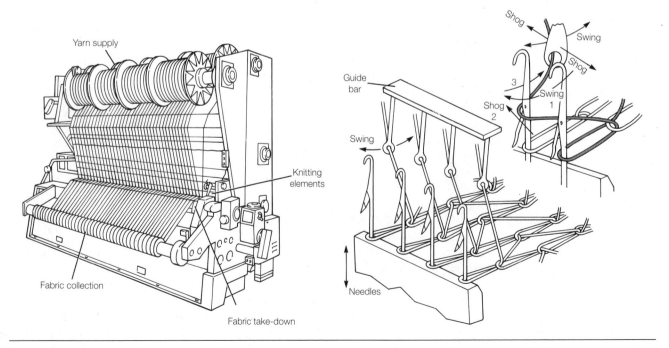

FIGURE 27.10 A two-bar tricot.

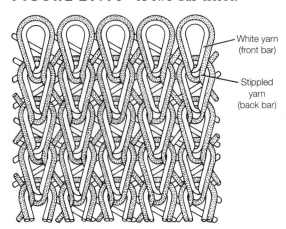

White yarn
(front bar)

Stippled
yarn
(back bar)

Warp knitting provides the fastest way to form fabric from yarns. Tricot machines with computer-controlled guide bars, electronic beam control, and computerized fabric take-up are able to knit 2000 courses/minute.

Tricot Knits

The largest quantity of warp knit is tricot (tree-ko′), a word that comes from the French word *tricoter,* meaning to knit. Tricot fabrics are composed solely of knit stitches (Detail View 27 and Figure 27.10). Wales are therefore seen on the technical face. A crow's foot appearance (rather than courses) results on the technical back due to the underlaps. Tricot fabrics, also called tricot jerseys, are available in widths up to 170 inches (432 centimeters). Filament yarns are usually used.

In the apparel market today, most tricot knits are used for underwear, nightwear, and lingerie, followed by dresses and blouses, and then other outerwear. Most growth in apparel uses is in outwear fabrics. Due to competition from woven fabrics, the amount of tricot used by lingerie manufacturers is decreasing. The major household use of tricot knit is sheets and pillowcases.

In industrial fabrics, the largest market of tricot knits is upholstery fabrics for car interiors.[3] They may be plain, loop-raised or corded, ribbed, cropped velour, or patterned designs. Warp-knit upholstery fabrics com-

pare favorably in performance to woven and weft-knit constructions. They are more comfortable than vinyl-coated fabrics because they are breathable.

One-, two-, three-, and four-bar tricot fabrics are named by the number of guide bars required in their manufacture. The name, therefore, also indicates the number of yarn systems in the fabric. One-bar or single-bar tricots (shown in Detail View 27) have one set of warp yarns forming all the loops. This tricot is seldom produced commercially because of its flimsiness, low strength, lack of dimensional stability, poor covering power, and distortion caused by loop inclination, as well as its limited patterning potential. The simplest tricots are, therefore, usually composed of at least two sets of warp yarns. The greatest quantity of tricot produced is two-bar, which is used extensively in a variety of end uses. Three- and four-bar tricots are used primarily for women's dresses and in men's wear.

One type of two-bar tricot knit, called locknit, is diagramed in Figure 27.10. The white overlaps and underlaps are formed by a front guide bar and the stippled overlaps and underlaps by a back bar. Upon close observation of this particular tricot structure, it is apparent that the white yarn makes a loop (overlap) in every other wale, whereas the stippled yarns make an overlap (loop) at each wale. The stippled yarn has shorter underlaps than the white yarn does. By changing the pattern of movement of the guide bars, tricot fabrics named full-tricots and sharkskin are made. These two-bar tricots have properties that differ from each other as well as from other tricots.

---

[3] Pile fabrics with a Raschel-knit construction are also used for automobile upholstery fabric, as well as for upholstered furniture.

Raschel Knits

Raschel knits are those structures in which columns of loops are connected by in-laid yarns traversing from column to column up the fabric (Figure 27.11). They split or come apart lengthwise when the laid-in yarn is removed.

This category of warp knits obtains its name from the French actress Elisabeth Raschel Felix, who charmed mid-19th century audiences with her dramatic acting and became a fashion oracle through her no less dramatic attire. Whatever she wore became instantly fashionable. Raschel Felix favored jackets with lace ruffles at the neck and sleeves. She also wore elaborate lace stoles. The large following attracted by her tastes created a huge demand for lace articles that could only be satisfied by newly developed machines. W. Barfuss, a French inventor, named one of his machines Raschel in honor of the actress who put this industry on the fashion map.

Any fabric produced on a Raschel knitting machine can correctly be called Raschel. Products as diverse as coarse sacking, carpets, and fine, delicate laces are possible. The three main types of Raschel fabrics are those with the basic structure, fall-plate Raschels, and pile Raschels.

Usually, *basic-structure Raschels* tend to be open and be composed of spun rather than filament yarns. The in-laid yarn tends to form the dominant vertical appearance; the yarn forming the pillar stitch is less visible. Different colors of in-laid yarns are often used to form multicolored vertical stripes. The photograph of the face and back of a Raschel knit in Figure 27.11 illustrates

these features. The largest markets for the basic-structure Raschels are apparel and casement (curtain) fabrics.

Fall-plate Raschels have raised or relief patterns on the effect side (the technical back). The fall-plate or relief yarns are not knitted (they do not make overlaps). The fall-plate yarns lie under the underlaps of the ground construction. They lie on the top of the technical back of the fabric between these points. For this reason, these yarns can be fancy and/or heavy. The largest markets for fall-plate Raschel fabrics are casement (curtain) and upholstery fabrics. A typical casement fabric is shown on the left in Figure 27.12.

Pile Raschel knits are easily recognized by the presence of the pillar and in-laid yarn features that appear distinctly on the reverse side of the pile fabric. As in other pile fabrics, the pile in a pile Raschel knit results from incorporating an additional yarn system into the basic structure.

Pile Raschel knits are used as simulated-fur for coats and coat linings and as upholstery for automobile applications and interior furniture. Artificial turf is also a pile warp knit. They are particularly suitable as upholstery fabrics because they are more stable than weft knits. Pile tufts are short and more securely bound into the backing structure than is the case with most woven velvets. Loss of complete pile tufts in use is almost unknown, as are creasing and pile shading due to compression. Extension and recovery renders the structure very easy to mold to conform to furniture cushions. In addition, Raschel-knit velvets contain a higher proportion of their total weight of fiber as pile than do woven velvets. Knit carpets have been produced but have not been a commercial success.

FIGURE 27.11   A Raschel warp knit.

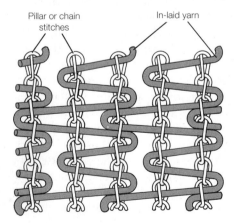

Pillar or chain stitches   In-laid yarn

FIGURE 27.12 Knitted laces.

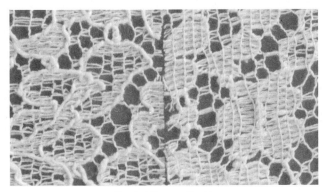

Raschel (face and back)

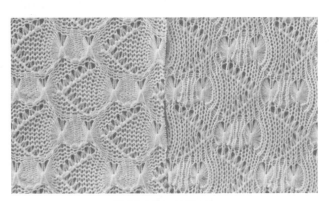

Weft knit (face and back)

They are cheaper to manufacture than woven carpets but not as inexpensive as tufted carpets because some of the expensive pile yarn has to be put into the back of the carpet in the form of overlap. Knit carpets can usually be identified by the appearance of chains of stitches on the underside.

Other Warp Knits

The majority of laces, nets (meshes), elasticized fabrics and banding, and tubular fabrics are produced on Raschel machines but they can also be successfully produced on tricot machines as well. Each has a distinctive appearance but retains the pillar and in-laid yarn structure typical of fabrics produced on Raschel machines.

Nets (Meshes) and Laces. Both net and lace are open fabrics. *Net* is "an open-mesh fabric in which a firm structure is ensured by some form of twist, interlocking, or knitting of the yarn." *Lace* "is a fine openwork fabric with a ground of mesh or net on which patterns may be worked at the same time as the ground is formed or applied later, and which is made of yarn." Most nets and laces today are products of warp knitting, but some are products of weft knitting (Figure 27.12).

Warp-knit nets have the advantage of enhanced slip resistance, dimensional stability, resistance to abrasion, and low drag in water when compared to other types of nets. Warp-knit nets are used for bags in industry and agriculture, for protective devices against coastal erosion, and for catching fish and land animals. Two to four guide bars are used in the production of knitted net.

Multi-bar Raschel (or tricot) machines are needed to produce laces. Increasing the number of guide bars (there may be as many as 56 bars that are individually controlled to provide the openwork patterns) as well as retaining the fall-plate mechanism are required for the intricate structures. Sophisticated patterning control is also necessary.

Elasticized Fabrics and Bands. Swimwear and foundation garments, as well as lingerie, active sportswear and leisurewear garments are made with elastic warp knits. The main difference between regular and elastic warp knits is the incorporation of the elastic yarn. Usually bare, core-spun yarns with a spandex core or covered yarns with a rubber core are used (Chapter 25). High-speed Raschel and tricot machines are used to form plain elastic fabrics and multiple guide-bar lace machines to form patterned elastic fabrics. Changes in the engineering of the knitting machine include needles that will not deflect under the tension of the elastic yarn and fabric take-up.

Power net is the most widely used fabric in foundation wear. Two bars knit the nylon ground and two bars inlay the elastic yarn. This structure may provide a lengthwise extension of 75–85% and a crosswise extension of 65–75%. Tricot can be made as stretch tricot using special lapping motions to insert spandex yarn.

Much elastic banding is also manufactured by warp knitting machines, usually called crochet machines. The banding is often the simple pillar and in-laid structure of Raschel knits. The in-laid yarn traverses from one side of the banding to the other.

Insertion Knits. *Insertion fabrics* are those in which additional yarns have been incorporated into the warp knit structure, spanning the fabric from side to side and/or from end to end.

In *weft-insertion knits,* a crosswise yarn is inserted between the face loops and the underlaps. Note that the inserted yarn crosses the entire width of the fabric and does not form loops. Also note that it is never "caught" in the stitching. This latter point is important when making a distinction between insertion fabric and the stitch-bonded nonwoven fabrics called Malimo (Chapter 29).

In *warp-insertion fabrics,* lengthwise yarns are inserted into a warp knit. Some insertion fabrics have yarns inserted in both the length and width. *Multiaxial fabrics* have yarns inserted diagonally as well as crosswise and lengthwise in the warp knit.

Yarns are inserted into warp knits for two primary purposes. One is the creation of interesting surface effects. The inserted yarn can be of virtually any size or structure; thus, the patterning potential is tremendously extended. Secondly, the insertion of yarns provides additional stability to the fabric. In some industrial uses, insertion is crucial to maintaining the strength of a fabric because insertion yarns are not subjected to the compression forces of interlacing or intermeshing.

The largest apparel use of weft-insertion knits is in interfacing fabric, though nonwoven and woven fabrics share this market. Industrial and consumer uses of conventional weft-insertion fabric are tarpaulins, screens, body protection, abrasives, carpet backing, blood dialysis filters, air ducts, tapes, interlinings, composites, and molded vehicle components. Household applications include dishcloths (a nylon yarn forms the pillars and a cotton yarn serves as the weft-inserted yarn) and curtain fabrics (such curtainings are of an openwork nature and contain very fancy weft yarns, that is, slubs, gimps, knops, etc.).

Tubular Warp Knits (Complete Garments and Other Products). Stockings, panty hose, tights, briefs, girdles, complete pockets, fire and irrigation hose, meat bags, packing bags and sacks, and even artificial arteries can be made by special warp knitting methods. Efforts are underway to produce complete casual trousers or slacks. An element of all these products is a seamless tube of fabric. A double-needle-bar Raschel machine is required to produce these tubular products.

Double-Face Warp Knits. Double-face warp knits have two layers of loops; one layer forms the face and the other the back. They tend to be heavier and more expensive than equivalent weft-knit double-fabrics. Double-face warp knits are products of either Simplex or double-bed Raschel machines.

Simplex knits are similar in appearance to tricot but are heavier and denser. End uses of the fabric are women's gloves, handbags, and simulated suede-textured apparel fabrics. Glove fabrics are given a suede finish (via sandpaper rollers) and then dyed.

Some thermal cloth for cold-weather underwear is a double-face knit produced on a double-Raschel knitting machine. The pockets between the fabric layers serve to trap a layer of heated air. Industrial and consumer uses of double-face knit from Raschel machines include sound insulation walls and geotextile applications such as gradient stabilization, drainage, and oil catchment.

CHAPTER SUMMARY

Knit fabrics are fabrics composed of intermeshing loops. They are either weft or warp knits. The yarn forming weft knits traverses the fabric crosswise; those yarns forming warp knits traverse the fabric lengthwise.

The three basic single weft knits are jersey, rib, and purl. These fabrics are composed of all knit stitches or of knit and purl stitches. They differ in appearance as well as performance due to their varying stitch structures. The incorporation of tuck and float stitches in the basic structure introduces a diversity of appearances and alters elongation and dimensions (length, width, and thickness). The two double knits, rib and interlock, are rib structures because they have alternating knit and purl stitches.

There are three major types of warp knits: tricot, Raschel, and nets and laces. Tricot is composed of all knit stitches and represents the "commodity" warp-knit product. Tricot fabrics vary in the number of sets of yarns in their structure. Most are two-bar tricots and are composed of multifilament yarns. Raschel knits are composed of vertical columns of chain stitches and an in-laid yarn that traverses the fabric horizontally between chain stitches. Raschel knits usually contain spun yarns in an open structure. Most lace and net fabrics in the marketplace today are the product of either Raschel or tricot knitting. Elasticized fabrics, pile fabrics, and double fabrics are also products of warp knitting.

Nonwoven Fabric Structures

Nonwoven fabrics are usually "made from extruded continuous filaments or from fiber webs or batts strengthened by bonding using various techniques: these include adhesive bonding, mechanical interlocking by needling or fluid jet entanglement, thermal bonding, and stitch bonding."

STAPLE-FIBER WEBS

Felt fabrics are nonwovens characterized by the entangled condition of most or all of the fibers of which they are composed, with the entanglement resulting from the application of heat, moisture, and agitation to a fibrous web.

Needlepunched fabrics are nonwovens characterized by the entangled condition of the fibers of which they are composed, with the entanglement resulting from the action of barbed needles. They may contain a scrim of yarns near the center.

Spunlaced fabrics are nonwovens characterized by the entangled condition of the fibers (usually polyester staple), with the entanglement caused by action of high-velocity water jets.

Wet-laid fabrics are paper-like nonwovens containing a random array of layered fibers, with the layering resulting from the deposition of the fibers from a water slurry.

Dry-laid fabrics are nonwovens containing layers of fibers, each layer containing randomly positioned or parallel fibers, with the fiber positioning resulting from deposition from an air stream or by carding. Bonding of the layers with an adhesive or by heat is necessary.

Melt-blown fabrics are nonwovens in which layers of microfibers of various lengths are bonded at fiber crossover points forming a fiber web with very small pores.

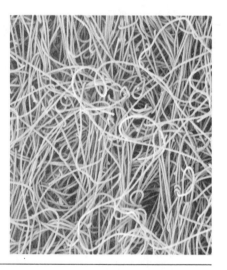

SPUNBONDED FABRICS

Nonwovens that contain a random web of manufactured filaments bonded at filament crossover points.

STITCH-BONDED FABRICS

Multicomponent fabrics in which one component is a series of interlooped stitches running the fabric length and the other component is a fiber web, yarns, or preformed fabric.

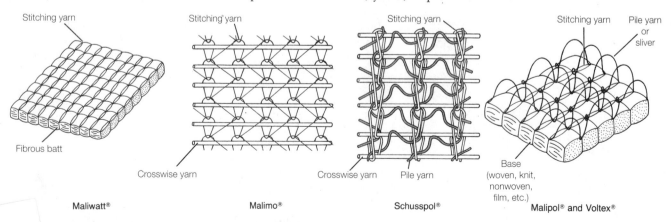

Stitching yarn

Fibrous batt

Maliwatt®

Stitching yarn

Crosswise yarn

Malimo®

Stitching yarn

Crosswise yarn   Pile yarn

Schusspol®

Stitching yarn   Pile yarn
or
sliver

Base
(woven, knit,
nonwoven,
film, etc.)

Malipol® and Voltex®

Nonwoven Fabrics

Tapa cloth, which is made from the fibrous inner bark of the fig tree in the Pacific Islands and Central America, and felt, which is made from wool fibers, are thought to represent the first nonwoven fabrics. They date back to biblical times. During the 1930s, textile engineers began to seriously experiment with ways to form other fabrics directly from fibers. They realized that such processes would yield great economic savings by permitting manufacturers to bypass the step of converting fiber to yarn before making fabric.[1] Within a few decades, engineers had developed an extensive range of nonwoven fabrics with performance properties to meet specific requirements. Entirely new applications, primarily in the consumer and industrial fabrics market, were created.

The term *nonwoven* may be interpreted to include all fabrics that are not woven. Knit fabrics (Chapter 27) and compound fabrics such as tufted (Chapter 29) would, therefore, be nonwoven fabrics. However, nonwoven usually refers to those fabrics that have not been produced by conventional methods such as weaving, knitting, tufting, and so on. Technically, nonwovens are "fabrics normally made from extruded continuous fila-ments or from fiber webs or batts strengthened by bonding using various techniques: these include adhesive bonding, mechanical interlocking by needling or fluid jet entanglement, thermal bonding, and stitch bonding."

Even with this technical definition, opinions vary about whether certain fabric structures should be classified as nonwoven. For example, the boundary between wet-laid fabrics and paper is not always clear (Chapter 1). Some stitch-bonded fabrics are clearly nonwoven, but others contain no fiber web; the latter, therefore, are not always classified as nonwoven fabrics. Felt as well as fibrillated film and foam are placed within the nonwoven sector by some experts but not by others.

Opinions also differ about the appropriate name for nonwoven fabrics. Other names that have been considered and are currently used are bonded fabrics, formed fabrics, engineered fabrics, and fiberwebs. The names and descriptions of nonwoven fabrics considered in this chapter are given in Detail View 28. The staple-fiber webs are listed in order from those that tend to be the thickest to those that tend to be the thinnest. The photomicrographs in the chapter show the arrangements of the staple fibers and the filaments within the fabrics. Cross-sectional views are included for the three thickest nonwovens because little structural difference can be seen in their surface photomicrographs. The magnification in each of these photographs is different because the fabrics differ in thickness. Surface photomicrographs are provided for the four thin nonwovens because structural differences are more evident than in the cross-section.

---

[1] Production of nonwoven fabrics is considerably faster than weaving and also faster than knitting. The average output of a shuttle loom is 6 square yards (5 square meters) of fabric per hour. The average output of a circular knitting machine is 4 times greater; that of a warp knitting machine, 16 times greater. Nonwoven fabric production is 38 to 2300 times the 6 square yards per hour base. Tufting yields a rate of output 500 times greater than a shuttle loom. See J. Lunenschloss and W. Albrecht, eds., *Non-Woven Bonded Fabrics* (New York: John Wiley and Sons, 1985), p. 25.

Photographs of the surfaces of six types of stitch-bonded fabrics are also provided.

PROPERTIES AND END USES

Nonwoven fabrics may be compact and crisp as paper or supple and drapable. They may be highly resilient or limp. The texture or feel ranges from soft to harsh. Their tensile properties range from barely self-sustaining to impossible to tear, abrade, or damage by hand.

The properties of nonwoven fabrics derive from the properties of the fibers themselves, the geometrical arrangement of the fibers in the web, and the manner in which the web has been stabilized (i.e., how it is held together). Performance is, therefore, engineered by selecting the appropriate fiber, geometrical web arrangement, and bonding substance.

Fiber composition influences performance far more for nonwoven fabrics than for fabrics containing yarns. The arrangement and bonding of the fibers within the web have a greater influence on fabric performance than does the arrangement of yarns on woven and knit fabrics. Usually performance can be engineered more readily into nonwoven fabrics than into woven and knit fabrics. High strength combined with softness is one of the most difficult property combinations to achieve in nonwoven fabrics because the geometrical factors that permit high strength also lead to increased stiffness. The explanation proceeds as follows: Bond density is the number of fiber-to-fiber bonds per unit area. Fabrics with high bond density are strong. However, a high number of bonds prevents fibers from moving as the fabric is flexed. The nonwoven fabric is, therefore, stiff. Low bond density yields a more supple fabric with lower strength.

The specific bonding agent used affects strength as well as hand and drape. Strong adhesives provide high fiber-to-fiber bonding but a coarse hand and stiff drape. Adhesives that are more elastic and yield as the web is flexed provide better drape but weaken the structure.

Nonwoven fabrics usually have high air and water vapor permeability. Their porous structure permits flow of air and water vapor between fibers.

Through nonwoven technology, textile fabrics with new combinations of properties opened up new applications, many of them in technical areas. Most nonwoven fabrics are not substitutes for woven and knit fabrics; rather, they are used where conventional fabrics do not provide the performance required for the application. The three major applications for nonwoven fabrics,

based on yardage used, are wipes and towels, feminine hygiene products, and cover stock for diapers and incontinence pads. Other uses include filters of many kinds, interfacing and interlining fabrics, durable "papers," carpet components, geotextiles, roofing and surgical pads, gowns, and accessories. Both disposable and durable uses are of importance.

TERMINOLOGY OF NONWOVENS

An important category of nonwoven terminology is words that describe the arrangement of the fibers in the web. *Oriented* usually indicates that the fibers lie primarily in the lengthwise direction of the fabric; *cross-laid*, that the fibers are oriented lengthwise and then crosswise in successive layers within the web; and *random*, that the fibers lie in all directions within the web. Terms conveying the method of web formation also indirectly indicate the orientation of the fibers or filaments in the web. In wet laying, staple fibers are suspended in water; when the water is removed, the staple fibers are deposited randomly. Dry laying by means of air also deposits staple fibers randomly, as rapidly circulating air mixes the fibers thoroughly until they fall from the air current onto the forming web. Carding, the same process introduced in the spun-yarn chapter, orients the fibers in the web. Cross-laid webs require an additional manufacturing step because they are usually formed by spreading oriented webs into layers, so that the resultant web has fibers oriented both lengthwise and crosswise.

The method of entanglement—hydroentangled or needlepunched—or the method of bonding—adhesive-bonded or thermally bonded—may also be part of the name of a nonwoven structure.

FELT FABRICS

Felt fabrics have been referred to as one of the oldest of modern engineering materials. It is "a textile fabric characterized by the entangled condition of most, or all, of the fibers of which it is composed." Most felt fabrics are composed of 100% wool or part-wool fibers that have matted due to the application of heat, moisture, and mechanical action (Figure 28.1). Some highly compacted *woven* fabrics are also called felts because they take on the appearance of the felts that are discussed here. Such woven fabrics do have yarns, however, making them readily distinguishable when the structure is examined.

Felts are noted for their resiliency, sound absorption, and moldability. They can be manufactured in highly ab-

FIGURE 28.1 Cross section of a typical felt fabric.

⊢——⊣ 500 μm

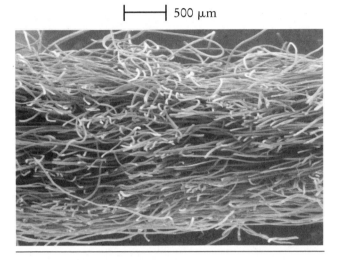

sorptive forms with unique wicking ability. They are able to isolate vibration, polish, seal, and absorb shock, as well as filter materials and provide thermal insulation. They do not fray or ravel. Limitations include the rather stiff nature of the fabric that does not allow it to fall gracefully into folds. Felts are not as strong as other fabrics, tear more readily, and are subject to pilling.

Felt has many industrial uses, some interior fabric uses, and a few clothing applications. Specifically, it is found in high-fidelity speakers and as an acoustic wall covering in auditoriums and public spaces. Felt is not used for fitted clothing but is widely used in hats, house slippers, and clothing decoration. Pennants are usually made of felt. In industry, it is found as pads for heavy production machinery, for isolating sensitive instruments from vibration in the environment, and for athletic equipment. It seals plumbing and marine gaskets and serves as weather stripping. The uses of felt are far too numerous to list.

In felting, cleaned wool fiber is carded, and a batt or web is formed by layering the carded webs. Next, the hardening process begins, with steam being forced through the web. A heavy, heated plate or rollers are then lowered onto the web and moved about to produce friction. The wool fibers interlock due to the combination of heat, moisture, and friction. The web passes through a solution of soap or acid that causes the fabric to shrink even further, and hardening is complete. At the "fulling" mill, the felt is subjected to further agitation, pounding, and shrinkage.

NEEDLEPUNCHED FABRICS

Needlepunched fabrics, also called *needled felts,* are those "nonwoven structures formed by the mechanical bonding of a fiber web or batt by needling" (Figure 28.2). Their structure is virtually identical to that of felt fabrics. However, any fiber can be mechanically entangled in a needlepunched fabric.

Fabric weights range from 1.7–10 ounces per yard^2 (40–237 grams per meter^2). Thicknesses range from 0.015–0.160 inches (0.4–4.0 millimeters). The mechanical entanglement process yields a web that is more dimensionally stable than that produced from the felting of wool fibers. Incorporation of a scrim, which is a lightweight, open-weave, coarse fabric, into the center of the web provides additional strength. Such a scrim can be seen in the photomicrograph of the needlepunch fabric in Figure 28.2.

Blankets and carpets may have a needlepunched structure. The fiber composition of needlepunched blankets is often acrylic or acrylic blends. Needlepunched indoor/outdoor carpeting made of olefin fibers is used extensively for patios, porches, and putting greens. A needlepunched fabric of olefin is used as the backing in a tufted carpet. The U.S. Army has a ballistics-protective vest for combat that is fabricated from needlepunched fabrics.

Synthetic fiberfill material may be needlepunched to prevent the fibers from shifting. In addition to fiber entanglement, fusing (melting) fibers at their crossover

FIGURE 28.2 Cross section of a typical needlepunched fabric.

⊢——⊣ 1000 μm

points may help limit the shifting of fibers. Other uses of needlepunched fabrics are filter media, coated fabric backing, apparel interlinings, road underlay, and auto trunk liners.

Needlepunching consists of passing a properly prepared (dry-laid) web over a needle loom as many times as necessary to produce the desired strength and texture. This process is relatively inexpensive. A needle loom is a board with barbed needles protruding 2–3 inches (5.0–7.6 centimeters) from the base. As the needle carrier pushes the blades of the barbed needles into and partially through the web, each barb catches one or more fibers and pushes them into or through the body of the web. When the motion of the needles is reversed and they start to withdraw from the web, the fibers that were pushed down come unhooked from the barbs. Unhooking occurs when that part of the tension in the fiber that was produced by the first motion of the needle is resisted by frictional forces built up between it and other fibers within the web. The resultant increases in fiber stresses and interfiber friction, combined with a degree of reorientation of the fibers within the web, produces an increase in the dimensional stability or strength of the web as a whole and an increase in web density. The cumulative effect of repeating this action many times in the same area of the web is the mechanical interlocking of fibers and the production of fabrics with a wide variety of useful characteristics. Heated needles may be used when synthetic-fiber batts are needlepunched. The heat facilitates fusing some of the fibers together.

SPUNLACED FABRICS

Spunlaced fabrics are nonwoven fabrics "made from a staple-fiber web or batt, in which entanglement by high-pressure water jets provides the bond." A photomicrograph of the cross section of a typical spunlaced fabric is shown in Figure 28.3. The fabric may have a uniform surface (see the photograph in Detail View 28) or be lace-like. Spunlaced fabrics are usually composed of staple polyester or olefin fibers.

The fiber arrangement is circular as a result of the subjection of the fibrous web to high-velocity water jets. A row of water jets positioned above the staple-fiber web sprays very fine jets of water at high pressure. The jets of water pull fibers into the web at the point of contact and whirl these new fibers around those already in the web. The entangled web is then dried and wound up. Additional measures, such as the use of an adhesive, must usually be taken to bond the fibers.

FIGURE 28.3   Cross section of a typical spunlaced fabric.

⊢ 100 μm

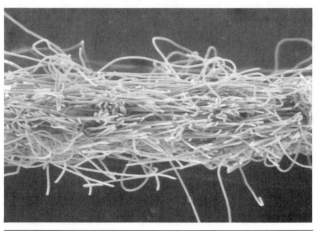

Spunlaced fabrics are soft and drapable. Strength and dimensional stability are limited. Fabric weights range from 0.7–2.2 ounces per yard^2 (1.66–5.21 grams per meter^2). Thicknesses range from 0.0035–0.025 inches (0.09–0.64 millimeters).

End uses of spunlaced fabrics are draperies and bedspreads, quilt backings, mattress pad tickings, the underlayer in coated fabric, interlinings, curtains, tablecloths, and apparel.

WET-LAID NONWOVEN FABRICS

Wet-laid nonwoven fabrics appear to be paper-like (Figure 28.4). Indeed, they are "made from a fiber sheet formed by papermaking techniques, normally followed by adhesive bonding. The material may contain a high percentage of non-textile fibers, e.g., wood pulp." The fibers are randomly arranged within the web, but the webs are the most uniform of the nonwoven structures. Fabrics weights range from 0.3–16 ounces per yard^2 (0.7–38 grams per meter^2). Thicknesses range from 0.0023–0.190 inches (0.06–4.8 millimeters). Typical end uses include laminating and coating base fabrics, filters, interlining, insulation, roofing substrates, adhesive carriers, wipes, battery separators, towels, surgical gowns, diaper cover-stock, and shoe components.

In the wet-forming process, natural or manufactured fibers are suspended in water to obtain a uniform distribution. As the fiber-and-water suspension flows onto a moving screen, the water passes through, leaving the

FIGURE 28.4 Surface of a typical wet-laid nonwoven fabric.

⊢─┤ 100 mm

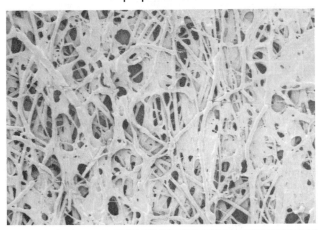

FIGURE 28.5 Surface of a typical dry-laid nonwoven fabric bonded with adhesive.

⊢─┤ 100 μm

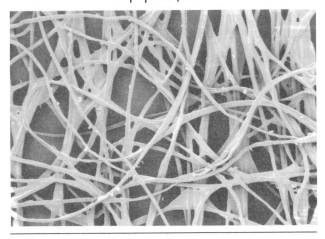

staple fibers laying uniformly as a web. Additional water is then squeezed out of the web and the remaining water is removed by drying. Bonding may be completed during drying or an adhesive may be added and the web cured.

DRY-LAID NONWOVEN FABRICS

The web structure of *dry-laid nonwoven fabrics* may be random, oriented, or cross-laid depending on the orientation of the fibers within the web (Figure 28.5). Those fabrics with random webs and cross-laid webs have uniform strength in all directions. Such webs do not have grain. Those fabrics with oriented webs are stronger in the direction in which the fibers are oriented, which is usually lengthwise. Fiber-to-fiber bonding is usually achieved by the addition of binders or by heat fusion. The binder chemicals are dried.

Dry-laid nonwovens usually have a soft hand and excellent drape, with greater strength lengthwise. Major end uses are interlinings, coated-fabric backings, carpet components, diaper cover-stock, wipes, and sanitary napkins.

MELT-BLOWN NONWOVEN FABRICS

Melt-blown nonwoven fabrics contain microfibers of varying lengths, all 2–4 micrometers in diameter (Figure 28.6). The fibers, usually olefin (polypropylene), are entangled and bonded at their crossover points. The non-

woven fabric formed is permeable, but contains very small pores.

In the formation of melt-blown nonwovens, polymer is extruded through a single-extrusion orifice into a high-velocity, heated-air stream. The fibers are thus broken into short pieces that are collected in a web on a moving conveyor belt.

Melt-blown fabrics have recently begun to be made with polyester fiber, olefin copolymers, and thermo-

FIGURE 28.6 Surface of a typical melt-blown nonwoven fabric.

├───────┤ 500 μm

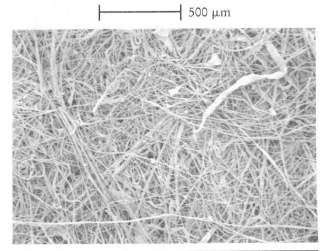

plastic polyurethanes. In addition, melt-blown non-woven fabrics are being layered (combined) with spunbonded fabrics to form spunbonded/melt-blown composites, called SMS fabrics.

SPUNBONDED FABRICS

A wide range of fabrics are called *spunbonded*. All, however, are composed of a web of randomly distributed filament fibers (Figure 28.7). They are "a nonwoven fabric made by the extrusion of filaments that are laid down in the form of a web and bonded." Fabric weights range from 0.3–6 ounces per yard^2 (0.71–14.22 grams per meter^2); fabric thicknesses, from 0.003–0.025 mils (3 × 10^{-6} to 2.5 × 10^{-6} inches or 7.6 × 10^{-5} to 6.3 × 10^{-4} millimeters). Fibers must be synthetic; polyester, nylon, and olefin are the primary fibers used.

Although the precise performance characteristics vary with the end use, spunbonded webs tend to have high tensile, high tearing strength, and low bulk. They are used for apparel interlining, carpet backing layers, bagging, packaging, filtration, wallcoverings, and charts and maps, in numerous geotextile applications, as house wrap vapor-barriers, and in protective apparel.

Spunbonding is a continuous process from extrusion of the fiber polymer to the finished product. As fiber cools, it is spread in random fashion over the surface of a moving conveyor belt. In the lay-down process, the desired orientation of the fibers is achieved by the rotation

FIGURE 28.7 Surface of a typical spunbonded nonwoven fabric.

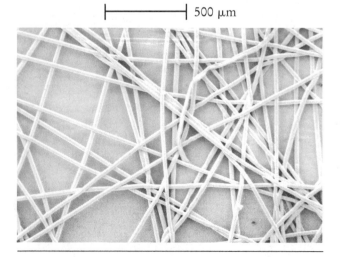

of the spinneret, electrical charges, or controlled air streams. The web is then bonded by thermal or chemical treatment.

STITCH-BONDED FABRICS

Stitch-bonded fabrics are "multicomponent, one component of which is a series of interlooped stitches running along the fabric length. The other components may be fiber web or batt, yarns, or pre-formed fabric." The components of the fabrics are marked in the diagrams of the structures in Detail View 28. Note the presence of columns of interlooped stitches in each of the stitch-bonded fabrics diagramed and in those fabrics pictured in Figure 28.8. Sometimes this structural feature is visible on both sides and sometimes on one side only. These fabrics are also called sew-knit, stitch-through, and knit-through fabrics.

Stitch-bonded fabrics are considered to be part of the nonwoven industry so are included in this chapter. However, they could be included in Chapter 29 because they are also compound fabrics.

Stitch-Bonded Webs

Of the six types of stitch-bonded fabrics, Maliwatt® and Malivlies® are the most closely related to other nonwoven fabrics because the base structure of each is a fibrous web. In *Maliwatt*® fabrics, the fibers in the web are bonded by rows of chain stitches made with a sewing thread (shown in the photograph) or by a tricot stitch. The stitching, which shows on both sides of the fabric, is so uniform, it appears that the fabric contains crosswise yarns. However, removing some of the stitching shows the fibrous nature of the fabric. The thickness of the web, the chain-stitch length and gauge (the distance between rows of stitches), and the type of stitch (such as tricot), may also be varied. These fabrics tend to have high tearing strength and relatively high bulk per unit weight, leading to good insulating ability. Their major end uses are interlinings for garment, shoe, and upholstery fabrics, decorative fabrics, textile wallcoverings, dishcloths, and backing fabrics for coating.

Threadless stitch-bonded fiber webs, fabrics in which the stitching loops are formed from the fibers of the web, are trademarked *Malivlies*® fabrics. The stitching loops appear on only one side of the fabric; the opposite side looks like a fiber web. Usually, these fabrics are lower in strength than those made with a stitching thread. End uses are backing layer for coated fabrics,

FIGURE 28.8 The six types of stitch-bonded fabrics.

Maliwatt®

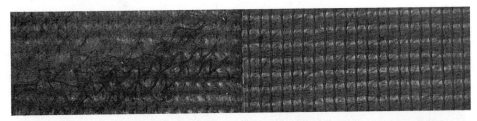

Malivlies®

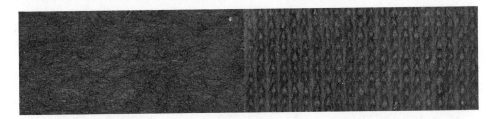

Malimo®

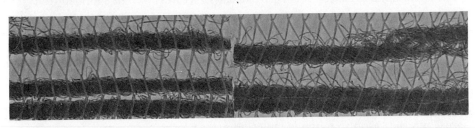

Schusspol®

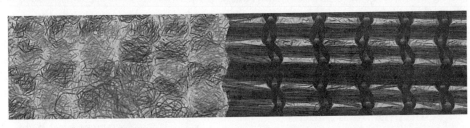

Malipol®

Voltex®

textile wallcoverings, decorative felts, packing materials, and insulating materials.

Stitch-Bonded Yarn Systems

Crosswise yarns, with or without lengthwise yarns lying over them, may be stitched together with a chain or tricot stitch to form a stitch-bonded fabric called *Malimo®*. The example shown in Figure 28.8 has one yarn system that is stitched together with a tricot stitch. Malimo® fabrics are nonwovens because the yarn systems do not interlace or intermesh in any way. The stitching yarns are usually fine and as inconspicuous as possible. The lengthwise yarns, when present, provide textural interest. Structural variation is achieved when the lengthwise yarns wave rather than lying straight. Fancy yarns often add interest.

Most Malimo® fabrics are fairly open structures. When the yarns are laid too closely together, the fabric becomes much too stiff and boardy for most end uses. Shrinkage tends to occur in the crosswise direction. Strength is good but the fabric is subject to tearing and breaking due to the use of delicate stitching yarns in a rather open structure.

The majority of Malimo® fabrics are used for draperies, but they are also found in tablecloths, dishcloths, and vegetable bags. All these end uses accommodate an open structure in which the yarns do not slip. Occasionally, outerwear, upholstery, textile wallcoverings, bed sheets, towels and dishcloths, and industrial and high technology fabrics are Malimo® fabrics.

Pile Stitch-Bonded Fabrics

Schusspol® fabrics are characterized by the addition of a yarn into the chain stitches of a basic Malimo® structure to form a looped surface. Note in the photograph in Figure 28.8 the presence of crosswise yarns held together by chain stitches on the fabric back that serve as the base of the structure—the fundamental Malimo® structure—and the lengthwise pile yarns on the face side. Carpeting

and upholstery fabrics are made with this fabric-forming process.

Malipol® *fabrics* are single- or double-faced pile fabrics in which pile *yarns* are held to a base structure by a chain or tricot stitch. In a single-sided pile fabric, as shown in Figure 28.8, stitch heads are seen on the fabric back (right) and pile loops on the fabric face (left). The base structure may be a nonwoven, a knit or woven fabric, a Malimo® stitch-bonded fabric, or a plastic film. The fabric in Figure 28.8 has a woven-fabric base. Usually there is an adhesive on the fabric back to hold the loops. Floor covering and "crushed" velvet-like fabrics for upholstery are the two main interior fabric uses. Simulated furs and pile lining fabrics are made for apparel applications. Terry towels and blankets are the household end uses.

Voltex® *fabrics* are characterized by deep, voluminous pile formed from slivers of fiber rather than yarn, a nonwoven for the base, and the presence of chain-stitch heads on the fabric back. The preformed sliver of fibers is "stitched" through the base web. Major applications are blankets, imitation furs, plush fabrics, and lining materials.

CHAPTER SUMMARY

Nonwoven fabrics are fabrics in which a fiber web or a yarn system is held together (bonded) by various means to form an integral fabric structure. Specific types of nonwoven fabrics are felt, needlepunched, spunlaced, wet-laid, dry-laid, melt-blown, spunbonded, and stitch-bonded. A major difference between the different nonwoven fabrics is whether they are composed of staple or filament fiber webs. Nonwoven fabrics, largely a product of 20th century fabric-forming technology, are engineered to fill markets not previously served by conventional fabrics. Major markets are various consumer and industrial applications including geotextiles, protective clothing, feminine hygienic products, disposable diapers, and towels and wipes.

Compound Fabric Structures

Compound fabrics are composed of two or more layers of fabric or of a fabric and another component (yarn, fiber, vinyl, film, etc.) held together by stitching, fusing, adhesive bonding, and other means.

QUILTED FABRICS

Fabrics in which the center or bottom layer is composed of a batt of natural fibers, a synthetic fiberfill, or down. Their two or three layers are either stitched together with sewing thread, fused or joined by adhesives at points along the surface.

TUFTED FABRICS

Fabrics that have "a pile consisting of tufts or loops formed by inserting yarn into a previously prepared backing fabric."

FLOCKED FABRICS

Fabrics composed of very short or pulverized fibers standing vertically on a base layer to form a velvet-like surface. Usually, adhesive secures the fibers to the base.

COATED FABRICS

Fabrics "composed of two or more layers, at least one of which is a textile fabric and at least one of which is a substantially continuous polymeric layer. The layers are bonded [joined] closely together by means of an added adhesive or by the adhesive properties of one or more of the component layers."

LAMINATED FABRICS

Fabrics "composed of two or more layers, at least one of which is a textile fabric, bonded closely together by means of an added adhesive, or by the adhesive properties of one or more of the component layers."

FUSION-BONDED CARPETS

Carpets in which the pile yarn is secured to a backing fabric by a layer of adhesive.

FOAM-AND-FIBER FABRICS

Fabrics comprised of a layer of foam and fiber or an entangled fiber web surrounded by a foam matrix.

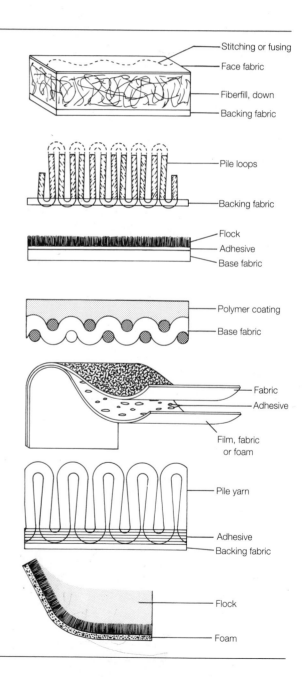

Stitching or fusing
Face fabric
Fiberfill, down
Backing fabric

Pile loops
Backing fabric

Flock
Adhesive
Base fabric

Polymer coating
Base fabric

Fabric
Adhesive
Film, fabric or foam

Pile yarn
Adhesive
Backing fabric

Flock
Foam

29

Compound Fabrics

The fabrics considered in this chapter are those in which two or more distinctive layers are present, with at least one of the layers being a conventional textile structure (yarns, fibers, or woven, knit, or nonwoven fabric). The manufacture of these fabrics involves bringing various materials such as previously formed fabrics, films, thin sheets of foam, and/or very short fibers together and joining them by various means, forming one structure. Definitions and diagrams of the seven fabrics considered are provided in Detail View 29.

QUILTED FABRICS

Quilted fabrics consist of a filler material sandwiched between two thin fabrics. These layers are fused or held together with stitching threads (Figure 29.1). A design—frequently diamonds or a wavy repetitive pattern—is formed. The filler material is often a thick nonwoven fabric composed of synthetic fibers. The filler material can also be down, feathers, wool, or cotton fibers.

Quilting Technology

Quilting is done on a sewing machine or with an ultrasonic quilting machine. The former uses thread to bind the components and the latter heat to fuse them.

Quilting done by guiding the fabric layers through a sewing machine by hand is very costly but makes any quilting pattern possible. Automated sewing machines

FIGURE 29.1 Quilted fabrics.

Machine-stitched quilted fabric
(layers joined by stitching)

Ultrasonically quilted fabric
(layers joined by fusing at
points along the surface)

speed the work and thus lower the cost, but they can make only continuous quilting lines. Face and backing fabrics of any fiber composition can be *machine-quilted*.

Ultrasonic quilting causes the layers to fuse together at points along the surface as high-frequency, ultrasonic vibrations generated in a stitching device heat the thermoplastic fibers in the assembled fabric. The thermoplastic fibers soften and adhere to each other. Only face fabric, backing fabric, and filling material with a high percentage of thermoplastic fiber content can be used.

End Uses

Many quilted fabrics are used for cold-weather garments. Quilted upholstery fabrics are popular. Most mattress pads and many bedspreads are quilted. Protective vests may also be quilted.

Quilted fabrics can fulfill several performance needs. They can trap body heat, provide soft padding, or provide a degree of safety by preventing penetration of sharp objects or projectiles. They are also produced for their beauty. Because the degree of thermal insulation provided is determined mainly by the thickness, uniformity, and compressional resilience of the fiberfill or batting, it is important that the quilted fabric layers do not separate due to stitching thread breakage or fuse point debonding. Wind resistance is provided by a closely constructed outer fabric. Some outer fabrics need to be "downproof" to prevent down or other filling materials from working through to the outside fabric.

Because the method used to join the layers is critical in the functional and aesthetic life of quilted fabrics, the thread type, stitch length, or bond points should be closely inspected before a purchase is made. A lock-type stitch with a strong, abrasion-resistant thread is considered best. Twistless nylon monofilament thread is, therefore, often used. Such thread is transparent as well, so it picks up the colors of the fabric. Ultrasonically quilted fabric should be inspected for potential tearing at the fused points.

TUFTED FABRICS

Tufted fabrics have "a pile consisting of tufts or loops formed by inserting yarn into a previously prepared backing fabric" (Figure 29.2). As in all pile fabrics, the yarn forming the pile stands vertical to a base or ground. The pile on tufted fabric may be cut (as shown) or uncut, and the backing fabric may be woven (as shown), knit, or nonwoven. Parallel rows of stitches can be seen on the back of tufted fabrics. Because the "stitches" are not interlocked, the pile yarn can be removed easily from the backing fabric. Therefore, a thin coating of adhesive is often applied to the back to hold the pile yarns in place, or a secondary backing is added (as shown in Detail View 29).

Tufted fabrics differ from each other in the distance between rows of stitches (called the gauge length), the stitch length, and the pile height. Pattern and texture can be achieved by cutting loops in selected areas, varying loop heights, and printing level-loop surfaces.

Tufting Technology

Tufting involves punching yarn through a previously formed fabric (the primary backing) to form a loop. In commercial tufting, a series of needles are used, each carrying a yarn from a series of spools held on a creel. The previously formed fabric is held horizontally and the needles, vertically. The needles move in unison through the primary backing, carrying the yarn with them. A hook called the loop former located behind the base moves forward to hold the loop as the needle is retracted. When the needles clear, the base moves forward a predetermined distance, and the action repeats itself. If the loops are to be cut, a knife attached to the hook cuts the loops as the needle retracts. Although the basic principle is simplistic, many refinements are necessary to produce an acceptable product. For example, mecha-

FIGURE 29.2　The face and back of a tufted fabric (left) and the process of tufting (right).

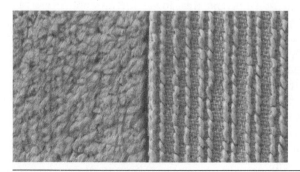

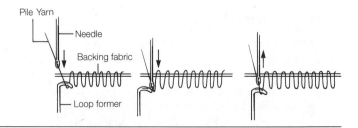

nisms must ensure that the needles do not lift the base as they pull forward, so that the formed loops are of uniform size. After the loops are formed and cut, the yarns are opened and fibers teased from the yarn. Cut tufts are held in place by this "blooming" of the yarn, by the shrinkage of the primary backing in finishing, and frequently by the use of an adhesive on the fabric back.

End Uses

More than 95% of carpeting today is tufted. Tufted carpets are less expensive than the woven carpets that they replaced because production rates are considerably higher, equipment costs are lower, and less-skilled labor can be used. Tufted carpeting can be produced at a rate of 645 yards^2 per hour (539 meters^2 per hour). An Axminster loom that weaves carpeting produces carpet at a rate of 14 yards^2 per hour (11.7 meters^2 per hour). By contrast, over 30,000 yards^2 (25,083 meters^2) of carpet can be tufted on one machine in one day.[1] These factors do not imply that a tufted carpet is of lower quality than a woven carpet because carpet performance depends more on fiber composition, yarn structure, backing, and its detailed construction (stitch length, pile height, etc.) than upon the basic construction (woven, tufted, or other).

----

[1]R.G. Turner, "What's New in Carpet Dyeing?" *Textile Chemist and Colorist* 19/8 (1987): 16.

Tufted upholstery fabrics are widely available. Candlewick bedspread fabrics are tufted. They are often called chenille spreads, though they do not contain chenille yarns (Chapter 25). Fur-like tufted fabrics are used for shells or linings of coats and jackets. Tufted blankets have been successful in Europe but are not produced or sold in the United States.

FLOCKED FABRICS

"Flocked products are made from very short or pulverized fibers which, when attached to cloth or paper, form a velvet-like surface and are used in the textile, furniture, and packaging industries as well as protective coating for metal and plastic."[2] *Flock*, "a material obtained by reducing textile fibers to fragments by cutting, tearing, or grinding, to give various degrees of comminution [pulverization]," is usually held to a base fabric with an adhesive. Flocked fabrics have flock adhering to the entire surface (Figure 29.3).[3] The base may be cloth (as shown) or foam. Rayon is the fiber most often used for the flock, but nylon, polyester, olefin, and acrylic are also used.

----

[2]Definition developed by the American Flock Association as stated in the *Encyclopedia of Associations*.
[3]Fabrics with flock applied in localized areas on a fabric surface are called flock prints; they are considered in Chapter 35. To make flock prints, flocking technology is modified so that the adhesive is printed onto the fabric surface with conventional or heat transfer printing processes.

FIGURE 29.3 **Cross section of a flocked fabric (left) and the beater-bar method of flocking (right).**

⊢ 100 μm

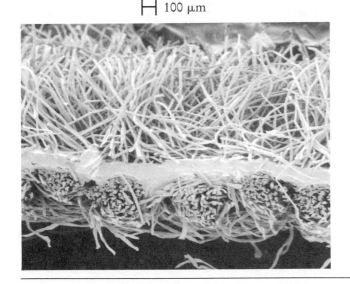

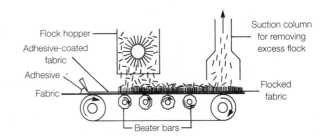

Flocked fabrics, a type of pile fabric, have a sueded-leather, woven-velvet, or plush-like appearance. Pile height varies from 0.008 inches (0.2 millimeters) for suede-like fabrics up to 0.32 inches (8 millimeters) for carpet pile.

Flocking Technology

The *beater-bar method* and the *electrostatic method* are two techniques used to flock flat fabrics. Both involve preparing the flock, storing the flock in a flock hopper, applying adhesive to the surface of the base fabric, directing the flock to the prepared surface, drying the fabric, and cleaning nonbonded fibers from the surface. Figure 29.3 shows the beater-bar method. Here the adhesive-coated fabric passes over a series of polygonal rollers that rapidly rotate to vibrate the fabric. The flock falls by gravity from the flock hopper and is driven into the adhesive by the vibration of the fabric. A diagram for electrostatic flocking would be very similar. In the electrostatic method, the beater bars are replaced with a grounded electrode and the flock falls straight toward the fabric surface because it is given a charge as it leaves the flock hopper. *Windblown flocking*, used for flocking three-dimensional objects such as the inside of latex gloves, delivers the fibers to an adhesive-coated surface with an air stream.

End Uses

Flocked fabrics have been used for several centuries in a number of end uses. Today, their largest use is household and interior textile items, including velvet-like upholstery fabrics, draperies, bedspreads, wallcoverings, and blankets. At one time, it was thought that flocked carpeting would establish itself in the market, but this never happened. The second largest end use is in children's and women's clothes. Flocked fabrics are also found as outer fabric for stuffed toys, air filters, nonslip patch fabrics on boat decks and swimming areas, handbags, and belts.

The performance of flocked fabrics is in large measure related to the adhesive used. For many years, the adhesives made the fabrics stiff and turned fabrics off-color as time passed. During laundering and drycleaning, the adhesive often dissolved and the flock was lost. Developments in flock technology in the 1960s permitted washable and drycleanable flock fabrics to be made. Today, flocked fabrics have good durability, drape, and hand. They are also colorless and free of undesirable odor.

Water-vapor and air permeability may be adversely affected because the adhesive can make the fabric almost completely impermeable.

COATED FABRICS

Coated fabrics are "composed of two or more layers, at least one of which is a textile fabric and at least one of which is a substantially continuous polymeric layer. The layers are bonded [joined] closely together by means of an added adhesive or by the adhesive properties of one or more of the component layers." The textile layer, which usually forms the base or ground layer, may be a woven, knit, or nonwoven fabric.

Conventional continuous polymeric materials such as rubber, polyvinyl chloride (PVC), and polyurethane, are used to make a coated fabric that is impervious to water as well as chemical solutions. These coated fabrics are typically found as upholstery fabrics, conventional waterproof fabrics, and chemical-protective clothing fabrics and in a variety of industrial uses. Coating materials, either hydrophobic and porous or hydrophilic and closed, are used to make coated fabrics that are pervious to water vapor but quite impervious to water and other liquids.

Note in Figure 29.4 how the coating flows into the surface of the base fabric, adhering to all of the surface fibers. The coating shown is hydrophilic and closed; the base is a woven polyester/cotton fabric. This coated fabric would be used in waterproof breathable rainwear.

Coating Technology

Coating is the application of a semiliquid material to one or both sides of a base fabric in such a manner that the material lies on the surface, without permeating the entire base. The coating solution is applied to the base fabric in a number of ways, two of which are shown in Figure 29.4. In *direct coating*, the base fabric is passed, horizontally and under considerable tension, beneath a stationary coating head that applies a thin, uniform coating of polymer solution to its upper surface. The simplest type of coating head consists of a knife, or doctor blade, accurately positioned at a preset clearance above the base fabric, which is supported by a roller. Polymer solution that is held in a reservoir behind the blade is forced through the preset knife gap by the forward motion of the base fabric, forming a continuous coating. Extremely small knife gaps (100 micrometers or less) are commonly used. Direct coating is usually car-

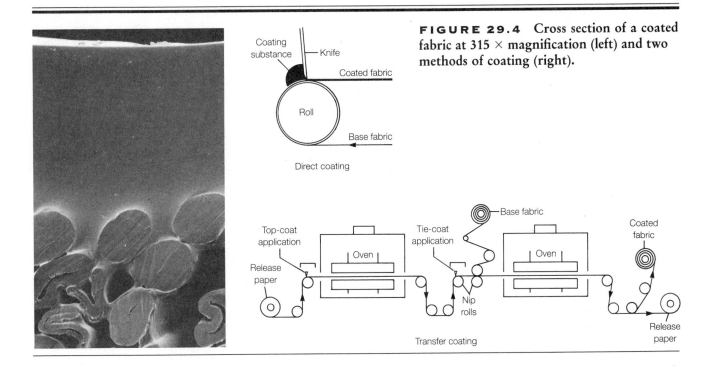

FIGURE 29.4 Cross section of a coated fabric at 315 × magnification (left) and two methods of coating (right).

ried out on closely woven fabrics constructed from filament yarns; these materials do not distort under the high tensions involved and they present a smooth surface at the coating head. The coated fabric then travels through an oven, where the coating is dried and cured, and is finally wound up.

In *transfer coating*, the coating layer is first prepared on release paper and then transferred to the base fabric. More specifically, a polymer solution is knife-coated onto a release paper. As it passes through an oven, the polymer is cured, becoming the prepared top-coat. A thin application of an adhesive is then added to form a tie-coat/top-coat/release-paper assembly. While the tie-coat is still tacky, it is brought in contact with the base fabric, and this new assembly is passed under pressure through nip rolls. The fabric/tie-coat/top-coat/release-paper assembly is passed through a second oven, where the tie-coat is dried and cured. The release paper is then stripped from the rest of the assembly. Transfer coating is particularly useful for dimensionally unstable fabrics such as loosely woven, knitted, and nonwoven fabrics. Hairy fabrics have the advantage that they afford better mechanical adhesion to the top-coat. The thickness of the coating, the thickness of the tie-coat, and the pressure influence the handle and drape of the final coated fabric.

Other technologies are (a) *dip coating*, in which the base fabric is passed through a vat containing the coating solution and the solution is spread by passing the fabric between rollers; (b) *roller coating*, in which the base fabric moves between two rollers, one of which is covered with the coating solution; and (c) *cast coating*, in which resinous material is cured by heated casting drums. In all cases, the coated fabric must be cured.

End Uses

There are numerous consumer and industrial uses for coated fabrics. Window shades, book covers, wallcoverings, and shoe liners are usually PVC-coated fabrics (polyvinyl chloride). Women's shoe uppers may be polyurethane-coated. Industrial tarpaulins are a heavyweight base fabric with a coating of polyurethane. Other applications are vinyl car tops, floor coverings, bandages, acoustical barriers, filters, soft-sided luggage, awnings, ditch liners, and air-supported structures.

Vinyl upholstery fabrics are coated fabrics. The most common combination is an expanded vinyl on a jersey knit base. The expanded vinyl, a PVC-polymeric material, has a thin top layer—with a maximum thickness of 0.004 inches (0.1 millimeters)—and a thicker inner layer—approximately 0.020–0.024 inches (0.5–0.6 millimeters) thick. The thinner layer is fairly solid; the thicker layer has a cellular structure, resulting in a much softer and more pleasant feeling fabric than could be obtained if the entire coating were like the top layer. The upholstery vinyl is usually embossed with a leather-like grain, photogravure-printed, or covered with lacquer.

Other upholstery fabrics have a polyurethane coat that is quite thin—only 0.0008–0.002 inches (0.02–0.04 millimeters)—yielding a very soft and bendable fabric. Compared with an expanded-vinyl coating, this thin coating needs a base fabric of much higher quality to support it and to provide the necessary strength and other performance requirements. The most commonly used base is an unmercerized cotton sateen with filling yarns that are raised and cropped to give a dense, close nap. The disadvantage of a very thin coating is that the weave pattern of the base fabric can become visible on the coated surface, causing considerable batch-to-batch differences in surface appearance. The advantages are softer, drier, and more flexible fabrics and a much more leather-like "break" (appearance when bent and flexed) than PVC-coated fabrics. Because the coating process is technically more difficult and several materials used in the past were not durable, polyurethane-coated fabrics are currently in limited use as upholstery fabrics.

Rainwear such as yellow rain slickers may be made with conventionally coated fabric (waterproof but not water-vapor permeable) or with fabrics coated with the more recently developed waterproof breathable (WB) polymer materials. WB-polymers, which may either be coated onto or laminated to a base, are discussed under laminated fabrics.

LAMINATED FABRICS

Laminated fabrics are "composed of two or more layers, at least one of which is a textile fabric, bonded [joined] closely together by means of an added adhesive, or by the adhesive properties of one or more of the component layers." In Figure 29.5, a base fabric, a film, and an adhesive holding the two layers together are visible. Three types of laminated fabrics are film laminates, foam laminates, and bonded fabrics.

Film Laminates

In *film laminates,* one component is film,[4] a thin, flexible sheet material composed of polymers that are not as well-oriented as in fibers. This film may be bonded with adhesive to a base fabric or between two fabrics.

Films in waterproof breathable fabrics (WBFs), whether laminated to or coated onto a base fabric, are of

---

[4]Heavy films can be used alone for shower curtains, tablecloths, shelf coverings, and waterproof rainwear. Tape yarns, discussed in Chapter 24, were initially films that were subsequently split or fibrillated.

FIGURE 29.5   Cross section of a film-laminated fabric at 315 × magnification (left) and process of film laminating (right).

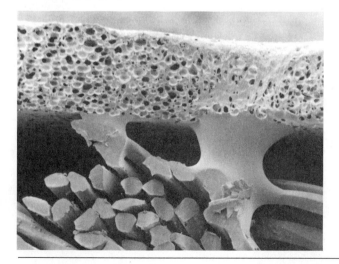

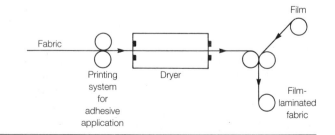

two types: one is hydrophilic and closed; the other is hydrophobic and porous. The latter films are often referred to as microporous membranes, and the fabrics containing them are microporous fabrics. The film in Figure 29.5 represents a hydrophobic and porous film. If the polymeric material in Figure 29.4 were laminated to the base fabric rather than coated to it, it would represent a hydrophilic and closed film.

The holes in *microporous films* or microporous coating materials are large enough for vaporous water to pass through but too small for liquid water droplets to pass. WBFs made with microporous films or coating materials are most effective when worn in cold, dry climates where there is a large difference in relative humidity between the inner and outer surfaces of the fabric. Because the inner surface will tend to be warm and moist, the gradient across a microporous WBF provides the driving force for removing perspiration. Prevailing winds assist in breathability by keeping the relative humidity at the outer surface at a constantly low level. Microporous WBFs are subject to clogging of the pores (due to detergent or drycleaning residues and salt from sea water). They do not have sufficient water-vapor permeability when the outer fabric is wet or when the atmosphere is very humid and the wind speed is low because water vapor can only diffuse when there is a difference in the vapor pressure gradient on the two sides of a fabric. Microporous fabrics, especially Goretex®, that contain an expanded polytetrafluoroethylene film, have enjoyed considerable success in outdoor activewear.

Hydrophilic and closed films or coatings move water vapor through a combination of chemistry and physics. The charges in the long polymer chains draw water-vapor molecules, which have a negative charge near the oxygen molecule, to the positive side of the film or coating. High vapor pressure on the body side also pushes the water-vapor molecules through the film or coating. Movement of vaporous water occurs even when the outside of the film or coating is wet because the temperature on the inside is still greater than that on the outside. There are no pores to become clogged. Sympatex®, manufactured by Akzo, is a fabric with a modified polyester polymer forming the hydrophilic and closed film or coating.

Foam Laminates

Foam laminates are those laminated fabrics in which a thin foam layer is present. Foam is a material characterized by small numerous air bubbles in a lofty, bulky, springy, elastic-like structure.[5] Thin, flexible layers of polyurethane foam, usually too weak to be used alone, serve as an insulating layer when joined to a fabric or sandwiched between two fabrics. Foam laminates are used in the manufacture of spring coats and bathrobes, where a warm and lightweight fabric is needed.

Bonded Fabrics

Bonded fabrics, which appeared in 1962, are those laminated fabrics in which a face fabric is joined to a backing fabric, such as tricot knit, with an adhesive that does not significantly add to the thickness of the combined fabrics.

Today, bonded fabric is found in some lined garments where the lining and fabric are one layer of fabric. In this application, the need for a separate garment lining is eliminated, as is the need for an interlining, an underlining, stay stitching, and seam finishing.

Bonding and Laminating Technology

Bonding involves the application of a wet adhesive or the use of foam that acts as an adhesive. In the *wet-adhesive method*, the adhesive is applied to the underside (technical back) of the face fabric, and the backing fabric is joined when the two layers are passed between rollers. The bonded fabric is heated twice, the first time to drive out the solvents and give a preliminary cure, and the second time to effect a permanent bond. In the foam-flame process, polyurethane foam as thin as $\frac{1}{15,000}$ inch ($\frac{1}{38,100}$ centimeters) is made tacky first on one side and then on the other by passing it by a gas flame. *Film laminating*, shown in Figure 29.5, is done either on a non-continuous basis by net-like or dot (punctiform) application of dissolved or fused adhesives, or by flame laminating, with fused foam serving as the adhesive.

The success of bonding and laminating rests with the adhesive. Unfortunately, textile mills began to bond fabrics before the development of suitable adhesives was achieved. Consequently, consumers encountered problems with bonded fabrics, including separation of the layers, puckering due to uneven (differential) shrinkage of the layers, and bleeding of the adhesive through to the surface of the face fabric. Many of the early bonded and

---

[5] Polyurethane flexible foam is used to form pillows, cushions on upholstered furniture, and foam mattresses and as a backing material for carpet tiles and kitchen carpets. Its use has been questioned because of its highly flammable nature, its emission of toxic fumes, and the quantity of smoke generated when burning. However, foam remains important because of its low cost.

foam-laminated fabrics were quite stiff. Soon, these fabrics had earned a poor reputation that has proved difficult to overcome.

Fusion-Bonded Carpets

Fusion-bonded carpets are those carpets in which the pile yarn is secured by a vinyl plasticizer, a bonding agent acting by solvent action on fibers (Detail View 29). The carpet has a continuous, impermeable vinyl back and a tuft lock superior to any other cut-pile carpet construction. Solid color, heather pile effects and printed fusion-bonded carpets are available.

In manufacturing, the pile yarn is inserted directly into a liquid vinyl plasticizer. The components are then fusion-bonded together.

FOAM-AND-FIBER FABRICS

Several fabrics are composed of fiber and foam that are either present in distinct layers or intimately mixed. An example of the first type of foam-and-fiber fabric is the Vellux® blanket, a trademark of West Point Pepperell, that is made of soft nylon fibers electrostatically joined to two layers of polyurethane foam. The foam layers are permanently sealed to a nylon scrim that lies between them. The blanket is lightweight and provides warmth to the user. It can withstand over 50 washings and dryings with no change in appearance if a gentle agitation cycle is used.

Examples of the second type of foam-and-fiber fabric are Facile®, Ultrasuede®, and Belleseime®. Of all suede-like textile structures, these are considered to be the most similar to natural sueded leather in appearance and hand. They are composed of microfibers surrounded by polyurethane foam; the arrangement of the fibers reproduces the microscopic structure of natural sueded leather. All surface fibers run in the same direction. The fabrics have a thin resin coating. The first two fabrics are distributed by the Skinner Division of Springs Mills and the third by the Kanebo Company of Japan.

Little is known about the details of the manufacture because the processes are proprietary. It is known that Ultrasuede® fabric, developed by Toray Industries of Japan, is formed using bicomponent-biconstituent fibers with a matrix-fibril configuration. These fibers are needlepunched to form a nonwoven fabric. Then the matrix portion of the fibers is dissolved, leaving a highly entangled web of microfibers. This entangled web is then impregnated with polyurethane foam.

These suede-like fabrics are used for coats, jackets, skirts, and other apparel items in which sueded leather is used, and for upholstery fabrics, wallcoverings, and luggage. Promotional materials state that these fabrics will not stretch out of shape, pill, fray, crock, wrinkle, or water spot. They are machine-washable and drycleanable using regular textile procedures (rather than leather drycleaning procedures) because they retain their softness and colorants during these processes.

CHAPTER SUMMARY

Seven types of compound fabrics—tufted, quilted, flocked, coated, laminated (film, foam, and bonded), fusion-bonded, and foam-and-fiber fabrics—were described in this chapter. All contain at least one textile layer but differ in the type of material used in each layer and the manner in which the layers are joined. Manufacturing and end uses of each fabric were also given.

UNIT

V

Chemical, Mechanical, and Thermal Treatments and Performance

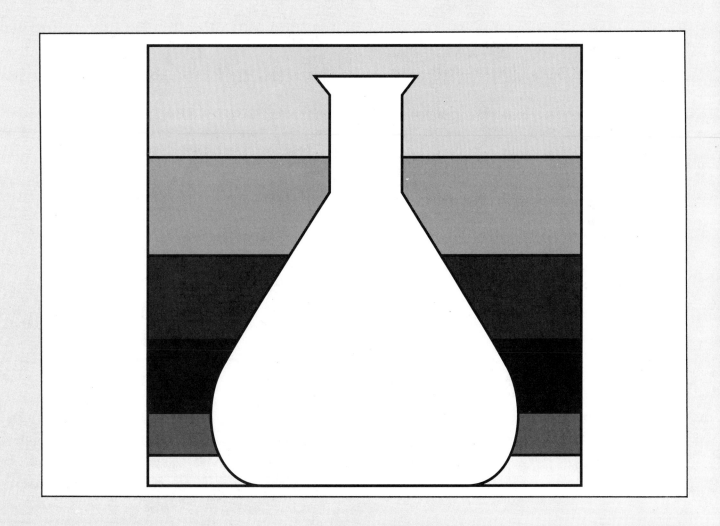

Chemical, Mechanical, and Thermal Treatments

FINISHED TEXTILES

Those textiles that have been converted from greige state into merchandise that is saleable to the ultimate consumer or textile product fabricator. Usually, it is fabrics that receive the finishing treatment but yarns or garments may also be processed. Finishes are chemical, mechanical, and/or thermal; visible or nonvisible; permanent, durable, semidurable, or temporary; and single- or multifunctional.

Chemical Finishes

Resins, gums, flame retardants, softeners, sodium hydroxide, ammonia, and many other chemicals may adhere to fiber surfaces, react with fiber polymers, or alter the fine structure of fibers and subsequently be extracted. Fabric interstices may be filled with finishing chemicals.

Topical   Internal

Geometric Alteration or Fibers and Yarns within a Fabric

Rearrangement of fibers and yarns within a fabric by mechanical or thermal manipulation (compaction, flattening, embossing, etc.).

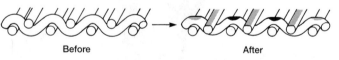

Before   After

DYED TEXTILES

Those textiles in which colorant (usually dye rather than pigment) is uniformly distributed within or on the surface of all fibers throughout yarns or fabric. Solid, heather, mottled, and mixed coloration, stripes, checks, and plaids, as well as colored motifs, are created.

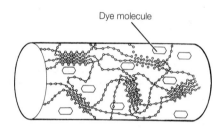

Dye molecule

PRINTED TEXTILES

Those textiles with designs resulting from the application of colorants (usually pigments rather than dyes) and certain other substances to localized areas on fabric or yarn surfaces. Designs range from simple dots to intricate motifs and patterns.

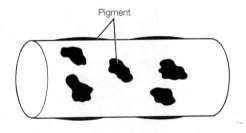

Pigment

Colorants

Substances, called dyestuffs and pigments, that "modify the perceived color of objects or impart color to otherwise colorless objects."

*M*OST COMMERCIALLY produced fabrics contain colorants and/or finishing chemicals. In 1987, 2.4 billion pounds of chemicals were added to unfinished fabric—called greige, gray, grey, or loom-state fabric—to alter aesthetics and functional performance.[1] An additional 137.8 million pounds of colorants were used.[2] Tens of thousands of yards of fabric were mechanically altered (brushed, napped, sheared, flatted, or compacted) and/or treated with heat following their formation. Devoid of these chemical, mechanical, and thermal treatments, the majority of fabrics would be unacceptable in aesthetics as well as functional performance.

WHAT ARE THE MAJOR FINISHES?

Finished textiles are those textiles that have been converted from greige state into merchandise that is saleable to the ultimate consumer or textile product fabricator (Overview V). *Greige fabrics* are fabrics just off the loom or knitting machine. They are in an unfinished state. It is usually fabrics that receive finishing treatments, but occasionally yarns are treated prior to fabric formation. Finishes alter a fabric by changing its geometry and/or its chemical nature. Finishes may be classified as (a) chemical, mechanical, and/or thermal, (b) visible or nonvisible, (c) durable, semidurable, renewable, or temporary, and (d) single- or multifunctional.

Chemically finished textiles are textiles that have been subjected to chemical compounds. Over 3000 finishing chemicals—including resins, gums, softening compounds, water repellents, antimicrobials, and flame retardants—are available for application to textiles.[3] Usually, the result of chemical treatments is the presence of the chemical(s) or its reaction product(s) in the purchased fabric. The chemical may adhere to fiber surfaces, forming a barrier or coating (a topical treatment),

or it may be absorbed into the fiber, where it may or may not react with fiber polymers (an internal treatment). These two types of treatments are illustrated in Overview V. The chemical may fill the fabric interstices (not shown). In some cases, the finishing chemical is absorbed into a fiber, alters the fiber's internal structure, and is subsequently extracted.

Mechanically and thermally finished textiles are textiles in which the geometry of the fabric or the polymer arrangement within fibers has been altered. As shown in Overview V by the use of before and after diagrams, such finished fabrics may have a flatter surface (causing enhanced luster) or have greater yarn crimp (causing reduced relaxation shrinkage) than the unfinished fabric. The finished fabric might also be more compact, more compressed, or bulkier than the unfinished fabric. Thermal treatments may cause the polymers in thermoplastic fibers to rearrange themselves or may cause fibers to crimp, increasing the bulk of the yarn and the fabric. Heat is also used to set or cure resins.

Visible finishes are those finishes applied to a fabric in order to change the fabric's appearance. An example is adding chemicals or mechanically polishing a fabric to make the surface shiny. *Nonvisible finishes,* which are usually chemical, require informative labeling for their presence to be known at the time of purchase. Labels will usually state the enhancement achieved, such as durable press or flame resistance. It is rare for the name of the specific reactant(s) or resin(s) to appear on labels. There are no federal or state laws that require fabric to be labeled with chemical finish information. When the specific chemical needs to be known, sale and production records must be traced or a sample of the fabric submitted to a laboratory for analysis. In the laboratory, sophisticated quantitative and qualitative procedures will usually identify the specific finishing chemical and determine the amount used.

Permanent, durable, semidurable, and *temporary* designate the length of time that a finish will maintain its effectiveness (the longevity of the finish).[4] Permanent finishes are those that do not decrease in effectiveness during the life of the fabric. They usually are chemical treatments that have permanently altered the fibers; for example, the mercerization of cotton fabric. Durable

---

[1] "2.4 Billion and Growing," *America's Textiles International* 17/4 (1988): 67.
[2] E.G. Hochberg, "Textile Dyebath Additives," *America's Textiles International* 13/5 (1984): 33–34, 36–39.
[3] A *resin* is a chemical used to modify textiles by (a) application of the chemical as a polymer to the textile; (b) self-polymerization of the chemical on the textile; (c) reaction of the chemical with the textile; or (d) a combination of these. American Association of Textile Chemists and Colorists, *1985 AATCC Technical Manual* (Research Triangle Park, NC: AATCC), p. 178.
   Gum is a very loosely applied term covering a wide range of substances. "Strictly, gums are carbohydrate high polymers, either soluble or dispersible in water, that are derived from vegetable origins. Loosely, the term *gum* is used to mean resins, saps, natural rubber, chicle, starch, cellulose derivatives, and many other products. In textile printing, the term refers to print-paste thickeners." Hoechst Celanese Corporation, *Dictionary of Fiber and Textile Technology* (Charlotte, NC: Hoechst Celanese Corporation, 199), p. 74.

---

[4] Finish longevity may also be expressed as finish durability. The latter terminology is not used in this text, as it may result in some confusion with the use of fabric durability, which is the ability of fabric to withstand repeated mechanical forces.

finishes usually last throughout the life of the textile but their effectiveness diminishes. For example, durable-press fabrics (those treated to reduce wrinkling) usually need some touch-up ironing after the 40th or 50th wash-and-use cycles, and certain antimicrobial finishes on carpet slowly diminish with each shampooing. Semidurable or renewable finishes are those which last through as few as 5–10 launderings or drycleanings. Examples of this type of finish include those that control static, impart softness and stiffness, and confer water repellency. Semidurable finishes can be renewed by the drycleaner or persons who do home laundry. Temporary finishes are those removed or substantially diminished the first time they are laundered or drycleaned. Starch, a stiffener that is soluble in water, is an example of a temporary finish.

Single-functional finishes enhance one fabric property. For example, a chemical used to increase the luster of cotton fabric would be a single-function finish. Multifunctional finishes enhance two or more performance properties. For example, the application of sodium hydroxide to cotton fabric increases luster, reduces fabric shrinkage, and enhances coloration.

Although finishes improve a certain property or properties of a fabric, they tend to detract from or reduce other aspects of fabric performance. For example, the application of durable-press resins enhances the wrinkle resistance of cellulosic fabrics, but durability, absorbency, and soil release, are lessened.

WHAT ARE THE MAJOR COLORANTS AND WHERE ARE THEY LOCATED?

Colorants, "those substances that modify the perceived color of objects, or impart color to otherwise colorless objects," are either dyes or pigments.[5] As shown in Overview V, dyes are usually absorbed into fibers, whereas pigments usually adhere to fiber surfaces. In dyed fabrics, dyes (and occasionally pigments) are uniformly distributed within (or on) each fiber. Coloration of a dyed fabric is dependent on the distribution of variously colored fibers or yarns in the fabric. In printed textiles, the colorant (usually pigments rather than dyes) adheres to those fibers lying close to the surface of a fabric in the design (localized) areas.

---

[5] F.W. Billmeyer, and M. Saltzman, Principles of Color Technology (New York: John Wiley & Sons, 1981), p. 111.

TERMINOLOGY

The primary sources for terms and definitions for finishing, dyeing, and printing processes were the American Association of Textile Chemists and Colorists' (AATCC) Glossary of Printing Terms (Research Triangle Park, NC: AATCC, 1992); the Textile Institute's Textile Terms and Definitions, 8th ed. S.R. Beech, ed. (Manchester, England, 1986), and Hoechst Celanese's Dictionary of Fiber and Textile Technology (Charlotte, NC, 1990). The descriptions of fabrics given different finishing treatments were compiled by the author of this text.

UNIT ORGANIZATION

The first four chapters of Unit V discuss about 55 different finishes. Chapter 30 focuses on preparatory and final finishes. Chapter 31 addresses finishes that contribute to comfort and protection; Chapter 32, those that enhance fabric maintenance; and Chapter 33, those that enhance the aesthetic appeal of fabric. There is not a chapter on finishes contributing to fabric durability because finishes are not effective in enhancing this aspect of fabric performance. Rather, finishes are likely to detract from a fabric's durability.

The Detail View for each chapter lists all applicable finishes. Those finishes that are multifunctional are listed in several Detail Views but discussed only in the chapter that focuses on that finish's most significant performance enhancement.

Dyed textiles are considered in Chapter 34 and printed textiles in Chapter 35. The Detail Views for these chapters characterize the coloration effects achieved or the print types.

LEARNING THE PERFORMANCE ENHANCEMENTS PROVIDED BY CHEMICAL, MECHANICAL, AND THERMAL TREATMENTS

Fortunately, the names of many of the finishes state the performance enhancement. For example, the purpose of a soil-release finish is to assist in the release of oily soil from fabric, and the purpose of a flame-retardant finish is to reduce the rapidity of burning of fabric. Table 34.1 provides a summary of the fastness of different classes of dyes to ultraviolet light, drycleaning solvent, and laundering.

OBJECTIVES

The primary objectives of Unit V are to

1. Provide information about the types of finishes that alter durability, comfort, aesthetic appeal, maintenance, and health/safety/protection aspects of fabrics.

2. Acquaint you with the coloration of dyed textiles and the methods by which various effects are achieved.

3. Familiarize you with the names of printed fabrics and the methods by which various prints are achieved.

Preparatory and Final Finishes

PROCESS NAME	PURPOSE AND METHOD
Singeing or Shearing	To remove protruding fibers from yarns or fabrics by passing them over a flame or heated copper plates (singeing) or by clipping (shearing), achieving a smooth fabric surface and reducing pilling propensity.
Desizing	To remove sizing (starches, gelatins, oils, waxes, and manufactured polymers such as polyvinyl alcohol, polystyrene, polyacrylic acid and polyacetates) that was added to yarns to aid in fabric formation by treating them in enzyme or mild alkaline solutions.
Scouring	To clean impurities and machine oils from fabrics containing cellulosic fibers by exposing them to a solution of sodium hydroxide and detergent.
Carbonizing	To eliminate plant debris from wool and specialty wool fabrics by subjecting them to sulfuric acid solutions or hydrogen chloride gas followed by heating. When the fabrics dry, the carbonized debris, which is dust-like, is removed.
Degumming	To remove the natural gum from silk fibers by boiling silk fabric in a mild alkaline solution.
Bleaching	To decolorize and remove colored matter from fabrics by exposing them to oxidizing and reducing chemicals.
Tentering	To realign yarns and extend fabrics to uniform width by using a tenter frame, a device that consists of a pair of endless chains on horizontal tracks. The fabric is held firmly at the edges by pins or clips on the chains that diverge as they advance through a heated chamber.
Calendering	To smooth and enhance the luster of fabric surfaces, to produce a more supple hand, or to make fabrics more compact (opaque) by subjecting them to heavy pressure while they pass between two or more heavy rollers that are sometimes heated.
Decatizing	To improve hand and remove wrinkles from fabrics by circulating hot water or blowing steam through fabrics that are wound tightly on perforated rollers.

Preparatory and Final Finishes

Before fabrics can be successfully finished to enhance a specific property, or be dyed or printed, some preparatory steps are almost always necessary. After functional finishes, as well as dyeing and/or printing, have been concluded, the fabric is almost always distorted. This condition must be rectified through yet another, final, finish. Detail View 30 lists and briefly defines nine preparatory and final finishes (also called general mill finishes).

SINGEING OR SHEARING

Singeing is the removal of free fiber ends from the surface of fabrics by burning. Cotton and staple-fiber rayon fabrics are customarily singed as the first preparatory process. Fabrics are passed very quickly over a row of gas flames or between heated metal plates and then immediately into a desizing solution (discussed in the next section).

When the fabrics are polyester/cotton blends or composed of synthetic staple fibers, singeing is not a preparatory step because it will cause the formation of globules of melted fiber that will interfere with uptake of dyes and chemicals in later treatment procedures. Singeing is, therefore, done at a later stage. Filament-yarn fabrics do not require singeing.

Worsted fabrics are usually sheared rather than singed to remove surface fibers. *Shearing* involves clipping fibers from the fabric surface, thus avoiding the strong sulfur odor created by the burning of wool fibers.

DESIZING

Desizing is the removal of a size to allow colorants and finishing chemicals to penetrate into fibers. Sizes are chemical compounds that are often added to warp yarns to provide them with sufficient abrasion resistance to withstand the action of the shuttle during weaving. Most types of yarns that are used in weaving, with the exception of wool, are sized. The most important sizing materials are modified corn starches, a range of hydrolyzed polyvinyl alcohols, acrylics, polyacrylic acid, polyesters, polyvinyl acetate, styrene maleic anhydride, and various other starches and cellulosics. When the sizing is a starch, agitation of the fabric in a solution containing enzymes removes the size. When the sizing is polyvinyl acetate (PVA), washing in a mild alkaline solution removes the size.

SCOURING, CARBONIZING, AND DEGUMMING

Scouring is a general term used to refer to the removal of impurities. Natural-fiber fabrics contain the greatest amount of impurities—waxes and gums, plant parts, and processing oils and soils. Manufactured-fiber fabrics usually require only the removal of machine oils and colorant added to aid in fiber identification. In scouring, the waxy coating on cotton fibers, as well as leaf and other vegetable matter between fibers, is removed by first exposing the fabric to aqueous solutions of concentrated sodium hydroxide containing detergents and then steaming and rinsing it. Five different processes are presently in use. The most drastic treatment removes virtually all impurities from cotton fabric, leaving only about 0.15% of the wax. Most methods leave up to 0.3% of fatty wax in the cotton fabric but remove most other impurities fairly completely. As much as 8% of fabric weight may be lost; usually it is in the range of 2.5–4%. The effect on the hand of a fabric varies with the scouring method used.

Carbonizing and degumming refer to the removal of foreign matter from wool and silk fabrics, respectively. Sulfuric acid carbonizes, or destroys, vegetable matter. Sometimes wool yarns are carbonized before fabrication into fabric. Degumming, the removal of the sericin surrounding the silk filaments, is accomplished by boiling silk fabric with a very mild alkali, usually soap.

BLEACHING

Bleaching is the process of applying oxidizing and reducing chemicals to decolorize and remove colored matter from fabrics. Greige fabrics that are composed of natural fibers are buff to off-white due to natural pigmentation in the fiber and/or the presence of foreign matter in the fabric. Thus, if they are to be sold as white, greige fabrics will be bleached. Fabrics that are to be dyed or printed are also bleached so that the colors will not be dull.

Bleaching of fabric has been practiced since the beginning of civilization, as evidenced by white wool and linen fabrics found in archeological excavations. Ancient Greeks and Romans soaked fabric in aqueous alkaline solutions and then placed it in sour milk and trampled on it to neutralize the alkaline treatment. They spread the treated fabric on the grass to be whitened by sunlight and moisture. Several months were required to obtain a white fabric. Around 1750, sour milk was replaced with sulfuric acid in this process. A bleaching solution of chlorine dissolved in potassium hydroxide was developed in the 1790s. At the beginning of the 19th century, potassium hydroxide was replaced with sodium hydroxide, which was less expensive. Today bleaching of fabric utilizes hypochlorite, chlorite, hydrogen peroxide, and sulfur derivatives.

For cotton fabric, bleaching follows desizing and scouring. The first step in bleaching a cotton fabric is saturating it with a solution of a bleach, usually hydrogen peroxide, buffered to maintain a pH of approximately 10.5. The padded fabric is steamed, to accomplish the bleaching action, and then rinsed. In the United States, sodium chlorite bleach is seldom used because of the emission of toxic chlorine dioxide gas.

Wool fabrics are bleached in sodium peroxide solutions. The sensitivity of wool fiber to alkali is carefully considered in selecting type of bleach and establishing the conditions under which bleaching is to occur. Fabrics containing synthetic fibers and fabrics that are blends of natural and synthetic fibers must be bleached differently than wool fabrics. When nylon 6,6 and acrylic fabrics need to be bleached, peracetic acid is usually used.

Washing is an integral part of bleaching because it stops the action of the bleach by removing the bleach chemical from the fabric. Washing, however, consumes vast quantities of water. Fabric may be washed in rope or open width form; the process used depends on the specific fabric.

TENTERING

Tentering is the process of drying fabrics to a specified width and placing the warp and filling yarns of woven fabrics back at right angles to each other. In other words, tentering places woven fabric on grain. Some relaxation in the warp direction of woven fabrics is accomplished on the tenter frame.

A tenter frame consists of a pair of endless chains on horizontal tracks (Figure 30.1). The fabric is held firmly at its selvage edges by pins or clips on two chains that diverge as they advance through a heated chamber. In this manner, a fabric is adjusted to the desired width and straightened. In Figure 30.1, the fabric is wider at position *b* than at position *a*. Electronic sensors are sometimes used to detect the positioning of the yarns so that the feed can be altered if necessary.

Fabrics may be tentered several times during their total finishing sequence. They are usually tentered as a final finishing process. Fabrics may accidentally be tentered off-grain. If a fabric is printed in an off-grain position, an off-grain print will result. If a fabric is resin-treated off-grain, it will be permanently off-grain.

CALENDERING

Calendering is similar to domestic ironing except that the pressure exerted on the fabric is much greater. A cal-

30.1   Tentering.

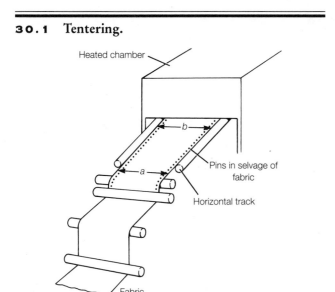

ender has two or more smooth, vertically stacked rollers that are hydraulically compressed against each other (Figure 30.2). The faces of the rolls are usually alternately steel and a composition product (paper). The steel rolls may be heated. When damp fabric passes between two rollers, the pressure at the nip can be as high as 1 ton/inch² (140 kilograms/centimeter²). Calenders are

FIGURE 30.2   Calendering.

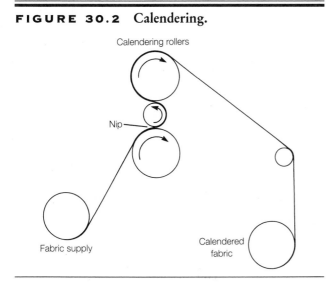

very expensive because there is very little tolerance of error in the manufacture of the rollers.

Calendering flattens fabric, which thus becomes smoother and more lustrous and acquires a more supple hand. When resins are added prior to calendering, cired and polished finishes are produced. These finishes are discussed in Chapter 32.

DECATIZING

Decatizing sets the luster on wool fabrics; it softens the hand and reduces the shine of silk and rayon fabrics. The dimensional stability of all these fabrics is improved. In a *wet-decatizing* process, first hot and then cold water is forced through fabrics. In a *dry-decatizing* process, fabrics are steamed and then cold air is forced through them. Pressing follows in both processes. The intensity of the heating/cooling cycles and the amount of pressure used in pressing are variable. The most intense procedure is called *full decatizing*, the least intense is decatizing, and intermediate is *semidecatizing*.

WET FINISHING

Wet finishing involves passing fabrics (sometimes yarns) through an aqueous bath containing the finish chemical(s). It is usually *not* a process that takes place in preparatory or final finishing of fabric. Perhaps, it should not be considered here. However, wet finishing is a general method for applying many of the chemicals that impart functional properties to a fabric. It is convenient to consider this general process here prior to considering the specific chemicals and the specific nature of their application in Chapters 31–33.

Wet finishing usually consists of a *pad-dry-cure sequence* (Figure 30.3). To *pad* means to apply a liquor (water plus chemicals) to a textile by passing it through a bath and subsequently through squeeze rollers. Fabric passes into a water bath containing the chemical finish in a concentration of 2–10%. The saturated fabric is squeezed through a pair of rollers to remove the excess solution; then the fabric is dried and the resin is cured. The wet pickup, or the increase in the weight of the fabric (usually expressed as a percentage of dry weight), depends on the fiber composition of the fabric and on the pressure at the nip of the pad rolls; at 60 pounds per inch² (40 newtons per cm²) even 100% cotton fabrics will have wet pickups of 65% or so.

The cost of removing water from fabrics led to the

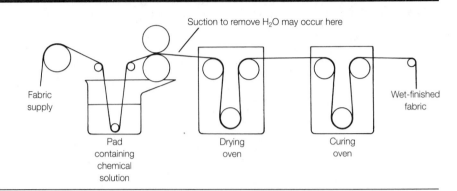

FIGURE 30.3 Wet finishing with the pad-dry-cure method.

development of foam and solvent finishing. In *foam finishing*, foam (a mixture of air and liquid) is spread evenly over the fabric surface. Wet pickup is kept at 15–35%, of which 75–90% is water. Despite the advantages claimed, foam finishing has been used only on a limited scale; the greatest use has been with tubular knits, corduroys, and fabrics requiring a different finish on each face. In *solvent finishing*, a solvent other than water is used. The cost of purchasing the solvents and reclaiming them has made this alternative less attractive than foam finishing.

In a *pad-extract-chemical-dry sequence*, the fabric is immersed in an aqueous solution containing a reactant that alters the structure of the fiber and is then completely removed. Mercerization is an example of this type of process.

CHAPTER SUMMARY

Nine preparatory and final finishes were discussed. The importance of adequate fabric preparation and final finishing cannot be overemphasized. The objective of finishing, whether removal of sizing, impurities, or loose surface fibers, depends on the specific fabric. Many synthetic fabrics are dyed without any preparation. Other fabrics may be scoured but not bleached.

Wet finishing was introduced in this chapter because of its important role in finishing processes in which special chemicals are added. The concept of padding entails the application of the liquor to the textile by passing it through a bath and subsequently through squeeze rollers.

Comfort and Protection Finishes

FABRIC NAME	DESCRIPTION
Water-Repellent-Finished Fabrics	Fabrics characterized by reduced spreading, wetting, and penetration of water due to the presence of water repellents, chemicals that increase the interfacial tension between a fabric's surface and water.
Hydrophilic-Finished Fabrics	Synthetic-fiber fabrics characterized by increased absorbency, wettability, and wicking, properties that have been achieved by treatment of the fabric with alkalies.
Mercerized Fabrics	Cellulosic-fiber fabrics that have slightly enhanced absorbency due to treatment with a sodium hydroxide solution. (Absorbency is not the primary reason for the finish to be done. Finish discussed in Chapter 32.)
Napped Fabrics	Fabrics that are warm to wear and feel warm because they have a fairly fuzzy surface achieved by raising fibers from low-twist yarns in a process called napping.
Brushed Fabrics	Fabrics that feel warm and soft because they have a slightly fuzzy surface achieved by raising fibers from twisted yarns in a brushing operation.
Temperature-Adaptable Fabrics	Fabrics that have the ability to alternatively store and release heat, depending on the environmental temperature, due to the presence of temperature-sensitive polymers called PEGs on the surfaces of the fibers in the fabric.
Flame-Retardant-Fabrics	Fabrics that meet established standards for ease of ignition, burning rate, heat generation, or other measures of burning behavior due to the presence of flame retardants on fiber surfaces.
Antimicrobial-Finished Fabrics	Fabrics on which the rate of growth and spread of microorganisms is reduced due to the presence of unbound or bound antimicrobials on the fibers of the fabric.
Antistatic-Finished Fabrics	Fabrics with increased electrical conductivity or, conversely, decreased static buildup, due to the presence of antistats on the surfaces of the fibers composing the fabric.

31

*C*omfort and Protection Finishes

Nine types of finishes may enhance the degree of comfort and protection provided by a fabric. Listed in Detail View 31 are the names of fabrics that have altered moisture, thermal, and protective properties due to chemical, mechanical, or thermal treatment. The descriptions of the fabrics highlight the specific enhancement and the means by which it has been achieved.

FABRICS FINISHED TO ALTER MOISTURE PROPERTIES

Chemical treatments may make fabrics more water-repellent and water-resistant, or they may increase the absorbency and wickability of fabrics.

Water-Repellent-Finished Fabrics

Water-repellent-finished fabrics are fabrics on which water beads up as a result of the topical application of a suitable chemical. The finish prevents water from spreading and penetrating the fabric because it increases the interfacial tension between the fabric surface and the water. Fabric must be closely structured for a water-repellent treatment to work successfully. Usually, water repellents do not prevent the penetration of water that falls forcefully onto the fabric surface.

Water repellents are hydrophobic chemicals that form hydrophobic films on fibers. They do not fill interstices.

The five main types of water-repellent chemicals differ in cost, longevity under washing and drycleaning, range of fibers and fabrics on which they can be successfully used, and simultaneous enhancement of oil repellency.

Wax-emulsion water repellents are the least expensive hydrophobic chemicals, but they give excellent water repellency, particularly on properly structured cellulosic fabrics. They are not durable under washing or drycleaning, so after several cleanings such treated fabrics must be re-proofed. Solvent-soluble wax emulsions are used by a drycleaner to restore water repellency. A tradename is Cravanette M–2®, manufactured by the Cravanette Co.

Pyridinium-based water repellents, long-chain fatty amides and wax resin mixtures, are durable under washing and drycleaning in hydrocarbon solvent. A tradename is Cravanette Long Life®, manufactured by the Cravanette Co.

Silicone water repellents can be applied to the widest range of fabrics. They are particularly suited to the treatment of filament fabrics. They are also excellent on wool and wool-blend fabrics. A high degree of water repellency is achieved and is durable under washing and drycleaning. These repellents are also applied to cellulosic fabrics, providing a degree of water repellency equivalent to that provided by wax emulsions. The silicone treatment is more expensive, however. Tradenames of this type of water repellent include Hydro-Pruf® and

Sylgard®, manufactured by Sandoz and Dow Corning, respectively.

Organic-chromium water repellents are excellent for synthetic-fiber fabrics and give good results on wool. They have good longevity under drycleaning and moderate longevity under washing.

Fluorochemical water repellents are unique in that they confer some oil repellency while providing durable water repellency. Tradenames of this type of chemical are Zepel® and Scotchgard®, manufactured by Du Pont and the 3M Co., respectively. These chemicals are discussed in greater detail in Chapter 33 because they are also used to achieve soil repellency. They are also called rain/stain protectors.

Hydrophilic-Finished Fabrics

Hydrophilic-finished fabrics are usually polyester or nylon fabrics that exhibit enhanced wicking of water over their surfaces (horizontal wicking or spreading) and/or through their thicknesses (vertical wicking), as shown in Figure 31.1. When placed in water, fabrics with hydrophilic finishes become wetter than unfinished fabric. Hydrophilic-finished fabrics are often used in exercise garments because they wick sweat away from the skin faster than unfinished fabric.

Polyester fabric may be made hydrophilic by finishing it in a sodium hydroxide solution. Degradation of the polymers at the fiber surfaces occurs, as shown in Fig-

FIGURE 31.1   Treating fabric to alter moisture properties.

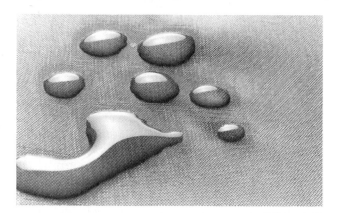

Polyester fabric (left) and fiber (right)
before treatment

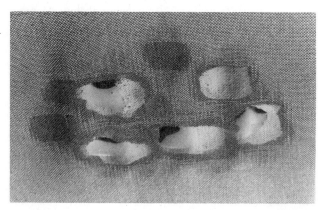
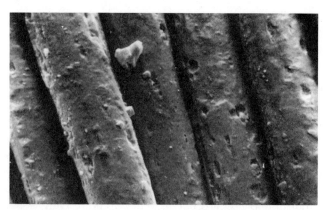

Polyester fabric (left) and fiber (right)
after treatment

ure 31.1. After the polymer fragments are washed away, an increased number of polar groups (hydroxyl and carboxyl) appear on the newly exposed fiber surfaces. These surfaces therefore become more hydrophilic. (The size of the fibers is slightly reduced.) Treated fabric is more wettable than untreated fabric because the exposed polar groups attract water and because the increased porosity of the fabric (due to its slightly smaller fibers) makes the fibers more accessible to water. When a drop of water is placed on the surface of treated fabric, it spreads and wets; when placed on the surface of untreated fabric, it beads up. A change in the interfacial tension has occurred. Hydrophilic-finished polyester fabrics have improved handle and drape, are less resistant to soiling, are less likely to pill, may have improved soil release properties, and have a reduced tendency to cling when wet.

Fabrics composed of naturally hydrophilic fibers are usually not finished with the primary intention of improving absorption or hydrophilicity, though finishing processes undertaken to achieve other objectives can affect this property. Mercerization is the only finish that does increase absorbency when applied to a cotton fabric. The primary aims of mercerization, however, are to enhance the acceptance of colorant by the fiber, increase fiber strength, and enhance luster. Chemical finishes applied to fabrics containing hydrophilic fibers are, in fact, more likely to decrease absorbency than enhance it. For example, the ability of cotton fabric to absorb moisture is reduced when it is treated with durable-press resins

and flame-retardant chemicals. Fabric softeners also reduce moisture absorbency; these softeners are chemically similar to pyridinium water repellents. Mechanical treatments that compact fibers and yarns decrease both absorbency and water vapor permeability.

FABRICS FINISHED TO ALTER THERMAL PROPERTIES

The amount of thermal insulation provided by fabrics can be enhanced by increasing the amount of dead air space in them through finishing processes called napping and brushing. The capability for heat storage and release can be achieved by adding temperature-sensitive polymers to a fabric.

Napped Fabrics

Napped fabrics have a relatively thick layer of fiber ends protruding from their surfaces. These fibers are raised from the base of the fabric with wire brushes during a mechanical process called napping (Figure 31.2).[1] The fibers may stand upright or lie primarily in one direction. Napped fabrics may be napped on one or both sides. A primary reason for napping fabrics is to increase their thermal insulative ability. A person stays warmer wear-

---

[1] Napped fabrics should not be confused with pile fabrics. Napped fabrics are similar in appearance to brushed fabrics, as well as sanded and sueded fabrics (Chapter 32).

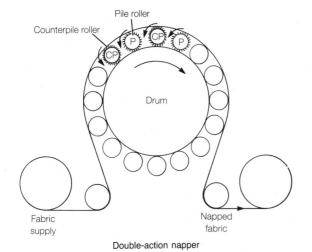

FIGURE 31.2 **Napping.**

Counterpile roller

Pile roller

CP

P

CP

P

Drum

Fabric supply

Napped fabric

Double-action napper

The appearance of a sweatsuit fabric before and after napping

ing a napped fabric than wearing an unfinished fabric due to the increased amount of dead air space in the body of the fabric and due to the thicker air layer formed at the skin surface. Napped fabrics also feel warmer than smoother-surfaced fabrics of comparable thickness; less fiber touches the skin, so less heat is conducted away. Napped fabrics are used for pajamas, shirts, coats, and dresses. Many woven and needlepunched blankets are napped. Some knit fabrics, usually jersey, are napped and used for sweaters and baby items. Napped fabrics usually contain low-twist spun yarns. In woven fabric, the low-twist yarns are usually filling yarns.

Napping, a mechanical finishing operation, involves passing a fabric over a series of rollers that are mounted on a large drum. Each roller is covered with a heavy fabric into which bent wires are embedded. The drum rotates in the direction of fabric movement. The rollers travel faster than the fabric to be napped so that fiber ends are raised. In single-action machines, the direction of the bent wires is the same on all the rollers. In double-action machines, every other roller is a counterpile roller. The wires on the counterpile rollers are bent in the direction opposite of those on the pile rollers. The counterpile rollers travel at a slower speed than the pile rollers. When the relative speeds of the rollers are reversed, a tucking action occurs, pushing the raised fibers back into the cloth and making a smoother surface.

Brushed Fabrics

Brushed fabrics have a raised fiber surface (Figure 31.3). In brushed woven fabrics, this surface is similar to a napped surface except that the density of the surface fibers is lower. An examination of the filling yarns in a brushed fabric will reveal that they have average twist, compared to low twist in napped fabric. Denim is sometimes brushed, and the brushed surface is usually placed to the inside of the garment when constructed. The brushed denim is warmer than an unbrushed denim because it creates a thicker boundary layer of air between the skin and the fabric surface. The fabric has a warmer feeling because the surface area of contact has been decreased. Brushed woven fabrics feel softer than comparable unbrushed fabrics.

Temperature-Adaptable Fabrics

Temperature-adaptable fabrics are fabrics capable of storing and releasing heat as the environmental temperature rises and falls. They can warm a cold person and cool a hot person.

FIGURE 31.3 Brushing.

Plain-woven fabric before and after brushing

Temperature adaptability is achieved using a class of chemicals called PEGs, or *polyethylene glycols.* PEGs store excess heat when the temperature rises and release it when the temperature drops. Adding a solution of PEG (molecular weights of 300–1000), dimethyloldihydroxyethylene urea (DMDHEU), and specific acid catalysts to fabrics and curing them creates a water-insoluble polymer that coats the fibers. The temperature-adaptable finish, trademarked Polytherm®, was developed at the USDA-ARS Southern Regional Research Center. Applications for temperature-adaptable fabrics include clothing worn next to the skin, such as T-shirts and thermal underwear; biomedical products, such as surgical gowns and dressings for medical personnel and patients; activewear, such as skiwear and socks; and protective fabrics for plants and animals.

Temperature-adaptable fabrics also have good to excellent resilience (particularly for cotton), soil release, antistatic performance, and pilling resistance. Water absorbency is markedly increased. Bacterial growth and foot odor are less on temperature-adaptable socks than on untreated socks. It is unusual and significant that thermal and several nonthermal properties are imparted to fibrous surfaces by one process. The finish is durable for 50 home launderings.

FLAME-RETARDANT FABRICS

Flame-retardant fabrics are fabrics that exhibit reduced burning behavior due to the use of *flame-retardant chemicals.*[2] A treated fabric that meets the criteria for flame resistance is called a flame-resistant fabric.

From 1972 to 1977, most children's sleepwear fabrics were finished with various flame retardants to pass the flame tests imposed by the Children's Sleepwear amendment to the Flammable Fabrics Act.[3] Millions of yards of 100% cotton and 100% polyester fabrics, as well as a more limited quantity of triacetate and acetate fabrics, were made flame-resistant by topically finishing them with flame retardants. In addition, some garments were made with inherently flame-resistant fibers such as modacrylic or vinyon/vinyl bicomponent-bigeneric fibers.

By 1978, almost all children's sleepwear containing flame retardants had disappeared from the marketplace. The major event leading to this drastic and swift action was the discovery that a flame retardant called tris (2,3 dibromopropylphosphate) might be a carcinogen. Although other flame retardants were not implicated, major retailers decided that they did not wish to offer such treated fabrics for sale. The market for chemically finished flame-resistant children's sleepwear fabric was lost. Today, flame resistance is achieved through inherently flame-resistant fibers, manufactured fibers modified by the addition of flame retardants during fiber spinning (flame-resistant rayon, acrylic, or olefin), or through engineered fabric composed of regular manufactured fibers. Most sleepwear fabrics are of the latter type; 100% polyester sleepwear is by far the most common.

Although fabrics destined for the apparel market are no longer topically finished to retard the spread of flame, fabrics to be used in protective clothing, theater curtains, carpeting, and aircraft interiors may be topically finished. Moreover, interest does continue in the development of a suitable flame-retardant finish for polyester/cotton blends because of their widespread use in apparel. As described in Chapter 24, polyester/cotton blends are more flammable than fabric composed of either fiber alone.

The only avenue by which cotton and wool fabrics can meet requirements for flame resistance is through topical finishing. In the case of cotton, chemical add-on at a level as high as 10–30% of unfinished fabric weight is necessary. At these high add-on levels, other aspects of fabric performance (for example, abrasion resistance and

FIGURE 31.4 Treating fabric with flame-retardant chemicals.

Protective suit made of flame-retardant wool fabric

hand) are affected. Extensive research and development have yielded finishes that allow cotton fabrics and wool fabrics to compete favorably in the protective clothing market (Figure 31.4). Fabric containing wool fiber can meet flame-resistance requirements with a lower add-on of flame retardant than fabric containing cotton fiber. Therefore, the total performance of wool fabric is not as seriously affected by the treatment as is cotton fabric. The chemistry involved in treating both wool and cotton fabric is highly complex.

Polyester and nylon fabric may be topically finished, or an additive may be added to the fiber spinning solution. Nylon tent fabrics tend to be given a topical finish in order to meet the voluntary flammability requirements established by tent manufacturers.

ANTIMICROBIAL-FINISHED FABRICS

Antimicrobial-finished fabrics—also called antibacterial-, bacteriostatic-, or antiseptic-finished fabrics—are fabrics that exhibit reduced microbial growth due to the presence of antimicrobial chemicals in the fabric. Figure 31.5 shows fungus growth on an untreated carpet and the absence of such growth on an antimicrobial-treated carpet. Such treatments can reduce bacterial counts by as much as 75–99%.[4] The probability that a person will

---

[2] The chemicals are flame *retardants;* the purpose of their use is to provide flame *resistance.*

[3] A general discussion of textile flammability, including the Federal Textile Flammability Laws and Standards, is found in Chapter 6.

[4] AATCC, Auburn University Student Chapter, "The Effectiveness and Cleanability of Antimicrobial Finishes on Carpet Tiles," *Textile Chemist and Colorist* 19/4 (1987): 27–31.

FIGURE 31.5   Treating fabric with antimicrobial chemicals.

Fungal growth on carpet without an antimicrobial treatment
after 10 days in a test chamber

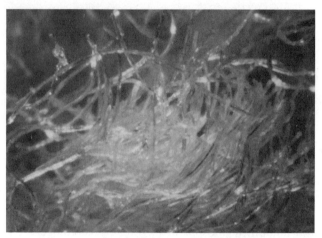

Lack of fungal growth on carpet with an antimicrobial treatment
after 10 days in a test chamber

contract an infection from carpeted areas is therefore considerably reduced.

In the United States, there is a growing concern about the dangers of microbial and viral contamination. Recent outbreaks of diseases such as Legionnaire's Disease and Acquired Immune Deficiency Syndrome (AIDS) have heightened awareness and concern. New markets for antimicrobial-treated textiles, particularly in institutional environments, have consequently developed. Health clubs, day-care centers, clinics, motels and hotels, and hospitals are turning more and more to antimicrobial-finished textiles, particularly sheets and carpets. Nonwoven surgical drapes and packs are often treated. In addition, there is renewed interest in skin-contact clothing (particularly socks and shoe lining fabrics) containing antimicrobials. There are no finishes that prevent the spread of viruses such as the AIDS virus.[5]

Trademarks for antimicrobial finishes for carpets include Sylgard® (Dow Corning), Intersept® (Interface Flooring, Inc.), Ultra-Fresh® (Bio-Dor Products, Ltd.), Halofresh® (Allied-Signal, Inc.), and Zeftron 5000ZX® (BASF Corporation). When carpet manufacturers use one of these antimicrobials with soil repellents, the carpeting may carry a trademark such as Bioguard® (Lees Commercial Carpet Co.). Bioguard® is also applied to socks.

Two types of antimicrobials, bound and unbound, are applied to fabric. *Unbound antimicrobials* must diffuse from the finished fabric and be consumed by the microorganism to be effective. They cannot, therefore, be bonded to a surface to function. Once inside the microorganism, the unbound antimicrobial acts like a poison, interrupting some key metabolic or life-sustaining process of the cell, causing it to die. During the use of a fabric, an unbound antimicrobial is slowly depleted because it diffuses or leaches from the substrate. As this diffusion continues, the concentration of the active ingredient becomes diluted below effective levels. Under these conditions, microorganisms have the ability to adapt or build up a tolerance to antimicrobials. Highly resistant strains can develop an immunity to what was once an effective finish. This adaptation process, as it is called, is of special concern to the health-care industry, which must continually develop new antimicrobials to combat more potent and highly resistant strains of disease-causing microorganisms. Unbound antimicrobials are very effective against specific microorganisms but usually have a limited ability to offer broad spectrum control. In other words, they may be effective against some, but not all, bacteria, or they may destroy all bacteria but be ineffective against fungi, yeasts, or algae. The safety and tox-

---

[5] Please refer to the discussion on the permeation resistance of fabric, found in Chapter 6, for ways in which textiles are effective in safeguarding health-care professionals and others from contact with the AIDS virus. Not mentioned in Chapter 6 is the use of Spectra® olefin fibers and Kevlar® aramid fibers in surgical gloves. These fibers resist tearing or being cut, thus helping to keep blood away from a surgeon's hands.

icity of unbound antibacterial treatments vary considerably, depending on the specific chemistry involved.

Bound antimicrobials remain chemically attached to the surface on which they are applied. They function by interrupting the delicate cell membrane of a microorganism, thus preventing it from carrying on vital life processes. Bound antimicrobials kill organisms on contact and can do so again and again. Bound antimicrobials function like a sword, which has an unlimited capacity to kill, whereas unbound antimicrobials function like a gun, which has limited ammunition. Because a bound antimicrobial is fixed to the fiber, rather than being depleted by continuously diffusing off the surface, the adaptation process cannot and does not occur. The unique mechanism by which bound antimicrobials exhibit their activity permits them to effectively control a broad spectrum of microorganisms. Bacteria, molds, mildew, fungi, yeast, and algae can all be controlled. All bound antimicrobials on the market today have a very favorable toxicological profile.

ANTISTATIC-FINISHED FABRICS

Antistatic-finished fabrics are usually those to which antistats—chemicals capable of preventing, reducing, or dissipating static electrical charges—have been applied. Nylon carpeting and lingerie fabrics are often given such a finish. Trademarks of antistatic agent products include 3M Brand Static Control® (3M Company) and X-Static® (West Chemical Products, Inc.). Aerosol sprays to control static are available in the laundry products section in grocery stores.

Acetate and triacetate fabrics may be finished by immersing them in a sodium hydroxide solution to reduce their static buildup. In a reaction called saponification, the polymers in the fiber "skin" are converted to cellulose. This process is known as S-finishing.

Other approaches to preventing static buildup are usually more effective than finishing, both initially and over longer periods of time. These approaches include adding antistats to the spinning solution during manufacture of synthetic fibers and incorporating fine metallic yarns among carpet face yarns. The use of fabric softeners when laundering garments is also an effective method of controlling static.

CHAPTER SUMMARY

The ability of fabric to provide the degree of comfort required or to possess the degree of protection necessary in certain end uses may be provided or enhanced by finishing processes. Nine finishes were discussed. Certain finishing chemicals make fabrics water-repellent (have hydrophobic surfaces); others make fabrics hydrophilic. Napping and brushing increase the insulative capability of fabrics; temperature-adaptable chemicals cause fabrics to absorb or emit heat. Flame retardants increase protection against skin burns, antimicrobials protect against the spread of microorganisms, and antistats protect against clinging and shocking.

Aesthetic Appeal Finishes

FABRIC NAME	DESCRIPTION
Ciréd Fabrics	Fabrics with a deep, glossy, patent-leather-like surface produced by the application of wax and the use of a friction calender.
Glazed or Polished Fabrics	Fabrics with highly lustrous surfaces produced by the application of starch, glue, paraffin, or shellac and the use of a friction calender.
Schreinerized Fabrics	Fabrics with luster enhanced by processing in a Schreiner calender.
Beetled Fabrics	Linen and cotton fabrics that are lustrous, flat-surfaced, closed, and firm from being pounded with wooden hammers.
Sanded, Sueded, and Emerized Fabrics	Fabrics that have a chamois-like appearance and hand or a suede-like texture because their surface fibers have been raised by abrasive action.
Pleated Fabrics	Fabrics with many folds created during passage through pleating machinery.
Sheared Fabrics	Pile and napped fabrics whose surfaces have been made even by cutting the surface fibers, tops of loops or tufts of yarn to a desired height with precision blades mounted on a shearing machine.
Embossed Fabrics	Fabrics that have figures or designs in relief produced by processing flat-surfaced fabrics through an embossing calender.
Moiré Fabrics	Fabrics, especially rib fabrics that have a wavy or watered effect created during passage through a calender.
Mercerized Fabrics and Yarns	Fabrics that dye to brighter, darker shades and are more lustrous, stronger, and more absorbent but somewhat stiffer due to immersion in cold sodium hydroxide solution while under tension, followed by neutralization in acid.
Liquid-Ammonia-Finished Fabrics	Fabrics that dye more deeply and are more lustrous, more absorbent, and softer due to treatment with liquid ammonia.
Prewashed Garments	Denim garments that are softer, have reduced relaxation shrinkage, and look slightly worn because they have been laundered prior to their sale.
Stonewashed Garments	Garments with a distressed appearance (fuzzy texture, puckered seams, and slight wrinkling) because they have been tumbled in cylindrical washers with stones.
Acidwashed	Garments with a distressed appearance and soft feel achieved by adding an oxidizing agent to the stones.
Stoneless-Washed (Enzyme Washed)	Garments with a distressed appearance and soft feel achieved by using enzymes that attack the surface of cotton fibers.
Optically Brightened Fabrics	Fabrics that appear brighter or whiter when placed under ultraviolet light due to the presence of optical whiteners on the fiber surfaces.
Softened Fabrics	Fabrics that have a slicker, smoother, softer feel due to the presence of softening compounds on the fiber surfaces.
Stiffened or Sized Fabrics	Fabrics that are stiffer and crisper due to the presence of stiffening compounds.
Fulled Fabrics	Woolen and worsted fabrics that are denser, more compact, softer, and bulkier because they have been subjected to moisture, heat, friction, chemicals, and pressure that cause matting and shrinkage.
Weighted Fabrics	Silk fabrics that are heavier and drape better due to the presence of metallic salts.
Silk-like Finished Fabrics	Fabrics, usually polyester, that have been subjected to sodium hydroxide for the purpose of decreasing the diameter of the fibers.
Parchmentized Fabrics	Fabrics that have a translucence and crispness characteristic of parchment paper as a result of being treated in sulfuric acid and then calendered.
Antiodor/Odor-Controlled/ Antimicrobial-Treated Fabrics	Fabrics that have a reduced rate of odor buildup (reduced rate of bacterial growth) due to the presence of antimicrobials.

32

Aesthetic Appeal Finishes

Numerous finishes applied to fabrics and garments enhance their appearance and feel. Over twenty fabrics, whose names reflect the nature of the aesthetic appeal finish they have received, are listed in Detail View 32. Their descriptions include information about the property enhanced and the method by which the enhancement has been achieved.

FABRICS FINISHED TO ALTER LUSTER

Fabrics can be made to have deep glossy or soft sheen surfaces by finishing. In this section of the chapter, fabrics with the shiniest surfaces are considered first and those with the least shiny are considered last.

Ciréd Fabrics

Ciréd fabrics are those with a deep, glossy, patent-leather-like surface. The fabric is usually taffeta (an unbalanced plain-woven fabric made of acetate filaments) or satin fabric composed of thermoplastic fibers. The deep luster results from application of wax and the use of a friction calender. A friction calender has a highly polished, heated steel roller that rotates at a higher surface speed than the softer roller against which it works. The deep gloss on ciréd fabrics is therefore the result of the wax, the difference in speeds of the rollers that have polished the waxed surface, and the pressure between the rollers that have flattened the fabric surface, thereby increasing the uniformity of light reflection.

Glazed or Polished Fabrics

Glazed or *polished fabrics* are usually cotton plain-woven fabrics with either a surface layer of starch or wax, in which case the finish is temporary, or a resin, in which case the finish is more durable. Polished cotton and chintz are common glazed fabrics. To glaze or polish a fabric, it is first immersed in a chemical solution containing the starch, wax, or resin and then is partially dried. Finally, it is passed through a friction calender (Figure 32.1).

Schreinerized Fabrics

Schreinerized fabrics are fabrics with luster enhanced by processing in a Schreiner calender, which flattens the yarns to create a smoother fabric surface (Figure 32.2). Many types of fabrics are Schreinerized, knits as well as wovens, and fabrics containing synthetic fibers as well as those composed of cellulosic fibers. More nylon than polyester knits are Schreinerized because polyester knits tend to firm up, causing an undesirable hand.

A Schreiner calender has one roller engraved with 150–350 diagonal lines/inch (50–150 lines per centimeter) at a 20° angle to either the vertical or the horizontal. The engraved roller is heated to a temperature of 300–320°F (149–160°C) and impinges on a plastic or fiber bottom-roller with a pressure of up to 120 tons.

The longevity of Schreinerizing depends on the fiber content of the fabric and whether or not a thermoplastic

FIGURE 32.1 Glazing.

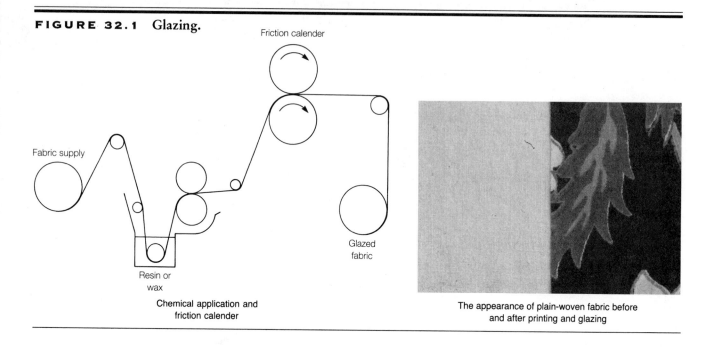

Friction calender

Fabric supply

Glazed fabric

Resin or wax

Chemical application and friction calender

The appearance of plain-woven fabric before and after printing and glazing

resin is used. Fabrics composed of thermoplastic fibers are durably Schreinerized. Cotton and linen fabrics without a resin treatment lose the Schreinerized luster during laundering because the yarns swell to a rounded configuration. With a treatment of cured resin, however, a durable finish is achieved.

Beetled Fabrics

Beetled fabrics are linen and linen-like fabrics that are lustrous, flat-surfaced, closed and firm from being pounded in a process called beetling. The yarns in a beetled fabric are visibly flatter and the woven structure closer after the beetling process than before it (Figure

FIGURE 32.2 Schreinerizing.

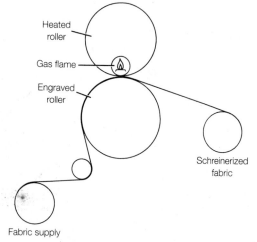

Heated roller

Gas flame

Engraved roller

Schreinerized fabric

Fabric supply

Schreiner calender

The appearance of a filament knit before and after Schreinerizing

FIGURE 32.3 Beetling.

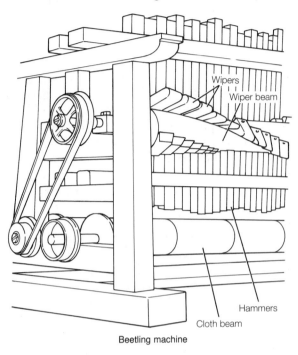

Beetling machine

The appearance of a linen fabric before
and after beetling

32.3). A beetled fabric is more absorbent and smoother as a result of the pounding.

Beetling is a noisy process because wooden hammers pound the fabric as it revolves slowly over a large wooden drum. Forty heavy wooden hammers arranged closely side-by-side and situated above the drum pound the many layers of fabric. A mechanism lifts the ham-

mers in rapid succession and allows them to fall under the action of gravity. The roller carrying the fabric regularly moves from side to side by a small amount so that the hammer strikes cover the entire fabric surface. The pounding may continue for 30–60 hours. The fabric is then turned over, so the inside layers are outside, and the beetling begins again.

FABRICS FINISHED TO ALTER TEXTURE

Many different textures are created either by mechanically altering the fabric surface or by applying chemicals.

Sanded, Sueded, and Emerized Fabrics

Sanded, sueded, and *emerized fabrics* have the look and feel of a natural suede or chamois (Figure 32.4).[1] The base fabric is the primary consideration in determining which of these methods to use to produce the surface appearance and feel.

Sanding is the process of abrading the fabric surface with sandpaper. It is a very skillful and delicate operation in which the tension, speed, and depth of the abrasive action must be precisely controlled. The fabric to be finished can easily weaken, become full of holes, or even disintegrate. Moreover, the dust generated during sanding must be continuously removed.

---

[1] Sanded, sueded, and emerized fabrics should not be confused with napped and brushed fabrics (Chapter 31).

FIGURE 32.4 Sanding.

The appearance of a warp knit before and after sanding

Sueded fabrics are those fabrics that most closely duplicate the appearance of natural suede. These fabrics were in great demand in the 1980s. Today, a considerable amount of warp-knit fabric, usually 70-denier high-filament-count polyester, is sueded. Some lightweight 40-denier polyester suede is also made, along with small quantities in triacetate, acetate, and nylon. Sueding also involves the use of sandpaper.

Emerized fabrics are lightweight and have the soft hand of chamois. Emerizing is a less vigorous process than either sanding or sueding because emery cloth is substituted for the sandpaper. As a result, emerized fabrics are more delicate.

Pleated Fabrics

Pleated fabrics, those with many folds or channels, have existed since at least the time of the Egyptians, who pleated cotton and linen fabrics by hand. Today, nylon and polyester fabrics are pleated with durable folds or creases using highly specialized machinery. These fabrics are mechanically folded and brought into contact with a heated roller to heat-set the pleats (Chapter 33). The depth, frequency and distribution of the pleats can be varied at will. Fashion dictates the availability of these fabrics.

Sheared Fabrics

Sheared fabrics are pile or napped fabrics with very even surfaces, resulting from the cutting of the yarn or fiber ends to a uniform length with precision blades (Figure 32.5). This process, called shearing, is also used to "carve" patterns or motifs into pile fabrics. Precise control of the blades is essential.

Embossed Fabrics

Embossed fabrics have a raised design or motifs that result from pressing fabric between engraved rollers on an embossing calender (Figure 32.6). Usually, the fabric to be embossed is plain-woven or satin. The embossed design may be crinkles (shown in Figure 32.6) or simulations of more complex dobby and Jacquard motifs. The embossed design is discernable due to the difference in light reflection between the raised and background areas. Printed fabrics may be embossed to raise certain portions of the print above the background. Both cotton and thermoplastic-fiber fabrics may be embossed.

An embossing calender has a hollow, engraved copper roller that is heated from the inside by a gas flame and a solid paper roller twice the size of the engraved roller. The pressure of the deeply engraved copper roller against the smooth paper roller produces the raised pattern. When a more raised, or relief, design is required, the paper roller is soaked in water and then rotated against an engraved roller (without fabric) until the pattern of engraving is pressed into the paper roller. The temperature is adjusted to suit the fabric and production begins. Embossed fabrics are expensive to produce. Very long production runs are required to make the fabrics economically feasible. However, a design is usually less expensive to emboss than to weave.

FIGURE 32.5 Shearing.

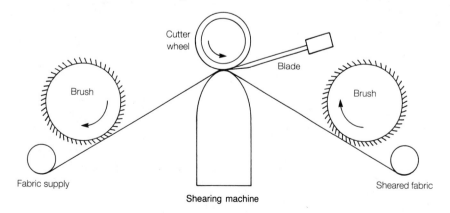

Fabric supply
Cutter wheel
Blade
Brush
Brush
Sheared fabric
Shearing machine

The appearance of a looped pile fabric before and after shearing

FIGURE 32.6 Embossing.

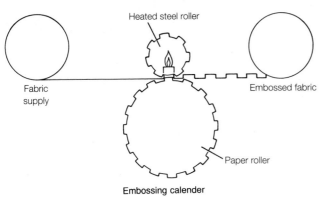

The appearance of a sheer, plain-woven polyester fabric before and after embossing

The longevity of an embossed design depends on the fiber content, the fabric structure, and the complexity of the design. Heat-set polyester fabrics that have been embossed will permanently retain the raised design. Embossing is usually semidurable on nylon fabric. When cotton fabrics are treated with a resin prior to embossing, the embossed design has longer longevity than when a resin is not applied. The recommended care procedures stated on embossed fabric labels should be followed.

Moiré Fabrics

Moiré fabrics have a wavy or watermark design (Figure 32.7). The fabric surface has highly lustrous areas surrounded by less lustrous areas, separated by a random and wavy boundary. *Moiré,* pronounced either mwa-ray or moy-ray, is a French word. The watermark motif may be achieved by two different finishing techniques or printed onto a fabric surface.

The watermark design on *true moiré fabrics* is an optical effect resulting from a complex interference between light reflected from two sets of reasonably parallel lines that are evenly spaced on the fabric surface. A true moiré finish is most commonly given to unbalanced plain-woven fabrics (such as taffetas, poplins, and failles) because they have fine crosswise ribs. The ribs constitute the parallel, evenly spaced lines that are essential to the true moiré effect. Unbalanced plain-woven fabrics composed of filament yarns of silk, acetate, and triacetate are given a moiré finish more often than fabrics composed of other fibers.

FIGURE 32.7 Moiré calendering.

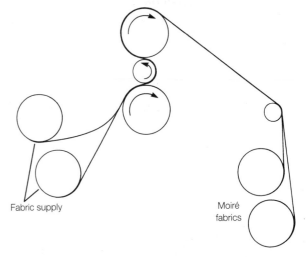

Moiré calender

The appearance of an unbalanced plain-woven fabric before and after passage through a moiré calender

To create the finish, two identical fabrics are placed face-to-face and fed into a calender with smooth, heated metal rollers, where a pressure of 8–10 tons causes the ribs of the top fabric to be pressed into the bottom fabric and vice versa. Each fabric consequently has two sets of nearly identical parallel lines on its surface: the original set of ribs and the set of lines impressed on the fabric during calendering. Great expertise and long experience is needed to produce moiré fabrics.

Great care must be taken in washing and cleaning true moiré fabrics. Acetate moiré has excellent longevity under drycleaning and washing in cold water. Rayon/cotton blend moiré fabrics are not durable to washing and will water spot unless a chemical finish has been applied. Nylon moiré fabrics have excellent longevity under pressing, ironing, and laundering.

Imitation moirés are the result of calendering with a metal roller engraved with the wavy pattern. The tops of the ribs in some areas of the fabric surface are thus flattened. The watermark design is visible because light is reflected differently from the flattened and the rounded rib areas. When the fabric is composed of thermoplastic fibers and the roller is heated, the finish is permanent. Imitation moiré fabrics can be distinguished from true moiré fabrics by the regular repeat on the surface on the imitation fabrics. True moiré fabrics have a nonrepeating pattern.

When in fashion, moiré fabrics are found in evening gowns, formal draperies, bedspreads, luggage linings, and dresses. Occasionally, upholstery fabric is a moiré.

FABRICS FINISHED FOR COLOR ALTERATION AND WHITENESS

Cotton fabrics may be finished to obtain deeper, brighter colors when they are subsequently dyed. They may also be mechanically and/or chemically finished to wash out color produced in a previous dyeing process. Fabrics of many fiber compositions are treated with optical whiteners to make them appear whiter.

Mercerized Fabrics and Yarns

Mercerized fabrics and yarns are those that dye to brighter and darker shades and are more lustrous because they have been mercerized, or treated under tension in cold sodium hydroxide solutions (Figure 32.8). Mercerization also enhances stiffness, strength, and absorbency. The primary motivation for mercerization today is to increase the dye affinity of cotton fibers in order to create fabrics with brighter and darker colors. Combed cotton fabrics are mercerized more often than carded cotton fabrics. Mercerized yarn may be labeled Lisle. Cotton sewing thread is often mercerized.

Mercerization involves placing fabric or yarn in a cold bath (25–45°F or −4–7°C) of 18–27% sodium hydroxide for a minute or less. After the fabric or yarn is rinsed several times, it is given a cold-acid sour-bath to neutralize any remaining alkali. More rinsing follows to ensure complete acid removal. The fabric or yarn must be

FIGURE 32.8 Mercerizing.

The appearance of cotton fibers before and after mercerization

The appearance of unmercerized and mercerized dyed knit fabrics

held under tension during the process to prevent shrinkage and develop luster.

Cotton fibers placed in a sodium hydroxide solution swell, breaking hydrogen and van der Waals bonds, thus freeing the polymers to rearrange, move further apart, and reorient. When the sodium hydroxide is removed, new bonds form between the reorganized polymers. Mercerized fibers are rounder in cross section, are more cylindrically shaped (the convolutions are nearly gone), and have a flatter lumen than unmercerized fibers, as shown in Figure 32.8. The fine structure of mercerized fibers is composed of smaller crystalline areas and has stronger internal bonds. Mercerized fibers and fabrics are therefore stronger because each fiber's polymers are arranged to share pulling forces more equally; they are more lustrous due to the rounder cross-sectional shape and decreased fiber twisting; and they are more absorbent and have greater affinity for dyestuff due to the expanded fiber structure (larger voids in the fiber for water and dyestuff to enter). Mercerized fabrics are less expensive to dye because they require only $\frac{7}{10}$ as much dyestuff as unmercerized fabrics to achieve a given shade.

Mercerization is often applied in conjunction with durable-press finishes (Chapter 33) to help fabrics maintain strength and abrasion resistance, which are considerably reduced by durable-press finishing. The costs involved in completely removing sodium hydroxide from the fibers and in recovering it from the reaction solution to prevent environmental pollution prompted textile scientists to find other swelling agents, such as liquid ammonia, that could be used.

Liquid-Ammonia-Finished Fabrics and Yarns

Liquid-ammonia-finished fabrics and yarns dye more deeply and are more lustrous, more absorbent, and softer due to treatment with liquid ammonia. Their degree of luster, brightness, and moisture absorption, however, is slightly less than that of mercerized fabrics. The difference in softness between these two types of fabrics is considerable because treatment with liquid ammonia decreases stiffness whereas mercerization increases stiffness. Increases in yarn strength may be greater than that achieved by mercerization. Abrasion resistance is less affected by liquid-ammonia finishing than by mercerization.

Liquid ammonia was identified in the 1930s as one of the strongest swelling agents for cotton fibers. It was not until the late 1960s, however, that this knowledge was applied in a commercial process. The process is sometimes called liquid-ammonia mercerization because the effect of the ammonia on the fine structure of cotton fibers is similar to that of sodium hydroxide in the mercerization process. Considerable difficulties had to be overcome to make liquid-ammonia finishing commercially feasible. A major problem was safely handling the liquid ammonia, a chemical that boils at $-27°F$ ($-33°C$), forms explosive mixtures with air, produces severe contact burns, and gives off a vapor with an extremely pungent and unpleasant smell. Nevertheless, the process is now considered to be safer and simpler than mercerization.

Liquid-ammonia finishing may be used in combination with compressive shrinkage control (Chapter 33) and durable-press finishing (Chapter 33). Cotton shirting fabrics treated with liquid ammonia require more durable-press resin than untreated shirting fabric to obtain satisfactory durable-press performance.

Prewashed Garments

Prewashed garments are garments that have been taken to commercial laundries prior to shipment to retail stores. Prewashing completely removes the sizing from the warp yarns, thereby softening the fabric. The process evens out the shade variations that appear because garment parts have been cut from various fabric bolts. In addition, it makes the garment more pleasant to try on (because it is softer) and provides the customer with a fit that the garment will closely retain after numerous home washings and dryings (because it preshrinks). Denim garments are usually prewashed, a trend that began about 20 years ago. Numerous other cotton apparel items made of other types of fabric are also prewashed.

Stonewashed Garments

Stonewashed garments are garments with a distressed appearance, including a fuzzy texture, puckering at the seams, and slight wrinkling, because they have been tumbled together with stones in large cylindrical washers. Stonewashed garments are usually made from indigo-dyed denim fabric.

Traditional denim fabric changes in coloration (wears) because it is a warp-faced twill fabric with blue warp yarns lying predominantly on the fabric face and white filling yarns lying predominantly on the fabric back. The blue warp yarns are usually dyed with indigo dyes in a process in which only the fibers near the surface of the yarn are dyed, leaving the fibers in the center of the yarn white. As the garment is worn and laundered, abrasion removes blue fibers, exposing more and more white fibers. The fabric surface is roughened and becomes fuzzier. Coloration is further altered by the indigo dye, which washes down to clear, bright blue shades. Because other dyes are often used alone or in combination with indigo dye, the manner in which denim fabrics change in coloration during wear and laundering varies.

In *stonewashing*, denim garments are tumbled in large cylindrical washers with stones, usually pumice stones, to abrade the fabric surface.[2] Pumice, a volcanic glass formed by the solidification of lava that is permeated with gas bubbles, is a colorless or light gray material with the general appearance of a rock froth. Different types, quantities, and sizes (2–10 inches in circumference) of pumice are used, and the length of tumbling time (1–5 hours) is varied to achieve different effects.

After stonewashing, abrasion is most evident on bulky puckered seam areas. The term *highlighting* is used to describe the selective abrasion. Stonewashing gives a speckled look to panel areas of a denim garment. The major drawbacks of stonewashing are the extent of physical damage to the fabric (Figure 32.9) and the presence of powdered pumice in pockets and cuffs. Abrasion can be so severe that 15–20% of garments require some fabric repair prior to sale. Processors must dispose of bags full of pumice powder and frequently replace equipment.

Acidwashed (Acid Stonewashed).

Acidwashed garments are stonewashed garments that have been tumbled with

pumice stones containing an oxidizing agent, such as sodium hypochlorite or potassium permanganate.[3] The use of an oxidizing agent in the stones decreases the amount of physical damage to the fabric because tumbling time can be decreased. The oxidizing agent oxidizes the molecules of the indigo dye, selectively destroying the ability of the molecules to reflect wavelengths of light in the blue range. The process of acidwashing is also called dry bleaching.[4] The size and porosity of the stones and the concentration of the bleach determine the appearance achieved. The garments are separated from the stones and wet processed to neutralize the bleach, remove debris, and soften the fabric. The bleach creates a yellow discoloration and the permanganate a brown hue in the whitened areas of the fabric. Considerable research has been undertaken to find the cause(s) of the discoloration and to correct the problem. Some acidwashing is being achieved by tumbling garments with pelletized permanganate (tablets of permanganate), a process that further reduces fabric damage and eliminates the need for stones and all the problems connected with their use.

Stoneless-Washed (Enzyme-Washed).

Stoneless-washed garments are garments that have been washed in a cellulase-based solution to obtain a fabric that appears stonewashed or acidwashed. The cellulase enzyme physically degrades the surface of the cotton fiber. With care-

---

[2] Stonewashing does not involve the use of water. The name likely reflects the fact that the effect achieved by stonewashing is similar to that traditionally produced by repeated washing of denim garments. The name may also be a reflection of the fact that garments are tumbled in large washers.

[3] Although this term implies the use of acid, in fact, no acid is used in stonewashing. Many finishers would prefer to see the term *acidwash* buried because it raises questions about the effect of this finish on the environment.

[4] Denim fabric/garments can also be liquor bleached. Usually sodium hypochlorite bleach is added to water in the washwheel. The quantity of bleach required to achieve a selected shade depends on the type of dye to be oxidized, the fabric weight, the active concentration of the bleach, the load size, and the time, temperature, and pH of the solution. No stones are used.

FIGURE 32.9 Prewashing, stonewashing, and stoneless washing.

Prewashed denim fabric

Stonewashed denim fabric

Stoneless-Washed denim fabric

ful control, fiber tenacity is not significantly deteriorated, and the highlighting of seams can be eliminated. The appearance and hand of the fabric are identical to those of stonewashed and acidwashed denims. At the microscopic level, however, the fabric surface is not as damaged as stonewashed or acidwashed fabric (Figure 32.9). Cellulase enzymes may be used with pumice stones.

Optically Brightened Fabrics

Optically brightened fabrics appear brighter or whiter (a blue white) when placed under ultraviolet light due to the presence of optical brighteners (also called optical whiteners) on the fiber surfaces. Optical brighteners are dye molecules that selectively absorb wavelenghts of light outside the visible region. More specifically, they absorb ultraviolet light (short, high-energy wavelengths), which is not visible to the human eye, and re-emit it as visible blue (longer, lower-energy wavelengths). Fabrics appear brighter or whiter because more visible light is reflected. These fabrics may also be called fluorescently brightened fabrics or optically whitened fabrics.

Optical brighteners are only moderately durable to laundering and are not durable to chlorine bleaching. They can, however, be renewed during laundry because most detergents contain optical brighteners. Wool fabrics that are optically whitened may develop brown discoloration from exposure to sunlight. Manufactured fibers may be modified by adding an optical brightener to the fiber spinning solution; the optical brightener is then durable to laundering.

FABRICS FINISHED TO ALTER HAND, BODY, DRAPE, AND TRANSLUCENCE

Dramatic alterations in hand, body, and/or drape occur when fabrics are given treatments to soften, stiffen, weight, full, or nap them, or to make them more silk-like.

Softened Fabrics

Softened fabrics are fabrics that feel slicker, smoother, and softer due to the presence of softening compounds on the fiber surfaces. When softened fabric is compressed in the hands, the fibers readily slide past each other and fingers slide readily across the fibers, resulting in a sensation of smoothness and softness. In the case of cotton and wool fabrics, softening compounds restore natural fats

that were removed from the fibers during processing. Softening compounds are also useful on fabrics with resin finishes (durable press, for example) and heat-set fabrics.

Anionic softeners, often used on cellulosic fibers and silk, are sulfonated, negatively charged fatty acids and oils. Because they lack affinity for the fibers, they are padded onto the fabric. Nonionic softeners, usually fatty acids, are also padded onto fabric. Cationic softeners, the fundamental ingredient in laundry fabric softeners, are not added commercially during manufacture of the fabric. They assist in static reduction on synthetic fibers. Overuse of cationic softeners will lead to buildup on fibers and then to yellowing with age. Absorbency can be decreased.

Stiffened or Sized Fabrics

Stiffened or *sized fabrics* are fabrics that are stiffer and crisper due to the presence of stiffening compounds. The fabrics become more difficult to bend and have reduced drapability. Starch is often used as a stiffener. It is temporary but can be renewed. At one time, cotton shirts were starched routinely prior to ironing by immersing them in a starch solution and allowing them to dry. When starching is necessary today, a spray starch is used at the ironing board. Durable stiffening compounds are available for cotton and rayon fabrics.

Fulled Fabrics

Fulled fabrics are woolen and worsted fabrics that are denser, more compact, softer, and bulkier because they have been subjected to moisture, heat, friction, chemicals, and pressure (Figure 32.10). Woven fabric can be fulled to such an extent (40–50% of unfulled dimensions) that the weave pattern is completely obliterated. The thickness and density of fabric that has been heavily fulled is thus greatly increased. Knitwear may be fulled, but never to such an extent that appreciable felting takes place.

Fulling was originally accomplished by pounding fabric with wet feet. People who performed this task were called walkers; hence, the origin of the surname Walker. Modern fulling is carried out in rotary fulling machines. The cloth, in rope form, passes between a pair of driven rollers and is compressed into a tunnel or spout with a tapering cross section, where the actual felting takes place. During fulling, the wool fabric is damp rather than wet, and the solution for damping the fabric contains either soap and sodium carbonate or sulfuric acid.

FIGURE 32.10 Fulling.

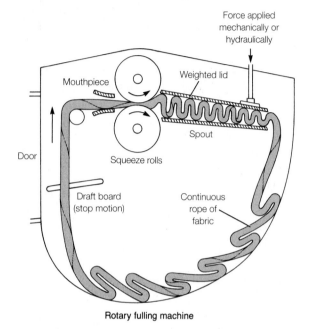

Rotary fulling machine

The appearance of a woolen twill fabric
before and after fulling

Acid fulling has certain measurable advantages over soap fulling, but the latter process is still widely practiced, mainly in the belief that fulling in soap gives the fabric a better hand.

Weighted Fabrics

Weighted fabrics are silk fabrics that have been treated with metallic (aluminum, iron, or tin) salts or other substances to replace the gum that was boiled off, leaving fabrics flimsy. The metals increase the weight of the fabric. The body, cover, and dye absorption of the fabric are also increased.

A moderate amount of weighting is necessary for all silk fabrics except those to be used in lingerie. Heavily weighted silks, however, are more sensitive to the effects of light and oxygen and deteriorate rapidly under certain circumstances, such as exposure to perspiration. Heavily weighted silks deteriorate even under good storage conditions and are especially likely to break at the folds.

Silk fabrics, other than black, that contain more than 10% of substances other than dye are labeled as weighted silks. Black silk may contain up to 15% of substances other than dye before it is labeled as weighted. Weighted silks must be drycleaned because the finish is removed in laundering.

In weighting, silk fabric is placed in the weighting solution for several hours. The fabric will absorb up to 10% of its weight. The fabric is dried, and if additional weight is needed, the process is repeated.

Silk-Like-Finished Fabrics

Silk-like-finished fabrics—also called denier-reduction or milled fabrics—are fabrics, usually polyester, that have been subjected to sodium hydroxide for the purpose of decreasing the diameter of the fibers. Finishing begins with heat-setting to stabilize the fabric to a controlled width, remove wrinkles, and impart wrinkle resistance. The fabric is immersed in a sodium hydroxide solution to dissolve a controlled amount of fiber surfaces. The effect of the sodium hydroxide on polyester-fiber surfaces was shown in Figure 31.1. A 50-denier yarn may be reduced to a 35-denier yarn. The fabric becomes thinner and the mobility of fibers within the yarns becomes greater, leading to a change in hand. All subsequent finishes are done with the fabric completely relaxed to achieve maximum weave crimp.

Parchmentized Fabrics

Parchmentized fabrics are fabrics that have a translucence and crispness characteristic of fine parchment paper as a result of being treated in a concentrated solution of sulfuric acid. A sheer, combed-cotton, plain-woven fabric called lawn is often selected for parchmentizing. First, the fabric is singed, desized, bleached, and mercerized. Then, it is dyed or printed with dyestuffs or pigments that will be unaffected by the parchmentizing to follow. The prepared fabric is immersed in a strong sulfuric acid solution for 5–6 seconds, partially dissolving the surfaces of the cotton fibers. As these surfaces reharden, a cellulose film forms. The fabric is neutralized in weak alkali, washed, and calendered to give more gloss to the surface. The resulting fabric is called organdy. Fabric left in the acid a second or two too long is severely weakened. Localized parchmentizing results when an acid resist is printed onto the fabric prior to its immersion in the acid solution.

FABRICS FINISHED FOR SOUND AND SMELL

The natural scroop of silk fabric can be increased by treating a silk fabric with an organic acid such as acetic or tartaric. Fabrics can be "taffetized" with a resin to obtain the rustle of taffetas.

Odor-control treatments are available to control the smells generated by bacteria on fabrics. Synthetic fibers are known to have greater retention of bacteria on their surfaces than natural fibers, so these fibers are more likely to be treated. Socks and underwear (next-to-skin garments) are often candidates for an odor-control treatment. Sanitized, Inc. pioneered the Sanitized® finish. Bioguard Odor Controller® by Burlington Industries is a more recent entrant in the market.

Finishes for odor control, for the reduction of microbiological deterioration, and for the control of the spread of such organisms are all based on the same chemical treatments. The major difference lies in the reason for the treatment. Antimicrobial treatments are discussed at length in Chapter 31.

CHAPTER SUMMARY

This chapter presented over 20 different finishes that enhance the aesthetic appeal of fabrics and garments through the application of chemicals or through mechanical manipulation. The majority alter color, fabric texture, and/or the degree of fabric luster.

Maintenance Finishes

FABRIC NAME	DESCRIPTION
Compressively Stabilized Fabrics	Cotton, HWM-rayon, flax, and cellulosic-blend fabrics that have reduced shrinkage because they have been mechanically manipulated in a compressive shrinkage control unit.
Liquid-Ammonia-Treated and Compressively Stabilized Fabrics	Cotton fabrics that have reduced relaxation shrinkage, are smooth drying, and are softer due to treatment with liquid ammonia and mechanical manipulation in a compressive shrinkage control unit.
Heat-Set Fabrics	Thermoplastic-fiber fabrics that have reduced relaxation shrinkage and increased wrinkle resistance due to the application of heat.
London-Shrunk or Sponged Fabrics	Worsted fabrics that have reduced relaxation shrinkage because they have been subjected to moisture, heat and pressure.
Washable Wool Fabrics	Wool fabrics that are machine-washable because felting shrinkage has been controlled by chlorinating the fibers, partially coating the fibers with polymers, or spot welding the fibers.
Machine-Washable Regular-Rayon Fabrics	Rayon fabrics that have reduced swelling shrinkage due to intrafiber crosslinking by a resin.
Washable Silk Fabrics	Silk fabrics that are machine-washable following treatment with a chemical process, the details of which are proprietary information.
Durable-Press Garments Cellulosic blends	Garments that have shape retention in wear and laundry, including smooth drying (when properly laundered), flat seams, and sharp pleats and creases, as well as increased rates of premature greying, lowered absorbency, reduced soil release, and increased stiffness, because cellulose polymers have been crosslinked with durable-press resins.
All cotton	Garments that share the same characteristics as durable-press cellulosic blends except that their wear life is significantly lower.
Permanent-Set Wool Fabrics	Wool fabrics that retain sharp pleats and creases during wear, laundering, and drycleaning because they have been chemically treated.
Durable-Press Wool Garments	Wool garments that retain sharp pleats and creases and have a smooth appearance due to the presence of special polymers.
Antipilling Fabrics	Fabrics, usually highly napped, that have reduced rates of pill formation due to the presence of proprietary bonding agents.
Soil-Repellent-Finished Fabrics	Fabrics that have reduced rates of soiling because water and/or oil (including the staining compounds they may contain) bead up on their surfaces, allowing time for these liquids to be blotted up, due to the presence of silicone or flurocarbon compounds on the fibers.
Soil-Release-Finished Fabrics	Fabrics from which oily soil is more easily removed due to the presence of soil-release agents.
Soil-Repellent-and-Release-Finished Fabrics	Fabrics that have reduced rates of soiling and are easily cleaned when oily soil does penetrate due to the presence of a unique block polymer on the fiber surfaces.
Stain-Resistant-Finished Fabrics	Fabrics, usually carpeting, that have increased resistance to staining by anionic compounds in artificially colored food and drink due to the presence of stain-resist agents.
Moth-Resistant-Finished Fabrics	Wool fabrics that have increased resistance to destruction by moth larvae due to the presence of mothproofing agents.
Mold- and Mildew-Resistant-Finished Fabrics	Cellulosic fabrics that have reduced growth rates of mildew and molds (increased resistance to destruction by these microorganisms) due to the presence of chemicals.
Light-Stabilized Fabrics	Fabrics that have reduced rates of disintegration from ultraviolet light due to the presence of light-stabilizing chemicals.

Maintenance Finishes

During the last 35 years, textile chemists have worked diligently to develop finishing processes that provide the type and level of maintenance performance demanded in the marketplace. In the 1950s, durable-press finishing provided ease-of-care performance for cellulose-fiber fabrics that matched the performance of synthetic-fiber fabrics. In the 1960s, machine-washable wool fabrics provided an alternative to dryclean-only wool fabrics. The discovery of fluorocarbons led to soil-repellent-finished fabrics. When textile chemists realized how tenaciously soil was held by certain resins they were applying to fabrics, they worked to discover how to get these resins to release soil. The 1980s brought significant strides toward the development of 100% cotton durable-press fabric, through the use of liquid ammonia, and toward the control of the spread of germs, through the application of antimicrobials to carpeting and fabrics. Detail View 33 names and describes 18 fabrics that have been finished to alter maintenance properties.

FABRICS FINISHED FOR DIMENSIONAL STABILITY

The relaxation, felting, and swelling shrinkage of fabrics, discussed in Chapter 5, may be substantially reduced by finishing processes. The specific process chosen depends on the type(s) of shrinkage to be controlled, the fiber composition of the fabric, and the structure of the fabric.

Compressively Stabilized Fabrics

Compressively stabilized fabrics are fabrics whose inherent tension has been alleviated in a mechanical finishing process called compressive stabilization (Figure 33.1). They, therefore, have reduced relaxation shrinkage; they shrink less during laundering as a result of the compressive stabilization process. Some residual shrinkage—shrinkage that remains even after treatment—may occur when compressively stabilized fabrics are laundered. A comparison of the structure of a woven fabric before and after compressive stabilization shows that yarn crimp increases in finishing (Figure 33.1). A similar comparison for weft knits would show that course loops become more compressed upon themselves as a result of finishing. Compressively stabilized fabrics are usually cotton, high-wet-modulus (HWM) rayon, or flax.

To compressively stabilize a woven fabric, it is mechanically manipulated (compacted) lengthwise and crosswise in the presence of heat and steam. The damp fabric is led over a guide roller and is drawn between a rubber blanket and a heated shoe. The shoe presses the fabric into intimate contact with the rubber blanket. During passage of the rubber blanket from A to B in Figure 33.1, the outer surface of the fabric is extended. The pressure of the shoe ensures that the fabric conforms to the rubber blanket. From B outward, the surface of the rubber blanket retracts and the fabric is physically forced to comply; the fabric is thus compressed or

FIGURE 33.1 Compressive stabilization.

The filling yarns of a woven fabric are compacted during compressive stabilization.

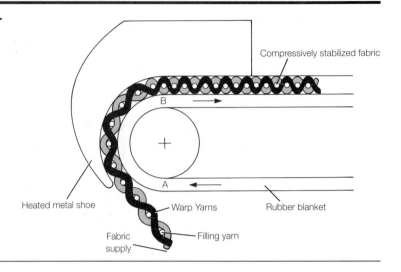

Compressively stabilized fabric

B

A

Heated metal shoe

Warp Yarns

Rubber blanket

Fabric supply

Filling yarn

shortened. The amount of stabilization is determined mainly by the thickness of the rubber blanket.

Cotton knits (usually tubular weft knits) are compacted using horizontal rollers. The knit is steamed to regain moisture and then introduced to the compacting rollers. The feed roller (first roller) turns at a faster speed than the retarding roller (the second roller). This speed differential, combined with a heated shoe placed between the rollers to confine the knit, forces the stitches to be compacted.

Trademarks of compressively stabilized fabrics are Sanforized® (for all cotton woven fabrics that are meant to be ironed), Sanforized-Plus-2® (for durable-press woven blends), and Sanfor-Knit® (for cotton and cotton blend knit fabrics). The Sanforized Company manages a certification program connected with these trademarks (Chapter 9). Woven fabrics on which the company's trademarks are found will not shrink more than 2%. Knit garments on which the Sanfor-Knit® trademark is present will keep their original comfort-fit for their entire wear life. Sanfor-Set® (woven cotton-bottom-weight fabrics) indicates a smooth drying performance in addition to shrinkage control. Pak-Nit® is a trademark of the Compax Corporation and indicates that a compressive shrinkage control treatment has been applied to a knit fabric.

Liquid-Ammonia-Treated and Compressively Stabilized Fabrics

In response to the American public's desire for cotton jeans that have a smooth appearance without ironing, to-gether with the softness and the faded, worn look that people expect, a new technology emerged. After four years of research, the processes of compressive shrinkage control and liquid-ammonia finishing (discussed in Chapter 32) were combined to produce the desired result (Figure 33.2).

Liquid-ammonia-treated and compressively stabilized fabrics result in garments that are smooth drying and maintain their fit after numerous washings and tumble dryings. The soft hand of cotton denim fabric is preserved; in fact, liquid-ammonia-treated and compressively stabilized denim is soft and tends to soften further with each washing. Fabric durability is superior to durable-press fabrics. The dye on the denim continues to fade.

Fabrics carrying the Sanfor-Set® label of the Sanforized Company exhibit these special attributes. In addition to denim, corduroys and chambrays are also treated. Efforts have been made to apply the technology to lighter-weight (particularly shirtweight) 100% cotton fabrics, but the desired level of performance has not yet been achieved.

Heat-Set Fabrics

Heat-set fabrics have reduced relaxation shrinkage and increased wrinkle resistance due to the application of heat. In heat-setting, fabrics (sometimes yarns) containing thermoplastic fibers are heated to temperatures greater than their glass transition temperature but considerably less than their melting temperature while they are held under tension. The heat-setting temperature of polyester fiber, for example, is about 400°F (215°C) and its melting point is about 518°F (270°C). The heat causes the molecules (polymers) within the fibers to move freely; the fine structure of the fiber changes, thus dissipating the stresses within the fiber. The tension on the fabric is maintained until the fabric cools. The fabric does not shorten during heat-setting, as is the case with the compressive stabilization of cellulosic fabrics.

Nylon, polyester, and acetate fabrics are routinely heat-set. The heat-setting temperature of fabrics containing olefin and acrylic fibers is so low that it can easily be surpassed by the consumer in home laundering, so these fabrics are usually not heat-set.

London-Shrunk or Sponged Fabrics

London-shrunk or *sponged fabrics* are worsted suiting fabrics that have been subjected to moisture to remove stress. Originally, worsted fabrics were laid out in fields near the city of London and the dew relieved the stresses, reducing the amount of relaxation shrinkage. The hand of the worsted fabrics also improved. Today, fine worsted suiting fabrics for men's wear (but not women's) may be London shrunk. Men's suit manufacturers all over the world may label garments "Genuine London Process" or similar wording when their fabric has been carefully processed according to the requirements established by a group of English textile companies.

In *London shrinking*, alternate layers of wet blankets and worsted fabric are built up on a long table. Sufficient weight is placed on top to force the moisture from the blankets into the wool, a process requiring about 12 hours. The damp fabric is hung over sticks and dried at room temperature. The next procedure is hydraulic pressing, in which preheated metal plates are inserted at intervals in the layers of fabric, as well as on the top and the bottom of the stack. This assembly is kept under 3000 pounds (1361 kilograms) of pressure for 10–12 hours.

Washable Wool Fabrics

Washable wool fabrics are wool fabrics whose felting shrinkage has been controlled by the application of specific chemicals, so that the fabric can be laundered in home washing machines. The treatment can be applied to both woven and knit fabrics. Washable wool fabrics tend to soil more readily and to hold the soil more tenaciously in laundering than untreated wool fabrics. An exception is chlorine/Hercosett® wool fabrics, which exhibit excellent soil release even when washed at 100.4°F (38°C).

Three different types of washable wool fabrics are made: chlorinated wools, polymer-coated or chlorinated/resin-treated wools, and spot-welded wools. Figure 33.3 shows the surfaces of wool fibers in three fabrics treated to make them washable and the surface of wool fiber prior to treatment.

Chlorinated Wool Fabrics. When wool fabric is steeped in a solution containing an oxidizing agent such as chlorine, the scale structure of the wool fibers is totally removed, but the fibers also sustain severe internal damage. When the chlorination process is carefully controlled, however, the chemical alteration occurs only at the fiber surface and the scale structure is not completely

---

FIGURE 33.2 Liquid ammonia/compressive stabilization.

The pair of denim jeans on the left is untreated, whereas the pair on the right has been given a liquid ammonia/ compressive stabilization treatment. Both appear following one home wash and tumble dry.

Untreated

With a liquid ammonia/compressive
stabilization treatment

FIGURE 33.3 Washable Wool Fabrics.

One of these wool fibers is untreated. The other three have been given various treatments to control felting shrinkage.

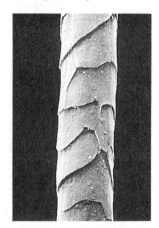

Chlorinated fiber   Polymer-coated fiber   Spot-welded fibers   Untreated fiber

destroyed. A highly satisfactory control of felting shrinkage is achieved, although the fabric does have a slightly harsher hand and is impaired to a degree in strength and abrasion resistance. About half of washable wool fabrics are chlorinated.

Felting shrinkage is reduced in chlorinated wool fabric because the difference in friction between the with-scale and against-scale directions of the treated fiber is less than for the untreated fiber. In other words, the directional frictional effect that was discussed in Chapter 5 is less. The greater the damage to the scale structure, the less difference there is in friction in the two fiber directions. Chlorination also reduces felting shrinkage by attacking the protein polymers. At low levels of chlorination (those that cause the least scale damage to the fiber), a degraded protein polymer is formed. When these mildly chlorinated fibers become wet, as during laundering, they behave like a gel or a viscous liquid and, consequently, are easily deformed. During washing, one fiber "ploughs" into another upon contact. Interfiber movement becomes difficult in any direction. Felting is thus controlled by this "ploughing" mechanism as well as by the reduction in the directional frictional effect.

Polymer-Coated Wool Fabrics. Wool fabrics can be made machine-washable by covering about 2% of the fiber surfaces with polymers. Polymer-coated wool fabrics are sometimes called chlorinated/resin-treated

fabrics because the fabric is treated with chlorine (or another chemical that attacks the scales) prior to resin application to ensure that the polymer will adhere to the fiber surfaces. These washable wool fabrics retain their hand and their strength and abrasion resistance. In some cases, the polymer impregnates the wool fibers in addition to forming a film on the outside surface, resulting in a more durable treatment.

The polymer may be applied as early as the fibrous stage or as late as the fabricated garment stage. Superwash Wool® (International Wool Secretariat) and H$_2$O Wools® (J.P. Stevens Company) are two trademarks found in the marketplace; Wurlan®, Dylan GR®, and chlorine/Hercosett® (Hercules Company) name specific manufacturing processes.

Reduced felting shrinkage of chlorinated/resin-treated fabrics results from masked scales, reduced friction between fibers, and/or from a "stand-off" mechanism. In dry Hercosett-treated wool fabrics, the even coating of polymer is too thin to mask the scales. However, the polymer film swells in water because it is very hygroscopic. The swollen polymer film is thick enough to mask the scales, and it also attracts water molecules. When two Hercosett-treated fibers are pressed together in water, there is no actual contact. The fibers are separated by layers of water molecules that act as a lubricant and reduce interfiber friction to very low levels.

A "stand-off" mechanism operates when the washable

wool fabric has a polyacrylate film. This film is not evenly distributed but rather exists as globules over the wool fiber surfaces. Because the globules are higher than the scale edges, they prevent the adjacent fibers from meshing, thus also preventing felting shrinkage. Polyacrylate does not swell greatly in water.

Spot-Welded Wool Fabrics. In spot-welded fabrics, a resin binds the fibers together at points along their lengths. The resin is never applied to fibers or yarns, only to fabric, because subsequent processing would break the spot-welds. After the resin is applied, the fabric is cured. Felting shrinkage is prevented because wool fibers cannot migrate. A wool fabric can be produced with acceptable levels of washability and other performance properties.

Machine-Washable Regular-Rayon Fabrics

Machine-washable regular-rayon fabrics are those in which shrinkage control is accomplished by the application of a resin. The resins form crosslinks in the amorphous areas within the fibers, reducing the swelling and elongation of the fibers. Resins that do not contain nitrogen, such as the aldehydes, are superior to other resins because they do not weaken the fabric, are nonchlorine-retentive, and have excellent wash longevity. Wash cycles should be gentle and short. Compressive treatments do not improve the dimensional stability of regular-rayon fabrics because much of the shrinkage is caused by the swelling of the fiber in water.

Washable Silk Fabrics

Washable silk fabrics are silk fabrics that have been chemically treated so that they can be washed successfully. Traditionally, silk fabric is treated with additives to restore the weight lost when the fabric is degummed. Most of the additives are water soluble, so the fabric must be drycleaned. Washable silk fabric is treated with a water-insoluble additive whose chemical composition is proprietary information. The yarn structure in washable silk fabric is also slightly altered, so that the fabric is duller, has a more distressed look, is softer, and is washable. Washable silk fabrics have found a market in casual and sporty wear for which the dressy, glossy finish of traditional silk is neither required nor even desired.

Some washable silk fabrics are machine-washable. It is recommended that they be spun dried without heat so that they do not stiffen. The alternative is to hang the fabrics for a short time and then iron them while they are still damp. Some silk importers and converters stress that washable silk fabrics are inevitably and irreparably changed once they encounter the heat and detergents of machine laundering. They say that washable silk fabrics can only be successfully hand washed in cool water with gentle soaps. The two points of agreement between proponents and detractors are that washable silk fabrics must be washed alone because of dye bleeding (the fabric both gives off and takes on color) and that washable silk fabrics must not be drycleaned.

FABRICS FINISHED FOR APPEARANCE RETENTION

Synthetic-fiber fabrics spoiled consumers because they were wrinkle-free during wear and emerged from laundering ready to hang in the closet without ironing. Pleats in skirts and creases in pants made from synthetic-fiber fabrics did not need to be reset. Scientists turned to the magic of chemistry to alter cotton and wool fibers to obtain the maintenance advantages of synthetic-fiber fabrics.

Durable-Press Cellulosic Garments

Durable-press cellulosic garments have smooth seams, retain sharp pleats and intentionally pressed-in creases, retain their press at hems and fabric folds, and are wrinkle free during wear and following home laundering and drying because they have been treated with durable-press resins. Durable-press finishing was heralded as one of the most significant textile developments of the 20th century. It eliminated the need to starch, line dry, sprinkle, and iron cotton fabrics to obtain a wrinkle-free appearance.

Durable-press garments must be laundered in a washing machine with a permanent-press or cool-down cycle, a cycle in which cold water is added before the garments are spun up against the sides of the washer during water extraction. They also require tumbling in a dryer rather than line drying for the smoothest and neatest appearance.

The terms *durable press* and *permanent press* may be used interchangeably; each reflects the exceptional appearance retention achieved. Durable press is usually the preferred terminology because it more realistically conveys the longevity of the finish. After about 50 wear and laundry cycles, touch-up ironing may be necessary.

Durable-press garment finishing evolved from wrinkle-resistant finishing and wash-and-wear finishing. "Wrinkle-resistant" finishes created *fabrics* that resisted wrinkling and recovered from wrinkling during wear but not in laundering. Wash-and-wear finishes filled this gap by adding smooth-drying ability to the fabric. Durable-press finishes lend the additional asset of shape retention to *garments.*

Most durable-press garments are made of fabrics that are blends of cotton or rayon with a synthetic fiber, usually polyester. Some 100% cotton fabrics are also available. Sheets and pillowcases, as well as most shirts, blouses, pants, jeans, pajamas, and robes, are durable-press finished. Trademarks found on durable-press garments include Conepress® (Cone Mills), Ameriset® (American Laundry Machinery Industries), and Creaset® (Creaset, Inc.).

Formation of Polymer Crosslinks. Cotton and other cellulosic fibers do not recover from bending deformation (Chapter 12). Durable-press finishing improves the wrinkle resistance of fabric containing cellulosic fibers because the chemicals used build crosslinks between cellulose polymers (Figure 33.4). A textile chemical supplier reacts urea (or a derivative of urea), a glyoxal, and formaldehyde. The product of this reaction is an N-methylol compound because a methylol (CH_2OH) group is attached to the urea nitrogen. Most of the N-methylol compound is in the form of a di-(N-methylol)

derivative with a little of the mono-form and even some free formaldehyde. The textile finisher adds this mixture to the fabric in a pad bath that also contains the appropriate catalyst, a softener, and a hand builder. The di-(N-methylol) compound reacts with the hydroxyl groups of two cellulose polymers to build a series of crosslinks. The most widely used di-(N-methylol) compound in durable-press finishing is dimethyloldihydroxyethyleneurea (DMDHEU).

Once formed and cured, the three-dimensionally crosslinked polymer system resists bending forces; the crosslinks are about 20 times stronger than the hydrogen bonds between cellulose polymer chains. When the bending force is released, the crosslinks pull the polymers back to the same formation, and no wrinkle is formed.

Precured and Postcured Durable Press. The terms *precure* and *postcure* relate to the point during the manufacturing process at which the resin impregnated in the fabric is cured to impart the durable-press performance (Figure 33.5). In the early years of durable-press finishing, the fabric was impregnated with resin, dried, cured, and washed before it was sent to the garment manufacturer or end-use product fabricator, where the product was cut, sewn, and pressed. Any shaping of the product had to be accomplished by the heat and pressure of the hot head press. The cured fabric, however, resisted the formation of creases because it had been set in a flat posi-

FIGURE 33.4   Durable-press resin.

Formaldehyde, a glyoxal, and urea are synthesized to create a durable-press resin that, in turn, forms crosslinks within a cellulosic fiber.

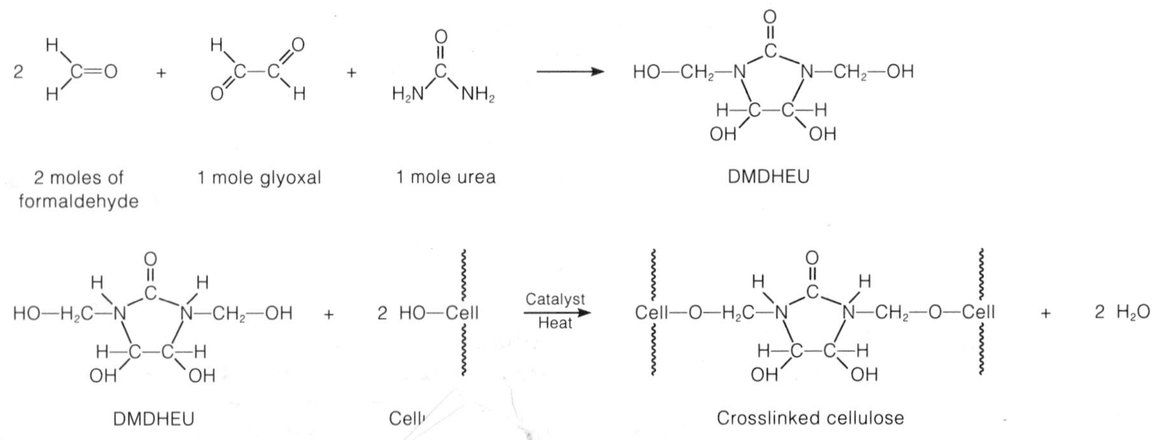

FIGURE 33.5   Durable-press finishing processes.

In the precuring sequence, the durable-press resin is cured before the garment is made. In the postcuring sequence, the resin is cured after the garment is made.

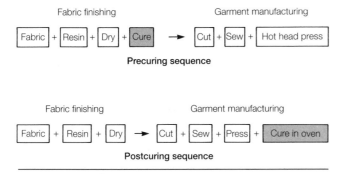

Precuring sequence

Postcuring sequence

tion. To overcome this problem, the textile industry developed the postcure process, in which the fabric is not cured until the product has been cut and sewn. Pleats and creases are sharply set on a hot head press and the rest of the fabric is set flat as the garment is hung on a hanger and placed in a curing oven. Garment alterations become difficult because the edges of the hems, sleeves, and seams are permanently creased. Today home sewing fabrics, tablecloths, curtains, and bed linens are precured. Most garments are postcured.

Performance Trade-offs. Although crosslinking improves the resilience of cotton fibers, it also reduces their elongation, tenacity, abrasion resistance, and flexibility and increases their stiffness. Durable-press finishing can reduce the strength of 100% cotton fabrics by as much as 50%, so durable-press resins are usually applied to polyester/cellulose blend fabrics. The polyester fibers, unaffected by the durable-press resin, compensate for the reduced durability of the cellulosic fibers. When durable-press resins are applied to 100% cotton fabrics, the fabrics are usually treated first with liquid ammonia to strengthen the cotton fiber.

Durable-press fabrics are excessive soil scavengers. In laundering, soil is redeposited on the fabrics, so they grey prematurely. Durable-press resins retain oily soil during laundering unless a laundry pretreatment product or a liquid detergent is applied.[1] In addition, the absorbency of durable-press garments is reduced enough

that some consumers detect a difference in their comfort. For some individuals, this discomfort is offset by the psychological comfort of a wrinkle-free appearance. Durable-press blended fabrics are also subject to frosting because the cotton fibers are preferentially abraded away.

Durable-press fabrics may contain free formaldehyde, and they may release formaldehyde as the crosslinks are broken.[2] Garment workers who handle durable-press fabrics and consumers who wear durable-press garments may therefore be exposed to formaldehyde. This presence of formaldehyde is of concern because it is a known contact allergen and is toxic. Allergic contact dermatitis to formaldehyde is common because formaldehyde is a strong allergen and is contained in many consumer products so exposure is high. However, in the United States very few cases of allergic contact dermatitis *due to working with, wearing, or using durable-press fabrics* have been documented. An individual who has such an allergic reaction must be highly sensitive because the release of formaldehyde under normal conditions is very slow in small quantities. No cases of toxic effects of durable-press fabrics are known.

Recommended Maintenance Procedures. Durable-press garments, sheets, pillowcases and other items should be laundered before they are used or worn in order to remove the small quantity of free formaldehyde that may be present. Manufacturers have always recommended that consumers wash durable-press textiles prior to use or wear.

Durable-press garments must be properly laundered for the garment to emerge and be acceptable to wear. Wash loads and dryer loads should be kept small; overcrowding will cause wrinkling to occur. A permanent-press wash and dry cycle should be used. For adequate soil removal, durable-press items should be washed frequently because the durable-press resin increases the fabric's affinity for oil and grease. Collars, cuffs, and any area where oily substances have been spilled need to be treated with a laundry pretreatment product unless the fabric was manufactured with both a durable-press and soil-release treatment.

The Search for Improved Overall Performance. Today, 100% cotton durable-press products do not meet all the performance requirements desired by consumers. Research continues in an attempt to find a procedure that

---

[1] Laundry pretreatment products include Spray and Wash®, a trademark of Dow Brands, Inc.; Shout®, a trademark of S.C. Johnson & Son, Inc.; and Clorox® Prewash®, a trademark of the Clorox Company.

[2] This breaking of the crosslinks over time is the reason that durable-press garments eventually need touch-up ironing.

will provide acceptable wear life and wrinkle-free performance for 100% cotton fabrics.

Current research in durable-press finishing also focuses on discovering commercially feasible formulations and processes that eliminate the need for use of formaldehyde. Tremendous strides have been made (a) in reducing the amount of formaldehyde present on fabrics when they are purchased and (b) in reducing the amount of formaldehyde released as the fabric is used.

Permanent-Set Wool Fabrics

Permanent-set wool fabrics are wool fabrics in which sharp pleats and creases have been permanently inserted. Permanent-set woven wool fabrics will also remain flat and unwrinkled during wear. The pleats and creases of permanent-set wool fabrics retain their sharpness during wear, drycleaning, and hand washing. More severe cleaning methods, however, result in the removal of the pleats and creases and in wrinkling. In addition, permanent-set wool fabrics are more dimensionally stable than those without set. Likewise, the twist in wool carpet yarns is set to give the carpet pile maximum compressional resilience.

The permanent set is the result of a chemical process in which the stresses within the wool fabric (fiber) are relaxed and the fibers are stabilized in a new, desired configuration. The chemical process of permanently setting wool fabric provides a means for the bonded protein chains to move in relation to each other. It involves breaking hydrogen and disulfide bonds and allowing them to reform in new positions when the fabric is placed in the desired configuration. Chemicals are applied to the fabric in the presence of heat and steam. The chemicals break the disulfide bonds, and the heat and the steam break the hydrogen bonds. If the fabric is wrinkle free when the bonds are allowed to reform, a permanently smooth fabric results. If it has been folded to form a pleat or crease when the bonds reform, then a sharp fold results. This process is very similar to that of giving a permanent wave to hair.

Durable-Press Wool Garments (Garment Setting)

Durable-press wool garments are garments that retain sharp pleats and creases and have a smooth appearance during wear and laundering due to the presence of special polymers. For a wool garment to achieve this durable-press performance, it must be shrink resistant to prevent felting and be set to maintain shape.

The most widely used process, developed by the International Wool Secretariat (IWS), involves applying polymers by padding. The fabric is dried, the polymer is cured, and the fabric finished in the normal manner. After a garment is made, it is set. For trousers, creases and side seams are sprayed with a special solution, and then steam pressing sets the fabric. Pleated skirt panels from the shrink-resistant wool are set by rolling them between paper formers and then steaming them in an autoclave. The other process, the CSIRO Solvent-Resin-Steam Process, relies on the observation that certain reactive polymers, when cured on the garment in the required shape, are capable of maintaining the shape while the free-hanging garment is set in steam.[3] After the polymer is applied to the garment, the garment is re-pressed to remove wrinkles and then hung in a steam oven for about two hours.

Antipilling Fabrics

Antipilling fabrics are fabrics, usually highly napped, that have reduced rates of pill formation due to the presence of proprietary bonding agents. The tendency of highly napped blankets to pill during laundering is often controlled by spraying the blanket with a proprietary bonding agent and then turning back the longer, protruding pile fibers by using an air stream. Passing the treated fabric through an infrared oven vaporizes the water. The individual fibers composing the outermost layer of the fabric are bonded or welded at their crossover points, forming a kind of flexible network. It is this flexible network that helps to eliminate the tendency to shed and pill. Blankets treated in this manner are slightly crisper than untreated blankets but are more lively and resilient and less likely to pill in laundering.

The routine process of singeing, done on most fabrics, helps to reduce pilling by reducing the number of free fiber ends. In many instances, though, modification of manufactured fibers to provide weak spots along their length is a preferable way to reduce pilling propensity.

FABRICS FINISHED FOR CLEANLINESS RETENTION

Four types of chemical finishes are used to assist in maintaining the cleanliness of a fabric during its use. One type shields individual fibers from absorbing oily

---

[3]CSIRO is the acronym for the Commonwealth Scientific and Industrial Research Organization.

soil, one type assists in the release of oily soil absorbed in fibers and in finishes, and another both shields and assists in releasing soil. The fourth finish prevents staining by liquids containing anionic compounds.

Soil-Repellent-Finished Fabrics

Soil-repellent-finished fabrics are fabrics that soil more slowly because water and/or oils bead up on their surfaces. Discolored areas are prevented because the oils and water, plus any dirt or staining substances they may contain, can be wiped away before they have time to spread over the fabric surface or penetrate the fabric.

Soil repellents, the chemicals that render a fabric soil repellent, may be applied at the textile mill, as post-treatments (by the consumer or retailer), or as after-market treatments (by the consumer, apparel drycleaners, or carpet and upholstery cleaners). The level of effectiveness differs considerably, depending on the chemical formulation, method of application, and fiber content of the fabric.

The Nature of the Chemical Shield. In the 1950s *fluorocarbon soil repellents*—also called *rain/stain protectors* or *fabric fluorodizers*—were introduced for use on apparel fabrics. Similar products were developed over 15 years ago for use on carpets containing synthetic fibers. Fluoropolymers, similar to those in Teflon® (a Du Pont trademark) nonstick cookware or others that impart a low-energy surface, surround the fibers within the treated fabric. They are strongly bound together and firmly "hook into" the fibers. The fluorine shield strongly repels water and oil. Thus, contact between oil or water and the fabric surface is minimized. Zepel® (Du Pont) and Scotchgard® (3M) are two well-known products. Each has a number of different formulations designed to meet different needs such as velvet protection, fabric protection, and upholstery protection. Treatments applied by the manufacturer are durable; aerosol products applied by the consumer are semidurable.

Silicone soil repellents impart resistance to waterborne soiling but provide little, if any, resistance to oilborne soiling. Mixtures of silicones and fluorocarbons are applied as soil repellents. Other important soil repellents are acrylic copolymers of various vinyl compounds.

Fabrics Treated. Soil repellents work well on nylon, polyester, wool, and acrylic fabrics and on cotton and synthetic/cotton blends. They are found on all kinds of apparel including rainwear, all-weather outerwear, skiwear, bikewear, hunting gear, uniforms, active sports-wear, and camping equipment. Slipcovers, upholstery fabrics, draperies, bedspreads, and carpet fabrics may have the protection of a soil-repellent finish because furniture and carpeting are constantly subjected to spills and other physical abuse. Also protected are marine covers, backpacks, luggage, and outdoor furniture.

Other Performance Considerations. Soil-repellent-finished fabrics are breathable because the soil repellents coat each fiber; they do not fill the voids in the fabric. Soil repellents do not usually alter fabric hand or appearance.

Periodic cleaning will remove dry soil that accumulates through normal use. Soaps and detergents, unless completely rinsed out, may temporarily mask the protective powers of soil repellents. Thorough rinsing is a must to retain the protective performance of the finish. Pressing or machine drying helps to keep the soil repellents operating at peak efficiency.

Problems with soil-repellent-finished fabrics occur when soil is not removed promptly or is forced down into the chemical shield. In the latter case, the shield tenaciously resists the removal of the soil because it keeps water from spreading, wetting the surface, and lifting the soil away.

Performance problems may arise when a siloxane post-treatment is applied over a fluorocarbon soil-repellent. The soil resistance of the fabric or carpet may be reduced. The co-application of siloxanes and fluorocarbons in manufacture also decreases oil repellency and soil resistance. After-market soil-repellents applied to carpeting do not tend to alter flammability or electrical resistivity, however. Treatments containing silicones adversely affect the flame resistance of polyester carpets.

Soil-Release-Finished Fabrics

Soil-release-finished fabrics are fabrics from which oily soil is more easily removed in home laundering, without pretreating with a liquid detergent or a laundry pretreatment product, due to the presence of soil-release agents. Durable-press fabrics and polyester fabrics are often given this treatment.

The soil-release finish was developed because consumers wanted the same degree of cleanliness they were accustomed to getting with 100% cotton fabrics without the bother of an additional laundering procedure. Before the advent of synthetic-fiber and blended fabrics, they were never concerned about "ring around the collar" because it did not exist.

A hangtag or label will usually indicate when a fabric has been treated to enhance soil release. Visa® (Milliken and Company, Inc.) is among the best-known trademarks; others include Come Clean® (Klopman Mills), X-it® (Graniteville Co.), and Scotchgard Stain Release® (3M). Soil release effectively lasts 20–50 home washings. For the most effective release, hot water should be used, and the fabric should be washed as soon as possible after the oil spot occurs. Carpet is also treated with soil release finishes. One of these is Scotchgard Stain Release® (3M).

Release of Tenaciously Held Soil. The methods used to give fabrics soil-release properties vary. Many processes use special soil-release chemicals that are applied simultaneously with or subsequent to durable-press finishes. Two general approaches have been taken to encourage hydrophobic surfaces to release oil. The first is to make the surface more hydrophilic (more wettable) by using certain poly(sodium acrylate) emulsions and hydrophilic copolymers. The other approach is to form a film or coat that protects the fibers from contact with oil; wash water then floats surface oils away. In this case, fluorocarbons can be used.

Other Performance Considerations. Soil-release chemicals that create a more hydrophilic surface on fabrics provide additional performance benefits. Comfort is improved (especially in hot weather) because the soil-release agents increase absorption of moisture and soften the fabric. The increase in moisture absorption also means a lower static buildup. Further, soil redeposition during laundering, which causes white and pastel fabrics to grey, is reduced. Likewise, pilling and fuzzing of fabric are reduced.

It should be noted that most soil-release chemicals do not prevent oil from entering the fabric. In fact, most soil-release-finished fabrics soil more heavily than unfinished fabrics.

Soil-Repellent-and-Release-Finished Fabrics

Soil-repellent-and-release-finished fabrics resist soiling and readily release any soil that may adhere to the fabric in normal home laundry. It is difficult to finish a fabric to make it both resistant to oily soiling and then willing to release oily soils inadvertently embedded within it because directly opposite types of surfaces are required. The enhancement of beading of water and oil demands a hydrophobic surface, whereas the release of embedded oil requires a hydrophilic surface.

The answer to this dilemma was the discovery of a block copolymer, a polymer with two distinctly different segments, that will change its orientation depending on whether it is in water or is exposed to the air (Figure 33.6). The fluorochemical segment (F) gives the fabric soil resistance during use in an air environment. The second segment of the polymer (O) is hydrophilic. In water,

FIGURE 33.6 Soil-repellent-and-release finishing.

The block polymer applied to fabrics/fibers changes its orientation to provide soil repellency in use and soil release during laundering.

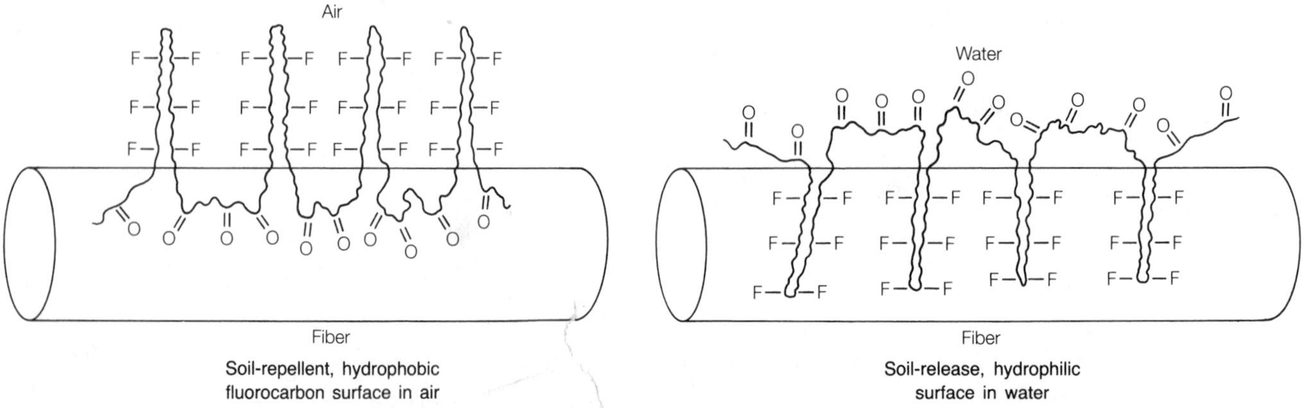

Soil-repellent, hydrophobic
fluorocarbon surface in air

Soil-release, hydrophilic
surface in water

it gives the fiber/fabric a more hydrophilic surface and functions as a soil-release agent. The orientation of the polymer does "flip-flops" when its environment changes. After the fabric is laundered and dried, the polymer is oriented with the fluorocarbon away from the fiber; in water, the fluorocarbon is toward the fiber.

By trademark, the finish containing this block copolymer is Dual-Action Scotchgard® (FC-218) by the 3M Company. It is applied to polyester/cotton blend fabric as well as to other synthetic fibers and fiber blends.

Stain-Resistant-Finished Fabrics

Stain-resistant-finished fabrics are those that resist staining by anionic compounds commonly found in artificially colored food and drink. Stain-resist agents are used in conjunction with soil repellents to impart soil (oil) resistance and anionic-stain resistance to nylon and wool carpets.

Nylon Carpets. Stain-resistant finishes for nylon carpets are considered to be one of the most significant developments in textiles in the last 20 years. The stain-resist agents are sulfonated aromatic aldehyde condensation products (SAC). It is believed that the stain resistance is due to the formation of a negatively charged surface barrier on or near the fiber surface. This anionic shield protects the fibers from immediate staining or dyeing by anionic stains or dyes in food and drink. Time is provided for the spilled liquid to be wiped up before the staining compound attaches itself to positively charged sites in the carpet fibers.

One of the problems encountered with stain-resist agents is yellowing. The resin (SAC) is naturally yellow. Manufacturers have created formulations of the resin to minimize potential yellowing.

Carpets of Du Pont nylon treated with a stain-resist agent as well as a soil repellent are sold under the Stainmaster® certification program. Likewise, carpet of Monsanto nylon is available with StainBlocker®, which has a Wear-Dated® guarantee.[4]

Wool Carpets. In February 1990, a stain-resist finish for wool fabric was announced. Invecta Wool Shield® is a chemical treatment that provides wool with a greater resistance to staining by acid-based food dyes. It provides stain resistance by covering microscopic fiber openings after dyeing and then coating again for lasting protection.

FABRICS FURNISHED FOR RETENTION OF PHYSICAL INTEGRITY

Literally hundreds of compounds have been tested for effectiveness in preventing textiles from disintegrating over time. The quest began as early as the time of the ancient Egyptians, who used herbs and spices to preserve their textiles. The Romans used cedar oil.

Moth-Resistant-Finished Fabrics

Moth-resistant-finished fabrics are wool fabrics that have increased longevity to destruction by moth grubs due to the presence of mothproofing agents. During the last 60 years, thousands of chemicals have been tried on wool fabric with the aim to poison or kill moth larvae. Only a few are effective and meet both toxicity and longevity requirements.

An old wives' tale held that green wool fabrics were more resistant to damage by moth larvae than wool fabrics of any other color. This tale was found to have a scientific basis when a dye called Martius Yellow, a component of green dye baths, was found to be a powerful mothproofing agent. DDT, very widely and successfully used on fabrics for years, is no longer employed because it may be toxic to humans. Other mothproofing formulations are presently used, but none are 100% effective.

Questions have been raised about the toxicity of mothproofing agents to humans. If the substance is toxic to insects that digest it, then is it also toxic to mammals, particularly humans? At the present time, there is no evidence of ill effects among either people who handle the chemicals in industry or people who wear or use fabrics to which they have been applied. Regardless, there is currently a search for mothproofing agents that are effective but less suspect. One commercial product is Permethryn®. The search also includes the discovery of chemicals that might prevent destruction of wool by moth larvae through a mechanism other than poisoning the larvae. It was suggested, for example, that the chemical structure of wool be changed so that the larvae cannot digest the fibers they chew. They would then cease to be interested in consuming wool fabrics. Complex chemicals have been developed to achieve this goal, but they are too expensive to be commercially feasible.

---

[4]Reduction of soiling and staining is an important feature of carpets and particularly for nylon carpet, since 90% of all carpeting is made from nylon fiber. SAC stain-resistant (blocking) finishes are only one approach. Fluorocarbons may be incorporated into nylon fiber at extrusion, producing Anso Worry Free® nylon carpeting (Chapter 16). Fluorocarbon finishes such as Zepel® and Scotchgard® (soil-resistant finishes) may be applied after carpet formation.

Mold- and Mildew-Resistant-Finished Fabrics

Mold- and mildew-resistant-finished fabrics are fabrics containing chemicals that slow or prevent mold and mildew growth. Salicylanilide is used on cellulosic and wool fabrics under the trademarks of Shirlan® and Shirlan NA®, respectively.

Light-Stabilized Fabrics

Light-stabilized fabrics are fabrics in which the degradation of fiber polymers by ultraviolet light and oxygen is slowed due to the presence of light stabilizers in the fabric. Photodegradation of textiles was discussed in Chapter 5. Ultraviolet screeners are reflective coatings which alter the appearance and hand of the textile. Ultraviolet light absorbers absorb UV light more strongly than the fiber polymer. They include colorants (some colorless) and carbon black. Excited-state quenchers combine very rapidly with the initial breakdown products (radicals) of the interaction of light with the polymer. Ultraviolet-stable antioxidants "kill off" some of the highly reactive chemical species formed by the action of light and oxygen before they can attack the polymer.

CHAPTER SUMMARY

This chapter presented 18 finishes that contribute to the maintenance of fabrics. Seven finishes reduce fabric shrinkage; the approach used depends on the type of shrinkage to be controlled and the fiber content of the fabric. Three finishes contribute to the appearance retention of cotton and wool fabrics, and an antipilling finish contributes to the appearance retention of highly napped fabrics. Four finishes—soil repellent, soil release, soil repellent and release, and stain resistant—facilitate the maintenance of fabric cleanliness. Three finishes maintain a fabric's physical integrity by preventing degradation from moth larvae, mildew and molds, and ultraviolet light.

Dyed Textiles

Dyed textiles are textiles in which colorant (usually dye rather than pigment) is uniformly distributed within or on the surface of all fibers throughout a yarn or fabric. A description of a dyed textile includes both its coloration and its dye process.

NAME	DESCRIPTION

COLORATION OR COLOR EFFECT

Solid	Having one color throughout; all fibers having the same color (hue) and shade (value).
Heather	Having fibers of different colors or shades of the same color blended within the yarns of a fabric.
Tweed	Having small spots of color randomly distributed over a fabric surface due to the incorporation of colored fibers in a random fashion into yarns.
Mottled	Having a spotted or blotched appearance.
Variegated or Mixed	Having many colors that blend together.
Muted	Having a softened, subdued, or deadened color by using strands of different colors in yarns or using yarns of different colors in the warp and filling directions of a woven fabric.
Iridescent	Having a sparkling effect created by the appearance of different colors at the peaks and valleys of folds when fabric is draped.
Design	Having motifs and patterns, including stripes, checks, plaids, color-and-weave designs, color-and-knit designs, computer-injection designs, and batik, shaped-resist, and ikat designs.

DYE PROCESSES

Producer Dyeing	Adding colorant to polymer spinning solutions during the processing of manufactured fibers.
Gel Dyeing	Adding colorant to wet-spun fibers while they are in the gel state (not yet fully crystallized or oriented).
Stock Dyeing	Adding dye to fibers in loose form.
Top Dyeing	Adding dye to top (a strand of straightened, paralleled, and separated wool fibers).
Tow Dyeing	Adding dye to filaments that are in the form of a rope (a tow) that will be cut to form staple fiber.
Yarn Dyeing	Adding dye to yarn before fabric formation.
Space Dyeing	Adding dye to yarn so that it has different colors at irregular intervals along its length.
Piece Dyeing	Adding colorant to fabric "in the piece."
Union Dyeing	Adding dye to fabrics that contain two fibers with different dyeing characteristics to achieve a solid-colored fabric by using a dye bath that contains several dyes capable of dyeing all the fibers to the same hue.
Cross Dyeing	Adding dye to blend and mixture fabrics to achieve heathers, stripes, checks, and plaids by using a dye formulation that contains different colored dyes, each having an affinity for a different fiber.
Tone-on-Tone	Adding dye to blend and mixture fabrics to achieve two or more shades of the same hue.
Reserve Dyeing	Leaving some fibers or yarns undyed while dyeing the others in blend or mixture fabrics by using dyes that have an affinity for the fibers to be colored but not for the fibers to be left white.
Computer-Injection Dyeing	Applying aqueous dye solution to the surface of carpet or tufted fabric through a series of microjets arranged transversely across and above the textile to be dyed.
Garment Dyeing	Adding colorant to garments or products, usually to obtain a solid color.
Batik Dyeing	Applying wax by hand to white fabric so that when the fabric is immersed in a dyebath, dye penetration is prevented in the waxed areas.
Shaped-Resist Dyeing	Dyeing fabric that has been folded, crumpled, stitched, plaited, plucked, or twisted and secured in a number of ways, such as binding and knotting.
Ikat	Applying a resist, such as wax or clay, to yarns and dyeing them so that dye cannot penetrate the areas on which the resist is applied.

34

*D*yed Textiles

The art of dyeing is thought to have originated in India or China earlier than 2500 B.C. Dyes capable of giving a full range of hues on linen were known by 1400 B.C. Mixing yellow, red, and blue dyes to give secondary and tertiary shades on fabrics was practiced before 150 A.D. The art of Oriental carpet making, resulting in a splendid variety of colors and designs, approached its peak by 1500 A.D.

Dyed fabrics remained a luxury for centuries. Even when they became widely available, some colors were reserved for the wealthy and influential. Color names such as "royal purple," "royal scarlet," and "royal blue" and the expression "born to the purple" are reminders that only royalty could afford such colors.

Efforts at dyeing fabrics with fast colors were greatly hampered until the Renaissance. The expression "true blue," which now means a constant or loyal person, is an old dyers' term, with "true" meaning colors that held fast as opposed to those that faded quickly. The discovery of mordanting—treating fabric with metallic oxides prior to immersion in dyebaths—increased the attraction of the dye for the fiber (called affinity). The natural dyes varied greatly in quality, and consequently, so did the dyed fabric. Bright colors were rarely possible. These conditions changed dramatically in 1856 when a teenage English chemist, William Henry Perkin, accidentally discovered the first synthetic dye, mauve, while attempting to make quinine from coal tar. Perkin recognized the importance of this discovery and went into partnership with his father and brother to manufacture both this dye and the chemicals needed to synthesize it. Perkin's discovery provided a springboard for a flood of investigations into the chemical composition of coal-tar products, which led to the development of the synthetic organic chemical industry. In these early investigations, it was learned that certain arrangements and groups of atoms caused color to result when the dye was placed in visible light. With this knowledge, it was possible to synthesize many dyes. The introduction of manufactured fibers spurred further development because many of them could not be satisfactorily colored with existing colorants. It has been estimated that three million chemically different dyes have been synthesized in major chemical (dye) manufacturers' laboratories since Perkin's discovery. Extensive equipment and process development has kept pace with dye and fiber development and has yielded methods that are faster and less costly.

The art of dyeing and printing became a science as more and more chemical principles were discovered. Today, a textile designer or colorist chooses a specific color or palette of colors for a particular fabric. A textile dyer is then responsible for matching the designer's color by selecting the proper colorants and applying them to the fabric. The dyer must also produce the required quantities of fabric economically and meet colorfastness requirements. The designer's work belongs to the world of artistry and creativity; the dyer's work, to the world of science and technology. Textile artists and dye chemists must cooperate to achieve the aesthetics and performance required.

Dyed textiles are textiles in which colorant (usually dye rather than pigment) is uniformly distributed within or on the surface of all fibers throughout a yarn or fabric. *Dye processes* involve the immersion of fibers, yarns, fabrics, or garments in the dyebath, a solution containing the colorant. The two primary topics of this chapter are fabric coloration and dye processes. Detail View 34 lists and defines 8 fabric colorations achievable by dyeing fibers, yarns, fabrics, and garments and 17 dye processes.

COLORATION OR COLOR EFFECTS

Consumers seek certain coloration or color effects, as well as specific colors, in fabrics. Figures 34.1–34.15 illustrate the types of coloration that are possible in dyed fabrics. Those color effects that are uniform over the fabric surface—such as solid, heather, and iridescent—may only be achieved or are best achieved through dyeing rather than printing. Designs may be created by dyeing textiles, but these are usually limited to stripes, checks, and plaids created by grouping colored (dyed) yarns and to colored motifs created by combining colored (dyed) yarns with figure, dobby, or Jacquard weaving.

Solid Coloration

In *solid coloration*, all of the fibers in a yarn, fabric, or garment are the same hue and value, as shown in Figure 34.1. Examination of solid-colored fabric reveals that each yarn and each fiber is identical in hue and shade (unless dyeing has been incomplete). Solid-colored fabrics are usually created by dyeing, but they may be made by printing, in which case the front and back of the fabric are not the same shade.

Heather Coloration

Heather coloration in textiles is traditionally characterized as having the purplish color of Scottish heather. This coloration results from blending fibers, usually wool, that are different shades of lavender into each yarn, as shown in Figure 34.2. Today, heather coloration includes the blending of fibers of different shades of colors (hues) other than lavenders.

Tweed Coloration

Fabrics with *tweed coloration* have small spots of color randomly distributed over the fabric surface due to the incorporation of colored fibers in a random fashion into yarns, as shown in Figure 34.3. Yarns may contain a blend of different colored fibers (a heather) to which random spots of color are added. A tweed coloration may be printed onto fabric, but this is unusual.

Mottled Coloration

Fabrics with *mottled coloration* have a spotted or blotched surface appearance. Yarns that have different colors along their length may be used to create this coloration, as is the case with the fabric in Figure 34.4. Certain fancy yarns, such as seed yarns, may also create a mottled coloration.

Variegated or Mixed Coloration

Fabrics with a *variegated or mixed coloration* are characterized as having many different colors, none of which dominates. Fancy yarns containing different colored strands often create this color effect. Yarns that differ in color along their length may also create this coloration when woven into a fabric, as shown in Figure 34.5.

Muted Coloration

Fabrics with *muted coloration* have a softened, subdued, or deadened appearance that often results from the presence of two different colored strands within the same yarn or different colored yarns in the warp and filling directions of woven fabrics, as shown in Figure 34.6. The degree of muting can be appreciated if one compares a fabric containing all dark-colored yarns to a fabric containing half dark-colored yarns and half white yarns.

Iridescent Coloration

Fabrics with *iridescent coloration* have a muted coloration when flat but a sparkling effect when they are draped because the peaks and valleys of the fabric folds appear to be different colors. These fabrics also change in coloration when they are rotated. Iridescence is often achieved by the use of different colored yarns (usually filament yarns) in the warp and filling directions of an unbalanced plain-woven fabric.

In Figure 34.7, the same unbalanced plain-woven fabric is shown on the left- and right-hand sides of the photograph. Only the positioning of the fabrics is different; the fabric on the right-hand side has been rotated 90°. The coloration on the left-hand side is redder be-

FIGURE 34.1   Solid coloration.

FIGURE 34.2   Heather coloration.

FIGURE 34.3   Tweed coloration.

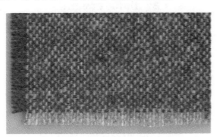

FIGURE 34.4   Mottled coloration.

FIGURE 34.5   Variegated or mixed coloration.

FIGURE 34.6   Muted coloration.

FIGURE 34.7   Iridescent coloration.

FIGURE 34.8   Striped design.

FIGURE 34.9 Checked design.

FIGURE 34.10 Plaid design.

FIGURE 34.11 Color-and-weave design.

FIGURE 34.12 Computer-injection design.

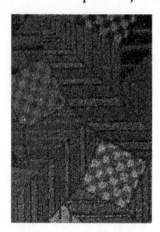

FIGURE 34.13 Batik design.

Face   Back

FIGURE 34.14 Shaped-resist design.

Face   Back

FIGURE 34.15 Ikat design.

Face   Back

cause the viewer sees predominately the red warp yarns forming the fabric surface. The blue filling yarns are not seen in this position. The coloration in the right-hand side appears bluer because the fabric is positioned so that the viewer can now see more of the blue filling yarns. When this fabric is draped, the viewer sees different proportions of warp and filling yarns at the peaks and valleys of the folds, thus bringing out the iridescent effect.

Striped, Checked and Plaid Designs

Striped fabrics have relatively long, narrow bands of color different from the rest of the surface. Stripes are formed in a woven fabric by grouping and alternating at least two different colors or shades of yarn. When the stripes are shades of the same hue arranged across the fabric width, the coloration is called *ombré*, as shown in Figure 34.8.

Checked fabrics have a pattern of squares. Grouping and alternating equal numbers of two different colored yarns in the warp and filling directions of a woven fabric creates the checked pattern (Figure 34.9). *Plaid fabrics* have colored stripes or bars that cross each other at right angles (Figure 34.10). Striped, checked, and plaid patterns can also be printed onto fabric.

Color-and-Weave and Color-and-Knit Designs

Color-and-weave and *color-and-knit designs* have a motif formed by colored *yarns* and a background formed by either white yarns or yarns of a different color than those in the motif. The designs may be small and contain few colors or be large and detailed and contain many colors. In Figure 34.11, a simple color-and-weave design is shown. Red yarns are used in both the warp and filling of the fabric. Yellow and green yarns are used for the figuring yarn that forms the floral motif in this figure-weave fabric. Larger and more complex designs result when the woven fabric is a dobby or Jacquard. In Jacquard knits, a colored yarn may be brought to the surface to create motifs and patterns.

Computer-Injection Designs

Computer-injection designs have intricate patterns—on either a small or large scale—and involve numerous colors, as shown in Figure 34.12. These designs rival color-and-weave designs, especially those resulting from Jacquard weaving with colored yarns or from a combina-tion of Jacquard and pile weaving. Computer-injection designs are found on pile fabrics, usually carpeting and tufted upholstery fabrics. The photograph shows a small section of a carpet that has a large repeat pattern. Although the entire repeat is not shown, the complexity of the coloration and patterning is readily apparent. Such designs are achievable by computer-injection dyeing, a process discussed later in this chapter.

Batik, Shaped-Resist, and Ikat Designs

True batik, shaped-resist, and ikat fabrics are made by textile artisans around the world who create designs by dyeing fabric. *Batik designs* are characterized by the presence of numerous cracked veins or lines and sharp-edged motifs (Figure 34.13). The special characteristic of *shaped-resist designs,* more commonly known as tie-dye designs in the United States, is a soft- or blurry-edged pattern (Figure 34.14).[1] *Ikat designs* also have hazy or blurred, indistinct edges, but they can be distinguished from shaped-resist designs because the edges of ikat designs follow yarns (Figure 34.15). The methods used to create these three types of designs are discussed in the next section of this chapter. The motifs and patterns of true batik, shaped-resist, and ikat are often simulated by printing.

COLORANTS

Textiles derive their color from colorants. The two types of colorants are dyes and pigments.

Dyes

Dyes or *dyestuffs* are organic chemicals that are able to selectively absorb and reflect wavelengths of light within the visible range of the electromagnetic spectrum. A dye molecule must have a conjugated system, that is, alternate double and single covalent bonds between the atoms that form its framework (Figure 34.16). Within this structure are specific groups called chromophores and auxochromes. Chromophores provide color; molecules without chromophores are colorless. Auxochromes intensify and deepen color.

---

[1] *Shaped-resist* is becoming the accepted term to indicate those fabrics that are embellished by shaping (folding, crumpling, stitching, plaiting, plucking, and twisting) and securing (binding or knotting) them before dyeing. *Shibori* (Japanese), *plangi* (Malay-Indonesian), and *banda* (Indian) are names of specific shaped-resist fabrics.

FIGURE 34.16   The chemical structure of dye molecules.

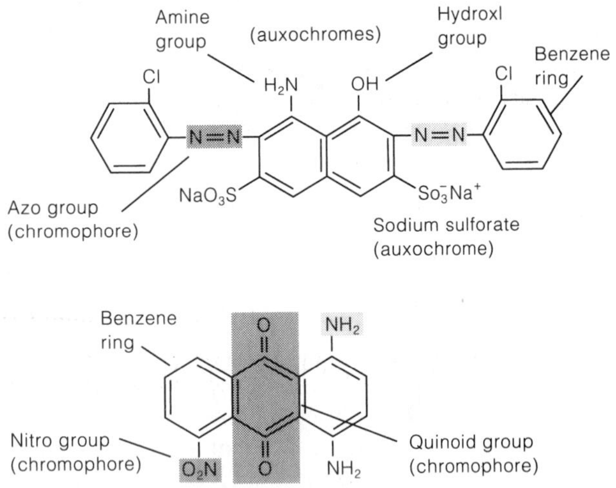

In a conjugated system, the electrons are held loosely enough that incident light in the visible range—which is low-energy radiation—can excite the electrons. Certain wavelengths of the incident light are absorbed as some of the energy of the incident light is expended in moving electrons from one energy level to another. The incident wavelengths that remain are reflected.[2] The color observed is a composite of all wavelengths not absorbed.

Dyes usually diffuse into the interior of a fiber from a water solution (the dyebath) and are retained in the amorphous areas within fibers. The auxochromes assist in the even uptake of dye because they make the dye more soluble in water. It is the auxochromes that enable forces of attraction to form between the dye and fiber polymer(s), thus improving the colorfastness of the dyed or printed textile. Dyes are usually retained within the fiber by hydrogen bonding, ionic bonding, or mechanical entrapment. Few dyes react with fiber polymers to form covalent bonds.

Dyes are relatively large molecules. Usually, the smaller the dye, the more readily it diffuses into fibers. The larger the dye, the better it stays in fibers when they are placed in water (wetfastness improves).

---

[2] When the dye is a solid powder on a table or in a bottle, as is described here, it does reflect the unabsorbed light. When the dye is in a textile, then the textile (not the dye) reflects the unabsorbed portion of the incident light.

The configuration of dyes has been described as similar to slips of paper; they have length and width but little thickness. This linear, coplanar configuration means that there are no bulky side groups to assist or hinder their absorption into fibers. The shape enables the dye to align itself between fiber polymers and assists the forces of attraction between dye and fiber. The degree of wetfastness is related to the intensity of these forces of attraction; the stronger the forces of attraction, the greater the wetfastness.

Natural and Synthetic Dyes. *Natural dyes* are dyes obtained from plant, animal, and mineral sources. Until 1856, all dyes were extracted from fruits, flowers, roots, insects, shellfish, and minerals. No two batches of natural dye are ever exactly alike in hue and strength. Colorfastness varies widely among natural dyes.

Synthetic dyes (synthetic organic dyes) are dyes synthesized from organic molecules in a dye-manufacturing facility. Good quality control in the manufacture of dyes provides a consistent product to the textile dyer and printer. Dyeing textiles so that color is identical from one batch to another requires great skill because a dye procedure contains many variables that influence the uptake of the dye by fibers. Commercially produced high-volume fabrics are usually dyed and printed with synthetic rather than natural dyes. Fabrics dyed by textile artisans may contain either natural or synthetic dyes.

Chemical and Application Classes. Dye manufacturers classify dyes by their chemical constitution, which indicates the method of their synthesis. For example, as shown in Figure 34.16, azo dyes contain one or more azo groups, -N=N-, and anthraquinone dyes are characterized by two aromatic (benzene) rings joined by two carbonyl groups:

$$>C=O$$

Each dye molecule within these chemical classes has a chemical constitution name.

The dyer at the textile mill is more interested in the application classification of a dye than the chemical classification. When classified by application, dyes requiring similar processes are grouped together, regardless of their chemical structures. Thus, all of the dyes within an application class will dye a specific group of fibers. Both anthraquinone and azo dyes are found in most of the synthetic-fiber dye application classes. Table 34.1 lists the major application classes and specifies which fibers each class can dye. For example, acid dyes are used to dye wool fibers and nylon fibers.[3]

Because only certain classes of dyes will dye certain fibers the dyer must carefully select which dyes to use when dyeing, for example, a polyester/cotton blend fabric to a solid coloration. The dye chemist, however, also cleverly utilizes the limited applicability of dye classes to economically achieve other colorations.

Colour Index Numbers and Brand Names. All textile dyes in commercial use are listed and cataloged in *The Colour Index.*[4] In volumes 1–3 where dyes are arranged according to application class, each dye has been assigned a five-digit colour index number (C. I. Number). Volume 4 cross references each dye to its chemical consti-

tution and volume 5, to its commercial and generic name. Often, several dye manufacturers make a dye with the same chemical constitution. The C.I. Number will be the same in these cases, even though the trademarks are different. At the beginning of each section, *The Colour Index* gives information concerning common application procedures, dyeing properties and fastness properties.

Pigments

Pigments are water insoluble, microscopic-sized color particles that are usually held on the surface of a fiber by a resin. The resin, rather than the pigment, unites or combines with the textile fiber. Therefore, any pigment can be used on any fiber. A wide variety of pigments are available in many colors.

The use of pigments to dye fabrics or garments is called *pigment dyeing*. In recent years, garment dyers have been using pigments to produce solid-colored gar-

---

[3] Both nylon, a polyamide, and protein fibers can be dyed with similar dyes due to the similarity of the polymer chemistry. Please refer to Chapters 9 and 16.
[4] Society of Dyers and Colourists, *The Colour Index* (Bradford, West Yorkshire, England: The Society, 1982).

TABLE 34.1   Dye application classes.

DYE CLASS	FIBERS DYED	DYE MECHANISM	LIGHT	FASTNESS TO WASHING	FASTNESS TO CROCKING	BLEACH
Acid	Nylon Wool	Strong (ionic) affinity	Good	Vary	Good	Fair
Basic (Cationic)	Acrylic Basic-dyeable polyester Basic-dyeable nylon	Strong (ionic) affinity	Vary	Excellent	Excellent	Poor
Disperse	Acetate Polyester Acrylic Nylon (all) Other synthetics	Simple solubility	Good	Good	Good	Good
Fiber Reactive	Cellulosic Wool	Chemical reaction with the fiber	Good	Excellent	Excellent	Poor

Mordant	Natural fibers
	    (Primarily cotton
	    and wool)
		Dye affinity
		    for mordant
		    (preapplied)
			Vary	Fair	Fair	Vary

Naphthol (Azoic)	Cellulosic	Entrapment, by reaction of dye	Excellent	Excellent	Excellent	Excellent
Pigment	All fibers	Binders	Excellent	Fair	Fair	Excellent
Sulfur	Cellulosic	Entrapment	Excellent	Excellent	Good	Poor
Vat	Cellulosic	Entrapment	Excellent	Excellent	Good	Excellent

ments. Pigment dyeing is relatively simple, involving padding, drying, and fixing. The addition of pigments to the spinning solution during the process of manufacturing fibers is called *mass pigmentation*. Pigments are much more widely used for printing apparel and bedding fabrics than for dyeing of fabric.

DYEING PRINCIPLES

In a full or partially automated dyehouse, an infinite variety of fibers and fabric structures must be dyed "on shade" in a minimum amount of time at a minimum cost. The colorfastness expectations and coloration desires of consumers must also be met. The dyer's task is a difficult one, even with assistance from the company laboratory, technical services from the dye manufacturers, color-measuring instruments, and computer-aided dye selection.

The dyer must know how to dye a wide array of fabrics composed of natural and manufactured fibers and various blends. Fiber manufacturers produce seemingly endless modifications of their fibers (various cross-sectional shapes, tenacities, etc.), and each modification alters the way the fiber behaves when it is dyed. Most fiber manufacturers also produce dye-variant fibers, such as "deep-dyeing" nylon fibers, which dye deeper shades with conventional acid dyes than do standard nylon fibers, and "basic-dyeable" nylon, which is dyeable with basic dyes rather than acid dyes. Similarly, polyester fibers, which are normally dyed with disperse dyes, can be modified to be dyed with basic dyes, and acrylic fibers, conventionally dyed with either disperse or basic dyes, can be given acid-dye capability. The dyer must also be familiar with the bewildering selection of dyes, too numerous for one dyer to maintain an exhaustive stock. Furthermore, equipment is continuously being developed to accommodate new fabrics and dyes. The dyer must continuously keep abreast of changes in the field in order to remain competitive.

Textiles are usually dyed by immersing them into a prepared aqueous dyebath. In most cases, the dyebath contains dyes that differ in the wavelength of light absorbed and reflected. When the yarn or fabric to be dyed contains different fibers, the dyebath may contain different classes of dye so that each type of fiber can absorb dye. The concentration of the dyebath may be as much as 8% or as little as 0.25% of the fiber (fabric) weight in dye. The deeper the shade needed, the greater the quantity of dye required in the bath and the longer the time the substrate

(fiber, yarn, fabric, garment) must be immersed. Dark shades, therefore, cost more than lighter shades.

The aqueous dyebath usually contains salts, acids or alkalies, and other auxiliary chemicals that cause the dye to have a greater affinity for the fibers than for the solution. They assist the migration of the dye from the solution to the fiber surfaces and aid the diffusion of the dye into the fiber.

Either the textile substrate or the dye solution must be agitated to promote uniform dyeing. The dyeing time varies from a few minutes to several hours. The temperature of the dyebath also varies; some baths are cooled with ice, whereas others are heated above the boiling point inside special pressurized equipment.

Variations of shade from batch to batch are inevitable. To match color shades, the textile dyer must be able to skillfully blend and formulate different dyes and understand the behavior of fibers and numerous chemicals required to carry out the processes. Each batch of dyed textile is unique because of slight differences in dye and chemical concentrations, in the fine structure of the fibers, or in the water used.

Dyeing is a chemical process involving the principles of migration, diffusion, and retention. First, the dye must migrate from the solution to the fiber surface and be adsorbed on the surface of the fiber. Then, the dye must diffuse from the surface toward the center of the fiber. Finally, fixation of the dye by covalent or hydrogen bonding or other forces must occur in order for the fiber to retain the dye.

DYEING PROCESSES

Most of the previously described color effects can be achieved in several different ways. For example, a solid-colored fabric could be made by dyeing loose fiber in a single color, spinning that fiber into yarn, and using that yarn to weave, knit, tuft, or otherwise form the fabric. However, the same fabric might be made by immersing white yarn into a dyebath and using that yarn to form the fabric. Likewise, a heather could be made by dyeing two batches of loose fiber different colors and blending the fibers prior to forming yarn, but it might also be achieved by immersing a blended *fabric* containing fibers with different dyeing behaviors into a dyebath that contains dyes from different dye classes, one for each type of fiber.

The textile substrate, or the material being dyed, can be the product of any stage in the formation of the textile, from loose fiber (for natural fibers) or polymer solution (for manufactured fibers) to the end-use item. The type of dyeing machinery used depends on the textile substrate. The dye solution can be circulated continuously within the equipment while the textile is stationary, the textile can be moved through a stationary dyebath, or both the textile and dye solution can be circulated (Figure 34.17).

As a rule, when the same color effect can be achieved at different stages of manufacture, the substrate closest to completion of the product is immersed in a dyebath. Production costs are usually lower, and the decision about the color of the textile can thus be delayed as long as possible, giving the textile manager flexibility in accommodating clients' desires. Colorant must be added to fibers at least 18 months prior to the sale of the end-use product, whereas color can be added to garments as orders are received.

Producer Dyeing

In *producer dyeing*—also called solution dyeing, dope dyeing, and spun dyeing—colorant is added to the spinning solution before the polymer mix is extruded and formed into a manufactured fiber. The colorant is therefore dispersed evenly throughout each fiber and constitutes an integral part of the fiber. The colorant becomes trapped between the fiber polymers as the fiber solidifies.

Fibers dyed in this manner are called *producer-dyed fibers,* and the fabrics in which they are subsequently used are called *producer-dyed fabrics.* The coloration of the yarns and fabrics depends on how the producer-dyed fibers are spun into yarns and how the yarns are incorporated into the fabric.

Producer-dyed fibers and fabrics are highly desirable when the color must be permanent and the fabric is exposed to conditions that normally cause color fading. Automotive seating fabrics, carpeting (interior and outdoor), and upholstery and drapery fabrics often contain producer-dyed fibers. When almost perfect color matching is required, producer dyeing may be done. Apparel fabrics rarely contain producer-dyed fibers because the level of colorfastness and wetfastness achieved with other dye processes is usually satisfactory, making the added expense of producer dyeing unjustifiable. Producer-dyeing is expensive due to the time necessary to clean the spinnerets when a different colorant is to be used.

Certain fibers are producer dyed because other techniques for adding colorant simply do not work. For example, olefin fibers are usually producer dyed because

their crystallinity and lack of dye-receptive sites prevents dye absorption. The use of olefin fibers in carpeting is expected to continue to expand because these producer-dyed fibers do not present the dye-related problems that accompany nylon and polyester fibers. This avoidance of dye-related problems is especially desirable for the contract carpet market, in spite of the fact that olefin may not have some of the other performance advantages of nylon.

Producer-dyed fibers and fabrics are readily identified on labels in the marketplace because the manufacturers want consumers to be aware that the additional colorfastness is the reason for the added cost. Some registered trademarks for producer-dyed fibers are Camalon® nylon (Camac Corporation), Chromspun® acetate (Eastman Chemicals Division of Eastman Kodak Co., Inc.), and Coloray® rayon (Courtaulds Fibres, Inc.).

Gel Dyeing

Gel dyeing involves the addition of dye or pigment to the liquid coagulating bath during the formation of wet-spun manufactured fibers. The dye or pigment is absorbed by fibers while they are still in the soft, gel stage. Upon complete coagulation, the colorant is trapped within the fibers.

Stock Dyeing

In *stock dyeing*, masses of loose fibers are placed in large drums called kiers, into which dye is pumped and circulated. When the fibers have absorbed the quantity of dye necessary to provide the color and shade desired, the fibers are removed, dried, and processed into yarns or directly into fabric. Stock dyeing is a relatively expensive process because it takes the manufacturer longer to dye loose fibers than it does to dye a comparable quantity of yarn or fabric. In addition, the dyeing process causes the fibers to clump together in a fibrous mass that must be reopened before yarn can be formed. More dye is used than in other dye processes because 10–15% of the dyed fibers are lost in further manufacturing steps. Furthermore, a strong element of fashion risk is involved because the decision about color is made at a very early stage of production, usually months before the fabric will be marketed.

Fibers that have been dyed in this manner are called *stock-dyed fibers.* Wool fibers to be used in making woolen fabrics are stock dyed more often than any other fibers. Wool fibers to be used in worsted fabrics are

FIGURE 34.17
Commercial dyeing processes for
textiles.

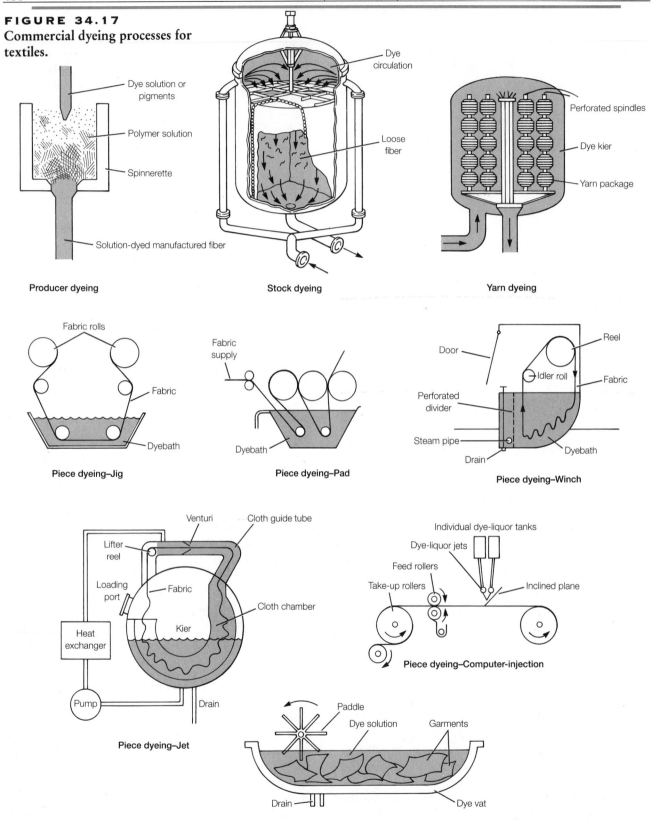

Producer dyeing

Stock dyeing

Yarn dyeing

Piece dyeing–Jig

Piece dyeing–Pad

Piece dyeing–Winch

Piece dyeing–Jet

Piece dyeing–Computer-injection

Garment dyeing

usually not stock dyed because the combing process removes too much of the dyed fiber, resulting in a product that is not competitive in price. Manufactured fibers and cotton are rarely stock dyed.

Stock-dyed fibers are usually used to form fancy yarns. Combining different colored stock-dyed fibers in varying proportions yields mottled, heather, and tweed colorations. The use of stock-dyed fibers to achieve heather and tweed colorations is shown in Figures 34.2 and 34.3, respectively. Some thick, solid-colored woolen fabrics contain stock-dyed fibers because stock dyeing ensures that each fiber is dyed. Although thick, white, wool fabrics could be immersed in the dyebath to produce solid-colored fabrics, the fibers at the center of the yarns may not be dyed at all or not to the same depth of shade as the outer fibers. When such a fabric is worn or used, the fibers at the center of the yarn tend to work their way outward, resulting in a worn look.

Top Dyeing and Tow Dyeing

Top dyeing involves the immersion of top—slivers of long wool fibers that have been straightened, paralleled, and separated from the short fibers by combing—into a dyebath. Similarly, *tow dyeing* involves the immersion of tow—ropes of filament fibers destined to be cut into short lengths—into a dyebath. Stock, yarn, or beam dyeing equipment may be used.

Top of two or more colors may be combined to form yarns with mottled coloration. Two or more strands of top of the same color may be combined together to form a solid-colored yarn. Worsted fabrics having various colorations (solids, checks, plaids, muted, etc.) are more likely to be formed following top dyeing than stock dyeing. Top dyeing is less expensive because all of the dyed fibers are used.

Yarn Dyeing

In *yarn dyeing*, yarns are immersed in a dyebath prior to their incorporation into fabric. Whether of a single-fiber or multiple-fiber composition the yarns are usually dyed to a solid color. Yarn dyeing is less costly than stock, top, or tow dyeing because more substrate can be dyed in a given amount of time. Excellent penetration of dye occurs and, thus, great clarity of color results.

There are three major approaches to yarn dyeing: *skein, package*, and *beam dyeing*. Most yarn is package dyed because it is the least costly and yet is satisfactory for most types of yarn used in knit and woven fabrics.

Skein dyeing requires rewinding the dyed yarn onto packages for further processing, thus increasing costs. However, the yarn is not distorted during dyeing, making the process suitable for the dyeing of soft, lofty yarns such as hand-knitting yarns. Yarn can be processed in smaller quantities in skein form than in package form. Beam dyeing, a larger version of package dyeing, is the most economical when all warp yarns are to be the same color because no transfer of dyed yarns from cones to beam is necessary.

Solid-color, muted, iridescent, striped (including ombré), checked, or plaid fabrics can be made with *yarn-dyed yarns*. The fabrics shown in Figures 34.6–34.10 illustrate the use of yarn-dyed yarns to achieve such coloration. Such yarns can also be used to make dobby, Jacquard, and figure-weave fabrics that have colored motifs and backgrounds, and striped jersey and Jacquard knits. Figure 34.11 shows a fabric in which yarn-dyed yarns were used in combination with figure weaving.

Different colored yarns may be combined into ply yarns, forming yarns with muted coloration. Strands of different colors may be brought together to form fancy yarns.

Although yarn dyeing is not commonly the route chosen to form a solid-colored fabric, it is used for high-quality, heavyweight, and densely woven fabrics—especially furniture coverings, as well as some fabrics for uniforms and children's wear. To avoid the look of worn fabric caused by the migration of uncolored fiber to the fabric surface, it is important that all fibers be well colored.

A special case of yarn dyeing is *indigo dyeing* of warp yarns for denim fabrics. Yarn to be used for denim is wound onto a special perforated warp beam, which is immersed in a dyebath. Only the surface fibers of the yarn are dyed. As the denim fabric is worn, the surface fibers are worn away and the white, undyed fibers at the center begin to show, producing the desired worn effect.

Space Dyeing

In *space dyeing*, yarns are dyed so that the color of the yarn varies along its length. This effect can be accomplished by (a) printing a knit fabric and then unraveling it in a knit-de-knit process, (b) squirting dye from a needle into a yarn package in a process called yarn package impregnation, or (c) spraying colorant into yarn skeins. Carpet yarn can also be space dyed by tufting, printing, then de-tufting. This latter technique is used extensively for contract carpets.

The use of *space-dyed yarns* in fabric usually creates mottled and variegated colorations. The knit fabric in Figure 34.4 shows the use of a space-dyed yarn to achieve a mottled coloration. The woven fabric in Figure 34.5 illustrates the use of space-dyed yarns to achieve a variegated coloration. Space-dyed yarns are used in carpeting to help disguise soil.

Piece Dyeing

Piece dyeing—also called fabric dyeing—involves dyeing fabrics "in the piece," rather than dyeing stock or yarn. Fabric is immersed in a dyebath. For centuries, the outcome of piece dyeing was a solid coloration. The fabrics were usually of a single-fiber composition and dye from only one application class was used in the dyebath, although two or more colors of dye were often included. For example, a green fabric could contain one dye that absorbs all incident light except yellow and one that absorbs all incident light except blue. The mixing of the reflected yellow and blue wavelengths would yield the green color. Alternatively, the green fabric could be produced by the selection of single dye that would absorb all wavelengths of light except green. The 100% cotton fabric shown in Figure 34.1 has been piece dyed. In this instance, dye did not penetrate all of the fibers; note the white areas in the lower fringe where the yarns crossed over.

As the blending of fibers became popular and more dyes were developed, dyers discovered that blended fabrics could be immersed into carefully prepared dyebaths to create color effects that were previously achievable only by dyeing loose fiber and yarn. Specific names—union, cross, tone-on-tone, and reserve dyeing—are given to piece dyeing of fabrics containing fibers that exhibit different dyeing characteristics.

Union Dyeing. In *union dyeing*, the intent is to dye to a solid color a fabric containing fibers that accept dyes from different classes. The fabrics can be either blends—in which all of the yarns in the fabric are intimate blends of two fibers, such as cotton and polyester—or mixtures—in which the warp yarns are made of one type of fiber, such as polyester, and the filling yarns of another, such as cotton. As shown in Table 34.1, disperse dye is required to dye the polyester (unless the polyester is modified to accept basic dyes). Mordant, naphthol, sulfar, or vat dyes are possible choices to dye the cotton fibers. To achieve a green polyester/cotton fabric, for ex-

ample, dyes of the same color, in this case green, could be selected from two suitable dye classes. Alternatively, two or more colors of dye from each dye class could be selected to produce the color in each type of fiber. For example, yellow and blue disperse dyes and yellow and blue naphthol dyes could be selected to dye the polyester/cotton fabric to a solid green.

Cross Dyeing. In *cross dyeing*, the intent is to produce a multicolored fabric. Muted and heather coloration, stripes, checks, and certain motifs can all be achieved. Fabrics may be composed of (a) fibers from different generic groups, (b) natural and manufactured fibers, or (c) manufactured fibers from the same generic group when one fiber has been modified to accept dyes from a different dye class. When the fibers are intimately blended and all the yarns in the fabric are the same, muted and heather coloration will result in cross dyeing. When some yarns are composed of one fiber and the other yarns composed of a second fiber, two-colored stripes, checks, and motifs are produced. The arrangement of the yarns in the mixture fabric determines which design results.

In theory, the advantages of cross dyeing as compared to stock and yarn dyeing to achieve the same color effect are speed, economy, and flexibility. White fabrics can be stored in the warehouse until the colors that are in fashion for a particular season have been determined. Dye houses and garment makers therefore commit themselves only to white fabric. They can arrange to have the goods cross dyed when they are needed. Color combinations can be speedily changed, although the design cannot, thereby minimizing the quantity of unwanted merchandise.

In practice, however, cross dyeing is difficult to implement. Even with stripes and checks, the fabric manufacturer must decide on the width of the stripes and the size of the checks. Therefore, little yardage is actually cross dyed.

Tone-on-Tone Dyeing. *Tone-on-tone dyeing* is a method of piece dyeing in which the intent is to achieve two or more shades of the same hue using blend and mixture fabrics. A *tone-on-tone fabric* is, therefore, one in which lighter and darker shades of the same hue are present. These fabrics are composed of fibers from the same generic group, but the fibers differ in their affinity to the dye. For example, two shades are achieved with the blending of regular- and deep-dye nylon, polyester, or acrylic fibers. Nylon is produced in both deep-dye and ultra deep-dye modifications, thus making three-tone coloration possible. Carpeting may be tone-on-tone to produce a heather coloration.

Reserve Dyeing. Reserve dyeing is a way of piece dyeing blend and mixture fabrics so that one type of fiber will remain undyed. The objective is accomplished by the use of dyes that are attracted to the fiber to be colored but not to the fiber to be reserved. Such reserve-dyed fabrics will contain white fibers or white yarns.

Reserve dyeing is also a method of piece dyeing single-fiber-composition fabrics. Certain yarns in the fabric or portions of the fabric (face or back for example) are treated so that they will remain undyed when the fabric is immersed in the dyebath. For example, 100% cotton denim fabric, which is traditionally made by yarn dyeing the warp yarns blue and using white filling yarns, might also be made by reserve dyeing. The cotton filling yarns would need to be treated so that the blue indigo dye in the dyebath did not dye them. Cotton and other fabrics can have a colored face and a white back by treating the back side prior to immersing of the fabric in the dyebath. Sides of different colors can be achieved by treating one side, piece dyeing, removing the treatment, applying the treatment to the dyed side, and piece dyeing again.

Production Methods. Piece-dyed fabrics (single-fiber-composition, union, cross, tone-on-tone, and reserve) are less costly than stock- or yarn-dyed fabrics because more fabric can be dyed per hour than an equivalent amount of loose fiber or yarn. Piece dyeing is also undertaken at a time closer to the point of sale of fabrics and thus involves substantially less fashion risk than the processes previously described.

Jig, pad, winch (also called beck or box), beam, and jet are methods for piece dyeing (Figure 34.17). The specific method depends on the fiber content, fabric weight, dye, and degree of penetration required, but the choice tends to be the process in which the fabric can be dyed the fastest under the given constraints.

Fabrics may be dyed in batches or continuously. Batch processes are those in which a group or unit is dyed. In continuous processes, large yardages are processed. Fabrics may be dyed in open width or rope form. Knit and woven fabrics that do not crease are usually dyed in rope form because the fabric can be bunched together and thus handled as a narrower entity.

Some of these processes (continuous dye ranges and becks) can be modified to dye carpets. Commercial contract carpet, however, cannot be piece dyed without unacceptable side shading. Carpet is dyed in both open width and rope form.

In *jig dyeing,* an open width of fabric is pulled back and forth through an open dye vat until the desired color and shade is obtained. The fabric passes continuously through the bath, from one side to the other, then back again many times. Only a yard or so is immersed at any given time. Thus any given yard segment is in the dyebath only once every 20 minutes or so. However, because the fabric is squeezed by layers of fabric wrapping around it on the roll, the dye solution is being continuously worked through the fabric layers, so the fabric is in contact with dye solution throughout the entire process. Approximately 4000 pounds (1815 kilograms) of fabric can be dyed in one batch. Jig dyeing is suitable for fabrics of fairly close weave because considerable tension is created. Since jig dyeing has a tendency to flatten fabric and decrease fullness of hand, it is used on acetate, rayon, and nylon taffetas and surahs for garment lining, where a full, soft hand is not required. It is economical only for large quantities of fabric. Shade variations from selvage to selvage as well as from end to end of the fabric are a problem.

In *pad dyeing,* the dye solution is applied by means of a padder or mangle. Fabric in open width is run through an open vat. The fabric enters the dye solution, passes between two rollers above the dyebath, reenters the dyebath, passes again between two rollers above the dyebath, and reenters the dyebath. This sequence is repeated several more times. In this manner, the dye is repeatedly absorbed and forced into the fabric and the appropriate amount of excess dye is squeezed out. Fabric is passed rapidly through the dyebath at speeds from 30 to 300 yards (27.5 to 275 meters) per minute, depending on the fabric and depth of color desired. Pad dyeing permits a uniform concentration and penetration of dye into the fibers. The fabric is subjected to tension and pressure, so only selected fabrics can be dyed. Smaller amounts of dye are used than in other methods, making pad dyeing economical.

Most pad dyeing is done as part of a continuous dye system in which large quantities of fabric are continuously run through a pad, into a heat or steam chamber to set the dye, and into washers, rinsers, and dryers before they emerge as completely dyed fabric. The method is used for both single-fiber-composition and blend fabrics.

Polyester and cellulose (usually cotton) blends are typically dyed in a continuous dye range. The configuration of the range depends on the class of dye (vat or reactive) chosen to dye the cellulose. A Thermosol unit is always included to dye the polyester fiber with disperse dyes. The mechanism of Thermosol dyeing has been the subject of speculation and study for many years. The general consensus is that the temperature in the unit softens the fiber, enlarging it slightly. As the disperse dye particles penetrate, they dissolve into the fiber, until dye has penetrated the entire fiber. As the fiber cools, it returns to its original size, and the dye particles are trapped.

The continuous processes are economical only for very large runs of a given color. One of the problems with the U.S. textile industry is that its operations are dominated by continuous dye ranges, limiting its ability to efficiently produce the short color runs that are needed to accommodate rapid shifts in fashion.

Winch dyeing places little tension on the fabric, which is processed in rope form. The ends of a length of fabric are sewn together to form an endless, circular rope, up to 1000 yards (915 meters) long, that is lifted in and out of a dyebath by a reel. In this process, only about 5–10 yards (4.5–9 meters) of the roll are *not* immersed in the dyebath at any given time. Dye penetration and desired shade are obtained by continuous immersion. Twelve ropes of fabric can be processed at one time. Winch dyeing is suitable for lightweight and loosely woven fabrics and knit fabrics. It is also used for heavy fabrics, especially woolens and crepe fabrics. The original softness and fullness of hand are maintained. In addition, winch dyeing is used for dyeing carpets. In this case, huge becks with winches capable of lifting extremely heavyweight carpet are necessary.

Beam dyeing of fabrics is practically the same as beam dyeing of yarns; the difference is that fabric, rather than yarn, is wound on the perforated beam. No tension or pressure is exerted on the fabric. Lightweight, fairly open-weave fabrics and tricot knits can be beam dyed; thick and closely woven fabrics cannot because the dye cannot be forced through. As much as 10,000 yards (9144 meters) or 4000 pounds (1815 kilograms) of fabric can be wound onto the beam.

Jet-dyeing machinery represents the most recent advance in fabric-dyeing equipment.[5] It allows polyester/worsted fabrics to be dyed more gently than in traditional winch dyeing. Jet dyeing is ideal for fabrics prone to felting when subjected to lengthy dye cycles and for fabrics that do not tolerate added dye for shade adjustment. Many 100% polyester woven fabrics and blended fabrics are jet dyed.

Jet dyeing is accomplished in a closed, tube-like system in which fabric in rope form passes through a fast-moving stream of pressurized dye liquor. Dye penetrates the fabric as it passes in front of a jet of dye. The dye is recirculated as the fabric moves or floats in a tension-free condition along the tube container at rapid speed. The movement of the fabric is controlled by the propulsive action of the dye liquid as it is forced through the jets. A low volume of water is used. Up to 1400 pounds (635 kilograms) of fabric can be dyed at one time.

Vacuum impregnation is designed to dye thick, heavy fabrics by providing a system in which there is good dye penetration. Corduroy, sateens, and heavyweight ducks are, therefore, often processed by vacuum impregnation. In this system, the fabric contacts a perforated stainless steel cylinder. A vacuum pump draws air into the cylinder while dye liquor is simultaneously applied to the fabric. Dye penetrates the fabric without tension and pressure.

Foam dyeing, a method for dyeing carpets, has been described as "spreading shaving cream over the face of the carpet." Foam bubbles break down and deposit dye over the wet carpet surface. Less time and energy are required to dry the dyed carpet than when other fabric-dyeing methods are used. Vat and sulfur dyes cannot be used.

Computer-Injection Dyeing

In *computer-injection dyeing*, the correct amount of aqueous dye solution is injected into the pile of carpet or upholstery fabric through a series of microjets. The microjets are positioned transversely and above the textile, with one row of jets per color. An eight-color, 4-meter-width computer-injection machine has approximately 13,500 jets, each of which is individually controlled by a computer. This method allows great design versatility. Tufted carpeting can be produced with complex designs and many different colors, as shown in Figure 34.12.

Different designs are produced by varying and combining (a) the number and size of the jets, (b) the arrangement and placement of the jets, (c) the amount of dye applied and the color extruded, (d) the movement of the fabric and the jets, and (e) the rate at which the fabric moves. No distortion of the pile surfaces occurs. Production speeds of more than 3600 yards (3290 meters) per minute make this method cost-effective only for large production runs.

Garment or Product Dyeing

Socks, sheer hosiery, and sweaters have been dyed in garment form since the turn of the century because this

---

[5]Jet-dyeing equipment should not be confused with the computer-injection dyeing system, which uses jets to deliver dye to a fabric surface and is sometimes called jet dyeing or jet printing.

method yielded the best product. In the 1980s, garment-dyed skirts, shirts, and slacks became available. To date, these garments are 100% cotton or woolens, but it is expected that polyester/cotton garments will soon be able to be processed in this manner.

The popularity of the "distressed" look in apparel, along with the need to quickly respond to orders for specific colors in apparel items, propelled the rapid increase in the quantity of garment-dyed apparel produced. This method presents both advantages and disadvantages to the consumer. First, garment-dyed apparel is more expensive than apparel manufactured from piece goods. The actual cost of garment dyeing, whether knits or wovens, ranges two to three times higher than the cost of piece dyeing. An advantage to the consumer is that garment-dyed items can be considered to be fully preshrunk, and they represent the latest in color fashion.

To the retailer and garment manufacturer, the advantages of garment dyeing are many. If a color is unpopular, it can easily be dropped from the line. Likewise, the volume of a popular color can easily be increased. Decisions on color assortments can be made the day the garment is scheduled for processing. In comparison, the color decision must be made two to three months prior to shipment for a garment made from a piece-dyed fabric. With garment dyeing, more colors can be offered, and both small and large lots can be handled easily. On the other hand, considerably more expertise is required to cut and sew a garment for subsequent dyeing than to make a similar garment from piece-dyed fabric. Pattern sizes must be altered to accommodate the shrinkage that will occur during the dye process. All garment parts must come from the same roll of cloth. Selection of compatible garment components is essential.

Paddle and extract dyeing methods are used in garment dyeing. *Extract-dyeing* equipment tumbles the fabricated product in the dye solution. It automatically scours the garment fabric, dyes it, extracts the dye, and dries the fabric. Precise shade repetition from lot to lot is readily achieved. *Paddle-dyeing* equipment consists of a large tub into which the fabricated product and dye solution are placed (Figure 34.17). A motor-driven paddle wheel placed over the tub has wide, short blades that move the product and dye solution continuously. This process, however, tends to misshape the garment/product.

Batik Dyeing, Shaped-resist Dyeing, and Ikat

Batik dyeing, shaped-resist dyeing, and ikat are not processes for dyeing mass-produced fabric; rather, they are methods used by artisans to create designs on fabric by dyeing. They are considered here because the motifs and designs created using these processes are often simulated by printing techniques such as resist and warp printing.

Batik dyeing involves the application of wax to those areas of a fabric where the artisan does not want dye to penetrate. In Indonesia, a small, spouted cup with a handle (called a *tjant*) is used. As the wax is heated, it melts and the liquid wax is poured from the cup onto the cloth. When the wax has solidified, the fabric is immersed in a cold dyebath. The wax tends to break as the fabric is placed into the dyebath, allowing dye to penetrate through the small cracks. In this way, the cracked line or veining appearance is created, as shown in Figure 34.13. Following dyeing, the wax is removed. When another color is to be added, the fabric is waxed in all areas in which the next dye should not be absorbed, and the fabric is again immersed in the dyebath and dyed. The wax is removed. This sequence continues until the planned design is achieved. The fabric is treated with a fixative (mordant) to make the colors fast.

Shaped-resist dyeing involves shaping (folding, crumpling, stitching, plaiting, plucking, and twisting) fabric and then securing (binding or knotting) it before dyeing. In this way, the artisan prevents dye from penetrating all portions of the fabric. In Figure 34.14, the artisan gathered small portions of fabric and clamped them.

Ikat involves the application of a resist to yarn prior to fabric formation. In Figure 34.15, both the warp and filling yarns were prepared with a resist (clay, wax, or tieing the yarn). Where the resist was used, the yarns are white. Where the white boxes appear, both the warp and filling yarns are white at that location along their length. In the flower petals, only the filling yarns are white along their length. For complex patterns, yarns are treated with resist and dyed several times.

PERFORMANCE

Color is usually the first attribute noticed in a textile and is often an influential factor in determining whether the textile will be purchased. An inappropriate or unattractive color may make a fabric unmarketable no matter how excellent the fiber, yarn, fabric structure, or finish. Similarly, a poor-quality fabric may become a heavy seller because of its color. In addition, the usual expectation of consumers is that the original color will be retained throughout the wear life of the fabric. Rarely, however, does a textile have perfectly fast color, that is, colorant that is resistant to change under any circumstances. Typically, the color changes as a fabric is worn or used. No colorant is colorfast to all destructive agents. The color can change with washing, shampooing, drycleaning, rubbing (crocking), exposure to ultraviolet light, exposure to heat, and exposure to 35 other known colorant-destroying agents. The fabric may become less colored, that is, fade or change "on tone." Some colors may become stronger or shift dramatically in shade.

A textile will usually have good colorfastness toward one or two destructive agents but poor colorfastness towards others. In order to obtain the desired serviceability, a consumer must select a fabric that is colorfast to the specific color-destructive agents that will be encountered in use. Maintenance of the color of a textile depends not only on how expertly dye chemists have applied appropriately selected dyes and pigments but also on the maintenance of the fabric by the user under end-use conditions.

On occasion, the purchaser wants the color to change or fade. Such is the case with denim. The sooner a worn, faded fabric results, the more desirable is the garment made from it. Denim is usually dyed with indigo. By today's standards indigo is a very poor dye because it has a low affinity for the cotton fiber. It exhibits relatively poor fastness to wet crocking and poor lightfastness. However, the dye is popular because it washes down to clear, bright-blue shades without staining the white filling yarns in a denim fabric. Another instance in which color change is desired is with Indian madras cloth. Indian madras cloth, often a plaid fabric with several different colored yarns, gains its beauty when the fabric is washed and the various colors bleed over it, giving a softened effect.

Color problems, many of which were discussed in Chapter 4, are the major complaint about textiles. Norris Little, executive vice-president of Shaw Industries, the largest carpet manufacturer in the world, said of carpet color problems, "the number one consumer complaint today is dye-related. This includes side match, dye streaks, color fade, dye spots, unlevel dyeing, crocking, poor penetration and off-shade. They account for 32% of customer quality complaints and number 51,000 annually, representing a loss of over $20 million. A very, very serious problem."[6]

Original color (shade, intensity, and brightness), the maintenance of that color (that is, colorfastness), and to a lesser extent any possible weakening of the fabric by

the dye or pigment are important performance considerations at point of purchase for most end-use situations. The nature of the colorant is the primary determinant of these performance outcomes.

Table 34.1 shows the colorfastness expectations of pigments and dyes by application class. Many pigment colors have excellent fastness to light and are used extensively for draperies and curtains. However, fabrics colored with pigments show loss of color and fading with each successive laundering or drycleaning because the resins holding the pigment become separated due to abrasion. The effect is more serious on dark than on pastel shades. Most colors show a distinct faded-out appearance by about the 15th to the 20th cleaning. Resins used in conjunction with the pigments cause stiffening of the fabric to which they are applied. The effect is minimal in light colors, but can be serious in dark shades. The use of fabric softeners in manufacture reduces the stiffness. Color loss by crocking (rubbing) occurs for pigment-dyed textiles. Again, the effect is minimal in light-colored fabric, but can be serious in dark shades. In addition, the color shades of pigment-dyed fabrics are easily matched from lot to lot. Mass-pigmented fabrics, in which the pigment is embedded within the fiber, possess extreme colorfastness to almost all environmental influences.

Dyes differ considerably in wetfastness, or washfastness. Wetfastness of dyes refers to the ability of the dyes to remain in the fiber when placed in water. Wetfastness is important both when the consumer washes the textile item and when a finish applied after dyeing requires that the fabric be placed in water.

Table 34.1 demonstrates that any dye application class does not give colorfastness in all categories. For example, cotton fibers dyed with reactive dyes can be expected to provide excellent fastness to washing and crocking (rubbing), but poor fastness to bleaching (chlorine). Thus, reactive dyes in cotton/spandex swimsuits will quickly fade.

In the marketplace, information about the type of colorant used or the colorfastness expected is rarely given. In the absence of such information, it is usually accepted that many color problems can be avoided by selecting fabrics according to the end-use applications intended by the manufacturer. The assumption is that fabrics are dyed or printed with colorants that are sufficiently fast for their intended end use. Problems are invited when fabrics are used for an unintended purpose. For example, if a beautiful voile that is intended to be fabricated into a blouse is instead fabricated into sheer cur-

---

[6]G.R. Turner, "Newest Development in Jet Dyeing Equipment," *Textile Chemist and Colorist* 20/10 (1988): 25–28.

tains, it will probably fade readily in sunlight. The manufacturer probably did not select dyes that would provide a high degree of fastness to sunlight because to do so would have involved added expense.

Likewise, care labels should be followed to avoid color problems introduced by inappropriate care procedures. For example, cotton fabrics labeled "dryclean only" might be so labeled due to the specific colorant on the fabric rather than fiber content or other fabric features. Washing fabrics in which the dyes are highly soluble in water will result in appreciable fading. Drycleaning fabrics that contain solvent-soluble dyes will likewise result in appreciable fading. Instructions pertaining to the use of bleaches should also be heeded. Chlorine bleach may fade a color that other bleaches, such as perborate, will not.

Textile products labeled "colorfast" should be regarded with great caution if the manufacturer fails to state the specific type of colorfastness. There are over 40 environmental factors known to alter color and, as has been indicated above, it is rare indeed that a dye will be fast to all of them. Likewise, labels or technical information that say "washfast" or perhaps "lightfast" should be questioned. The degree of fastness should be specifically given and interpreted in terms of the amount required for a specific end use.

In selecting a textile product for which colorfastness is critical and definitive information is not provided on a label or in technical literature, the information should be sought directly from the manufacturer. It may be necessary for a textile laboratory to test the fabrics under consideration. The interpretation of the results should be clearly communicated. In all situations, buyers must familiarize themselves with the conditions under which such tests are done and the interpretation of the results of these tests. One can always conduct "practical" tests to determine colorfastness under simulated conditions.

CHAPTER SUMMARY

Dyeing is the process of adding colorants (dyes and pigments) to fibers. In all cases except producer dyeing and computer-injection dyeing, the substrate to be dyed (the fiber, yarn, fabric, or fabricated product) is immersed in a dyebath. In producer dyeing, colorant is added to a fiber spinning solution. In computer-injection dyeing, dye is injected from above the fabric surface. In all cases, the colorant is absorbed into the fiber or adheres to its surface.

The intent of dyeing is to achieve certain color effects. Fabrics described as solid-colored, heather, tweed, mottled, mixed or variegated, muted, iridescent, striped, checked, ombré, and certain other design motifs may be the result of dyeing.

Terms such as stock dyeing, top and tow dyeing, yarn dyeing, piece dyeing, and garment dyeing refer to a substrate that was immersed in the dyebath. Coloration of the fabric is dependent on how the fibers are incorporated into the yarns and the yarns into the fabric. In piece dyeing, the fiber composition of the fabric and the types of dyes in the dyebath largely determine the coloration. Fabrics are said to be union dyed, cross dyed, reserve dyed, or tone-on-tone dyed, depending on the nature of the fiber composition and the dyebath. When portions of a yarn or fabric are covered with a substance that resists the penetration of dye, ikat, batik, and shaped-resist designs are achieved.

Printed Textiles

Printed textiles are textiles with designs resulting from the application of colorants (usually pigments rather than dyes) and certain other substances to localized areas on fabric or yarn surfaces. A description of a printed fabric includes the print pattern, the print type, and the print process.

NAME	DESCRIPTION
PRINT PATTERNS	
Realistic or Naturalistic Designs	Depict real objects—human, animal, plants, or other objects—in a natural manner.
Stylized Designs	Exaggerate or simplify objects and use colors and proportions that are not natural.
Geometric Designs	Incorporate circles, squares, ovals, rectangles, ellipses as design elements.
Abstract Designs	Little or no reference is made to real objects. Often geometric in form but less rigid.
PRINT TYPES	
Application Prints	Characterized by a white background with colored motifs.
Overprints	Characterized by a colored background that is the same depth of shade on the fabric face and the back and by colored motifs over the dyed ground which is usually a light rather than deep shade.
Blotch Prints	Characterized by a background color and motif colors that are deeper in shade on the face than on the back.
Discharge Prints	Characterized by a dark background that is the same depth of shade on the face and the back and usually by widely spaced motifs. On white discharge fabrics, the white motifs appear on both the face and the back. On color discharge fabrics, the area where the motif occurs is usually filled with vibrant colors and the motif area on the fabric back is nearly white.
Resist Prints	Characterized by white designs and a dyed background or by a colored design and a dyed background.
Warp Prints	Characterized by hazy-edged motifs ranging from simple to complex. An examination of the yarns in the fabric usually will show that the filling yarns are of a solid color but the warp yarns vary in color along their length.
Duplex or Register Prints	Characterized by being printed on both sides.
Flock Prints	Characterized by the fact that the motif(s) is composed of short lengths of fiber (white or colored) standing upright on the fabric surface.
Burn-Out Prints	Characterized by the presence of transparent and opaque areas on the fabric, one forming the motif and the other the background.
PRINT PROCESSES	
Roller Printing	A method of applying print paste to yarn or fabric by transferring it from the engraved areas of metal rollers to the textile.
Flatbed Screen Printing	A method of applying print paste to yarn or fabric by forcing it through open (untreated) portions of a flat screen to the textile.
Rotary Screen Printing	A method of applying print paste to yarn or fabric by forcing it from the interior of a cylindrical screen, portions of which are closed, to the textile.
Heat-Transfer Printing	A method of transferring dye from preprinted paper to fabric composed of polyester or other thermoplastic fibers by placing the paper in contact with the fabric surface and heating to cause the dyes to sublime.

(handwritten annotation: using sulfuric Acid to burn it out.)

(handwritten annotation: Application)

*P*rinted Textiles

Printing of fabrics is thought to have extremely ancient roots originating in the Far East. Early designs were crude and were probably produced by block printing or stencil printing. In *block printing*, a wooden block is carved to form raised pattern areas, the carved surface is placed in a dye paste, and the block is pressed against a fabric surface. In *stencil printing*, a design is cut from paper, the paper is placed on the fabric surface, and dye paste is brushed over the open design areas. The paper protects the remaining areas of the fabric surface from the paste. In the 16th and 17th centuries, block-printed cotton and silk fabrics were imported in such great quantities into Europe that British home producers of woolen cloths induced Parliament to pass an act in 1621 banning their import. The British print manufacturers' rationale was that the import of these prints was damaging their trade. The act remained in force for over 50 years. Block and stencil printing are still done by artisans throughout the world, and their motifs and patterns are simulated on modern printing equipment.

In the 1780s, mechanization of printing, with the introduction of roller printing, revolutionized the printed-fabric market. The prints produced by roller printing were distinguished by delicacy of design, fine lines, and good fit (registration), in sharp contrast to the crude, wide-line designs with ill fit between pattern repeats produced by block and stencil printing. Demand for printed fabrics increased markedly. New printing methods continued to be introduced to keep pace with developments in fiber technology, fabric formation technology, and colorants.

Of the 87.5–98.5 billion yards (80–90 billion meters) of fabric produced each year, about 18.6 billion yards (17 billion meters), or about one-fourth, are prints.[1] About 56% of this quarter are printed for apparel and 33% for home furnishings.[2] The largest portion of printed apparel fabric is used in the manufacture of women's and children's wear, but each year, more printed fabrics appear in men's garments—a market that traditionally has not used prints. Upholstery and drapery fabrics are often printed, as well as many household items, especially sheets and pillowcases, bedspreads, and some towels. In recent years, there has been an interest in printing warp and weft knits.

Printed textiles are textiles with designs resulting from the application of colorants (usually pigment rather than dyes) or certain other substances to localized areas of fabric or yarn surfaces. *Printing* is a process for producing a pattern on yarns, fabric or carpet by any of a number of methods. The colorant or other substances (solvent, adhesive, discharge paste, resist) are deposited onto the fabric or yarn in a paste form. The yarns or fabric are usually treated with steam, heat, or chemicals for fixation.

[1]T.D. Fulmer, "Printing: Where it is Now—Where Will It Go?" *America's Textiles International* 18/12 (1989): 64.

[2]T.D. Fulmer, "World Class Printing for the '90s," *America's Textiles International* 20/2 (1991): 66.

When pigment is printed onto fabric, the fabric is called a *pigment print*. When dye paste is printed on, the fabric is called a *wet print*. In both cases, the print paste is carefully formulated to ensure proper flow of the colorant during application and to ensure that it remains in place from the time it is printed onto the fabric until it dries. Pigment prints are by far the most common. Wet prints are typically special-purpose prints, such as cotton upholstery or slipcover fabric and drapery fabric that are matched using vat dyes.

Most printed fabrics are *direct prints* because colorant is applied directly to the surface of a white or previously dyed fabric. It is the largest category of printed fabrics. Some prints are *discharge prints,* so named because the intent is for the substance applied—a discharge paste—to remove color from localized areas of the fabric to create the design. *Resist prints* are prints in which the intent is for the substance—a resist—to prevent coloration in the areas to which it is applied.

Other terminology for printed fabrics is presented in three groups in Detail View 35; the terminology of print patterns, print types, and printing processes. A complete description of a printed fabric would include terms from all three groups.

PRINT PATTERNS

Print stylists search endlessly for that new concept in pattern, that exquisite variation to an established pattern that will give their fabric a selling edge. American printers acknowledge the creativity of the Europeans in the conceptualization of designs. The trend-setters for print styles are found in the ateliers of Europe. Ateliers are professional studios in which a number of designers or colorists gather to produce new designs, called coquis, for sale to the textile printers. These designs are purchased as drawings that, in the majority of cases, are modified by the in-house designers who tailor the more generalized remittal of the original designers to fit the market requirements and production capabilities of the textile printers.

Designs can be grouped into four categories. *Realistic* or *naturalistic designs* depict real objects—human, animal, plants, or other objects—in a natural manner. *Stylized designs* distort real objects, but the original source of inspiration to the artist is still obvious. Distortions can be introduced by exaggerating or simplifying the object or by using colors and proportions that are not natural. *Geometric designs* are designs created using circles, squares, ovals, rectangles, ellipses and other geometrical

forms. Lastly, *abstract designs* have little or no reference to real objects. Often they are geometric but are less rigid. Designs have one or more motifs, distinctive and recurring forms, shapes, and figures. The color photographs of fabrics in this chapter show realistic and stylized designs using flowers as the motif. Fabric designs do not always fall neatly into one of these four categories. They may have elements of two or three of the categories.

The language of fabric designs also includes words such as toile de Jouy, calico, rococo, and baroque (broque). *Toile de Jouy* indicates that the design is a pastoral or historical scene presented like a pen-and-ink drawing using one color on a white or off-white fabric. *Calico* describes a fabric with small flowers over the entire fabric surface. *Rococo* designs consist of motifs of delicate, pastel flowers (natural or stylized) with some oriental influence presented in the style of 18th-century French fabrics. *Baroque* designs use leafy prints, foliage, flowers, and fruit motifs as well as full, flowing, curved lines in the style of 17th-century Italian fabrics. The terminology of design, however, is beyond the scope of this book.

PRINT TYPES

Print types indicate whether the fabric or yarns were printed, how many sides of the fabric were printed, what substance was applied, and whether the textile has been both dyed and printed. Clarity or vibrancy of color, pattern edge clarity (resolution), and darkness of background color are among the design features indicated by the print type. Photographs of fabrics representing the print types are provided in Figures 35.1–35.10. **In each photograph, the face of the fabric is shown on the left-hand side and the back of the fabric on the right-hand side.**

Application Prints

Application prints are prints in which a design has been printed over a white fabric. Figure 35.1 shows a typical application print. Many printed fabrics are of this type. Application prints are direct prints and pigment prints because pigment has been applied directly to a fabric surface.

Overprints

Overprints are prints in which a design has been printed over a previously dyed fabric (Figure 35.2). They are

FIGURE 35.1
An application print.

Face   Back

FIGURE 35.2
An overprint.

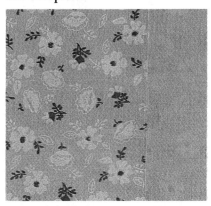

Face   Back

FIGURE 35.3
A blotch print.

Face   Back

FIGURE 35.4
A white discharge print.

Face   Back

FIGURE 35.5
A color discharge print.

Face   Back

FIGURE 35.6
A resist print.

Face   Back

FIGURE 35.7
A warp print.

Face   Back

FIGURE 35.8
A duplex print.

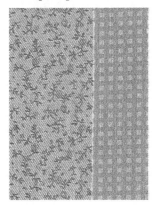

Face   Back

FIGURE 35.9
A flock print.

Face   Back

FIGURE 35.10
A burn-out print.

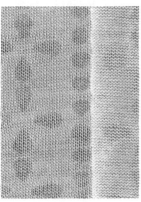

Face   Back

direct prints. The design is usually darker than the background. Since the fabric is dyed, the background color is the same depth of shade on both the front and the back of the fabric. Usually, the background color is off-white or pastel to ensure that the background colorant does not interfere with the colorant in the design motif by "reflecting" through. Any print process may be used to apply the design over the dyed fabric.

Blotch Prints

Blotch prints are prints in which both the background and the motif have been printed onto the fabric (Figure 35.3). The background may be a light or a dark shade. Usually, there is an obvious difference in the intensity of the background color between the face and the back of the fabric. When the fabric is thin, however, dye may be forced through the fabric, lessening this difference in color intensity. Blotch prints are direct prints.

One problem with blotch prints is that large background areas may not be the same depth of color from edge to edge. The overall appearance can almost be a washed-out look rather than a full, rich cover. Blotch prints made on screen-printing equipment may have more even color in the background areas than those made on roller-printing equipment. In screen printing, the print paste is pushed into the fabric rather than laid onto it, as in roller printing. Another problem with blotch prints is that minute uncolored areas sometimes appear between the sections of background color and the design motif. Blotch-printed fabrics colored with pigments rather than dyes may have an objectionable stiff or "boardy" hand.

Discharge Prints

Discharge prints are prints that have a dark background (such as black, navy, or maroon), widely spaced motifs, and a rich, vibrant, expensive look. Motifs may range from simple polka dots to very intricate patterns. Print designs inspired in the 1950s are typical.

White discharge prints are those in which the design motif is white (Figure 35.4); *color discharge prints* are those in which the design motif has many colors (Figure 35.5). In today's market, modified rayons in crepe and challis constructions are often discharge printed. Some cottons and wools are discharge printed.

In the manufacture of discharge prints, the fabric is first piece dyed. A discharge paste is printed onto the fabric with rollers (see the later section on roller print-

ing). This paste contains sodium sulfoxylate formaldehyde, a chemical capable of reducing the dye in the fabric, causing the dye to lose its ability to selectively absorb and reflect light. Thus, the fabric is not colored in areas where the paste comes into contact with the dye. If the discharge paste also contains dyes, usually vat dyes, that are not themselves reduced, then a colored motif results because the color-destroying chemical removes the previously dyed background color while the vat dye color is simultaneously printed. The fabric is subsequently steamed at 214–215°F (101.1–101.6°C).

The vat colors remain water soluble at this stage of manufacture. Chemical reactions fix the colorant, but the final shade is not yet discernable. Next, in a highly critical step, the vat colors applied in the print paste are reoxidized. If not done properly, the colorants are irreversibly washed out.

The identification of discharge prints is usually accomplished by inspecting the back of the fabric for small specks of background color under the design motif. These specks result from the incomplete removal of the background color by the reducing agent in the print paste.

Discharge prints are not widely found. Production is more costly than for blotch prints because it is necessary to dye the fabric prior to printing. Moreover, the long and delicate process must be very carefully and precisely controlled. Improper discharge procedures result in either poor color removal, poor shades, or even weakening and destruction of the fabric in the pattern area. Such a tendered area, when it occurs, may not be evident until the fabric has been laundered two or three times or drycleaned. In recent years, blotch prints that rival discharge prints in vibrancy have become available through the use of automatic and rotary screen methods.

Resist Prints

Resist prints are characterized by white designs and a dyed background (the fabric has the same color in the background areas on the face and the back) or a colored design with a dyed background (Figure 35.6). To produce these prints, either (a) a paste containing a resist (a substance that will prevent dye penetration) is printed onto a white fabric or (b) a paste containing a resist and dye is printed onto white fabric. In both cases, the fabric is dyed after the paste is applied. When the paste contains only a resist, the pattern motifs are white and the background is dyed or the motifs are dyed and the background white, depending on whether the motifs or the background areas are treated with the resist. When the paste contains both a resist and dye, the color of the pattern motifs is not affected by subsequent dyeing of the fabric background.

Warp Prints

Warp prints have a hazy edge to the design motif and many have a white or off-white background (Figure 35.7). The design effect is often described as soft, shadowed, and low-key. The motif or print pattern can be simple but is often complex. Warp prints are direct prints.

All colorant is found on the warp yarns; none is found on the filling yarns. Further, the colored areas along the length of a warp yarn are usually limited to the top surface of the yarn.

Warp prints are created by printing the warp yarns prior to fabric formation. Each warp yarn must remain aligned with adjacent yarns during weaving or a flaw will appear in the motif. Until recently, warp-printed fabrics—produced by roller or screen printing the warp yarns—were rather costly. Heat-transfer printing has significantly reduced the cost of warp-printed fabrics made of polyester fiber.

Warp prints should not be confused with ikat or fabrics containing space-dyed yarns (Chapter 34). Both warp prints and ikat are characterized as having hazy-edged motifs. Ikat motifs are usually simpler than those of warp printing and tend to be true to the traditional designs of the art form. Warp prints usually contain more colors than ikat fabrics, although warp printing is also used to simulate traditional ikat motifs and patterns. A close inspection of the yarns in simulated ikat fabrics, that is, warp prints, will show that only the surface fibers of each yarn are colored and a rather sharp demarkation appears between the colored sections on each yarn.

Distinguishing between warp prints and fabrics containing space-dyed yarns is easier than distinguishing between warp prints and ikat. Although both fabrics contain yarns with different colors along their length, space-dyed yarns usually cannot be used to form motifs, either with or without hazy edges.

Duplex or Register Prints

Fabrics may be printed on both sides instead of one (Figure 35.8). These are called *duplex* or *register prints*. The motifs on the two sides can be the same or different. Duplex prints may simulate coloration usually achieved by dyeing yarns, but inspection of the yarns clearly shows the fabric to be a duplex print because the yarns in duplex prints have surface spots of color; those in yarn-dyed or cross-dyed fabrics have a solid color throughout.

Flock Prints

Flock prints are prints in which short lengths of fiber (about $\frac{1}{10}-\frac{1}{4}$ inches or 2.54–6.4 millimeters) stand upright on the fabric surface to form a design (Figure 35.9). An adhesive material rather than a colorant is applied to the fabric surface. The short fibers are then directed to the adhesive through either a mechanical or electrostatic process, the details of which were considered in Chapter 29.

Practically all manufactured fibers can be used for the flock. Rayon and nylon are the most popular, however. The flock fiber is usually dyed prior to its application to the fabric. The fabric is also dyed prior to flocking.

Whether or not the flock-printed fabric will withstand drycleaning and/or laundering depends on the adhesive. Many high-quality adhesives are used by textile processors. When feasible, it is suggested that the flock-printed fabric be checked by laundering or drycleaning the fabric according to the manufacturer's care instructions prior to purchasing large yardages.

Burn-Out (Etched or Pattern-Milled) Prints

Burn-out prints, also called *etched* or *pattern-milled prints,* result from the destruction of some of the fibers in the fabric by a chemical printed onto certain areas. On flat fabrics, the intent is to produce a design by rendering some areas more translucent than others (Figure 35.10). The difference in light reflection creates the motif. On pile fabrics, the intent is to produce a raised design on a sheer background.

Sulfuric acid, mixed into a colorless print paste, is the chemical most often used. This acid, in the strength used for burn-out prints, will destroy (dissolve) cellulosic and nylon fibers but leave most others unaffected. A print paste composed mainly of aluminum chloride or sulfate will also induce etching of the cellulosic component when printed onto a mixture fabric (a nylon ground and a rayon or cotton face), dried, and cured at high temperature. Fabric containing acetate can be etched using acetone to dissolve the acetate fibers from the fabric. The market for such pattern-milled products is currently limited. Certain types of drapes are pattern milled to obtain interesting effects that are not available through any other means.

PRINTING PROCESSES

Printing processes, the methods used to place the colorant paste, adhesive, resist, or other substances onto fabric or yarn surfaces, determine the size of the design repeat (the single pattern unit that is repeated to cover the entire length of fabric), the fineness of detail (thinness of lines), character edge definition (resolution), and the maximum number of colors. Print processes differ in what type of fabric can be printed and in speed of printing. The cost of printing a fabric also varies with the printing process.

Roller Printing

Roller printing has remained essentially unchanged since its inception in 1783. A roller-printing machine consists of engraved printing rolls, color boxes, furnish rolls, doctor blades, a backing and blanket, and a main cylinder (Figure 35.11). There is one print roll, one furnish roll, and one doctor blade for each color to be applied. Most roller-printing machines have 8 print rolls but some have 16.

In roller printing, the areas of the design that require a certain color are etched or "carved out" on a copper roll, with one roll for each color. These etched areas on a print roll are continuously filled with print paste from a smooth-surfaced furnish roll that picks up the paste from the color box. A doctor blade removes any print paste from the raised surface of the print roll, thus leaving print paste only in the etched areas of the print roll. This print paste is transferred to the fabric as the fabric moves continuously between the print roll and the central cylinder. The blanket and back grey cloth absorb excess print paste, so that it does not become deposited on the drum. Fabric moves at rates up to 6000 yards per hour, or over 100–150 meters per minute.

When pigments are used, the fabric is subjected to dry heat at temperatures up to 400°F (204°C) for several minutes to set the resin that holds the pigment. Further processing is not necessary for pigment prints. When a dye is used, the steps necessary to complete processing depend on the type of dye. For example, nylon fabric that has been printed with acid dyes are steamed or autoclaved. Fabric printed with vat dyes must first be treated to reoxidize the dye and then washed.

Production Considerations. Once prepared, the print roll can be used to print millions of yards of fabric. Roller printing is an expensive process due to the high cost of engraving the copper rolls (though many advances have been made in the engraving process) and placing them into the printing machine. Only lengthy runs of the same pattern are cost effective. Roller printing requires skilled labor and heavy manual work to change the color boxes and the print rolls.

Types of Fabrics that Are Roller Printed. Currently, less than one-fourth of printed fabrics in the United

FIGURE 35.11 Roller-printing equipment.

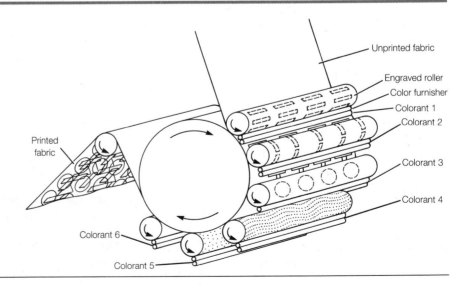

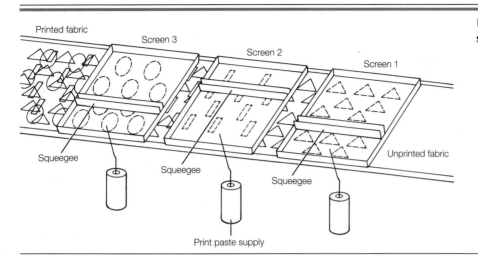

FIGURE 35.12 Flatbed screen-printing equipment.

States are roller printed. On a worldwide basis, less than one-half are roller printed.[3] Roller printing is most suitable for woven fabrics. It remains highly successful in printing of woven cotton and cotton blend fabrics, especially those used for sheets. Knit fabrics are not usually roller printed due to the potential elongation of the knit fabric as it is led from one print roll to the next.

Characteristics of Roller Prints. Roller-printing equipment can produce almost any design motif and pattern. Until recently, fabrics that had detailed, fine-line, multi-colored patterns were easily identified as roller prints because roller printing was the only way to achieve these design elements. Heat-transfer printing and rotary screen printing now rival roller printing in the production of such designs. Fabrics with high-quality tonal designs are probably the result of roller printing; roller printing is unrivaled on this point. Patterns with large background areas are avoided.

Roller prints usually have a design repeat less than 16 inches (40.6 centimeters) long. The size of a design repeat is limited by the circumference of the print rolls. Colorant tends to penetrate deeper into fabrics that have been roller printed compared to those that have been rotary screen printed because the pressure of the rollers forces colorant into the fabric. More colorant is therefore necessary to roller print a fabric to the same depth of shade as a rotary-printed fabric. The additional colorant needed adds to the cost of a roller-printed fabric.

[3]C.B. Smith, "ATI's Dyeing and Printing Guide," *America's Textiles International* 18/2 (1989): 32–52.

Flatbed Screen Printing

Manual (hand) screen printing, the forerunner of flatbed screen printing, began in the United States in the mid-1930s. In the 1940s, the process became mechanized and was called flatbed screen printing.

Flatbed screen-printing equipment consists of a long table over which a continuous rubber belt moves, fabric positioning rolls, flat screens that are mounted above the table, and a squeegee in each screen (Figure 35.12). The fabric to be printed enters the printing area at one end of the table, where it is positioned to align with the screens, and emerges at the other end. During printing, a wide rubber belt moves the fabric an established distance, the fabric and belt stop moving, the prepared print screens are lowered, and the squeegee moves across the screen, forcing print paste through the open areas of the screen. The screens are then raised, and the fabric moves forward the established distance. About 500 yards (457 meters) of fabric can be printed per hour.

The design and color are determined by the print screens. The mesh of each screen is prepared, so that there are open areas and closed areas. The open areas allow print paste to be pushed through onto the fabric surface, and the closed areas prevent print paste from being pushed through the screen. One prepared screen is required for each colorant applied.

Originally, screens were made from silk and the process was called silk screen printing. Today, screens are made from nylon, polyester, or metal. Screens for commercial screen printing are often prepared by a photochemical process similar in many ways to the process used for acid etching of copper rolls, but screens cost much less to prepare than the copper rolls for roller-printing equipment. To prepare a screen, it is coated with a light-sensitive lacquer, covered with a negative of the design, and exposed to light. The light-exposed areas become water insoluble and the shielded areas remain water soluble. Subsequent washing, followed by application of protective coatings to the insoluble lacquer, yields a screen with the design areas left open to the passage of color.

Types of Fabrics that Are Flatbed Screen Printed. Today, about one-tenth of commercial fabric printing is flatbed.[4] Typical flatbed-screen-printed products include tablecloths, towels, T-shirts, and scarves that require discrete noncontinuous patterns. In addition, designer items, limited prints, prototype patterns, and specialty patterns with very large numbers of colors (over 10) are often created through flatbed screen printing. All types of fabric structures, including wovens, knits, and nonwovens, can be flatbed screen printed.

Characteristics of Flatbed Screen Prints. When a print fabric has a large design repeat, it probably is the result of flatbed screen printing. The design repeat can be up to 240 inches (6 meters) long. Flatbed screen prints do not have the fine-line design detail that is possible with roller printing, rotary screen printing, and heat-transfer print-

---

[4]C.B. Smith, "ATI's Dyeing and Printing Guide," *America's Textiles International* 18/2 (1989): 32–52.

ing because the print paste is forced through a screen that has been partially blocked with resin. The finest detail results from screens with a mesh on the order of 200 × 200 holes per inch (80 × 80 holes per centimeter). Patterns with lengthwise stripes generally are not flatbed screen printed.

Rotary Screen Printing

Rotary screen-printing equipment consists of a table and screens that are shaped into seamless cylinders or rolls (Figure 35.13). Print paste is pumped into the center of a cylindrical screen and pushed through by a squeegee inside the cylinder. The fabric is moved on a wide rubber belt under the rotary screen cylinders, which are in continuous motion. Production rates of 2500–3500 yards of fabric per hour (25–100 meters per minute) are possible.

Rotary screen printing was introduced in 1963. It has several production advantages compared to roller printing: Fewer out-of-register patterns are produced; changeover times are faster; pattern changeovers are easier because the screens weigh about 10 pounds (4.5 kilograms), compared to 200 pounds (91 kilograms) for copper rolls; and less dye is required for the same depth of shade. Moreover, there is a shorter apprentice time for printers and less chance for human error. Rotary screen printing is efficient for long as well as moderately small (1000 yard or 914 meter) production runs. The screens, however, do not last as long as copper print rolls.

FIGURE 35.13 **Rotary screen-printing equipment.**

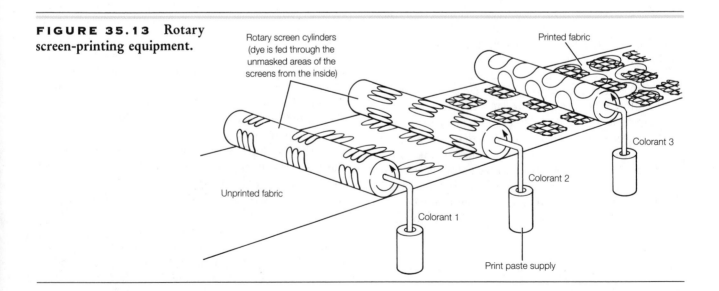

Rotary screen cylinders (dye is fed through the unmasked areas of the screens from the inside)

Printed fabric

Unprinted fabric

Colorant 1

Colorant 2

Colorant 3

Print paste supply

Types of Fabrics that Are Rotary Screen Printed.
Approximately two-thirds of printed fabric in the United
States and about one-third worldwide are rotary screen
prints.[5] Typical products include apparel, sleepwear,
sheeting and shirting, curtains, and upholstery. Carpets
can be printed on rotary screen-printing machines.

Characteristics of Rotary Screen Prints. Rotary screen
prints are difficult to distinguish from roller prints. One
difference is the maximum size of the design repeat. Rotary screen prints have a maximum design repeat of 36
inches (0.9 meters) long compared to 16 inches (4.6 meters) long for roller prints. A second difference is the
number of colors; the maximum number is 16 for a rotary screen prints compared to 8 (typically) for roller
prints. The colorant on a rotary screen print lies closer
to the fabric surface than it does on a roller-printed fabric. Thus, rotary screen prints may have brighter colors
than roller-printed fabrics with the same amount of colorant applied.

Heat-Transfer Printing

In France in the late 1960s, a method of printing onto
full-fashioned knitwear and garment panels was developed. By a simple heat process, a design printed on a
piece of paper was transferred to the fabric using modified garment presses. The dyes used were capable of va-
porizing under the heat conditions of the presses and
had a high affinity for the fibers composing the fabric.
The process is called *heat-transfer printing*, sublimation
printing, or sublistatic printing.

At about the same time, polyester was predicted to become the most important manufactured fiber. It presented coloration difficulties to both the dyer and
printer. In particular, the fixation of screen-printed designs required a degree of precision too great to make
mass production feasible.

When the basic heat-transfer technique was modified
it was found to be ideal for printing polyester fabrics, especially circular polyester knits, enabling these base fabrics to be converted into desirable printed fabrics. Continuous calenders running at elevated temperatures have
also been adapted (Figure 35.14). Continuous rolls of
preprinted paper and fabric are held face to face passing
between a central heated cylinder and a continuous porous blanket. Only light pressure is required. Tempera-

FIGURE 35.14 Heat-transfer-printing
equipment.

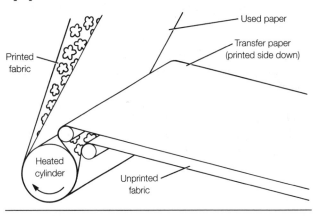

tures in the range of 392°F (200°C) are applied for periods of 15–20 seconds. Under this high temperature, the
disperse dyes on the paper sublime and are absorbed into
the polyester, acrylic, nylon or acetate fibers in the fabric.[6] After dye transfer, no further processing is required,
so no environmental pollution results. Print defects,
which run as high as 5–10% of the yardage processed on
roller- and screen-printing equipment, are avoided because the print paper can be inspected prior to the transfer of the dye to fabric. Heat-transfer-printed fabrics
have an unmatchable sharpness and clarity of design.
The used paper retains the original design in very muted
colors and is sold as wrapping paper to consumers or
made into bags and sold to specialty stores.

Warp yarns, rather than fabric, may also be heat-
transfer printed. When these yarns are formed into fabric, the fabric takes on the characteristic of warp-printed
fabric.

Heat-transfer printing of 100% cotton and cotton/
polyester blend fabrics may become a reality in the 1990s
as a result of research on chemical carriers that move special inks from the transfer paper to cotton fabric. This
development will permit the production of printed cotton knits with the fine-line detail motifs that are characteristic of heat-transfer-printed polyester knit fabrics.
Currently, less than one-tenth of all printing is by heat
transfer.[7]

[5]C.B. Smith, "ATI's Dyeing and Printing Guide," *America's Textiles International* 18/2 (1989): 32–52.

[6]Sublime means to change from a solid to a gas without becoming a liquid. The
alternative name for heat-transfer printing, sublistatic, is derived from this characteristic of the dyes used.

[7]C.B. Smith, "ATI's Dyeing and Printing Guide," *America's Textiles International* 18/2 (1989): 32–52.

Special Applications or Experimental Printed Fabrics

Some printing methods are used in specialty applications or are experimental.

Carpet Printing. Until the early 1970s, few advances were made in equipment to produce printed carpet. By this time, most carpet was tufted rather than woven and, consequently, the intricate patterns of woven carpets had been replaced by color effects obtainable through yarn and piece dyeing. Interest in a return of patterned carpets to simulate woven Axminster designs spurred the development of printing machinery.

The earliest efforts were in roller printing. Attempts were made to apply a continuously dyed background with designs of one to four colors. The goal of ensuring color penetration to the full depth of the carpet at commercially acceptable speeds was never realized. The industry turned to flatbed screen printing and then quickly to rotary screen printing. This change involved huge capital investment that only the largest companies could afford. Computer-injection systems (Chapter 34), introduced in the late 1970s, proved to be even more expensive. Economic considerations ushered in a new class of printing equipment that can be incorporated into existing finishing lines. Many of these units are based on drip-dye techniques in which streams of color are directed onto the carpet in a programmed fashion. The drip-dye method produces a seemingly random or simple design repeat in several colors. Future development efforts will remain minimal until printed carpets constitute a significant part of the carpet market.

High-Resolution Ink-Jet Printing. High-resolution ink-jet printing is one of the most recent printing developments. It may facilitate the printing of extremely delicate fabrics and pile fabrics because there is no contact between the fabric and the printer. Patterns can be made and transmitted as electronic data between locations that have compatible Computer-Aided Design systems. Patterns can be modified and duplicated swiftly and easily. Resolutions approaching photographic quality are expected.

CHAPTER SUMMARY

Printed fabrics are fabrics with designs resulting from the application of colorants (usually pigments rather than dyes) or certain other substances to localized areas on fabric or yarn surfaces. A complete description of a printed fabric includes information about the design, the type of print, and the printing process. Nine different types of prints were defined and illustrated to show their distinctive features. The four major print processes, roller, flatbed screen, rotary screen, and heat-transfer printing were presented. For each process, information was included about production considerations, design advantages and limitations, and the types of fabrics that are printed.

The objectives of this epilogue are to
1. Restate the goal of this textbook and briefly summarize how the information presented relates to achievement of that goal.
2. Clarify the contributions of fiber composition, yarn construction, fabric construction, and porosity, finishes, and colorants toward the attainment of fabric performance.
3. Provide direction toward further study of fabric performance.

OBJECTIVE 1

The goal of this book is to assist individuals in improving their ability to select the most appropriate fabric for a specified end-use situation. The book begins by recognizing that fabrics are composed of fibers, which are usually formed into yarns, and that these yarns are interlaced, interlooped, or otherwise formed into porous, planar structures. In addition, it is noted that fabrics may contain colorants and finishing chemicals. The point is made that each component of a fabric—its fiber composition, yarns, fabric construction, porosity, colorants, and finishing chemicals—contributes to total, or overall, performance, with some components contributing more significantly than others toward the attainment of specific properties.

Unit I focuses on the set of textile terminology that states and delineates the types of properties fabrics may have. These properties are grouped into the categories of durability, comfort, aesthetic appeal, maintenance, and health/safety/protection. Over 50 properties, including strength, wrinkle resistance, insulative ability, combustibility, and water vapor permeability, are discussed. Complete lists of fabric properties are provided in Detail Views 2 through 6. By the end of Unit I, the reader is familiar with the nature of fabric performance—with what properties consumers may seek when purchasing textile fabrics and products.

Unit II describes macroscopic, microscopic, and fine structures and the chemical nature of natural and manufactured fibers. It characterizes the unique combination of properties for each fiber (refer to the fiber property tables in Chapters 10 through 20) and relates each property to aspects of the fiber's structure and chemical nature. Unit III discusses yarn structures that are marketed today and explains how geometrical arrangements of fibers within various yarns (such as ring-spun yarns, air-jet-spun yarns, flat filament yarns, and textured filament yarns) influence yarn strength, yarn flexural rigidity, and other aspects of yarn performance. Similarly, Unit IV portrays fabric constructions (woven, knit, nonwoven, and compound) and focuses on how interlacement and interlooping of yarns or fiber entanglement and/or bonding affect fabric performance. Finally, Unit V addresses how fabric performance can be modified through various chemical, mechanical, and thermal treatments and how the appearance of fabric can be enhanced by the application of colorants.

Upon completing Units II through V, the reader should be well informed about the variety of fibers, yarns, fabric constructions, colorations and designs, and finishes available today. The reader should also be knowledgeable about the relationship of fiber structural features to fiber properties, yarn structural features to yarn performance, and fabric construction features to performance. Utilization of this knowledge in the marketplace helps substantially in assessing the suitability of fabric for a particular end-use situation.

Consider the selection of a T-shirt for jogging. The knowledgeable consumer can recognize the terms on a label that specify the fiber composition of the T-shirt. For example, cotton, polyester, polyester/cotton, and olefin will be recognized as common or generic names of different fibers. Terms such as Pima and Merino will be recognized as a type of cotton and wool fiber, respectively, and terms such as Dacron® and Trevira® as trademark names of polyester fiber produced by manufactured-fiber companies. The knowledgeable consumer can also translate fiber composition information into an assessment of expected performance. For example, wicking of sweat and quick drying are anticipated performance aspects of T-shirt fabric composed of olefin or polypropylene fiber. Other label information on a T-shirt label such as *mercerized, combed,* or *pigment dyed* will also be recognized as providing definitive information about expected performance. The knowledgeable consumer knows, for example, that *combed* means the shorter fibers have been removed from the yarn in processing and maximum effort was made to align the fibers in the yarn to produce a smooth, strong yarn. A T-shirt with combed yarns is thus considered to be "of better quality" than one with carded yarns. Observation of fabric construction can also be translated into expected performance. A jersey knit that has more stitches per inch (the gauge or cut is greater) may be expected to hold its shape better than one with fewer stitches per inch.

OBJECTIVE 2

In evaluating fabric performance at the time of purchase, it is essential that the purchaser know what performance is required and/or desired and then know what fabric components influence those aspects of expected performance. Table E.1 provides an at-a-glance view of the origin of fabric performance; it illustrates the relationship between a fabric's components and its performance. In this table, fabric properties found in Detail Views 2 through 6 are listed in the left-hand column, and the components of fabric established in Detail View 1 are listed across the top. Three symbols—an open circle, a blackened circle, and a half-blackened circle—are used to indicate degrees to which a component influences a property. If a component has no influence on a fabric property, an empty circle appears in the appropriate row and column position. If a fabric component plays a major role in the attainment of a fabric property, a black circle appears. Half-blackened circles indicate an intermediate degree of influence.

From Table E.1 it is clear that a fabric's fiber composition exerts the most influence on its performance because the greatest number of blackened and half-blackened circles appear in the fiber composition column. There are only a few properties for which no in-

fluence by fiber composition is indicated. At the other extreme, white circles predominate in the columns headed porosity and dyes and pigments; the least number of properties are altered as a consequence of the percentage of fabric volume occupied by air or as a consequence of the specific dye or pigment in the fabric. Treating fabric with chemicals or subjecting fabric to mechanical finishing treatments can significantly influence many fabric properties, but only when the correct or appropriate finish is applied. This situation is conveyed in the table by the symbolic notation ○-●, the ○ indicating that most finishes would not alter a specific property and the ● indicating that there is a finish that can enhance a specific aspect of a fabric's performance. The significant number of blackened and half-blackened circles under the columns of yarn construction and fabric construction shows those components to be important determinants of fabric performance, ranking after fiber composition in number of properties influenced.

Using the table, one can discern which fabric components are the most important determinants of specified aspects of performance. Porosity, for example, exerts an important influence on thermophysiological comfort—heat and moisture transport—provided by fabrics, surpassing the influence of fiber composition. Likewise, colorants are extremely important in determining the visual aspects of a fabric's aesthetic appeal even though they are relatively unimportant in terms of numbers of properties influenced.

It is also apparent from Table E.1 that most fabric properties are determined by several of a fabric's components. In fact, 39 of the 66 properties listed are influenced by 3, 4, or 5 components, and an additional 6 properties are influenced by 6 or 7 components. Fifteen of the 66 properties are determined by 2 components. Only 6 of the 66 properties originate from one fabric component (in each of the 6, that component is the fiber composition). When thinking about a fabric's performance, one must remember to consider all relevant aspects of its structure.

OBJECTIVE 3

In the highly competitive textile marketplace, fabric performance often needs to be quantified. Quantification allows buyers to specify performance requirements and provides buyers a means to determine that the goods they receive are what they requested (quality control). Quantification also makes it possible for manufacturers and retailers to certify that a product has certain perfor-

TABLE E.1 Origin of Fabric Performance

Fabric Properties	Fabric Components						
					Finishes		
	Fiber Composition	Yarn Construction	Fabric Construction	Porosity	Chemical	Mechanical and Thermal	Dyes and Pigments
Durability							
Breaking strength	◐	●	●	○	O-●	O-●	○
Tearing strength	○	●	◐	○	O-●	O-●	○
Bursting strength	◐	●	●	○	O-●	O-●	○
Elongation	●	●	●	○	O-●	○	○
Elastic recovery	●	●	●	○	○	○	○
Abrasion resistance	●	◐	◐	○	O-●	O-●	○
Flexibility	●	◐	◐	○	O-●	O-◐	○
Comfort							
Insulative ability (thermal resistance)	◐	◐	●	●	O-◐	O-●	○
Air permeability (windproofness)	◐	◐	●	●	O-●	O-◐	○
Water vapor permeability (breathability)	◐	◐	◐	●	○	O-●	○
Wickability	●	●	●	●	O-●	○	○
Water content (regain)							
Absorbency	●	○	○	○	O-●	○	○
Adsorbency	◐	●	●	○	○	O-●	○
Imbibed water	◐	◐	◐	●	○	O-●	○
Drying rate	●	◐	◐	◐	O-●	O-◐	○
Water repellency	◐	◐	●	○	O-●	O-◐	○
Water resistance and waterproofness	◐	◐	●	●	O-◐	O-◐	○
Prickliness/itchiness	◐	◐	◐	○	○	O-◐	○
Roughness	◐	◐	◐	○	O-◐	O-●	○
Thermal character (warm/ cool feeling)	◐	●	◐	○	O-●	O-●	○
Electrical resistivity (cling and shock)	●	○	○	○	O-◐	○	○
Stretch	●	●	●	○	O-◐	○	○
Weight	●	◐	◐	○	O-◐	○	◐
Pressure/compression	●	●	●	○	○	O-◐	○
Aesthetic Appeal							
Translucence/opacity (covering power)	●	●	●	●	O-◐	O-◐	◐
Luster/dullness	●	●	◐	○	O-●	O-●	○
Pattern and texture	○	◐	●	○	O-●	O-●	○
Color	◐	◐	◐	○	○	O-◐	●
Drapability (shear resistance)	○	◐	●	○	O-●	○	○
Flexural rigidity (stiffness/ softness)	◐	●	●	○	O-●	O-◐	○
Colorfastness	●	○	○	○	○	○	●

(continued)

TABLE E.1 *(continued)*

Fabric Properties	Fabric Components						
					Finishes		
	Fiber Composition	Yarn Construction	Fabric Construction	Porosity	Chemical	Mechanical and Thermal	Dyes and Pigments
Crocking resistance	●	○	○	○	○	○	●
Frosting resistance	●	○	○	○	○	○	●
Bleeding resistance	●	○	○	○	○	○	●
Yellowing	●	○	○	○	O-●	○	○
Wrinkle resistance and recovery	●	◐	◐	○	O-●	○	○
Compressional resilience (loft)	◐	●	◐	○	○	O-●	○
Shape retention	◐	◐	◐	○	O-●	○	○
Crease retention	●	◐	◐	○	O-●	○	○
Pilling propensity	◐	●	◐	○	O-◐	O-●	○
Snagging propensity	◐	●	●	○	○	○	○
Body	●	◐	◐	○	O-●	○	●
Hand	●	●	●	○	O-●	O-●	●
Odor absorption and release	●	○	○	○	O-●	○	○
Maintenance							
Soiling propensity	●	◐	◐	●	O-●	O-◐	○
Soil release	●	○	○	○	O-●	○	○
Stain resistance	●	○	○	○	O-●	○	○
Dimensional stability (shrinkage and growth)	●	◐	●	○	O-●	O-●	○
Light resistance	●	○	○	○	O-◐	○	○
Biological resistance	●	○	○	○	O-●	○	○
Chemical resistance	●	○	○	○	○	○	○
Heat durability and resistance	●	○	○	○	O-●	○	○
Health/Safety/Protection							
Potential as irritants, allergens, or carcinogens	●	○	○	○	O-●	○	●
Potential to hold bacteria	●	◐	◐	○	O-●	○	○
Potential as incendiary spark generators	●	○	○	○	O-◐	○	○
Combustibility (flammability)	●	◐	◐	◐	O-●	O-◐	○
Permeation resistance	○	◐	●	●	○	O-◐	○
Ultraviolet light penetration resistance	◐	◐	●	●	○	O-◐	○
High energy impact penetration resistance	●	◐	●	○	○	○	○
Filtration efficiency	○	○	●	●	○	○	○
Ability to absorb toxic gases, air pollutants	●	○	○	○	○	○	○
Sound absorption ability	○	◐	●	●	○	○	○
Biologic compatibility	●	○	○	○	○	○	○
Biodegradability	●	○	○	○	○	○	○
Ultrafiltration ability	●	○	○	○	○	○	○
Light transferability	●	○	○	○	○	○	○

mance capabilities. Fabric performance data can be used to determine whether a new product has superior performance features compared to the old product or to competing products.

An area of study called fabric performance evaluation, or more broadly textile testing, considers the quantification of fabric properties. One learns about instruments used, laboratory and wear study procedures, and the analysis and interpretation of test data. Many universities offering programs of study in textiles or merchandising offer a couse in textile evaluation or testing. The American Association of Textile Chemists and Colorists (AATCC) offers several workshops throughout the year. Three journals that report the findings of fabric performance studies are the *Textile Research Journal, Textile Chemist and Colorist*, and *Textile and Clothing Research Journal*. Several excellent books and manuals are available:

American Association of Textile Chemists and Colorists. *AATCC Technical Manual.* Research Triangle Park, NC: AATCC, 1992.

American Society for Testing and Materials. *Annual Book of ASTM Standards.* Philadelphia, PA: ASTM, 1992.

Booth, J.E. *Principles of Textile Testing* (3rd ed.). New York: Chemical Publishing Co., 1969.

Cohen, A.C. *Beyond Basic Textiles.* New York: Fairchild Publications, 1982.

Fourt, L., and N.R.S. Hollies. *Clothing: Comfort and Function.* New York: Marcel Dekker, 1970.

Grover, E.B., and Hamby, D.S. *Handbook of Textile Testing and Quality Control.* New York: Wiley-Interscience, 1960.

Lyle, Dorothy. *Performance of Textiles.* New York: John Wiley & Sons, 1977.

Merkel, Robert S. *Textile Product Serviceability.* New York: MacMillan, 1991.

Best wishes for further textile study.

Kathryn L. Hatch

Credits (continued)

Technology Group of Manchester, England. **Figure 7.17** Data obtained from *Manufactured Fiber Producers Handbook* and *Fiber Organon*, Vol 62(4), 1991, p. 71 and used with permission of the Fiber Economics Bureau, Inc., 101 Eisenhower Pkwy., Roseland, NJ 07068. **Figure 7.18** Data obtained from *Fiber Organon*, Vol 61(9), 1990, p. 1 and used with permission of the Fiber Economics Bureau, Inc., 101 Eisenhower Pkwy., Roseland, NJ 07068. **Figure 8.1** (right-hand graph) Data obtained from the *Journal of the Textile Institute*, Vol 47, 1956, p. T58–T101. Reproduced by kind permission of the Textile Institute of Manchester, England. **Figure 8.1** (left-hand graph) Fiber stress-strain curves reprinted from the *Journal of the Textile Institute*, Vol 36, 1945, p. T122. Reproduced by kind permission of the Textile Institute of Manchester, England. **Figure 8.2** Model stress-strain curve reprinted from *Industrial & Engineering Chemistry*, Vol 44, 1952, p. 2121 with permission of the American Chemical Society of Washington, DC. **Figure 8.3** Elastic-recovery curves reprinted from the *Journal of the Textile Institute*, Vol 36, 1945, p. T162. Reproduced by kind permission of the Textile Institute of Manchester, England. **Figure 8.4** Data obtained from "1991 Man-Made Fiber Properties Chart" inserted into *Textile World*, Vol 141, 1991 and used with the permission of Maclean Hunter of Chicago, IL. **Figure 8.5** Data obtained from *Polymer Engineering and Science*, Vol 29(24), 1989, p. 1744 and used with permission of the Society of Plastics Engineers of Brookfield Center, CT. **Figure 8.6** Nylon fiber, silk fiber, and rayon fiber absorption curves reprinted from the *Journal of the Textile Institute* with the nylon curve appearing in Vol 40, 1949, p. T171; silk fiber curve in Vol 40, 1949, p. T166; and the rayon fiber curve in Vol 23, 1932, p. T165. Reproduced by kind permission of the Textile Institute of Manchester, England. Wool fiber absorption curve reprinted from the *Journal of the Society of Chemical Industries*, Vol 49, 1930, p. 210T with permission of the Society of Chemical Industry of London, England. Colloidal fiber absorption curves reprinted from *Transactions of the Faraday Society*, Vol 22, 1926, p. 188 with permission of the Royal Society of Chemistry of Cambridge, England. Synthetic fiber absorption curves reprinted from R. Hill, *Fibres from Synthetic Polymers*, 1953, p. 443 with permission of Elsevier Publishing Co. of New York, NY. **Figure 8.7** Data obtained from the *Textile Research Journal*, Vol 17, 1947, pp. 96–98 and used with permission of the Textile Research Institute of Princeton, NJ. **Figure 8.8** Data obtained from "1991 Man-Made Fiber Properties Chart" inserted into *Textile World*, Vol 141, 1991 and used with the permission of MacLean Hunter of Chicago, IL. **Figure 8.9** Data obtained from the Journal of the Textile Institute. Reproduced by kind permission of The Textile Institute of Manchester, England. Cotton fiber data appeared in Vol 39, 1948, p. T361; data for wool, silk, Orlon acrylic, and drawn nylon in Vol 44, 1953, p. T591; and for flax and rayon in Vol 40, 1949, p. T501. **Figure 8.10** Curve reprinted from *Man-Made Textile Encyclopedia*, 1959, p. 542 with permission of Interscience Publishers, Inc. of New York, NY. **Figure 8.11** Graph reprinted from the *Journal of the Textile Institute*, Vol 44, 1953, p. 61. Reproduced by kind permission of The Textile Institute of Manchester, England. **Figure 8.12** Graph reprinted from the *Journal of the Textile Institute*, Vol 44, 1953, p. T142. Reproduced by kind permission of the Textile Institute of Manchester, England. **Figure 8.13** Data obtained from the *1990 AATCC Technical Manual*, p. 47 and used with permission of the American Association of Textile Chemists and Colorists, P.O. Box 12215, Research Triangle Park, NC 27709. **Table 8.1** Data obtained from DuPont technical bulletin X-142, September 1961 and used with permission of E. I. DuPont de Nemours of Wilmington, DE. **Table 8.2** Ranking obtained from the secondary source W. E. Morton and J. W. S. Hearle, *Physical Properties of Textile Fibres*, London: Heinemann and the Textile Institute, 1975, p. 436. **Table 8.3** Table constructed from descriptive (qualitative) data found in the soil removal technical literature. **Table 8.4** Melting temperatures obtained from *1990 AATCC Technical Manual*, p. 47 and used with the permission of the American Association of Textile Chemists and Colorists, P.O. Box 12215, Research Triangle Park, NC 27709. Other temperature data compiled from the secondary sources D. R. Jackman and M. K. Dixon, *The Guide to Textiles for Interior Designers* (2nd edition), Peguis Publishers Limited, Winnipeg, Canada, 1990, p. 120, and J. Yeager, *Textiles for Residential and Commercial Interiors*, Cambridge: Harper & Row Publishers, Inc., 1988, p. 102. **Table 8.6** Table reprinted from *1992 AATCC Technical Manual*, p. 47 with permission of the American Association of Textile Chemists and Colorists, P.O. Box 12215, Research Triangle Park, NC 27709. **Table 8.7** Table reprinted from M. Lewin and E. M. Pearce (eds.), *Handbook of Fiber Science and Technology: Volume IV*, 1985, pp. 305–306 by courtesy of Marcel Dekker, Inc. of New York, NY. **Figure 9.4** Silk trademark reprinted with permission of the International Silk Association of Lyon, France, and New York, NY. Mohair trademark reprinted with permission of the Mohair Council of America of New York, NY, and San Angelo, TX. Wool trademark reprinted with permission of the American Wool Council of Englewood, CO. **Figure 9.5** Wool certification marks reprinted with permission of the Wool Bureau, Inc. of New York, NY/U.S. Division of the International Wool Secretariat. Linen certification mark reprinted courtesy of the International Linen Confederation of Paris, France. The seal of cotton is a registered trademark/service mark of Cotton Incorporated of New York, NY, and is reprinted with permission of Cotton Incorporated. Carpet certification mark reprinted with permission of the Carpet and Rug Institute of Dalton, GA. "Floor tested" certification mark reprinted with permission of Hoechst Celanese Corporation of Charlotte, NC. And the four Sanforized marks reprinted with permission of Cluett, Peabody, & Co., Inc., of New York, NY. **Detail View 10** Photograph provided by Stock of Boston, MA. **Figure 10.1** Data obtained from *Fiber Organon*, Vol 61(9), 1990, p. 1 and used with permission of the Fiber Economics Bureau, Inc., 101 Eisenhower Pkwy., Roseland, NJ 07068. **Figure 10.2** Photograph printed from slide F1 in Shirley Institute's collection of Slides of Textile Fibres with permission of the British Textile Technology Group of Manchester, England. **Figure 10.3** Drawing reprinted from E. P. G. Gohl and L. D. Vilensky, *Textile Science* (2nd ed.), 1983, p. 73 with permission from Longman Cheshire Pty Limited of South Melbourne, Victoria, Australia. **Figure 10.7** Photographs reprinted from the *Textile Chemist and Colorist*, Vol 22(8), 1990, pp. 23–25 with permission from the American Association of Textile Chemists and Colorists, P.O. Box 12215, Research Triangle Park, NC 27709. **Detail View 11** Drawings reprinted from H. R. Mauersberger (ed.), *Matthew's Textile Fibers* (6th ed.), 1954, New York: John Wiley & Sons, p. 752. **Figure 11.1** Photograph printed from slide F14 in Shirley Institute's collection of Slides of Textile Fibres with permission of the British Textile Technology Group of Manchester, England. **Figure 11.2** Photograph printed from slide F15 in Shirley Institute's collection of Slides of Textile Fibres with permission of the British Textile Technology Group of Manchester, England. **Figure 11.3** Photograph courtesy of

R. M. Robson and M. G. Dobb, Department of Textile Industries, University of Leeds, Leeds, United Kingdom. **Figure 11.5** Drawing reprinted from W. E. Morton and J. W. S. Hearle, *Physical Properties of Textile Fibres* (2nd ed.), 1975, p. 54 with permission of the Textile Institute of Manchester, England. **Detail View 12** Drawings reprinted from "The Story of Cotton," p. 10 with permission of the National Cotton Council of America of Memphis, TN. **Figure 12.1** Data obtained from and used with permission of The National Cotton Council of Nashville, TN. **Figure 12.2** Photograph printed from slide F16 in Shirley Institute's collection of Slides of Textile Fibres with permission of the British Textile Technology Group of Manchester, England. **Figure 13.1** Photograph printed from slide F19 in Shirley Institute's collection of Slides of Textile Fibres with permission of the British Textile Technology Group of Manchester, England. **Figure 13.2** Photograph courtesy of the International Linen Promotion Commission of New York, NY. **Figure 13.3** Photograph printed from slide F27 in Shirley Institute's collection of Slides of Textile Fibres with permission of the British Textile Technology Group of Manchester, England. **Figure 13.4** Photograph printed from slide F22 in Shirley Institute's collection of Slides of Textile Fibres with permission of the British Textile Technology Group of Manchester, England. **Figure 14.1** Data obtained from *Manufactured Fiber Producers Handbook* (1990 data sheets) and used with permission of the Fiber Economics Bureau, Inc., 101 Eisenhower Pkwy., Roseland, NJ 07068. **Figure 14.2** Photograph printed from slide F39 in Shirley Institute's collection of Slides of Textile Fibres with permission of the British Textile Technology Group of Manchester, England. **Figure 14.3 and 14.4** Graphs reprinted from M. Lewin and E. M. Pearce (eds.), *Fiber Chemistry*, 1985, pp. 979–980 with permission of Marcel Dekker, Inc. of New York, NY. **Figure 14.5** Photographs courtesy of ITT Rayonier of Stamford, CT. **Figure 14.6** Photograph printed from slide F34 in Shirley Institute's collection of Slides of Textile Fibres with permission of the British Textile Technology Group of Manchester, England. **Figure 14.7** Photograph courtesy of Courtaulds Fibers Inc. of Axis, AL. **Figure 15.1** Photograph printed from slide F32 in Shirley Institute's collection of Slides and Textile Fibres with permission of the British Textile Technology Group of Manchester, England. **Figure 15.2** Photograph printed from slide F38 in Shirley Institute's collection of Slides of Textile Fibres with permission of the British Textile Technology Group of Manchester, England. **Figure 16.1** Data obtained from *Manufactured Fiber Producers Handbook* (1990 data sheets) and used with permission of the Fiber Economics Bureau, Inc., 101 Eisenhower Pkwy., Roseland, NJ 07068. **Figure 16.2** Photograph printed from slide F48 in Shirley Institute's collection of Slides of Textile Fibres with permission of the British Textile Technology Group of Manchester, England. **Figure 17.1** Data obtained from *Manufactured Fiber Producers Handbook* (1990 data sheets) and used with permission of the Fiber Economics Bureau, Inc., 101 Eisenhower Pkwy., Roseland, NJ 07068. **Figure 17.3** Photograph printed from slide F51 in Shirley Institute's collection of Slides of Textile Fibres with permission of the British Textile Technology Group of Manchester, England. **Figure 17.5** Drawing courtesy of Hoechst Celanese of Charlotte, NC. **Figure 17.6** Photographs courtesy of Teijin Limited of Osaka, Japan. **Figure 17.7** Photographs courtesy of E.I. DuPont de Nemours of Wilmington, DE. Cross-sections of Coolmax* and Thermax* Fibers courtesy of the DuPont Company. (* is the DuPont certification mark for high performance fabrics.) **Figure 18.1** Data obtained from *Manufac-*

tured Fiber Producers Handbook (1990 data sheets) and used with permission of the Fiber Economics Bureau, Inc., 101 Eisenhower Pkwy., Roseland, NJ 07068. **Figure 18.4** Photograph printed from slide F54 in Shirley Institute's collection of Slides of Textile Fibres with permission of the British Textile Technology Group of Manchester, England. **Figure 19.1** Data obtained from *Manufactured Fiber Producers Handbook* (1990 data sheets) and used with permission of the Fiber Economics Bureau, Inc., 101 Eisenhower Pkwy., Roseland, NJ 07068. **Figures 19.3 and 19.4** Photographs printed from slides F41, F42, and F43 in Shirley Institute's collection of Slides of Textile Fibres with permission of the British Textile Technology Group of Manchester, England. **Figure 19.5** Graphs reprinted from Rosenbaum, S., *Journal of Applied Polymer Science*, Vol 9, pp. 2077 and 2078, Copyright © 1965 John Wiley & Sons, Inc. Reprinted by permission of John Wiley & Sons, Inc. of New York, NY. **Figure 19.6** Drawings courtesy of National Spinning Co., Inc., of New York, NY. **Figure 19.8** Drawing courtesy of Kanebo, Ltd., of New York, NY. **Figure 20.1** Photograph printed from slide F57 in Shirley Institute's collection of Slides of Textile Fibres with permission of the British Textile Technology Group of Manchester, England. **Figure 20.2** Right-hand photograph printed from slide F58 in Shirley Institute's collection of Slides of Textile Fibres with permission of the British Textile Technology Group of Manchester, England. Left-hand photograph courtesy of Globe Manufacturing Co. of Fall River, MA. **Figure 20.3** Drawing reprinted from E. P. G. Gohl and L. D. Vilensky, *Textile Science* (2nd ed.), 1983, p. 100 with permission from Longman Cheshire Pty Limited of South Melbourne, Victoria, Australia. **Table 20.1** Table reprinted from M. Grayson (ed.), *Encyclopedia of Textiles, Fibers, and Nonwoven Fabrics*, p. 151, Copyright © 1984 John Wiley & Sons, Inc. Reprinted by permission of John Wiley & Sons of New York, NY. **Figure 21.1** Modacrylic fiber photograph printed from slide F46 in Shirley Institute's collection of Slides of Textile Fibres with permission of the British Textile Technology Group of Manchester, England. Saran fiber courtesy of Pittsfield Weaving Co., Inc., of Pittsfield, NH, and photograph kindly prepared by Phillips Fibers Corporation of Greenville, SC. **Figure 21.2** Meta-aramid fiber photograph printed from slide F70 in Shirley Institute's collection of Slides of Textile Fibres with permission of the British Textile Technology Group of Manchester, England. PBI photograph courtesy of Hoechst Celanese of New York, NY. Cross-section photomicrograph of Ryton* Sulfar fibers made by Phillips Fibers Corporation of Greenville, SC. (*Ryton is a registered trademark of Phillips Petroleum Co.) **Figure 21.3** Para-aramid fiber photograph printed from slide F71 in Shirley Institute's collection of Slides of Textile Fibres with permission of the British Textile Technology Group of Manchester, England. Photograph of high-tenacity, high-modulus organic fiber (Spectra®) courtesy of Allied Fibers of Petersburg, VA. **Figure 21.4** Photographs printed from slides F59, F62, F63, F68, and F69 in Shirley Institute's collection of Slides of Textile Fibres with permission of the British Textile Technology Group of Manchester, England. **Unit III opener** Artwork courtesy of Brentwood Yarns of South Grafton, MA. **Figure 22.1** Open-end spun-yarn photograph courtesy of American Savio Corporation. Air-jet yarn courtesy of Murata of America, Inc., of Charlotte, NC. Photographs of ring-spun and air-jet spun-yarn courtesy of the University of Arizona Electron Microscopy Facility, Division of Biotechnology. **Figure 22.2** Data courtesy of Rieter Spinning Systems of Zurich, Switzerland. **Figure 22.3** Yarns courtesy of Dixie Yarns, Inc., of Chattanooga, TN. Photographs courtesy of the University of Arizona Electron Microscopy Facility, Division of Biotechnology. **Figure 23.1 and 23.2** Photographs courtesy of Allied Signal, Inc., of Petersburg, VA. **Figure 23.3** Drawing reprinted from *Textiles*, 6(3), 1977, p. 59 with permission of the British Textile Technology Group of Manchester, England. **Figure 23.4 and 23.5** Drawings reprinted from B. C. Goswami, J. G. Martindale, and F. L. Scardine, *Textile Yarns*, 1977, pp. 394 and 447 with permission of John Wiley & Sons, New York, NY. **Figure 23.6** Yarn from the University of Arizona textile collection and photograph courtesy of the author (K. L. Hatch). **Figure 24.3** Photographs reprinted from *Textile Chemist and Colorist*, Vol 22(12), 1990, p. 12 with permission of the American Association of Textile Chemists and Colorists of Research Triangle Park, NC, and Akzo NV of Arnhem, Netherlands. **Figure 24.6** Drawings reprinted from *Textiles*, Vol 7(1), 1978, p. 11 with permission of the British Textile Technology Group of Manchester, England. **Figure 24.7** Stress-strain curves of polyester fibers courtesy of Hoechst Celanese Corporation of New York, NY. **Figure 25.2** Upper right-hand drawing reprinted from Coats & Clark "Core Thread" brochure with permission of Coats and Clark, Inc., of Toccoa, GA. Lower left-hand drawing reprinted from Leesona Textile Machinery advertisements for Coverspun yarn with permission of Leesona Textile Machinery of Burlington, NC. **Figure 25.3** Photographs reprinted from the *Textile Research Journal*, Vol 59, 1989, p. 14 with permission of the Textile Research Institute of Princeton, NJ. **Figure 25.4 and 25.5** Yarns obtained from the textile collections at the University of California—Davis and the University of Arizona at Tucson, AZ. Photographs courtesy of the author (K. L. Hatch). **Unit IV opener** Artwork courtesy of Henkel Textile Chemicals Corporation of Charlotte, NC. **All figures in Chapter 26 with a photograph** Fabrics obtained from textile collections at the University of California—Davis, Colorado State University in Fort Collins, CO, and the University of Arizona in Tucson, AZ. Photographs courtesy of the author (K. L. Hatch). **Figure 26.13** Drawings courtesy of Karastan-Bigelow of Greensboro, NC. **Figure 26.16** Drawings reprinted from *Textiles*, 5(1), 1976, p. 14 with permission of the British Textile Technology Group of Manchester, England. **Figure 26.17** Triaxial drawing reprinted with permission of Nissho Iwia Corporation, Howa Machinery, Ltd., Sakase Adtech Co., Ltd., and Wayne C. Trost, Triaxial Weaving Consultant. **Figure 27.1** Drawings reprinted from J. A. Smirfitt, *An Introduction to Weft Knitting*, 1975, p. 10 with permission of Merrow Publishing Company, Limited, of Watford Herts., England. **Figure 27.2** Drawings reprinted from P. Schwartz, T. Rhodes, and M. Mohamed, *Fabric Forming Systems*, 1982, pp. 99, 105, and 111 with permission of Noyes Publications of Park Ridge, NJ. Author added drawings of the back views of the 1 × 1 rib and 1 × 1 purl structures. **Figure 27.3** Left-hand drawing reprinted from P. Schwartz, T. Rhodes, and M. Mohamed, *Fabric Forming Systems*, 1982, p. 98 with permission of Noyes Publications of Park Ridge, NJ. Right-hand drawing reprinted from D. J. Spencer, *Knitting Technology* (2nd ed.), 1989, p. 20 with permission of Pergamon Press of Oxford, England. **Figure 27.4** Drawing reprinted from D. J. Spencer, *Knitting Technology* (2nd ed.), 1989, p. 56 with permission of Pergamon Press of Oxford, England. **Figure 27.5** Drawing reprinted from D. J. Spencer, *Knitting Technology* (2nd ed.), 1989, p. 65 with permission of Pergamon Press of Oxford, England. **Figure 27.6** Pile jersey knit drawing reprinted from International Bulletin World Edition (Knitting, Hosiery, Embroidery, and Making-Up), 3/78, p. 95 with permission of the International Textile

Service of Zurich, Switzerland. Plated jersey knit, fleece jersey knit, Jacquard jersey knit, and openwork knit drawings reprinted from D. J. Spencer, *Knitting Technology* (2nd ed.), 1989, pp. 47, 148, 90, and 47, respectively, with permission of Pergamon Press of Oxford, England. **Figure 27.7** Drawings reprinted from D. J. Spencer, *Knitting Technology* (2nd ed.), 1989, pp. 202 and 203 with permission of Pergamon Press of Oxford, England. **Figure 27.8** Interlock double-knit drawings reprinted from D. J. Spencer, *Knitting Technology* (2nd ed.), 1989, p. 61 with permission of Pergamon Press of Oxford, England. **Figure 27.9** Drawings reprinted from P. Schwartz, T. Rhodes, and M. Mohamed, *Fabric Forming Systems*, 1982, pp. 127 and 140 with permission of Noyes Publications of Park Ridge, NJ. **Figure 27.10** Drawing reprinted from D. J. Spencer, *Knitting Technology* (2nd ed.), 1989, p. 291 with permission of Pergamon Press of Oxford, England. **Figure 27.11** Drawing reprinted with permission of the National Knitwear and Sportswear Association of New York, NY. Fabric from the textile collection at the University of Arizona and the photograph courtesy of the author (K. L. Hatch). **Figure 27.12** Fabrics from the textile collection at the University of Arizona. Photographs courtesy of the author (K. L. Hatch). **Detail View 28** Fabric courtesy of the Association of the Nonwovens Fabrics Industry of Cary, NC. Photograph courtesy of the University of Arizona Electron Microscopy Facility, Division of Biotechnology. **Figures 28.1 through 28.7** Fabrics courtesy of the Association of the Nonwoven Fabrics Industry of Cary, NC, and photographs courtesy of the University of Arizona Electron Microscopy Facility, Division of Biotechnology. **Figure 28.8** Fabrics courtesy of Malimo Maschinenbau of Chemnitz, Germany, and their American representative, Chima, Inc., of Reading, PA. Photographs courtesy of the author (K. L. Hatch). **Figure 29.1** Machine-stitch quilted fabric courtesy of Sauerer Textile Machinery Group of Greensville, NC, and photographs courtesy of the author (K. L. Hatch). **Figure 29.2** Fabric from the University of Arizona textile collection and photograph courtesy of the author (K. L. Hatch). **Figure 29.3** Fabric courtesy of the American Flock Association (AFA) of Boston, MA, and photograph courtesy of the University of Arizona Electron Microscopy Facility, Division of Biotechnology. Drawing reprinted from "Design with Flock in Mind," a brochure of AFA with permission of the American Flock Association. **Figure 29.4** Photograph reprinted from *Textiles*, Vol 20(4), 1990, p. 15 with the permission of the British Textile Technology Group of Manchester, England. Drawings reprinted from *Textiles*, Vol 14(1), 1985, p. 3 with the permission of the British Textile Technology Group of Manchester, England. **Figure 29.5** Photograph reprinted from *Textiles*, Vol 20(4), 1990, p. 16 with the permission of the British Textile Technology Group of Manchester, England. Drawings reprinted from *Textiles*, Vol 14(1), 1985, p. 3 with the permission of the British Textile Technology Group of Manchester, England. **Unit V opener** Artwork courtesy of C. H. Patrick of Charlotte, NC. **Figure 30.1** Drawing reprinted from P. Carty and M. S. Byrne, *The Chemical and Mechanical Finishing of Textile Materials* (2nd ed.), p. 14 with permission of P. Carty. **Figure 31.1** Photographs courtesy of Sperotto Rimar Spa of Malo, Italy. The fabrics, which appear on the photographs, have been treated on "Debaca" installation manufactured by Sperotto Rimar Spa, Italy. **Figure 31.2** Fabric courtesy of Tompkins Bros. Co., Inc., of Syracuse, NY, and photograph courtesy of the author (K. L. Hatch). **Figure 31.3** Fabric courtesy of Bolliger Corporation of Spartanburg, SC, and photograph courtesy of the author (K. L. Hatch). **Figure 31.4** Photograph courtesy of Stock of

Boston, MA. **Figure 31.5** Photographs courtesy of AEGIS Environmental Management, Inc., of Midland, MI.   **Figure 32.1** Fabric from the University of Arizona fabric collection and photograph courtesy of the author (K. L. Hatch).   **Figure 32.2** Fabrics courtesy of Greenville Machinery Corporation of Greenville, SC, and photograph courtesy of the author (K. L. Hatch).   **Figure 32.3** Drawing and fabric courtesy of Wm. Clark & Sons, Ltd., of Londonderry, North Ireland. Photograph courtesy of the author (K. L. Hatch).   **Figure 32.4** Fabric courtesy of Curtin–Herbert Co., Inc., of Gloversville, NY, and photograph courtesy of the author (K. L. Hatch).   **Figure 32.5** Photograph courtesy of Heusch GmbH & Co. KG, of Aachen, Germany, The World's Oldest Factory of Shearing Knives.   **Figure 32.6 and 32.7** Fabrics courtesy of Symphony Fabrics Corporation of New York, NY. Photographs courtesy of the author (K. L. Hatch).   **Figure 32.8** Left-hand photographs printed from slides F16 and F17 in the Shirley Institute's collection of Slides of Textile Fibres with permission of the British Textile Technology Group of Manchester, England. Fabrics in right-hand photograph courtesy of Batson Yarn and Fabrics Machinery Group, Inc., of Greenville, SC, and photograph courtesy of the author (K. L. Hatch).   **Figure 32.9** Photomicrographs courtesy of Ecolab, Inc., of St. Paul, MN.   **Figure 32.10** Fabrics courtesy of Pendleton Woolen Mills of Portland, OR. Photograph courtesy of the author (K. L. Hatch).   **Figure 33.2** Photographs reprinted from "Sanforset" brochure with permission of Sanforized Co. of New York, NY.   **Figure 33.3** Photographs courtesy of The Wool Bureau Inc./U.S. Division of the International Wool Secretariat. **Figures 34.1 through 34.15** Photographs courtesy of the author (K. L. Hatch). Fabric containing space dyed yarns in Figure 34.5 courtesy of Franetta Fabrics, Inc., of New York, NY. The computer injection dyed carpet sample for Figure 34.12 was produced by Millitron® Technology, which is proprietary to Milliken & Company. The carpet sample was courtesy of Milliken & Company, Interior Furnishings Division of LaGrange, GA. Japanese warp-and-weft ikat fabric for Figure 34.15 is from the collection of Joan Teer Jacobson of Tucson, AZ. Fabric for Figure 34.7 is from the fabric collection at the University of Nevada—Reno. All other fabrics are from the fabric collection at the University of Arizona in Tucson, AZ.   **Figure 34.16** Dye formulas reprinted from E. P. G. Gohl and L. D. Vilensky, *Textile Science* (2nd ed.), 1983, p. 122 with permission of Longman Cheshire Pty Limited of South Melbourne, Victoria, Australia.   **Figures 35.1 through 35.10** All fabrics except those in Figures 35.4 and 35.6 courtesy of Cranston Print Works Company of Cranston, RI. Fabrics in Figures 35.4 and 35.6 are from the fabric collection at the University of Arizona, Tucson, AZ. Photographs courtesy of the author (K. L. Hatch). **Figures 35.11 through 35.14** Illustrations by Michael D. Pitts, from *Textiles: A Handbook for Designers*, by Marypaul Yates. © 1986 Marypaul Yates.